Internet and Distributed Computing Advancements:

Theoretical Frameworks and Practical Applications

Jemal H. Abawajy
Deakin University, Australia

Mukaddim Pathan
CSIRO, Australia

Mustafizur Rahman
IBM, Australia

Al-Sakib Khan Pathan
International Islamic University, Malaysia

Mustafa Mat Deris
Universiti Tun Hussein Onn, Malaysia

Managing Director:	Lindsay Johnston
Senior Editorial Director:	Heather Probst
Book Production Manager:	Sean Woznicki
Development Manager:	Joel Gamon
Development Editor:	Hannah Abelbeck
Acquisitions Editor:	Erika Gallagher
Typesetter:	Russell Spangler
Cover Design:	Nick Newcomer, Lisandro Gonzalez

Published in the United States of America by
Information Science Reference (an imprint of IGI Global)
701 E. Chocolate Avenue
Hershey PA 17033
Tel: 717-533-8845
Fax: 717-533-8661
E-mail: cust@igi-global.com
Web site: http://www.igi-global.com

Library of Congress Cataloging-in-Publication Data

Internet and distributed computing advancements: theoretical frameworks and practical applications / Jemal H. Abawajy ... [et al.].
    p. cm.
  Includes bibliographical references and index.
  Summary: "This book is a vital compendium of chapters on the latest research within the field of distributed computing, capturing trends in the design and development of Internet and distributed computing systems that leverage autonomic principles and techniques"--Provided by publisher.
  ISBN 978-1-4666-0161-1 (hardcover) -- ISBN 978-1-4666-0162-8 (ebook) -- ISBN 978-1-4666-0163-5 (print & perpetual access) 1. Electronic data processing--Distributed processing. 2. Internet. 3. Autonomic computing. I. Abawajy, Jemal H., 1982-
  QA76.9.D5I647 2012
  004.67'8--dc23
                                        2011042025

British Cataloguing in Publication Data
A Cataloguing in Publication record for this book is available from the British Library.

All work contributed to this book is new, previously-unpublished material. The views expressed in this book are those of the authors, but not necessarily of the publisher.

To Ziad and Mam – Jemal

To my lovely wife Ziyuan for her warmth, patience, and understanding while I was busy editing this book. This book would not have come to light without her continuous support – Mukaddim

To my parents – Mustafiz

To my family; parents and all others – Sakib

To my parents, wife, and children – Mustafa

Table of Contents

Section 1
Internet and Distributed Computing Systems

Section 2
Wireless Sensor Networks

Chapter 11

Detailed Table of Contents

Section 1
Internet and Distributed Computing Systems

The aim of this chapter is to discuss the main TCP issues and challenges that influence TCP performance, within different wireless data packet communication networks, taking into consideration the specific characteristics of each of them. In this chapter, the authors have presented the work done in order to improve TCP performance and to cope with new data transmission network technologies and topologies (such as Wi-Fi, WiMAX, cellular, wireless, mobile, ad-hoc, mesh, and vehicular networks). This chapter also discusses related research challenges that should be studied and evaluated within such wireless networks.

This Chapter discusses the integration of classical e-learning paradigms with new advancements of distributed computing, such as: the usage of Peer-to-Peer (P2P) techniques to produce network-independent overlays, also by enabling direct student-to-student exchanges; the integration, through grid-based middleware, of real or virtual devices, plants and Sensors Network (SN) within the e-learning environment; and the adoption of a distributed e-learning system to spread culture through mobile devices, with an emphasis on satellite communications.

Chapter 3

Hairulnizam Mahdin, University of Tun Hussein Onn, Malaysia
Jemal Abawajy, Deakin University, Australia

This chapter addresses reliability and dependability issues of RFID systems. RFID components such as the readers are prone to failures with serious consequences to the overall system. It presents an approach that detects the faulty readers with the aim to minimize the impacts of the faulty readers on the system reliability and dependability. Performance evaluation of the approach against other techniques is presented to show that it performs reasonably well in the presence of faulty readers.

Chapter 4

Harinda Sahadeva Fernando, Deakin University, Australia
Jemal Abawajy, Deakin University, Australia

This chapter presents a conceptual framework for analyzing the threats, attacks, and security requirements pertaining to networked RFID systems. The vulnerabilities of, and the threats to, the system are identified using the threat model. The security framework itself consists of two main concepts: (1) the attack model, which identifies and classifies the possible attacks, and (2) the system model, which identifies the security requirements. The framework gives readers a method with which to analyze the threats any given system faces. Those threats can then be used to identify the attacks possible on that system and get a better understanding of those attacks. This chapter also allows readers to easily identify all the security requirements of that system and identify how those requirements can be met.

Chapter 5

Bellarmine Ezumah, Murray State University, USA
Suraj Olunifesi Adekunle, Lagos State University, Nigeria

This chapter serves as a collection of works that were done in the area of cybersecurity in Africa—with a focus on four countries representing the Cardinal points in Africa: Kenya, Nigeria, Egypt, and South Africa. Detailed information is presented on the legislative framework proposed and implemented by these countries to combat and control cybercrimes. These legislative measures were commended, criticized, and factors that militate their implementation are also discussed in this chapter. Finally, the chapter posits areas that the African nations can improve in their quest to make cyberspace safer.

Section 2
Wireless Sensor Networks

Chapter 6

Mukaddim Pathan, Australian National University, Australia & Telstra Corporation Limited, Australia
Doug Palmer, CSIRO ICT Centre, Australia
Ali Salehi, CSIRO ICT Centre, Australia

This chapter presents a survey of existing programming models for sensor networks and classifies them by following a layered approach, based on their level of abstractions. It establishes the fact that using the right programming model can have enormous impact in the development, deployment, and maintainability of sensor networks. This chapter also endeavors to lay out a clear guideline to choose the right approach for programming sensor networks for application development, thus potentially alleviating the heavy burden for programmers.

Chapter 7

Dennis P. Mirante, Hofstra University, USA
Habib M. Ammari, University of Michigan – Dearborn, USA

This chapter takes a representative survey of the types of security attacks WSNs may be subjected to. Additionally, steps that may be taken to mitigate these attacks are also discussed. Intrusion Detection Systems, a paradigm for monitoring network activities for malicious behavior, are introduced and specific examples of them are discussed. This chapter also establishes the fact that the introduction of new types of WSN applications will result in new types of security attacks and that WSN researchers and designers will always be playing catch up in their attempts to find and plug the latest security holes used by attackers.

Chapter 8

Enamul Haque, Bangladesh Agricultural University, Bangladesh
Norihiko Yoshida, Saitama University, Japan

This chapter focuses on context aware clustering techniques that carry a great deal of importance among WSN routing protocols. It describes noteworthy context aware routing protocols such as: Context Adaptive Clustering, Data-Aware Clustering Hierarchy, Context-Aware Clustering Hierarchy, and Context-Aware Multilayer Hierarchical Protocol. Insights based on comprehensive investigations and analyses of these protocols have been included in this chapter with useful remarks. Since context awareness is considered an integral part of Body Sensor Networks (BSN), a kind of WSN, this chapter also discusses issues related to context aware techniques used in BSN.

Chapter 9

Anar Abdel Hady, Electronics Research Institute, Cairo, Egypt

Sherine M. Abd El-kader, Electronics Research Institute, Cairo, Egypt

Hussein S. Eissa, Electronics Research Institute, Cairo, Egypt

Ashraf Salem, Ain Shams University, Cairo, Egypt

Hossam M.A. Fahmy, Ain Shams University, Cairo, Egypt

This chapter provides a detailed description of the characteristics of routing in wireless sensor networks; it describes the routing protocols used in these networks, pointing out the advantages and disadvantages of each. It states the fact that wireless sensor networks have several restrictions, e.g. limited energy supply, limited computing power, and limited bandwidth, and hence, one of the main design goals of WSNs is to carry out data communication while trying to prolong the lifetime of the network and prevent connectivity degradation by employing efficient energy management techniques.

Chapter 10

Yupeng Hu, Hunan University, China

Rui Li, Hunan University, China

This chapter discusses the key elements of MAC design with an emphasis on energy efficiency. Furthermore, it reviews several typical MAC protocols proposed in the literature, comparing their energy conservation mechanisms. Particularly, it presents a Collaborative Compression-Based MAC (CCP-MAC) protocol, which takes advantage of the overheard data to achieve energy savings. Finally, it compares the performance of CCP-MAC with related MAC protocols, illustrating their advantages and disadvantages.

Chapter 11

Basma M. Mohammad El-Basioni, Electronics Research Institute, Egypt

Sherine M. Abd El-Kader, Electronics Research Institute, Egypt

Hussein S. Eissa, Electronics Research Institute, Egypt

Mohammed M. Zahra, Al-Azhar University, Egypt

This chapter proposes a routing protocol inspired by an energy-efficient cluster-based routing protocol called Energy-Aware Routing Protocol (EAP). The new enhanced protocol that is called Low Loss Energy-Aware Routing Protocol (LLEAP) enhances the performance of EAP in terms of some quality of service parameters by adding a second iteration for constructing the tree structure for multi-hop communication among cluster heads, by modifying the used weights of the cluster heads and parent node selection, and finally by selecting suitable aggregation methods to decrease losses and delays. Simulation results showed that LLEAP significantly outperformed EAP in terms of packet loss percentage by on average 93.4%.

Preface

Internet is an essential tool in modern life. Though the initial use of Internet was restricted to the people in touch with technology only, now-a-days all kinds of people from different backgrounds and areas need Internet for their specific areas of interest as well as for daily life. It is a remarkable achievement that Internet is now used for trading, business, education, banking, searching, advertising, auctioning, research works, politics, movements, conferencing, and many other purposes related to our day-to-day living. New concepts related to Internet are also emerging or getting clearer shapes day by day like Future Internet, Next-Generation Internet, Internet of Things (IoT), Internet for tiny embedded system like sensors, etc. Side-by-side, the use of mobile and wireless devices such as PDA, laptop, and cell phones for accessing the Internet has paved the way for related distributed computing technologies to flourish through recent developments.

In general terms, a distributed system is defined as a system that consists of several autonomous computers that communicate through a computer network. Usually there is a common goal that all these networked computers try to achieve. A computer program that runs in a distributed system is called a distributed program, and distributed programming is the process of writing such programs. The same definitions could be rewritten by considering different types of computing devices instead of only computers in traditional sense. With the advancements of micro-electronics, many low-resource computing devices have been devised that can form useful distributed systems. One of the most recent attractive technologies is wireless sensor networks. Sensors are small computing devices that form a distributed system or network over a target area to collect and process required data. The workloads and network traffic in such type of distributed system could be divided among the participants. Thus, sensor network becomes a major type of distributed system. Other commonly known distributed systems are various types of telecommunications networks like; telephone networks and cellular networks, computer networks such as the Internet, World Wide Web (WWW) and Peer-to-Peer (P2P) networks, multiplayer online games network and virtual reality network, distributed database network, distributed information processing network (e.g. airline ticket reservation system), aircraft control system, industrial control system, clustered and grid systems.

Despite the rapid advancements, the increasing scale, complexity, heterogeneity, and dynamism of Internet and distributed computing systems with respect to communication networks, resources and applications have made such systems brittle, unmanageable and insecure. This scenario calls for innovative solutions to deal with the complexity, dynamism, heterogeneity, and uncertainty of distributed systems and provide a holistic approach for the development of systems that can meet the requirements of performance, fault tolerance, reliability, security, and Quality of Service (QoS). Given all the works done so far and the facts and figures, it is necessary to compile in a single volume what we have achieved so far, what is going on currently in academic and industry environments for developing the tools and concepts, and what we could expect in the coming days or after a good number of years from now.

This book entitled *Internet and Distributed Computing Advancements: Theoretical Frameworks and Practical Applications*, focuses on theoretical frameworks and practical applications. It is an attempt to put together some of the critical aspects of Internet and Distributed Systems from theoretical to practical issues. The book was envisioned to be a premier reference source for the academics, students, researchers, readers, and knowledge seekers in the related fields. We have focused on including chapters that can easily explain a particular topic, sometimes even a complex issue. After a rigorous review process, 11 chapters have been finally selected for inclusion in this book. The reviewers and editors who handled the review processes are the experts in the relevant fields.

The sequence of chapters in the book is important to mention. We divided the accepted 11 chapters into 2 sections: (1) Internet and Distributed Computing Systems and (2) Wireless Sensor Networks.

In the first section, we start with the chapters dealing with Internet and Distributed Computing systems. The aim of the introductory chapter titled "*TCP for Wireless Internet: Solutions and Challenges*" is to discuss the main TCP issues and challenges that influence TCP performance, within different wireless data packet communication networks taking into consideration the specific characteristics of each of them. In this chapter, Ghaleb-Seddik et al. have presented the work done in order to improve TCP performance and to cope with new data transmission networks technologies and topologies (such as Wi-Fi, WiMAX, cellular, wireless, mobile, ad-hoc, mesh, and vehicular NETWORKS). This chapter also discusses related research challenges that should be studied and evaluated within such wireless networks. In the 2nd chapter, "*Enhancement of e-Learning Systems and Methodologies through Advancements in Distributed Computing Technologies*," Caviglione and Coccoli discuss the integration of classical e-learning paradigms with new advancements of distributed computing, such as: the usage of Peer-to-Peer (P2P) techniques to produce network-independent overlays, also by enabling direct student-to-student exchanges; the integration, through grid-based middleware, of real or virtual devices, plants and Sensors Network (SN) within the e-learning environment; and the adoption of a distributed e-learning system to spread culture through mobile devices, with emphasis on satellite communications. Mahdin and Abawajy in 3rd chapter "*An Approach to Faulty Reader Detection in RFID Reader Network*," address reliability and dependability issues of RFID systems. RFID components such as the readers are prone to failures with serious consequences to the overall system. It presents an approach that detects the faulty readers with the aim to minimize the impacts of the faulty readers on the system reliability and dependability. Performance evaluation of the approach against other techniques is presented to show that it performs reasonably well in the presence of faulty readers. Fernando and Abawajy in the chapter, "*A Security Framework for Networked RFID*," present a conceptual framework for analyzing the threats, attacks and security requirements pertaining to networked RFID systems. The vulnerabilities of, and the threats to the system are identified using the threat model. The security framework itself consists of two main concepts: (1) the attack model: which identifies and classifies the possible attacks and (2) the system model which identifies the security requirements. The framework gives readers a method with which to analyze the threats any given system faces. Those threats can then be used to identify the attacks possible on that system and get a better understanding of those attacks. This chapter also allows readers to easily identify all the security requirements of that system and identify how those requirements can be met. Finally, Ezumah and Adekunle write the fifth chapter of the first section titled, "*A Review of Privacy, Internet Security Threat, and Legislation in Africa: A Case Study of Nigeria, South Africa, Egypt, and Kenya*". This chapter serves as a collection of works that were done in the area of cybersecurity in Africa - with a focus on four countries representing the Cardinal points in Africa: Kenya, Nigeria, Egypt, and South Africa. Detailed information is presented on the legislative framework proposed and implemented by these countries to combat and control cybercrimes. These legislative measures were commended, criticized and factors that militate their implementation are also discussed in this chapter. Finally, the chapter posits areas that the African nations can improve in their quest for making the cyberspace safer.

The second section focuses on wireless sensor network related issues. "*A Walk through Sensor Network Programming Models*" by Pathan et al. presents a survey of existing programming models for sensor networks and classifies them by following a layered approach, based on their level of abstractions. It establishes the fact that using the right programming model can have enormous impact in the development, deployment and maintainability of sensor networks. This chapter also endeavors to lay out a clear guideline to choose the right approach for programming sensor networks for application development, thus potentially alleviating the heavy burden for programmers. Then a survey chapter by Mirante and Ammari "*Wireless Sensor Network Security Attacks: A Survey,*" takes a representative survey of the types of security attacks WSNs may be subjected to. Additionally, steps that may be taken to mitigate these attacks are also discussed. Intrusion Detection Systems, a paradigm for monitoring network activities for malicious behavior, are introduced and specific examples of them are discussed. This chapter also establishes that fact that the introduction of new types of WSN applications will result in new types of security attacks and that WSN researchers and designers will always be playing catch up in their attempts to find and plug the latest security holes used by attackers. Haque and Yoshida present "*Clustering in Wireless Sensor Networks: Context-Aware Approaches*" which focuses on context aware clustering techniques that carry a great deal of importance among WSN routing protocols. It describes noteworthy context aware routing protocols such as: Context Adaptive Clustering, Data-Aware Clustering Hierarchy, Context-Aware Clustering Hierarchy, and Context-Aware Multilayer Hierarchical Protocol. Insights based on comprehensive investigation and analyses of these protocols have been included in this chapter with useful remarks. Since context awareness is considered as an integral part of Body Sensor Networks (BSN), a kind of WSN, this chapter also discusses issues related to context aware techniques used in BSN. Hady et al.'s "*A Comparative Analysis of Hierarchical Routing Protocols in Wireless Sensor Networks*" provides a detailed description of the characteristics of routing in wireless sensor networks; it describes the routing protocols used in these networks pointing out the advantages and disadvantages of each. It states the fact that wireless sensor networks have several restrictions e.g. limited energy supply, limited computing power and limited bandwidth, and hence, one of the main design goals of WSNs is to carry out data communication while trying to prolong the lifetime of the network and prevent connectivity degradation by employing efficient energy management techniques. Hu and Li, in their chapter, "*Energy-Efficient MAC Protocols in Distributed Sensor Networks,*" discuss the key elements of MAC design with an emphasis on energy efficiency. Furthermore, it reviews several typical MAC protocols proposed in the literature, comparing their energy conservation mechanism. Particularly, it presents a collaborative compression based MAC (CCP-MAC) protocol, which takes advantage of the overheard data to achieve energy savings. Finally, it compares the performance of CCP-MAC with related MAC protocols, illustrating their advantages and disadvantages. The final chapter of this section is the chapter 11 titled, "*Low Loss Energy-Aware Routing Protocol for Data Gathering Applications in Wireless Sensor Network*" by El-Basioni et al.

Acknowledgment

This book came into existence thanks to the direct and indirect involvement of many researchers, academicians, developers, designers, and industry practitioners. Therefore, we acknowledge and thank the contributing authors, research institutions, and companies whose papers, reports, articles, notes, Web sites, and study materials have been referred to in this book. Furthermore, many of the authors have acknowledged their respective funding agencies and co-researchers, who made significant influence in carrying out their research. Throughout the working period of the book, its organization, selection of chapters for specific sections, we were constantly involved in discussions to fine tune our work. We have directed the authors to provide high quality manuscripts with minimal errors within the texts.

With the contributions from authors, we have tried to make this book as rich as possible within our capacity. We thank the Almighty who allowed us to complete this work within the given schedule. Alongside the valuable time and efforts from the editors of this book, the authors contributed significantly with their valuable works and opinions during the book editing phase. Because of the rigorous review process and selection policy enforced by the editorial board, we could not include all the submitted chapters. However, we also thank those authors whose contributions could not be selected for the final book. Besides these, we are very thankful to Kristin M. Klinger, Director of Editorial Content and Erika Carter, Acquisition Editor of IGI Global for accepting our book proposal and giving us the opportunity to work on this book project. Last but not least, we are thankful to the Editorial Assistant from IGI Global, Hannah Abelbeck, for the continuous support and cordial assistance during our work on the book to keep it in line with the publisher's policies and key dates.

Prior technical sources are acknowledged at appropriate places in the book. We hope that this book will serve as a valuable text for students, especially at graduate level, and reference for researchers and practitioners working in the Internet and distributed computing systems and its emerging consumer applications.

Jemal Abawajy
Deakin University, Australia

Mukaddim Pathan
CSIRO, Australia

Mustafizur Rahman
IBM, Australia

Al-Sakib Khan Pathan
International Islamic University, Malaysia

Mustafa Mat Deris
Universiti Tun Hussein Onn, Malaysia

Section 1
Internet and Distributed Computing Systems

Chapter 1
TCP for Wireless Internet:
Solutions and Challenges

Alaa Ghaleb-Seddik
Ecole Nationale Superieure d'Informatique pour l'industrie et l'Entreprise (ENSIIE), France

Yacine Ghamri-Doudane
Ecole Nationale Superieure d'Informatique pour l'industrie et l'Entreprise (ENSIIE), France

Sidi Mohammed Senouci
University of Bourgogne, France

ABSTRACT

The importance of TCP as a transport control protocol comes from its wide usage in most implemented data packet communication networks all over the world. Because TCP was mainly developed to be implemented within wired networks, the continuous development and enhancements of its functionality and its control algorithms to catch up with the on-going development of different and new data packet communication networks, topologies, and technologies has represented non-stop work and effort.

The authors aim in this chapter is to discuss the main TCP issues and challenges that influence TCP performance, within different wireless data packet communication networks, taking into consideration the specific characteristics of each of them.

The authors present, in this chapter, the work done in order to improve TCP performance and to cope with new data transmission network technologies and topologies (such as Wi-Fi, WiMAX, cellular, wireless, mobile, ad-hoc, Mesh, and Vehicular networks). They also discuss the remaining research challenges that should be studied and evaluated within such wireless networks.

DOI: 10.4018/978-1-4666-0161-1.ch001

INTRODUCTION

TCP is known, nowadays, as the most popular and widely implemented transport protocol. Although TCP was mainly developed to be used within wired data networks, the evolution of data networks technologies and topologies had not affect its popularity or its implementation as the researches are continuing to keep studying and enhancing its ability to cope with these new technologies. The development of TCP to meet these new technologies was a crucial milestone and a hard-working task in the domain to keep it still in the track. Over several years, many TCP variants were developed and implemented to keep up with the continuous communication technology evolution that invades our lives.

The development of TCP takes different scales. Some researchers were concerned by its development over wired data networks while others were oriented towards solving the challenges raised from wireless data networks. Certainly, dealing with each type of networks requires specific and well adapted solutions as the challenges and problems within each data network type are not the same. For example, within wireless cellular data networks, the main problem resides in the wireless link characteristics representing the last hop within the network configuration. Wireless links introduce new challenges to traditional TCP processes. These challenges are often expressed in terms of new data packet loss situations due to the specific characteristics of these networks. These new challenges require TCP enhancements and modifications for its embedded functional algorithms and sometimes its calculation processes. This is made with the aim to get an optimal behavior from TCP in terms of bandwidth usage.

The modifications proposed for wireless cellular data networks still does not satisfy the requirements of wireless multi-hop data networks, as almost all the communication links are wireless links, which amplify the wireless link challenges to TCP within such networks. Thus, solutions or TCP enhancements that address wireless cellular data networks problems are different from those dealing with multi-hop wireless data networks. Consequently, new TCP enhancement solutions were also proposed, implemented and analyzed as soon as new wireless data network technologies and topologies came into prospective (e.g. mobile ad hoc networks, wireless sensor networks …).

In this chapter, we are concerned by the development of TCP within wireless data networks. We start by explaining the different concepts of each data network topology/technology and the challenges that could affect TCP performance within such networks and then detailing the state-of-the-art solutions proposed to overcome these challenges within each of such wireless data networks. The research challenges that are still open will also be detailed. More precisely, in this chapter, we intend to discuss and compare different TCP variants and mechanisms that had been mainly developed to enhance the data packet transmission process over different single or multi-hop wireless data networks. Some of these variants are developed through a microscopic (i.e. details oriented) point of view manner while others were dealing with the macroscopic (i.e. global problem addressing) point of view.

We will start by introducing each wireless data packet network type and showing its main characteristics and the new challenges that may affect TCP performance when implemented within it. Then, we discuss, in details, the existing TCP solutions that are proposed and developed in order to enhance TCP performance within such networks. Finally, we investigate the possible remaining or new challenges to TCP that might be in perspectives to be discussed and dealt with within the discussed wireless data networks.

The discussed wireless data packet networks, in this chapter, include: (1) infrastructure single-hop networks (Wi-Fi or 802.11 Wireless LANs, WiMAX networks, and mobile cellular networks), (2) infrastructure-less multi-hop networks (mobile ad hoc networks, wireless sensor networks, wireless mesh networks, and vehicular wireless networks).

In the next section, we discuss TCP, in general, and its main characteristics within wireless data networks and some of the proposed solutions and algorithms that tend to enhance its performance within different wireless networks configurations and topologies.

TCP WITHIN WIRELESS DATA NETWORKS

The Transmission Control Protocol (TCP) is a reliable transmission protocol that provides an ordered delivery of a stream of bytes over the communication link between the sender and the receiver. TCP was originally designed to be deployed within wired networks where the communicating nodes are connected through physical cables. Physical cables are considered as reliable transmission media where congestion is the most common cause of data packet losses. That's why TCP is a congestion-control-oriented algorithm. TCP deploys flow control mechanism through its implemented algorithms (Slow-Start and Congestion Avoidance). These algorithms tend to better utilize the available bandwidth and to avoid congestion episodes over the connection through the CWND (Congestion WiNDow) and SSThresh (Slow-Start Threshold) parameters.

As stated earlier, TCP had been initially designed in order to cope with congestion-related packet losses in wired data networks. However, nowadays the networks include more and more wireless links. In the following, we discuss briefly TCP performance problems within wireless mobile network environments, and the proposed solutions to overcome them. Let's take the case of wireless mobile networks, which are infrastructure networks that use wireless radio channels as the last hop connection. Cellular Networks where a mobile host is connected to the fixed network with the help of Base Stations, is the most com-

mon form of wireless networks. Even that this type of networks contains only one wireless link, the performance of TCP is highly affected. A key factor for that unsatisfactory performance is the wireless radio channel quality that can fluctuate greatly in time due to channel fading and user mobility, leading to a high variability of transmission time and delay as well as to data packet losses. Furthermore, the possibility to handoff from one base station to another may lead to sudden and high increase of data packets delay over the connection and a burst data packet loss episode. In addition to data packet losses due to the wireless channel inefficiencies, high fluctuations of RTT (Round Trip Time) values over the connection may lead the TCP Retransmission Time-Out (RTO) to expire. This will invoke the TCP sender to trigger its congestion control algorithm. This leads to TCP data packets retransmission; although that the retransmitted packet is not actually lost but simply delayed. As a result, TCP decreases its CWND to minimum and under-utilizes the available bandwidth unnecessarily. In addition, TCP sender consumes more energy to retransmit the considered to be lost data packets without need (redundant retransmission). Within wireless mobile networks, losses are often due to wireless link channel errors such as interference, variable RTT delays, or nodes' mobility. All the above reasons lead to TCP performance degradation in such environments as it was mainly developed to deal with congestion over wired networks and not other data packet loss types (such as those due to wireless radio channels). In order to improve the performance of TCP within such networks, many proposals were introduced. These solution proposals can be categorized as follows: (1) Split-connection approaches, (2) Link layer related approaches, and (3) End-to-end approaches.

The split-TCP (Kopparty, Krishnamurthy, Faloutsos, & Tripathi, 2002) approach divides the end-to-end TCP connection between the mobile node and the corresponding node into two separate and independent connections with a proxy, serving as a common point between the two connections. This proxy is usually located at the base station. The main idea in this approach is to isolate impacts of wireless link errors and variable RTT delays over it from the impact of the wired connection (mainly congestion in this second). Consequently, TCP congestion control, timeout and retransmission mechanisms in the wired link will not suffer from the fluctuating quality of the wireless radio channel. Even that this approach can optimize the wireless link performance, this approach introduces extra TCP protocol overhead over the connection (extra buffer required for each connection, and higher overall delay), which in turn causes performance degradation. This also, complicates the handoff process over the network. Also, the main idea of the split-TCP violates the end-to-end semantics of TCP.

Many other approaches, such as SNOOP (Balakrishnan, Seshan, & Katz, 1995; Balakrishnan, Padmanabhan, Seshan, & Katz, 1997) was developed for networks with high wireless channel errors. In this approach, all the modifications are done at the base station side. The main idea of SNOOP is very similar to that of split-TCP. SNOOP tends to hide and isolate the wireless channel errors and looses from the wired network, and avoids the frequent fast retransmit triggering at the other end of the TCP connection (the wired network). This action leads to faster recovery due to the local data packets retransmissions, and hence to better throughput performance than in the split-TCP solution. However, the problems of TCP performance degradation in case of nodes' mobility are not treated or considered in this solution.

The third approach proposed in order to enhance the performance of TCP within wireless mobile networks applies Explicit Loss Notification (ELN) (Balakrishnan, et al., 1997) messages to distinguish between congestion-induced and non-congestion-induced losses. However, the transmission of such messages leads to more computational complexity at the TCP node as it introduces more protocol overheads over the TCP connection.

The Wireless Transmission Control Protocol (WTCP) (Sinha, Venkitaraman, Sivakumar, & Bhargavan, 1999) is an example of the end-to-end approaches. WTCP is an end-to-end TCP modification to improve its performance within wireless mobile networks. In this TCP variant, the detection of losses due to congestion is done at the receiver side through the measured inter-packet separation delay. Hence, most of the congestion control computations are done at the receiver side. Even that, WTCP shows the ability to detect and handle both loss types. The fact that most of the calculations are done at the receiver side increases the complexity of the approach and requires protocol modification at both sides (sender and receiver).

All the above solutions may help enhancing TCP performance within wireless mobile networks where only the last communication hop is a wireless channel. However, if all the communication channels are wireless such as within wireless ad hoc networks, we expect that TCP performance would be dramatically influenced. In the following section, we discuss the main issues that may influence TCP performance within different wireless network environments. We also discuss some of the proposed solutions in order to improve its performance within such networks.

TCP OVER WI-FI (IEEE 802.11 WLANS)

IEEE 802.11, also known as Wi-Fi, denotes a set of Wireless LAN (WLAN) standards developed by the working group number 11 of the IEEE LAN/MAN (IEEE 802) Standards Committee. The low cost of such networks, their convenience, as well as the ease of their integration with other networks, are the main reasons for their popularity and wide usage. WLAN stands for Wireless Local Area Network which normally consists of two computers, at least, that are connected together through wireless links. This network configuration permits the users to move around freely within a certain area of coverage and still be connected to the same network. This technology was developed to be used within home/small office networks configuration and can be viewed as an extension to any existing wired networks where cable extension facilities are not possible.

The main characteristics of wireless communication link are the following:

1. Limited bandwidth,
2. High latencies and delays over the connection,
3. Noticeably high bit-error rates,
4. Temporary disconnections due to wireless signal loss

All the above characteristics should be treated by the implemented network protocols and/or applications. Additionally, according to the configuration of the wireless network, there might be more concerns that the network protocols and/or applications have to deal with, such as wireless station mobility from one base station to another one within the network (handoff).

There are two modes of WLAN networks configurations: Infrastructure mode and Ah-Hoc mode. In Infrastructure mode, the wireless users, known as Wireless Stations (WSs) or Mobile Hosts (MH), are connected to a wired network through an Access Point (AP), also known as Base Station (BS), and all the traffic between the wireless users goes through that access point (AP) which is considered as the connecting point between the wired and wireless sections of the network. While in Ad-Hoc mode, the wireless users are totally and directly connected through wireless links without the use of an access point.

In this section, we discuss the WLAN Infrastructure configuration mode, and we will discuss the WLAN Ad-Hoc mode in details in an upcoming section (see Figure 1).

WI-FI NETWORKS CHALLENGES

Though, the above mentioned advantages of WLAN networks, there are some important challenges that can influence its design, implementation as well as its functionality. Most of these challenges are highly related with the inherited limitations of the wireless links nature. We present, in this section, some of these challenges and discuss how these challenges might influence TCP performance when implemented within such networks (Crow, Widjaja, Kim, & Sakai, 1997).

Frequency Band Allocation and Used Range

According to the standards, the operation of such networks requires that all the wireless users should be able to communicate over the same frequency band. Thus, licenses should be approved in order to use the requested frequency bands. In addition, the range of the used IEEE 802.11 standard is not sufficient to be used within large network structures.

Mobility of Wireless Stations and Available Bandwidth

The mobility of wireless LANs terminals needs adequate handoff mechanisms between transmission boundaries as well as routing algorithms. In addition, wireless terminals mobility represents a new challenge for TCP within Wi-Fi networks, as data packet delays and even losses increase over the network links during handoffs. In fact, the delay needed by the transmission of wireless information between the base stations might be long enough to invoke TCP congestion control algorithm. In this situation, TCP invokes its congestion control algorithm and decreases its data transmission rate to minimum leading to low network throughput. The available bandwidth of WLANs is normally lower than that of wired networks due to the limited and scarce resources of wireless links. Hence, if

Figure 1. Wireless wi-fi network

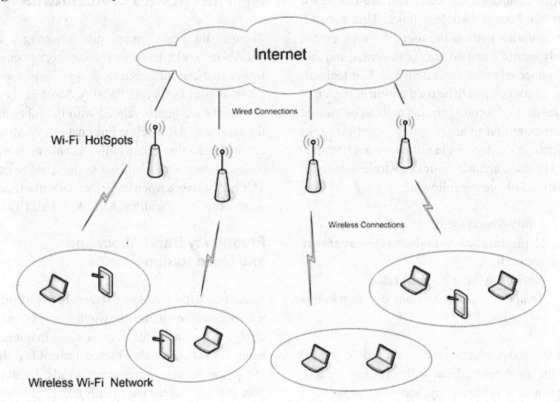

we imagine a network with high mobility rate, we conclude that the overall network throughput will always stay at low level which is considered as a bad performance and, in the mean time, waste of network's scarce resources (bandwidth).

Interference over the Wireless Links and Channel Errors

Using wireless links makes the communication between the users susceptible to data collisions, interference, and propagation effects as all the users are sharing the same frequency band. Also, the relatively high bit error rates over wireless links due to multipath fading and shadowing may corrupt packets in transmission. In addition, the well known "Hidden Terminal" problem, where a certain user or terminal start transmitting data without perceiving that there is another ongoing transmission over the wireless link, leads to data

collisions and interference over the network links. All these situations have a negative influence on TCP performance within the network. The corrupted data packets will force TCP to invoke its congestion control algorithm unnecessarily as there is no any congestion over the links.

Energy Efficiency

As the main apt of Wireless LANs is to provide free mobility to its users, it is expected that these users would use portable devices (such as laptops or mobiles). Hence, one of the most requirements of such networks terminals or devices is to be energy-efficient devices. As a result, all the protocols and applications developed to be used within such networks must deal with this concern.

Data Security

Again, the use of wireless transmission links makes it difficult to have secure data transmission sessions over the network. That is due to the fact that any user within the sender terminal transmission range can receive the transmitted data. However, in order to secure data transmission over the network, encryption is highly needed and recommended. Otherwise, though it is recommended using encryption for security concerns, this will increase the cost of network deployment and penalize its performance.

PROPOSED TCP SOLUTIONS FOR WI-FI NETWORKS

Unlike wired networks, where the main challenge for TCP is to react properly to data packet losses due to network congestion episodes, TCP faces more challenges when implemented within wireless networks. This is due to the fact that TCP must deal with more data packet loss episodes, other than network congestion, over the wireless links. In order to improve TCP performance within Wi-Fi networks, new TCP algorithms were developed to meet the requirements of such networks. In this section, we discuss the most known proposed solutions developed to be used within wireless networks.

We can categorize the work done in this domain into four major categories (Chen, Zhai, Wang, & Fang, 2002):

1. Split-Connection solutions,
2. Proxy-based solutions,
3. Link Layer solutions, and
4. End-to-End solutions.

We will detail here the proposed TCP solutions developed in each category and their main specifications.

Split-Connection Solutions

In this category, the proposed solutions apt for enhancing TCP performance by splitting each TCP connection into two connections at the base station side. This means that there will be one connection between the wireless station and the base station, which is a wireless connection, and another one from the base station to the other end of the connection, which is a wired connection in most cases. This configuration helps better tune the wireless connection in order to get better performance over the wireless links. In addition, splitting TCP connection into two connections helps to differentiate the problems due to wired links from those due to wireless links and consequently better deal with each one separately and more easily. For example, the wired part of the connection will stay unaware of the data losses due to wireless signal imperfections on the wireless part of the connection. Finally, this approach leads to improve the performance of TCP over the end-to-end connection, the connection from the TCP sender to the TCP receiver.

The idea of splitting the end-to-end connection was presented for the first time in (Badrinath, Acharya, & Imielinski, 1993). In this paper, the authors propose Split-Connection solution in order to improve wireless Internet access performance. Few years later, Indirect-TCP (I-TCP) was developed (Bakre & Badrinath, 1995; Bakre, 1996). M-TCP (Brown & Singh, 1997) is another example of TCP Split-Connection approach. We will see in the followings sections, the differences between these two approaches and the advantages/ disadvantages of each of them.

Indirect-TCP

Indirect-TCP (I-TCP) (Bakre & Badrinath, 1995) protocol is a Split-Connection solution, in which any TCP connection is split into two distinct TCP connections. One connection is the link between the wireless station and the base station or the access point over the wireless network and the other is between the base station and the fixed station on the wired network.

I-TCP protocol works as follows: the base station is the splitting point over the TCP connection between the wireless station and the fixed station. Any packet sent to the wireless station will be received firstly by the base station and then will be forwarded to the wireless station after sending an acknowledgement to the fixed station, and the same will be done when there is a packet sent to the fixed station. However, the fixed station does not recognize or even notice this process at the base station. As mentioned above, this process helps separate the problems caused by the wireless links from those caused by the wired links and better deal with them. In addition, this approach provides transparent handoffs of the wireless stations between different base stations, from the point of view of the fixed station, as each base station maintains all the necessary information of each wireless connection and transfers it to the new base station in case of handoff.

Though the above mentioned advantages of the I-TCP protocol, the main drawbacks of it are:

1. It breaks up the end-to-end semantics of TCP design aspects, as each part of the split connection (wired and wireless) has its own acknowledgement algorithm.
2. The control overhead of maintaining all the required information of each wireless connection at the base station in order to over relay this information to the new base station in case of handoff may lead to a performance degradation over the whole end-to-end TCP connection. This effect may be recognized as an extra delay over the network in case of wireless station handoff.

M-TCP

M-TCP (Brown & Singh, 1997) is another Split-Connection TCP protocol that functions mainly as I-TCP. It splits the TCP connection into two distinct ones, one connection between the wireless/mobile station and the base station and the other one is between the base station and the fixed station. Even though the main functionality of M-TCP is based on the same approach as I-TCP, the authors in Brown & Singh (1997) propose many enhancements in order to overcome the main drawbacks within I-TCP algorithm. Firstly, they manage to maintain the end-to-end semantics of TCP protocol by adding a new element that is called Supervisor Station within the network configuration. The main rule of that Supervision Host (SH) is to serve as a gateway that is connected to the wired network and to collect all the necessary information from the connected base stations. This configuration helps reduce the number of handoffs within the network as well as the performance degradation problems related to the handoff process. This is due to the fact that, in the above mentioned network configuration; one Supervisor Host is in charge of several base stations. Hence, the switching from a base station to another cannot be considered, and indeed does not invoke handoff process, as the two base stations belong to and are controlled by the same Supervision Host.

M-TCP works as follows: Unlike I-TCP protocol, in M-TCP, the Supervision Host does not acknowledge received data packets before receiving the corresponding acknowledgement from the wireless station. This is how M-TCP preserves TCP's end-to-end semantics. In the absence of the acknowledgement from the wireless station, M-TCP presumes that there is a wireless link problem or loss and consequently, it sends an acknowledgement with a zero window size to the sender side. The sender side, upon receiving this acknowledgement, enters freeze state where it freezes or stops all its ongoing transmissions as well as its RTO and congestion window parameters. The wireless station notifies the Supervision Host with a greeting packet when the wireless link is recovered. Accordingly, the Supervision Host notifies the sender side which, in turn, resumes its data transmission process starting from frozen state. The fact that M-TCP freezes its data transmission and maintains the same performance parameters as before losing the wireless link helps improve TCP performance over the network connection and avoids wasting the networks scarce resources (network bandwidth) as it avoids invoking the congestion control algorithm of TCP. In addition, it has been shown that M-TCP performs well within wireless networks that suffer from frequent wireless signal loss or disconnections between the wireless station and the base station.

Proxy-Based Solutions

Proxy-Based Solutions idea is to implement an intelligent agent at the network base stations. These agents aim to detect data packet losses over the wireless links and take the most adequate reactions to recover from these losses and to ensure better performance over the wireless links. These reactions may include duplicate acknowledgement suppression and/or local data retransmission. This approach helps separate the wireless data losses and its negative effects on the performance of the entire TCP connection as the implemented proxy agent at the base station handles the losses locally and without need of any interaction from the fixed station side. We present in this work SNOOP as an example of Proxy-Based solutions developed to enhance TCP performance within wireless networks.

SNOOP Protocol

SNOOP protocol (Balakrishnan, et al., 1995) is developed in order to improve TCP performance by introducing a SNOOP agent at the network-layer of the base station within the network. SNOOP protocol aims at preserving end-to-end TCP semantics. SNOOP agent monitors every packet that passes through the base station in both directions and caches them for performance improving as we will see later.

SNOOP protocol works as follows: TCP packets sent from the fixed station to the wireless station, and are not acknowledged yet, will be cached by the SNOOP module. Meanwhile, SNOOP agent keeps track of all the acknowledgments that are originating from the mobile station. The detection of data packet losses is recognized at the base station through either duplicate acknowledgments or local time-out expiration. In case of data packet loss, the SNOOP agent suppresses the duplicate acknowledgment, if any, and locally retransmits the lost data packet from its cache. According to this approach, packet losses problems due to wireless link imperfections stay hidden from the fixed station and the wired part of the connection as they are handled locally at the base station. The advantage here is that, as the fixed station has no knowledge about the packet loss over the connection, this avoids the unnecessarily invocation of TCP congestion control algorithm that may lead to TCP performance degradation over the network. In fact, invoking TCP congestion control algorithm for data packet losses that are not due to network congestion is considered as an aggressive reaction as well as waste of network resources.

However, TCP SACK option can be used to inform the sender of the lost data packets sent from the wireless stations to the fixed stations. Selective ACKnowledgment is sent to the wireless station by the base station when it notices a gap in the sequence numbers of the sent packets from the wireless station. Upon the reception of this selective acknowledgement, the wireless station retransmits the lost data packets to the base station.

SNOOP uses multicast groups and intelligent buffering in nearby base stations in order to ensure smooth handoffs and minimize its cost in terms of the connection performance. The base stations near any wireless station perform a multicast group and start buffering the latest data packets sent from the fixed station towards the wireless station. This process starts at the reception of a control message from the wireless station stating that a handoff process is initiated and that a certain base station is selected to handle the handoff and forward sent, by the fixed station, data packets to the wireless station. Choosing the base station that will handle the handoff is the responsibility of the concerned wireless station. This is done according to its signal strength and its communication quality with this base station. During handoff process, the chosen base station will proceed in transmitting data packets while the other base stations (in the multicasting group) will keep buffering data packets. This approach tends to minimize data losses and handoff delays and consequently, enhance end-to-end TCP performance over the network. However, although that the SNOOP protocol can enhance the performance of TCP within wireless networks during handoff situations, the overhead due to multicast information exchange within the base stations multicast group cannot be neglected.

Link Layer Solutions

The solutions of this category tend to hide the adverse characteristics and consequently the problems of wireless links from TCP through providing a reliable link layer configuration and sometimes error correction approaches at the link layer. The main advantage of such approach is to improve the reliability of communication independently of the higher-level protocol, such as TCP. Many link layer solutions had been developed in the literature (Chen, et al., 2002; Balakrishnan, et al., 1997). The proposed solutions can be classified into two main classes:

1. Error correction approaches (such as Forward Error Correction or FEC),
2. Data packets retransmission (Automatic Repeat reQuest messages or ARQ)

However, there are some link layer solutions that combine both the above classes such as AIRMAIL (Ayanoglu, Paul, LaPorta, Sabnani, & Gitlin, 1995) and TULIP (Parsa & Garcia-Luna-Aceves, 1999), discussed with some extent in the following sections. The gain from implementing both approaches, error correction approaches as well as link layer retransmissions, together is to get better performance in terms of both connection throughput and latency through correcting the wireless link errors and local retransmissions.

AIRMAIL

Since high bit error rate of the wireless link is one of the major problems for TCP over wireless networks, it could be a good idea to hide such problems or errors for TCP. This can be done through reliable link layer protocol that helps TCP to avoid unnecessary invoking its congestion control algorithm and wasting network resources in order to recover from such losses. This, indeed, leads to better TCP performance over the network. An example of such a reliable link layer protocol is AIRMAIL (AsymmetrIc Reliable Mobile Access In Link-layer) (Ayanoglu, et al., 1995). As mentioned above, AIRMAIL uses two well-known link error recovery approaches, FEC and ARQ. Asymmetry in the design of the protocol tends to decrease the processing overhead at the wireless stations and to put most of the data and acknowledgement processing at the base station side. This is due to the fact of power constraints and limited processing capabilities of the wireless stations.

We notice that there are three levels of FEC included within AIRMAIL protocol, in order to provide high level of data error correction within different wireless error rates over the connection. These levels are:

1. Bit level FEC,
2. Byte level FEC,
3. Packet level FEC.

The problem with AIRMAIL proposed solution, though its ability to deal with wireless link errors; is its inability to handle long disconnections due to wireless devices handoffs. This leads to TCP congestion control algorithm invocation and thus TCP performance degradation within the network.

TULIP

As its name states, Transport Unaware Link Improvement Protocol, TULIP is a TCP unaware link layer protocol (Parsa & Garcia-Luna-Aceves, 1999; Parsa & Garcia-Luna-Aceves, 2000). The main idea of TULIP approach is the usage of link layer selective acknowledgement algorithm in order to invoke data retransmission process. This is done locally at the link layer to recover from data lost packets due to wireless links imperfections. In order to have fast recovery action over the wireless link, these selective acknowledgements have a higher priority level than the other data packets over the connection. This approach helps avoiding TCP duplicate acknowledgement generation for out of order data packets arrival. Hence, it improves the TCP performance over the end-to-end connection. The approach of TULIP based on a local recovery from data packet losses is similar to the approach used within SNOOP solution, as both of them tend to hide the wireless links problems from the rest of the network and mainly from TCP.

The main drawback of most link layer proposed solutions could be their negative effect on TCP functionality as they could result in unnecessary TCP fast retransmission algorithm invocation at the TCP sender side. This is due to the fact that link layer protocols have much finer retransmission timeout granularities than TCP timers. In addition, link layer protocols do not guarantee an in-order data packets delivery over the link. This link layer protocols behavior leads to an out-of-order data packets reception at the TCP receiver side, and consequently TCP duplicate acknowledgements generation, and unnecessary fast retransmission algorithm invocation at the TCP sender side. This means that, TCP sender will send the out-of-order data packets that are already had been locally retransmitted by the link layer causing redundant double retransmissions over the connection. The above process could result in TCP performance degradation over the network links in terms of network bandwidth.

End-to-End Solutions

Unlike the above mentioned solutions, end-to-end solutions tend to modify TCP functions and algorithms in order to resolve the wireless links problems or to recover from data packet losses due to wireless links imperfections directly by TCP itself. End-to-end solutions are transport layer solutions. TCP SACK or Selective AC-Knoweledgement option is one of those kinds of solutions (Chen, et al., 2002). The TCP SACK aim is to recover from multiple data packet losses within the network faster than within the traditional TCP recovery algorithm. Other solutions tend to predict imminent handoffs within the network attempting to avoid unnecessary TCP congestion control invocation. Fast Retransmission/Fast Recovery algorithm, TCP SACK, and Freeze-TCP are some examples of end-to-end TCP performance enhancement solutions within wireless networks.

Fast Retransmit

TCP Fast Retransmit algorithm can be considered as one of the first and simplest end-to-end solutions that aim to enhance TCP performance within wireless networks. We mention here that Fast Retransmission algorithm was proposed in (Caceres & Iftode, 2001) in order to overcome the problem of high latency and data packet losses over network links during handoff process. The main idea of Fast Retransmit algorithm is to respond to the received duplicate acknowledgements at the TCP sender side by immediate retransmission of the corresponding lost data packet without waiting the TCP timer to expire. This action leads to better and faster recovery of data losses and better usage of the available network bandwidth.

Selective Acknowledgement

TCP selective acknowledgement or TCP SACK enables a TCP SACK-enabled terminal to acknowledge multiple data packets lost using only one acknowledgement packet. Upon the reception of such acknowledgement, TCP SACK sender sends all the lost data packets mentioned in the received acknowledgement. This is done in only one RTT without need to wait for the TCP timer to expire. In (Balakrishnan, et al., 1997) the authors show that TCP SACK is a good solution over wireless links where data packet losses occur in bursts (losing multiple data packets at the same time).

Freeze-TCP

Freeze-TCP (Goff, Moronski, Phatak, & Gupta, 2003) is an end-to-end solution that does not rely on any other intermediate node (such as the base station) within the network and does not need any modification of the network's nodes. In this approach, the wireless station keeps observing the strength of its received signal in order to predict an imminent disconnection due to signal fading or a handoff situation. If this is the case, the wireless station sends an acknowledgement that notifies the fixed station with a zero window size. In its turn, the fixed station, upon the reception of such acknowledgement stops all the ongoing transmission and freezes all its timers, including the retransmission one. However, when the wireless station recognizes the wireless link recovery, it sends three duplicate acknowledgements to the fixed station, in order to invoke its fast retransmission algorithm. Though that, Freeze-TCP helps improve the performance of TCP connection over wireless networks without the need of any modification or interaction of intermediate nodes. The accuracy of the wireless station to notice or recognize the wireless link disconnection is the master key of its performance improvement or enhancement.

DISCUSSION

As Wi-Fi networks were one of the most first technology that is used to connect wireless users to the wired Internet, the proposed solutions divide the TCP connection into two different ones and deal with each one separately according to its communication media characteristics.

In addition to TCP end-to-end semantics violation by such approaches, the network security concern as encrypting data communication over the TCP connection could not be achieved within networks that implement such approaches. With encrypted data packets over the connection, the base station will not be able to access the data packets and hence to react properly. In addition, the high control overhead at the network base station may lead to network bottleneck at heavy traffic situations and consequently extra delay over the connection. This would result in TCP performance degradation over the connection.

We also cannot neglect the negative effect of some of these approaches (such as link layer proposed ones) on TCP performance due to the link layer local retransmissions algorithm and the big differences in the timers' granularity between link layer and TCP algorithms. This again could result in TCP performance degradation over the connection.

TCP OVER WIMAX

IEEE 802.16e, also known as WiMAX (Worldwide Interoperability for Microwave Access), denotes a set of standards for high performance Metropolitan Area Networks (MANs). In addition, it is, sometimes, considered as a last mile access solution for the Internet users. Consequently, it is important to consider the performance of TCP within such networks, given that most of the Internet traffic is TCP/IP. WiMAX was mainly developed to provide high data rate services, high users' mobility, and wide coverage at low cost.

WiMAX might be viewed as wireless networks extension or even a less expensive alternative for cable and DSL broadband access configurations.

WiMAX standards define both Physical (PHY) and Medium Access Control (MAC) layers of the wireless interfaces. MAC layer of WiMAX standard supports both point-to-multipoint and mesh topology networks and is capable to deal with shared access links, such as wireless links. For example, in point-to-multipoint network configurations, the network is configured in a base station/subscriber stations model, such as wireless cellular networks. Theoretically, WiMAX can reach data transmission rate of 120Mbps or more over 50 km coverage area, according to the modulation algorithm used as well as the wireless frequency range used (Halepovic, Wu, Williamson, & Ghaderi, 2008). WiMAX does not support Quality of Service (QoS) features itself, as a standard, but it gives the possibilities to network administrators to employ QoS policies over the network. This possibility is due to the fact that MAC layer is connection-oriented. Thus the connection between the base station and the wireless station can be mapped to different MAC connections according to the required services. For example, a TCP connection could be mapped into two MAC connections, one for each TCP communication transfer direction.

Even that WiMAX might be considered as an extension of the Wi-Fi technology over wireless networks, WiMAX is developed for long-range infrastructure networks and not for short-range home/office networks as Wi-Fi. In addition, as mentioned above, WiMAX is capable of supporting QoS policies over the networks, which is not available in Wi-Fi technology (see Figure 2).

WIMAX NETWORKS CHALLENGES

WiMAX networks are wireless networks, meaning that they are subjected to most wireless environment related problems. High bit error rates over the communication links, signal fading, weather effects, and signal disconnections are some of these problems. However, the most important problem that influences TCP performance within such networks is the asymmetry of WiMAX networks configuration. For example, in a point-to-multipoint WiMAX configuration, the base station controls all the data packets exchange between the network's base station and the connected wireless stations. Data packets transmission is done through two unidirectional connections. The one transmitting packets from the wireless station to the base station is called the uplink, and the other that transmitting packets from the base station towards the base station is called the downlink. However, the base station is charged of allocating the required bandwidth for each wireless station uplink upon the reception of bandwidth request message from the concerned wireless station (Park, Kim, Kim, & Kim, 2008).

Having two different communications links for sending data packets and receiving acknowledgements does not really reflect the actual network conditions for data packets transmission. This in turn, can lead to TCP congestion control algorithm misbehavior as it depends on the acknowledgements arrival at the sender side in order to increase its data transmission rate or its congestion window. In addition, if the downlink, where the acknowledgments are received by the wireless station, experiences high delay, the delayed acknowledgments may lead to TCP sender side congestion control algorithm invocation and thus unnecessarily TCP performance degradation. However, these unacknowledged data packets might be correctly received at the receiver side. Thus, we may conclude, from the above, that the performance of TCP within WiMAX networks depends not only on the characteristics of the uplink but also depends on those of the downlink used to receive acknowledgements.

Figure 2. Wireless WiMAX network

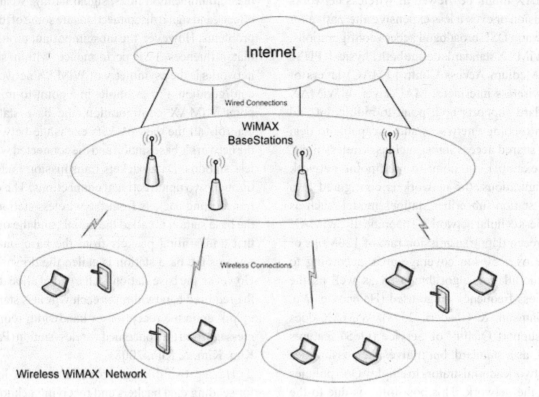

PROPOSED TCP SOLUTIONS FOR WIMAX NETWORKS

Many TCP variants were developed and proposed in order to enhance TCP performance within heterogeneous wired-wireless networks such as WiMAX. Most of these variants tend to distinguish data packet loss cause over the TCP connection (congestion related or wireless related losses) and react differently in front of each data packet loss cause in order to recover from data losses. Most of these proposed variants incorporate bandwidth estimation algorithms that tend to estimate the available bandwidth over the TCP connection. Some of these proposed TCP algorithms are discussed briefly in this section. We notice that these TCP variants can also be used within other wireless data networks, such as wireless ad hoc networks.

TCP-Jersey

TCP-Jersey (Xu, Tian, & Ansari, 2004) is a TCP variant that is capable of differentiating between data packet losses due to wireless channel errors from those due to network congestion. TCP-Jersey incorporates two components: the Available Bandwidth Estimator (ABE), and the Congestion Warning (CW) router configuration. The Available Bandwidth Estimator (ABE) within the TCP sender tends to estimate the connection available bandwidth through monitoring the rate of received acknowledgements. According to the estimated bandwidth, TCP-Jersey re-adjusts its data transmission rate or the congestion window size. TCP-Jersey calculates and re-adjusts its data transmission rate once per each RTT. While, the Congestion Warning (CW) is a configuration of network routers. Within such configuration, the routers notify the wireless stations of an imminent congestion over the TCP connection through marking the data packets travelling towards the wireless station. These marks help TCP sender to differentiate between losses due to congestion and losses due to wireless channel errors. When the TCP-Jersey sender recognizes that there is an imminent congestion over the TCP connection, it re-adjusts its data transmission rate and its slow-start threshold to the estimated congestion window size. TCP-Jersey keeps most of the TCP-Reno implemented algorithms, and replaces only TCP-Reno's Fast Retransmit mechanism with an explicit retransmit mechanism. The main difference between these mechanisms is that TCP-Jersey does not halve its congestion window size after data loss episode within the connection, as does TCP-Reno's Fast Retransmit mechanism.

TCP-Vegas

Another enhancement of TCP's congestion control algorithm is the network congestion avoidance algorithm implemented within TCP Vegas (Brakmo, O'Malley, & Peterson, 1994). TCP-Vegas relies on measured RTT values of sent packets to extend Reno's retransmission mechanisms. According to this measurement, the RTO value is updated. When a duplicate acknowledgement is received, Vegas checks if the difference between the current time and the timestamp recorded for the first unacknowledged segment (i.e. its round trip time) is greater than the timeout value. If so, then it retransmits the segment without having to wait for three duplicate acknowledgements. Also, TCP-Vegas uses round trip time values to calculate the actual transmission rate in the network. Hence, by comparing this value with the expected throughput in the network, TCP-Vegas decides how to adapt its transmission rate.

TCP-Vegas still contains Reno's coarse-grained timeout code as a fallback mechanism. Notice that the congestion window should only be reduced due to losses that happened at the current sending rate, and not due to losses that happened at an earlier higher rate. In TCP-Reno, it is possible to decrease the congestion window more than once for losses that occurred during one RTT interval. In contrast, TCP-Vegas only decreases the congestion window if the retransmitted segment was previously sent after the last decrease. Any losses that happened before the last window decrease do not imply that the network is congested for the current congestion window size, and therefore, do not imply that it should be decreased again. This change is motivated by the fact that TCP-Vegas detects losses much sooner than TCP-Reno (Brakmo, et al., 1994).

TCP-Westwood

Another way to improve the performance of TCP was to implement a bandwidth estimation algorithm as in TCP-Westwood (Mascolo, Casetti, Gerla, Sanadidi, & Wang, 2001) variant. The bandwidth estimation algorithm tends to estimate the available bandwidth over the connection through measuring and averaging the rate of the returning acknowledgements. TCP-Westwood then adapts its data transmission rate according to the available bandwidth over the connection. This enhancement improves TCP performance over wireless data networks as it optimizes the usage of the available bandwidth.

TCP-Westwood is a sender-side modification of the TCP congestion window algorithm that is intended to bring performance improvements to TCP New-Reno and TCP-Reno in wired as well as wireless networks. In fact, there are two variants of TCP-Westwood, one is based on TCP-Reno and the other is based on TCP New-Reno. The improvement is also targeted to be more significant in wireless networks with lossy links. TCP-Westwood (Mascolo, et al., 2001) relies on end-to-end bandwidth estimation to identify the cause of packet loss (congestion or wireless channel effect), which is a major problem in TCP New-Reno, and then adapts the congestion window size accordingly. This loss cause identification process is based on measured round trip time values. When the pipe size, calculated by multiplying the estimated bandwidth (*BWE*) by the minimum round trip time value (*RTT min*) is smaller than congestion window, it is more likely that packet losses are due to congestion. This is because the connection is using a congestion window value much higher than its share of pipe size, thus congestion is likely to be the cause of packet losses. On the other hand, when the condition "*BWE×RTTmin*" >*congestion window* is satisfied, it indicates that wireless channel errors are more likely to be the cause of the packet losses. The key idea of TCP-Westwood is to exploit TCP acknowledgement packets to derive rather sophisticated measurements as follows. First, the source performs an end-to end estimation of the bandwidth available along a TCP connection by measuring and averaging the rate of returning acknowledgements. Second, after a packet loss episode (i.e. the source receives three duplicate acknowledgements or a timeout) the source uses the measured bandwidth to properly set the congestion window and the slow-start threshold. By backing off to congestion window and slow-start threshold values that are based on the estimated available bandwidth (rather than simply halving the current values as TCP New-Reno does), TCP-Westwood avoids overly conservative reductions of congestion window and slow-start threshold; and thus resulting in achieving higher throughput.

TCP-Veno

TCP-Veno (Cheng & Soung, 2003) is another TCP variant that tends to improve TCP performance within the wireless networks through distinguishing the data packet loss cause within the network. It differentiates between network congestion induced losses and wireless related losses. TCP-Veno incorporates a congestion control algorithm similar to that used in TCP Vegas in order to classify the cause of data packet losses over the connection. However, TCP-Veno is a congestion

control enhancement transport protocol that reacts after a loss episodes and not a congestion avoidance algorithm as in TCP-Vegas.

TCP-Veno uses a threshold value in order to represent the network conditions (congestion or non-congestion). Then, when TCP-Veno recognizes data packet loss over the connection, it refers to that threshold to identify the data packet loss cause according to these two factors.

However, TCP-Veno may misinterpret the data packet loss cause in case of frequent and consecutive data packet losses over the connection.

DISCUSSION

We have seen that in order to enhance TCP performance within WiMAX networks new TCP variants had been proposed to estimate the available bandwidth over the connection. The new proposals can be considered as a new step towards more intelligent TCP algorithms. These proposed bandwidth estimation algorithms tend to help TCP to recognize data packet loss cause over the connection (congestion induced or wireless related problems). Distinguishing data packet loss cause within the network is an important step in the TCP evolution and enhancement process as it overcomes the main challenge that TCP faces when implemented within wireless or heterogeneous data networks. In fact, TCP is not capable of differentiating between data packet loss causes over the connection and consequently not able to deal with wireless environment induced losses.

In addition, TCP loss differentiation capable variants have the advantage of maintaining the TCP end-to-end semantics.

We notice that most of these variants depend on bandwidth estimation algorithms over the connection in order to differentiate between different data packet loss causes within the network (mainly congestion and non congestion induces losses). These algorithms prove to enhance the performance of TCP within wireless environments, where the error bit rates over the communication path are noticeably high and occur frequently. However, in some TCP proposals, considering a congestion avoidance algorithm that aims at detecting imminent congestion episodes over the connection would help improving TCP performance through avoiding frequent TCP congestion control algorithm invocations and consequently leads to better utilization of the available network and nodes resources (Bandwidth and energy).

TCP OVER MOBILE CELLULAR NETWORKS

Nowadays, millions of people around the world are using their mobile devices to make phone calls, to surf the Internet, or to check their mails. And this can be done wherever we are and while moving without losing the connection. Cellular networks are an infrastructure networks that helps wireless devices connect to the traditional switched telephone network. The development of Cellular networks has been through three different generations, each with different applied technology:

1. Analog voice,
2. Digital voice,
3. Digital voice and data.

In the first generation, cellular networks implemented analog technologies to accomplish voice transmission. In order to increase the cellular network capacity, digital technologies were used in the second generation (2G). Using both digital Time Division Multiple Access (TDMA) and Code Division Multiple Access (CDMA) technologies helps increasing the number of wireless users within the cellular network configuration. In addition to the increasing number of cellular network users, the networks of the second generation are more secure as the digitization of voice signals can be coded and encrypted.

The third generation (3G) has incorporated both voice and data services for the wireless users though high speed packet-switching for data transmission and circuit-switching for voice transmission. The technologies used in the third generation cellular networks helped the wireless device users to connect to internet through there devices and while moving without interrupting the provided service (see Figure 3).

MOBILE CELLULAR NETWORKS CHALLENGES

The main challenges of Mobile Cellular networks are almost the same ones within other wireless networks. The main challenges within such networks arise from their wireless communication links. Thus, wireless high bit error rates or wireless links imperfections, weather conditions, multipath interference, urban obstacles all represent important challenges for TCP performance within mobile cellular networks. In addition to all these challenges, we mention also the mobility of the wireless users which is one of the most important aspects and characteristics within such networks. This mobility leads to frequent handoffs and temporary disconnections of the wireless users. Taking into consideration the reaction of TCP in front of disconnection situations, by invoking its congestion control algorithm, the wireless connection and the communication between users might be prolonged due to its backing off algorithm. This action can be considered as aggressive from TCP and, at the same time, unnecessary. Each failed attempt to retransmit TCP data packets or acknowledgements during the disconnection period of time will increase the TCP sender's timer. This is because TCP increases its retransmission timer exponentially after each failed retransmission attempt. This phenomenon is known as a "serial time-out" and leads to high TCP connection inactivity and unnecessary waste of network

Figure 3. Wireless cellular network

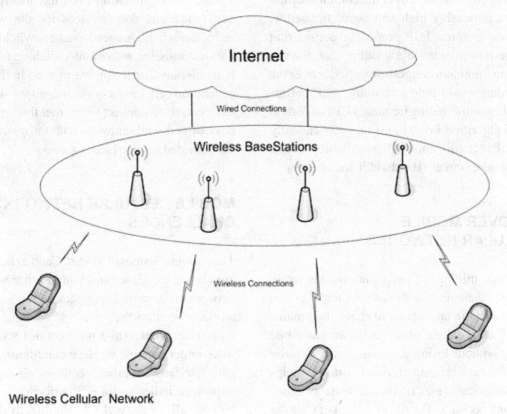

resources as it underutilizes the networks' available bandwidth.

Link asymmetry within the network represents the case when the communication passes through two different paths in each direction (forward and reverse directions), in which the characteristics and transmission capacitances are not the same (Balakrishnan, et al., 1997). For TCP connections, this type of communications might cause performance degradation problems within the network, due to the different delays and available bandwidth over each communication path. One of the most reasons of some TCP variants performance degradation is its self-clocking algorithms dependency on the received acknowledgements. In such algorithms, loosing acknowledgements leads to malfunctioning and sometimes misbehavior of TCP algorithms. For example, the misinterpretation of a data loss due to wireless link imperfections

as a network congestion condition should lead to unnecessarily low throughput over the network and consequently TCP performance degradation as well as network resources waste.

PROPOSED TCP SOLUTIONS FOR MOBILE CELLULAR NETWORKS

TCP suffers from performance degradation when implemented within heterogeneous networks (mixed wired and wireless networks) such as wireless cellular networks. Thus, many TCP enhancements were proposed in order to improve its performance within such networks. Some of these proposed TCP solutions are based on the idea of data packet loss differentiation algorithms. Such algorithms aim at explicitly informing the TCP sender of the cause of data packet losses over the connection. Within cellular networks, the main two causes of data packet losses are network congestion and wireless link imperfections. According to the identified data packet loss cause, TCP sender should react properly in order to recover from this loss and better use of the network available resources.

We mention here, that most of TCP enhancements proposed to be implemented within wireless networks (such as Wi-Fi, and WiMAX) could be used within cellular networks as the main characteristics of such networks are the same.

Freeze-TCP (Goff, et al., 2003) is one of the end-to-end proposed solutions that tend to improve TCP performance within wireless networks, such as cellular networks. Freeze-TCP, as discussed earlier in this chapter, does not imply any modifications on the intermediate nodes within the network. It has been showed that, Freeze-TCP, can handle the problems caused by wireless devices handoffs or wireless signal loss due to obstacles, and improve TCP performance in terms of throughput within the network. Freeze-TCP is described earlier in this chapter.

Also, TCP New-Reno, TCP SACK, TCP-Vegas, and TCP Westwood are other TCP enhanced variants to improve TCP performance within wireless cellular networks.

TCP New-Reno

Another modification of TCP congestion control algorithm is TCP New-Reno (Floyd, Henderson, & Gurtov, 2004). TCP New-Reno deploys partial acknowledgements that help to notify the TCP sender that the following segment in the sequence number is lost. This approach leads to less data packets retransmissions over the connection, and hence a better utilization of the available bandwidth. In TCP New-Reno, partial acknowledgements do not take TCP out of Fast Recovery. Instead, partial acknowledgements received during Fast Recovery are treated as an indication that the packet immediately following

the acknowledged packet in the sequence space has been lost, and should be retransmitted. Thus, when multiple packets are lost from a single data window, TCP New-Reno can recover without a retransmission timeout. It retransmits one lost packet per Round-Trip Time (RTT) until all of the lost packets from the window have been retransmitted. TCP New-Reno remains in Fast Recovery until all of the outstanding data, ever since Fast Recovery was initiated, are acknowledged (Fall & Floyd, 1996). This way the TCP New-Reno sender avoids to retransmit the entire congestion window that contains the lost packets; it resends only the lost ones and eliminates the unnecessary retransmissions. This approach enables TCP to better deal with the problem of multiple random data losses within the same congestion window, as it does not decrease its data transmission rate after each lost packet. Instead, it decreases its data transmission rate only once at the beginning of the Fast Retransmit/ Fast Recovery phase. TCP New-Reno stays in this phase until retransmitting all the lost data packets. TCP New-Reno can recover from multiple losses, and is therefore well suited for the mobile wireless environment, where multiple data packet losses are likely to occur during the same transmission window. However, during this recovery, the TCP New-Reno sender retransmits only one packet per RTT, since it must wait for the partial acknowledgement from the receiver side to know the next packet to be retransmitted. Consequently, when multiple losses occur, TCP New-Reno usually recovers after a considerable delay, which is a major drawback (Michel, Nelson, & José, 2003).

TCP SACK

Traditional TCP implementations use an acknowledgement number field that contains cumulative acknowledgement, indicating that TCP receiver has received all of the data up to the indicated byte. A Selective ACKnowledgement (SACK) option allows receivers to additionally report non-sequential data they have received. The SACK option is used within an acknowledgement packet to indicate which packets were received precisely (Fall & Floyd, 1996) and thus allows the sender to deduce which packets had been lost. This option aims to speed up the retransmission of lost packets and avoids retransmitting the whole data window. Adding SACK to TCP does not change the basic underlying congestion control algorithms. TCP SACK implementation showed to be robust in the presence of out-of-order packets and uses retransmit timeouts as the recovery method of last resort. The main difference between TCP SACK and TCP New-Reno is the behavior when multiple packets are dropped from one data window (Fall & Floyd, 1996). TCP SACK sender maintains a list of segments deemed to be missing (based on all the SACKs received) and sends new or retransmitted data when the estimated number of packets in the path is less than the congestion window. When a retransmitted packet is itself dropped, the SACK implementation detects the drop with a retransmission timeout, retransmitting the dropped packet and then slow-starting. TCP SACK exits Fast Recovery under the same conditions as TCP New-Reno. The SACK option of TCP will acknowledge the packets that have been correctly received and the sender will deduce the lost packets from the received SACK coming from the receiver side. This algorithm improves data packets transmission over the connection. On the other side, it complicates the calculation process at the sender side as it should retain a complete list of sequence numbers of all the transmitted data packets in order to deduce the numbers of lost ones when needed. This complexity might affect the overall TCP performance.

Both TCP-Vegas (Brakmo, et al., 1994), and TCP-Westwood (Mascolo, et al., 2001) were discussed earlier in this chapter.

DISCUSSION

Wireless cellular networks add a new challenge for TCP performance due to the mobility of nodes that induces temporary wireless signal disconnections. However, the wireless connection still represents only one-hop within the overall network configuration. Thus, the efforts were oriented to enhance TCP variants that were developed for Wi-Fi and WiMAX networks in order to achieve higher throughput and minimize the unnecessary data retransmissions over the TCP connection.

Taking into consideration nodes' mobility of wireless cellular networks, the energy consumption of such nodes becomes a new concern when developing and implementing new communication protocols within such networks. Saving the wireless nodes energetic resources (batteries) through minimizing its energy consumption due to transmitting/receiving data packets helps keeping them operational much longer. While minimizing the energy consumption in data packets transmission/reception process is a hard task, reducing or minimizing unnecessary data packet retransmissions over the connection may play an important role in achieving that purpose. Hence, the proposed solutions that aim at improving TCP performance within wireless cellular networks, even that these solutions were mainly concerned by enhancing the network achievable throughput, the proposed algorithms help minimize TCP end-points energy consumption through avoiding unnecessary data packets retransmissions over the TCP connection.

TCP OVER MOBILE AD HOC NETWORKS

As mentioned in the beginning of this chapter, Mobile Ad Hoc networks are classified within the ad hoc wireless networks category. These networks are known as infrastructure-less, decentralized administration networks, and their

Figure 4. Wireless ad hoc network

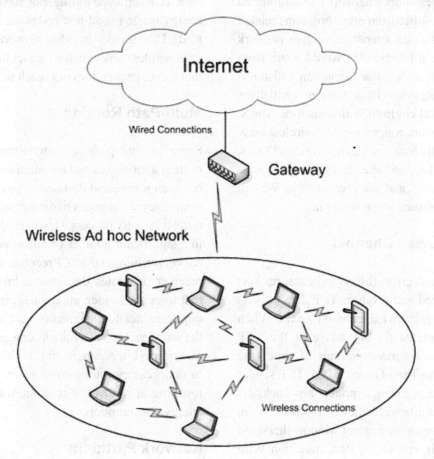

devices are characterized by independency and self-organization capabilities.

Wireless Mobile Ad hoc networks are wireless networks where all the terminals are totally connected to each other through wireless links. In such networks no infrastructure cables are needed, which makes it a good solutions for networking purposes in temporary places or wherever infrastructure deployment is difficult to accomplish or even not possible to be done. The communication within such networks is realized in a multi-hop fashion. The configuration of these networks forces each station within the network to act as a terminal, switch, router and even server for the rest of the stations over the network. The multi-role of each of the network's terminals and the independency of each of them makes them

inexpensive and easy to implement, as there is no need for special network devices (such as routers, switches, or servers) or any infrastructure requirements (see Figure 4).

MOBILE AD HOC NETWORKS CHALLENGES

As all wireless networks, Mobile Ad Hoc Networks are prone to many challenges that may influence its performance as well as that of the TCP when implemented within it. First of all, Mobile Ah hoc networks inherit all the challenges and problems of the wireless links. However, these challenges are amplified, as all the communication links within ad hoc networks are wireless and not only the last hop as in wireless mobile networks. In addition, ad hoc networks suffer from other problems related to their specific characteristics, such as network partitions, route failures that would result from nodes mobility, node battery depletion, and multi-hop communications. Thus, the new challenges that TCP would confront within such networks, other than network congestion, are: wireless lossy channels, multi-path routing, network partitions, network topology and the surrounding environment, link failures, and power constraints. We will discuss these issues in the following.

Wireless Lossy Channel

Wireless channel errors (bit errors) cause packets to get corrupted and result in TCP data packets (segments or acknowledgements) losses. When acknowledgements do not arrive at the TCP sender within a certain amount of time (the Retransmission Time-Out or RTO), TCP sender retransmits the segment, exponentially backs off its retransmission timer for the next retransmission, reduces its congestion control window threshold (SSThreshold), and closes its Congestion Window (CWND) to one segment. Frequent wireless channel errors lead to having continuously small congestion window at the sender side resulting in low connection throughput (Liu & Singh, 2001). The appropriate behavior in such situation is to simply retransmit lost packets without shrinking the congestion window to avoid the delay and the energy consumed and in turn to increase the congestion window size. It is important here to mention that, in the case of CSMA/CA (802.11) based networks, there will be an error correction algorithm; meaning that not all the packets will be lost. In fact, some of them will be corrected and resent again correctly while other will not reach the destination. Furthermore, the CSMA/CA correction action introduces some delay in the network and in the mean time will waste some of the bandwidth resource. Obviously, the delay introduced will increase the RTT value resulting in

poor TCP achieved throughput and also a certain energy waste (as ad hoc nodes are battery operated). This situation in ad hoc networks happens on each wireless link which increases the probability that a data packet does not reach the destination.

Multi-Path Routing

Some routing protocols implement multi-path routing approaches and maintain multiple routes between source and destination pairs, in order to minimize the frequency of route re-computation or route discovery process. However, this may result in a significant number of out-of sequence data packets arriving at the TCP receiver side. The TCP receiver generates duplicate acknowledgments that force the sender, upon the reception of three duplicate acknowledgments that acknowledge the same packet, to invoke its congestion control algorithm (Liu & Singh, 2001). This action leads to unnecessary retransmissions by TCP sender, resulting in bandwidth resource waste and high energy consumption.

Network Partitions

Wireless ad hoc networks may periodically get partitioned for several seconds at a time. If the TCP sender and receiver find themselves in different partitions, all the data packets will be dropped. Hence, TCP sender invokes its congestion control algorithm. If the network remains partitioned for an important amount of time relatively to the Retransmission Time-Out, the situation gets even worse because of phenomena called serial timeouts. A serial timeout is a condition wherein multiple consecutive retransmissions of the same segment are transmitted to the TCP receiver while it is disconnected from the sender side. All these retransmissions are thus lost. Since the retransmission timer at the sender side is doubled with each unsuccessful retransmission attempt (until it reaches 64 sec), several consecutive failures can lead to inactivity that might last for one or two minutes even when the sender and receiver get reconnected (Liu & Singh, 2001). However, the most adequate solution here is to stop the data transmission (to avoid flooding the network with packets that cannot be delivered) until the TCP sender gets reconnected to the receiver.

Topology and Environment

Nodes location and the nature of their surrounding environment determine which nodes can contact each other and the amount of interference from other nodes (Westin, 2003). If the nodes are located close to each other, there will be a greater chance that the data will not have to make as many hops as in a network where the nodes are further apart. It is clear that the energy consumption of a mobile node increases with the distance between the two communicating nodes. For that, it is better that the nodes communicate through a minimum number of hops. Also, networks with a dense concentration of nodes will experience more contention for the available capacity and hence more collisions and interferences leading to high TCP data packet losses and thus frequent TCP sender congestion control algorithm triggering. In addition, the environment affects TCP performance in a similar way. Actually, walls and other objects that hinder radio transmissions will lower the effect of high node density.

Link Failures

In case of nodes' mobility, each node might move out of the communication range of old neighbors or into the communication range of new ones. This leads to break the established routes (link failures) and also to trigger the establishment of new ones within the network. The implemented ad hoc routing protocol is the one in charge of recovering from the link failure allowing maintaining the communication session between the involved end points. Usually, a broken route results in performance degradation, since no data can be

exchanged during the time where the new route is not yet available. To overcome this problem the network layer should find a new route as quickly as possible to resume the dropped communication. In fact, high mobility is not always a bad thing for ad hoc networks. Some authors have observed that mobility can increase performance by distributing traffic more evenly over the network (Johansson, Larsson, Hedman, Mielczarek, & Degermark, 1999). The problem with TCP in the case of link failure situation is that after resuming data communication session, TCP sender starts from the Slow-Start phase, with minimum CWND threshold over the links. Indeed, during a link failure multiple data packets can be lost in a burst fashion. TCP sender shrinks its CWND to minimum considering that the loss is due to congestion. However, in case of link failure, the new discovered route might have higher link capacity compared to the old lost one. Thus, TCP sender will waste the available bandwidth (which is a scarce network resource) over the connection.

Power Constraints

Within wireless ad hoc networks, the devices are independent and battery operated. Thus, in order to ensure the network connectivity, it is obvious to increase the network nodes lifetime as long as possible. Increasing the nodes' battery lifetime can be done through minimizing the node's energy consumption. In addition, losing a node due to battery depletion leads to broken communication sessions (link failure) even if the node is not the sender or the receiver side of that session. This is because each node within the network forwards data packets of its neighbors when it participates to multi-hop path. Thus, we get the same effect on TCP performance as in link failure case.

Proposed TCP solutions for Mobile Ad hoc Networks

All the above factors affect the performance of TCP within wireless ad hoc networks in different ways. They are all having a great influence on both TCP connection throughput and may also have an influence on node's energy consumption. Let us now discuss the main TCP enhancement approaches to improve its performance within wireless ad hoc networks. There are many proposals introduced in order to improve the TCP performance within wireless ad hoc networks. Some proposals dealt directly with enhancing TCP, others dealt with other OSI layers such as network layer and link layer. Also, some other proposed solutions that improve TCP performance through cross layer interactions. We discuss in the following the main proposed solutions to improve TCP performance within wireless ad hoc networks while dividing them into two categories:

1. TCP enhancements at the transport layer proposals,
2. TCP enhancements through cross layer proposals.

Transport Layer Solutions

Many proposals that only deal with the transport layer were introduced in order to enhance TCP performance within wireless ad hoc networks. Fixed-RTO (Dyer & Boppana, 2001) and TCP DOOR (Wang, Valla, Sanadidi, Ng, & Gerla, 2002) are examples of those proposals. We discuss here the main idea of both mechanisms and their issues within such networks.

Fixed RTO (Dyer & Boppana, 2001) is a sender side based mechanism that does not imply feedback messages over the connection. This mechanism is able to distinguish between link failure induced and congestion induced data packet losses. When two consecutives retransmission timeout expiration occurs, the TCP sender interprets the loss as a

link failure induced loss. Hence, it retransmits the unacknowledged data packet but keeps the RTO value un-changed. Remind having the same situation in the case of standard TCP implementation leads to using "exponential" back-off algorithm. In Fixed-RTO, the RTO values remains fixed until the failed link is recovered and the retransmitted data packet is acknowledged. The assumption that any two consecutive retransmission timeouts are the exclusive results of link failures requires more investigations, as it may be also the case with persistent network congestion. In addition, this solution takes into consideration only two of the wireless ad hoc network data packet loss cases, and ignores the wireless channel related losses which are also common within such environments.

TCP Detection of Out-of-Order and Response (TCP DOOR) (Wang, et al., 2002) is an end-to-end TCP enhancement solution that does not imply any intermediate nodes cooperation. TCP DOOR deals mainly with out-of-order data packets over the connection. The reception of out-of-order data packets is interpreted as an indication of link failure over the connection. In order to detect the out-of-order data packets, another mechanism is needed, either at the TCP sender or receiver side. The TCP sender side based mechanism profits from the non-decreasing property of the acknowledgements' sequence number to detect the out-of-order data packets. In case of duplicate acknowledgements arriving at the sender side, they all have the same sequence number. However, this is not enough for the TCP sender to detect the out-of-order data packets. Hence, the TCP sender uses a one byte option that is added to acknowledgement packets and called Acknowledgement Duplication Sequence Number (ADSN). The ADSN option is incremented and transmitted with each duplicate ACK. On the other side, when implementing a receiver side based mechanism to detect the out-of-order data packets; the TCP receiver requires an additional two-bytes TCP option that is called TCP Packet Sequence Number (TPSN). The TPSN option is incremented and transmitted with each transmitted TCP data packet (including retransmitted packets). When the TCP receiver detects out-of-order data packets, it uses a specific option bit within the acknowledgement packet header to notify the TCP sender. At the reception of this notification at the TCP sender side, it disables its congestion control algorithm, and enters into congestion avoidance phase. The mechanisms implemented within TCP-DOOR take into consideration only the out-of-order data packets, and ignore other data packet loss causes over the wireless ad hoc network. Also the modifications implemented with the TCP data packet header may cause some incompatibility problems with other TCP existing variants in case the sender or receiver does not support TCP-DOOR.

Cross Layer Solutions

Cross layer proposed solutions are mainly based on the explicit exchange of notification messages between the TCP sender and receiver. Here, we introduce some of these proposed solutions.

TCP Feedback (TCP-F) (Chandran, Raghunathan, Venkatesan, & Prakash, 2001) is a feedback based approach that deals with route failures within wireless ad hoc networks. This approach helps the TCP sender to distinguish losses due to route failures from those due to network congestion. When the TCP node's routing agent detects the disruption of a route over the connection, it explicitly sends a Route Failure Notification (RFN) packet to the TCP sender. At the reception of the RFN packet, TCP sender enters into a snooze state: stops data packet transmission and freezes all its connection variables (e.g. timers and congestion window size). The TCP sender stays in this snooze state until the routing agent recovers from the link failure. In this case, the routing agent sends a Route Reestablishment Notification (RRN) packet to the TCP sender side. When the TCP sender receives the RRN packet, it leaves the snooze state and resumes data packet transmission using the previ-

ous sender window and timeout values. In order to avoid that the TCP sender stay blocked in the snooze state, it triggers a route failure timer at the reception of a RFN packet. This way, when this timer expires the TCP sender leaves the snooze state and triggers its congestion control algorithm. It is clear that this approach can only be used in the specific case of ad hoc network using a reactive routing approach.

Another TCP feedback based approach is the Explicit Link Failure Notification technique (ELFN) (Holland & Vaidya, 1999). This later had been designed in order to distinguish the cause of data packet loss and to avoid a wrong interpretation of TCP as if it is due to network congestion. To do so, ELFN uses a real interaction between TCP and the ad hoc routing protocol. This is done through informing the TCP sender of the route failure by messages like "host unreachable" Internet Control Message Protocol (ICMP) message. Then, the TCP sender disables its retransmission timers and enters into a "standby" mode. During the standby period, the TCP sender probes the network to check if the route is recovered or not. When the TCP sender receives the acknowledgment of the probe packet, it leaves the standby mode, resumes its retransmission timers, and continues its communication session. Feedback messages consume nodes' as well as network resources. As for node's resources, sending feedback leads to supplemental energy consumption. Using feedback messages increases the TCP protocol messages overhead over the connection and consumes part of the available bandwidth. In addition, some researches (Anantharaman, Park, Sundaresan, & Sivakumar, 2004; Monks, Sinha, & Bharghavan, 2000) show that ELFN performs badly within wireless ad hoc networks (worse than the standard TCP implementation) especially in case of high network loads (for example in case of 25 TCP connection over the network).

Ad Hoc Transport Control Protocol (ATCP) (Liu & Singh, 2001) also employs network layer feedback messages. ATCP tries to deal with both wireless channel related problems and link failure problems. The TCP sender can switch between four different connection states according to the cause of the data packet losses: normal state, persist state, congestion control state, or retransmit state. In this proposal, a layer called ATCP is inserted between the TCP and IP layers of the TCP sender side. At the beginning of the connection, ATCP is always in the normal state. ATCP listens to the network state information provided by the ECN messages (Ramakrishnan, Floyd, & Black, 2001; Floyd, 1994) and ICMP "Destination Unreachable" message; then ATCP chooses the appropriate connection state to be in. At the reception of a "Destination Unreachable" message, TCP sender perceives that there is a link failure over the connection and enters into the persist state. During this state, the TCP sender stops data packets transmission until finding a new route towards the destination (this is done by probing the network). ECN is used in order to notify the TCP sender about network congestion situation over the TCP connection. When the TCP sender receives the ECN packet, it triggers its congestion control algorithm without waiting for the retransmission timeout timer to expire. This is called the congestion control state. Wireless channel induced data packet losses are detected through the reception of three duplicate acknowledgements. ATCP then switches to the persist state and quickly retransmits the lost packet from TCP's buffer (this is known as the retransmit state). After receiving the next ACK, ATCP leaves the persist state to the normal state. Even that ATCP show better performance than standard TCP implementation, the feedback messages used within ATCP have the same drawbacks as in the above mentioned ELFN mechanism, especially when implemented within high load wireless ad hoc networks. This leads to high TCP protocol messages overhead and more energy consumption at the TCP nodes.

TCP-WELCOME (TCP Variant for Wireless Environment, Link Losses, and Congestion Packet Loss Models)

In order to enhance the performance of TCP in front of the different data packet loss situations within wireless ad hoc networks, TCP must be able to react differently when confronted with each of them. TCP- WELCOME (Seddik Ghaleb, Ghamri Doudane, & Senouci, 2009) is a new TCP variant that tends to improve TCP performance within wireless ad hoc networks through differentiating the data packet loss cause and reacting accordingly. It guarantees data packet recovery, achieves good throughput, and saves the nodes' energetic resources. TCP-WELCOME is able to handle data packet losses due to network congestion, wireless link imperfections and errors, link failures, and temporary wireless channels disconnections. In the case of high BER over the wireless communication channels within the network, it is unnecessary to stop data transmission or to decrease TCP's transmission rate after experiencing a loss event. While, in case of link failure within the network (i.e. a broken route between the connection's end points), it will be sufficient to stop data transmission till an alternative route towards the destination is found. The transmission rate here will be adjusted according to the available bandwidth of the new route. It is obvious that, the length and the load of the communication path have an impact on the Round Trip delay Time (RTT) between the end points. Hence, it would be necessary, in this case, to recalculate both TCP data transmission rate (CWND) and Retransmission Time Out (RTO) values according to the characteristics of the new route (e.g. length and load of the new route). When there is a congestion situation in the network, TCP keeps its normal behavior. It reacts according to how the congestion had been detected (3 Duplicate Acknowledgements or RTO). In all congestion cases, TCP stops data transmission during a certain period of time and resumes it afterwards with a reduced data transmission rate. TCP-WELCOME incorporates two algorithms that interacts together in order to get the best TCP performance within the network taking into consideration the actual network conditions in the moment where the data loss occurred:

1. Loss Differentiation Algorithm (LDA),
2. Loss Recovery Algorithm (LRA).

In order to decrease the execution overhead of TCP algorithms and the interaction with the intermediate nodes within the network, both LDA and LRA algorithms are end-to-end and sender side modifications. In addition, TCP-WELCOME relies on the evolution of RTT samples of sent packets at the sender side in order to take its decisions. The evolution of RTT samples history is an efficient indication of the loss cause over the connection.

TCP-WELCOME: Loss Differentiation Algorithm (LDA)

In order to get the best TCP performance within wireless ad hoc networks, we need to have an adapted LDA algorithm that enables TCP to correctly classify the cause of data packet losses within wireless ad hoc networks. This algorithm should differentiate between the most common data packet loss situations within the network (wireless link related losses, network congestion, and link failure related losses). The main idea in the proposed algorithm is based on observing the history of RTT samples evolution within the network and the way in which TCP identifies the data packet loss. According to the evolution of RTT samples over the connection, TCP should be able to identify the cause of data packet losses.

1. Wireless channel related losses: three Duplicate Acknowledgements and RTT values that are almost constant mean that

data packet losses over the connection are due to wireless channel errors,
2. Link failure loss events: Retransmission Time Out and RTT values that are almost constant mean that data packet losses over the connection are due to link failure,
3. Network congestion event: Retransmission Time Out and RTT values that are increasing gradually mean that data packet losses over the connection are due to network congestion.

TCP-WELCOME: Loss Recovery Algorithm (LRA)

The behavior of TCP-WELCOME Loss Recovery Algorithm (LRA) depends on the identified data packet loss cause through the Loss Differentiation Algorithm (LRA), and differs in front of each of the different data packet loss cases within a wireless mobile ad hoc network (Ghaleb, et al., 2009). For example, in case of wireless channel errors, TCP-WELCOME will calculate the slow-start threshold and verify that the congestion window is not greater than the allowed slow-start threshold over the connection. Yet, RTO will stay unchanged. Whereas, in case of network congestion induced data loss, TCP-WELCOME will decrease its congestion window in proportion to the calculated slow-start threshold (to avoid decreasing the congestion window to minimum as in traditional TCP), in order to enhance the TCP throughput and saves the node's energy. When there is a link failure within the route between the communicating end points, TCP-WELCOME will adjust its parameters taking into consideration the characteristics of the lost and the new discovered route (RTT values).

DISCUSSION

According to the description of a wireless ad hoc network as a multi-hop wireless network, the earlier developed TCP variants for Wi-Fi, WiMAX, and cellular networks, were shown not to perform well in such environment. Additionally, a new concern was added to the TCP challenges, which is the TCP energy consumption. Even that this concern has been already shown up within wireless cellular networks, it is more crucial within wireless ad how networks, as losing an ad hoc node affects not only this communicating node or its communication session but it affects other nodes communication sessions within the network and consequently all the TCP communication sessions performance within the network. This is due to the fact that each wireless ad hoc node takes part of other TCP communication sessions through relaying data packets between other communication sessions end-points. We can, then, imagine a TCP node that breaks down and disappears due to its energetic resources depletion could lead to the following problems within the network:

1.   The lost of the TCP communication session in which this node where involved as an end-point,
2.   The interruption of all the TCP communication sessions in which this node was involved as an intermediate relaying or forwarding data packet node,
3.   The failure of all the wireless communication links that were connecting this node with the surrounding ad hoc network nodes and consequently the interruption of multiple TCP communication sessions again. This effect is called a link failure situation within the network.

All the above mentioned states are TCP data packet loss inducing situations within the network and thus an overall TCP performance degradation factors.

From the above, we conclude that, unlike the wireless cellular networks where losing a wireless node affects only that node and its communication session, conserving the TCP nodes energy consumption is a big concern within wireless ad hoc networks as it affects all the network performance. From which, arises the importance of avoiding unnecessary data retransmissions over the connection as well as optimizing the available bandwidth utilization in order not to waste the energetic resources of the network's nodes.

In addition, new TCP data packet loss cause is shown up within such networks configuration which is the link failure case. Most TCP proposed solutions differentiate between only congestion and non-congestion induced losses. This classification cannot be considered adequate to improve TCP performance as it deals with all non-congestion induced losses (wireless related or link failure related) similarly. This might be considered as a misinterpretation due to the big difference of these two data packet loss causes and the totally different reactions needed to recover from each of them.

However, few TCP variants were developed to distinguish data link failure induced losses within wireless networks, and these algorithms are considered as an Intelligent, more advanced and more wireless environment aware TCP variants due to their ability to distinguish and deal with each data packet loss cause within the wireless ad hoc environments.

TCP OVER WIRELESS SENSOR NETWORKS

Wireless Sensor Networks (WSNs) are consisting of autonomous devices or sensors that are supposed to monitor various environmental conditions at different locations, especially those where human access is not permitted or difficult to be achieved. In fact, wireless sensor networks can be viewed as a wireless ad-hoc network where the network devices (sensors) are static in most cases, thus we may call it wireless Static Ad-hoc NETworks (SANETs). Within such networks, sensors are connected to a central device or server

Figure 5. Wireless sensor network

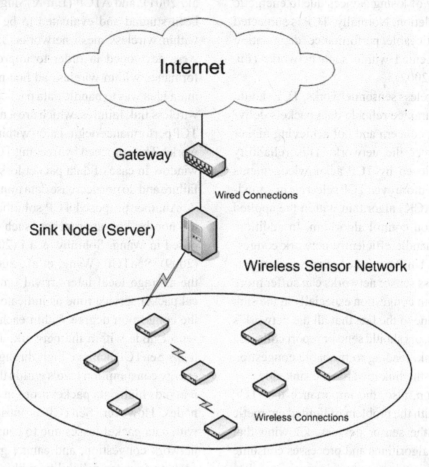

named sink, through wireless channels, in order to send the collected data (such as environmental temperature, sounds, pressure, motion, etc.). The small size of such sensors puts some limitations on its available resources, such as energy (they are equipped by batteries), memory capacity, computational abilities, and available bandwidth. This resource limitations especially in terms of energy leads to a new communication problems within the network, as the depletion of sensor's batteries will interrupt the connection between this sensor and its neighborhood. Additionally, it may disrupt other connections within the sensor network, as all the nodes or sensors are relaying packets and route information within the network. This introduces a new challenge for TCP within such networks that we may call it link failure situ-

ation. In fact, sensor networks applications would prefer reliable and fast data packets delivery rather than having high throughput (Lien, 2009). In the next section, we will see the most challenges that could affect TCP performance within wireless sensor networks (see Figure 5).

WIRELESS SENSOR NETWORKS CHALLENGES

Within wireless sensor networks, TCP should handle the traditional wireless environment challenges. These challenges include, wireless channel imperfections or high bit error rates, interference over the wireless links, signal fading and limited bandwidth resources. Also, we note the possibility of losing devices due to energetic resources depletion. Normally, TCP is subjected to highly noticeable performance degradation when implemented within such networks (Fu, Meng, & Lu, 2002).

Within wireless sensor networks, TCP should be able to guarantee reliable data packets delivery as its first concern and not achieving higher throughput over the network. This reliability could be achieved by TCP acknowledgements mechanism or more even TCP selective acknowledgement (SACK) algorithm within the applied TCP congestion control algorithm. In addition, TCP should handle efficiently network congestion episodes. Unlike most of other wireless networks, wireless sensor networks can suffer more frequently from congestion especially at the sink side. This is due to the fact that all the network's devices or sensors should send or report collected data to the sink, leading to probable congestion situation over the link towards the sink side.

We mention, also, the importance that TCP should deal with the problem of limited energetic resources of the sensor devices, knowing that TCP running algorithms and processes consume energy each time the sensor sends or receives data packets. In the next section, we will discuss the most TCP enhancements done in order to improve TCP performance within wireless sensor networks.

PROPOSED TCP SOLUTIONS FOR WIRELESS SENSOR NETWORKS

As mentioned above, wireless sensor networks are some sort of wireless ad-hoc networks. Thus, TCP variants that were developed to be implemented within wireless ad hoc networks might be a good choice to be employed within wireless sensor networks.

Many TCP variants had been proposed for other wireless data packet networks, such as TCP-ELFN (Holland & Vaidya, 1999; Bakshi, Krishna, Vaidya, & Pradhan, 1997), TCP-F (Chandran, et al., 2001), and ATCP (Liu & Singh, 2001), had been studied and evaluated to be implemented within wireless mesh networks. These variants were developed in order to improve TCP performance within wireless ad hoc networks. The main idea was to handle data packet losses due to wireless link failures, which are a major factor to TCP performance degradation within wireless networks. They proceed by freezing TCP congestion window in case of data packet losses due to link failure and do not decrease data transmission rate.

Another proposed TCP solutions category is the hop-by-hop approaches, such as those proposed in Wang, Sohraby, & Li (2005) and Lien (2009). SenTCP (Wang, et al., 2005) uses both the average local inter-arrival time and the local packet service time as indicators to estimate the congestion degree within each intermediate sensor node within the network. This approach helps SenTCP achieve high throughput and low energy consumption levels within the network, as it avoids high data packet drops at the network's nodes. However, SenTCP is incapable to deal with data packet losses due to causes other than network congestion, and cannot guarantee data packets transfer reliability within the wireless sensor networks.

The proposed hop-by-hop approach in Lien (2009), aims at (1) Improving the end-to-end packet delivery time as well as the achievable throughput over the network, and (2) Minimizing both the network congestion episodes and data packet retransmissions within the network.

The proposed approach consists of two main algorithms: an End-to-End TCP algorithm that is applied on both the TCP sender and receiver sides, and One-Hop TCP that is implemented on the intermediate nodes within the network. Taking into consideration the limited computational and memory resources of the sensor devices, the One-Hop TCP algorithm is designed to be a light version of TCP as well as efficient at the same time. This is done by removing some TCP features from One-Hop TCP algorithm, such as packetizing option and also the congestion control mechanism. This proposed algorithm might be considered as a link layer enhancement to recover from link failures within the network.

DISCUSSION

The main concern of TCP within wireless sensor networks is to guarantee reliable data packet delivery over the connection. Due to the fact that sensor nodes send periodically large amount of collected data or information over the network links, congestion might be considered as one of the most important challenges to be dealt with over the communication path. From that point of view, TCP congestion control algorithm is totally capable to manage such congestion related losses.

However, energy consumption of wireless sensor network nodes must be taken into consideration as the sensor nodes are totally dependent on their batteries and the depletion of their batteries might influence the network performance. Thus, the proposed algorithms those aim at freezing the TCP connection status or using explicit notifications to inform the TCP sender about the data packet loss cause were considered as good solutions to overcome the above mentioned problems. This propositions force TCP not to react aggressively, by invoking its congestion control algorithm, in front of non-congestion data packet losses.

However, studying the effect of such feedback messages overhead over the network and its influence on TCP performance should be put into consideration as it might lead to TCP performance degradation.

TCP OVER WIRELESS MESH NETWORKS

Wireless mesh networks are multi-hop wireless communication networks that aim to connect wireless end users or stations to the wired Internet access point. Unlike flat ad hoc networks, wireless mesh networks have a hierarchical configuration. Wireless mesh routers are implemented in order to provide data forwarding services between wireless stations and between wireless stations and network access points. Wireless mesh networks are networks where each node takes part in the communication process through relaying data packets from and to other nodes within the network, as in wireless ad hoc networks.

Data packets within such networks might be flooded over the network or routed hop-by-hop until reaching the destination side, according to used routing algorithm. A fully connected wireless mesh network is a wireless network where all its nodes are connected to each other through wireless channels. Like wireless ad hoc networks, mesh networks are characterized by their low cost, quick deployment and re-configurability. Thus, they could be a good choice within places where temporary networks connectivity is required and cable deployment is not available or difficult to achieve.

Wireless mesh networks can be distinguished, according to the wireless station rule within data packet relay process, into two different networks (Ramachandran, Buddhikot, Chandranmenon, Miller, Belding-Royer, & Almeroth, 2005):

1. Client mesh networks: in such networks, each wireless station takes part in the packet relay process between all the networks' nodes. This type of networks is decentralized as no need for a managing server within the network configuration (Luo, Ramjee, Sinha, & Erran, 2003; Papadopouli & Schulzrinne, 2001; Zhao, Ammar, & Zegura, 2004).
2. Infrastructure mesh networks: in this category, networks' wireless stations do not relay data packets within the network and separate multi-radio relay nodes are deployed within the network (Zhao, et al., 2004).

Figure 6. Wireless mesh network

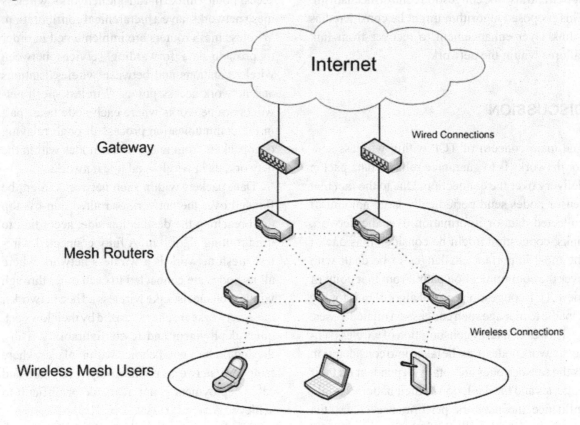

In the following, we state briefly the major advantages of wireless mesh networks: (1) Low deployment costs: unlike other wireless access technologies, such as WI-FI networks that need large number of hot spots or access points due to its limited distance coverage, wireless mesh networks deployment costs are not high as mesh networks configuration needs less number of connection to be connected to the wired network (Internet), (2) Large distance coverage at higher speed than other wireless LANs technologies, (3) The wireless mesh network configuration helps having multiple available paths between each two end-points. This provides data communication reliability within the network. In addition, this helps faster recovery from wireless link failure problems (i.e. due to obstacles within the communication path)

within the network. This behavior guarantees that, the wireless stations will always have an output point towards the wired network, and (4) One of the most important features and advantages of such networks is the independency and self-management abilities of their nodes (exactly as within wireless ad hoc networks). Thus, adding new wireless stations to the network configuration does not interrupt its functionality nor demand any pre-configuration for the new added nodes. Each new node that joins the wireless mesh network will automatically discovers the available wireless routers and the available routes towards the wired network. Consequently, the wireless mesh network can be expanded without any extra effort needed or waste of time (see Figure 6).

WIRELESS MESH NETWORKS CHALLENGES

We have seen earlier that in this chapter that TCP suffers from performance degradation when implemented within one-hop wireless networks due to its inability to deal with wireless link errors and data packet losses related to wireless environment and configurations. Thus, it is obvious that TCP suffers more and performs worse within multi-hop wireless networks such as wireless mesh networks and wireless ad hoc networks. The most common challenges that TCP faces within such networks are the following:

1. Wireless channel errors or high bit error rates over the wireless connections within the network. TCP misinterpretation of wireless channel induced data packet losses as a congestion episode leads to low bandwidth utilization and waste of nodes' energetic resources (batteries). Taking into consideration frequent losses due to wireless bit errors over the communication link, we can imagine the severe performance degradation of TCP within the network,

2. In case of data packet out-of-order arrival at the TCP receiver side (due to multipath data forwarding within the network), TCP congestion control algorithm invokes unnecessary data packets retransmissions and consequently causes performance degradation and waste of network and nodes scarce resources,

3. As mentioned above, wireless mesh networks are multi-hop wireless networks. Thus, we expect that the problems and challenges related to wireless channels will be intensified as the communication is handled over multiple wireless channels (each one has a different characteristics and different bit error rates). As a result, the developed TCP

variants to handle data packet losses related to wireless channels within one-hop wireless networks cannot cope with data packet losses within multi-hop wireless networks, such as wireless mesh networks,

4. We cannot neglect also that within wireless mesh networks, there might be network congestion induced losses as the wireless channels are shared between wireless stations and mesh routers,

5. Hidden and exposed terminal problems within such networks could lead to data packet losses TCP packets contention over the connection.

6. The asymmetry of communication links within the network, as the TCP sender might send the data packet over wireless link and receive its acknowledgement over another one.

PROPOSED TCP SOLUTIONS FOR WIRELESS MESH NETWORKS

As discussed above, TCP suffers from severe performance degradation when implemented within wireless networks, such as mesh networks. However, TCP variants that had been developed to improve TCP performance within wireless ad hoc networks were studied in order to evaluate its performance within wireless mesh networks. TCP-F (Chandran, et al., 2001), and TCP-ELFN (Holland & Vaidya, 1999) are two of these studied TCP variants. These two variants are feedback-based TCP algorithms that tend two differentiate data packet losses due to wireless channel imperfections from those due to network congestion episodes over the connection. However, designing an adequate TCP variant and loss differentiation algorithm for wireless mesh networks is still in progress and more future studies are needed.

DISCUSSION

Within wireless mesh networks, we notice that most of the problems and challenges are due to wireless environment characteristics. Thus, the earlier TCP variants that were developed for wireless ad hoc networks and aim at differentiating between congestion and non-congestion or wireless channel induced data packet losses are studied and evaluated in order to be implemented within wireless mesh networks. Most of these studied algorithms implement feedback messages in order to inform the TCP sender of the data loss cause. These algorithms are proved to enhance the performance of TCP within the network.

We notice, also, that the configuration of wireless mesh networks helps reducing the effect of link failure situations on TCP as it avoids the single point of failure issue, as mesh routers and wireless mesh clients are connected in an ad hoc network topology.

However, the overhead of such feedback messages over the connection is the main drawback of such algorithms. Also, the asymmetry of wireless communication links between the sender ans the receiver leads to RTT values fluctuations and TCP performance degradation. Thus, the effect of feedback messages overhead and that of the communication link asymmetry on TCP performance within wireless mesh networks need to be re-evaluated and studied.

TCP OVER WIRELESS VEHICULAR NETWORKS

Wireless Vehicular Ad hoc NETwork (VANET) (Fussler, Schnaufer, Transier, & Effelsberg, 2007) is a new technology that deploys communication and information technology over moving vehicles. In such network, each vehicle or node acts as an end point as well as a wireless router, helping nearby cars to be connected together forming a wide range communication network. During nodes' mobility (movement of cars) existing connections might be dropped as cars get out of the wireless signal range, and new connections can be established as new cars join the network or enters the wireless signal range. That is how the wireless mobile Internet is established within such networks. We may imagine the importance of such technology in situations where police or emergency services vehicles can communicate and exchange information in order to accomplish their missions. In fact, the applications developed for such network were mainly used for exchanging road traffic and safety related information messages. And most of these applications are not TCP based solutions.

Wireless vehicular networks support different data communication configurations (Fussler, et al., 2007):

1. Inter-Vehicle Communication: within such network communication configuration, road traffic and safety related information is transmitted through multi-hop broadcast messages. In fact, there are two different broadcasting mechanisms. The first one is called naïve broadcasting algorithm in which the senders broadcast regular and periodical messages. The receiver in such configuration ignores the messages received from behind vehicles. While, it broadcasts the messages received from the vehicles in front of it. Though that naïve broadcasting messages guarantee the reception of the messages at all the vehicles in the forward direction, naïve broadcasting mechanism overloads the wireless communication links with large numbers of broadcasting messages and leads to data packets collisions and losses within the network (Bickel, 2010). The second broadcasting mechanism is called intelligent broadcasting. In such mechanism, if a vehicle receives the same message from two vehicles (one behind it and one in front of it), it assumes that the message has been

Figure 7. Wireless vehicular network

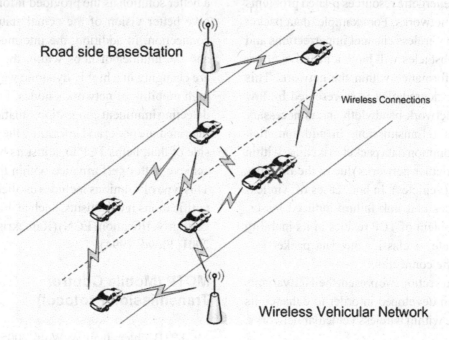

already reached the behind vehicles and decides not to broadcast it. This action helps alleviate the overhead caused by the regular and periodical broadcasting messages over the network connections (such as within the naïve broadcasting mechanism).

2. Vehicle-to-roadside Communication: Vehicle-to-roadside communication configuration is a single-hop broadcast. In this communication configuration the roadside unit transmits road traffic and safety messages to all the nearby vehicles through high bandwidth links between the roadside units and the nearby vehicles. In order to guarantee high data transmission rates during heavy road traffic periods, the roadside units are located at equal distances (within one kilometer between neighboring roadside units). Broadcasting road speed limits is one example of such broadcasting messages. In addition, a warning message could be transmitted from the roadside unit to any vehicle that might exceed the speed limits.

3. Routing-based Communication: Routing-based communication configuration implements multi-hop unicast messages propagation model. When a vehicle receives a request, from another vehicle within the network, to gather some information, it answers with the required data and returns the message to the sender. The other vehicles within the network are charged by forwarding the messages between the two communication vehicles in a multi-hop unicast propagation way.

We discuss in the following section, the most common challenges that may affect TCP performance within wireless vehicular networks (see Figure 7).

WIRELESS VEHICULAR NETWORKS CHALLENGES

The main problems of TCP within wireless vehicular networks include frequent disconnections, high speed mobility of nodes. However, there are no energetic resources related problems within such networks. For example, data packet losses due to wireless channel imperfections and temporary obstacles will have a negative effect on TCP performance within the network. This performance degradation is represented by low achievable network bandwidth and unnecessary data packets retransmission. In addition, link failure is a common data packet loss cause within wireless vehicular networks due to the mobility of its nodes (vehicles). In both cases of wireless induced losses and link failure induced losses, the main problem of TCP resides in its inability to differentiate or classify the data packet loss cause over the connection.

In the next section, we present the TCP variants that had been developed in order to enhance its performance within wireless vehicular networks.

PROPOSED TCP SOLUTIONS FOR WIRELESS VEHICULAR NETWORKS

According to the above challenges that might affect TCP performance within wireless vehicular networks, the proposed solutions could be classified into:

1. Solutions that aim at modifying TCP congestion control algorithm,
2. Solutions that are based on the information provided by intermediate nodes within the network.

The proposed solutions that aim at modifying the TCP incorporated mechanisms (such as Slow-Start and Congestion Avoidance) are mainly based on the available local information within TCP network nodes in order to predict imminent congestion episodes within the network. However, these solutions do not provide a complete information status of the wireless connection within the network. Thus, using information from intermediate nodes within the network might be

a better solution as the provided information can give better vision of the actual status over the connection. In addition, the intermediate nodes and the number of hops within the connection are changing in a highly dynamic way due to the high mobility of network's nodes. For example, detecting imminent congestion situation by a TCP intermediate node, and informing the TCP sender side of that, helps TCP to adjust its behaviour to achieve better performance within the network. This type of solutions includes explicit loss cause notifications mechanisms, such as Explicit Congestion Notification (ECN) (Ramakrishnan, et al., 2001; Floyd, 1994).

MCTP (Mobile Control Transmission Protocol)

MCTP (Bechler, Jaap, & Wolf, 2005) is a proxy based communication architecture that allows mobile vehicles to get access to the Internet through a fixed proxy that is implemented within the Internet wired network. MCTP is developed as a sub-layer between both the Transport (TCP) and the Network layers (IP). The main idea of MCTP is to observe the feedback and notification messages received from intermediate nodes within the network to differentiate between different data packet loss causes over the connection. For example, the reception of an ECN notification from the network intermediate nodes indicates that a congestion episode is detected over the connection. And ICMP destination unreachable message indicates a network partition situation within the network.

MCTP allows multi-hop communications between mobile vehicles as well as between mobile vehicles and the fixed proxy, while the communication between the fixed proxy and Internet server uses standard TCP. MTCP aims at avoiding TCP to invoke the slow start mechanism after data losses due to wireless channel related problems. In order to achieve this purpose, MCTP reactions differ according to the loss notification received from the networks' intermediate nodes. MCTP can handle four different data loss situations within the network:

1. Wireless related losses: when MCTP receives two duplicate acknowledgements or when its retransmission timer times out, it enters the LOSS state and forces TCP to stop transmitting data and freeze its timers. MCTP retransmits the unacknowledged data packets and waits for the corresponding acknowledgement. When MCTP receives the acknowledgement, it forwards it to the TCP sender. Then TCP starts transmitting data again from its freezing state and MCTP returns to its NORMAL state.

2. Congestion related losses: in this case, when MCTP receives an ECN notification from the intermediate nodes, it enters the CONGESTED state and invokes TCP to deal with this situation. In fact, TCP handles such situation efficiently as its congestion control algorithm is a congestion oriented mechanism. MCTP returns to NORMAL state, after that the TCP sender starts transmitting new data after loss recovery.

3. Network Partitioning related losses: in case of link failure within the network, intermediate nodes notify MCTP through an ICMP destination unreachable message. Upon the reception of that notification, MCTP enters PARTITIONED state and again forces TCP to freeze. MCTP then starts probing the connection periodically, and upon the reception of one duplicate acknowledgement, it recovers TCP and invokes its slow-start mechanism but without decreasing the slow-start threshold value.

4. Wireless Disconnection related losses: when a mobile vehicle disconnects from the network, a notification is sent to MCTP which, in turn, enters DISCONNECTED state and tells TCP to stop data transmission and freeze its retransmission timers. Both MCTP and

TCP stay inactive until a new notification is received by MCTP telling the availability of a new connectivity within the network. Hence, MCTP recovers TCP and returns to NORMAL state. Here again, MCTP does not decrease the slow-start threshold value.

DISCUSSION

Wireless vehicular networks have particular TCP challenges compared to other wireless data packet networks; such as high speed mobility of its nodes (vehicles). Unfortunately, few TCP studies were done in this domain and most of these studies consider the TCP variants that were developed for wireless ad hoc networks. This is because that most VANET applications are not TCP based solutions.

However, some other transmission protocols, other that TCP, were developed in order to enhance its performance within such networks. Some of these protocols, such as MCTP that is discussed in the previous section, are proxy based solutions and interact with TCP algorithms in order to control its congestion control algorithm. Such proposed solutions help TCP to react properly in front of each data packet loss cause over the TCP connection and consequently improving its performance within the network.

FUTURE RESEARCH DIRECTIONS

Even that most of TCP challenges within wireless data packet networks had been studied and there are many proposals in order to deal with them effectively and improve TCP performance within such networks, there are, still, other open research issues that should be considered and investigated. One of these issues is the effect of the communication link asymmetry on TCP performance within the network. This problem arises from the fact that TCP sends its data packets over a wireless link that is different from the one over which it receives its acknowledgements. As TCP algorithms and timers are based on the acknowledgements reception from the receiver side, the fluctuation of the round trip time values within the network may lead to misbehaviour of TCP and consequently TCP performance degradation within the network.

Another open research issue that should be considered is the overhead of feedback and loss notification based TCP algorithms as that might negatively affect TCP performance. This messaging overhead could lead to congestion episodes over wireless links and hence under utilization of the wireless channel available bandwidth. Additionally, transmission and reception of such messages invoke energy consumption of the nodes, which consequently influence their batteries life. As seen before, losing a wireless node, especially within mobile ad hoc networks; influences TCP performance within the entire network. Thus, considering TCP solutions those are not based on feedback or explicit notifications help improving TCP performance.

Also, the interaction between the link-layer based solutions developed to improve TCP and TCP congestion control algorithm within the network might need more investigation. This interaction could lead to performance degradation over the connection instead of enhancing it. In fact, the local link-layer data packet retransmissions and the large difference of timers' granularities between link-layer and transport layer forces TCP to unnecessary invoke its congestion control algorithm and eventually redundant data packet retransmissions over the TCP connection.

However, as long as there will be new data networks technologies and topologies/configurations, there will be new challenges and issues that TCP should recognize and deal with. The evolution of TCP as a Transport Control Protocol will not stop at this point. Otherwise, its definition could be changed as it is no longer an oriented congestion related control protocol; it might be called data

packet loss recovery protocol, whatever the data packet loss cause could be.

CONCLUSION

The main problem of TCP within the new wireless data networks configurations and technologies is the fact that it was mainly developed for wired data networks. Then, it was mandatory using TCP within wireless data networks in order to connect wireless users to Internet. The most severe part of that configuration is that TCP should be able to handle data packet losses due to two different data networks technologies that are connected together.

Taking into consideration the quick and non-stop growth and development of data networks topologies and technologies puts TCP in a real challenge, since it is supposed to deal with and handle all existing and upcoming new data networks configurations and all the upcoming data packet loss causes within such networks. TCP has to evolve to be capable of identifying and dealing with different loss causes, while at the same, it has to maintain the core TCP functionalities; in order maintain backward compatibility with earlier wired and wireless data packet communication networks.

Firstly, the proposed solutions aimed at isolating the wireless channel characteristics and related problems over the wireless part of the hybrid network, from the wired network part and to handle data packet losses over each part separately according to the network conditions. These solutions are TCP-Proxy-based algorithms that require the involvement of an intermediate node within the communication process. We should note that, such a solution violates the end-to-end TCP semantics as it divides the TCP connection into two, wired and wireless parts.

These proposed solutions and algorithms are proved to enhance the performance of TCP within wireless static data packet networks.

After that, new and more intelligent TCP solutions were proposed. These solutions aimed at dealing with both data network types, wired and wireless, without separating them or isolating one part from the other. In addition, these propositions took into consideration new wireless data packet networks configurations with wireless mobile nodes, as the networks' nodes are moving during the TCP communication session. This new feature (nodes' mobility) within the wireless network imposes new data packet loss causes (congestion, wireless channel, link failure and disconnections) and consequently new TCP capabilities to distinguish and deal with them.

These TCP variants algorithms can be categorized into two main categories:

1. Algorithms that implement feedback based mechanisms in order to explicitly inform the TCP sender about data packet loss and its cause,
2. Algorithms that implement bandwidth estimation mechanisms in order to distinguish between different data packet loss causes over the connection.

Most of these proposed algorithms are studied and evaluated within different wireless data packet networks, and most of them could be considered efficient to deal with data packet losses within wireless environments. However, the main concern that must be taken into consideration, when implementing the feedback-based solutions is the effect of such messages overhead within the network on TCP performance.

In this chapter, we have presented the evolution of TCP congestion control algorithm in order to enhance its performance within new data packet network technologies and topologies. We discussed the main challenges that lead to TCP performance degradation within different types of wireless data packet networks, and the TCP algorithms proposed to overcome such challenges and improve TCP performance within such networks.

REFERENCES

Anantharaman, V., Park, S.-J., Sundaresan, K., & Sivakumar, R. (2004). TCP performance over mobile ad hoc networks: A quantitative study. *Journal of Wireless Communications and Mobile Computing*, *4*(2), 203–222. doi:10.1002/wcm.172

Ayanoglu, E., Paul, S., LaPorta, T., Sabnani, K., & Gitlin, R. (1995). Airmail: A link-layer protocol for wireless networks. *Wireless Networks*, *1*(1), 47–60. doi:10.1007/BF01196258

Badrinath, B., Acharya, A., & Imielinski, T. (1993). Impact of mobility on distributed computations. *ACM Operating Systems Review*, *27*(2), 15–20. doi:10.1145/155848.155853

Bakre, A., & Badrinath, B. R. (1995). I-TCP: Indirect TCP for mobile hosts. In *Proceedings of the 15th International Conference on Distributed Computing Systems (ICDCS)*. IEEE Press.

Bakshi, B., Krishna, P., Vaidya, N. H., & Pradhan, D. K. (1997). Improving performance of TCP over wireless networks. In *Proceedings of ICDCS*. Baltimore, MD: IEEE Press.

Balakrishnan, H., Padmanabhan, V., Seshan, S., & Katz, R. H. (1997). A comparison of mechanisms for improving TCP performance over wireless links. *IEEE/ACM Transactions on Networking*, *5*(6), 756–769. doi:10.1109/90.650137

Balakrishnan, H., Padmanabhan, V. N., & Katz, R. H. (1997). The effects of asymmetry on TCP performance. In *Proceedings of ACM/IEEE Mobicom*, (pp. 77–89). IEEE Press.

Balakrishnan, H., Seshan, S., & Katz, R. (1995). Improving reliable transport and handoff performance in cellular wireless networks. *ACM Wireless Networks*, *1*, 469–482. doi:10.1007/BF01985757

Bechler, M., Jaap, S., & Wolf, L. (2005). An optimized TCP for Internet access of vehicular ad hoc networks. *Lecture Notes in Computer Science*, *3462*, 869–880. doi:10.1007/11422778_70

Bickel, G. (2010). *Inter/intra-vehicle wireless communication*. Retrieved from http://userfs.cec. wustl.edu/~gsb1/index.html#toc.

Brakmo, L. S., O'Malley, S. W., & Peterson, L. L. (1994). TCP Vegas: New techniques for congestion detection and avoidance. In *Proceedings of ACM SIGCOMM 1994*, (pp. 24-35). ACM Press.

Brown, K., & Singh, S. (1997). M-TCP: TCP for mobile cellular networks. *ACM Computer Communication Review, 27*(5).

Caceres, R., & Iftode, L. (2001). Improving the performance of reliable transport protocols in mobile computing environments. *IEEE Journal on Selected Areas in Communication, 19*(7).

Chandran, K., Raghunathan, S., Venkatesan, S., & Prakash, R. (2001). A feedback based scheme for improving TCP performance in ad-hoc wireless networks. *IEEE Journal on Personal Communications, 8*(1), 34–39. doi:10.1109/98.904897

Chen, X., Zhai, H., Wang, J., & Fang, Y. (2002). A survey on improving TCP performance over wireless network. *ACM Computing Surveys, 34*(3), 357–374. doi:10.1145/568522.568524

Cheng, P. F., & Soung, C. L. (2003). TCP Veno: TCP enhancement for transmission over wireless access networks. *IEEE Journal on Selected Areas in Communications, 21*, 216–228. doi:10.1109/JSAC.2002.807336

Crow, B. P., Widjaja, I., Kim, L. G., & Sakai, P. T. (1997). IEEE 802.11 wireless local area networks. *IEEE Communications Magazine, 35*(9), 116–126. doi:10.1109/35.620533

Dyer, T., & Boppana, R. (2001). A comparison of TCP performance over three routing protocols for mobile ad hoc networks. In *Proceedings of ACM MOBIHOC*, (pp. 56–66). ACM Press.

Fall, K., & Floyd, S. (1996). Simulation-based comparison of Tahoe, Reno, and SACK TCP. *ACM Computer Communications Review, 5*(3).

Floyd, S. (1994). TCP and explicit congestion notification. *ACM Computer Communication Review, 5*(5).

Floyd, S., Henderson, T., & Gurtov, A. (2004). The NewReno modification to TCP's fast recovery algorithm. *RFC 3782*. Retrieved from http://www.ietf.org.

Fu, Z., Meng, X., & Lu, S. (2002). How bad TCP can perform in mobile ad-hoc networks. In *Proceedings of IEEE ICNP 2002*. Paris, France: IEEE Press.

Fussler, H., Schnaufer, S., Transier, M., & Effelsberg, W. (2007). Vehicular ad-hoc networks: From vision to reality and back. In *Proceedings of IEEE Wireless on Demand Network Systems and Services*. IEEE Press.

Goff, T., Moronski, J., Phatak, D. S., & Gupta, V. (2003). *Freeze-TCP: A true end-to-end TCP enhancement mechanism for mobile environment*. Paper presented at IEEE INFOCOM 2000. Tel-Aviv, Israel.

Halepovic, E., Wu, Q., Williamson, C. L., & Ghaderi, M. (2008). TCP over WiMAX: A measurement study. In *Proceedings of MASCOTS*, (pp. 327-336). IEEE Press. Holland, G., & Vaidya, N. (1999). Analysis of TCP performance over mobile ad hoc networks. In *Proceedings of the 5th ACM/IEEE International Conference on Mobile Computing and Networking*, (pp. 219-230). IEEE Press.

Johansson, P., Larsson, T., Hedman, N., Mielczarek, B., & Degermark, M. (1999). Scenario-based performance analysis of routing protocols for mobile ad hoc networks. In *Proceedings of the Fifth Annual ACM/IEEE International Conference on Mobile Computing and Networking*, (pp. 195–206). IEEE Press.

Kopparty, S., Krishnamurthy, S. V., Faloutsos, M., & Tripathi, S. K. (2002). Split TCP for mobile ad hoc networks. In *Proceedings of IEEE Global Communications Conference GLOBECOM,* (vol 1), (pp. 138- 142). IEEE Press.

Lien, Y.-N. (2009). Hop-by-hop TCP for sensor networks. *International Journal of Computer Networks & Communications.* IJCNC.

Liu, J., & Singh, S. (2001). ATCP: TCP for mobile ad hoc networks. *IEEE Journal on Selected Areas in Communications, 10*(7).

Luo, H., Ramjee, R., Sinha, P., & Erran, L. (2003). Unified cellular and ad-hoc network. In *Proceedings of ACM Mobicom.* ACM Press.

Mascolo, S., Casetti, C., Gerla, M., Sanadidi, M. Y., & Wang, R. (2001). *TCP Westwood: Bandwidth estimation for enhanced transport over wireless links.* Paper presented at the 7th Annual International Conference on Mobile Computing and Networking. Rome, Italy.

Michel, M., Nelson, L. S., & José, F. (2003). On the performance of TCP loss recovery mechanisms. In *Proceedings of IEEE International Conference on Communications,* (vol. 3), (pp. 1812- 1816). IEEE Press.

Monks, J., Sinha, P., & Bharghavan, V. (2000). *Limitations of TCP-ELFN for ad hoc networks.* In Proceedings of Mobile and Multimedia Communications. ACM Press.

Papadopouli, M., & Schulzrinne, H. (2001). A performance analysis of 7DS a peer-to-peer data dissemination and prefetching tool for mobile users. In *Advances in Wired and Wireless Communications: IEEE Sarnoff Symposium Digest.* Ewing, NJ: IEEE Press.

Park, E. C., Kim, J. Y., Kim, H., & Kim, H. S. (2008). *Bidirectional bandwidth allocation for TCP performance enhancement in IEEE 802.16 broadband wireless access networks.* Paper presented at the IEEE 19th International Symposium on Personal, Indoor and Mobile Radio Communications, PIMRC 2008. Cannes, France.

Parsa, C., & Garcia-Luna-Aceves, J. J. (1999). TULIP: A link-level protocol for improving TCP over wireless links. In *Proceedings of the Wireless Communications and Networking Conference,* (pp. 1253-1257). New Orleans, LA: IEEE Press.

Parsa, C., & Garcia-Luna-Aceves, J. J. (2000). Improving TCP performance over wireless networks at the link layer. *ACM Mobile Networks and Applications, 5.*

Ramachandran, K., Buddhikot, M. M., Chandranmenon, G., Miller, S., Belding-Royer, E., & Almeroth, K. (2005). On the design and implementation of infrastructure mesh networks. In *Proceedings of WiMesh 2005.* Santa Clara, CA: IEEE Press.

Ramakrishnan, K., Floyd, S., & Black, D. (2001). The addition of explicit congestion notification (ECN) to IP. *RFC 3168.* Retrieved from http://www.ietf.org.

Seddik Ghaleb, A., Ghamri Doudane, Y. M., & Senouci, S. M. (2009). TCP WELCOME: TCP variant for wireless environment, link losses, and congestion packet loss models. In *Proceedings of the 1st International Conference on Communication Systems and Networks, COMSNETS 2009.* Bangalore, India: IEEE Press.

Sinha, P., Venkitaraman, N., Sivakumar, R., & Bhargavan, V. (1999). WTCP: A reliable transport protocol for wireless wide-area networks. In *Proceedings ACM MOBICOM,* (pp. 231–241). ACM Press.

Wang, C., Sohraby, K., & Li, B. (2005). SenTCP: A hop-by-hop congestion control protocol for wireless sensor networks. In *Proceedings of IEEE INFOCOM 2005*. Miami, FL: IEEE Press.

Wang, R., Valla, M., Sanadidi, M. Y., Ng, B. K. F., & Gerla, M. (2002). Efficiency/friendliness tradeoffs in TCP Westwood. In *Proceedings of the Seventh IEEE Symposium on Computers and Communications*. IEEE Press.

Westin, O. (2003). TCP performance in wireless mobile multi-hop ad hoc networks. *SICS Technical Report T2003:24*. Stockholm, Sweden: Swedish Institute of Computer Science.

Xu, K., Tian, Y., & Ansari, N. (2004). tcp-jersey for wireless ip communications. *IEEE Journal on Selected Areas in Communications*, 22(4), 747–756. doi:10.1109/JSAC.2004.825989

Zhao, W., Ammar, M., & Zegura, E. (2004). A message ferrying approach for data delivery in sparse mobile ad hoc networks. In *Proceedings of ACM Mobihoc 2004*. Tokyo, Japan: ACM Press.

ADDITIONAL READING

Allman, M., Paxon, V., & Stevens, W. (1999). TCP congestion control. *RFC 2581*. Retrieved from http://www.ietf.org.

Barman, D., & Matta, I. (2002). *Effectiveness of loss labeling in improving TCP performance in wired/wireless networks. Technical Report*. Boston, MA: Boston University Press.

Biaz, S., & Vaidya, N. (1998). Distinguishing congestion losses from wireless transmission losses: A negative result. In *Proceedings of Seventh International Conference on Computer Communications and Networks*, (pp. 722-731). IEEE Press.

Biaz, S., & Vaidya, N. H. (1999). Discriminating congestion losses from wireless losses using inter-arrival times at the receiver. In *Proceedings of the IEEE Symposium on Application-specific Systems and Software Engineering & Technology*, (pp. 10–17). IEEE Press.

Capone, A., & Martignon, F. (2001). Bandwidth estimates in the TCP congestion control scheme. In *Proceedings of Tyrrhenian International Workshop on Digital Communications*, (pp. 614–626). ACM Press.

Cen, S., Cosman, P. C., & Voelker, G. M. (2002). End-to-end differentiation of congestion and wireless losses. *In Proceedings of MMCN 2002: SPIE Multimedia Computing and Networking*, (vol. 4673), (pp. 1-15). IEEE Press.

Chiu, D.-M., & Jain, R. (1989). Analysis of the increase and decrease algorithms for congestion avoidance in computer networks. *Journal of Computer Networks and ISDN Systems*, 17(1), 1–14. doi:10.1016/0169-7552(89)90019-6

Dykeman, D., Kaiserswerth, M., Meister, B.W., Rudin, H., Williamson, R., & Doeringer, W. (1990). A survey of light-weight transport protocols for high-speed networks, 38(11), 2025–2039.

Garcia, J., & Brunstrom, A. (2003). Transport layer loss differentiation and loss notification. In *Proceedings of First Swedish National Computer Networking Workshop (SNCNW)*. SNCNW Press.

Grieco, L. A., & Mascolo, S. (2002). TCP Westwood and easy RED to improve fairness in high-speed networks. In *Proceedings of the Seventh International Workshop on Protocols for High-Speed Networks*. ACM Press.

Hoe, J. (1995). *Start-up dynamics of TCP's congestion control and avoidance scheme*. Master Thesis. Cambridge, MA: MIT Press.

Jacobson, V. (1990). Modified TCP congestion avoidance algorithm. *End2end-Interest Mailing List.* Retrieved from ftp://ftp.isi.edu/ end2end/ end2end-interest-1990.mail.

Jacobson, V. (1998). Congestion avoidance and control. *ACM SIGCOMM, 18*(4).

Karn, P., & Partridge, C. (1987). Improving round-trip time estimates in reliable transport protocols. In *Proceedings of ACM SIGCOMM 1987.* ACM Press.

Kim, T., Lu, S., & Bharghavan, V. (1999). *Improving congestion control performance through loss differentiation.* Paper presented at the International Conference on Computers and Communications Networks 1999.

Mathis, M., Mahdavi, J., Floyd, S., & Romanow, A. (1996). TCP selective acknowledgement options. *RFC 2018.* Retrieved from http://www.ietf.org.

Nagle, J. (1984). Congestion control in IP/TCP internetworks. *RFC 896.* Retrieved from http://www.ietf.org.

Ott, T., Kemperman, J., & Mathis, M. (1997). *Window size behavior in TCP/IP with constant loss probability.* Paper presented at the Fourth IEEE Workshop on the Architecture and Implementation of High Performance Communication Systems (HPCS 1997).

Ramarathinam, V., & Labrador, M. A. (2002). Performance analysis of TCP over static wireless ad hoc networks. In *Proceedings of ISCA 15th International Conference on Parallel and Distributed Computing Systems, PDCS 2002.* ISCA Press.

Samaraweera, N. K. G. (1999). Non-congestion packet loss detection for TCP error recovery using wireless Links. *IEEE Proceedings Communications, 146*(4), 222–230. doi:10.1049/ip-com:19990597

Seddik-Ghaleb, A., Ghamri Doudane, Y. M., & Senouci, S.-M. (2006). *A performance study of TCP variants in terms of energy consumption and average goodput within a static ad hoc environment.* Paper presented at the 2nd ACM International Wireless Communications and Mobile Computing Conference, IWCMC 2006. Vancouver, Canada.

Seddik Ghaleb, A., Ghamri Doudane, Y. M., & Senouci, S. M. (2006). *Effect of ad hoc routing protocols on TCP performance within MANETs.* Paper presented at the IEEE International Workshop on Wireless Ad-hoc and Sensor Networks.

Seddik-Ghaleb, A., Ghamri Doudane, Y. M., & Senouci, S.-M. (2007). Emulating end-to-end losses and delays for ad hoc networks. In *Proceedings of IEEE International Conference on Communications.* IEEE Press.

Singh, H., Saxena, S., & Singh, S. (2004). Energy consumption of TCP in ad hoc networks. *Journal of Wireless Networks, 10*(5). doi:10.1023/B:WINE.0000036456.85213.45

Stéphane, L., Ghamri Doudane, M. Y., & Pujolle, G. (2006). *Cross-layer loss differentiation algorithms to improve TCP performances in WLANs.* Paper presented at the 11th IFIP International Conference on Personal Wireless Communications.

Tobe, Y., Aida, H., Aida, Y. X., & Tokuda, H. (2001). Detection of congestion signals from relative one-way delay. *IPSJ Journal, 42*(12).

Wang, B., & Singh, S. (2004). Computational energy cost of TCP. In *Proceedings of IEEE INFOCOM 2004.* IEEE Press.

Wang, F., & Zhang, Y. (2003). Improving TCP performance over mobile ad hoc networks with out-of-order detection and response. In *Proceedings of ACM MOBIHOC,* (pp. 217–225). ACM Press.

Xylomenos, G., Polyzos, G. C., Mahonen, P., & Saaranen, M. (2001). TCP performance issues over wireless links. *IEEE Communications Magazine*, *39*(4), 52–58. doi:10.1109/35.917504

KEY TERMS AND DEFINITIONS

Acknowledgement (ACK): A packet message, used in the Transmission Control Protocol that is sent by the receiver to acknowledge the sender the receipt of a certain packet(s).

Congestion Avoidance: A phase where TCP enters after Slow-Start phase. In this phase, the TCP CWND increases slowly in order to avoid network congestion.

Congestion Window (CWND): The maximum amount of data bytes that can be sent out over the connection without being acknowledged.

Congestion: A saturation of communication links due to much data transmitted simultaneously by the network's nodes. This results in both data packet loss and extra transmission delays over the connection.

Duplicate ACK (DUPACK): TCP receivers generate a duplicate acknowledgment when out-of-sequence segment is received. This one acknowledges only some of packets outstanding at the start of the Fast Recovery.

Retransmission Time out (RTO): RTO is the maximum time that TCP waits for the data acknowledgment before declaring that the packet is lost.

Round Trip Time (RTT): RTT is the delay that corresponds to the time needed by the TCP sender after sending a data packet to receive its acknowledgment.

Slow Start Threshold (SSThresh): The slow-start threshold that is used to define the transition from slow-start phase to congestion avoidance phase.

Chapter 2
Enhancement of e-Learning Systems and Methodologies through Advancements in Distributed Computing Technologies

Luca Caviglione
Institute of Intelligent Systems for Automation (ISSIA), Italy

Mauro Coccoli
University of Genoa, Italy

ABSTRACT

The evolution of the Internet, distributed architectures, and Grid-oriented frameworks can change the way people acquire and disseminate both knowledge and experience, thus the way they learn. Therefore, one can envisage new e-learning models, based on a more efficient users' interaction, that also empowers the hands-on experience. This will improve learning outcomes, while reducing the need of physical devices and removing the inherent boundaries. Moreover, this reduces costs by promoting the sharing of resources and learning assets. From this perspective, the chapter discusses the integration of classical e-learning paradigms with new advancements of distributed computing, such as: 1) the usage of Peer-to-Peer (P2P) to produce network-independent overlays, also by enabling direct student-to-student exchanges; 2) the integration, through grid-based middleware, of real or virtual devices, plants and Sensors Network (SN) within the e-learning environment; and 3) the adoption of a distributed e-learning system to spread culture through mobile devices, with an emphasis on satellite communications.

DOI: 10.4018/978-1-4666-0161-1.ch002

INTRODUCTION

The continuous advancements in the field of Information and Communication Technology (ICT) lead to fast changes in the scenario of content management and sharing. New systems influence the way people acquire knowledge and disseminate their experience. Nevertheless, such evolution enhances how individuals achieve results by means of e-learning systems and services, in education and at work (Rosenberg, 2001). As a consequence, also e-learning environments are experiencing a paradigm shift. This can happen owing to many important technological enablers. We mention, among the others: the mobile and broadband Internet, distributed computing architectures, Grid-oriented frameworks, and the Peer-to-Peer (P2P) communication paradigm. Therefore, it is possible to envisage new models for sharing both knowledge and information. As an example, an intrinsic *added value* concerns the efficient circulation and delivery of ideas, which can be produced or consumed by different bodies, e.g., Universities, Companies, and "common" people. Additionally, the sharing can be not limited only to knowledge, but it can be also extended to "machineries," in order to perform hands-on experiences to grant a more successful learning process.

To give a better understanding, we perform a short introduction of architectural blueprints and components commonly adopted for e-learning purposes. In standard set-ups a well-defined centralized entity, usually defined as the Learning Management System (LMS), is responsible of: 1) providing basic functionalities for the e-learning services, such as authentication, accounting and monitoring; 2) allowing data delivery, for instance the digital contents for educational purposes. Such learning assets are made available in the form of Learning Objects (LOs) (Ip, Morrison, & Currie, 2001), and they can be locally archived into a Learning Content Management System (LCMS), or distributed among different Learning Object Repositories (LORs). The most adopted solution relies upon a unique LCMS. Notwithstanding, if multiple LORs are employed, each LOR must have at least indexing and archiving functionalities, to handle specific policies, ranging from requirements of data protection, to the widest possible diffusion of the knowledge. To this aims, people as well as software applications, can access LORs, simply with a Web browser (thus requiring a proper server-side Web-oriented logic), or through duly developed access interfaces.

In this perspective, the engineering of the LMS can be a complex task, since it could embrace different constraints. In fact, it should be properly tweaked for specific user needs (e.g., the desired level of interaction among students and accessibility issues), the chosen learning strategies (i.e., associative, cognitive, or situative), and the specific pedagogical model (i.e., constructivism, constructionism, or reflection). Depending on the chosen approach, different applications are feasible and must be made available. To handle such a variety of choices, the LMS platform is designed to deliver a set of standard services, which can be further composed to provide more sophisticated functionalities. However, they could not be sufficient, and then an Application Programming Interface (API) is often supplied, to inter-connect with external tools and third-party products, and to allow access to internal data and services. This concept can be further pushed owing to Web 2.0 technology, used to merge the LMS with other "full-featured" services or with remote devices/laboratories, exported through standard interfaces, such as Web-Services (Okon, et al., 2006). As an example, the integration of a LMS can range from a static link to a forum or a blog, to the transparent internetwork with complex social network platforms. At the same time, the functionalities provided by the *mashup* concept, allow the retrieval and the aggregation of heterogeneous contents published outside the LMS.

Additionally, the LMS must guarantee a proper degree of scalability. In fact, the required software architecture can be run on a single machine for small projects (e.g., mainly to act as a Course Management System), while for the delivery of e-learning activities in more complex organizations (e.g., Universities), the LMS requires the adoption of a scalable architecture. This is needed to cope with two different complexities: 1) to support the access to a large population of students and 2) to sustain the requirements imposed by the increasing size of the assets used for learning activities (e.g., ranging from multimedia components to sophisticated and bandwidth intensive applications). Consequently, the most complex LMS could be highly distributed, remotely interconnected through the Internet, and resource consuming. At the same time, an open LMS can assure the proper degree of interoperability.

To effectively pursue such vision, advancements in distributed systems can be used to face with many different problems, ranging from resource aggregation/search/publishing to the possibility of interacting through a networked environment with real or virtual devices, also augmented with multimedia feedbacks (Adorni, Coccoli, Fadda, & Veltri, 2007). In fact, modern e-learning platforms are requested to:

1. Distribute LOs to remote learners (according to the classical distance-learning paradigm), and to interconnect remote users also by aggregating them into virtual classes. In this case, P2P-based frameworks can be adopted for the implementation of distributed services to overcome lacks of performance and limited bandwidth capabilities of a centralized LMS. In such environment, LOs have to be indexed by some entity, so that they can be easily retrieved, also by exploiting P2P to perform scalable look-ups. We point out that LOs can be not limited to digital data, but also devices and laboratories, e.g., as already happens in the Internet of Things. Besides, a different case is when learning happens freely over the Internet, i.e.,

outside of traditional education institutions and duties. In this setting, resources can be "tagged" rather then indexed (Macgregor & McCulloch, 2006) and potentially exchanged on-demand by the users themselves;

2. Perform computing intensive learning activities. In many cases, learning strategies are based on the simulation of complex systems, also by using virtual worlds. More in general, to achieve specific learning objectives it is not uncommon that some computing intensive tasks have to be accomplished. Also, the demand of computing power for e-learning is discontinuous, since it is connected to the schedules of specific lectures. Therefore, it may be convenient to rely on frameworks capable of allocating resources in a scalable and highly dynamical way, in order to reduce issues due to over-provisioning, expenditures and underutilization of resources. Additionally, grid-based middleware can be also used to "publish" complex devices, or machineries (Caviglione, et al., 2009), thus making them remotely accessible through the e-learning environment, as a sort of enhanced-LOs;

3. Enable the continuous interaction among learners, and among learners and teachers, in a collaborative fashion, which can be also mobile. In the latter case, learning is done through personal devices (e.g., tablets and smart-phones) that are part of everyday life. This reflects into a new archetype, commonly defined as "*m-learning.*" This is even truer in *developing Countries* (or rural areas), where wired networks are almost absent, and the lack of connectivity is recovered through satellite communications.

To these aims, we envisage the adoption of ideas already enhancing distributed systems, to effectively implement a Distributed Learning Environment (DLE) (Alavi, 2004). This also conforms to the most cutting-edge trends, aiming at the so-called e-learning 2.0 (Downes, 2005), in which the social aspects of teaching and learning are emphasized by the availability of highly collaborative technologies. Owing to the presence of Web 2.0 applications, and well-defined APIs or interfaces, such services are integrated within the LMS itself. Nevertheless, the exploitation of external services makes the overall architecture intrinsically layered and distributed. We underline that the goal of this Chapter is not investigating implementation issues, or providing a numerical performance evaluation. Rather, it is explaining how distributed computing technologies can enhance e-learning systems and methodologies, enabling new learning paradigms. Also, it discusses how pre-existent functionalities can offer access to and control of complex systems and machineries. Summarizing, we concentrate on the "space of possibilities" achievable through different features granted by technologies such as, P2P overlays, grid-oriented middleware and mobility support. Moreover, the Chapter resumes the authors' experience in the field of e-learning enhanced through distributed computing technologies, and some results have been partially borrowed from Caviglione and Coccoli (2010) and from Caviglione, Coccoli, and Punta (2010).

In the remainder of the chapter, we firstly describe the usage of the P2P communication paradigm to build the next-generation of scalable and distributed e-learning platforms. Then we propose ideas, and reference architectures to join real and virtual devices to empower the learning experience of remote students, as well as to support a new class of hands-on practices. Moreover, we discuss about the usage of grid-related technologies to make such vision feasible and simple, upon reusing the huge variety of pre-existent grid middleware. Next we outline new trends in technology-enhanced learning, also proposing a vision for future e-learning applications, i.e., networked systems to push the paradigm of "ubiquitous learning," with emphasis on satellite communications and possible related issues.

Lastly, we conclude the Chapter and showcase the future works.

APPLYING P2P TO E-LEARNING FACILITIES

As introduced, new models to produce and share knowledge are becoming widely adopted for different purposes. Among the others, this is due to the availability of high-speed Internet connectivity for home users, such as Asymmetric Digital Subscriber Loop (ADSL) or Fiber To The Home (FTTH) broadband accesses. Additionally, the increasing power of personal computers and a generalized reduction of costs (i.e., in terms of hardware, software, as well as the availability of flat-rate network accesses, especially for mobile devices), allow users to actively participate to the production of the knowledge they consume. In this respect, the P2P communication paradigm can be profitably applied to the learning process for both content sharing and collaboration purposes, thus reducing potential *bottlenecks* in the delivery phase and nurturing *social* aspects.

Before introducing *distributed* e-learning systems based on P2P, we will briefly showcase the main aspects concerning P2P networking. Put briefly, the migration of many client-server architectural frameworks towards more distributed ones occurred owing to: 1) users being able to exploit more powerful *access networks*; 2) the more heterogeneous nature of the Internet; 3) the increased demand for multimedia contents, accounting for strict scalability requirements, and 4) the need of hiding copyright infringements. As a consequence, in many content delivery frameworks, the centralized components are now reduced to the minimum, or simply employed for coordination purposes, such as to provide users paging facilities. Therefore, the core duties are managed by all the network participants. This paradigm leads to P2P systems, where all the involved entities have (about) the same capabilities and responsibilities.

As to emphasize this characteristic, all nodes are called *peers*. Additionally, P2P technologies are mainly placed at the application layer (i.e., ISO/OSI L7), thus being able to "juxtapose" a virtual network over the physical infrastructure. Such a virtual environment is called *overlay*, and it is composed by the transport-layer connections (i.e., ISO/OSI L4) spawned by all the peers. Users are commonly placed at the border of the network, so they can connect according to different strategies, as to create an overlay, which can be almost arbitrary. In this perspective, it can be said that overlays can be used to provide applications with a *"network independent environment."* Being overlays decoupled from the physical deployment, they can be also employed to recover to design limitations of the underlying network, e.g., to overcome the lack of multicast support. In a nutshell, services based upon a P2P blueprint reflect in a very cooperative architecture, which exhibits highly autonomic and scalability properties. As a consequence, P2P-based infrastructures offer an intrinsic resistance against *churn* (i.e., the continuous process of peers arrival and departure) and shutdown attempts. For these reasons, this kind of organization is commonly utilized when scalability is one of the main concerns. As a typical use-case, earlier adoptions of P2P were used to empower file-sharing applications (Sen & Wang, 2004) and (Karagiannis, Broido, Brownlee, Claffy, & Faloutsos, 2004).

The majority of P2P overlays available today can be roughly grouped in *three* different kinds:

- **Unstructured:** peers organize themselves without any external enforcement, resulting in an overlay without a well-defined structure. Hence, it is hard to develop efficient look-up algorithms, both to find users and resources. A typical example is Gnutella;
- **Structured:** peers are organized in a well-defined manner, as to optimize the look-up phase. But, an overhead is present in terms of signaling traffic and storage in nodes. Popular structured systems are the ones based on Distributed Hash Table (DHT) principles, such as Chord (Dabek, et al., 2001) and Kademlia (Maymounkov & Mazieres, 2002);
- **Hybrid:** such class conjugates the best features of centralized (i.e., client-server) and P2P systems. The most popular application is BitTorrent.

As a result of the presence of a centralized entity, which guarantees an easy deployment, BitTorrent has gained popularity, becoming one of the most used applications for content delivery over the Internet. Basically, it is composed of two different architectural blueprints: the *tracker*, which is the centralized component, and the *distribution swarm*, which is the P2P portion of the overall system. One of its main characteristics is the ability to handle *flash crowds*. Such peaks happen when a large amount of peers simultaneously request a specific content; this behavior has been extensively studied and analyzed by Yang and de Veciana (2004). Besides its scalability properties, rooted into the presence of the P2P swarm, the usage of the tracker allows to: *i*) quickly adapt user policies and *ii*) simply develop AAA (Authentication Authorization and Accounting) and CAC (Call Admission Control) mechanisms. Since in e-learning frameworks information and learning assets are bundled inside digital resources, we will showcase how to enhance the delivery process by means of P2P architectures.

P2P Delivery Method

As briefly explained, any learning resource (or activity) over the Internet can be made available in the form of a LO, which is handled by the LMS, that can serve as a LCMS too. To this aim, the latter stores LOs in a suited database and/or repository. LMS are fully standardized, both in terms of information models (e.g., LOM - Learning Object Metadata) and software interfaces and components (e.g., SCORM - Shareable Content Object Reference Model). However, they are usually deployed according to a "walled-garden" flavor. To augment the degree of interoperability, the activity of international standardization in this area has been making important progresses (Friesen, 2005). Therefore, the number of LORs (e.g., Merlot), as well as the availability of trusted learning assets, is rapidly growing. To face to the intrinsic limitations of the adoption of server-centric repositories (Kronsteriner, Weippl, Ibrahim, & Kotsis, 2003) some projects have been developed in the direction of using P2P networks for sharing learning resources (Bulkowski, Nawarecki, & Duda, 2008; Jin, et al., 2005; Duval, Vandepitte, & Ternier, 2002; Zualkernan, 2005; Nejdl, et al., 2002). However, most of them are based on the Edutella framework, which uses standard metadata already defined for the WWW (e.g., the Dublin Core element set). Furthermore, it also defines an additional RDF-based metadata infrastructure to support basic functionalities of P2P applications, and relying upon the JXTA protocol suite, for network-oriented purposes. As a result, the adoption of P2P can introduce additional complexities and requirements, especially within the client-interface devoted to handle the proper logic. We underline that, in the case of JXTA, the resulting "overheads" in terms of protocols and functionalities can be non-negligible. Summing up, overlay networks built via the P2P paradigm can be exploited to disseminate LOs and to set-up collaborative learning communities and educational activities. This also enables the creation of collaborative spaces of learners, driven by similar interests, where it is possible to exchange knowledge, opinions, and experience. Besides, traditional e-learning activities based on the mere transmission of LOs can take great benefits from such a collaboration handle. In this way people can nurture new knowledge and develop social capital while actively participating to the learning

process. All together, they can create a community of practice to learn in an emotional space.

For what concerns the state-of-the-art of P2P file-sharing application, many of them offer ("for free") additional functionalities to make communications among peers possible, e.g., Network Address Translation (NAT) traversal mechanisms. This makes them suited for the integration within a LMS. As an example, they could communicate in order to detect and to avoid fake or corrupt files, or simply discuss technical quality or reliability of LOs. In this way users can really build a technical solidarity (Dagiral & Dauphin, 2005), also increasing the quality of shared LOs and, consequently, of their learning outcome. In fact users can: 1) add metadata to LOs to have a better description available (Or-Bach, 2005); 2) introduce proper indexing information to make them retrievable; 3) produce and share new Los, and 4) annotate the existing ones, based on a collaborative construction model. The activities reported in (1-4) can enhance the learning process, since they allow improving the quality of contents, as well as they ease the process of selection of the best resources. This can be regarded as an incentive to enforce cooperation, necessary because many experiences with P2P architectures show that most of peers only consume the resources offered by the rest of the population of the system. Moreover, due to the technical constraints of e-learning systems, and restrictive digital rights management policies, the educational resources or learning materials cannot be easily shared with other people outside a given LMS. To overcome such issue, it could be necessary to introduce a Trusted Collaboration Infrastructure (TCI) (Yan & Holtmanns, 2007).

Regarding the content to be managed, as already stated, a LO is a file intended to be used for educational purposes, which includes, either internally or via association, indications or suggestions on the appropriate context where it has to be utilized (Sosteric & Hesemeier, 2002). This is done through *metadata*, accounting for the management, indexing, searching and sharing (Littlejohn, 2004). The use of metadata enriches any resource on the Web, like tags and comments commonly do for unstructured information. While pages and documents on the Web are mainly retrieved and accessed through search engines, other multimedia resources cannot be found easily if they do not have already an appropriate description to enable indexing (e.g., when publishing/retrieving photos and videos over the Web). The same applies to LOs. Thus, the successful distribution and re-use of LOs strictly depend on how resources can be found, screened, and retrieved to be used in different instructional contexts (Richards & Hatala, 2005). To make the interoperability possible, among a LMS and any LOR, a specific metadata framework is needed and many exist (Broisin, Vidal, Meire, & Duval, 2005; Maarof & Yahya, 2008; Fertalj, Hoić-Božić, & Jerković, 2009).

In the perspective of adopting P2P capabilities in e-learning systems, the BitTorrent metadata mechanism can be used to enhance, from the users' point of view, the aforementioned ones, while also relying upon a simpler protocol architecture, for instance if compared with JXTA. This is mainly due to: 1) BitTorrent natively support metadata files to handle contents to be distributed and 2) according to specific architecture, the control portion can be co-located within pre-existent e-learning deployments, thus reducing the efforts for its possible integration. In order to share a LO with a BitTorrent-like application, a proper *.torrent* file populated with data for handling the content must be prepared. Then it can be published and exchanged among peers. However, both the name of the LO or of the *.torrent* are not sufficient for a meaningful description of the LO itself. An additional set of metadata, besides those needed to operate the file-sharing service, allows users to give a complete description of the resource itself, e.g., *author, language, description, scope,* and *educational model.*

Figure 1 depicts the basic architectural blueprint, which relies upon a P2P file-sharing service

Figure 1. Reference architectural blueprint based on BitTorrent. Solid lines represent the P2P interactions (i.e., for direct data exchange), while dashed ones are related to client-server communications (e.g., for user paging, AAA, and CAC purposes).

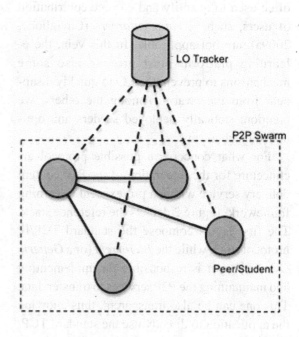

to support the delivery of LOs. Put briefly, it has a direct lineage into the BitTorrent framework. Henceforth, the tracker has been defined as *LO Tracker*, as to emphasize its duties in coordinating a swarm exchanging a LO. It could be implemented by using a standard BitTorrent tracker with some additional layers to wrap its core functionalities, or within the e-learning platform, specifically at the content provider side. The same applies for peers, which are students consuming e-learning services, also running a proper client-interface. Consequently, all the students sharing the same LO compose the swarm. In order to be effective the usage of a P2P content delivery mechanism must be transparent to the user.

As it happens in common file-sharing platforms, to assure a satisfactory performance and a proper degree of scalability, users should share the content as long as possible. As an example, this happens when a student attending a course switches from a lesson to another one, thus actively using a different LO. Anyway the previous one must remain available in the P2P system for the other users. However, standard techniques often used to quantify and enforce contribution of users, such as *ratio enforcers* (Caviglione, 2009a), are not applicable. In this vein, the e-learning platform must provide also some mechanisms to prevent the LO to quickly disappear from the swarm. Among the others, we mention: statically deployed seeders and optimized mechanisms.

For what concerns a possible protocol architecture for the integration of the P2P content delivery service within a pre-existent e-learning framework, Figure 2 depicts the reference stack. The first layers compose the standard TCP/IP protocol suite, while the *BitTorrent* (or a *Generic Overlay*) layer is responsible for implementing and maintaining the P2P services to transfer data. This one can be also transparent, thus allowing the application to directly use the standard TCP/UDP transport services, for instance via a *socket()* syscall. The *Application*, which both implements the e-learning environment and protocols, can directly interact in a transparent manner with the P2P service, or be "mediated" by the e-learning layer. The latter exploits all the rules and mechanisms needed to access the rest of the framework, also hiding the origin of the LOs. Nevertheless, one might imagine this layer: 1) monolithically embedded within the application; 2) partially split across the P2P service and the rest of the framework; 3) merged within the P2P portion of the system offering an API specifically tweaked for the e-learning environment.

Figure 3 depicts a more heterogeneous deployment spanning across different swarms. We define such reference scenario as the *Federated LO* case. In fact different institutions (e.g., Universities) can deploy their own LOs, related to given lectures and according to specific needs and capabilities,

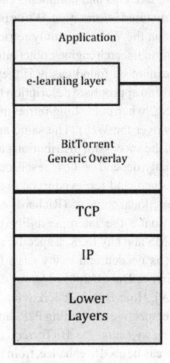

Figure 2. The reference protocol architecture of the P2P infrastructure for the delivery of LO. Lower layers are the merge of the OSI L1 and L2.

differing from already published ones. Therefore, we can imagine a *multi-tiered* approach, where we can compose a complete course by dynamically aggregating LOs, coming from different sources, to produce a federated (or, aggregated) educational content. This can be done in different manners, specifically:

- **Tracker-Side Mechanisms:** an additional layer can be deployed within the LO Trackers, thus being able to process and route requests to retrieve sub-LOs from the proper swarms. This solution implies to change core mechanisms of the protocol, becoming highly unpractical;
- **Client-Side Mechanisms:** ad-hoc implementations of the P2P file-sharing service can be developed to support the proposed vision. But, this increases the complexity

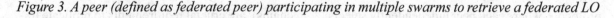

Figure 3. A peer (defined as federated peer) participating in multiple swarms to retrieve a federated LO

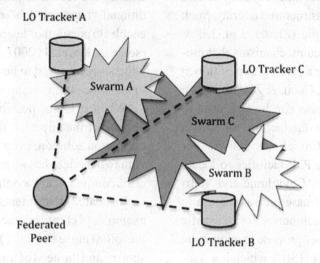

and reduces the usage of well-known and tested P2P algorithms and libraries;

- **Meta-Data Wrapping:** this allows to wrap all the needed *.torrent* files, which describe each LO, into an application specific one, e.g., *.torrent.course*. Then, owing to the "decoupled" architecture presented in Figure 2, the resulting metadata can be parsed by the application or by the e-learning layer, according to the specific needs, and spawn parallel retrievals from the needed swarm (as depicted in Figure 3).

Multimedia and Look-up

More and more frequently, distance-learning activity is made through video lessons, accounting for bandwidth provisioning and availability issues. Furthermore, the resource-consuming nature of multimedia can reflect into possible bottlenecks at the servers' side. Educational systems can greatly benefit of the progress in video capture, analysis and delivery, combined with the rapid adoption of broadband communication. In addition, new trends in content delivery to hand-held devices or advanced approaches for the automatic analysis of multimodal signals, offer novel opportunities for

teaching and learning, as reported, for instance, by Friedland, Hrst, and Knipping (2007) and by Bolettieri, Falchi, Gennaro, and Rabitti (2007). Another topic of interest concerns Video-on-Demand (VOD) systems in which users can obtain the desired teaching materials through the network by using a computer or, alternatively, a television with a Set-Top-Box (Zhang, Liu, & Zou, 2008). VOD learning systems are useful for learners who cannot attend a lecture in real-time, or for those who want to review it later. The VOD systems are already widely used in specific education programs, such as in the field of Evidence Based Medicine (EBM) (Bridge, Jackson, & Robinson, 2009).

Nevertheless, the increasing diffusion of broadband accesses, such as the aforementioned FTTH or Fiber To The Building (FTTB), spawned also many P2P applications for streaming multimedia data. Many of them are already deployed in the Internet. Among the others, we mention *Zattoo*, *PPStream* and *GridMedia* (Zhang, Zhang, Sun, & Yang, 2007). Obviously, the real-time constraints enforced by the need of streaming contents, impose to implement protocols and algorithms different from those employed for file sharing. The most popular ones are called *pull-based* streaming protocols, where each peer independently selects neighbors creating an unstructured overlay. Such protocols are very simple (Zhang, Liu, Li, & Yum, 2005) but enhanced mechanisms that create multiple (i.e., one for a given group of flows) spanning trees exist (Li, Chou, & Zhang, 2004).

Lastly, P2P frameworks can be also used to provide a scalable look-up facility for different kind of resources (Caviglione, 2009b). For the perspective of using P2P facilities to locate devices and laboratories, Caviglione and Veltri (2006) introduce a DHT-based infrastructure to publish and retrieve machineries for scientific experiments. Besides, they propose to exploit the Session Initiation Protocol (SIP), which is a standard signaling solution, to easily support different solutions, which can be also highly heterogeneous. Moreover, the SIP can be used as a "raw" signaling mechanism to set-up devices and instruments, as well as to carry commands and results. Having standardized frameworks like SIP, also accounts for creating sophisticated naming or numbering planes also in the perspective of unifying devices, learning facilities, and multimedia subsystems adopted for communication, conferencing, and presence purposes.

VIRTUAL LABORATORIES, INSTRUMENTATION, AND COMPLEX SYSTEMS

Key aspects of learning strategies involve the replication of experiences, environments, and machineries. In technology enhanced learning, this is achieved by means of *virtualization* and *simulation* techniques, adopting highly distributed computing systems cooperating through a networked environment. This also enables the implementation of "virtual laboratories," where users can operate remote plants and/or simulated devices and systems. The remote control of and access to devices (despite being real or simulated), as well as laboratories (or complex measurement

chains), are crucial requirements to replicate traditional "hands-on lab" experiences. The latter enables to pursue the "learning by doing" paradigm (see, e.g., Ko, et al., 2001, as a possible example), which is recognized to be a powerful educational model since it traces the way the people learn.

When it is not possible to operate physical devices or machineries, the use of simulators is a common solution, even if the direct interaction with real devices has no equivalent. In fact, powerful computers are available at low cost, while sophisticated instruments are not. As possible examples of complex machineries, let us consider the following use cases: 1) hospital equipment for surgery and the need of training doctors to operate them, and 2) to practice on experimental set-ups in the field of robotics, as well as in industry or in hostile environments.

Then, possible trade-offs, becoming practical thanks to the advancements in the field of distributed systems, networking and grid frameworks, are: 1) to accurately emulate a complex hardware deployment, thus exchanging "real hardware" for distributed computing power, reflecting in a *virtual device* or 2) to make remotely available a real plant through the Internet, resulting in a *remote device*. Accordingly, the definition of *remote* or *virtual laboratory* is then straightforward. In the perspective of equipping e-learning platforms with the aforementioned features, the use of grid is a suitable solution, also to cope with performance issues. In fact, it offers computing as utility, making the simulation (or the emulation) of complex systems feasible (Foster & Kesselman, 1999). Szczytowski and Schmid (2006) present an example of mixed usage of a traditional e-learning environment with a simulated laboratory relying on a grid middleware, which exploits the grid to run separate experiments, or several instances of a simulation task. The intrinsic scalability of grids guarantees building complex and rich distributed environments that can be also extended with additional elements. Okon et al. (2006) report on general concepts and key architectural elements of virtual laboratories. Both laboratories and related facilities are core components in the education of students, especially for what concerns the scientific disciplines (Corter, et al., 2007).

Given the general characteristics and capabilities of grid-based distributed systems, two different grid paradigms are adopted for the aforementioned goals, specifically:

- **Computational Grid:** for providing access to a shared pool of resources so that high throughput applications can be performed over distributed machines;
- **Data Grid:** for handling data storage as the shared resource. In this type of grid, the storage capacity can be enhanced and uniquely accessed by also exploiting different types of permanent storage systems and devices.

To develop a virtual laboratory, depending on the specific configurations and the required features, a suited architecture has to be identified, as to provide an appropriate access and control to the remote hardware, as well as the requested functionalities. A common solution exploits a Web-based facade mimicking control panels and instruments, which may optionally include reports of measurements, data or audio/visual feedbacks, e.g., a live Web-cam showing the effects of remote control on a device. We also mention the possibility of creating sophisticated Graphical User Interfaces (GUIs) relying upon Web 2.0 paradigms, such as the Asynchronous Javascript And XML (AJAX) one. However, this pushes additional requirements to the network and can be endangered when in presence of high delays or intermittent connectivity, e.g., when accessing instrument from a satellite or a mobile link.

More sophisticated requirements could be: 1) multiple experiments and equipment must be managed; 2) the facility must be operated by a large amount of users; 3) the software must be equipment-independent, thus parameterized and

reusable on different set-ups (see, e.g., Bochicchio & Longo, 2009, for a prototypal implementation with such properties). Since the grid heavily relies upon the network infrastructure, we can envisage its adoption also for additional services. For instance, to use a portion of the available bandwidth to implement learning strategies based on strict interactions among students, which is a very important part of the learning process when conducted through laboratory experimentation. Therefore a proper network (an overlay or a Virtual Organization - VO) infrastructure empowers this aspect and can duly support the student-to-equipment, student-to-student, and student-to-instructor relationships (Lowe, Murray, Lindsay, & Liu, 2009).

Simulation and Emulation of Complex Systems

As said, through simulation one can achieve real-time interactive experience and the ability of working in safe and controlled environments. It is also possible to realize a wide variety of use-cases and scenarios, also by mixing multiple learning strategies and styles. Additionally, a simulated environment guarantees many important features, such as: reliability, reproducibility of experiments, and availability of feedback signals. Also, it allows operations of data collection and analysis, and the adoption of trial and error methodologies. As a consequence, students are motivated and willing to work in remote labs (Ma & Nickerson, 2006). According to classical educational models, a simulation allows learners to perceive an event as real, with the main objectives (Alessi & Trollip, 1991) of:

1. Contextualizing the learning process in a real-life scenario (e.g., learners may face it on the job);
2. Providing a safe virtual environment where learners have the opportunity to practice their skills without fear of real-life consequences;

3. Utilizing remedial feedback to explain the consequences of mistakes and to reinforce best practices;
4. Simplifying and controlling the reality by properly abstracting complex systems existing in real life. So, the learner can focus on the knowledge to be learnt effectively and efficiently.

To simulate physical phenomena and systems' dynamics, suited mathematical models must be designed. To this aim the support of computing resources is needed, which increases with the complexity of the phenomena to be investigated and the relevant models to be implemented. With the objective of simulating complex systems, also the real world devices composing them must be modeled, even if some approximations can be accepted, according to their dynamics and the required commands, as well as input signals. Subsequently, they must be properly arranged (or merged) together, to reflect the overall system. The more the system is complex and the sampling rate is high, the more accurate is the model, thus the more powerful the computing infrastructure has to be. When real-time simulation is needed, all of these aspects are further amplified. Another key point is the memory required by the control system and the relevant control and decision strategies. In fact, they are often derived from the "past history" of the system to be controlled, thus a large amount of data has to be collected and delivered across the network and has to be continuously/iteratively processed.

To make this vision feasible, we identify grid computing and distributed architectures as the solution to have the needed "rough" power in a scalable and cost-effective manner. Many industrial companies and institutions have shown interest in exploiting the possibilities offered by the virtual laboratories not only for training but also for activities supporting the development and the design of complex systems. Performing the control over a network has some attractive benefits, even

if the networked nature of the set-up introduces additional hazards due to network delays, jitter, and dynamics introduced by the protocol architecture in the control loop. Among the others, the presence of complex layered software architectures, as it happens in grid systems, accounts for additional delays, e.g., data percolation across multiple software modules. For a preliminary performance evaluation of control systems remotely operated through the network for educational purposes see, e.g., Caviglione et al. (2010).

A Design Pattern Analysis of e-Learning through Plants and Devices

In this section, we introduce paradigmatic use-cases, i.e., common situations in the daily practice of performing e-learning activities in the field of controlling remote plants or access to complex devices. Depending on the available equipment, the hardware and network resources, various configurations can be met. One can simulate the control strategy for the real plant or it may be necessary to train personnel on the use of equipment via remote controllers. Such approach resembles the design pattern one employed in software engineering. Specifically, we present *three* paradigmatic cases of possible usage patterns of grids in remotely operated laboratories, for simulation/emulation purposes and for designing controls for remote plants and complex systems.

The first use-case deals with the remote control of a real plant. The idea at the basis of this "pattern" is the availability of a complex system to be used for educational purposes, such as experimental activities or training of specialized personnel. The input signals for the real plant are provided by a suited control system, designed according to the specific needs. It can be a real device or an emulated one, too. To make such operations feasible, we propose the reference system architecture presented in Figure 4.

Figure 4. Remote control of a real plant through a simulated complex control system

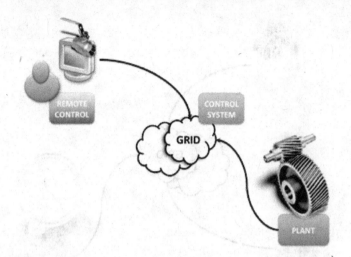

Additionally, let us consider the case in which, for research and/or training purposes, the control system is simulated. The required performances in terms of sampling frequency and response time may cause very high computational requests, and non-negligible usage of network resources. The grid architecture is exploited so that the computational activity can be distributed over the grid itself, thus reducing the load per single node. Nevertheless, it also allows to exploit load-balancing policies, or to aggregate the needed computing resources, which are not available locally. For what concerns the network, we can imagine having proper mechanisms for providing the needed degree of Quality of Service (QoS) to specific flows, or to the control strategies, which have to be sent to the plant.

The second case describes the remote access to a Sensor Network (SN), as depicted in Figure 5. We consider the SN as the source of external data driving the behavior of the plant, also by sharing the same network infrastructure. We point out, that our aim is not to investigate all the possibilities and related interoperability issues of joining SN and grid. Rather, we would like to discuss, even if in an abstract flavor, how distributed systems originated from the coupling of SN and grid can enrich learning facilities and virtual laboratories.

This allows underlining the access to a peripheral device, which can be also the resulting aggregation/composition of a complex set of machineries. In this perspective, a prototypal example can be found in a SN. In fact, SNs are often remotely accessed in order to acquire data from the field, to be used for different purposes. Nevertheless, this also highlights the following technological aspects:

- SNs are commonly implemented by using wireless technologies, such as the IEEE 802.11 family of standards, Bluetooth and ZigBee. Consequently, joining one or several SNs accounts for a more heterogeneous network deployment. Being grid-based infrastructures often deployed over wired technologies, this requires adopting countermeasures, both in terms of protocols and infrastructural elements;
- SNs are usually "hidden" by an ad-hoc software infrastructure, as well as architectural components (e.g., a centralized data sink or collector) in order to perceive them as a standard data source, gathered via well-known paradigms, e.g., Web-Services or event-driven protocols. Thus, to access SNs' data, proper software components or

Figure 5. A reference deployment where data is provided by remotely accessing a sensor network

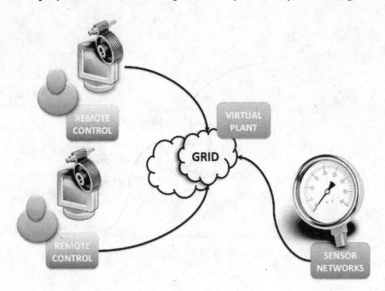

protocol adapters must be present within the overall grid architecture.

In a nutshell, a SN can be the data provider for a plant. The stimuli can be routed through the grid infrastructure to the virtual plant, in order to use them to feed particular educational models or practical experiments, for instance, those aiming at understanding the tuning of critical parameters. Conversely, SN can be also emulated to enable people to gain more comprehension on what can happen when using data provided by such environments.

A very simple "virtual" SN can be roughly done via a database, which can be remotely accessed with the proper protocols and mechanisms. However, since SNs are complex tools, jointly with the dynamics injected by the remote access, a simple database cannot be sufficient to mimic battery-draining issues or network outages due to wireless channel conditions. To this aim, the impact of having a complex remote sensing infrastructure can be "simulated" by having a recorded data set that can be delivered to the virtual plant upon some specific processing. For instance, data can be pruned as to represent malfunctioning of

some sensors, delayed or completely lost, sent in irregular bursts as to simulate problems in the data bearer devoted to deliver the quantities of interest. With respect to "race conditions," we can also imagine to share a real SN to feed multiple virtual plants, allowing students to do their learning assignments by using real data. But, in the case of "races" over the SN, we can introduce the following procedural countermeasures: 1) using multiple databases to "emulate" the availability of different SNs or 2) using a real SN and use it to feed a database farm to solve all race issues. We point out that another possible application of a grid integrated with SNs is related to data fusion and analysis.

As a final consideration, we underline that the joint utilization of SN and grid environments for e-learning purposes (e.g., to enrich virtual laboratories) has been already partially investigated in literature. Concerning issues in performing experiments on SNs in grid-based virtual laboratories, Christou, Efremidis, Tiropanis, and Kalis (2007) deal with both the pedagogical and technical challenges when deploying a distributed laboratory for didactical aspects of SNs. Moreover, Panda, Panigrahi, Khilar, and Panda (2010) discuss the

Figure 6. Remote multiple access to simulated devices and/or control systems

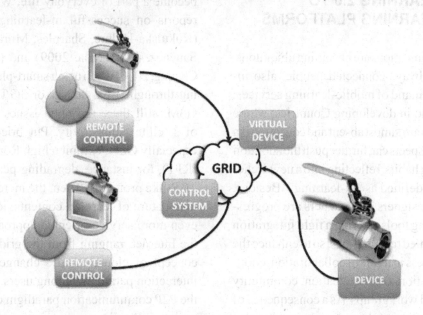

case of Wireless Sensor Networks (WSN). This scenario is significant for e-learning purposes, e.g., when a merge between wireless technologies and virtual systems must be provided to learners. Lastly, Li, Sun, Gao, Yu, and Cai (2009) (and references therein) survey the usage of wireless grids to facilitate e-learning tasks, also by taking into account interactions and contact points with WSNs.

The last case proposed is depicted in Figure 6, and it represents a scenario in which plants or devices are not directly available to users, i.e., the remote multiple access to simulated devices. To cope with this, a simulated instance is implemented, based on mathematical models and known dynamics. Then, by using our reference model, the access to the facility is granted, even if in a virtualized flavor, through a grid-based infrastructure, which makes it possible to create as many instances as needed. This way guarantees the remote multiple accesses to device or plant. The reference architecture discussed in this use-case can also "embed" (and, consequently implement) the control system within the same environment. Additionally, also the devices to be controlled, or

automatically operated, can be real or emulated. In this case lean Internet clients can be used to drive and control the simulated plant, reflecting in a full virtualization of the deployment.

Concluding, the development of middleware to publish and integrate real devices and instrumentation within grid services is a hot research topic. Besides, many projects already demonstrated its feasibility, as well as provided prototypal implementations. Among the others, the most relevant attempts (also in the field of empowering the grid with instruments for training purposes) are: the Grid Enabled Remote Instrumentation with Distributed Control and Computation (GRIDCC) Project, aiming at extending the grid technology to the real-time access and control of instrumentation and the National Science Foundation supported CIMA (Common Instrument Middleware Architecture) Project, which is oriented to the definition of a standard interface methodology across a broad range of instrument types and the abstraction of instrument capabilities. Interested readers can find more details in the work by Caviglione et al. (2009) and the references therein.

FROM E-LEARNING 2.0 TO MOBILE LEARNING PLATFORMS

Mobile communications are becoming ubiquitous, reflecting in always-connected people, also increasing the demand of mobile-learning services. This is true also in developing Countries, where wired networks are almost absent and education is a priority. Such aspects can further push the adoption of new learning habits, reflecting into a new archetype, which is defined as "m-learning." Besides, instructional designers and teachers are progressively exploiting tools offering a tight integration with social-related technologies, so to enhance the education process in terms of collaboration, cooperation, interaction, communication, community of practice, and workgroups. As a consequence of the more user-centric nature of such frameworks, contents are possibly distributed over the network. To dynamically retrieve and compose them, we can employ mashup techniques, which can lead great benefits to the users' experience. Therefore, the learning process is more successful, also by involving people in collaborative processes, activities, relationships, and communications. At the present, most of the e-learning happens through the so-called e-learning 2.0 paradigm, that can further change the level of personalization of the services, the number of interactions and communication channels. According to this, the learning activity can be carried on at home, as well as at school and the mobile-learning techniques can be used for unconventional education purposes too, such as empowering the immersive experiences at museums, keeping up-to-date at workplaces, and for improving tourism.

The m-learning is usually performed trough the usage of a cellular network, or by Wireless LANs (WLANs) connected to a wired data bearer. Alternatively, satellite communications can be used, to enable the delivery of multimedia learning materials and recover to the *digital divide*. In this vein, mobile learning through personal devices (e.g., tablets, smart-phones) is going to become a part of everyday life. While literature reports on successful m-learning applications (Kukulska-Hulme, Sharples, Milrad, Arnedillo-Sanchez, & Vavoula, 2009) and (Lam, Yau, & Cheung, 2010) when using smart-phones connecting through IEEE 802.11 or 3G/UMTS/GPRS/GSM, still there are open issues on the usage of satellite connectivity. Put briefly, satellites, especially GEO, exhibit a high Round Trip Time (RTT), for instance, degrading performances of TCP-like protocols. Then, the increasing distributed nature of learning contents, jointly with an even more service-oriented approach applied to the Internet, ranging from the grid to the recent concept of cloud, require changes also in the interaction paradigm among users. For instance, the P2P communication paradigm can be used to empower the direct user-to-user interaction, also in the perspective of providing a network support to the more social-oriented flavor of e-learning 2.0 applications. Moreover, one can observe that communication and information exchange may happen among people or with well-defined content provider regardless the type of connection used. In this way, mobile devices increase the overall complexity, since they can have different connection capabilities, if compared to wired accesses (e.g., ADSL).

To clarify these concepts, we will present possible relapses of the m-learning paradigm on learning systems, models and strategies. Also, we will consider those aspects related to the high interactivity to keep into account when designing distributed learning systems and services. Lastly, due to growing interest in the field of satellites communication and to the overcome of the digital divide in developing Countries, the role of satellite technology in e-learning is considered.

Mobile Learning

People are increasing their attitude of consuming digitized materials and about any modern portable device with networking capabilities can be used for m-learning purposes, making it profitable. Obviously, the learning model can be influenced by the characteristics of the access network employed. For instance, 3G or IEEE 802.11 connectivity guarantee a rich set of features (also, with some kind of multimedia content support), while slower accesses, such as the plain GPRS, allow a less sophisticated user experience. Besides, different devices offer different capabilities, for instance in term of display size or resolution. Consequently, providers must be able to deliver contents in a scalable manner, according to a "functional space" constrained by devices and network requirements. According to this paradigm, learning may happen even in non-formal and non-structured environment. Among the others, we can mention: 1) outside of Universities or schools; 2) at home or at the workplace, in lifelong learning projects (Adorni, Battigelli, & Coccoli, 2007); 3) in museums, to disseminate information and knowledge about art, architecture or history; 4) in a urban scenario, to apply the same pattern presented in *iii*) and to implement a "context-aware" learning path, also by gathering stimuli from the surrounding environments (for instance by exploiting Near Field Communication - NFC, Radio Frequency IDentification - RFID, or QR Code technologies). Nevertheless, since contents are consumed through personal devices, rather than on "serialized" devices, they can be further personalized according to individual preferences and attitudes.

Despite being an enabler for innovative paradigms, m-learning can be considered both as a brand new model or the revamping of the former idea of distance-learning. The original approach aimed at exploiting the mobility of learners in order to proficiently use idle periods experienced by learners, especially while moving (e.g., traveling time) (Evans, 2008). Nowadays, at least in *developed countries*, portable multimedia communicators (e.g., smart-phones, mp3 players, portable network appliances with audio/video play-backs) are widely diffused. Then, the

m-learning has the opportunity of becoming an embedded part of life, even if at an unconscious level. The m-learning can be exploited through *three* different implementations:

- A new *learning paradigm* that leads to design new learning strategies and contents constrained by the limited resources of mobile devices. In this respect, mobile learning can be considered as an add-on to standard e-learning activities (e.g., quizzes);

- A new *interaction mode* in existing distributed learning environments, that can be accessed by users via their mobile personal devices relying upon networking technologies or even satellite connections. Additionally, the e-learning 2.0 is empowered by the almost-constant on-line presence of people participating to the social learning activities, thus reflecting in increased bandwidth requirements;

- A new *system* mostly based on the use of mobile technologies, for instance to avoid the interruption of learning activities in case of disasters, especially where wired connectivity maybe no longer available. In this case, wireless and satellite connections are commonly the only possible communication infrastructures. Then, the system must be suitably designed to be effective and reliable, also to be employed in Public Safety and Disaster Recovery (PSDR) situations.

Interactivity Requirements and Issues

To provide interactive environments, e-learning 2.0 tools are expected to adopt "classical" features already deployed in Web 2.0 applications. Among the others, we cite the AJAX technique based on the *XMLHttpRequest* JavaScript object. This introduces a kind of "synchronous logic" (e.g., the periodical synchronization of data in

SaaS—Software as a Service—applications, status updates about known contacts in social network applications, as well as presence information). Also, it reflects in repetitive traffic patterns and background traffic. Interested readers can find more details about this model in a work by Caviglione (2009c).

Summarizing, a service relying on the aforementioned methodology can produce a throughput having the form:

$$T(t) = I(t) + B_K(t - KT), \text{ for } K = 1,2,3,...,$$

where: $T(t)$ is the throughput of the traffic produced by the e-learning 2.0 application at time t, $I(t)$ is the interactive traffic generated by users browsing through contents, or produced by specific responses to stimuli applied to the user interface, $B_K(t-KT)$ is the *background contribution*, which is present despite operations performed by users, and T is the time period at which the synchronization happens (usually, it is constant and bounded *a-priori*). As an example, the background contribution could be related to periodical synchronization of data between the student's browser and the remote e-learning facility, for instance for quantifying her/his degree of attention or participation. This continuous traffic must be taken into account, especially when utilizing e-learning 2.0 services through mobile devices, e.g., UMTS terminal. In fact, many users do connect on a pay-per-volume basis, thus reflecting in additional costs. Also, the presence of Comet or AJAX-based objects to assure the constant update of content can be endangered when using mobile terminals, which are often affected by intermittent connectivity due to geographical constraints or multi-path fading. Nevertheless, when in presence of high-delay accesses (such as satellites), calibrating the timeouts could be complex, thus reflecting in misbehaviors especially for what concerns the delivery of the background contribution.

The Role of Satellites in e-Learning

Satellite links are one of the most important tools for the advancement of the Internet and the development of distributed services, such as those related to e-learning. Owing to their deployment characteristics, they can speed-up the globalization, thus contributing to reduce the digital divide (e.g., in developing countries or rural areas), as well as to pursue the "anywhere-anytime" paradigm (Caviglione, Collini-Nocker, & Fairhurst, 2008). GEO accesses are also widely adopted to overcome the lack of wired Internet infrastructures, for instance, after disasters. Such deployments can really take advantages from being reached by an e-learning service, providing a recover or a "back-up" to cope with local deficiencies.

However, even if satellites introduce great benefits (e.g., they allow to deploy multicast in a simple and efficient manner), their joint usage with new technologies empowering e-learning 2.0 frameworks can raise some issues. Firstly, let us discuss possible hazards due to the intrinsic aggregation characteristics of Web 2.0 technologies. In fact, they rely upon data dynamically retrieved from different remote sources (e.g., web-servers, distributed content providers, etc.). This evolves to the mashup, which is the dynamic composition and aggregation of distributed data to produce a brand new content. Figure 7 depicts a reference deployment where the host retrieves components to complete a mashup via heterogeneous network accesses.

Thus, the presence of a satellite link in the path (or in the access network) will reflect into: 1) a reduced performance due to the additional delay in the data transfer phase, if TCP-like protocols are employed; 2) being web contents dynamically composed from "chunks" delivered through portions of the network with different characteristics, this impedes the adoption of a unique enhancement or countermeasure; 3) the presence of satellite links with high and varying delays reflects in difficulties in calibrating HTTP timers; 4) the

Figure 7. Reference scenario of a host accessing a web resource exploiting the mashup technique. Different remote content providers of learning resources are accessed: two deliver contents via a wired access, while one via a satellite link. Notice that content providers can be also students.

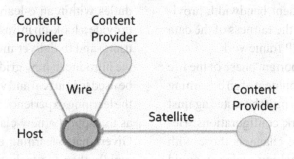

level of security could be technology dependent; 5) due to the heterogeneous characteristic of the mixed wired-wireless environment, users could have incomplete mashups.

In order to make e-learning 2.0 applications interactive, also by using a GUI, bandwidth and real-time requirements from the underlying network must be assured. In other words, a proper QoS guarantee is needed to maintain a proper degree of usability and interactivity. Also, it is possible to put in place some specific tweaks in the application to cope with hazards introduced by well-defined network environments. Specifically, in the case of satellite, data can experience intermittent connections and excessive delays. This is even true for GEO satellite channels, which are characterized by a high *bandwidth delay* product.

For what concerns innovative paradigms characterizing e-learning 2.0 platforms, which can be empowered by the adoption of satellite communication, Caviglione (2009c) explains how they can help in building an "Internet of People." This is the case of e-learning when students have to strictly interact in order to achieve better results. Moreover, video embedding/distribution is another important requirement to bring e-learning services to the next-step. Satellite could provide the proper technology enabler to empower, at a reduced cost, the delivery of multimedia contents and the required social connectivity to a huge

population of individuals (sometimes in the order of hundred millions). In this vein the "social" nature of e-learning 2.0 applications can mix with distribution opportunities made available by satellite technologies. In fact, in e-learning platforms users tend to aggregate according to scholar or business relationships, which often happen among people living in the same area, or in the same Nation. Therefore, GEO satellites can be employed to develop data delivery to well-defined groups of users arranged into a circumscribed area, e.g., a kind of "socialcast" (i.e., the possibility of mapping social relations over the broadcast nature of satellites in order to develop well-aimed content distribution disciplines) (Caviglione, 2009c). Another possible satellite-based learning model uses the satellite TV for the transmission of huge learning contents in the form of video and multimedia. Then, it is possible to interact with a low-bandwidth cable access or a Plain Old Telephone Switching (POTS) Internet connection (Issa, Hussain, & Al-Bahadili, 2010).

The joint usage of satellite and P2P-based applications can introduce some hazards (Caviglione, Davoli, Asorey-Cacheda, & Gonzalez-Castaño, 2005). The main drawbacks are: 1) performance degradations, especially those of TCP, are often mitigated by using Performance Enhancing Proxies (PEPs), which break the end-to-end semantics of P2P; 2) more generally, the presence of middleboxes (and also NATs) can interfere with the highly symmetrical nature of P2P communications, and 3) satellite links commonly offer asymmetrical, time-varying and intermittent bandwidth provisioning, which can reduce the fairness of the data exchanged through the P2P framework.

Lastly, testing is an important phase of the life cycle concerning the development of an e-learning platform or services, which must be tested against the most disparate network configurations. Besides, being GEO satellite channels those with a RTT of about 520 ms, making trials can avoid unpredictable misbehaviors (e.g., disconnections or expiring timeouts). Therefore, a simple and cost-effective solution is the Linux-based software emulator NIST Net. Starting from the kernel branch 2.6, its core functionalities have been integrated in *netem*, which can be used to emulate different wide area network behaviors, e.g., delay, packet delay and Bit Error Rate (BER). Netem is controlled through the *tc* (Traffic Control) command and it is part of iproute2, a collection of utilities for controlling the TCP/IP networking on Linux. Opposite from NIST Net, *netem* does not perform rate control or packet classification, since the kernel already has functionalities to exploit queuing disciplines. Configuring and using *netem* is simple, but a limitation applies: it is only able of emulating traffic for outcoming packets. To overcome such restriction, thus correctly emulating a satellite link, it is sufficient to create a new Intermediate Functional Block (IFB) pseudo device and attaching the emulation disciplines on its incoming packets.

CONCLUSION

This chapter presented how different advancements in distributed computing technologies can be profitably exploited to enhance e-learning systems and methodologies. Specifically, we analyzed the usage of the P2P communication paradigm as a scalable content delivery method for LOs,

also increasing the degree of interaction among learners and teachers. Additionally, we briefly discussed how overlays could be used for other duties within an e-learning platform, such as to provide a look-up infrastructure for resources and users, and to deliver multimedia contents. Then, we introduced how grid-related technologies can be used to join real and virtual devices to empower the learning experience of remote students, as well as to support a new class of hands-on practices. Given that e-learning environments evolve less rapidly than the technology they rely on, many different solutions are possible and only some opportunities have been outlined, reflecting more recent successful implementations in the field of distance education, mostly related to e-learning 2.0 applications. Besides, being satellites a key tool to provide Internet access for developing Countries, we also discussed the role of satellite communication within e-learning platforms, with emphasis on issues and possible hazards when jointly used with two key components for such new systems, i.e., Web 2.0 and P2P architectures.

Further developments of e-learning platforms and services may be connected to the rapid development of the so-called Next Generation Network (NGN), which allows the support in a simple and unified manner of mobility issues, as well as the ubiquitous provision of services to learners and teachers. To this purpose, future work aims at enriching the set of use-cases, and to produce prototypal testbeds or analytical models to conduct performance evaluation campaigns. Specifically, both usage and traffic patterns must be investigated, in order to quantify the needed network requirements, as well as the technological constraints imposed by users' devices. In this perspective, the adoption of scalable "learning profiles," i.e., LO varying according to specific users' requirements and needs, are part of ongoing research related to the field of adaptive systems and interfaces. This is particularly challenging, since in the proposed "enriched" e-learning vision, LOs can be classical assets (e.g., slides or e-books) as well as applications and virtual or real devices.

REFERENCES

Adorni, G., Battigelli, S., & Coccoli, M. (2007). Beyond learning management systems in lifelong learning. In *Proceedings of the 13rd International Conference on Distributed Multimedia Systems - Workshop on Distance Education Technologies, DMS-DET 2007,* (pp. 159-164). San Francisco, CA: IEEE Press.

Adorni, G., Coccoli, M., Fadda, C., & Veltri, L. (2007). Audio and video conferencing tools in learning management systems. In *Proceedings of the 3rd IEEE International Conference on Automatic Production of Cross Media Content for Multi-channel Distribution - AXMEDIS 2007,* (pp. 123-129). Barcelona, Spain: IEEE Press.

Alavi, M. (2004). Distributed learning environments. *Computer, 37*(1), 121–122. doi:10.1109/MC.2004.1260733

Alessi, S. M., & Trollip, S. R. (1991). *Computer based instruction: Methods and development.* New York: Prentice Hall.

Bochicchio, M. A., & Longo, A. (2009). Hands-on remote labs: Collaborative web laboratories as a case study for it engineering classes. *IEEE Transactions on Learning Technologies, 2*(4), 320–330. doi:10.1109/TLT.2009.30

Bolettieri, P., Falchi, F., Gennaro, C., & Rabitti, F. (2007). A digital library framework for reusing e-learning video documents. In Duval, E., Klamma, R., & Wolpers, M. (Eds.), *EC-TEL 2007: Lecture Notes in Computer Science (Vol. 4753,* pp. 444–449). Berlin, Germany: Springer.

Bridge, P. D., Jackson, M., & Robinson, L. (2009). The effectiveness of streaming video on medical student learning: A case study. *Medical Education Online, 14.* Retrieved July 5, 2011, from http://www.med-ed-online.org.

Broisin, J., Vidal, P., Meire, M., & Duval, E. (2005). Bridging the gap between learning management systems and learning object repositories: Exploiting learning context information. In *Proceedings of Telecommunications* (pp. 478–483). IEEE Press.

Bulkowski, A., Nawarecki, E., & Duda, A. (2008). Peer-to-peer dissemination of learning objects for creating collaborative learning communities. In *Proceedings of the World Conference on Educational Multimedia, Hypermedia and Telecommunications,* (pp. 1874–1878). IEEE Press.

Caviglione, L. (2009a). *File-sharing applications engineering.* New York: Nova Science Publishers.

Caviglione, L. (2009b). Enabling cooperation of consumer devices through peer-to-peer overlays. *IEEE Transactions on Consumer Electronics, 55*(2), 414–421. doi:10.1109/TCE.2009.5174402

Caviglione, L. (2009c). Can satellites face trends? The case of Web 2.0. In *Proceedings of International Workshop on Satellite and Space Communications (IWSSC 2009),* (pp. 446-450). Siena, Italy: IEEE Press.

Caviglione, L., Berruti, L., Davoli, F., Polizzi, M., Vignola, S., & Zappatore, S. (2009). On the integration of telecommunication measurement devices within the framework of an instrumentation grid. In Davoli, F., Mayer, N., Pugliese, R., & Zappatore, S. (Eds.), *Grid Enabled Remote Instrumentation* (pp. 283–300). Norwell, MA: Springer.

Caviglione, L., & Coccoli, M. (2010). Peer-to-peer infrastructures to support the delivery of learning objects. In *Proceedings of the 2nd International Conference on Education Technology and Computer (ICETC 2010)*, (pp. 176 – 180). Shangai, China: IEEE Press.

Caviglione, L., Coccoli, M., & Punta, E. (2010). *Education and training in grid-enabled laboratories and complex systems.* Paper presented at the INGRID 2010 Workshop, Instrumenting the grid. Poznań, Poland.

Caviglione, L., Collini-Nocker, B., & Fairhurst, G. (2008). FIRST: Future internet - A role for satellite technology. In *Proceedings of IEEE International Workshop on Satellite and Space Communications (IWSSC 2008)*, (pp.160-164). IEEE Press.

Caviglione, L., Davoli, F., Asorey-Cacheda, R., & Gonzalez-Castaño, F. J. (2005). P2P in satellite networks: A tutorial on related problems and some possible solutions. In *Proceedings of 2nd International Symposium on Wireless Communication Systems*, (pp. 733-736). IEEE Press.

Caviglione, L., & Veltri, L. (2006). A P2P framework for distributed and cooperative laboratories. In F. Davoli, S. Palazzo, & S. Zappatore (Ed.), *Distributed Cooperative Laboratories - Networking, Instrumentation and Measurements*, (pp. 309-319). Norwell, MA: Springer.

Christou, I. T., Efremidis, S., Tiropanis, T., & Kalis, A. (2007). Grid-based virtual laboratory experiments for a graduate course on sensor networks. *IEEE Transactions on Education, 50*(1), 17–26. doi:10.1109/TE.2006.886447

Corter, J. E., Nickerson, J. V., Esche, S. K., Chassapis, C., Im, S., & Ma, J. (2007). Constructing reality: A study of remote, hands-on, and simulated laboratories. *ACM Transactions on Computer-Human Interaction, 14*(2).

Dabek, F., Brunskill, E., Kaashoek, M. F., Karger, D., Morris, R., Stoica, I., & Balakrishnan, H. (2001). Building peer-to-peer systems with chord: A distributed lookup service. In *Proceedings of the 8th Workshop on Hot Topics in Operating Systems*, (pp. 81-86). Elmau-Oberbayern, Germany: IEEE Press.

Dagiral, E., & Dauphin, F. (2005). P2P: From file sharing to meta-information pooling. *International Journal on Digital Economics, 59*, 35–51.

Downes, S. (2005). E-learning 2.0. *ACM eLearn Magazine, 10.*

Duval, E., Vandepitte, P., & Ternier, S. (2002). LOMster: Peer-to-peer learning object metadata. In P. Barker & S. Rebelsky (Eds.), *Proceedings of World Conference on Educational Multimedia, Hypermedia and Telecommunications 2002*, (pp. 1942–1943). IEEE Press.

Evans, C. (2008). The effectiveness of m-learning in the form of podcast revision lectures in higher education. *Computers & Education, 50*(2), 491–498. doi:10.1016/j.compedu.2007.09.016

Fertalj, K., Hoić-Božić, N., & Jerković, H. (2009). Analysis of e-learning repository systems and frameworks with prepositions for improvements. In *Proceedings of the ITI 2009 31st International Conference on Information Technology Interfaces*. IEEE Press.

Foster, I., & Kesselman, C. (1999). *The Grid: Blueprint for a new computing infrastructure.* San Francisco, CA: Morgan Kaufmann.

Friedland, G., Hrst, W., & Knipping, L. (2007). *Educational multimedia systems: The past, the present, and a glimpse into the future.* Paper presented at the ACM Workshop on Educational Multimedia and Multimedia Education. Augsburg, Germany.

Friesen, N. (2005). Interoperability and learning objects: An overview of e-learning standardization. *Interdisciplinary Journal of Knowledge and Learning Objects, 1*, 23–31.

Ip, A., Morrison, I., & Currie, M. (2001). What is a learning object, technically? In *Proceedings of WebNet2001 Conference.* Orlando, FL: IEEE Press.

Issa, G. F., Hussain, S. M., & Al-Bahadili, H. (2010). A framework for building an interactive satellite TV based m-learning environment. *International Journal of Interactive Mobile Technologies, 4*(3).

Jin, H., Yin, Z., Yang, X., Wang, F., Ma, J., Wang, H., & Yin, J. (2005). APPLE: A novel P2P based e-learning environment. In *Distributed Computing, IWDC 2004: Lecture Notes in Computer Science,* (vol 3326), (pp. 52–62). Berlin, Germany: Springer.

Karagiannis, T., Broido, A., Brownlee, N., Claffy, K. C., & Faloutsos, M. (2004). Is P2P dying or just hiding? In *Proceedings of IEEE Globecom 2004 - Global Internet and Next Generation*, (pp. 1532 – 1538). IEEE Press.

Ko, C. C., Chen, B. M., Hu, S., Ramakrishnan, V., Cheng, C. D., Zhuang, Y., & Chen, J. (2001). A web-based virtual laboratory on a frequency modulation experiment. *IEEE Transactions on Systems, Man, and Cybernetics, 31*(3), 295–303. doi:10.1109/5326.971657

Kronsteriner, R., Weippl, E. R., Ibrahim, I. K., & Kotsis, G. (2003). Can P2P deliver what web repositories promised: Global sharing of e-learning content? In *Proceedings of the 5th International Conference on Information and Web-Based Applications*. IEEE Press.

Kukulska-Hulme, A., Sharples, M., Milrad, M., Arnedillo-Sanchez, I., & Vavoula, G. (2009). Innovation in mobile learning: A European perspective. *International Journal of Mobile and Blended Learning, 1*(1), 13–35. doi:10.4018/jmbl.2009010102

Lam, J., Yau, J., & Cheung, S. (2010). A review of mobile learning in the mobile age. In *Hybrid Learning, Lecture Notes in Computer Science (Vol. 6248,* pp. 306–315). Berlin, Germany: Springer.

Li, G., Sun, H., Gao, H., Yu, H., & Cai, Y. (2009). A survey on wireless grids and clouds. In *Proceedings of International Conference on Grid and Cloud Computing,* (pp. 261- 267). IEEE Press.

Li, J., Chou, P. A., & Zhang, C. (2004). Mutualcast: An efficient mechanism for one-to-many content distribution. In *Proceedings of ACM SIGCOMM - Asia Workshop.* ACM Press.

Littlejohn, A. (2004). *Reusing online resources: A substantial approach to e-learning.* London: Routledge Falmer.

Lowe, D., Murray, S., Lindsay, E., & Liu, D. (2009). Evolving remote laboratory architectures to leverage emerging Internet technologies. *IEEE Transactions on Learning Technologies, 2*(4), 289–294. doi:10.1109/TLT.2009.33

Ma, J., & Nickerson, J. V. (2006). Hands-on, simulated, and remote laboratories: A comparative literature review. *ACM Computing Surveys, n.d.*, 38.

Maarof, M. H. S., & Yahya, Y. (2008). LORIuMET: Learning object repositories interoperability using metadata. *International Symposium on Information Technology, 3*, 1–5.

Macgregor, G., & McCulloch, E. (2006). Collaborative tagging as a knowledge organization and resource discovery tool. *Library Review, 55*(5), 291–300. doi:10.1108/00242530610667558

Maymounkov, P., & Mazieres, D. (2002). Kademlia: A peer-to-peer information system based on the XOR metric. In *Proceedings of the 1st International Workshop of Peer-to-Peer Systems*. IEEE Press.

Nejdl, W., Wolf, B., Qu, C., Decker, S., Sintek, M., & Naeve, A. ... Riscj, T. (2002). EDUTELLA: A P2P networking infrastructure based on RDF. In *Proceedings of the 11th International Conference on World Wide Web*, (pp. 604–615). IEEE Press.

Okon, M., Kaliszan, D., Lawenda, M., Stoklosa, D., Rajtar, T., Meyer, N., & Stroinski, M. (2006). Virtual laboratory as a remote and interactive access to the scientific instrumentation embedded in grid environment. In *Proceedings of 2nd IEEE International Conference on e-Science and Grid Computing*, (pp. 124-128). IEEE Press.

Or-Bach, R. (2005). Educational benefits of metadata creation by students. *SIGCSE Bulletin, 37*(4), 93–97. doi:10.1145/1113847.1113885

Panda, M., Panigrahi, T., Khilar, P. M., & Panda, G. (2010). Learning with distributed data in wireless sensor network. In *Proceedings of 1st International Conference on Parallel Distributed and Grid Computing*, (pp. 256-259). IEEE Press.

Richards, G., & Hatala, M. (2005). Linking learning object repositories. *International Journal of Learning Technology Molecular Biology, 1*(4), 399–410. doi:10.1504/IJLT.2005.007151

Rosenberg, M. (2001). *E-learning: Strategies for delivering knowledge in the digital age*. New York: McGraw Hill.

Sen, S., & Wang, J. (2004). Analysing peer-to-peer traffic across large networks. *IEEE/ACM Transactions on Networking, 12*(2), 219–232. doi:10.1109/TNET.2004.826277

Sosteric, M., & Hesemeier, S. (2002). When is a learning object not an object: A first step towards a theory of learning objects. *International Review of Research in Open and Distance Learning, 3*(2).

Szczytowski, P., & Schmid, C. (2006). Grid technologies for virtual control laboratories. In *Proceedings of 2006 IEEE International Conference on Control Applications*, (pp. 2286-2291). IEEE Press.

Yan, Z., & Holtmanns, S. (2007). Trust modeling and management: From social trust to digital trust. In *Computer Security, Privacy and Politics: Current Issues, Challenges and Solutions*. Hershey, PA: IGI Global.

Yang, X., & de Veciana, G. (2004). Service capacity of peer to peer networks. In *Proceedings of the 23rd Annual Joint Conference of the IEEE Computer and Communications Societies*, (pp. 2242–2252). IEEE Press.

Zhang, M., Zhang, Q., Sun, L., & Yang, S. (2007). Understanding the power of pull-based streaming protocols: Can we do better? *IEEE Journal on Selected Areas in Communications, 25*(9), 1678–1694. doi:10.1109/JSAC.2007.071207

Zhang, P., Liu, W., & Zou, X. (2008). A study of video-on-demand learning system in e-learning platform. In *Proceedings of the 2008 International Conference on Computer Science and Software Engineering*, (pp. 793– 796). IEEE Press.

Zhang, X., Liu, J., Li, B., & Yum, T.-S. P. (2005). Coolstreaming/donet: A data-driven overlay network for efficient media streaming. In *Proceedings of IEEE INFOCOM*. IEEE Press.

Zualkernan, I. A. (2005). HYDRA: A light-weight, SCORM-based P2P e-learning architecture. In *Proceedings of the 5th IEEE International Conference on Advanced Learning Technologies*, (pp. 484–486). IEEE Press.

ADDITIONAL READING

Adlnet. (2004). *Shareable content object reference model, SCORM 2004* (4th ed). Retrieved July 5, 2011, from http://www.adlnet.gov/ Technologies/ scorm/ SCORMSDocuments.

Caviglione, L., & Cervellera, C. (2007). Design of a peer-to-peer system for optimized content replication. *Computer Communications Journal, 30*(16), 3107–3116. doi:10.1016/j.comcom.2007.05.041

Devresources. (2011). *Netem project*. Retrieved July 5, 2011, from http://devresources. linuxfoundation. org/ shemminger/ netem/ faq.html.

Dublin Core. (2011). *The Dublin core® metadata initiative*. Retrieved July 5, 2011, from http:// dublincore.org/ metadata-basics.

Linuxfoundation. (2011). *Using intermediate functional block pseudo device to attach Netem disciplines on incoming packets*. Retrieved July 5, 2011, from http://www.linuxfoundation.org/ en/Net:Netem.

SNAD. (2011). *NIST net emulation package*. Retrieved July 5, 2011, from http://snad.ncsl. nist.gov/ nistnet.

KEY TERMS AND DEFINITIONS

Churn: The continuous process of nodes arrivals and departures.

Learning Content Management System (LCMS): A LMS with content management capabilities.

Learning Management System (LMS): A software platform specifically designed to provide the basic functionalities for the e-learning services, to deliver educational content, and to monitor users' activity.

Learning Object (LO): A standardized form for digital learning assets.

Chapter 3
An Approach to Faulty Reader Detection in RFID Reader Network

Hairulnizam Mahdin
University of Tun Hussein Onn, Malaysia

Jemal Abawajy
Deakin University, Australia

ABSTRACT

Radio Frequency Identification (RFID) technology is becoming increasingly popular as an automated tool for object monitoring and identification in a cost-efficient manner. RFID systems are made up of heterogeneous components consisting of both hardware and software. RFID components such as the readers are prone to failures with serious consequences to the overall system. Thus, issues such as reliability and dependability of RFID systems are receiving attention recently. This mandates fault management that includes monitoring the health of RFID readers and accessing the RFID reader configurations remotely. Therefore, an approach that detects the faulty readers with the aim to minimize the impacts of the faulty readers on the system reliability and dependability is of paramount importance. In this chapter, the authors discuss an approach to detect faulty readers in networked RFID system environments. Performance evaluation of the approach against other techniques is presented and shows that it performs reasonably well in the presence of faulty readers.

DOI: 10.4018/978-1-4666-0161-1.ch003

INTRODUCTION

RFID is gaining popularity as a technology of choice for object identification. RFID automates many tedious processes that were done manually previously (Bradley & Guerrero, 2010). RFID is being deployed in many application areas including supply chain management, military applications, retail store and transportation (Liu, et al., 2010a; Thiesse, et al., 2009; Kim & Garrison, 2010). The market value for RFID is expected to grow up to $26 billion by 2016 (Das & Harrop, 2010). One of the reasons that RFID is in the limelight is because of the advantages it offers as compared to the traditional barcode. RFID can store more data, monitor multiple tagged objects at a time and does not need line of sight for detection (Fu, et al., 2010). Unlike barcodes, it provides a timestamp on each reading which is useful to visualize the object movement. The use of RFID in retail store for inventory-taking saved 87% of time compared to barcode (Thiesse, et al., 2009).

Unfortunately, the RFID system is prone to fault due to the harsh environment and the possibility of hardware malfunction (Fritz, et al., 2010). As RFID is increasingly used in many types of applications, some of which are critical, dependability aspects of RFID (fault-tolerance, reliability, etc.) is becoming apparent. One of the RFID system components that is vulnerable to failure is the RFID reader that can originated from many factors such as power failures, hardware or software defects, misplaced antennas, signal interference, weak antenna electromagnetic fields, and fast moving tagged objects (Kamoun, 2009). RFID reader failure is unavoidable (Rao & Chandranr, 2009) and should be detected and as soon as possible to ensure the system reliability.

In many RFID application domains, such as supply chain management and logistics, there are many RFID readers distributed across factories, warehouses, and distribution centres capturing RFID data that need to be disseminated to a variety of applications (Floerkemeier, et al., 2007).

For example, networked of readers are used baggage handlings at the airport to help minimize lost baggage (Ouyang, et al., 2008; Saygin & Natarajan, 2010; Johnstone, et al., 2010; Zhang, et al., 2008; Saygin & Natarajan, 2010) and for security reasons (Harrison, 2010; Roach, 2011). Without RFID, the air travel industry made 30 million error in misrouting the destination of the baggage and it have cost the industry $2.5 billion (Flint, 2007). In order to prevent such tragic events and to reduce the cases of lost baggage, RFID is used to track baggage, its owner and destination to prevent misrouting.

In this chapter, we focus on mechanisms for detecting faulty readers in the networked RFID system environment with the aim to minimize the failure effects on the operation and dependability of the system. With RFID's primary roles in critical applications such as patient monitoring (Corchado, et al., 2008) and assets safeguarding (Dang, et al., 2009), an approach to validate the readers correctness is becoming paramount importance. To address this problem, we propose an approach based on interval fusion algorithm (Marzullo, 1990). The reader's readings were fused together and generate an interval that is agreed by majority of the readers. Reader that did not agree with the majority is considered as faulty. We also compared the performance of the algorithm with other statistical approach that has been used in literature and experimental results show that algorithm performs better than the others. The next section presents the background information in RFID, faulty detection and motivating application.

NETWORKED RFID SYSTEM ARCHITECTURE

Figure 1 shows a high-level RFID system architecture. The system components are tags, readers, middleware and back-end servers and enterprise applications. In this chapter, we assume that the system is composed of $R = \{R_1, R_2, ..., R_n\}$ in-

Figure 1. RFID networks system architecture

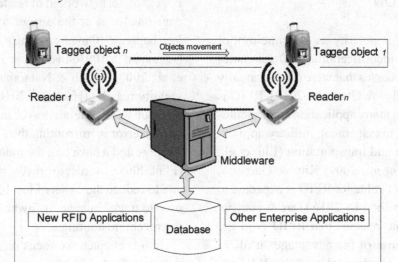

terconnected homogenous readers and $T = \{T_1, T_2, ..., T_m\}$ tags such that $n \ll m$. An RFID tag is attached to an object and each tag contains unique ID known as Electronic Product Code (EPC). RFID tags can be passive, active or semi-active. An active tag has its own on-board power source and transmitter. Active tags always beacon their signal. In contrast, passive tags do not have a power source and solely depend on an external electromagnetic field generated from the reader to initiate a signal transmission. Semi-active tags have a small battery on board that is activated when in the presence of an RFID reader. Active tags are the most expensive while passive tags are less expensive and widely used (Clampitt, 2006). The RFID tags have different frequency ranges from low to Ultra High Frequency (UHF).

The *R* networks of readers are strategically placed to monitor the movement of the same tagged objects from one checkpoint to another. The number of the objects detected also will be the same at each reader in a given time frame. This is because the conveyor is moving at a constant velocity (Lee & Foong, 2008; Shin, et al., 2009) and will carry the same amount number of objects passing the readers. For example, several

RFID readers are used to monitor and track objects at a manufacturing plant with objects moving along the conveyor belt and passed a number of checkpoints (Tan, et al., 2008; Liu, et al., 2010b). At each checkpoint, there is a reader that will read the tagged object. Based on the reading, the system will determine the action that would be taken on that object. For example, the reading will determine the color that will be sprayed on the object based on the code read by the reader. If the reader fails to read the tag correctly, the wrong color will be sprayed on the component. The longer the times to realize this fault, the more components will possibly be sprayed with wrong color. It is very costly to correct such mistakes in the production line especially when involving expensive material.

RFID readers can be either stationary or mobile. A reader will read tags that are reachable by their antenna (e). The more antennas the reader has, the wider its interrogation zone will be. RFID readers use different methods to communicate with RFID tags depending on whether the RFID system is passive or active. Passive and semi-passive tags use passive backscatter to communicate. The signal is generated by the interrogator and radiated through the antenna. The signal is then demodulated by the tag to decode the reader's commands. The reader requested data is reflected back to the interrogator through the modulated signal. Thus an active tag does not have to wait for the interrogator to transmit a signal. This tag can send its data or "beacon" at certain intervals as defined by the system. A system usually has a number of readers that forms a network to monitor the tags movement from one node to another (Dang, et al., 2009; Liu, et al., 2010b; Wang, Luo & Wong, 2010; Kim & Garrison, 2010). Besides reading tags, readers also can perform other functions such as writing data, setting password, locking data and killing tag (Dashevsky & Sokolov, 2009).

The middleware is responsible for handling data coming from the readers before it is send to the backend system. Data processing at middleware includes cleaning, aggregation, joining and generalization. A middleware also can control the reader state in reading the tags (Clampitt, 2006) such as the time lapses between tags reading and time of readings. After middleware process the data, it will be send to the database or enterprise application like Supply Chain Management (SCM) and Customer Relationship Management (CRM). Applications at this layer will transform the data into meaningful information as required by users. It is important to ensure that only correct data be sent to this layer to ensure the reliability of the system. Therefore, unreliability that exist at previous layers need to be detected and filtered quickly in order to ensure correct system state.

FAULTY READERS PROBLEM

Although RFID has many advantages, there are some problems with this system. One such problem is that RFID readers can malfunction for a number of reasons. Generally speaking, fault is the incorrect state of hardware or a program as a consequence of a failure of an RFID system component. Faults can be classified as perma-

nent fault or intermittent fault or transient fault. Permanent faults are the ones resulting from systems failure. For example, RFID reader may die due to battery depletion. An intermittent fault is one that occurs due to unstable characteristic of the RFID hardware components. A transient fault is one that is the consequence of temporary environmental impact on otherwise correct RFID hardware components. For example, the change in environment may cause incorrect RFID reading.

We focus on the problem of faulty reader detection with emphases on an RFID system with a faulty reader that generates faulty readings. The reader can be permanently or temporarily faulty depending on the source of fault. Faulty readings might occur in every functioning readers because an RFID reader cannot be hundred percent correct all the time. This is due to factors such as interference and weak signal (Derakhshan, et. al., 2007). Faulty readers should be detected and repaired to get the system working as expected. Otherwise, the faulty readers will be continuously sending faulty readings for the whole period when the failures occurred.

Faulty readers commonly generate faulty readings with serious consequences. Faulty reader report incorrect readings that will cause excessive order for the items stock (Park, et.al., 2008) or miss reading the tags (Derakhshan, et.al., 2007). The type of faulty readings generated depends on the type of the failure experienced by the reader. For example, if there is power outage, there will be no reading at all from the reader. The following are the two common reading errors due to faulty RFID reader:

- **Incorrect reading:** Incorrect readings are the readings that return incorrect data from the tag to the reader. This is due to interference, signal collision or weak signal. Reader's defect also can generate incorrect reading where it did not encode the signal correctly to get the data. The incorrect reading creates new ID that actually did not exist in the reader vicinity. The incorrect reading can make the system response incorrectly regarding the tagged object.

- **Missed reading:** Faulty readers can miss reading the tagged objects due to a number of reasons. The reader might have been worn out, which makes its beacon not to have enough signals to power up the passive tag in its vicinity. Also, it might have been infected with malware, which decreases it reading speeds and render it to miss reading the tagged objects. The virus also can cause the reader to temporarily sleep and not to do any readings at all.

There is little work on the problem of detecting faulty readers in networked RFID system environments. There are no established methods to manage and monitor RFID readers that were distributed widely in the network (Park, et al., 2008). Faulty readers are one of the sources for unsuccessful readings (Ilie-Zudor, et al., 2011). Siror et al. (2010) observed that the RFID reader recorded failures 77 times in updating the status of the electronic seal on the cargo send to Kenya. The reader failures along with other failures such as GPS failures contribute 33.5% trips that contain error and alerts from the overall trips. The failure is considered high and must be addressed to increase system efficiency and to minimize loss.

A simple method to check the correctness of the reader is by using a reference tag, which is located near the reader (Ni, et al., 2003). As long as the reader can read the tag, the reader is considered working correctly. However, the reference tag itself can be faulty. If the reader cannot read the reference tag, it does not necessarily mean that the reader is faulty. This approach leads to duplicate readings problems and in the case of moving tags like in the baggage handling scenarios, the reference tag could not indicate that the reader is working correctly because the reading static tags is easier as compared to readings moving tags. The moving tags might disappear from the reader vicinity before it has the chances to be read by the reader.

Redundant readers could be used to mask faulty reader (Chetan, et al., 2005; Zhou, et al., 2007). More than one reader can be used to monitor the same vicinity. When one of the readers fails, the backup readers will step in and do the reading of the tagged objects. More than one tag also can be attached to the object hopping that at least one of the tags could be read properly by the reader. This approach also suffers from the redundant reading problems. One of the interesting issues is how to provide the backups after faulty reader has been identified. Lin et al. (2009) specifies a number of logical relationships between the readers in the RFID network. Based on the relations, backup reader can be specified when a faulty reader is detected. The most common relationship that can be found in the RFID readers is the sequence relation. Sequence relation is in the application where the tag will be moving from one reader to another in a predefine path, which is similar for objects moving on the conveyor belt. Figure 2 shows the logical relation between readers and the tag movement through the reader derived from the work by (Peng, et al., 2008; Lin, et al., 2009). The logical relations that can be implied in this figure can be sequence, direction and location which are based on the motive of tags movement (Lin, et al., 2009). Tags maybe moved along a set of readers (sequence), based on the movement of the bearer (direction) or moved from location to location that already set for them (location). The tags are moved through *Reader1* and end up at either *Reader8* or *Reader9*. Based on the logical relations, the faulty readers detected can be covered by other readers in the relation. For example if *Reader1* failed it can be covered by *Reader2* because all the tags will move to *Reader2* after the *Reader1*.

Peng et al. (2008) introduced peer to peer data cleaning that is based on this logical relation. In this approach they identify the Data Cleaning Cluster (DCC) which is the path that will be travelled by the tags through the readers. The

Figure 2. Logical relation among the readers and tags movement

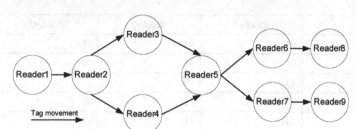

readers are sitting next to each other which form the sequence logical relation. Reading at one reader can be validated by the reading from previous and next reader. If tag is not detected at the current reader but detected at the previous and next readers, then the reading at the current reader will be corrected. Based on this approach, if one reader is detected to be faulty, we can replace the readings from its neighbouring readers.

Many research for detecting faulty sensors have been presented in the literature (Marzullo, 1990; Ding, et al., 2007; Ni, et al, 2009). Ding et al. (2007) proposed an algorithm that computes the median of signal measurements to identify faulty sensor nodes and filtered out extreme measurement by faulty sensors. Median can be used to represent the centre of readings and can show the extreme readings from faulty sensors. Other statistical measures that are commonly exploited for these purposes are the mean and variance (Ni, et al., 2009). Rajasegarar et al. (2010) used median and mean to filter out extreme values in the data. Similarly, Jeffery et al. (2006) used the mean across both temporal and spatial windows to correct faulty sensor values. Faulty sensors can be identified by monitoring measurement deviations from the joint mean, median and others (Zug, et al., 2011). The Marzullo's Interval Fusion (MIF) algorithm (Marzullo, 1990) finds an interval that is agreed by the majority of the readings. MIF has been used in other areas such as the Network Time Protocol (Mills, 2003) to find the correct sources in synchronizing clock time among the nodes in the network. We will use the MIF to identify faulty readers in RFID network by comparing the readings with each other. In the paper, we will compare the performance of Marzullo's algorithm with median and mean to identify readings that produced by faulty readers.

FAULTY READERS DETECTION APPROACH

The premise we start with is that faulty readers will generate incorrect readings or generate no readings at all. Specifically, after t time of tagged moving objects reading, the number of object reads by the faulty readers can be zero or lower than the functioning readers. We will adapt the Marzullo's interval fusion algorithm (Marzullo, 1990) to identify the faulty readers.

As a way of illustration, we use the data shown in Table 1 from four readers: *Reader1, Reader2, Reader3* and *Reader4*. Each reader reads a number of objects at every reading cycle. After 10 reading cycles, we summarize the lowest (*lb*) and the highest number (*hb*) of tagged objects read by each reader. We then generate interval (*lb, hb*) based on the majority of the readers. will be separated to form a new tuple which is *<offset, type>*. To distinguish between *lb* and *hb*, *type* in *<offset, type>* is used to mark the differences. The *lb* will be marked by negative *type* (-) the while *hb* is marked by a positive *type (+)*.

The value for *type* is always 1. The *offset* represent the value of *lb* in the form of *c-r*, while *hb* in the form of *c+r*, where *r* is the difference

Table 1. Number of objects read by each reader

Time	Reader1	Reader2	Reader3	Reader4
100 secs	93	98	108	61
200 secs	91	96	90	65
300 secs	83	99	89	74
400 secs	95	112	80	68
500 secs	104	118	114	61
600 secs	121	99	124	67
700 secs	92	109	107	69
800 secs	115	90	95	68
900 secs	102	84	106	69
1000 secs	90	117	101	72
Lower bound (*lb*)	**83**	**84**	**80**	**61**
Higher bound (*hb*)	**121**	**118**	**124**	**74**

from the centre of the interval c to either *lb* or *hb* and computed as follows:

$$r = \frac{hb - lb}{2} \qquad (1)$$

In contrast, c is the centre of the interval that can be calculate from the following equation:

$$c = hb - r \qquad (2)$$

For example, the interval for *Reader1* is (83,121). The value of r for this interval is r=(hb-lb)/2=(121-83)/2=19 and the value of c is hb-r=121-19=102.The *lb* for this interval (83,121) will be written as <102-19,-1> and the *hb* is <102+19,+1>. All the intervals from Table 1 will be converted to this form. The tuples then will be sorted as shown in Table 2.

The interval fusion algorithm now can be used to detect the faulty reader based on the readings consensus. The algorithm will produce interval that is agreed by the majority of the readers. A reader with a reading value that intersects with this interval is considered as a properly functioning reader while those readers that do not fall

Table 2. The tuple <offset, type> from Table 1 after sorted ascending

Index i	<*offset, type*>	Description
0	<67.5-6.5,-1>	Reader 4 lower bound
1	<67.5+6.5,+1>	Reader 4 higher bound
2	<102-22,-1>	Reader 3 lower bound
3	<102-19,-1>	Reader 1 lower bound
4	<101-17,-1>	Reader 2 lower bound
5	<101+17,+1>	Reader 2 higher bound
6	<102+19,+1>	Reader 1 higher bound
7	<102+22,+1>	Reader 3 higher bound

within the range of the intervals are considered as faulty readers.

From Table 2, the interval is (84, 118). Based on this interval, *Reader4* is considered faulty because its interval (61, 74) does not intersect with the derived interval (84, 118) chosen by the majority of the readers.

As an illustration, we plot each reader readings and their intersections with the intervals as shown in Figure 3. The grey area shows the readings of the properly functioning readers that intersect with interval produced by the algorithm.

Figure 3. Illustration of interval intersection

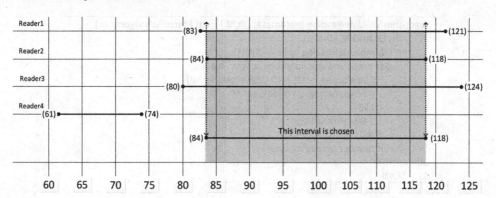

To ensure that only functioning reader will send their reading to the middleware, the interval (*lb, hb*) from the fusion process is sent back to each reader. The readers will compare their readings locally with this interval from the fusion process to validate their readings. If the interval does not intersect with each other, the reader is regards as faulty and is prevented from sending the readings to the middleware. This can save energy consumption by performing the validation locally where it reduces the network load from being used to send faulty readings.

To perform this, we used *ValidateReading* algorithm as shown in Figure 4. At step 1, the algorithm starts by receiving the readings from the tags. In step 2 and step 3, after a number of reading cycles specified by the application is true, the interval from the readings will be produced. In step 4, if the interval's low bound is equal or smaller than the *lb*, and the interval's higher bound is equal or higher than *hb*, the readings for the whole cycle is considered as correct. At step 5 the readings is sent to the middleware. Otherwise, the readings will be discarded from the reader and this indicates a faulty reader (step 7). The number of reading cycle will be reset to start the process again.

PERFORMANCE ANALYSIS

In this section, we present experimental results conducted to study the performance of the approach discussed in this chapter. As in (Derakhshan, et al., 2007), we model faulty readers having low read rate as compare to the properly functioning readers. As in Tang et al. (2009), Li et al. (2008), and Alani & Elmirghani (2009), tag readings are generated based on Poisson process. We will use false positive and false negative to examine the performances of the Marzullo-based algorithm as compared to median and mean (Rajasegarar, et al., 2010) approaches to study their accuracy and the robustness. The median and mean are commonly used to identify outliers in a data as shown in. The outliers can intuitively represent the readings that produced by faulty readers.

Comparative Analysis

In this experiment, we want to investigate the false positive rate under different percentage of faulty readers. In the experiment, the number of faulty readers was varied from 20% to 50%. The tag arrival rate is varied from 90 to 110 tags per cycle for functional reader while 30 to 50 tags per cycle for the faulty readers.

Figure 5 shows the result for false positive rates under different percentages of faulty readers. The Marzullo-based algorithm is the most accurate and

Figure 4. ValidateReading algorithm

Algorithm ValidateReading (parameter (lb,hb) from Marzullo's algorithm)
1   INCOMING READING
2   IF (Number of Reading Cycle == TRUE)
3   Get lowbound and upperbound from readings
4   IF (lowbound <= lb) AND (highbound >= hb)
5   Send readings to middleware
6   ELSE
7   Discard readings
8   END IF
9   Reset number of reading cycle
10   ENDIF
11   END

Figure 5. False positive rate comparison under different percentage of faulty reader

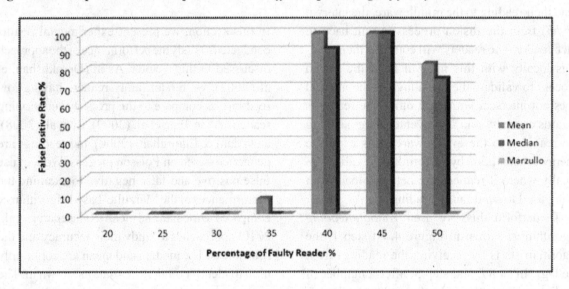

robust with no false positives on all samples. In contrast, the *mean* and *median* algorithms have very high false positive rates, especially when the number of faulty readers reaches 50% of readers in the system. As the percentage of the reader increases, the intervals produced by Marzullo-based algorithm become smaller. The interval produced by Marzullo-based algorithm tends to represents the majority of readings by the functioning readers. This makes readings from faulty readers to rarely lie within the intervals and subsequently lead to detection of the faulty readers. However, the *median* and *mean* algorithms always represent the center of all readings and disregard the sources whether it is majority or not. This tendency led the *median* and *mean* algorithms to fail capturing faulty readings from the faulty reader beginning with the number of faulty readers reach 40% in the sample. For Marzullo-based approach, even when the faulty reader is 50%, there are no false positive readings because the faulty readers' readings have short interval ranges (because of low tag arrival) that do not intersect with the derived intervals.

Figure 6 shows the false negative rate under different percentage of faulty readers. Marzullo-based algorithm has the lowest rate as compared

Figure 6. False negative rate comparison under different percentage of faulty reader

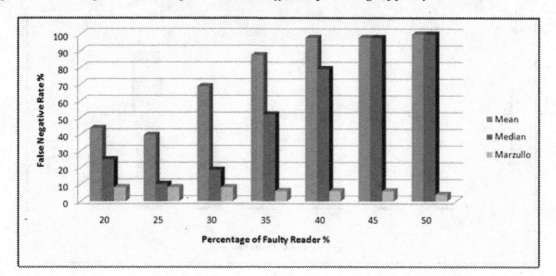

to the *median* and *mean* algorithms. The *median* and *mean* algorithms show a big drop in their performance where the false negative increased almost linearly with the addition of faulty readers. This happens because some of the correct readings have very high read rate that left them from being in the majority readings. When we run the algorithms, these correct readings with very high rate do not intersect with the interval produced. Although Marzullo-based algorithm also have the false negative but the false negative is still low compared to the *median* and *mean* algorithms. When the number of faulty readers increased, there are many correct readings undetected as correct by *median* and *mean* algorithms as compared to Marzullo-based approach.

Sensitivity to Tag Detection Rate

In this experiment we want to test the robustness of the approach under different tag arrival rate. In the experiment, we fixed the number of faulty reader at 30% but changed the arrival rate for the tags from 10 to 80. Figure 7 shows the false positive rate under different tag detection rate by faulty readers. The Marzullo-based approach has about 24% false positive when the tag detection rate is 70. This is because some of the readings from faulty readers have reading rate that are nearly at the same rate with the functioning readers. This allows the faulty readers readings to intersect with the interval produced. Figure 7 also shows that the result we get in Figure 5 is consistent where there are no false positive for all the approach when the number of faulty readers is at 30%.

The false positive starts to show on the *mean* algorithm when the tag detection rate for the faulty readers is increased to 60. This is because the centre of readings generated by the *mean* algorithm has decreased making it intersects with the readings from the faulty readers. In contrast, the median and Marzullo-based approaches are only affected when the tag detection rate for the faulty readers is at 70. However Marzullo-based approach still performs better than the *median* algorithm because it takes into account both the majority of the readings and each intervals of the reading individually. The *median* algorithm does not look at the readings individually but only consider the centre of the readings based on the number of appearances.

Figure 8 shows the false negative rate under different tag detection rate. The *mean* approach generated the highest false negative, followed

Figure 7. False positive rate comparison under different tag arrival rate

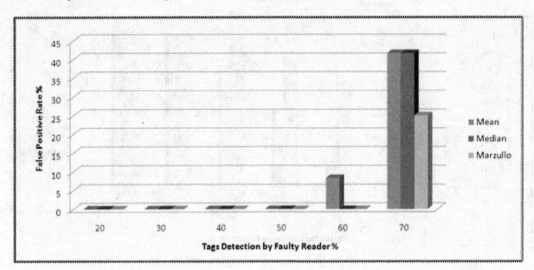

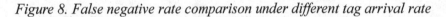

Figure 8. False negative rate comparison under different tag arrival rate

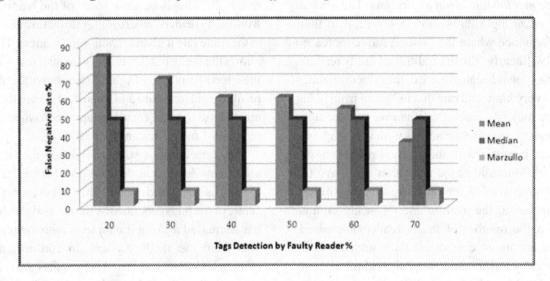

by the *median* algorithm and Marzullo-based approach. The later remains stable throughout the different tag detection rate and generated below 10% false negative. There is false negative in Marzullo-based approach because there are sample readings that generate correct readings. This is because the Poisson process generates the reading randomly and causing some of the readings that meant for correct reader to appear and have the same rate with faulty readers readings. However

the performance of Marzullo-based algorithm is better compared to *median* and *mean* in all sample readings.

From all these experiments, we conclude that the interval generate from the Marzullo-based algorithm is more suitable to be used to identify correct faulty sources as compared to the *median* and *mean* approaches. The *mean* does not depict the majority of agreed sources. It takes the center of all readings including correct and faulty readers readings. The *median* performs better than *mean* when the majority of the data is reading from functioning readers. However, it cannot perform better than Marzullo because Marzullo-based considered each reading interval individually that make it more accurate to represent the center of the correct readings.

FUTURE RESEARCH DIRECTIONS

For future works, we plan to work on expanding the research to provide the fault tolerance mechanism in RFID. We also want to perform the interval fusion process dynamically. The process should be done only when there are incorrect readings in the reader's readings. By this we can reduce the work load instead of doing it periodically. We also aim to modify the proposed approach for usage in applications that do not have constant movement of objects like in retail store. For the time being the Marzullo's algorithm cannot be applied directly because the number of objects passing by each reader is varies. There is also opportunity to solve faulty readings problem including noise, missed and duplicate reading using the approach.

CONCLUSION

In this paper we proposed an approach to detect faulty readers in a system composed of networked RFID readers. From the experimental results, we concluded that Marzullo's algorithm is suitable to be used in solving the problem of detecting faulty readers in RFID networks. Faulty readers need to be detected early to ensure the reliability of the system is not affected. The mechanism to detect faulty readers must be done automatically instead of manually checking, which is not efficient .One of the ways to do this is by using the Marzullo's algorithm as proposed in this chapter.

REFERENCES

Alani, O., & Elmirghani, J. (2009). Mix queues approach for indoor network traffic modelling. In *Proceedings of the Fifth International Conference on Networking and Services*, (pp. 438-443). IEEE Press.

Bai, Y., Wang, F., & Liu, P. (2006). Efficiently filtering RFID data streams. In *Proceedings of the CleanDB Workshop*, (pp. 50-57). IEEE Press.

Bradley, J. R., & Guerrero, H. H. (2010). A framework for RFID deployment in supply chains. *IT Professional*, *12*(4), 44–50. doi:10.1109/MITP.2010.43

Chetan, S., Ranganathan, A., & Campbell, R. (2005). Towards fault tolerance pervasive computing. *IEEE Technology and Society Magazine*, *24*(1), 38–44. doi:10.1109/MTAS.2005.1407746

Clampitt, H. G. (2006). *RFID certification textbook*. Houston, TX: PWD Group.

Corchado, J. M., Bajo, J., de Paz, Y., & Tapia, D. I. (2008). Intelligent environment for monitoring Alzheimer patients, agent technology for health care. *Decision Support Systems*, *44*(2), 382–396. doi:10.1016/j.dss.2007.04.008

Dang, Q., Hong, L., Liu, S., Su, Z., & Yu, J. (2009). RFID application in IT assets management. In *Proceedings of the International Conference on Microwave Technology and Computational Electromagnetics*, (pp. 29-32). IEEE Press.

Das, R., & Harrop, P. (2010). RFID forecasts, players and opportunities 2011-2021. *IDTechEx Inc Report*. Retrieved 10 December 2010 from http:// www.idtechex.com.

Dashevsky, V., & Sokolov, B. (2009). New concept of RFID reader networks structure: Hardware and software architecture. In *Proceedings of the International Conference on Ultra Modern Telecommunications & Workshops*, (pp. 1-4). IEEE Press.

Derakhshan, R., Orlowska, M. E., & Li, X. (2007). RFID data management: Challenges and opportunities. *IEEE International Conference on RFID*, (pp. 175-182). IEEE Press.

Ding, M., Liu, F., Thaeler, A., Chen, D., & Cheng, X. (2007). Fault-tolerant target localization in sensor networks. *EURASIP Journal on Wireless Communications and Networking, 1*, 19.

Flint, P. (2007). Baggage asphyxia. *Air Transport World, 44*(3), 5.

Floerkemeier, C., Lampe, M., & Roduner, C. (2007). Facilitating RFID development with the Accada prototyping platform. *IEEE Systems Journal, 1*(2), 495–500.doi:10.1109/JSYST.2007.909778

Fritz, G., Beroulle, V., Nguyen, M. D., Aktouf, O., & Parissis, I. (2010). Read-error-rate evaluation for RFID system on-line testing. In *Proceedings of the IEEE 16th International Mixed-Signals, Sensors and Systems Test Workshop (IMS3TW)*, (pp. 1-6). IEEE Press.

Fu, P., Li, Y., & Tian, Y. (2010). Research on the compatibility of RFID middleware reader. In *Proceedings of the 2nd International Conference on Computer Engineering and Technology*, (vol 4), (pp. 16-18). IEEE Press.

Harrison, J. (2010). Supply chain security and international terrorism. In Thomas, A. (Ed.), *Supply Chain Security* (*Vol. 1*, pp. 7–53). Santa Barbara, CA: ABC-CLIO.

Ilie-Zudor, E., Kemeny, Z., Blommestein, F. V., Monostori, L., & Meulen, A. V. D. (2011). A survey of applications and requirements of unique identification systems and RFID techniques. *Computers in Industry, 62*(3), 227–325.doi:10.1016/j.compind.2010.10.004

Jeffery, S. R., Garofalakis, M., & Franklin, M. J. (2006). Adaptive cleaning for RFID data streams. In *Proceedings of the 32nd International Conference on Very Large Data Bases (VLDB 2006)*, (pp. 163-174). IEEE Press.

Johnstone, M., Creighton, D., & Nahavandi, S. (2010). Status-based routing in baggage handling systems: Searching verses learning. *IEEE Transactions on Systems, Man, and Cybernetics, 40*(2), 189–200.doi:10.1109/TSMCC.2009.2035519

Kamoun, F. (2009). RFID system management: State-of-the art and open research issues. *IEEE Transactions on Network and Service Management, 6*(3), 190–205.doi:10.1109/TNSM.2009.03.090305

Kim, S., & Garrison, G. (2010). Understanding users' behaviors regarding supply chain technology: Determinants impacting the adoption and implementation of RFID technology in South Korea. *International Journal of Information Management, 30*(5), 388–398.doi:10.1016/j.ijinfomgt.2010.02.008

Lee, K.-M., & Foong, S. (2008). Lateral optical sensor with slip detection of natural objects on moving conveyor. In *Proceedings of the IEEE International Conference on Robotics and Automation*, (pp. 329-334). IEEE Press.

Li, Z., Chu, C.-H., & Yao, W. (2008). SIP-RLTS: An RFID location tracking system based on SIP. In *Proceedings of the IEEE International Conference on RFID*, (pp. 173-182). IEEE Press.

Lin, X., Pan, J., Liang, J., & Wang, D. (2009). An RFID reader coordination model for data process. In *Proceedings of the Second International Symposium on Computational Intelligence and Design*, (pp. 83-86). IEEE Press.

Liu, L., Chen, Z., Yang, L., Lu, Y., & Wang, H. (2010a). Research on the security issues of RFID-based supply chain. In *Proceedings of the International Conference on E-Business and E-Government*, (pp. 3267-3270). IEEE Press.

Liu, W. N., Zheng, L. J., Sun, D. H., Liao, X. Y., Zhao, M., Su, J. M., et al. (2010b). RFID-enabled real-time production management system for Loncin motorcycle assembly line. *International Journal of Computer Integrated Manufacturing*.

Marzullo, K. (1990). Tolerating failures of continuous-valued sensors. *ACM Transactions on Computer Systems*, 8(4), 284–304. doi:10.1145/128733.128735

Mills, D. (2003). A brief history of NTP time: Confessions of an internet timekeeper. *ACM Computer Communications Review*. Retrieved from http://www.eecis.udel.edu/~mills/database/papers/history.pdf.

Ni, K., Ramanathan, N., Chehade, M. N. H., Balzano, L., Nair, S., Zahedi, S., … Srivastava, M. (2009). Sensor network data fault types. *ACM Transaction on Sensor Networks, 5*(3).

Ni, L. M., Liu, Y., Lau, Y. C., & Patil, A. P. (2003). *LANDMARC: Indoor location sensing using active RFID*. Paper presented at First IEEE International Conference on Pervasive Computing and Communications. Dallas-Fort Worth, TX.

Ouyang, Y., Hou, Y., Pang, L., Wang, D., & Xiong, Z. (2008). An intelligent RFID reader and its application in airport baggage handling system. In *Proceedings of the International Conference on Wireless Communications, Networking and Mobile Computing*, (pp. 1-4). IEEE Press.

Park, N., Song, Y., Won, D., & Kim, H. (2008). Multilateral approaches to the mobile RFID security problem using web service. In *Proceedings of APWeb 2008,* (vol 4976), (pp. 331–341). IEEE Press.

Peng, X. Z. Ji, Z., Luo, Z., Wong, E. C., & Tan, C. J. (2008). *A P2P collaborative RFID data cleaning model*. Paper presented at the 3rd International Conference on Grid and Pervasive Computing – Workshops. Kunming, China.

Rajasegarar, S., Leckie, C., Bezdek, J. C., & Palaniswami, M. (2010). Centered hyperspherical and hyperellipsoidal one-class support vector machines for anomaly detection in sensor networks. *IEEE Transactions on Information Forensics and Security*, 5(3), 518–533.doi:10.1109/TIFS.2010.2051543

Rao, K. S., & Chandranr, K. R. (2009). Efficient method for identifying location and removal of data redundancy for RFID data. *International Journal of Recent Trends in Engineering, 2*(1).

Roach, K. (2011). The Air India report and the regulation of charities and terrorism financing. *The University of Toronto Law Journal, 6*(1), 45–57.doi:10.3138/utlj.61.1.045

Saygin, C., & Natarajan, B. (2010). RFID-based baggage-handling system design. *Sensor Review, 30*(4), 324–335.doi:10.1108/02602281011072215

Shin, I. S., Nam, S.-H., Roberts, R., & Moon, S. (2009). A minimum-time algorithm for intercepting an object on a conveyor belt. Industrial Robot. *International Journal (Toronto, Ont.), 36*(2), 127–137.doi:10.1108/01439910910932586

Tan, J., Wang, H., Li, D., & Wang, Q. (2008). A RFID architecture built in production and manufacturing fields. *International Conference on Convergence and Hybrid Information Technology, 1*, 1118-1120.

Tang, S., Yuan, J., Li, X.-Y., Chen, G., Liu, Y., & Zhao, J. (2009). RASPberry: A stable reader activation scheduling protocol in multi-reader RFID systems. In *Proceedings of the 17th IEEE International Conference on Network Protocols*, (pp. 304-313). IEEE Press.

Siror, J. K., Guangun, L., Kaifang, P., Huanye, S., & Dong, W. (2010). Impact of RFID technology on tracking of export goods in Kenya. *Journal of Convergence Information Technology, 5*(9).

Thiesse, F., Al-Kassab, J., & Fleisch, E. (2009). Understanding the value of integrated RFID systems: A case study from apparel retail. *European Journal of Information Systems, 18,* 592–614. doi:10.1057/ejis.2009.33

Wang, J., Luo, Z., & Wong, E. C. (2010). RFID-enabled tracking in flexible assembly line. *International Journal of Advanced Manufacturing Technology, 46,* 351–360.doi:10.1007/s00170-009-2102-z

Zhang, T., Ouyang, Y., & He, Y. (2008). Traceable air baggage handling system based on RFID tags in the airport. *Journal of Theoretical and Applied Electronic Commercial Research, 3*(1), 106–115.

Zhou, S., Luo, Z., Wong, E., Tan, C. J., & Luo, J. (2007). Interconnected RFID reader collision model and its application in reader anti-collision. In *Proceedings of the IEEE International Conference on RFID,* (pp. 212-219). IEEE Press.

Zug, S., Dietrich, A., & Kaiser, J. (2011). An architecture for a dependable distributed sensor system. *IEEE Transactions on Instrumentation and Measurement, 60*(2), 408–419.doi:10.1109/TIM.2010.2085871

ADDITIONAL READING

Hassan, T., & Chatterjee, S. (2006). A taxonomy for RFID. In *Proceedings of the 39th Annual Hawaii International Conference on System Sciences (HICSS 2006),* (vol 8), (p. 184b). HICSS Press.

Jalote, P. (1994). *Fault tolerance in distributed systems.* Upper Saddle River, NJ: Prentice-Hall.

Marzullo, K. (1989). *Implementing fault-tolerant sensors. Technical Report TR 89-997.* Ithaca, NY: Cornell University Press.

Nguyen, M.-D., Fritz, G., Aktouf, O.-E.-K., Beroulle, V., & Hély, D. (2011). Towards middleware-based fault-tolerance in RFID systems. In *Proceedings of the 13th European Workshop on Dependable Computing (EWDC 2011),* (pp. 49-52). IEEE Press.

KEY TERMS AND DEFINITIONS

False Negative: Data that not being detected in the experiment while it's actually exists.

False Positive: Data that being detected in the experiment while it's actually not exists.

Faulty Reader: A reader that generates no readings at all, all faulty readings or low number of readings compare to the other reader in the system.

Interval Fusion Algorithm: Algorithm that fuse sensors data to produce intervals that can represent the majority of the data.

Middleware: Software that receives readings from the readers and performs filtering and aggregation to the raw data before sending it to the enterprise and database application.

Poisson Process: A stochastic process in which events occur continuously and independently of one another. For example bus arriving at the bus station.

RFID: Stands for Radio Frequency Identification. A technology that uses radio waves to transmit data from a tag to a reader

Chapter 4
A Security Framework for Networked RFID

Harinda Sahadeva Fernando
Deakin University, Australia

Jemal Abawajy
Deakin University, Australia

ABSTRACT

In the last decade RFID technology has become a major contender for managing large scale logistics operations and generating and distributing the massive amount of data involved in such operations. One of the main obstacles to the widespread deployment and adoption of RFID systems is the security issues inherent in them. This is compounded by a noticeable lack of literature on how to identify the vulnerabilities of a RFID system and then effectively identify and develop counter measures to combat the threats posed by those vulnerabilities. In this chapter, the authors develop a conceptual framework for analysing the threats, attacks, and security requirements pertaining to networked RFID systems. The vulnerabilities of, and the threats to, the system are identified using the threat model. The security framework itself consists of two main concepts: (1) the attack model, which identifies and classifies the possible attacks, and (2) the system model, which identifies the security requirements. The framework gives readers a method with which to analyse the threats any given system faces. Those threats can then be used to identify the attacks possible on that system and get a better understanding of those attacks. It also allows the reader to easily identify all the security requirements of that system and identify how those requirements can be met.

DOI: 10.4018/978-1-4666-0161-1.ch004

INTRODUCTION

Radio Frequency Identification (RFID) is an automatic identification technology that is based on a contact-less, proximity based communication method (radio waves). The potential applications of RFID systems are diverse and RFID networks already exist in a large range of environments and applications. The proliferation of RFID networks has been rapid in the last decade (Schuster, et al., 2007). One specific area in which the use of RFID technology has become increasingly popular is in massively networked logistics applications such as global supply-chain management systems. The use of RFID tags instead of barcodes allow for the automated identification and tracking of the tagged objects. In addition RFID systems can generate a vast amount of transactional data concerning the tagged objects that can then be shared in real time with the other partners of the system. But, as with all technologies there are a number of issues that prevent its widespread adoption. In RFID the main current barrier to adoption is the large number of security concerns about networked RFID systems and the additional performance overhead placed on the system when generating and sharing such a vast quantity of data.

Networked RFID systems are a relatively complex type of RFID system. This complexity arises from some of its features such as wireless communication, mobile data containers (RFID tags), highly distributed nature and the presence of multiple independent entities that are authorized to access the system. Due to its wireless communication method and distributed nature networked RFID systems are vulnerable to a great number of malicious attacks at the edge of the system (tags, readers and wireless communications). These attacks can range from simple ones such as passive jamming and eavesdropping to more sophisticated attacks such as physical cloning of tags, man in the middle attacks and even RFID malware (Karygicmnis, et al., 2006). In RFID systems these threats can be mounted either through physical or logical access to system components. In addition, networked RFID systems can be attacked by internal partners as well as external attackers. Therefore the security threats and attacks that are faced by RFID networks are both numerous and extremely diverse. To successfully manage and eliminate all these different types of threats a large number of security requirements must be implemented.

Due to the large number and different types of attacks and threats facing a RFID system, fully securing it is a very complex task. This task is made even more difficult by the number of different components that must be protected and the large number of security concepts that must be upheld. Currently one of the biggest barriers to the widespread adoption of networked RFID systems is the unresolved security issues inherent in them (Juels, 2006). Without a proper security framework to reference most companies have no method with which to reliably access the vulnerabilities of their system. Nor do they have a method with which to decide how best they can remove those vulnerabilities and fully secure their RFID systems. Due to this fear over RFID system security most companies are still reluctant to implement RFID based solutions even though the benefits they pose are great. Therefore the need for a RFID security framework that will allow developers to successfully identify, manage and secure against the threats and attacks faced by RFID systems is currently very acute. But if such a framework is to be successfully developed a few challenges must first be overcome. Networked RFID systems, while seemingly similar to normal networked systems, differ quite significantly from them. Therefore the most important challenge is analysing how the security requirements of networked RFID differ from the security requirements of typical networked systems.

There is a currently number of security frameworks that are available in literature. But a majority of the current existing security frameworks are aimed at general networked systems (Jeong &

Haas, 2007; McGee, et al., 2004). Because the architecture of massively networked RFID applications is significantly different from typical IT networks and standalone RFID systems (further discussed in section 2) these frameworks do not take into account the differences of a networked RFID system and therefore cannot be fully applied to those systems. In addition some of the frameworks only look at the possible threats and do not look at how those threats can be mitigated, while some others only look at standalone RFID and not at networked RFID (Rotter, 2008). Therefore most of these frameworks are either not applicable to networked RFID systems or they are insufficiently detailed to fully secure a networked RFID system.

If a security framework for networked RFID was successfully developed it would ensure that the companies that are implementing RFID solutions could easily analyse and verify the security of those systems leading to higher adoption rates for networked RFID. Therefore in this chapter we develop and present "A networked RFID security framework." As a precursor to developing the security framework we develop a threat model which analyses the threats faced by networked RFID systems, the vulnerabilities they exploit and the attacks that result. The actual framework will be composed of two main components (1) The attack model: which identifies and classifies all possible attacks on networked RFID systems, and (2) the system model which identifies all security requirements needed to protect a networked RFID system. The developed security framework will create a systematic path to identifying all the potential threats to any given RFID application, better understanding the attacks that can be mounted on the system and also identifying the security requirements for securing the system.

The remainder of this chapter is organized as follows: The next section presents the conceptual model for a networked RFID system and identifies the key differences between networked RFID systems, standalone RFID systems and general networked systems. It also illustrates what a net-

worked RFID system is by using a RFID enabled global supply chain management system as an example. The following section presents the current research in the area and identifies some key weaknesses we are trying remover. The section titled Threat model presents and analyses the threat model that applies to this type of system. The section titled security framework contains the developed security framework for networked RFID while the section after that shows how the framework can be applied to a RFID system. Next we identify some possible future research direction for the work presented in this section as well as other possible research areas we have identified as being important. The final section presents the conclusions of this chapter.

BACKGROUND

In this section we will describe the basic conceptual model of a networked RFID system and its operation. We also clearly differentiate it from normal networked RFID systems and standalone RFID systems by identifying the differences between these different types of systems. We will also present the threat model specific to the system in question

Networked RFID System Model

The most important component of a networked RFID system is the RFID tag. RFID tags used in networked systems are typically low cost passive tags with update functionality. The items in the system are tagged with a RFID tag when they are first manufactured. The tag will always hold a unique identifier which allows the system to associate data stored in the backend databases with the attached item. When a new RFID tag is entered in the system the manufacturer of the item allocates its identification number. He then stores any data concerning that item in a secure database that can be accessed by any partner who needs

Figure 1. Networked RFID architecture

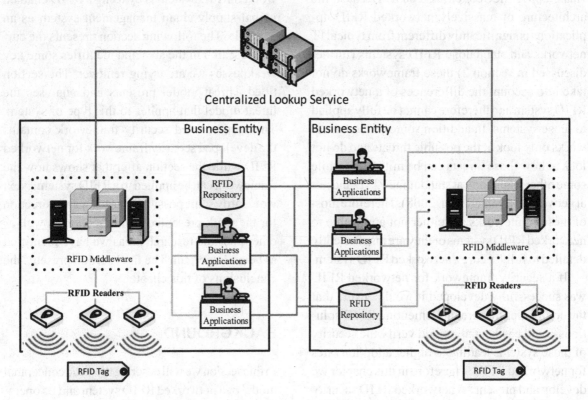

that data. Because the RFID tags are physically attached to objects they are relatively less secure that typical data storage devices in networked IT systems (Glover & Bhatt, 2006). In addition, most large networked RFID system need to use very low cost RFID tags. Therefore the amount of resources available on those tags (both performance and power wise) is considerably low and it is nearly impossible to implement the standard cryptographic security measures employed in IT networks on those tags. But because the RFID tags contain a memory module that contains sensitive data it's still imperative that the data stored on the tag be secure from both logical and physical access (see Figure 1).

The tagged items are then transported along the network while passing from one partner to another. Along the way these tags items will come in contact with the RFID readers of partners of the system. RFID readers are used to read and

write data to and from RFID tags. They are composed of three main parts: the receiver, transmitter and controller (Hassan & Chatterjee, 2006). A RFID reader needs to manage the large number of simultaneous transmissions it may receive and respond to them (Tajima, 2007). In systems that employ passive RFID tags the readers must also provide power to the tags (Glover & Bhatt, 2006). The readers also need to read the identifier and any additional data stored on any authenticated tags within reader distance and update the data on the when necessary (Ranasinghe, et al., 2005). When an authorized reader comes in contact with a RFID tag it first retrieves the identifier of the tag. That identifier and any other data stored on the tag is then passed on to the RFID middleware of the system.

The RFID middleware is arguably the most complex component of the system. It needs to carry out a number of different tasks to ensure that the overall RFID system functions correctly. The middleware filters and collects the data received from RFID tag as low cost RFID tags are notorious for bad and false reads. The middleware also needs to carry out most of the security tasks to ensure the integrity and authenticity of the tags and the data received from them (Juels, 2006). Systems employing the EPCGlobal architecture translate the EPC and data retrieved according to the tag data specification as data is stored in binary format on the tag. The middleware also aggregates, filters and formats RFID tag data as required by the enterprise applications. The middleware also generates transaction data based on business events (Christian & Matthias, 2005). Therefore when it receives tag data from readers the middleware first filters it to ensure that they are not false or bad reads. Then any security functionality is carried out to ensure that the data is safe to be used. The middleware then locates any additional data locations using a lookup service and retrieves any required information from those partners' data servers. It then uses preset business rules to generate transaction data, associates that data with the identifier and stores that data in the system database. The middleware also communicates with other applications that require RFID data and retrieve that data; either from the local database or from partners databases and forwards it to them. This architecture is very different from normal networked systems which typically do not have a dedicated middleware component, as different partner applications communicate directly with each other as required.

The centralized lookup service is what allows different independent partners to locate and communicate with each other (Schuster, et al., 2007). In some very large networked RFID systems all the partners of the system may not even directly know each other or of each other's existence (Tajima, 2007). This is normally different from networked IT systems as in those systems all partners who communicate with each other directly know each other as well. Therefore networked RFID systems

require a method with which the partners can locate all the data stored in the overall system concerning a specific tag. This service is normally run by an independent entity that is trusted by all partners. In EPCGlobal systems this service is provided by the EPCGlobal ONS service. The lookup directory needs to have the identification numbers of all the RFID tags of the system. It also needs to know the location of all the data concerning each specific RFID tag and the details on how to contact that data server.

The RFID repository is where the data concerning the tagged objects are stored. In some systems the data servers are only accessible by the RFID middleware, and internal or external applications which need to access that data need to do so through the RFID middleware. In other systems these servers can be directly accessed by partner applications (Armenio, et al., 2007). Either way the RFID repository needs to allow more access to its data by external entities and programs than is typically allowed in IT systems. In addition the data stored in the RFID data servers are stored in as granular a form as possible to preserve as much of the information as possible. It is up to the querying middleware or the business applications to extract the required information from the raw data and format it in a way that can be used by the business applications.

The business applications use the data received from the RFID system to carry out existing business processes (Floerkemeier & Lampe, 2005). They may also update the data stored in the repository or the RFID tags based on their processes. These applications are mostly pre-existing ones that have been modified to integrate with the RFID system and use the information supplied by the RFID middleware (Asif & Mandviwalla, 2005). They retrieve information as required by either going through the middleware or by directly communicating with the external and internal RFID data repositories. Therefore in networked RFID systems the business applications must be modified to directly communicate with either the middleware of the system or other partners RFID repositories. Unlike in typical networks where the different partners have data format and storage standards and agreements the business applications using a networked RFID system may be required to use data stored in a number of different formats and granulites by different partners. The retrieved data is then used to automate, improve and streamline existing business processes.

As in any networked system all these different components have to be connected by a communication network. The networks used in RFID systems can be divided into two main parts: the internal network and the external network. The internal network (shown in the green lines above) connects the components of a single partner together. This part of the network typically consists of a LAN or WAN and is protected from outside intrusion by the partner's firewall and intrusion detection and prevention software. The external network on the other hand connects the components of different partners together, as well as connecting the middleware of the systems with the centralized lookup service for the overall system (Li & Ding, 2007). This part of the network is generally implemented over the internet and typically has very little security other than what's provided at each end.

Networked RFID Example

The best example for a truly large scale networked RFID system is the global supply chain management systems being deployed by large retailers such as Wal-Mart. The RFID systems in this case spans all the way from the initial raw materials manufacturer to the final retailer who sells the end product to the consumer and in some cases even continues past sales. When raw materials are first generated and packed those packages are attached with a RFID tag. Then the manufacturer stores static information such as date, batch number, and price and expiry date of that package on either the tag itself or the backend database. He may also

associate transaction data such as who bought that package, and to where it should be delivered with the specific RFID tag as they become available. When the logistics get that package they use that data to properly deliver that package. They also update the data in their backend database with details such as unit's current location and the shipment and transport truck it's been attached to. This kind of 'transactional data" is automatically generated and will be constantly updated in a large number of different repositories as new readers pick up that specific RFID tag and the middleware associates new business processes with that item.

When the final product producer receives that item he unpacks it and uses the raw materials contained inside to create products. These products each have new RFID tags but those tags are also linked with the tags of the raw materials packages they were developed from. Once again the producer stores static information on either the tag or the back end and then the final products starts moving alone the supply chain moving from each partner to partner. At different points in this chain each partner generates more and more transactional data concerning the products attached to each tag and stores them in his personal RFID repository. As can be imagined most of time each partner is only aware of the partner directly up and down chain of him. (e.g., a logistics company moving goods between the producer and the distributor only know about those two partners, Likewise the final retailer is only aware of the distributor he received the goods from not the logistic companies that did the transport at each leg of the journey). But while they may not know the other partners they still need to access all the transactional data that was generated by each partner if the full power of the RFID system is to be leveraged. Therefore they need to be able to locate all the data repositories that contain information about any given RFID tag. This is where the EPCGlobal comes in. The EPCGlobal provides services that allow partners to identify the data repositories anywhere in the world that contain information about any given tag. Different companies use different business applications and place more importance on different types of data. Therefore the data stored in each repository must not only contain as much information as possible but it must also be able to carter to the data format requirements of a large number of different business applications.

CURRENT RESEARCH ISSUES

As the following sections illustrate RFID systems have the following unique features that set them apart from typical IT network systems: (1) unlike most IT systems which are accessible by a single authorized entity, the RFID tags of the system need to need to be fully accessible by all partners in the network. (2) Unlike other data storage devices in IT systems the RFID tag is much more physically accessible by attackers. (3) Low security resulting from the lack of resources available on RFID tags makes the wireless communications of the system highly vulnerable to attackers. (5) The mobile nature of RFID tags make it possible to invade the privacy of the system without ever gaining access to the communications or the memory modules of the system. (6) Even the internal components such as the RFID repository and the middleware needs to allow considerably more external access compared to internal components of a normal networked system. (7) The data storage and data the formatting may be completely different from partner to partner and (8) Some of the different partners of the system may not even know each other at all (Li & Ding, 2007).

Additionally networked RFID systems also have a few main features that set them apart from standalone RFID systems. (1) Networked RFID systems have a number of users while standalone RFID systems have only one user. (2) The tags of networked RFID systems are comparatively a lot more mobile and physically accessible by attackers than the tags of a standalone RFID system and

(3) overall system structure for standalone RFID is considerably simpler than the system structure for a networked RFID system. Therefore when developing a security framework specifically for networked RFID systems these differences must be taken into consideration. Currently no security framework has been developed for networked RFID systems. But there exists a number of generic security and network security frameworks as well as some classifications of RFID attacks and defences that present some interesting insights in to this research area. In the following section we will examine some of those papers and analyse their weakness in context of the security of networked RFID systems.

In Ayoade (2007) the authors present a 'Roadmap to solving security and privacy concerns in RFID systems.' This paper identifies some of the potential threats and attacks possible on RFID systems. It then goes on to present some proposed technical solutions as well as some policy propositions that can be used to neutralize the identified threats and attacks. Unfortunately the security threats identified are in no way comprehensive and it fails to mention some of the more dangerous threats such as RFID malware or RFID cloning. The list of proposed technical solutions presented is short and in some cases not viable due to practical or performance issues.

In Rotter (2008) the authors present "A framework for assessing RFID System Security and Privacy Risks.' The work presented contains a lot of information about the potential security and privacy threats faced by a large number of different types of RFID systems. Unfortunately it makes no mention of some of the threats and issues specific to networked RFID systems with multiple partners. This paper also contains no information about the security functionality required to defend against the identified threats. While the framework is suitable for standalone RFID systems it's too simple for networked RFID systems.

'Framework for ensuring network security' (McGee, et al., 2004) has been built around a

Figure 2. Threat model for networked RFID

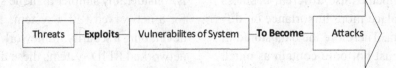

threat model using a modified version of the C.I.A threat model. It uses a layering technique to ensure that all areas of the system's security have been covered whether it's at hardware level or at application level. It also contains a list of the security requirements to secure an IT network and a number of cross analysis tables mapping the security requirement, the threat model and the different layers of the network to identify what needs to be done at each layer to negate each threat identified in the threat model. It also compares the developed framework with some other popular security frameworks. The biggest issue with this framework is that's it's developed for typical network systems and not networked RFID systems. Therefore this framework overlooks some threats specific to networked Multi-entity RFID systems as well as some threats that all RFID systems face. Also some of the preventive measures discussed are not possible in a RFID system due to the differences in its architecture compared to a normal wired IT network.

The 'Integrated security framework' presented in (Jeong & Haas, 2007) is also of the same nature but even more generic framework than the one presented in Rotter (2008). This framework has been developed to apply to all types of wirelesses networks ranging from complex and high powered cellular networks to basic RFID networks employing low cost RFID tags. While the authors discuss the basic security concepts that apply to all wireless systems (Confidentiality, Authentication, Integrity, Availability and Non-repudiation) it does not mention any of the RFID specific attacks such as data leakage, cloning or tag tracking.

'Classification of RFID attacks' (Mitrokotsa, et al., 2010) classifies a majority of the currently possible attacks on RFID systems based on the layer at which the attack is targeted at. The taxonomy contains all the common RFID threats such as replay attacks, impersonation attacks and denial of service attacks. It also discusses some of the lesser known attacks such as malicious code injection and traffic analysis. While this classification is helpful in securing a majority of RFID systems it still does not look at some of the threats uniquely present in networked multi-entity RFID systems such as repudiation, unauthorized data modification by partners and corporate data theft. It is also taxonomy rather than a security framework and therefore focuses more on identifying and classifying threats rather than identifying how to secure the system against them.

THREAT MODEL FOR NETWORKED RFID

The distributed and collaborative nature of networked RFID along with the use of low cost RFID tags which employ wireless communications mean that there are a large number of threats faced by these types of systems. These threats exploit vulnerabilities in the system to become attacks. The threat model we develop and present in this section will identify and discuss the common threats faced by networked RFID systems. It will then analyse how those threats exploit certain vulnerabilities that can exist in the system to become specific attacks that that compromise the security of the system (see Figure 2).

The two most common threats faced by RFID systems are the possibility of an attacker intercepting or changing the wireless communications between tags and readers. Because low cost RFID tags do not contain sufficient resources for standard security functionality most networked RFID systems cannot implement strong authentication, confidentiality or integrity verification. Therefore potential attackers can exploit the lack of these security mechanisms to mount a number of attacks on the system. These attacks allow them to either gain access to confidential information or allow them to exchange sensitive data so as to harm the system. In eavesdropping the attacker exploits the lack of confidentially in the system to listen to a legitimate conversation between readers and tags. This allows the attacker to gain access to confidential information. Data leakage attacks: a more complex form of eavesdropping, are mounted by eavesdropping on a large number of authenticated communications between a tag and a reader and using that data to gain confidential information (Mitrokotsa, et al., 2010). Another common attack which exploits lack of proper mutual authentication in RFID communications is the man-in-the-middle attack. This attack is a form of active eavesdropping in which the attacker makes independent connections with a reader and tag that is communicating while making them believe that they are talking directly to each other. The attacker then proceeds to change valuable data or steal confidential information as it's transmitted through him between the reader and the tags (Rotter, 2008). Lack of strong mutual authentication is also exploited to mount replay attacks. Here the attacker uses previously used responses by a tag or a reader in a challenge-response protocol to initiate a new session with the tags or readers of the system. This allows the attacker to access either the reader or tags as a legitimate component and steal information or wrongly update data stored on the system. Attackers can also exploit the weak encryption techniques used in RFID systems using low cost tags to mount

crypto attacks on those systems. Crypto attacks use various mathematical methods to break through the weak encryption in communications and gain access to the information that's being communicated.

Another major threat faced by networked RFID systems is the attacker introducing false objects into the system. These types of threats primarily exploit the lack of proper mutual authenticate between tags and readers. Tag cloning, tag spoofing and reader impersonation are all attacks that result from this type of threat being successfully leveraged into an attack. In tag cloning the attacker replicates all the identification details of a legitimate tag on to a forged tag and introduces it in to the system. In tag spoofing, rather than creating a new tag, the attacker just transmits the identification information of legitimate tags in the vicinity of readers using a transmitting device. In reader impersonation the attacker impersonates a reader of the system, rather than a tag, and tries to access tags by initiating a conversation with them (Rotter, 2008). All three of these attacks enable the attacker to either feed false data to the system or retrieve confidential data from the backend database while posing as a legitimate component of the system.

The threat of RFID malware has only been recently brought to the attention of RFID researchers (Rieback, et al., 2006). These attacks are mounted by exploiting poor mutual authentication or storage integrity checks to store malicious code on the tags or to create cloned tags with malicious data and introduce them into the system. When these tags are read by readers the malware either corrupts the data in the backend databases or compromises the middleware of the system by infecting it. In buffer overflow attacks, which are a simpler version of malware attacks, the attacker makes a tag try and send the same block of data repeatedly till it overflows a memory buffer in either the readers or the middleware of the system thereby corrupting data or even crashing that component or even the whole system (Rieback, et al., 2006). The threat of RFID malware is very severe because it not only corrupts data but it can also spread from tag to system to tag and affect a very large amount of tags and back end databases very quickly. More complex RFID malware can even infect the business applications or open breaches in the firewalls protecting the internal system allowing attackers access the internal components of the system directly.

Another type of threat to networked RFID systems is the invasion of privacy enabled by tracking tags. Here the attacker sets up a network of RFID readers and exploits the mobility of the tags and the fact that most tags reply with their unique identification number on being queried by any reader. By identifying the tag at regular intervals they can then build a map of their movement over time thereby tracking either the person or the object the tag is attached to (Weis, et al., 2003). Tag constellation tracking is a more complex form of tag tracking where the attacker tracks a combination of tags rather than a single tag (Mitrokotsa, et al., 2010). Additionally most radio transmitting devices have what is known as a radio fingerprint which is created at manufacture and is unique to each tag. By exploiting this attackers can sometimes track individual tags even if they don't have access to its identification number.

Another threat faced by RFID systems is the attacker rendering components or even the whole system unavailable my various means. The successful completion of such an attack can cause part of or even the whole system to become unavailable. This in turn affects the performance of not only the RFID system but also that of the business applications of both the company in question and external partners that rely on the RFID system for information. The easiest Denial of Service (DOS) attacks to mount on RFID systems are signal jamming and physical destruction of system components. Signal jamming takes advantage of the fact that wireless communications use a broadcast medium and floods the channel with powerful signals using the same frequency. This makes it

impossible for the relatively weak RFID signals to propagate through thereby effectively rendering the tags unavailable to be read by the readers (Rotter, 2008). The attacker can also exploit limited amount of resources available on readers and tags and bombard a specific reader or tag of the system with data requests thereby overloading that tags or the reader's capability to reply (Mitrokotsa, et al., 2010). Attackers can also exploit the relatively lower physical security available to RFID tags to just physically damage or destroy the tag thereby shutting down the system. A more complex DOS threat that can be mounted on some RFID systems is the de-synchronization of tags with the backend components. Here the attacker takes advantage of the temporary pseudonyms used by certain RFID protocols to de-synchronize the tags next response from the response expected by the rest of the system. This makes it impossible for the tag and reader to communicate till they are manual re- synched (Li and Deng, 2007). Attackers can also exploit the built in KILL or LOCK commands on certain RFID tags to disable those RFID tags thereby rendering them useless till they are reactivated (Juels, 2006).

In RFID systems with multiple partners the possibility of a partner compromising the overall system for his own profit is an ever-present threat. The possibility of attacks by partners jeopardizes the trust the users have in the system thereby reducing the overall advantages that can be gained by implementing a networked RFID system. Here the partners take advantage of either there authorized access to the system or the lack of proper access controls to mount attacks which compromise the system for other users. Repudiation attacks happen when an entity sends a communication or changes system data but later denies doing so (Fernando & Abawajy, 2009). In RFID this can be in the form of changed tag data to forged tag broadcasts. Another threat in this environment is partner de-synchronization. This attack is a carried out by an authorized independent partner of the system and would typically de-synchronize

Table 1. Networked RFID threat model

Threat	Exploits weaknesses:	And results in
Interception or modification of system data and communications	Lack of secure mutual authentication	Replay attacks
	Lack of secure mutual authentication and confidentiality	Eavesdropping attacks Data leakage
	Lack of secure mutual authentication, integrity verification and confidentiality	Man-in-the- middle,
	Lack of sufficiently strong encryption	Crypto attacks,
	Lack of storage confidentiality Poor physical security of tags	Physical reading of tags
	Lack of storage integrity Poor physical security of tags	Physical writing to tags
Introduction of false objects into system	Lack of strong and secure mutual authentication	Tag cloning Tag spoofing Reader masquerading
Invasion of privacy	Mobility of tags lack of proper mutual authentication	Tracking (Forward and Backward) Tag constellation tracking
	The mobility of the tags and the easily identifiable radio fingerprint on low cost tags	Radio fingerprint tracking
Denial of service	Lack of physical security	Physical destruction of components
	Low resources available on tags	Active jamming
	Broadcast mechanism of communications	Passive jamming,
	Use of pseudonyms of some security protocols	De-synchronization of tags
	Built in lock and kill commands and lack of mutual authentication	Unauthorised tag locking or killing
RFID malware	Lack of strong and secure mutual authentication lack of storage integrity. Weak anti- malware protection on backend servers	RFID malware (worms, viruses, SQL and Script injection)
	Lack of strong and secure mutual authentication Lack of proper buffer control in readers	Buffer overflow
Attacks by internal partners	Lack of access control	Elevation of privileges (reading)
	Lack of data ownership	Elevation of privileges (writing)
	Lack of non-repudiation	Repudiation of actions
	Lack of access controls Lack of non-repudiation	Partner de-synch, killing or locking tags for partners

the RFID tag with the backend databases and readers of the other partners in the network. In a multi entity RFID network some companies may want to use the RFID tags to store data that is confidential or the capabilities of some companies may be limited (e.g., can read tag data but cannot update it or can read just some of the tag data and not all of it). By exploiting the lack of proper access controls a partner can mount an elevation

of privileges attack and increase the access he has to the tags of the system to gain confidential information on the partners business processes and intents or to even update or delete RFID data without proper authorization (Mitrokotsa, et al., 2010) (see Table 1).

Figure 3. Attack model for networked RFID

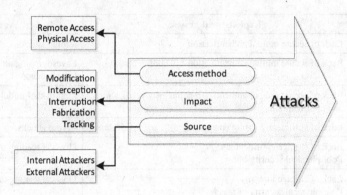

SECURITY FRAMEWORK

When developing a security framework for any system there are two main areas that have to be explored and analysed: (1) the possible attacks to the system and their features and (2) the important system components that must be protected. Therefore our security framework is composed of two main parts: the attack model and the system model.

Attack Model

The attack model analyses the possible attacks on the system and classifies them based on various different criteria. The attack model allows readers to get a better understanding of all the attacks that can possibly be mounted on a networked RFID system. The attack model analyses the attacks in three ways. It looks at the source of the attack, the negative impact the attack will have on the system if successful and the method by which the attack access the system components it's attacking (see Figure 3).

Access Methods

One of the most important aspects of any attack is how that attack is actually mounted on the system. For networked RFID applications we identify two main access methods with which

attackers can attack the system: logical access and physical access.

The main method of communication between tags and readers in a RFID system is wireless communication. Therefore potential attackers can exploit this communication method to gain logical access to either the memory modules of the system or even the information that is being remotely communicated between the tags and readers. Unauthorized logical access to the system can be gained in a number of different ways (Mitrokotsa, et al., 2010). The attacker can pretend to be an authorized tag or reader and gain access to the system. They can also try and intercept the wireless transmissions between the readers and tags and decrypt them to gain the information stored in them. Eavesdropping, tag tracking and replay attacks are some common types of logical access attacks.

In normal IT systems the data is stored in a physically secure location such as a data server in a server room. Whereas RFID systems store some of its sensitive data on the RFID tag itself, which is in turn affixed to physical objects that travel along the physical network (Tajima, 2007). IN addition the RFID readers may also be mounted in relatively unsecure locations such as warehouses and transport vehicles. Therefore some of the components in networked RFID systems have relatively low physical security compared to the components of a normal network. Physical access

Table 2. Mapping of attack classification to Microsoft STRIDE model

	Spoofing	Tampering	Repudiation	Information Disclosure	Denial of Service	Elevation of Privilege
Modification		Y	Y			Y
Interception				Y		Y
Interruption					Y	Y
Fabrication	Y	Y	Y			
Tracking				Y		Y

attacks are mounted by attackers who gain physical access to the tags or the readers of the system. Physical destruction of tags and physical reading and writing of tags are some common physical access attacks. (See Table 4 for details of access methods of all identified attacks)

Attack Impact

Another important aspect of any attack is the impact it will have on the system. We categorize the attacks possible on networked RFID systems into 5 main groups based on the negative impact they will have on the system: (1) Modification, (2) Interception, (3) Interruption, (4) Fabrication and (5) Tracking. The impacts we have identified are slightly different from the STRIDE developed my Microsoft. Table 2 maps our impacts to the STRIDE model for comparison.

Interception and modification attacks are the most common attacks possible on any IT system. In interception attacks the attacker intercepts data while it's stored or being communicated and gains access to confidential information. In modification attacks the attacker changes, deletes or creates data in the system without authorization (Fernando & Abawajy, 2009). In RFID systems these attacks can be carried out with either remote or physical access. The wireless nature of RFID means communications can be easily intercepted as they are travelling between tags and readers allowing for remote modification and interception. The storage of sensitive data on a mobile RFID tags means the system can also be subject to

modification and interception attacks via physical access to the tags (Fernando & Abawajy, 2009). Replay-attacks, man-in-the-middle attacks, eavesdropping, data leakage and crypto attacks are all common interception attacks on RFID systems. Modification attacks while harder to mount also have a much greater impact on the system if they are successful. If a modification attack is successful then critical data that's not available elsewhere may be lost or corrupted in the process. If the system is to continue working there must be a way in which the system can identify and recover from these attacks. Successful modification attacks mounted via replay attacks or man in the middle attacks can be further leveraged to carryout RFID malware or buffer overflow attacks (Rieback, et al., 2006). Data integrity of the tag can also be compromised by natural causes such as electromagnetic fields and physical shocks (Fernando & Abawajy, 2009) (see Table 3).

Ensuring the availability of any IT system is of paramount importance. An interruption attack renders the system unusable by blocking access to some or all parts of the system or by ensuring that different parts of the system can't properly identify or communicate with each other (Fernando and Abawajy, 2009). The availability of RFID systems are of vital importance to corporations using them as unavailability of the RFID systems leads to the unavailability of all the applications that rely on it. In RFID systems interruption attacks can vary from simple active radio jamming attacks to complex attacks that desyn-

Table 3. Attacks by their possible impact on system

	Modification	Interception	Interruption	Fabrication	Tracking
Replay attacks	Y	Y			
Eavesdropping attacks		Y			
Data leakage		Y			
Man-in-the- middle,	Y	Y			
Crypto attacks		Y			
Physical reading of tags		Y			
Physical writing to tags	Y				
Tag cloning	Y	Y	Y	Y	
Tag spoofing	Y	Y	Y	Y	
Reader masquerading	Y	Y	Y	Y	Y
Tracking (Forward and Backward)					Y
Tag constellation tracking					Y
Radio fingerprint tracking					Y
Physical destruction of components			Y		
Active jamming			Y		
Passive jamming,			Y		
De-synchronization of tags	Y		Y		
Unauthorised tag locking or killing			Y		
RFID Malware (worms, viruses, SQL and Script injection)	Y	Y	Y		
Buffer overflow	Y		Y		
Elevation of privileges (reading)		Y			
Elevation of privileges (writing)	Y				
Repudiation of actions	Y				
Partner de-synch,				Y	
Killing or locking tags for partners			Y		

chronize tags with the central database in RFID systems using pseudonyms (Karygicmnis, et al., 2006). The availability of RFID systems can also be compromised by physical or logical destruction of tags or their data and the use on unauthorized kill/lock attacks to stop the functionality of the tags.

In addition to the above common types of attacks RFID systems are subject to two more types of attacks: fabrication attacks and tracking attacks. Fabrication happens when the attacker inserts new messages or items into the system without the knowledge or authorization of the system owners (Pfleeger, 1997). In RFID systems these attacks mainly manifest as cloning or spoofing attacks where the attacker inserts fabricated tags into the system. The attacker may also try to carry out a fabrication attack by pretending to be an authorized reader and querying tags for their information as well. Like with modification attacks successful fabrication attacks can be further leveraged to mount malware attacks on the system or in some cases cloned tags can be used to authenticate false object as their real counterparts (medicines and other designer consumer goods). Tracking attacks are possible on networked RFID systems due to the mobile nature of the tags. By tracking the movement of individual tags along the physical network the attacker can gain insight into the structure of the network as well other information such as location of specific vehicles or people and the efficiency of physical network and the business processes that support it. Tracking can also carried out my physically or logically compromising a tag and then using the information gained to identify the past or future transmissions of that tag (forward tracking and backward tracking) (Mitrokotsa, et al., 2010).

Source of Attack

Another important part of any attack is the source of that attack. In networked RFID systems, unlike in standalone RFID systems, the attack can originate from one of two different sources: External attackers and internal attackers (see Table 4).

External attackers are persons or organizations that have no authorized access to the system

Table 4. Attacks by access method and attack source

	Access Method		Attack Source	
	Logical	Physical	External	Internal
Replay attacks	Y		Y	
Eavesdropping attacks	Y		Y	
Data leakage	Y		Y	
Man-in-the- middle,	Y		Y	
Crypto attacks	Y	Y	Y	
Physical reading of tags		Y	Y	
Physical writing to tags		Y	Y	
Tag cloning	Y	Y	Y	
Tag spoofing	Y		Y	
Reader masquerading	Y		Y	
Tracking (Forward and Backward)	Y		Y	
Tag constellation tracking	Y		Y	
Radio fingerprint tracking	Y		Y	
Physical destruction of components		Y	Y	
Active jamming	Y		Y	
Passive jamming,	Y		Y	
De-synchronization of tags	Y	Y	Y	
Unauthorised tag locking or killing	Y	Y	Y	
RFID Malware (worms, viruses, SQL injection)	Y	Y	Y	
Buffer overflow	Y	Y	Y	
Elevation of privileges (reading)	Y	Y		Y
Elevation of privileges (writing)	Y	Y		Y
Repudiation of actions	Y	Y		Y
Partner de-synch	Y	Y		Y
killing or locking tags for partners				Y

but try and gain some or complete access to the system by various means. These attackers have a number of motivations for these attacks including stealing restricted information, changing system data, stealing the goods the tags are affixed to, tracking the tags as they travel long the physical network, cloning the RFID tags for counterfeiting and spreading malicious malware into the system thereby disrupting its performance (Rotter, 2008). Internal attackers on the other hand are authorized users of the system who try and gain more access than they are entitled to (a partner who is only allowed to read tag data updates it) or try to disrupt the system in such a way as to harm other users of the system. Because networked RFID systems are typically used by a number of independent entities who are simultaneously partners and competitors, internal attacks are a major concern for these types of systems (Li & Visich, 2006). There are a number of attacks that internal attackers can carry out on networked RFID systems including creating data/ updating tags and then denying they made those changes (repudiation) and gaining access to private data stored on the tags by other partners in the supply chain (Elevation of privileges [reading]) as well as changing data they are not authorized to change (Elevation of privileges [writing]).

System Model

In the previous section we discussed the attack model component of the security framework. In this section we will discuss the system model component of the security framework. The system model identifies the key system components that need to be protected and analyses the security concepts that must be preserved to fully secure the system and the security requirements that result.

System Components

In a networked RFID system the system components include RFID tags, RFID communications, readers, middleware, and backend data storage and business applications. In RFID systems the edge components: namely the readers and tags are implemented on non-standard devices and they communicate using a non-secure channel. The other components on the other hand are all implemented and connected by standard IT infrastructure. Therefore in our framework we separate the components into three groups: The tags, the wireless communications and the backend components (see Figure 4).

Tags in standard large scale networked RFID applications typically comprise of an electronic memory module, a logic module and a communication antenna. The memory module of the tag can consist of memory which can be read only, write once or updatable. The logic module of low cost RFID tags consists of between 500 to 10000 gates. The tags can be powered with either passive a semi-passive power source or an active power source (Hassan & Chatterjee, 2006). In any RFID systems the tags hold the identifier of the object it's attached to as well as additional data such as brand, product, expiry date and price of the object it's attached to. Unlike other IT components RFID tags are extremely mobile and have very low physical security.

Wireless communications are how tags and readers of a networked RFID system communicate. The wireless signals are communicated via an insecure channel and is transmitted using a broadcast mechanism. The range of a RFID transmission depends on the frequency of the radio wave used and the power applied. One of the main concerns in securing RFID systems is providing adequate security to the wireless communications given the limited power and computing capabilities available on low cost tags and the throughput required. Currently most RFID communications are secured using relatively weak security protocols. These protocols normally employ low resource operations such as bitwise XOR and one way hashing to try and secure the communications.

Figure 4. Components of networked RFID

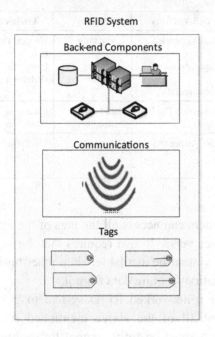

Figure 5. Applying the security concepts to the components

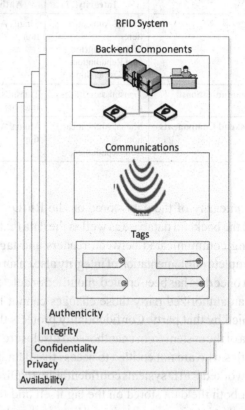

The backend components compose of the readers, middleware, RFID repository and business applications. RFID readers are used to read and write data to and from RFID tags. RFID readers do not normally store any data or translate any data. They just act as a messenger between the RFID middleware and the RFID tags and relay raw binary information from the middleware to the tags and vice versa. The middleware filters, translates and formats the data to the RFID repository that then stores that data from future retrieval from either the middleware or by business applications (Tajima, 2007).

Security Concepts

Security concepts are core requirements that must be met to ensure the security of any given application. The security concepts for an application depend on the system architecture and its functionality. In networked RFID systems we identify five key security concepts that must be met to ensure the security of the system: authenticity,

integrity, confidentiality, privacy and availability (see Figure 5).

Authenticity ensures the validity of the claimed identities of the components participating in a communication. It ensures that no entity is actually trying to masquerade as someone or something they are not (McGee, et al., 2004). In networked RFID this means that all readers must be able to identify each tag as being who it claims to be and that all tags can identify each reader as being part of the system.

Integrity ensures the correctness and accuracy of data, whether its stored data or data being communicated, against unauthorized creation, modification and deletion. It also provides an indication if the data has been compromised in this manner and in some cases allows for the retrieval of the correct data from the corrupted version (McGee, et al., 2004). For networked RFID this requires

Table 5. Networked RFID security requirements

	Integrity	Authenticity	Confidentiality	Privacy	Availability
Tags	Mutual Authentication, Storage Integrity, Non Repudiation, Data Ownership	Mutual Authentication	Mutual Authentication, Storage Confidentiality, Access Control	Anonymity	Physical Protection, Electronic Protection
Communications	Transmission Integrity	Transmission Integrity	Transmission Confidentiality	Data Leakage Protection	Electronic Protection
Backend Components	Mutual Authentication, Non Repudiation,	Mutual Authentication	Mutual Authentication,	N/A	Electronic Protection

the integrity of the data stored on the RFID tag and the backend database as well as the data that's being communicated between readers and tags. Complete implementation of integrity also ensures that once data has been created, modified or deleted by an authorized party those changes cannot be denied by that party. Confidentiality protects the data of the system from unauthorized disclosure to parties who are not entitled to access that data. In networked RFID systems confidentiality requires that both the data stored on the tag itself and the data that is being communicated between readers and tags is secure from unauthorized access by outside parties. It also requires that the authorized partners do not gain access to data that they are not allowed to access.

In addition to the above mentioned requirements, full security of a RFID system requires that the concepts of privacy and availability be assured. Privacy provides for the protection of information that might be derived from observing system activities (Rotter, 2008). In networked RFID systems this protects against attacks such as tracking of tag movements and the use of traffic analysis to derive information about the data that's being communicated. The final security concept, availability ensures that that there is no denial of access or service by any component of the system to other authorized parties or components of the system (McGee, et al., 2004). For networked RFID applications this requires that

all readers can access all the tags of the system and vice versa. It also requires that the overall RFID system be available when other business applications require data from it.

For a networked RFID system to be fully secured all of the above mentioned security concepts must be fully assured for each group of components in the system. Therefore the five core security concepts of authenticity, integrity, confidentiality, privacy and availability must be separately assured for the tags, communications and backend components of the RFID system.

Networked RFID Security Requirements

The security requirements are the security functionality that needs to be implemented to secure the system. As explained above, each security concept for each component must be separately secured before the overall system can be considered secure. Therefore we identify that the all following security requirements must be implemented to ensure that all the security concepts for each component is fully secured (see Table 5).

Mutual authentication allows the two communicating entities to verify the identity of the entity they will be communicating with (Pfleeger, 1997). In RFID systems mutual authentication is required to ensure that the readers and tags that are communicating are of the same network and have access to that information and are authorized to do the data modifications they request. Proper mutual authentication not only ensure the authenticity of the components but also provides confidentiality and integrity for the data stored on the backend components by ensuring that only authorized entities can access that data. Secure mutual authentication is also required as a base to implement a majority of the remaining security requirements and is therefore the most important security requirement in networked RFID. Most RFID security protocols implement mutual authentication as part of its security features. Some important protocols that implement mutual authentication are (Chien, 2007; Peris-Lopez, et al., 2008; Zhang & Baciu, 2008).

Because RFID systems use wireless communications it is easy for potential attackers to intercept them. Transmission confidentially ensures the security of data while it's been broadcast by ensuring that it cannot be understood by an attacker who intercepts it (McGee, et al., 2004). Transmission confidentiality typically uses various encryption methods to ensure that attackers cannot understand data intercepted in this manner. The protocols in (Chien, 2007; Peris-Lopez, et al., 2008; Zhang & Baciu, 2008) all provide for transmission confidentiality. Storage confidentiality ensures the security of data while it's stored on the tag or the backend components. In networked RFID systems the tag is easily accessible by attackers. Hence it is important that tag data be secure in case of physical or logical compromise of the tag (Fernando & Abawajy, 2009). Unfortunately storage confidentially is an area that has received very little research attention till now.

Complete data integrity requires the two security requirements of transmission integrity and storage integrity to be implemented. In RFID not only can potential attackers intercept wireless communications but they can also modify those communications compromising there integrity. Ensuring that communications that have been illegally modified can be identified and the original

data recovered is done by transmission integrity Transmission integrity in RFID typically employ various low cost encryption methods and message digests/hashes to enable the detection and recovery of RFID communications that have been externally modified (Mohan, et al., 2006). The protocols presented in (Chien, 2007; Peris-Lopez, et al., 2008; Zhang & Baciu, 2008) all provide communication integrity but not data recovery. RFID broadcast data recovery still remains an area open for research. Storage integrity ensures the integrity of data while it's stored on the tag. The relative physical and logical accessibility of RFID tags on which sensitive data is stored dictates that storage integrity is a high priority, especially in systems which store additional sensitive data on the tag (Fernando & Abawajy, 2009). Both encryption methods and journaling systems such as the ones presented in (Han & Chao-Hsien, 2008; Yamamoto, et al., 2008) can be used to ensure some storage integrity but currently they are not sufficiently strong or compete enough. Currently storage integrity of RFID tags is an area with very little research contributions. Because current applications store a majority of data on the backend database rather than the tag this is not currently an issue. But in the future as more and more systems store data on the tag itself this will become a high priority security requirement.

In a multi-entity RFID system some partners may like to store data on the tags that is accessible only to them (Fernando & Abawajy, 2009). Therefore the security functionality of the system must protect that data from unauthorized access by internal partners. If other partners gain access to private data this can lead to confidentiality issues as well as create trust problems among them. The security requirement of access control ensures that partners can only gain access to data that they are authorized to do so. While the confidentiality of private partner data is assured by access control its integrity is assured by data ownership. Data ownership guarantees that entities can only modify data that they are authorized do so. Both access

Figure 6. Networked RFID security framework

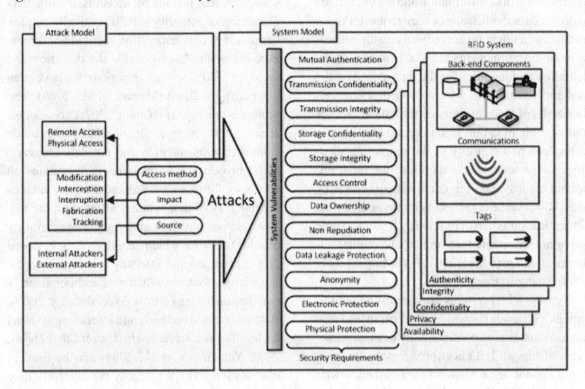

control and data ownership requires granular data storage based on the network partner who owns it. They also require that finely grained controls are implemented to ensure that data on the tags can only be accessed or modified by partners based on a predefined set of access and update rules. If done successfully multiple independent partners can have read and write access to the RFID tags while ensuring that access is limited to the data they are actually authorized to access or modify. RFID tag access control and data ownership are research areas which have very little work done in them.

Non repudiation is a security requirement that ensures the identification of the origin of data and the assurance of the genuineness of that data (Pfleeger, 1997). For example a partner, who is authorized to do so, may change the price stored on the RFID tag then deny doing so. Non-repudiation ensures that this cannot happen. By ensuring that a record of what data is modified by

which entity is kept, non-repudiation guarantees accountability of those partners increasing overall trust in the system (Yamamoto, et al., 2008). Non-repudiation techniques for backend database exist but no non-repudiation techniques have been developed for securing the data stored on RFID tags (see Figure 6).

In networked RFID systems attackers are able to invade the privacy of the tag holder by tracking their movement (Juels, 2006). Anonymity ensures that tracking attacks cannot be mounted on the tag. There are a number of tracking attacks possible on RFID systems including tag tracking, forward and backward tracing, and radio fingerprint tracking as well as tag constellation tracking (Juels, 2006). The protocols presented in (Chien, 2007; Peris-Lopez, et al., 2008; Zhang & Baciu, 2008) all use a system of pseudonyms to ensure the privacy of the tags. This system also provides a limited form of protection against forward and backward tracking as well. The privacy of RFID systems can also be compromised by data leakage. Data leakage happens when attackers intercept communications or other information about the system over a long period of time and gradually use that data to derive information about the system and the data being communicated by it (Mitrokotsa, et al., 2010). Common data leakage attacks include traffic analysis as well as attacks on confidentiality of the system via a large number of eavesdropping attacks on weakly encrypted communications. Data leakage protection requires that the attacker is unable to derive any information about system data or system security over the course of multiple eavesdropping sessions. Data leakage protection can be implemented by using techniques such as implementation of more advanced hardware configurations and ensuring that all communications are strongly encrypted. The protocols presented in (Chien, 2007; Peris-Lopez, et al., 2008; Zhang & Baciu, 2008) all claim strong and secure encryption which makes data leakage attacks impossible.

Networked RFID systems availability can be disrupted through physical or electronic means. The security requirements of physical protection and electronic protection secure the system against these types of attacks. Physical protection will protect the system against attacks such as physical tag destruction, removal of tags from the tagged items or the use of items such as aluminium foil to mask tag signals. Physical protection is easily provided by ensuring that physical access to RFID tags is limited to authorized parties when possible and by having deterrents such as electronic surveillance present when unauthorized parties can access the tagged items. Electronic protection is required to protect the system from denial of service attacks mounted through electronic means. These attacks include overwriting/destroying tag data through strong electronic magnetic pulses, disruption of communications through radio frequency jamming, overloading of the system capability with repeated requests or by de-synching the tags with the authorized readers through message blocking.

To combat these types of threats, functionality such as filtering of tags or readers which repeatedly send the same request and multiple frequency transmissions can be implemented. Also the use of RFID tags that can simultaneously transmit in several different wireless frequencies or move between a few preset frequencies can make passive jamming attacks much more difficult.

APPLICATION OF THE FRAMEWORK

In this section we will evaluate the developed framework by applying it to a real world networked RFID application. We will demonstrate that our framework allows for the methodical identification of the threats faced by the system in question and that it also allows the user to easily identify all the possible attacks on the system and analyse their impact, point of origin and access method. We will also demonstrate how the framework makes identifying the security requirements that need to be implemented to protect against those threats easy.

RFID in E-Passports

An area in which the use of networked RFID is rapidly becoming more common is the use of RFID tags in passports. Many countries—including the USA, Australia and all European Union members—recently introduced e-passports containing RFID chips. The tags are normally embedded in the photo page of the passport and also contain all the information displayed on the photo page. When interrogated by authorized readers, the tags transmit personal and biometric data of the holder to the reader. For example the Australian e-passports contain all the data that's displayed on the photo page of the passport: namely the digitized photograph, name, gender, date of birth, nationality, passport number, and the passport expiry date. The stored information is only broadcast when an authorized reader requests for that information, requests by unknown readers are ignored. One key feature of this system is that a majority of the static data of the object is stored on the tag itself and not on a back end database. Because the data stored on the RFID tag is unchanging the readers and tags are typically only read enabled and that data cannot be updated. In addition data is communicated in one way with no data being broadcast from the reader to the tag other than its authentication info. The main differences between the RFID tags used in RFID enabled passports and other common RFID applications such as patient tracking and global supply chains is that the tags used are typically a lot more expensive. Because personal and biometric data are particularly sensitive, attackers might be highly motivated to copy e-passports or use their data for identity theft. The consequences of an attack could be serious, including personal and biometric data theft, tracking of the e-passport's owner, illegal border crossings or even detonating a bomb designed for a specific country of origin or for a specific individual, based on information emitted by the chip in his or her passport (McGee, et al., 2004).

Applying the Threat Model to Scenario

Now let's consider the threat model for this type of system: Out of the 6 types of threats possible on networked RFID systems only 4 of are of concern to this particular system. The threats (1) interception and modification of system data and communications (2) introduction of false objects into system (3) invasion of privacy and (4) denial of service still remain. But the threat of (5) RFID malware and (6) attacks by internal partners can be disregarded. The threat of RFID malware can be disregarded because these systems use read-only RFID tags which make storing malware on them impossible. Even if an attacker managed to use a cloned or spoofed RFID tag to feed malware to a reader it would only affect that reader and terminal and would not be further propagated to other systems or tags as the tags used in the system

are not updatable. Therefore the use of malware would become data integrity and authentication issue rather than a malware problem. The threat posed by internal partners can be disregarded for a number of reasons. All authorized partners are allowed to read all the data stored on the system and none of the partners can update the data stored on the tag making non repudiation and elevation of privileges impossible. In addition only reliable and trustworthy government law enforcement agencies are authorized to read the tags removing any trust issues between the partners. Therefore by applying the threat model to the system in question we can determine the threats, exploits and the attacks of the system (see Table 6).

Understanding the Attacks on the System

Now that we have identified all possible attacks on the system it's time to understand how those attacks can affect this particular system. This is done by applying the attack model tables to the attacks that can affect this particular system. To do this we first disregard any attacks that were eliminated when we analysed the threats to the system. Then we look at the remaining attacks and identify which of their possible impacts are applicable for the system in question (see Table 7).

In Table 7 the Ys represent impacts that can affect the system. An impact that cannot affect the system in question has been removed (e.g., possibility of data modification from attacks other than man-in-the-middle can be disregarded for this system as tags data cannot be updated). The final row of the table shows the total number of attacks that have each type of impact on the system.

By comparing the possible attacks on the system to Table 4 we identify the number of attacks that use each access method and the number of attacks that originate from each source (see Table 8).

Table 6. Threats, weaknesses, and attacks applicable to e-passport systems

Threat	Exploits weaknesses:	And results in
Interception or modification system data and communications	Lack of secure mutual authentication	Replay attacks
	Lack of secure mutual authentication and confidentiality	Eavesdropping attacks Data leakage
	Lack of secure mutual authentication, integrity verification and confidentiality	Man-in-the- middle,
	Lack of sufficiently strong encryption	Crypto attacks,
	Lack of storage confidentiality Poor physical security of tags	Physical reading of tags
	Lack of storage integrity Poor physical security of tags	Physical writing to tags
Introduction of false objects into system	Lack of strong and secure mutual authentication	Tag cloning Tag spoofing Reader masquerading
Invasion of privacy	Mobility of tags lack of proper mutual authentication	Tracking (Forward and Backward) Tag constellation tracking
	The mobility of the tags and the easily identifiable radio fingerprint on low cost tags	Radio fingerprint tracking
Denial of service	Lack of physical security	Physical destruction of components
	Low resources available on tags	Active jamming
	Broadcast mechanism of communications	Passive jamming,
	Use of pseudonyms of some security protocols	De-synchronization of tags
	Built in lock and kill commands	Unauthorised tag locking or killing

Identifying Security Requirements and Solutions

Finally we will use the system model of the security framework to identify the required security requirements and the possible methods with which to implement them based the systems architecture and use. As can be seen in Table 9, a number of the identified security requirements for networked RFID systems is not required for this system due to some of its features.

Next we decide how each of the security requirements identified above can be implemented for the system under review taking into consideration the system architecture and the attacks that the system is vulnerable to. Therefore we first look at the system architecture and identify any important and unique features of the system that may affect how the security requirements may be

implemented. In this system we notice a few important features: (1) the tags are only contacted by authorized readers at very specific points (airport immigration areas) and the owner of the tag is well aware of these areas. (2) The tags need only contain static non changing data (3) the data flow in the system is only from tags to readers and (4) the tags are imbedded in expensive passports and therefore can be high cost tags with more resources available on them. Based on the vulnerabilities and the identified features of the application the following steps can be taken to implement the security requirements (see Table 10).

The analysis done using the framework suggests that non electronic methods may allow for a much greater increaser to security at a lower price. The use of a simple sleeve to ensure that the tag cannot communicate will easily eliminate

Table 7. Impact that the attacks can have on system in question

	Modification	Interception	Interruption	Fabrication	Tracking
Replay attacks		Y			
Eavesdropping attacks		Y			
Data leakage		Y			
Man-in-the- middle,	Y	Y			
Crypto attacks		Y			
Physical reading of tags		Y			
Physical writing to tags					
Tag cloning		Y		Y	
Tag spoofing		Y		Y	
Reader masquerad-ing		Y		Y	Y
Tracking (Forward and Backward)					Y
Tag constellation tracking					
Radio fingerprint tracking					Y
Physical destruction of components			Y		
Active jamming			Y		
Passive jamming,			Y		
De-synchronization of tags			Y		
Unauthorised tag locking or killing			Y		
1		9	5	3	3

most tracking, reader impersonation and replay attacks. The use of tags with very short transmission ranges will make attacks such as eavesdropping, man-in-the-middle and replay much more difficult. The more expensive nature of the tags employed allow for the use of more traditional and power security primitives such as tag side PRNG and encryption algorithms that make the implementation of secure and strong mutual authentication and transmission confidentiality and integrity relatively straightforward. The use of write only tags will ensure storage integrity and storing the data on the tag in encrypted form will ensure storage confidentiality.

FUTURE RESEARCH

During the research conducted for this paper we identified a number of key areas in RFID security which can benefit from future research. One of these areas is in actually implementing some of the security requirements identified in this framework. Out of the security requirements identified in this framework a large number already has significant

Table 8. Access methods and attack sources of attacks on system

	Access Method		Attack Source	
	Logical	Physical	External	Internal
Replay attacks	Y		Y	
Eavesdropping attacks	Y		Y	
Data leakage	Y		Y	
Man-in-the- middle,	Y		Y	
Crypto attacks	Y	Y	Y	
Physical reading of tags		Y	Y	
Physical writing to tags				
Tag cloning	Y		Y	
Tag spoofing	Y		Y	
Reader masquerading	Y		Y	
Tracking (Forward and Backward)	Y		Y	
Tag constellation tracking				
Radio fingerprint tracking	Y		Y	
Physical destruction of components		Y	Y	
Active jamming	Y		Y	
Passive jamming,	Y		Y	
De-synchronization of tags	Y	Y	Y	
Unauthorised tag locking or killing	Y	Y	Y	
14		5	16	0

Table 9. E-passport security requirements

	Integrity	Authenticity	Confidentiality	Privacy	Availability
Tags	*N/A – Tag data cannot be modified in a meaningful manner*	Mutual Authentication	Mutual Authentication, Storage Confidentiality, *Access Control (not required as all partners have access to all data)*	Anonymity	Physical Protection, Electronic Protection
Communications	Transmission Integrity	Transmission Integrity	Transmission Confidentiality	Data leakage protection	Electronic Protection
Backend Components	Mutual Authentication	Mutual Authentication	*N/A – Backend data is not transmitted to the tags and therefore cannot be requested by attackers*	N/A	Electronic Protection

Table 10. Defences for RFID enabled passport systems

Security requirement	Recommendation on how to implement	Removes or reduces vulnerability to
Transmission Integrity	Use data integrity verification techniques (simple one way hashing is a good recommendation) to verify the integrity of broadcasts. If any corruption is detected request a retransmission	Man-in-the-Middle, Desynch Attacks,
Mutual Authentication	Requires a secure mutual authentication mechanism that allows readers and tags to reliably authenticate each other. Can be implemented using mechanisms such as BAC (Basic Access Control) or EAC (Extended Access Control) which have been standardised for passport security. Lock commands using the MRZ (Machine Readable Zone) is also a possibility but not recommended. The use of plastic sleeves to prevent unauthorised remote access is also possible	Reader Masquerading, Cloning, Spoofing, Data Leakage, Man-in-the-Middle, Replay Attack, Eavesdropping Kill/Lock Commands, Desynch Attacks, Active jamming
Storage Confidentiality	Because the owner of the passport may try and access the data stored on the tag to clone it or spoof the system storage confidentiality must be implemented - Storing the data in encrypted form on the tag and allowing only secured access to the keys required to decrypt that data is a option	Physical reading of tags, Crypto attacks
Transmission Confidentiality	Extremely important – needs to implement some method of secure encryption. Can be implemented using traditional security primitives due to the high cost of the tags employed. Because tag polling is done at very specific areas and only required when the tag is in close proximity of the reader tags that specifically have extremely short transmission ranges can also be employed.	Man-in-the-Middle, Data Leakage, Replay Attack, Eavesdropping, Crypto Attacks
Anonymity	Extremely important because passports allows the holder to be tracked. While strong mutual authentication and rotating pseudonyms can make tracking harder the nature of the system allows for a much simpler system. Using a plastic sleeve that blocks all communications to protect the passport till the owner arrives at an area where the tag needs to be read is possible. Lock commands using the MRZ (machine readable zone) is also a possibility	Tag tracking, Forward tracing, Backward tracing Radio finger print tracking,
Data Leakage Protection	Not really required as nature of the application means tags are polled only very infrequently making data leakage a very low threat. Also the tags can be built to be pretty sophisticated making radio fingerprint tracking harder	Radio finger print tracking, Data leakage
Physical Protection	Already at an acceptable level due to readers being in secure areas and the tags being attached to important objects (passports) which are secured by the owner. Physical protection from owner cannot be implemented.	Physical destruction of components
Electronic Protection	Use multi frequency RFID tags and short range transmissions to reduce the chance of jamming, Use lockout mechanisms to ensure active jamming is not possible	Passive jamming Active jamming

work done in their area. There are a large number of publications that implement the security requirements of mutual authentication, transmission integrity and confidentiality, anonymity and data leakage protection. But the amount of research done concerning non repudiation, access control and storage confidentiality and integrity for networked RFID systems is very little. Therefore continued research in implementing these key security requirements is of high priority and we recommend that researchers focus their efforts on these areas. In addition the development of a security protocol that allows for the transmission of tag data other than the EPC and associated identifiers is a major research priority that has not been fulfilled. In the future as more and more networked RFID systems store additional data other than the identifier and associated keys on the tag itself, communication of that data via a secure means would become a very important requirement. Therefore this is also another area in RFID security which could benefit from more research efforts.

The validation in the last part of this paper using the real life case study indicates that there are non-electronic means of security that can be easily implemented which provide networked RFID systems with high security with very low overhead in terms of technology and cost (physical sleeves to protect the RFID embedded page of electronic passports) and that policy changes can increase security very easily with minimum cost and disruption to the system (use of read only tags instead of updatable tags). Therefore we also recommend that more research be conducted on possible non-technical security measures and on the possibility of policy and management changes which can help improve overall RFID application security.

While the security framework presented in this chapter has been developed specifically developed for networked RFID systems there are a number of other systems which greatly resemble this type of system. For example sensor networks have a large number of similarities with networked RFID systems: they both use mobile, low cost hardware components that have relatively low physical security. The components in both can be shared by different independent partners, the data generated by the system are used for different purposes by different users, both systems are highly constrained in terms of the amount and power and computation capacity available on the mobile nodes and both systems use wireless communications for communicating between the low cost mobile nosed and the more traditional IT components. Therefore it is our belief that the framework presented here can be easily translated to apply to some other similar systems such as sensor networks with minimum modification to the core concepts developed in this framework. This type of research will not only help secure another type of system but it may also help further enhance this framework in relation to security it affords to networked RFID systems.

CONCLUSION

Even though the deployment of networked RFID systems has greatly accelerated in the last few years there are still major concerns about the security available in systems using low cost tags. These concerns arise because of the inherent differences in various types of RFID systems and the large amount of security threats they are subject to. Even though there a large number of security frameworks focused on how best to assess and secure IT systems implemented using typical infrastructure next to no work has been done in developing a comprehensive security framework for networked RFID systems.

In this paper we develop and present a conceptual security framework that can be used for (1) accessing the vulnerabilities of RFID systems, (2) identify the attacks possible on them and (3) identify the security requirements to fully secure that system. Our framework is composed of two main parts: the attack model and system model. There is also a threat model which is used identify the vulnerabilities of the RFID system. Overall the framework developed provides a methodical manner in which possible attacks and threats on a given RFID system can be analyzed and allows the user to easily identify the manner in which those threats can be removed for that particular system. The presented framework is applied to real world networked RFID system. The application of the framework illustrates how the framework can be used to assess and improve the security of networked RFID systems

REFERENCES

Armenio, F., Barthel, H., Burstein, L., Dietrich, P., Duker, J., Garrett, J., et al. Williams, J. (2007). *The EPC global architecture framework*. Retrieved February 12th, 2009, from http://www.epcglobalinc.org/ standards/ architecture/ architecture_1_2-framework- 20070910.pdf.

Asif, Z., & Mandviwalla, M. (2005). Integrating the supply chain with RFID: A technical and business analysis. *Communications of the Association for Information Systems, 15*(24), 393–426.

Ayoade, J. (2007). Roadmap to solving security and privacy concerns in RFID systems. *Computer Law & Security Report, 23*(6), 555–561. doi:10.1016/j.clsr.2007.09.005

Chien, H.-Y. (2007). SASI: A new ultralightweight RFID authentication protocol providing strong authentication and strong integrity. *Transactions on Dependable and Secure Computing, 4*(4), 337–340. doi:10.1109/TDSC.2007.70226

Christian, F., & Matthias, L. (2005). RFID middleware design: Addressing application requirements and RFID constraints. In *Proceedings of the Joint Conference on Smart Objects and Ambient Intelligence: Innovative Context-Aware Services: Usages and Technologies,* (pp. 219 - 224). New York: ACM Press.

Fernando, H., & Abawajy, J. (2009). A RFID architecture framework for global supply chain applications. In *Proceedings of the 11th International Conference on Information Integration and Web Services,* (pp. 213-320). New York: ACM Press.

Floerkemeier, C., & Lampe, M. (2005). RFID middleware design: Addressing application requirements and RFID constraints. In *Proceedings of the 2005 Joint Conference on Smart Objects and Ambient Intelligence: Innovative Context-Aware Services: Usages and Technologies*. New York: ACM Press.

Glover, B., & Bhatt, H. (2006). *RFID essentials*. New York: O' Reilly Media.

Han, S., & Chao-Hsien, C. (2008). Tamper detection in RFID-enabled supply chains using fragile watermarking. In *Proceedings of the 2008 IEEE International Conference on RFID,* (pp. 111-117). IEEE Press.

Hassan, T., & Chatterjee, S. (2006). A taxonomy for RFID. In *Proceedings of the 39th Annual Hawaii International Conference on System Sciences,* (pp. 184b - 184b). IEEE Press.

Jeong, J., & Haas, Z. J. (2007). An integrated security framework for open wireless networking architecture. *IEEE Transactions on Wireless Communications, 14*(2), 10–18. doi:10.1109/MWC.2007.358959

Juels, A. (2006). RFID security and privacy: A research survey. *IEEE Journal on Selected Areas in Communications, 24*(2), 14. doi:10.1109/JSAC.2005.861395

Karygicmnis, A., Phillips, T., & Tsibertzopoulos, A. (2006). RFID security: A taxonomy of risk. In *Proceedings of the First International Conference on Communications and Networking in China,* (pp. 1-8). IEEE Press.

Li, S., & Visich, J. K. (2006). Radio frequency identification: Supply chain impact and implementation challenges. *International Journal of Integrated Supply Management, 2*(4), 407–424. doi:10.1504/IJISM.2006.009643

Li, T., & Deng, R. H. (2007). Vulnerability analysis of EMAP-An efficient RFID mutual authentication protocol. In *Proceedings of the International Conference on Availability, Reliability and Security,* (pp. 10-13). New York: ACM Press.

Li, Y., & Ding, X. (2007). Protecting RFID communications in supply chains. In *Proceedings of the 2nd ACM Symposium on Information, Computer and Communications Security,* (pp. 234-241). New York: ACM Press.

McGee, A. R., Vasireddy, S. R., Xie, C., Picklesimer, D. D., Chandrashekhar, U., & Richman, S. H. (2004). A framework for ensuring network security. *Bell Labs Technical Journal, 8*(4), 7–27. doi:10.1002/bltj.10083

Mitrokotsa, A., Rieback, M. R., & Tanenbaum, A. S. (2010). Classification of RFID attacks. *Information Systems Frontiers.* Retrieved from http://www.cs.vu.nl/~ast/publications/iwrt-2008.pdf.

Mohan, M., Potdar, V., Chang, E., & Perth, W. A. (2006). Recovering and restoring tampered RFID data using steganographic principles. In *Proceedings of the IEEE International Conference on Industrial Technology (ICIT 2006),* (pp. 15-17). IEEE Press.

Peris-Lopez, P., Hernandez-Castro, J. C., Estevez-Tapiador, J. M., & Ribagorda, A. (2006). RFID systems: A survey on security threats and proposed solutions. In *Proceedings of the 11th International Conference on Personal Wireless Communications,* (pp. 159 - 170). Berlin, Germany: Springer.

Peris-Lopez, P., Hernandez-Castro, J. C., Tapiador, J. M. E., & Ribagorda, A. (2008). Advances in ultralightweight cryptography for low-cost RFID tags: Gossamer protocol. In *Lecture Notes in Computer Science* (pp. 56–68). Berlin, Germany: Springer.

Pfleeger, C. (1997). *Security in computing.* Upper Saddle River, NJ: Prentice Hall.

Ranasinghe, D. C., Leong, K. S., Ng, M. L., Engels, D. W., & Cole, P. H. (2005). A distributed architecture for a ubiquitous RFID sensing network. In *Proceedings of the Second International Conference on Intelligent Sensors, Sensor Networks and Information Processing,* (pp. 7-12). IEEE Press.

Rieback, M., Tanenbaum, A., & Crispo, B. (2006). Is your cat infected with a computer virus? In *Proceedings of the Fourth Annual IEEE International Conference on Pervasive Computing and Communications,* (p. 10). IEEE Press.

Rotter, P. (2008). A framework for assessing RFID system security and privacy risks. *IEEE Pervasive Computing / IEEE Computer Society [and] IEEE Communications Society, 7*(2), 70–77. doi:10.1109/MPRV.2008.22

Schuster, E. W., Allen, S. J., & Brock, D. L. (2007). *Global RFID.* Berlin, Germany: Springer.

Tajima, M. (2007). Strategic value of RFID in supply chain management. *Journal of Purchasing and Supply Management, 13*(4), 261–273. doi:10.1016/j.pursup.2007.11.001

Weis, S. A., Sarma, S. E., Rivest, R. L., & Engels, D. W. (2003). Security and privacy aspects of low-cost radio frequency identification systems. *Lecture Notes in Computer Science, 28*(8), 201–212.

Yamamoto, A., Suzuki, S., Hada, H., Mitsugi, J., Teraoka, F., & Nakamura, O. (2008). A tamper detection method for RFID tag data. In *Proceedings of the IEEE International Conference on RFID,* (pp. 51-57). IEEE Press.

Zhang, X., & Baciu, G. (2008). Low cost minimal mutual authentication protocol for RFID. In *Proceedings of the IEEE International Conference on Networking, Sensing and Control,* (pp. 620-624). IEEE Press.

KEY TERMS AND DEFINITIONS

Attack Model: A conceptual model of a system which focuses on identifying and classifying the different attacks that can be mounted on that system.

Networked RFID Application: A RFID system which has components spread over a wide geographic area and have a number of different independent partners using and sharing the system components and information.

RFID: Radio Frequency Identification

Security Framework: A conceptual model of a system which takes into account the above three types of models to build a complete framework of the systems security requirements.

System Model: A conceptual model of a system which focuses on identifying its different components and how they communicate and the key security concepts required for each component.

Threat Model: A conceptual model of a system which focuses on identifying the threats that the system faces and analyzing how those threats can be leveraged to mounts attacks on the system.

Chapter 5
A Review of Privacy, Internet Security Threat, and Legislation in Africa:
A Case Study of Nigeria, South Africa, Egypt, and Kenya

Bellarmine Ezumah
Murray State University, USA

Suraj Olunifesi Adekunle
Lagos State University, Nigeria

ABSTRACT

This chapter serves as a collection of works that were done in the area of cybersecurity in Africa—with a focus on four countries representing the cardinal points in Africa: Kenya, Nigeria, Egypt, and South Africa. It presents detailed information on the legislative framework proposed and implemented by these countries to combat and control cybercrimes. Notable among them are the Egypt's e-Signature Law 15, Kenya's e-Transaction Bill, Nigeria's Computer Security and Critical Information Infrastructure Protection Bill, and South Africa's Electronic Communications and Transaction Act. Equally, these legislative measures were commended, criticized, and factors that militate their implementation are discussed. The ultimate realization is that cybercrime can never be abolished; rather, every effort aims at combating and controlling it in some way. Finally, the chapter posits areas that the African nations can improve in their quest for making cyberspace safer.

DOI: 10.4018/978-1-4666-0161-1.ch005

INTRODUCTION

Arguably, the 21st century is characterized by an unprecedented deluge of Information and Communication Technologies (ICTs) which are interconnecting the world instantaneously and defying the inhibition of time and geographical space. These ICTs especially with Internet component are providing opportunities for information creation, sharing, pilfering, and consumption that transcend earlier innovations. Africa has seen a phenomenal growth in Internet connectivity in recent years. With the increasing availability of broadband connections and the decrease in subscription fees, the number of new online users in Africa is on the increase. But, with this proliferation of ICTs, comes the byproduct of internet scam, cybersecurity, and their like. Cybercrime, whether occurring in, or originating from Africa or elsewhere is a global problem because its effect reverberates worldwide. As Chawki (2009) observed, Nigerian 419 scam is a major concern for the global community. The Symantec Internet Threat First Quarter Report of 2010 ranks Nigeria as 70th on the Global Internet crime watch and 43rd in the EMEA (Europe, Middle East and Africa) Countries. Nigeria is first in Africa, followed by Ghana and South Africa. According to 2007 Internet Crime Report prepared by the National White Collar Crime Centre and the Federal Bureau of Investigation (FBI), Nigeria currently ranks third in the world with 5.7% of perpetrators of cybercrime (2007 Internet Crime Report) after United Kingdom and The United States of America. A 2004 estimate suggests that annual losses due to activities of cybercrime in South Africa are in the region of R100 million (approximately $ 16.5 million USD). However, as rightly noted by Olowu (2009), South Africa is equally home to all forms of cybercrime activities. According to Olowu, South African Police estimated that their country is home to more than 190 criminal organizations, many of which are even more sophisticated with international dimension that is far wider in scope than their Nigerian coun-

terparts. In South Africa, spam alone is reported to cost business "between R7 billion and R13 billion yearly in lost productivity" (Tladi, 2008, p. 183). Equally disturbing is the fact that Egypt according to Ojedokun (2005) is also reputed to be one of the most phished countries in the world with about 2000 phishing incidents.

Social network sites are conduits for cyber criminal activities in Africa. Africa is home to numerous social networking sites such as Facebook and MySpace for communications, friendships, blogging and other activities which provides ample opportunities for hackers and cyber criminals to carry out their nefarious activities of redirecting internet users to phishing websites consequently making it possible for them to steal user's passwords, accounts and opening security holes in the victim's machine. Thus, it became easier for them to carry out identity theft and malicious activities against home users and employees in both private and public sectors since local social networks in Africa are not secured enough to protect users' or members' privacy and sensitive information. As rightly noted by Dejo (2009), the risk is very high not only in social networks but also in peer-to-peer networks, Web 2.0, chatting and popular applications that can be exploited.

This chapter serves numerous purposes; first, it is a collection of selected works in the area of cybercrime and cyber security in Africa with a concentration in Nigeria, Egypt, South Africa, and Kenya. Second, it defines cyber crime, tabulates efforts and initiatives that were established in and for Africa and by Africans for the purposes of combating cybercrimes. Third, the chapter lists factors that challenge legislative efforts and addresses the nature of cybercrimes that are inherent in Africa. Fourth and finally, it posits ways that the cyber highway can be made safer for people in Africa and beyond.

BACKGROUND

Internet Penetration in Africa: Historical Account

Although Africa was the last continent to embrace Information and Communication Technology (ICT) especially the Internet component of ICTs, but it has experienced insurmountable growth in Internet usage for the past decade. While the rest of the world is reporting a 420.5% growth in internet use, Africa geometrically leaped to a 2,357.3% growth between 2000 and 2010 (IWS, 2011). Similar increase also exists in the use of mobile phones and has permeated to numerous spheres of life such as e-schooling with distance education and numerous educational materials available online, e-commerce with the introduction of online banking, ATMs, Credit and Debit Cards allowing for instantaneous money transfer and access to bank accounts, e-government, telemedicine with doctor-patient consultation done via telephone or e-mail, teleconferencing, teledemocracy as evidenced in the 2009 Kenyan Post-election War and 2011 Egyptian 18-day protest that ended the 30 year regime of President Mubarak. Unfortunately, either by design or by chance, the ubiquity of information technology in Africa consequently led to the abuse of the ICTs in terms of criminal activities including identity theft, scam, abuse and molestation, infringement of copyrights, and many others.

The success and proliferation of cyber crimes in Africa has overtime been traced to the absence or limited scope of anti cybercrime laws, both locally, regionally and at a continental level. To this end, most African nations are taking time to shore up legislations to strengthen national cyber laws and also seek for a harmonized international law against cybercrime owing to the absence of geographically defined boundaries in cyber space. A common thread in relation to some of these laws is the proposal for an individual country law to deal with cybercrime which we believe might not go far enough in dealing with cybercrime in Africa. A study that was reported at the June 2009 ITU Regional Cybersecurity Forum for Africa and Arab States in Tunis demonstrated that only 38% of respondents among African countries have cybersecurity laws and that include Egypt, Nigeria, Ghana, Benin, Senegal, Sudan and Zambia. Also, 45% have national guidelines for preventing, detecting and responding to cybercrimes and they include Egypt, Nigeria, Ghana, Benin, Cote d'Ivoire, Gambia, Mali, Niger, and Senegal. Interestingly, 60% of countries who responded to this study have guidelines for overcoming obstacles to the effective use of electronic documents and transactions, including electronic means of authentication and those countries include Egypt, Nigeria, Kenya, Congo, Ethiopia, Ghana, Madagascar, Mozambique, Niger, Senegal, and Sudan. Finally, 55% have guidelines on the right to privacy, data and consumer protection and those countries include Egypt, Nigeria, Kenya, Ethiopia, Gambia, Ghana, Madagascar, Mozambique, Senegal, and Sudan. In essence, among our countries of focus, Egypt and Nigeria demonstrated highest effort in their quest for a safer cyberspace, followed by Kenya. Subsequent sections will discuss in detail the legislative efforts made to combat cybercrime.

Some East African countries are in the process of formulating unified computer crime legislations. Also, the first West African Cyber Crime Summit was convened on 30th November to 2nd December, 2010 in Nigeria's capital, Abuja. The summit focused on the theme, "The Fight against Cybercrime: Towards Innovative and Sustainable Economic Development," by the Nigeria's Economic Financial Crime Commission (EFCC) in collaboration with United Nations on Drugs and Crime (UNODC), the Economic Community of West African States (ECOWAS), Council of Europe (CoE), INTERPOL, US Federal Bureau of Investigation, US Federal Trade Commission, US Department of Homeland Security, European Union and FRANCOPOL and Microsoft. Over 450 people attended from across the world including countries such as Togo, Guinea, Guinea Bissau, Gambia, Ghana, Senegal, Ivory Coast, Niger, Austria, UK, France, USA, Turkey, South Africa, UAE, Tunisia and Nigeria. The forum allowed participants from all over the world to consider local and international cybercrime strategies and policies with a view to strengthening international cooperation and developing a regional roadmap to tackle cybercrime and fosters economic growth. Specifically, the summit focused on how to: Position the fight against cybercrime as a national priority to help the economic development in the region and to showcase best practices and case studies of partners organization in combating cybercrime. It is expected that this ongoing regional initiatives will eventually lead to amendment of current African laws that will eventually replace the current proposed laws of individual countries to form a common Africa's Cybercrime Framework. This we envisaged will provide for generic and understandable laws across the African continent with anticipation of the effect of new technologies on the horizon that will not render the framework obsolete when eventually passed.

Computer Crime: Cyberspace and Cybercrime—Definition and Concept

Cyberspace is a convenient but fictitious notion describing "the network of networks" constituting the internet, the communication and services provided through it. Some scholars (Bequai, 2001; Johnson & Post, 1996) are of the opinion that Gibson's definition probably explains why it has been extremely difficult for countries and their law enforcement agencies to trace, apprehend and punish perpetrators of cybercrimes beyond their respective territories since by the very nature of international law, a State's sovereignty is limited to its territory and the Cyber space, through which these crimes are perpetuated is not defined by political or geographical boundaries, thus amending laws to curb crimes becomes a challenge. In other words, we envisaged that effective law

enforcement will be hampered by transnational nature of the cyberspace. Moreover, this informs probably why there is lack of legal and technical resources to address the obvious complexities of the cyberspace. As a result, the mechanism for cooperation across national borders in solving and prosecuting cybercrimes are complex and slow. The laws generally do not accommodate all possible cyber crimes and this is due to the fact that the laws applicable in the physical world are in many respects inapplicable in virtual world.

While scholarly consensus on a single definition of cybercrime is yet to be achieved, it would appear that writers and law drafters are more comfortable with describing various elements constituting cybercrime than in defining it. According to the Council of Europe (COE, 2004), for instance, cybercrime involves "action directed against the confidentiality, integrity and availability of computer systems, networks and computer data as well as the misuse of such systems, networks and data." Casey (2004) offered another definition of cybercrime as "any crime that involves computers and networks, including crimes that do not rely heavily on computers" (p. 8). Other authors have resorted to simply describing the role of computers and the internet in the promotion of crime (Collier, 2004; Bazelon, Choi, & Conaty, 2006) while others sought to classify cybercrime into computer-related and content-based species (Chawki, 2009; Lewis, 2004) or between *true cybercrime* referring to dishonest or malicious acts that would not exist outside online environment and e-enabled crime, that is, criminal acts already known to the world but now promoted through the internet (Burden, Palmer, & Lyde, 2003). Yet, there have been debates about whether unlawful activities involving computers and the internet should be classified as crimes or civil wrongs (Barton & Nissanka, 2003) especially when one observes that the effectiveness of legal framework in the authorization and management of digital signatures is inadequate and deterrence in respect of cybercrime is weak. On the other hand,

Table 1. Internet penetration and growth (2000 – 2010)

Country	Population (2010)	Internet Users (Latest Data)	Penetration (% Population)	User Growth 2000-2010 (%)
Egypt	80,471,869	17,060,000	21.2	3,691.1
Kenya	40,046,566	3,995,500	10.0	1,897.8
Nigeria	152,217,341	43,982,200	28.9	21,891.1
South Africa	49,109,107	5,300,000	10.8	120.8

Source: Internet World Stats (2011)

Computer crime can broadly be defined as criminal activity involving an information technology infrastructure including illegal access or unauthorized access; illegal interception that involves technical means of non-public transmissions of computer data to, from or within a computer system; data interference that include unauthorized damaging, deletion, deterioration, alteration or suppression of computer data; systems interference that is interfering with the functioning of a computer system by inputting, transmitting, damaging, deleting, deteriorating, altering or suppressing computer data; misuse of devices, forgery (ID theft), and electronic fraud (Taylor, 1999).

Cyber Security then, entails all measures taken proactively and actively to prevent and ensure safety from cyber attacks. Cyber attacks vary and evolve daily with advances in technology. Amongst the common cyber threats include but are not limited to the following; Cyber theft, Cyber terrorism, Cyber stalking, E-mail Forgery / Spoofing, Online Auction fraud/Online fraud, Phishing, Online Child Pornography, Malicious Codes-Viruses/Worms/Trojans, Hacking/Computer Intrusions, Identity Theft, Intellectual Property Rights (IPR) matters, Economic Espionage (theft of Trade Secrets) and Cyber laundering/ Cyber Contraband. Cybersecurity is imperative because some have considered it critical to national security (Cole, Chetty, LaRosa, Rietta, Schmitt, & Goodman, 2008), an effort that are both sensitive and occupies the central seat in most nations' agenda especially in this 21st Century.

MATERIALS AND METHODS

It would pose a daunting task to confine information on all 53 countries of Africa in a single chapter and the vast uniqueness of each country makes it even harder to choose points of focus for this discussion. After much deliberation, we decided on our countries of focus because, in addition to representing the cardinal points of Africa, Kenya, Nigeria, Egypt and South Africa ranked among the highest Internet users in Africa. These countries also, always manage to make the list of countries with highest rate of cybercrimes and sometimes appear to be the originating points of cyber crimes to other parts of the world. Additionally, according to Internet World Stats (IWS, 2011) these four countries demonstrate remarkable growth in internet usage in the last decade (see Table 1).

For the purpose of this chapter, we investigated and carried out a critical review of cybercrime laws in Africa especially countries like Nigeria, South Africa, Egypt and Kenya. Also an investigation was carried out on various cybercrimes and unlawful online activities that are peculiar to Africa, various means by which individual and corporate African organizations protect themselves from various crimes that are perpetrated through the internet and review of African legislative regulations with the aim of determining their effectiveness in curbing cybercrimes over the years. The paper also reviews the definition of privacy in Africa and how various government interventions have violated the issue of personal and corporate privacy in Africa. The perceptions of African citizens to cyber security and to what degree of security consciousness they have come to imbibe. In addition, review of fraudsters' web-like structure that made internet users a constant prey despite repeated warnings was also examined. We equally examined the inadequacies of the existing laws in combating cybercrime in Africa with the aim of proffering possible solution.

Various Cybercrimes and Other Unlawful Activities in Africa

Cybercrime is acknowledged to be on the rise globally and Internet users are bashful or ignorant when it comes to reporting crimes. Even for a developed country like the United States of America, the number of internet crime complaints is very low; the Internet Crime Complaint Center (IC3) 2010 report indicated that IC3 received 303,809 complaints and the top three categories include non-payment or non-delivery of merchandise (14.4%), Scams impersonating the FBI (13.2%) and followed by Identity theft (9.8%). However, this may not pose an accurate statistics for cybercrime because reporting cybercrimes is not a regular activity of cyber users and several crimes go undetected (Cassim, 2009). According to Hale (2002) only about 10% of all cybercrimes committed globally are actually reported and fewer than 2% result in a conviction, against the backdrop of ill-trained police and security agents. And in the absence of cybercrimes records or conduits such as the US IC3, one can only conjecture that the statistics of reporting and conviction will inevitably be lower for Africa (Ojedokun, 2005).

Notwithstanding the low statistics of reported cases of cybercrimes in Africa, Baraka (2009) had listed cybercrimes inherent in Egypt to include intimidation, sabotage, threats of embezzlement, rumors, copyright issues, credit card theft, defamation, unlicensed network, immoral content, hacking, impersonation, child exploitation, forgery, and unlicensed activities. Longe, Ngwa, Wada,

Mbarika, and Kvasny (2009) equally listed as common to Nigeria are e-mail scams, phishing, internet based prostitution, child trafficking and advanced fee fraud.

Advanced Fee Fraud (a.k.a 419): An important factor making Africa a source and target of much cyber-criminal activity is the growth of international banking and money-laundering. The unique opportunities of a quickly developed financial infrastructure allowing anyone to transfer monetary fund to any State, anonymously and through tangled routes have caught the attention of cyber-criminals. Electronic transfers are an efficient tool for concealing sources of money intakes and laundering illegally earned money. As reported by Ojedokun (2005), there are many well-known online money laundering cases involving victims in Africa who were tricked in order to steal their identity or transfer money from their real accounts using phishing and scams. The operation of cybercrime in Africa is somehow discernible in pattern. According to Wall (2007), Advanced Fee Frauds commence with the receipt of an official-looking letter or email, usually purporting to be from the relative of a former senior government official, who, prior to their death, accrued a large amount of money which is currently being held in a bank account within the country from which the letter was being sent. The sender of the 419 letter invites the recipients to assist with the removal of the money by channeling it through his or her bank account. In return for collaborating, the recipient is offered some reasonable amount of money, certain percent of the money to be transferred. Once recipients respond to the sender, an advanced fee is sought to pay for banking fees and currency exchange. As the victim becomes more embroiled in the scam and pays out money, it becomes harder to withdraw. Needless to say, the majority according to Wall (2007), if not all, of these invitations are bogus and are designed to defraud the respondents, sometimes for considerable amounts of money Another technique employed by the scammers is to invite the victim to visit the scammers in their home country to explain their situation in person and ask for money and assistance. This ploy is relatively uncommon, though it can lead the victim to be held hostage or killed (Holt & Graves, 2007). Another method is to persuade the victim to provide the scammer with personal information such as their name, address, employer, and bank account information. The initial request may be made under the guise of assuring the sender that the recipient is a sound and trustworthy associate (Holt & Graves, 2007). However, the information is surreptitiously used by the sender to drain the victim's accounts and engage in identity theft. According to Brenner (2004), Chawki, and Abdel-Wahab (2006), Phishing and pharming are two popular forms of fraud that aim to dupe victims into believing they are at a trusted Website such as their banks, when in fact they have been enticed to a bogus Website that intends to steal their identity and drain their financial resources.

Spyware: While spyware has occupied the center stage of late, it is but one of the tools behind today's rash of cybercrime in Africa. Deceptive Trojan horses, multi-purpose bots, and spyware programs form the crimeware arsenal of today's African hackers are regularly bought and traded on the illicit market. The price tag of crimeware is often based on their ability to steal sensitive data such as bank and credit cards while remaining undetected by the victim. Whatever the case, it is obvious that spyware may be targeted against natural persons, property, or institutions. Nigeria in an effort to redeem the image that cybercrime in form of spyware has tarnished, is now targeting internet access points such as Cybercafés where spyware cybercrimes are being perpetrated. However, majority of the spyware cybercrimes perpetrated in Nigeria generally are targeted at individuals and not necessarily computer systems, hence according to Longe and Chiemeke (2008), they require less technical expertise.

Hucksters: According to Longe and Chiemeke (2008), the hucksters do perpetrate their criminal

activities through the use of e-mail address harvesting software called harvesters (web spiders) such as Mail Extractor Lite1.4. It has been observed that these tools can automatically retrieve e-mail addresses from web pages by a slow turnaround from harvest to first message (typically at least one month), followed by a large number of messages typical product based Spam (i.e. Spam selling an actual product to be shipped or downloaded even if the product itself is fraudulent).

Fraudsters: The fraudsters are characterized by an almost immediate turnaround from harvest to first message (typically less than 12 hours) involving only a small number of messages sent to each harvested addresses. According to Longe and Chiemeke (2008), Fraudsters often harvest e-mail addresses using tool such as mailing address extractors. Their mode of operation is to send only a message to their victims all at a particular time. Fraudsters have been found to be typical of Nigerian cyber criminals (Longe & Chiemeke, 2008).

Piracy: Piracy has been found to flourish in Nigeria than any other African countries. The illegal reproduction and distribution of software applications, Games, movies and audio CDs can be done in a number of ways. Usually, Longe and Chiemeke (2008) observed that pirates buy or copy from the Internet an original version of a software, movie or game and illegally make copies of the software available online for others to download and use without the notification of the original owner of the software. This classified Internet piracy appears to be the modern day piracy into which conventional piracy have metamorphosized. Internet piracy may be less dramatic or exciting but it must be acknowledged that it is far subtler and more extensive in terms of the monetary losses the victim faces. This particular form of Cyber crime may be the hardest of all to curb as the common man typified by high poverty rate in Africa also seems to be benefiting from it. Nigeria is typically notorious for piracy despite the unrelenting effort by the Nigerian government to combat the menace.

Hacking: Average young Africans are excited about the prospect of trying to crack security codes for e-commerce, ATM cards and e-marketing product sites with astonishing results despite their low level of education and computer literacy. Phishing which refer to imitating product and e-commerce web pages in order to defraud unsuspecting users is also becoming popular cyber crimes in Africa as criminals simulate product websites to deceive innocent Internet users into ordering products that are actually non-existent. This method is used mostly to obtain credit card numbers. Longe and Chiemeke (2008) had observed that in Nigeria some cybercafés do dedicate a number of systems to fraudsters (popularly referred to as "yahoo boys") for the sole purpose of hacking and sending fraudulent mails. However, due to the effort of EFCC, these criminal activities appear to have been reduced to some categories of hackers who acquire systems and share bandwidth (popularly referred to as home use) with some cybercafés for home use in order to perpetuate cybercrimes from their homes.

Economic Reasons for Cyber Crime / Cybercafé Serving as Conduit for Cybercrimes in Africa

Cybercrime has advanced from mere pranks by computer geeks to conscious effort with monetary motives. Kshetri (2006) cited an article published by PC World with a quote from a Russian hacker who asserted "there is more of a financial incentive now for hackers and crackers as well as for virus writers to write for money and not just for glory or some political motive" (p. 36). Little wonder that recent hackers target financial institutions and credit card industries. According to Card Systems Solutions, 40 million Credit Card numbers were hacked in 2004; the Boston Globe of March 28, 2007 reported 45.7 million Credit and Debit Card numbers were stolen from TJX group of companies including T. J. Maxx, BJ's Wholesale Club, OfficeMax, Barnes and Noble

bookstore, although the Associated Press of October 24, 2007 doubled the number to 94 million credit cards amounting to hundreds of millions in US dollars (Hashem, 2009).

Besides, most African countries are contending with high unemployment problems; the numbers are increasing daily and this we envisaged might be one major reason for alarming growth of cybercrimes in the continent. According to the World Bank, African States face great challenges to generate 100 million new job opportunities by the year 2020 or the region's instability will increase (World Bank, 2008). Statistics reveal that the unemployment rate is very high among youth in Africa most are university graduates with computer and Internet competency. With cybercafés becoming readily available throughout the region at relatively low rates for Internet access, the stage appears set for a new generation of local hackers and cybercriminals majority of which are script kiddies working for financial motives. Careful investigation revealed that these script kiddies do not have deep programming knowledge like experienced hackers who can create their own malware or viruses, but they take advantage of many websites available for free that help them understand the basics behind hacking techniques with links to underground hacking sites and even free tools to use.

Efforts to Combat Cybercrimes and Promote Cybersecurity

It is imperative to ensure the security of cyberspace as it has become one of the common spaces for humans, next to land, air, sea, and outer space (Schjolberg, 2010). Definitely, a global intervention is necessary and to an extent, has been initiated. Yet, on a local level, Africa as a continent ought to device means of making the cyberspace safe. Although this is a daunting task because cybercrime occurs seamlessly across countries, regions, and continents and adding to the challenging aspect of combating cybercrime is the issue of jurisdiction; unlike traditional crimes in which case, one can be confined to a geographical location, the fluidity of cybercrime renders any law or policy impotent because of jurisdictional difficulties and challenge of tracking down the origin of the crime. In any case, some laws are better than none and as Cassim (2009) noted, "law enforcement officials cannot prosecute cyber criminals unless countries have adequate laws in place outlawing such criminal activities" (p. 40). However, it is disturbing to note that most African States do not have Internet-specific laws, although some are beginning to initiate laws in this direction. For instance, countries, such as Botswana, Egypt, Lesotho, Mauritius and South Africa are trying to shape new legislation and legal definitions for cybercrime. While this effort might be commendable, there is still need for more specific laws for combating cybercrime activities in Africa. Even in many of the few countries with specific legal framework against cybercrimes, one observed that the existing laws lack the potential to tackle the transnational aspects of the phenomenon.

Egypt: Egypt enjoys the reputation of the only northern African state with a "formal legislation against cybercrimes and a public key infrastructure" (Cole, et al., 2008, p. 15). The legal measure in Egypt for curbing cybercrimes dates back to the Penal Code No. 58 of 1937; newer laws and policies include Child Law 126 of 2008, Telecom Act 10 of 2003, e-Signature Law 15 of 2004 and the Intellectual Property Law 82 of 2002. Baraka (2009) noted that Egypt considers online child safety a priority and upholds such effort through Child Helpline 16000, a helpline that receives and records complaints and provides protection for children against violence, neglect and abuse. The Egyptian government also established Ministry of State for Family Population and creates awareness of cyber threats through training prosecutors about the rights of a child. Other technical measures as noted by Baraka (2009) include requiring Internet Service Providers (ISPs) to include safety applications that would provide filters, classification

systems for sites, ratings, and age verification systems. On an international level, Egypt has reached out and sought help from international organizations and institutions including the United Nations, International Telecommunication Union (ITU), and non-governmental organizations such as International Centre for Missing and Exploited Children (ICMEC) and eNASCO in capacity building and enforcing the laws and policies.

Egypt is one of the advanced African countries in terms of ICT usage and has made history with their adeptness in social network usage. Many have attributed the victory of forcing President Hosni Mubarak out of office after 30 years to the power of social networking sites like Facebook, Twitter, and other networking tools including the cellular phones which allowed Egyptian youth to organize tumultuous protest that lasted for 18 days with a resignation of President Mubarak on February 11, 2011. Beyond the social networking efforts, Egypt prides itself of several initiatives geared towards building digital bridges including launching a national ICT plan in 1999 that provides access and infrastructure, establishing ICT Club Initiative in 2000, instituting a subscription-free internet initiative and PC for every home in 2002, promulgating Smart Village in 2003, the Egyptian Information Society initiative of 2003, Broadband project of 2004, ITIDA was also established in 2004, Arabic E-content initiative of 2005, Education initiative of 2006, ICT Export Strategy was established in 2006 also and Cybersecurity initiative promulgates between 2007 and 2009 (Hashem, 2009).

The E-Signature Law of 2004 with Public Key Infrastructure (PKI): In April 2004, Egypt passed the E-signature Law alias Law 15 to regulate electronic signatures under the authority of the Information Technology Industry Development Agency (ITIDA) and that is entirely managed by highly trained Egyptian staff on a 24-hour basis. In a global sense, this law supports commercial transactions in and with Egypt by establishing a secured e-signature of contracts without the cost and delay of signing the documents in person. In addition to e-commerce and on a national level, this secured Public key Infrastructure (PKI) can also be used in e-government applications as well as in private sectors. This in essence creates the National Root Certifying Authority which issues and manages electronic credentials, certificates and signature through the PKI system. The certificate authorities or service providers which can include private and public sectors as well as international bodies must be certified by the ITIDA which is the Egyptian government and any certification breach incurs an exorbitant amount of fine up to 100,000 Egyptian pounds (Arab Republic of Egypt, Law 15 of April 2004).

Nigeria: Efforts at preventing financial Cyber crime in Nigeria are at entrepreneurial, private and public pedestal. For cyber café owners, notices are pasted on walls warning of possible arrests of scammers who send fraudulent mails. While in the USA and Western Europe, the term cybercafé refers often to true cafes offering both internet access and beverages, in Africa, cybercafés can refer to places offering public internet access in places like restaurants or hostels, or at locations that are wholly set aside for public access internet services (Adomi, 2007). Cybercafés in Nigeria provide overnight browsing, a special internet service offered from 10:00 p.m. to 6:00 a.m. This shift as Adomi (2007) observed, offers lower fees to internet users. Although overnight browsing is very important and useful to cybercafé users, it was banned by the Economic and Financial Crimes Commission (EFCC) with the collaboration of the Association of Cybercafé and Tele centers Owners - Association of Telecommunications Company Of Nigeria (ATCON) in Nigeria (Adomi, 2008). The ban was promulgated in response to attempts by the EFCC to combat cybercrime.

Other decisions of EFCC and Association of Telecommunication Companies of Nigeria (ATCON) reached to combat cybercrime as noted by Adomi (2008) include:

- Undertaking international awareness programs for the purpose of informing the World of Nigeria's strict Policy on Cybercrime and to draw global attention to the steps taken by the Government to rid the country of Internet 419 in particular and all forms of cybercrimes;
- Mandating each sector of the telecom industry, namely the global system for mobile communication operators, private telecomm operators and cybercafés to institute a due care document that would be a standard guide and proffer measures for the effective policing of cybercrime in Nigeria;
- Requiring all cybercafés to register with the Corporate Affairs Commission, National Communications Commission (NCC) and EFCC;
- Introducing membership system for cybercafé as opposed to pay-as-you-go;
- Requiring all cybercafés to install acceptable hardware surveillance;
- Architectural setting of cybercafés must be done such that all computer screens are visible to staff
- ATCON members must subscribe to registered and licensed Internet Service Provider in the country;
- Each cybercafé is expected to be a watchdog to others, as they have been detailed to have direct access to EFCC

The Federal government of Nigeria authorized EFCC to arrest and prosecute individuals and organizations suspected to be involved in the promotion of cybercrimes. As at the period of writing, there are virtually no known technical measures implemented for combating cybercrime in Nigerian cybercafés. Hopefully he EFCC is working on something along this line. Besides curbing cybercrimes through cybercafés initiatives, the Nigerian government has over the years enacted far-reaching laws aimed at combating transnational organized crime and punishing the perpetrators of these crimes. Among these numerous efforts are the Criminal Code Act, Economic and Financial Crimes Commission Act 2004, Computer Security and Critical Information Infrastructure Protection Bill 2005 and Advance Fee Fraud and other Fraud Related Offences Act 2006. Advance fee fraud scam under the Nigerian Criminal Code Act, qualifies as a false pretence (section 418), while a successful Internet scam would amount to a felony under section 419. Furthermore, a suspect could alternately be charged under section 421 of the Criminal Code Act.

However, as noted by Oriola (2005), the Criminal Code Act provisions on advance fee fraud are ill-suited for cyberspace criminal governance because of the fluidity of the jurisdiction under which the crime was committed. Oriola (2005) succinctly explained that:

Although section 419 of the Criminal Code Act deems advance fee fraud a felony, the provision that an advance fee fraud suspect cannot be arrested without a warrant, unless found committing the offence, does not reflect the crime's presence or perpetration in cyberspace. Only in rare circumstances could a suspect be caught in the act because most of the scam emails are sent from Internet cafes. (p. 241)

Another related law on Internet scam regulation in Nigeria is the Money Laundering (Prohibition) Act 2004. It makes provisions to prohibit the laundering of the proceeds of crime or an illegal act. Although advance fee fraud is not expressly mentioned in the Act, proceeds of the scam would appear covered under section 14(1) (a) which, prohibits the concealing or disguising of the illicit origin of resources or property which are the proceeds of illicit drugs, narcotics or any other crime. The Act also implicates any person corporate or individual who aids or abet illicit disguise of criminal proceeds. Section 10 Subsection (1) places a duty on every financial institution to report within seven days to the Economic and Financial

Crimes Commission and the National Drug Law Enforcement Agency any single transaction or transfer that is in excess of N1m (or US$7,143) in the case of an individual or N5million (US$35,714) in the case of a body corporate (Chukwuemerie, 2006). Any other person may under sub-section (2) also give information on any such transaction, or transfer. Under sub-section (6) even if a transaction is below US$5,000 or equivalent in value, but the financial institution suspects or has reasonable grounds to suspect that the amount involved in the transaction is the proceed of a crime or an illegal act it shall require identification of the customer.

On an international level, the Nigeria Government and Microsoft Corp signed a Memorandum of Understanding defining a framework for cooperation between Microsoft and the Economic and Financial Crimes Commission (EFCC) of Nigeria with the aim of identifying and prosecuting cyber criminals, creating a safe legal environment and restore hundreds of millions of dollars in cost investment. This agreement is the first of its kind between Microsoft and an African government and gives the EFCC access to Microsoft technical expertise information for successful enforcement. The Memorandum combats issues such as spam, financial scam, phishing, spyware, viruses, worms, malicious code launches and counterfeiting. Microsoft is expected to instruct Nigerian investigators on techniques of extracting useful information from PCs compromised by botnet attacks, how to monitor computer network to detect such attacks, and how to identify the people behind them. Under this contract also, Microsoft will also provide leads on spam emanating from Nigeria, enabling the authorities to pursue investigations more quickly and successfully (Adomi, 2008).

Similarly, the Anti-Drug Network (ADNET) is a computer network with powerful capabilities for the storage and retrieval of data concerning Nigerian crime (Chawki, 2009). ADNET is a secure system and can be accessed through dedicated ADNET terminals in the task force cities. In conjunction with the Nigerian Crime Initiative

(NCI) working group, an outside private contractor trains and provides support to investigators working Nigerian crime cases (Chawki, 2009). ADNET terminals are also located in Lagos, Nigeria, and Accra, Ghana, so that data can be accessed close to sources of much of the Nigerian crime activities. Several federal law enforcement agencies contribute and access ADNET data. In the last two years the number of records in the NCI database has increased dramatically, making the network a potentially valuable resource to law enforcement agencies. Some of this data consists of information collected from prior criminal investigations, including aliases used by persons involved in Nigerian criminal activities (Chawki, 2009)

Another relevant legislative measure in the fight against advance fee fraud on the Internet is the Advance Fee Fraud and other Fraud Related Offences Act 2006. This is a replacement of an Act of the same title passed in 1995. Section 2 makes it an offence to commit fraud by false representation. Subsection (2) (a) and (2) (b) clarify the representation must be made with intent to defraud. Section 3 makes it an offence if a person who is being the occupier or is concerned in the management of any premises, causes or knowingly permits the premises to be used for any purpose which constitutes an offence under this Act. This section provides that the sentence for this offence is the imprisonment for a term of not less more than 15 years and not less than five years without the option of a fine. Section 4 refers to the case where a person who by false pretence, and with the intent to defraud any other person, invites or otherwise induces that person or any other person to visit Nigeria for any purpose connected with the commission of an offence under this Act. The sentence for this offence is the imprisonment for a term not more than 20 years and not less than seven years without the option of a fine.

South Africa: The South African government considers cybercrime a serious issue that requires government intervention. President J. G. Zuma of South Africa included this topic in his 2009 State of the Nation address "Amongst other key initiatives, we will start the process of setting up a Border management Agency; we shall intensify our efforts against cyber crime and identity theft, and improve systems in our jails to reduce repeat offending." (Grobler & van Vuuren, 2009). However, necessary legislations such as Section 86(1) of South Africa's Electronic Communications and Transaction Act (ECTA) provides that, subject to the Interception and Monitoring Prohibition Act, 1992 (Act 127 of 1992), a person who intentionally accesses or intercepts any data without authority or permission to do so, is guilty of an offence are proving worthwhile in these regards. To avoid issues of unnecessary red-tape which may hamper a prosecution, Cyber inspectors in terms of Section 83 of the Act are also empowered to access and inspect the operation of any computer or equipment forming part of an information system-used or suspected to have been used in an offence and require any person in control of, or otherwise involved with the operation of a computer to provide reasonable technical assistance. However, there are constitutional concerns with regards to the search and seizure provisions (in particular section 14 of constitution-privacy) which still need to be addressed by the South African courts.

Three of the most important legislative interventions in South Africa, include the Electronic Communications and Transactions Act (ECTA) 25 of 2002, the Regulation of Interception of Communications and Provision of Communication-related Information Act 70 of 2002 (the RICPCIA), and the Electronic Communications Act 36 of 2005. Also, the current voluntary regime governing the collection of private and personal information obtained by means of electronic transactions, in future, will be substituted by privacy and data protection legislation of which due cognizance has to be taken. E-commerce in South Africa is governed primarily by the Electronic Communications and Transactions Act (ECTA) 25 of 2002, which came into force on 30 August 2002, as South Africa's first comprehensive e-commerce legislation (Sibanda, 2009). The process of establishing the country's first e-commerce law was initiated in 1999 by the Department of Communications, which sought to identify and determine the existing contract-specific or related legislation and decide on its appropriateness to e-commerce. The ECTA is modeled partly on the United Nations Commission on International Trade Law Model Law on E-Commerce (UNCITRAL Model Law) of 1996, which provides national legislatures with a basic legal framework for enacting or revising their e-commerce laws (Faria, 2004; Sibanda, 2009).

Section 45(1) of the ECTA only regulates the unsolicited commercial communications to consumer. In effect, this means that any unsolicited communication that is not regarded as *commercial* will not fall within the ambit of the regulation. The term commercial being an elusive and fluid concept, it does mean that a communication offering a commercial transaction will obviously be covered by the ECTA. However, this is yet to give an answer to communication which does not amount to offering a contract, but which nonetheless has some vague commercial features. Furthermore, the regulatory protection of section 45 cannot be extended to legal persons. This is because the ECTA defines a consumer as "any natural person who enters or intends entering into an electronic transaction with a supplier as the end user of the goods or services offered by the supplier." The implication of this law as it now stands could mean that a legal person, for example a company that receives unsolicited commercial communication is precluded from having recourse to section 45 of the ECTA. The ECTA employs an approach of regulation rather than the prohibition of spam, subject to some penalties, including 12 months imprisonment, for non-compliance with the requirements of section 45(1).

Kenya: In the Eastern Africa region, cyber-security effort is mostly undertaken by the East African Community (EAC) which comprises of Kenya, Uganda, Tanzania, Rwanda, and Burundi, although to a lesser extent, individual states are promulgating some legislatives. Kenya's effort to institute a national cyber legislature has been a collaborative effort of the Kenyan Government and other international bodies including, The United States Agency for International Development (USAID) and Washington' Economic Growth Agriculture and Trade / Information Technology and Energy (EGAT / IT&E) Bureau, and the Academy for Educational Development (AED). The 2007 proposed Kenyan e-Transactions Bill is similar to Egypt's e-Signature Law with the PKI system. According to e-Government Kenyan website (http://www.e-government.go.ke) the e-Transactions Bill aims at creating an enabling legal environment for consumers, businesses, investors and Government that:

- Recognizes the importance of the information economy to the future economic and social prosperity of the Republic of Kenya;
- Facilitates the use of electronic transactions;
- Promotes business and community confidence in the use of electronic transactions;
- Enables business and the community to use electronic communications in their dealings with government;
- Provides effective protections against cybercrimes through appropriate judicial measures including penalties;
- Adheres to and supports international best practices in electronic transactions (e.g. United Nations Commission on International Trade Law (UNCITRAL) including E-commerce, digital signatures, data protection, cyber crime).
- Comply with the proposed East African cyber laws framework; and any other legal, legitimate and productive activities per Kenyan laws related to electronic transactions and electronic government.
- Encourages the use of e-government and e-commerce services as well as to protect the privacy of the public and the interests of consumers and clients due to potential mis-

use and unauthorized use of Information and Communication Technology.

An October 1, 2007 report by USAID on the final policies of Kenya's proposed e-Transaction Bill descried the pros of the bill with five distinguished qualities: *Comprehensive* because it addresses holistically electronic transaction such as e-signature, privacy and security, e-contracts, cybercrime, offences and punishments relevant to e-transactions; *Provide Legal Clarity*, the report commended the Bill as a stand-alone legislature which attracts outsourcing partnership; *Boost Investor Confidence*: in the sense that Investors will be rest assured that transactions with Kenya are both legal and secure; *Competitive Advantage* over other countries with no such legislature; and *Captures e-Commerce across Sectors* this initiative is expected to benefit all sectors of Kenya economy such as tourism, M-Pesa, BPO and Contact Centers especially with the proposal of The East African Marine System (TEAMS), a fiber optic cable project that is expected to provide faster and less expensive internet service to the Eastern African region (Ng'ang'a, 2009).

The Kenyan Communications Act of 2009 finally passed the e-Transaction bill and it addresses cybercrime among other issues and is regulated by the Communications Commission of Kenya (CCK). It guards against unauthorized access to computer data, access with intent to commit offences, unauthorized access to and interception of computer services, damaging or denying access to computer systems, unlawful possession or devices and data, electronic fraud, tampering with computer source document and phishing obscene material in electronic form (section 83 W-Z & Section 84 A-F). The Communications Commission of Kenya provides succinct answers to frequently asked questions about the e-Transaction Bill at http://www.cck.go.ke/licensing/e_transactions/faqs.html.

WEAKNESSES OF POLICIES AND LEGISLATIVE MEASURES

Despite many efforts that the government of Egypt has invested in providing a safer cyberspace, several challenges still abound and to some extent cripple the efforts. Hashem (2009) listed challenges to include providing better security challenges and policies, legal framework and regulations, systems and processes, technologies, tools, skills, gaining the cooperation of networks and creating better awareness for cyber threats.

The major challenge for Kenya's e-Transaction Bill seems to lie on its strength which is the stand-alone component. The East African Community (ECA) has always collaborated in several national and international efforts especially with regards to ICT and international relations. The USAID 2007 report quoted earlier noted that Kenya could face insurmountable competition if the other four countries of ECA (Tanzania, Rwanda, Burundi, and Uganda) decide to communally set up a challenging e-Transaction Bill as well. Therefore, it was recommended that Kenya consider regional trade integration. While Kenyan e-Transaction Bill has been promoted as a brilliant economic venture as earlier indicated, the major challenge that face the nation is the minimal or lack of adequate knowledge of ICT. At the September 2008 meeting in Mombasa, Kenyan Minister for Information Hon Samuel Poghisio noted that the ICT sector is not well understood in Kenyan and proposes that ICT should be demystified so as to be understood by *mwanachi*– a Swahili word meaning the common man. We equally believe that this observation applies to Africa in general.

African countries are criticized as ill-equipped to fight cybercrime as they lack the personnel, intelligence, and infrastructure (Cassim, 2009). Others argue that lack of IT knowledge to understand the intricacies of cybercrime and using the old law which is based on tangible crimes to fight cybercrimes which are based on intangible actions are other challenges that face the African states. For instance, reviewing the Nigerian Cybersecurity and Information Protection Agency Bill of 2008, and drawing comparative analysis between the Bill, European and US computer crime and data protection legislations identifies a number of gaps. Notable of which are the following; No definition of what constitutes personal data; no identification of the right to privacy; no definition of what constitutes data subjects rights; no appointment of a regulatory body to redress breach (i.e. a Data Protection Commissioner); no identification of the fact that organizations can also breach data protection rules; no provision for circumstances where the personal data needs to be utilized without the consent of the data subject; and finally, there was no provision, definition, or mandatory requirement of technical measures to mitigate data protection breaches. Furthermore, the Bill does not provide independent monitoring of the law enforcement agencies carrying out the provisions, nor does the Bill define law enforcement agency or lawful authority. Finally the Bill does not distinguish between serious offenses and emergencies or minor misdemeanors. As a result it may conflict with Article 37 of Nigeria's Constitution, which guarantees the privacy of citizens including their homes and telephone conversations, present a threat on national security, public health, morality, or the safety of others.

Further analysis of the bill revealed that Section 15 (1) of the bill which relates to data retention has some concerns associated with it that needed to be discussed. Firstly, Nigeria does not have a Data Protection Legislation. It is to be noted that one of the principles of Data Protection is that personal data should not be kept for longer than is necessary. This then brings to question the absence of Data protection requirements within the draft Bill. Bearing in mind that the Bill provides for the establishment of an Information Protection Agency, one would have thought that requirements about how personal information is to be handled from a legal perspective are spelt out. It is therefore recommended that a section should

be introduced within the Bill, which makes it a requirement for organizations to adhere to Data Protection principles. This should then be followed with a section within the Bill that introduces Data Protection principles and the penalties for none compliance. Now bearing in mind that processing of personal data constitutes a large segment of outsourcing, it makes a clear cut case for Nigeria to implement the legislation on data protection. This becomes highly imperative due to the ongoing telephone SIM and voter's registration cards in Nigeria.

Another point to note is that the Bill does not provide guidelines stipulating how long various types of data may be retained. The impact of the data retention section is that in the event that time-frames for keeping data types are not set in stone, ISP's and other organizations will need to ensure they have adequate backup and data storage facilities including policies and procedures for keeping information. This will without a doubt raise privacy, security and cost issues. In relation to costs, the key question is who will bear the burden of these costs, the government or the organizations requested to retain the data? ISP'S will therefore need to look at how this piece of legislation will impact their operations from a cost perspective. An immediate impact of the retention issues will be in relation to the SIM Card registration directive. For example, in the event that a subscriber is no longer a customer of a telecommunications service provider, how long should their data remain with that service provider? Under Data Protection Laws, we feel the information should be deleted once the customer notifies the service provider of this fact. This draws our attention to Subsection (4) of the bill, which states that ISP data retrieved for law enforcement agencies, shall not be utilized without consent of the individual to whom the data applies is quite intriguing. It is not clear if this section meant that if a suspect under investigation by law enforcement agencies does not consent to their data being accessed, then that data cannot be used or otherwise. Also, Section

18 introduces obligations on service providers to assist law enforcement agencies in identifying offenders. It should be noted that due to the fact that many breaches are internal breaches, there should also be an obligation on all organizations to develop, implement and ensure enforcement of industry standard policies, processes and procedures for computer related breaches.

One of the most controversial section in this Bill and one which should raise National security concerns is Section 24. This section stipulates that information about critical infrastructure will be published in a gazette. Placing critical infrastructure information in a gazette is not a smart idea. Rather it shows a lack of understanding of the risk, threats and vulnerabilities that may accrue to critical systems. Instead, the government should rather adopt a *need to know* policy in relation to government systems whereby only persons who have been vetted appropriately would have access to such information. Similar observation can be made to Section 24 (2b) which mentions procedural rules and requirements for securing the integrity and authenticity of data or information. We are of the opinion that this should be amended to include the confidentiality and availability of information. It has often been argued that confidentiality, integrity and availability are the cornerstone principles for information security and will need to be identified when carrying out impact assessments in relation to any system. There also needs to have an obligation placed on organizations that suffer security breach to personal information to be made to declare such breaches. This will allow persons affected to take necessary actions to prevent further loss and negative impact on them.

Equally, the ECTA of South Africa does not clearly define spam. As a result, it might not be out of point to state that South African spam regulation seems to maintain an *opt-out* approach. In other words, it does appear that the ECTA leaves it to the recipient to opt to cancel communication of unsolicited communication (see ECTA 45[1] [a]). Perhaps this state of affairs may be explained by

the fact that the ECTA primarily focuses on the functional equivalence of e-commerce and paper-based commerce and probably when the ECTA was drafted in 2001, spam was not viewed as a serious problem in South Africa. Be that as it may, opting out of unsolicited e-mails may be a costly onus for the consumer to discharge, and does not act as a real disincentive to the spammers. Nonetheless, South Africa's approach to spam ignores the fact that spam is a growing menace in South Africa, and can be offensive and intolerable which is in confirmation to an interview study conducted with scholars at the University of Cape Town, South Africa on six Internet Service Providers (IPS) which averaged the amount of spam received daily to be approximately 50% of incoming email. The study also revealed that 51% of the people interviewed found spam offensive (Chigona, Bheekun, Spath, Derakhashani, & Van Belle, 2005). Unfortunately, technology service providers in South Africa, such as the Wireless Application Provider Association (WASPA) which regulates the South African SMS messaging industry, had eagerly implemented the opt-out approach as the preferable approach as contained in section 5 of its Code of Conduct (Wireless Application Service Providers' Association Code of Conduct, 2008)

After many years of legal uncertainty, South African Parliament enacted the Electronic Communications and Transactions Act (2) (ECT) which comprehensively deals with cybercrimes and has now created legal certainty as to what may and may not constitute Cybercrime. Section 3 of the ECT (its interpretation clause) does not exclude any statutory or common law from being applied to, recognizing or accommodating electronic transactions. In other words, the common law or other statutes in place wherever applicable is still in force and binding which has the result that wherever the ECT has not made specific provisions for criminal sanction such law will be applicable. Denial of Service (DOS) attacks also popularly known as Disk Operating System attacks, are attacks that cause a computer system to be inaccessible to legitimate users. Denials of service attacks disrupt service to legitimate users for a period of time (Kufa, 2008). Section 86(5) states that, "any person who commits any act described in Section 86 with the intent to interfere with access to an information system so as to constitute a denial, including a partial denial of services to legitimate users is guilty of an offence." The act or conduct is fashioned in such a manner that it is widely defined and consist of any of the action criminalized in Sections 86(1) and Section 86(4). The actions include unauthorized access, unauthorized modification or utilizing of a program or device to overcome security measures (Kufa, 2008). Section 87 of the ECT also introduced the Cyber crimes of Extortion, Fraud & Forgery. Section 87 of the ECTA has introduced the Cybercrimes of E-Extortion as per section 87(1), E-Fraud as section 87(2) and E-Forgery as section 87(2). Section 87(1) provides an alternative to the common law crime of extortion. Kufa (2008) states that pressure is therefore exerted by threatening to perform any of the acts criminalized in section 86. Kufa also criticizes this section as "wet behind the ears" (p. 21) as its common law equivalent applies to both forms of advantage of propriety and non-propriety form. He suggests that this provision is wanting and will require redress.

FACTORS MILITATING CYBER POLICY ENFORCEMENT

For developed nations, cybersecurity is viewed along the prism of national security and thus considered a vital, sensitive, and priority issue to tackle. Equally, an effectively cyber secured space requires complicated infrastructures, digital militaries, a dedicated set of highly digitally intellectual force, and a robust funding. These, as Cole et al., (2008) observe, are lacking in developing countries as most developing countries fail to recognize the link between cybersecurity

and national security. Interestingly, the computer operating systems in Africa also renders them prone to frequent hackers and other cyber crimes. Grobler and van Vuuren (2009) noted that 93.40% of Operating System in Africa is Windows, 4.1% is Mac, 1.02% Linux, 0.25% java ME, 0.24% iPhone, 0.11% is Symbian, and *Others* constitute 0.13%. Windows are regarded as targets of cyber criminals and prone to many threats since the criminals themselves operate with Windows for easier compatibility. Furthermore, sensitive bio-data information such as name, date of birth, social security number, or mother's maiden name is used when applying for documents that are used to identify an individual such as driver's license or passport and for the provision of services, bank accounts or utility services contribute to this challenge. The problem lies in the manner in which these documents are issued and also the verification process used to gain access to such services. It has been identified that the process for issuing passports and driver's licenses in Africa can sometimes be manipulated. It has been well documented that criminals have been able to successfully produce counterfeit passports and licenses. When this is coupled with stolen personal information, it is easy to forge a person's identity to obtain goods and services or use it to commit criminal activity.

Call centers have equally being discovered as ideal places for identity thieves to thrive, as they represent personal information rich environments. Organizations customer relationship management systems are used to identify their customers in many African call centers. Some perpetrators of this crime usually referred to in Nigeria as "yahoo boys" are taking advantage of e-commerce system available on the internet to defraud unsuspected victims who are mostly foreigners thousands and sometimes millions of dollars. They fraudulently represent themselves as having particular goods to sell or that they are involved in a loan scheme project. They may even pose to have financial institution where money can be loaned out to prospective investors. In this regard, many persons have become victims.

RECOMMENDATIONS

In general, Africa as a continent lags behind in the effort to ensure a relatively secured cyberspace. We propose that efforts should be made in the following areas; first, as noted by Cassim (2009) since cyber criminals are using sophisticated computer technology to avert government traps, cyber education and expertise are imperative. With Blaise Compaore, President of Burkina Faso as the Patron of Global Cybersecurity Agenda, an international cooperation in cyber security, African countries could solicit the expertise of the International Criminal Police organization (Interpol) and other international organizations including the ITU. While tailoring legislative measures, African countries should be aware of the dichotomy between safeguarding the cyberspace and respecting the privacy and rights of its users. A typical example of the Nigerian effort of abolishing the use of cybercafés at night as a measure of warding off cyber criminals while depriving other innocent users who may be very busy during the day of the opportunity to use the cybercafé is a good example.

Many works on cybercrime that we reviewed proffered various ways that the cyberspace can be relatively secure. Countries that do not have any form of legislation ought to work toward setting up one that is both practical and balanced. Etges and Sutcliffe (2008) listed some examples of principles that could aid in combating cybercrime. They encouraged the use of cross-functional teams consisting of researchers, investigators, policymakers, business leaders, and security standard experts. Similarly, they emphasized the importance of Computer Emergency Response Team (CERT) and promoting its use among the citizenry, the use of both law enforcement and civilian personnel in crime investigation, treating

cybercrime solely as a national and international threat and not a branch the general criminal activity, alerting the general public of various online cyber crimes and establishing global channels and collaborative efforts.

It is also advisable that the current Computer Security and Critical Information Infrastructure Protection Bill be totally revised to consist of separate legislations comprising Data Protection Legislation, Computer Misuse Legislation, Information Security Legislation and Lawful Interception. These will then form the Nigerian Cyber Crime Legislative Framework to which it can be recognized as having appropriate legislature to combat computer related crime and Identity theft. However, since Nigeria and most African countries are considering Freedom of Information Act, we wish to state that Data Protection Legislation and Freedom of Information Act should be seen as compatible and not conflicting.

Furthermore, we observed that the Human Capital requirements to effectively monitor cyberspace would be huge and the demands unlimited, as cybercrime is a daily challenge. We therefore urge the provision of relevant sections of the Bill to address human capital requirements. It is also important that there should be standardization in computer security and cybersecurity education. A Standing Accreditation Body should therefore be endowed with the responsibility of accrediting Computer Security and Cybersecurity educational institutions, to ensure that the knowledge base and resource pool are actually relevant to the needs of the country. The Bill should also encourage the development of local security software using open source alternatives for developing information security expertise and solutions in Africa.

In reviewing data privacy issue in Africa, we wish to draw the attention of African Government to the fact that African countries who wish to be considered or partake as outposts for outsourcing services should note that development of sufficient laws and practices similar to those of the European Union must be put in place. This once again calls for harmonization of African countries cyber laws which should facilitate business transaction and cooperation with their international counterparts. In other words, African cyber crime laws must have an international dimension; signing relevant treaty with other regional bodies might just be a way forward.

In light of the many challenges identified in the experiences of other inter-governmental organizations concerning the subject of cyber-crimes, it would appear that two options are available for Africa's engagement with the menace. One, African States could decide to accede into the Convention on Cyber Crime (CCC) while they are considering the possibility of a cybercrime treaty tailored for Africa. This path is particularly commendable judging by the fact that, multiple provisions are included that allow divergent treatment of the procedural or substantive legal provisions by the individual member countries. According to Dejo (2009), these were included on matters that were recognized by the Convention's drafters as possible sources of conflicts among States. Moreover, the Convention allows for any nation at the time of signing or at ratification or accession, to submit declarations or reservations with respect to obligations under any provision of the Convention (Dejo, 2009). Besides, African governments could begin to engage the option of an immediate formulation of an Africa-specific anti-cybercrime treaty similar to what obtains under the Countries of Europe (CoE) regime. This approach is also commendable due to the fact that a country that exercises jurisdiction in a self-centered manner will not only contravene rules of international law but may also upset the international legal order and generate reprisals in the attempt to track and prosecute cyber criminals. To this end, Dejo (2009) is of the opinion that the African Union (AU), through its numerous technical agencies and commissions could assume responsibility for designing the framework for a continent-wide legal approach. This is because, purely domestic solutions are proving inadequate because cyberspace has no geopolitical borders and more so, computer systems can be stealthily accessed or compromised from any location in the world. Establishing and implementing effective and cybercrimes specific regulations should therefore be of concern to all African governments and peoples.

CONCLUSION

A unanimous agreement among all scholars of cybercrime is that it can never be solved entirely all that can be done is to fight it, minimize it, or just corner the criminals. This sad realization is based on many factors that we discussed all through this chapter. Unfortunately, cybercrime involve the Internet which is ubiquitous, cutting across several jurisdictions and involving various geopolitical and socio-economic considerations (Tushabe & Baryamureeba, 2005; Lovet, 2009). On another platform, is the issue of liberty and privacy which obviously conflicts with some security measures. The effort then turns out to be the proverbial double-edged sword and resonates with Benjamin Franklin's statement "any society that would give up a little liberty to gain a little security will deserve neither and loose both." However, cyber security lies along the continuum of other securities—national, human, economic therefore, numerous writers, policymakers and law enforcers have called for stringent and innovative laws to prevent and punish computer crimes. However, the right to privacy is often a complex and contentious issue, one dependent upon many variables that can range from the constitutional guarantees against government intrusion into individual rights to the rights of individuals against those who would, for whatever reason, invade their privacy. Sixty years after the UN's Human Rights declaration was launched in December 1948, many scholars within different jurisdictions have engaged in a continuing debate about the definition of privacy but while this debate has yielded many valuable insights there is yet no universally agreed definition for a universal value such as privacy.

Despite active international co-operation on cybercrimes, Africa still has a lot of work to do to secure a significant spot in the global scheme of legal approaches against the problem. Apart from the obvious apathy among majority of African States to critically engage the cybercrime phenomenon in a cogent way, one formidable possibility to formulating a comprehensive regional agenda against cybercrimes could be the question of limited jurisdiction to pursue cyber criminals across borders. South Africa as well as countries like Nigeria and Egypt has taken legislative arms to deal with these new crimes. The crimes as stated in these countries cybercrime bills, proposals and bills are however not exempted from scrutiny. For example, the enforceability of the ECTA provisions are still to be tested in South African courts and some legal practitioners and adjudicators (magistrates and judges) need to be educated and mentally conditioned to embrace the cyber crime provisions of the ECTA. Given the borderless nature of the internet and the challenges it poses in terms of jurisdictional questions, international cooperation and uniformity, it is of the utmost importance that African states learn from each other's efforts to deal with cybercrime and create an international cybercrime code to be applied across the continent if any significant success is to be achieved in combating cybercrime in Africa.

Also, many African States have witnessed a rise in outsourcing functions to Asian countries, which have recently enacted data protection legislation. Not enacting appropriate legislation to cater for data protection and identity theft in Africa means there is possibility of Africa being left out in the lucrative outsourcing deals which not only brings job opportunities but also the numerous opportunities that African legislative and technical services that are available. Currently, only three African countries have been identified for outsourcing, these being Egypt, South Africa and Ghana. A major disadvantage of not

implementing the legislation is the fact that many Africans who legitimately wish to purchase goods online are barred from doing so due to credit card companies blacklisting some African IP addresses which can be attributed to a lack of evidence that appropriate technical and legislative measures are available to protect personal data.

Finally, any cybersecurity effort ought to use the template of the 2002 UN Resolution of 57/239 as reported by Sund (2008), which identifies nine elements in the quest for a global culture of cybersecurity. They include awareness, responsibility, response, ethics, democracy, risk assessment, security design and implementation, security management, and reassessment.

REFERENCES

Adomi, E. (2007). Overnight internet browsing among cybercafé users in Abraka, Nigeria. *Journal of Community Informatics*, *3*(2). Retrieved February 20, 2010 from http://ci-journal.net/ index.php/ ciej/ article/ viewFile/ 322/351.

Adomi, E. (2008). Combating cybercrime in Nigeria. *The Electronic Library*, *26*(5), 716–725. doi:10.1108/02640470810910738

Baraka, H. (2009). *Empowerment and safety for children in a knowledge society: Egyptian experience.* Paper presented at the APEC-OECD Symposium. Singapore.

Barton, P., & Nissanka, V. (2003). Cyber-crime criminal offence or civil wrong? *Computer Law & Security Report*, *19*(5), 401–405. doi:10.1016/S0267-3649(03)00509-0

Bazelon, D. L., Choi, Y. J., & Conaty, J. F. (2006). Computer crimes. *The American Criminal Law Review*, *43*, 259–310.

Bequai, A. (2001). Organised crime goes cyber. *Computers & Security*, *20*(6), 475–478. doi:10.1016/S0167-4048(01)00604-6

Brenner, S. (2004). Cybercrime metrics: Old wine, new bottles. *Virginia Journal of Law and Technology, 9*(6), 537–584.

Burden, K., Palmer, C., & Lyde, B. (2003). Cybercrime: A new breed of criminals? *Computer Law & Security Report, 19*(3), 222. doi:10.1016/S0267-3649(03)00306-6

Casey, E. (2004). *Digital evidence and computer crime*. St. Louis, MO: Elsevier Press.

Cassim, F. (2009). Formulating specialised legislation to address the growing spectre of cybercrime: A comparative study. *Preservation Education & Research, 12*(4), 35–79.

Chawki, M. (2009). Nigeria tackles advance fee fraud. *Journal of Information, Law and Technology, 1361-4169*.

Chawki, M., & Abdel-Wahab, M. (2006). Identity theft in cyberspace: Issues and solutions. *LexElectronica, 11*(1), 1–41.

Chigona, W., Bheekun, A., Spath, M., Derakhashani, S., & Van Belle, J. (2005). Perceptions on SPAM in a South African context. *Internet and Information Technology in Modern Organisations: Challenges and Answers*. Retrieved March 3, 2011 from http://www.commerce.uct.ac.za/ InformationSystems/ Staff/ PersonalPages/ jvbelle/ pubs/ IBIMA05% 20Cairo% 2069.pdf.

Chukwuemerie, A. (2006). Nigeria's money laundering (prohibition) act 2004: A tighter noose. *Journal of Money Laundering Control, 9*(2), 173–190. doi:10.1108/13685200610660989

Cole, K., Chetty, M., LaRosa, C., Rietta, F., Schmitt, D. K., & Goodman, S. E. (2008). *Cybersecurity in Africa: An assessment*. Unpublished.

Collier, D. (2004). Criminal law and the internet. In Buys, R. (Ed.), *Cyberlaw @ SA* (2nd ed.). Pretoria: Van Schaik Publishers.

Etges, R., & Sutcliffe, E. (2008). An overview of transnational organized cyber crime. *Information Security Journal: A Global Perspective, 17*, 87-94.

Faria, J. A. E. (2004). E-commerce and international harmonization: Time to go beyond the functional equivalence. *Journal of Information, Law & Technology (JILT)*. Retrieved February 22, 2011 from http://www2.warwick.ac.uk/ fac/ soc/ law/ elj/ jilt/ 2008_2/ sibanda/ sibanda.pdf.

Gibson, W. (1984). *Neuromancer*. New York: HarperCollins.

Grobler, M., & van Vuuren, J. J. (2009). *Combating cyberspace fraud in Africa*. Johannesburg, South Africa: CSIR.

Hale, C. (2002). Cybercrime: Facts and figures concerning the global dilemma. *Crime and Justice International, 18*(65), 5–26.

Hashem, S. (2009). *Towards an Egyptian framework for cybersecurity*. PowerPoint presentation. Retrieved from http://www.itu.int/ ITU-D/ cyb/ events/ 2009/ tunis/ docs/ hashem-cybersecurity-framework-egypt-june-09.pdf.

Holt, T., & Graves, D. (2007). A qualitative analysis of advance fee fraud email schemes. *International Journal of Cyber Criminology, 1*(1), 137–154.

Johnson, D. R., & Post, D. G. (1996). Law and borders-the rise of law in cyberspace. *Stanford Law Review, 48*, 1367–1404. doi:10.2307/1229390

Kshetri, N. (2006). The simple economics of cybercrimes. *IEEE Transactions on Security and Privacy, 4*(1), 33–39. doi:10.1109/MSP.2006.27

Lewis, B. C. (2004). Prevention of computer crime amidst international anarchy. *The American Criminal Law Review, 41*, 1353–1356.

Longe, B., & Chiemeke, S. (2008). Cyber crime and criminality in Nigeria: What roles are internet access points playing? *European Journal of Social Science, 6*(4), 132–139.

Longe, O., Ngwa, O., Wada, F., Mbarika, V., & Kvasny, L. (2009). Criminal uses of information & communication technologies in sub-Saharan Africa: Trends, concerns and perspectives. *Journal of Information Technology Impact, 9*(3), 155–172.

Lovet, G. (2009). Fighting cybercrime: Technical, juridical and ethical challenges. In *Proceedings of the Virus Bulletin Conference,* (pp. 63-76). VBC Press.

Ng'ang'a, A. M. (2009). Toward a regional ITC hub: Need for cyber laws in Kenya. *Information Security Journal: A Global Perspective, 18*, 47-50.

Ojedokun, A. A. (2005). The evolving sophistication of Internet abuses in Africa. *The International Information & Library Review, 37*(1), 11–17. doi:10.1016/j.iilr.2005.01.002

Olowu, D. (2009). Cyber-crimes and the boundaries of domestic legal responses: Case for an inclusionary framework for Africa. *Journal of Information, Law & Technology.* Retrieved February 2, 2011 from http://www2.warwick.ac.uk/ fac/ soc/ law/ elj/ jilt/ 2009_1/ olowu/ olowu.pdf.

Oriola, T. (2005). Advance fee fraud on the internet: Nigeria's regulatory response. *Computer Law & Security Review, 21*(3), 237–248. doi:10.1016/j. clsr.2005.02.006

Schjolberg, S. (2010). *A cyberspace: A United Nations convention or protocol on cybersecurity and cybercrime.* Paper presented at the Twelfth United Nations Congress on Crime Prevention and Criminal Justice. Salvador, Brazil: United Nations Press.

Sibanda, O. S. (2009). *Anti-spam: A comparative appraisal of Canadian, European Union, and South African regulatory regimes.* Paper presented at the Lex Informatica Conference. Pretoria, South Africa. Retrieved February 02, 2011 from http://www.thefreelibrary.com/ Anti-spam: a comparative appraisal of Canadian, European Union, and...-a0197857850.

Snail, S. L. (2008). Cyber crime in context of the electronic communications act. *Juta Business Law, 6*(2), 65. Retrieved February 20, 2011 from http://www.allbusiness.com/ crime-law/ criminal-offenses-cybercrime/ 12956172-1.html.

Tladi, S. (2008). The regulation of unsolicited commercial communications (SPAM): Is the opt-out mechanism effective? *South African Law Journal, n.d.,* 178–183.

Tushabe, F., & Baryamureeba, V. (2005). Cyber crime in Uganda: Myth or reality? In *Proceedings of World Academy of Science, Engineering and Technology.* WASET Press.

UNECA. (2009). *ECA cooperative actions on cybersecurity.* Paper presented at the ITU Regional Cybersecurity Forum for Africa and Arab States. Tunisia, Tunis.

Wall, D. (2007). *Cybercrime: The transformation of crime in the Information age.* Cambridge: Polity Publishers.

World Bank. (2008). *Global monitoring report 2008.* Washington, DC: World Bank.

KEY TERMS AND DEFINITIONS

Cyber Security: It entails all measures taken proactively and actively to prevent and ensure safety from cyber attacks.

Cybercrime: It refers to any crime that involves a computer and a network. The computer may have been used in the commission of a crime, or it may be the target.

Cyberspace: Cyberspace is the electronic medium of computer networks, in which online communication takes place.

Section 2
Wireless Sensor Networks

Chapter 6
A Walk through Sensor Network Programming Models

Mukaddim Pathan
Australian National University, Australia & Telstra Corporation Limited, Australia

Doug Palmer
CSIRO ICT Centre, Australia

Ali Salehi
CSIRO ICT Centre, Australia

ABSTRACT

The widespread use of sensor networks in a range of applications has given rise to various programming approaches. It is a long standing concept that the application programmer of a sensor network should be shielded, as much as possible, from the questions of communications and systems architecture, that is, the low level details. In this chapter, the authors survey existing programming models for sensor networks and classify them by following a layered approach, based on their level of abstractions. With their approach they endeavor to lay out a clear guideline to choose the right approach for programming sensor networks for application development, thus potentially alleviating the heavy burden for programmers.

INTRODUCTION

Today, cheap and smart devices with multiple on-board sensors, networked with wireless links are available from research groups and companies. Due to the small size of these devices (also known as motes) pervasive computing concept is now far from just an imaginary idea. Sensor networks (Akyildiz, et al., 2002a; Yick, et al., 2008) gather data from the physical world and deliver it to a central node or sink where the data can be processed and analyzed. There are many applications of sensor networks, ranging from environmental monitoring to precision agriculture, animal tracking, volcano monitoring, weather forecasting, military situation awareness, structural monitoring, coal mine safety, medical emergency management, and traffic control. A sensor network typically has the following characteristics:

DOI: 10.4018/978-1-4666-0161-1.ch006

- Homogeneous or heterogeneous structure, comprising a large number of sensor devices, a small processing unit, and a wireless communications mechanism.
- Deployment of cheaper devices, rather than more powerful devices since data density and redundancy are key requirements (Costa, et al., 2007).
- Little or no infrastructure, beyond base station data sinks (Yick, et al., 2008).
- Short, low speed communication range between devices and the use of multi-hop routing to deliver messages. Communications may be asymmetric and unreliable (Woo, et al., 2003).
- Battery-powered devices with a limited energy budget, possibly backed by energy scavenging and solar cells (Estrin, 2001; Yick, et al., 2008).
- Unreliable devices that may stop functioning either due to physical damage or because they have run out of energy.
- Dense, overlapping data sets and in-network processing of data to reduce network contention and energy consumption.

With a fast moving world of building powerful sensors, the processing cost is becoming cheaper every day. Sensor devices are powerful enough to act like small computers autonomously managing their own resources and collaborating with other wireless nodes to provide detailed observations of the physical world. To rapidly build flexible sensing programs, researchers have proposed various programming models. A programming model is simply a development platform which constitutes a compiler for a domain specific language and a set of services. Services introduced by a programming model are the ones that are commonly required by the applications in which the programming model is intended to be used. As an example services which might be provided by a programming model are execution model (thread-based or event-based), routing algorithm

and time synchronization. Research community has proposed a number of programming models for the wireless sensor networks. One of the most well known contributions of the research community to the programming models used for wireless sensor networks is the TinyOS system. Using the right programming model can have enormous impact in the development, deployment and maintainability of sensor networks. As for instance, choosing a programming model that is event-based requires a different set of expertise and imposes different type of restrictions compared to a thread-based programming model.

Motivation and Contributions

Existing literature reports a few reviews of prominent programming models for sensor networks. In early works (Hadim & Mohamed, 2006; Römer, 2004), authors have taken a broader view of sensor networks and attempt to develop a taxonomy and comparison of different approaches. Mottola and Picco (Mottola & Picco, 2010) present a survey of programming approaches for sensor networks and identify the fundamental requirements programming platforms must deal with. Rubio et al. (2007) provides a broader middleware-support classification by covering a range of approaches and highlighting some open research challenges and future directions. Chatzigiannakis et al. (2008) provide a categorization of middleware platforms for sensor networks, using functionalities and challenges that will play a crucial role in sensor network software development. In another work, Henricksen and Robinson (2006) undertake a survey of programming approaches for sensor networks focusing on software engineering abstractions. Most of the existing surveys are based on a taxonomy with only a few dimensions, by centering around node-centric programming and macroprogramming model. In this chapter, we present a goal-based categorization of sensor network programming models, i.e. what are the low to high-level system goals achieved by

Figure 1. Layered categorization of programming models for sensor network

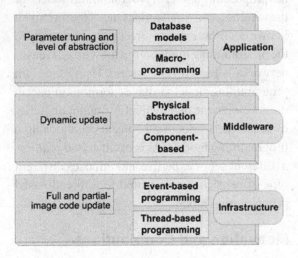

programming a sensor networks, as well as we provide the level of abstractions of realized through sensor network programming models. Our work draws similarity with the survey by Sugihara and Gupta (2008), who present a classification and survey of programming models based on the level of abstractions.

Figure 1 presents the layered categorization of programming models for sensor networks. We classify the existing approaches according to infrastructure, middleware, and application-based models. The programming goals for these three layers are code-update, dynamic update and parameter tuning, respectively. Our layered approach is also reflective of the level of abstractions in programming models. Infrastructure-based models include event and thread-based programming; middleware-based models comprise physical abstraction and component-based programming; whereas, application-dependent models include database programming and macroprogramming. Based on this classification, in this chapter, we provide a survey of existing research works. The main contributions of this chapter are:

- A layered classification and comprehensive survey of programming models for

sensor networks. It provides a basis for categorizing related solutions and techniques in this area.
- Outlining an effective programming model to lay out future research directions.

The rest of the paper is structured as follows. We start with providing a coverage of sensor network services that are vital for programming a sensor network. Then we survey the existing programming models by categorizing them according to our layered approach. It is followed by our findings on an effective programming model and future research directions. Finally, the paper is concluded with a summary of contributions.

SENSOR NETWORK SERVICES

Underlying any programming model for sensor networks is a layer of services that manage the system state and metadata, routing information, synchronization, and code management. In this section, we briefly describe some of the services that play an integral part in employing a particular programming model within a sensor network.

Routing

A routing strategy specifies how messages will be communicated within a sensor network. It should adapt to the specific characteristics of a sensor network, such as unreliable and redundant nodes, limited energy, high node count and limited memory (Al-Karaki & Kamal, 2004). Choosing the routing strategy is largely dependent on the nature of a given sensor network application.

Simple Routing: The simplest routing strategy is to flood a message over the network, with each node re-broadcasting any message that it has not seen before. Paradoxically, flooding is often unreliable, since the amount of radio noise generated can mean that some nodes never hear an undistorted message (Cardell-Oliver, 2004). Another simple routing protocol is a gradient-based method (Intanagonwiwat, et al., 2000). The target node is given a level of 0. A gradient is then established by recursively broadcasting a node's level to its immediate neighbors, which then take a level greater than the broadcast level. When a message is sent, it is broadcast and nodes which a level below the broadcasting node re-broadcast the message. Multiple copies of the message may arrive at the target.

Point to Point Routing: This protocol allows a node to send a message across multiple hops to a specific destination. To do this, a route has to be established between the two nodes and the route needs to be maintained across network failures for the duration of the communication. There are many existing point to point routing protocols, such as Ad-hoc On-demand Distance Vector (AODV) routing (Perkins, et al., 2003) and Greedy Perimeter Stateless Routing (GPSR) (Karp & Kung, 2000).

Spanning Tree Routing: Many sensor network applications, particularly data-gathering applications, route back to a central sink for storage and further analysis. In such a case, building a spanning tree over the network provides an energy-efficient way of delivering data back to the sink. Spanning trees are also useful when dealing with duplicate-sensitive aggregations and they naturally fit the dataflow programming models that are often associated with functional programming. Constructing a spanning tree essentially requires building a gradient towards the sink and then allowing nodes to select a parent node from a list of candidates (Woo, et al., 2003). Alternately, the spanning tree can be semi-statically constructed to provide some sort of global optimization (Krishnamachari, et al., 2002).

Content-Based Routing: Rather than publish or subscribe to simple channels or subjects, receivers can advertise a predicate that describes the content of the messages that should be delivered (Carzaniga & Hall, 2006; Carzaniga & Wolf, 2002). A predicate may be probabilistic, giving fuzzy matches. Similarly, senders can advertise a predicate that describes the sort of messages that the sender will produce. Routing becomes an issue of selectively forwarding messages based on matching receiver predicates. The routing nodes can combine and approximate predicates to provide space and matching efficiency.

Neighborhood Routing: Neighborhood routing (Awan, et al., 2007; Fok, et al., 2005), usually associated with supporting middleware is based on the idea that most in-network processing is performed in contiguous regions of sensors connected to some physical region. Logical neighborhood (Mottola & Picco, 2006) takes some form of content-based routing by following a predicate-based approach to define broadcast groups of sensors. Node templates describe lists of node attributes, which can be either static or dynamic. Neighborhood templates describe parameterized predicates over node templates, hop count and application-defined cost measures.

Synchronization

There is a distinction between an event's valid time (when an event happened) and transaction time (when an event appears in a database). Since analysis of sensor data often depends on comparing events over multiple nodes, there needs to be an adequate level of time-stamping on the events. While nodes typically have an internal clock, the clocks are subject to differing degrees of drift. Wisden (Paek, et al., 2005) uses low-overhead time stamping that does not require global clock synchronization. As packets move to a common node, they acquire enough timing information to allow the common node to assign a source time to the packet using. The amount of time a sample spends at a node, i.e. residence time, is calculated using the node's internal clock. Ganeriwal et al. (2003) suggest an explicit timing synchronization protocol that can synchronize to 20-50µs. A reference node, synchronized to an accurate clock, is assigned level 0. The reference node's neighbors then become level 1, their neighbors level 2, and so on. Nodes exchange packets with timestamps, and the timestamps can then be used to build a drift rate for the node's internal clock.

Virtual Machines

Virtual machines (VMs) (Costa, et al., 2007) can be used to provide a consistent interface to heterogeneous hardware and provide the sort of memory and multitasking protections unavailable on most devices. VMs also provide efficient way of reprogramming both because the bytecode programs are shorter than an entire image and because application-specific VMs can be used to reduce the number of bytecodes needed for certain operations (Koshy & Pandey, 2005). Generally, VMs provide consistent abstractions to allow either infrastructure-level programming or a single program to run on all nodes. Costa et al. (2007) provide an overview of VM models for sensor networks.

The earliest sensor network VM was Maté (Levis & Culler, 2002). A Maté virtual machine consists of three contexts: the clock, send and receive contexts. Each context operates independently and has an operand and a return stack. Each context is scheduled in response to an appropriate event: a clock timeout, a message to send or a received message. A single word heap can be used to communicate between contexts.

The original Maté VM is very restricted. To extend it, the concept of application-specific VMs was developed (Levis, et al., 2004). The extended version of Maté can have multiple contexts, shared resources and customizable operations drawn from a library of operations. A specification draws together the various elements and builds and application-specific VM. A concurrency manager provides race and deadlock-free access to shared resources. Application-specific virtual machines are a key component of subsequent sensor network development.

Dynamically Extensible Virtual Machines (DVM) (Balani, et al., 2006) go a step further by using the SOS incremental code update mechanism (Han, et al., 2005) to allow incremental modification of the VM at run-time. The VM* (Koshy & Pandey, 2005) system is based on the Java instruction set. Once an application has been compiled, the output bytecodes are analyzed for types, instructions, runtime support, devices, utilities and resources. Similarly, the node capabilities are analyzed and suitable support algorithms, such as heap management and garbage collection are selected. A constrained VM can then be built to support the specific program and node requirements; these machines can be extended in-network. VM* makes use of generative programming (Czarnecki, et al., 2002) to build families of systems.

An alternative approach to VM generation is to use an existing implementation and specialize it for a specific program by feature and reachability analysis. This approach has the advantage that it is not necessary to maintain the base VM code, since it is a specialization of a framework that is already being maintained. Application-specific VMs may not have a human-oriented source programming language, such as a scripting language. Instead, code can be generated directly from some intermediate-level form generated by a program- or query-analyzer. These VMs are often specialized towards a specific programming model.

Code Management

Once a sensor network has been physically deployed, it becomes increasingly difficult to maintain and reprogram the sensors. Since the nodes are in contact with each other, distributing code updates via the wireless network becomes attractive. Code management systems can be either homogeneous (all nodes are homogeneous and receive the same code and data) or heterogeneous (nodes may be heterogeneous or individually programmed).

Simple code management schemes use a global, reconfigurable runtime. A small enough reconfiguration, i.e. a monolithic binary image, can then be fitted into a single packet and then distributed throughout the network. This approach is called full-image code update (Stathopoulos, et al., 2003). It is commonly used for upgrades of TinyOS (Levis, et al., 2005) applications. While this approach provides maximum flexibility by allowing arbitrary changes to functionalities, it incurs high update cost. COSMOS (Awan, et al., 2007) allows in-network reprogramming by assuming that implementations of all components are already present. Reprogramming then becomes a matter of providing a new interaction assignment. TinyDB queries follow a similar pattern, with the query being flooded across the network and the TinyDB runtime performing local database operations.

To reduce energy consumption, a difference-based mechanism (Reijers & Langendoen, 2003) can be used, where only the differences between the new and old code are sent instead of sending the entire image. This approach is called partial image code update, which calculates differences to be delivered to target nodes and then integrated into the program image (Jeong & Culler, 2004). The heavy-duty calculation of re-linking and delta generation is performed at the gateway, at the cost of the gateway needing to know the state of the program at each node. An alternative approach is to either use a compressed dynamic linking system to allow dynamic linking on the node (Dunkels, et al., 2006) or to use efficient modularization of a program and operating system into location-independent modules with well

defined interfaces, a system used by SOS (Han, et al., 2005) and Contiki (Dunkels, et al., 2004). VM systems limit update cost by allowing split-level updates. A common runtime can be maintained by heavyweight, homogeneous code management techniques. VM programs are then smaller and can be delivered by more data-like delivery protocols. Many highly updatable virtual machine systems use SOS to allow mixtures of virtual machine and VM program updates (Balani, et al., 2006; Horré, et al., 2008).

Homogeneous Code Management: If both the sensor network is homogeneous and the nodes run identical copies of a program, then code delivery can simply be via nodes copying code. Viral code techniques, such as Trickle (Levis, et al., 2004) then become attractive. Trickle uses a polite gossip approach. Nodes transmit metadata summaries of the versions of code (or other information) that they have and listen to other node's summaries. If a node detects that its metadata is subsumed by the existing transmissions, then it remains silent. If a node detects another node with an earlier version of an object, it transmits the new version. If a node detects another node with a later version of the object, then it sends its own metadata, triggering a transmit. Deluge (Hui & Culler, 2004) is a build off Trickle to allow the dissemination of a large object, such as a new binary image throughout a sensor network. Objects are partitioned into pages and nodes maintain page registries for partially completed objects. At intervals, nodes broadcast summaries of their page registries and neighbors can then request pages to be transmitted in the form of a sequence of packets. If the object is a program, the node can completely load the program and then transfer to the new program. Impala (Liu & Martonosi, 2003) provides another viral update model for larger applications, capable of handling incomplete and inconsistent updates. Components (called modules) are given a version number. Sensor nodes compare version numbers with their immediate neighbors and request fragments of newer components.

Heterogeneous Code Management: The key difficulty in heterogeneous code management is accurate, energy- and time-efficient delivery of multiple code images to subsets of the network. This requirement means that the semi-flood algorithms used in homogenous code management will be inefficient. Pump Slowly, Fetch Quickly (PSFQ) (Wan, et al., 2005) can be used on top of a point to point routing scheme or content-based routing to deliver messages to subsets of nodes. Several sensor network platforms use mobile code techniques. Agilla uses agents that can copy or move themselves across the network to distribute Maté VM code (Fok, et al., 2005). Code migration is also used in MagnetOS (Liu, et al., 2005) and smart messages (Borcea, et al., 2003).

Aggregate Construction

Wireless sensor networks tend to use in-network processing wherever possible, since radio energy costs tend to swamp any processing costs. One of the simplest forms of in-network processing is the construction of aggregates for WSN queries, similar to that of SQL. Nodes that route data for several client nodes (or groups of nodes) can produce partial aggregates, rather than sending the raw data back to the sink for processing.

The TAG architecture (Madden, et al., 2002) provides the building blocks for producing a variety of different aggregates, not limited to common, SQL-based constructs. Instead, suitable functions can be built into a generic aggregation architecture. If the application is designed to work with noisy and inaccurate data, aggregates can be approximate. Readings taken from sensors may be unreliable and noisy and it may be necessary to build a best estimate from a number of sensors. Maximum-likelihood estimation can be made locally by diffusing estimates to participating nodes and a global best-estimate made. The aggregate functions used in TAG assume either duplicate insensitive aggregations, e.g. the maximum value aggregate, or a state record routing system that eliminates duplicates.

Metadata Management

Sensor networks produce a large amount of dense, in-situ data about an environment. Since the sensor network data provides a snapshot of the conditions in the network boundaries, the gathered data can be re-used and re-analyzed by scientists other than the original investigator. Collected sensor data from heterogeneous sensor networks is often archived or streamed as raw data, but it has to be associated with metadata, describing its meaning. The underlying reasons for enhanced meaning of sensor data are to enable situation awareness, ongoing citation and access to data, unaffected by changes in storage and services that data might undergo over its lifespan. Metadata annotation, i.e. providing meaning to sensor data, includes the feature of interest, the specification of measuring instruments, accuracy, location, condition, and scenario of measurements (Dawes, et al., 2008).

Creating metadata and keeping it up-to-date and usable is part of the strategy for the long-term management of sensor network data for e-research (Jeung, et al., 2010). This is particularly important as environmental scientists use sensor network deployments for detailed monitoring of the physical world and these deployments generate unprecedented quantities of data. Managing these data effectively is essential to support the full lifecycle of the e-research endeavor, from concept formulation and outlining of the research activity itself, to data collection, processing, metadata annotation, provenance, curation, discovery, analysis, and dissemination of research results.

Moreover, metadata management is essential when the user is confronted with large numbers of sensors and sheer volume of collected sensor data. When a user is not clear about what is available, he/she can start a general search of relevant concepts and narrow it down based on semantic descriptions and their relations.

External Visibility

The data gathered from sensor networks needs to be presented into a form that can be integrated into larger-scale processes, such as Semantic Reality or simply presented in a human-readable form. Captured data streams can also be centrally processed, a good option if multiple cross-references in the data would mean a great deal of in-network routing and delivery. Fjords (Madden & Franklin, 2002) collect all sensor data and then processes inputs on a powerful system using sequences of dataflow-like operators. Individual sensors are represented by sensor proxies. Captured data can also be processed to provide context information—semantic information on what a collection of sensor readings mean. The resulting context data can then be presented to other systems or be fed back into the sensor network itself for management and actuation. An example context system is the Gaia context management infrastructure (Ranganathan & Campbell, 2003). This infrastructure uses semantic web techniques—resource descriptions, ontologies and first-order predicate logic— to build context information.

From a scientific perspective, the use of sensor networks in sciences characterized by fieldwork, such as environmental science, creates big-science levels of data. Borgman et al. (2007) studied the data gathering processes of the Center for Embedded Networked Sensing (CENS) from the perspective of digital library support for the data and identified the use of campaigns to gather data. Campaigns involve an iterative approach to data gathering where short bursts of field sensing are then analyzed and experiments re-designed

in a cycle of: experimental design, calibration, data capture, data derivation, data integration, analysis, publication and preservation. In the data integration phase, the gathered data is often manually synchronized and cleaned. This cycle means that it is difficult to present the data in a standard, one-size-fits-all schema and captured data needs to be associated with a considerable amount of meta-data if it is going to be useful to other researchers. For a single environment, sensor data can be captured in a database, linked to sensor meta-data tables and calibration information and displayed as web pages using tools such as PHP. Suitable plugins for Google Earth can be used to provide spatial displays.

The Global Sensor Networks (Aberer, et al., 2007) platform allows sensor networks to presented as black-box entities, with virtual sensors described by XML documents. Virtual sensors present as streams that can be accessed by a number of methods, such as query, email notification or SMS. The virtual sensors can be built from a number of different data sources, including direct sensor streams, historical data and combined streams of data.

PROGRAMMING MODELS

In this section, we detail on the layered categorization of the sensor network programming models. Our survey of existing approaches is presented in a bottom-up approach according to Figure 1. Under each category, we list the relevant programming models and provide a summary of their technical details.

Infrastructure-Level Programming Models

In the infrastructure-level programming approach, an operating system provides a basic level of services and task management, however, without protection such as true multi-tasking and memory protection. Programs are generally assembled on a server by combining application specific code, library routines, configuration information, and operation system into a single image that can be delivered to a node. The programming models belonging to this category uses both full- and partial-image code update.

Event-based Programming: Most infra-structure-level sensor network programs are essentially reactive, with nodes responding to network messages, sensor data and timer events. As such, event-based programming is a natural sensor networking programming model and the main sensor network programming language is nesC (Gay, et al., 2003). nesC allows program-mers to write components with an interface specification. The components are connected together by a wiring specification, which the nesC environment uses to assemble an image from the requested components. nesC tasks and events are essentially non-preemptive units of work that can be invoked upon components, with events being able to preempt tasks. Long-latency operations, such as reading a sensor, require a split-phase execution with a request that returns immediately, followed by an event when the read completes. Event-based programming model is also used in Impala (Liu & Martonosi, 2003), SOS (Han, et al., 2005) and in Contiki (Dunkels, et al., 2004). Contiki also permits preemptive multithreading as an option for long-running processes, such as cryptography. Impala, SOS and Contiki all allow modular code management schemes to enable efficient reprogramming.

Event-based messaging systems are often built around active messages (von Eicken, et al., 1992). An active message conceptually contains the handler that should be invoked on the message by the receiver; in practice this is the name of the handler. The body of the message is decoded by the handler, freeing the message queue for the next message.

An event-based programming model often suffers from the level of complexity, such as split-phase execution is hard to get right; it is difficult to share code between components, leading to du-plication; component interfaces do not guarantee compatibility; components are not configurable; and memory is static, with components of the same class sharing state. Primitive event-based programming requires manual stack management, the need to keep global or heap-allocated variables between events and manual flow control, the need to use states as conditional switches.

Thread-based Programming: This approach provides a more programmer-friendly program-ming model than event-based programming at the expense of having to explicitly request informa-tion about external events. Lightweight fibers are implemented on top of TinyOS and consist of a non-blocking system fiber and blocking applica-tion fibers (Welsh & Mainland, 2004). Each fiber has a context consisting of its register values. Ap-plication fibers block by switching to the system fiber, which can then schedule another fiber. The Fleck Operating System (FOS) uses a blocking, thread-based model, with context switches com-ing either from explicit yields or from calls to blocking system services (Sikka, et al., 2007). An ingenious approach to thread programming is the t-kernel (Gu & Stankovic, 2006). The t-kernel provides preemptive multitasking and virtual memory management by modifying code as it is loaded, inserting yields and memory indirection at run-time. The resulting code runs 1.5 to 3.0 times more slowly than pure native code but the environment provides the sort of guarantees usu-ally associated with virtual machines.

Middleware-Level Programming Models

Middleware approaches to sensor network pro-gramming abstract infrastructure-level program-ming by providing abstractions for handling component and node interaction. Programming models in this category differ based on a number of features, as summarized in Table 1. Enterprise

Table 1. Desirable middleware features

Features Middleware	Distribution	Correctness	Modularity	Dynamic updates	QoS	Resource limitations	Cooperative applications	Physical abstraction
Abstract regions	√							
Agilla	√		√	√				
COCOS	√						√	√
COSMOS	√	√	√					
Hood	√							√
Impala	√		√	√	√			
SNACK		√					√	
Spatial programming	√							√
TeenyLIME	√						√	

middleware platform generally allow hot deployment and replacement of new applications, as well as component reconfiguration, also known as dynamic updates.

Inherent Distribution and Physical abstraction: Inherently distributed middleware describes a distributed environment, rather than a set of local environments. This generally means that data abstractions can be accessed and updated by a programmer with only minimal awareness of the location of the data. Physical abstraction allows applications to be written in terms of the physical location and qualities of the information desired, rather than in terms of individual nodes. TeenyLIME (Costa, et al., 2006) provides a tuple space to allow components to communicate. Tuple spaces are federated across nodes, with reactions allowing subscriptions to matching tuples in a similar manner to content-based routing. Agilla (Fok, et al., 2005) also provides a neighborhood tuple-space and network neighborhood communication for local agent-based algorithms. Mobile Agent Platform for Sun SPOT (MAPS) (Aiello, et al., 2011) is a Sun SPOT-based middleware-level programming model that enables agent-oriented programming of sensor network applications. It is based on components that interact through events. Each component offers a minimal set of services to mobile agents

that are modeled as multi-plane state machines driven by ECA rules. In particular, the offered services include message transmission, agent creation, agent cloning, agent migration, timer handling and easy access to the sensor node resources (sensors, actuators, input switches, flash memory and battery). The COCOS (Krüger, et al., 2007) framework provides a sensor space abstraction. Any nodes that detect a defined phenomenon join the space. A node within the space can then initiate an operation across the space. Spatial Programming (Borcea, et al., 2003) treats an entire network as a virtual address space. Primitive space regions are circular spaces within a physical space, with more complex regions composed by union or intersection and by relative references to other regions. Hood (Whitehouse, et al., 2004) provides reflective memory, where updated values are reflected to neighbors in a specific neighborhood, using a mixture of hop count and content-based filters. Abstract regions (Welsh & Mainland, 2004) allow regions to be formed out of simple neighbor, mesh or spanning-tree primitives. Shared variables, either retrievable on request or copied and cached are used for communication within each region. COSMOS (Awan, et al., 2007) uses composition of functional components. The components specify their inputs and outputs, along with the characteristics the host node needs to have to work properly. An interaction assignment wires the inputs to outputs, with intra- and inter-node data transfers being handled transparently.

Some middleware platforms are specifically designed to allow replacement or reconfiguration of components with the use of Virtual Machines (VMs). A VM executes application scripts in response to particular events. Maté (Levis & Culler, 2002), Application Specific Virtual Machines (ASVM) (Levis, et al., 2005), and VM* (Koshy & Pandey, 2005) are examples of systems enabling dynamic extensibility of the VM at runtime. VM programs are smaller and allow split-level updates. Essentially it allows the users to define the abstraction boundary between the native code and VM script on the fly. VMs provide a more cost efficient approach to update application level functionality of the system. However, the VM scripts are highly restricted in the flexibility of updates.

Component-based Programming: Component-based approaches allow programmers to assemble applications from individual components with well-defined interfaces (Clemens, et al., 1998). Aspect-oriented programming (Elrad, et al., 2001) allows separation of concerns, where application code is separated from cross-cutting concerns, such as event notification, security, logging, and so on. Middleware that uses these techniques, as opposed to a simple abstracting API, has an assembly phase, where components and aspects are woven together using generative programming (Czarnecki & Eisenecker, 1999) techniques. The advantage to these techniques is that the elements of the final application can be chosen on the basis of other features within the middleware, such as quality of service.

Access to sensor metadata also allows composition with an eye to the physical attributes of the network and with application-specific configurations. A temporal logic based program generates language functional components. These can be used to build load control elements. To interact correctly, components need to be assured of the correctness of the other components with which they interact. Simple interface definitions do not provide enough semantic information to guarantee expected behavior. However, design-by-contract allows some guarantees of semantic correctness. COSMOS (Awan, et al., 2007) allows design-by-contract between components. Contracts can also be added to TinyOS interfaces by weaving contact specifications into a nesC program. As an alternative to static assembly, Impala (Liu & Martonosi, 2003) allows dynamic components. Components are accessed via adapters to allow behavior to be switched between applications, based on the current state of the node.

Application-Level Programming Models

The programming models in this category assists in building applications on top on a sensor network infrastructure, but using the network as a logical resource and thus provide application-level abstractions. They often use a parameter update procedure to provide the least expensive and least flexible way for software update. An example framework supporting this approach is SNMS (Tolle & Culler, 2005) that updates parameters of TinyOS components written in NesC (Gay, et al., 2003) programming language. Parameter update can be aided with an SQL-like query framework, such as TinyDB (Madden, et al., 2005) that allows reprogramming by providing a new interaction assignment. Specifically, the TinyDB framework gather date from sensor networks by flooding queries across the network and the TinyDB runtime performing local database operations. Software update is performed by moving around points of data aggregation in the network.

Database Model: A database abstraction for a sensor network is an attractive model for purely data gathering sensor networks. A single query can be given to the network as a whole and a dataflow constructed that will stream the data back to the sink. Acquisitional Query Processing

(ACQP) (Madden, et al., 2005) in TinyDB uses the fact that sensors themselves have control over where, when and how data is acquired. However, the pure Database Management System (DBMS) model is not particularly well-suited to the nature of the data produced by sensor networks, mainly due to the following reasons:

- The data from sensor networks is in the form of correlated streams of data, rather than rows in a table.
- Queries occur over a bounded period of time, rather than the snapshot view of traditional database systems.
- Queries often represent samples of an underlying continuous variable.
- The rate of data production in a sensor network does not match the assumptions of most DBMSs.

Streaming data can be handled by dataflow approaches, with filters, aggregation and stream merging (Bonnet, et al., 2001). This approach works well when the merge key is the timestamp or order of the data in streams and is similar to the functional reactive programming (Field & Harrison, 1988). However, it is often necessary to perform joins over data from different time periods or sort records on arbitrary keys. Both the Continuous Query Language (CQL) (Arasu, et al., 2006) and TinyDB (Madden, et al., 2005) allow the creation of table-like segments of stream data, a process called materialization in TinyDB, that can then be joined over or sorted. Cougar (Bonnet, et al., 2001) builds query processing out of a set of operators similar to the standard RDBMS operators. Time in Cougar is divided into quanta and records associated with a particular time period are treated as a unit.

TinyDB introduces a number of specialized clauses in its query language to allow time-bounded queries. Queries can have a specific run time and have an id so that they can be stopped. Events allow data collection to be initiated or stopped

in response to some function, reducing polling. Queries may also be signal events. TinyDB tends to optimize over one query. If there are multiple queries, it is possible to optimize over the complete set of queries by forming synthetic queries out of multiple queries. The results represent a superset of the queries and are de-convolved at the sink. Since combining queries reduces the number of messages sent between nodes, the savings can be quite significant. Queries can also be optimised by using application semantics (Tanin, et al., 2007).

Macroprogramming: Macroprogramming (Awan, et al., 2007; Newton, et al., 2005; Pathak & Prasann, 2006) involves writing a single program for the entire network, rather than for individual nodes in the network. The program is then deglobalized by the compiler to convert the program into elements that can be distributed to individual nodes. A macroprogramming system should have the following features—the ability to specify the program and network topology in a high-level way; fast compilation; built in fault tolerance; energy efficiency and energy balance; and methods to allow a programmer to tune the system. There are several macroprogramming approaches as described below:

Middleware-like macroprogramming: Middleware-like macroprogramming essentially allows programs to be composed out of a set of components, but gives the compiler more latitude than more traditional middleware approaches. MagnetOS (Liu, et al., 2005) allows programs to be constructed out of collections of event handlers without specifying the location of the event handler. Event handlers can be automatically migrated to the most appropriate location by the system in a manner similar to Agilla. Event handlers tend to migrate towards sources of data packets, reducing the number of hops required to perform a computation. Hood (Whitehouse, et al., 2004) allows node-specific code generation for neighborhoods. Both GME and ATaG use the generic modeling environment (Davis, 2003) framework to allow graphical descriptions of the program.

Serializable programming: Serializable programming allows a programmer to write a macroprogram as a program with a single thread of control. During delocalization, any loops over sets of nodes are unwound and, if possible, parallelized. If there is a dependency between two nodes, then the operations are kept sequential, with state and the thread of control being passed from node to node. An existing language, such as Python for Kairos (Gummadi, et al., 2005) or C for Pleiades (Kothari, et al., 2007), is extended by primitives that allow iteration over sets of nodes and consistent read and write of distributed variables. Pleiades also includes deadlock detection and loop restarting.

Shared state space: State spaces allow the state of the entire network to be encoded in a set of application-specific state variables. The DESAL (Arora, et al., 2007) system is based on visible state variables and rule-based programs. Annotations provide methods to allow tuning. State variables can be dynamically shared between nodes by the action of binding a variable to a remote variable; variables can be unbound when a binding is no longer required. Guarded commands are used to specify rules. Another rule-based language (Sen & Cardell-Oliver, 2006) maps conditions onto actions, with duty-cycles specifying sampling rate and shared channels providing network-wide communication. The SPIDEY (Mottola & Picco, 2006) framework allows iteration over a logical neighborhood. Nodes broadcast data to help build a distributed state space, with messages distributed via content-based routing. A local node accumulates the tuples that it needs to perform a calculation over a logical neighborhood.

Functional programming: Functional programming (Field & Harrison, 1988; Newton & Welsh, 2004) provides a convenient macroprogramming paradigm for a variety of reasons. Pure functional programming hides state from the programmer, allowing the compiler and runtime to determine where the state resides in the network. Side-effect free functions can be migrated, replicated and parallelized easily. Functional programs tend to use the functional reactive programming (FRP) paradigm. In this approach, values are treated as continuous behaviors that have a value at a given time and functional programming elements are composed as dataflows, with serial, parallel and looping constructs. The Regiment macroprogramming (Newton, et al., 2007) language provides a purely functional language for expressing programs over regions, composable spaces of nodes, similar to spatial programs. Flask (Mainland, et al., 2008) is designed to allow the use of Haskell and AFRP to compose sensor network programs. Flask makes use of the arrow-processing facilities of the Haskell compiler to reduce the program to a set of residual program fragments that can be reduced to nesC and located on individual nodes.

Declarative programming: Declarative programming (Chu, et al., 2007; Loo, et al., 2005) concentrates on the what of a program, rather than the how. The logic of the program is separated from the control flow of the program. The programmer specifies the logic of the program, typically in some variant of first order logic. The programmer then leaves it up to the execution engine to supply a control flow that implements the logic. Since the execution engine may re-order, parallelize or otherwise manipulate the program execution, provided that it respects the specified logic, declarative programming provides a convenient paradigm for macroprogramming. The Declarative Sensor Network (DSN) model uses a Datalog-like declarative programming language called Snlog (Chu, et al., 2007). Datalog is a derivative of Prolog that only allows constants, removing recursive data structures. Datalog programs have the property that they can be reduced to relational database operations. Snlog is derived from declarative models for overlay networks (Loo, et al., 2005) and effectively treats the collections of facts associated with predicates as a sort of mixed table/stream. Predicates limit the number and lifetime of facts that they cache at a location and incoming facts cause excess facts to be evicted. The limited number of facts also allows elegant treatment of predicates that update, such as counters, by using recursive definitions and causing the predicate the evict the old value when the new value arrives.

DISCUSSION

An effective programming model should have the ability to shield application programmers from the complexity of communications and architecture as much as possible. It should allow the programmer to express an application program using a vocabulary drawn from the application domain. It should also naturally express the kinds of applications that are to be written, even if this means multiple "small" domain-specific language architectures. From our survey we have found that in the sensor network domain, a programming model should satisfy the following requirements:

- It should reflect the data gathering requirements in a sensor network.
- The programming model should allow state variables (knobs) to fine tune the system. This will provide implicitly declarative expression of non-functional requirements for software engineering. Typical knobs would be: completeness, accuracy, consistency, availability, latency, longevity and data density.
- It should allow efficient in-situ reprogramming of the sensor network.
- There should be provision for automatic management of network topology (and topology changes).
- The used programming model should allow automatic management of redundancy, in- and out-network processing, together with sensors and metadata, as sensors are automatically calibrated and clustered as needed.

- It should have the ability to naturally express trigger events that cause behavior changes.
- An effective programming model should demonstrate the ability to run more than one application program on the network.

An outline of a programming model that aims to satisfy these requirements is show in Figure 2. The nodes in the sensor network run a set of modular VMs. These VMs can have their instruction sets reprogrammed as well as receiving new virtual machine programs. Inputs are a program and a document describing the program settings. The sensor network maintains a database of metadata, which may include dynamic metadata such as location and power consumption. The programming system also maintains a database of existing programs in the network. Libraries of algorithms for specific services, such as routing and aggregation, are maintained, along with descriptions of the characteristics of the algorithms. A library of primitive descriptions is also maintained with information about the possible things that might be treated as first-class objects within the program. The program is then processed and deployed in the following way:

1. The program is concretized by combining it with primitive descriptions and setting up the knobs to fine tune the system.
2. The program is then subjected to deglobalization. The program is mapped onto a dataflow graph and a set of abstract operations. A set of algorithms that implement the operations is chosen, based on the metadata and program settings. If necessary, parts of the dataflow graph may be duplicated or repositioned to match the algorithm or to take advantage of an existing operation. The vertices of the dataflow graph are assigned to specific network nodes or groups of nodes. The result is a set of local programs for each node.

Figure 2. Outline of an effective programming model

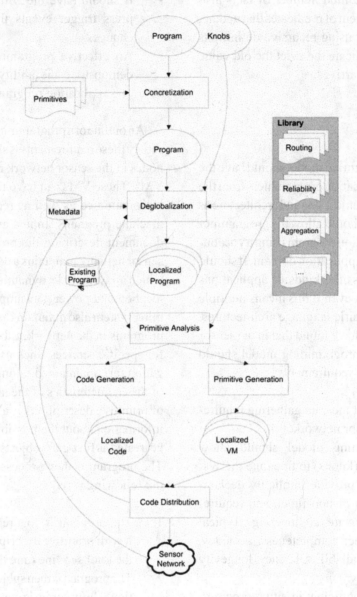

3. The local programs are analyzed for operations that should be treated as primitive operations, e.g. sending a message or merging an aggregate. This analysis is combined with the requirements of existing programs.

4. The local programs are compiled into VM code. If the VMs need new instructions, then they are also rebuilt.

5. The new set of VMs and associated programs are distributed to the underlying sensor network.

FUTURE RESEARCH DIRECTIONS

While conducting this survey, we identify the a few future research directions that will have implications for sensor network programming models. They are listed in the following:

Heterogeneity of sensor networks: Recent trends in sensor network applications exhibit that more heterogeneity in hardware platform is in existence than early mote-based systems. In order to address this issue, programming models have to effectively take into account these heterogeneous devices. In addition to physical heterogeneity, each sensor node needs to behave differently to carry out application-specific tasks. Future developments in programming models should also consider such logical heterogeneity. Future research on this topic can explore the existing approaches (Frank & Römer, 2005; Gnawali, et al., 2006; Han, et al.; Liu, et al., 2003) to address the heterogeneity of sensor networks.

Support for QoS: In many sensor network applications, various types of QoS such as accuracy and latency is essential (Sugihara & Gupta, 2008). The quality of collected data by a sensor network depends on a number of factors such as data collection method, QoS support, accuracy of measurement, physical network infrastructure and robustness of the underlying algorithms. Depending on the application, a sensor network must also support certain application and network specific QoS (Chen & Varshney, 2004; Iyer & Kleinrock, 2003; Romer & Mattern, 2004) to ensure high quality data. Some of them are: *real-time constraints*—a physical event must be reported within a certain period of time; *robustness*—the network should remain operational even if certain well-defined failures occur; *tamper-resistance*—the network should remain operational even when subject to deliberate attacks; *eavesdropping-resistance*—external entities cannot eavesdrop on data traffic; *unobtrusiveness or stealth*—the presence of the network must be hard to detect. Future

research in this direction should see the emergence of new programming model that will support these QoS attributes.

Modularization: Very few programming approaches support modularization, i.e. to be used as a building block so that different programming abstractions collaborate into a single, coherent framework (Mottola & Picco, 2010). The modularization feature could provide generic, reusable support for higher-level functionality and work as an enabling factor for wider adoption of sensor network technologies. Research in this direction can seek idea from existing work, such as the Embedded WiSeNts Project (Marrón, 2006).

Capturing low-level system details: It has been found that programming for sensor networks can be made effective by manipulating low-level aspects of the network in order to optimize resource consumption (Akyildiz, et al., 2002b). However, existing state-of-the-art programming models do not provide the facility to have access to the underlying system layers. This is due to the difficulties faced by sensor network programmers to understand and tune the low-level system parameters. Therefore, new and innovative programming model can be developed that will provide an abstraction to low-level layers and possibly provide an interface to access them. Interested researchers can explore related literature (Buonadonna, et al., 2005; Ceriotti, et al., 2009; Whitehouse, et al., 2004) to pursue research in this direction.

Plug-and-Play Configuration of Sensor Networks: Due to various environmental and contextual changes, typically in an uncontrollable environment, services from a sensor network are often required to adapt to changes such as signal quality degradation, isolated failures, resource addition, and sensor movement. These variations can happen either as random, periodic events or gradual evolutionary changes in the system. The burden of programming a sensor network, as a consequence of these changes, can be alleviated with a plug-and-play approach that allows dynamic adaptation of sensor network services. A new programming model for sensor networks can be developed that allows dynamic reconfiguration of sensor network services and adaptation to these changes, in order to make use of new context information and resources, and provide a plug-and-play environment for sensors and sensor nodes. Research on this topic can potentially explore the ongoing works (Botts, et al., 2008; Bröring, et al., 2009; Pathan, et al., 2010; Usländer, 2005) that are present in sensor network literature.

CONCLUSION

Wireless sensors are now available off-the-shelf from numerous vendors around the world. These new emerging computers are providing the basis to enable the integration of the physical and the digital world. However, programming and application development is still one major hurdle for the wide adoption of sensor network technology. There is still the need for an efficient programming model for sensor network that provides the right abstraction and simplify programming. In this chapter we provide a survey of programming models that will help researchers to choose the right kind of programming approach useful for their work. We have categorized the existing approaches using a layered technique, based on low to high-level goals, as well as the level of abstractions. Based on the survey, we have also identified potential directions for further research and point out relevant works. We have also listed the requirements for an effective programming model and outlined an associated framework that addresses those requirements. The work presented in this chapter should assist the research community

to build flexible and yet powerful programming models for highly distributed and heterogeneous sensor network deployments.

REFERENCES

Aberer, K., Hauswirth, M., & Salehi, A. (2007). Infrastructure for data processing in large-scale interconnected sensor networks. In *Proceedings of the International Conference on Mobile Data Management (MDM 2007)*. IEEE Press.

Aiello, F., Fortino, G., Gravina, R., & Guerrieri, A. (2011). A java-based agent platform for programming wireless sensor networks. *The Computer Journal*, *54*(3), 439. doi:10.1093/comjnl/bxq019

Akyildiz, I., Su, W., Sankarasubramaniam, Y., & Cayirci, E. (2002a). A survey on sensor networks. *IEEE Communications Magazine*, *40*(8), 102–114. doi:10.1109/MCOM.2002.1024422

Akyildiz, I., Su, W., Sankarasubramaniam, Y., & Cayirci, E. (2002b). Wireless sensor networks: A survey. *Computer Networks*, *38*(4), 393–422. doi:10.1016/S1389-1286(01)00302-4

Al-Karaki, J., & Kamal, A. (2004). Routing techniques in wireless sensor networks: A survey. *IEEE Wireless Communications*, *11*(6), 6–28. doi:10.1109/MWC.2004.1368893

Arasu, A., Babu, S., & Widom, J. (2006). The CQL continuous query language: Semantic foundations and query execution. *The VLDB Journal—The International Journal on Very Large Data Bases*, *15*(2), 121-142.

Arora, A., Gouda, M., Hallstrom, J., Herman, T., Leal, W., & Sridhar, N. (2007). A state-based language for sensor-actuator networks. *ACM SIGBED Review*, *4*(3), 30. doi:10.1145/1317103.1317108

Awan, A., Jagannathan, S., & Grama, A. (2007). Macroprogramming heterogeneous sensor networks using cosmos. *ACM SIGOPS Operating Systems Review*, *41*(3), 172. doi:10.1145/1272998.1273014

Balani, R., Han, C. C., Rengaswamy, R. K., Tsigkogiannis, I., & Srivastava, M. (2006). Multi-level software reconfiguration for sensor networks. In *Proceedings of the International Conference on Embedded Software (EMSOFT 2006)*, (pp. 121-130). IEEE Press.

Bonnet, P., Gehrke, J., & Seshadri, P. (2001). Towards sensor database systems. In *Proceedings of the International Conference on Mobile Data Management (MDM 2001)*, (pp. 3-14). IEEE Press.

Borcea, C., Intanagonwiwat, C., Saxena, A., & Iftode, L. (2003). Self-routing in pervasive computing environments using smart messages. In *Proceedings of the 1st IEEE International Conference on Pervasive Computing and Communications (PERCOM 2003)*, (pp. 87-96). IEEE Press.

Borgman, C., Wallis, J., Mayernik, M., & Pepe, A. (2007). Drowning in data: Digital library architecture to support scientific use of embedded sensor networks. In *Proceedings of the 7th ACM/IEEE Joint Conference on Digital Libraries (JCDL 2007)*, (pp. 269-277). IEEE Press.

Botts, M., Percivall, G., Reed, C., & Davidson, J. (2008). OGC® sensor web enablement: Overview and high level architecture. *GeoSensor Networks*, 175-190.

Bröring, A., Janowicz, K., Stasch, C., & Kuhn, W. (2009). Semantic challenges for sensor plug and play. *Web and Wireless Geographical Information Systems*, *5886*, 72–86. doi:10.1007/978-3-642-10601-9_6

Buonadonna, P., Gay, D., Hellerstein, J., Hong, W., & Madden, S. (2005). Task: Sensor network in a box. In *Proceedings of the 2nd European Conference on Wireless Sensor Networks*, (pp. 133-144). IEEE Press.

Cardell-Oliver, R. (2004). *Why flooding is unreliable in multi-hop, wireless networks. Technical Report*. Washington, DC: US Government Press.

Carzaniga, A., & Hall, C. (2006). Content-based communication: A research agenda. In *Proceedings of the 6th International Workshop on Software Engineering and Middleware (SEM 2006)*, (pp. 2-8). IEEE Press.

Carzaniga, A., & Wolf, A. (2002). Content-based networking: A new communication infrastructure. In. *Proceedings of the NSF Workshop on an Infrastructure for Mobile and Wireless Systems*, *2538*, 59–68. doi:10.1007/3-540-36257-6_6

Ceriotti, M., Mottola, L., Picco, G. P., Murphy, A. L., Guna, S., & Corra, M. .... Zanon, P. (2009). Monitoring heritage buildings with wireless sensor networks: The Torre Aquila deployment. In *Proceedings of the 8th ACM/IEEE International Conference on Information Processing in Sensor Networks (IPSN 2009)*, (pp. 277-288). IEEE Press.

Chatzigiannakis, I., Mylonas, G., & Nikoletseas, S. (2008). 50 ways to build your application: A survey of middleware and systems for wireless sensor networks. In *Proceedings of the International Conference on Emerging Technologies and Factory Automation (ETFA)*, (pp. 466-473). IEEE Press.

Chen, D., & Varshney, P. (2004). QoS support in wireless sensor networks: A survey. In *Proceedings of the International Conference on Wireless Networks (ICWN 2004)*, (pp. 227-233). IEEE Press.

Chu, D., Popa, L., Tavakoli, A., Hellerstein, J. M., Levis, P., Shenker, S., & Stoica, I. (2007). The design and implementation of a declarative sensor network system. In *Proceedings of the 5th International Conference on Embeded Networked Sensor Systems (SenSys 2007)*, (p. 188). IEEE Press.

Clemens, S., Dominik, G., & Stephan, M. (1998). *Component software: Beyond object-oriented programming*. Reading, MA: Addison-Wesley.

Costa, N., Pereira, A., & Serodio, C. (2007). Virtual machines applied to WSN's: The state-of-the-art and classification. In *Proceedings of the 2nd International Conference on Systems and Networks Communications (ICSNC 2007)*, (p. 50). IEEE Press.

Costa, P., Mottola, L., Murphy, A., & Picco, G. (2006). TeenyLIME: Transiently shared tuple space middleware for wireless sensor networks. In *Proceedings of the International Workshop on Middleware for Sensor Networks (MidSens 2006)*, (pp. 43-48). IEEE Press.

Czarnecki, K., & Eisenecker, U. (1999). Components and generative programming. *ACM SIGSOFT Software Engineering Notes, 24*(6), 19. doi:10.1145/318774.318779

Czarnecki, K., Østerbye, K., & Völter, M. (2002). Generative programming. In J. Hernández & A. Moreira (Eds.), *Proceedings of the Object-Oriented Technology Workshop (ECOOP 2002), LNCS 2548,* (pp. 15-29). Berlin, Germany: Springer.

Davis, J. (2003). GME: The generic modeling environment. In *Proceedings of the International Conference on Object Oriented Programming Systems Languages and Applications*, (pp. 82-83). IEEE Press.

Dawes, N., Kumar, K., Michel, S., Aberer, K., & Lehning, M. (2008). Sensor metadata management and its application in collaborative environmental research. In *Proceedings of the 4th International Conference on e-Science*, (pp. 143-150). IEEE Press.

Dunkels, A., Finne, N., Eriksson, J., & Voigt, T. (2006). Run-time dynamic linking for reprogramming wireless sensor networks. In *Proceedings of the 4th International Conference on Embedded Networked Sensor Systems (SenSys 2006)*, (pp. 15-28). IEEE Press.

Dunkels, A., Gronvall, B., & Voigt, T. (2004). Contiki: A lightweight and flexible operating system for tiny networked sensors. In *Proceedings of the 1st IEEE International Workshop on Embedded Networked Sensors*. IEEE Press.

Elrad, T., Filman, R., & Bader, A. (2001). Aspect-oriented programming: Introduction. *Communications of the ACM, 44*(10), 29–32. doi:10.1145/383845.383853

Estrin, D. (2001). Wireless sensor networks: Application driver for low power distributed systems. In *Proceedings of the International Symposium on Low Power Electronics and Design*, (p. 194). IEEE Press.

Field, A., & Harrison, P. (1988). *Functional programming*. Reading, MA: Addison Wesley Publishing Company.

Fok, C., Roman, G., & Lu, C. (2005). Mobile agent middleware for sensor networks: An application case study. In *Proceedings of the International Symposium on Information Processing in Sensor Networks (IPSN 2005)*, (pp. 382-387). IEEE Press.

Frank, C., & Römer, K. (2005). Algorithms for generic role assignment in wireless sensor networks. In *Proceedings of the 3rd International Conference on Embedded Networked Sensor Systems*, (pp. 230-242). IEEE Press.

Ganeriwal, S., Kumar, R., & Srivastava, M. (2003). Timing-sync protocol for sensor networks. In *Proceedings of the 1st International Conference on Embedded Networked Sensor Systems (SenSys 2003)*, (pp. 138-149). IEEE Press.

Gay, D., Levis, P., Von Behren, R., Welsh, M., Brewer, E., & Culler, D. (2003). The nesC language: A holistic approach to networked embedded systems. In *Proceedings of the ACM SIGPLAN International Conference on Programming Language Design and Implementation (PLDI 2003)*, (p. 11). ACM Press.

Gnawali, O., Jang, K. Y., Paek, J., Vieira, M., Govindan, R., & Greenstein, B. … Kohler, E. (2006). The tenet architecture for tiered sensor networks. In *Proceedings of the 4th International Conference on Embedded Networked Sensor Systems (SenSys 2006)*, (pp. 153-166). IEEE Press.

Gu, L., & Stankovic, J. (2006). T-kernel: Providing reliable OS support to wireless sensor networks. In *Proceedings of the 4th International Conference on Embedded Networked Sensor Systems (SenSys 2006)*, (p. 14). IEEE Press.

Gummadi, R., Gnawali, O., & Govindan, R. (2005). Macro-programming wireless sensor networks using kairos. *Distributed Computing in Sensor Systems*, 126-140.

Hadim, S., & Mohamed, N. (2006). Middleware: Middleware challenges and approaches for wireless sensor networks. *IEEE Distributed Systems Online, 7*(3).

Han, C., Kumar, R., Shea, R., Kohler, E., & Srivastava, M. (2005). A dynamic operating system for sensor nodes. In *Proceedings of the 3rd International Conference on Mobile Systems, Applications and Services (MobiSys 2005)*, (pp. 163-176). IEEE Press.

Han, C. C., Goraczko, M., Helander, J., Liu, J., Priyantha, B., & Zhao, F. (2006). *Comos: An operating system for heterogeneous multi-processor sensor devices*. Retrieved from http://research.microsoft.com/apps/pubs/default.aspx?id=55991.

Henricksen, K., & Robinson, R. (2006). A survey of middleware for sensor networks: state-of-the-art and future directions. In *Proceedings of the 1st ACM International Workshop on Middleware for Sensor Networks (MidSens)*, (pp. 60-65). ACM Press.

Horré, W., Michiels, S., Joosen, W., & Verbaeten, P. (2008). DAViM: Adaptable middleware for sensor networks. *IEEE Distributed Systems Online, 9*(1).

Hui, J., & Culler, D. (2004). The dynamic behavior of a data dissemination protocol for network programming at scale. In *Proceedings of the 2nd International Conference on Embedded Networked Sensor Systems (SenSys 2004)*, (pp. 81-94). IEEE Press.

Intanagonwiwat, C., Govindan, R., & Estrin, D. (2000). Directed diffusion: A scalable and robust communication paradigm for sensor networks. In *Proceedings of the 6th International Conference on Mobile Computing and Networking (MobiCom 2000)*, (pp. 56-67). IEEE Press.

Iyer, R., & Kleinrock, L. (2003). QoS control for sensor networks. In [*)*. IEEE Press.]. *Proceedings of the International Conference on Communications, ICC*, 2003.

Jeong, J., & Culler, D. (2004). Incremental network programming for wireless sensors. In *Proceedings of the 1st Annual IEEE Communications Society Conference on Sensor and Ad Hoc Communications and Networks (SECON 2004)*, (pp. 25-33). IEEE Press.

Jeung, H., Sarni, S., Paparrizos, I., Sathe, S., Aberer, K., & Dawes, N. ... de Lausanne, E. (2010). Effective metadata management in federated sensor networks. In *Proceedings of the IEEE International Conference on Sensor Networks, Ubiquitous, and Trustworthy Computing (SUTC 2010)*. IEEE Press.

Karp, B., & Kung, H. (2000). GPSR: Greedy perimeter stateless routing for wireless networks. In *Proceedings of the 6th International Conference on Mobile Computing and Networking (MobiCom 2000)*, (pp. 243-254). IEEE Press.

Koshy, J., & Pandey, R. (2005). VM*: Synthesizing scalable runtime environments for sensor networks. In *Proceedings of the 3rd International Conference on Embedded Networked Sensor Systems*, (p. 254). IEEE Press.

Kothari, N., Gummadi, R., Millstein, T., & Govindan, R. (2007). Reliable and efficient programming abstractions for wireless sensor networks. In *Proceedings of the ACM SIGPLAN International Conference on Programming Language Design and Implementation (PLDI 2007)*, (p. 210). ACM Press.

Krishnamachari, L., Estrin, D., & Wicker, S. (2002). The impact of data aggregation in wireless sensor networks. In *Proceedings of the 22nd International Conference on Distributed Computing Systems (ICDCS 2002)*, (pp. 575-578). IEEE Press.

Krüger, M., Karnapke, R., & Nolte, J. (2007). Controlling sensors and actuators collectively using the COCOS-framework. In *Proceedings of the 1st ACM Workshop on Sensor and Acton Networks (SANET 2007)*, (p. 54). ACM Press.

Levis, P., & Culler, D. (2002). Maté: A tiny virtual machine for sensor networks. *ACM SIGARCH Computer Architecture News, 30*(5), 95.

Levis, P., Gay, D., & Culler, D. (2004). *Bridging the gap: Programming sensor networks with application specific virtual machines. Technical Report.* Washington, DC: US Government Press.

Levis, P., Gay, D., & Culler, D. (2005). Active sensor networks. In *Proceedings of the NSDI 2005*. IEEE Press.

Levis, P., Madden, S., Polastre, J., Szewczyk, R., Whitehouse, K., Woo, A., ... Brewer, E. (2005). Tinyos: An operating system for sensor networks. *Ambient Intelligence*, 115-148.

Levis, P., Patel, N., Culler, D., & Shenker, S. (2004). Trickle: A self-regulating algorithm for code propagation and maintenance in wireless sensor networks. In *Proceedings of the 1st Symposium on Networked System Design and Implementation (NSDI 2004)*, (p. 2). IEEE Press.

Liu, H., Roeder, T., Walsh, K., Barr, R., & Sirer, E. (2005). Design and implementation of a single system image operating system for ad hoc networks. In *Proceedings of the International Conference on Mobile Systems, Applications and Services (MobiSys 2005)*, (pp. 149-162). IEEE Press.

Liu, J., Chu, M., Reich, J., & Zhao, F. (2003). State-centric programming for sensor-actuator network systems. *IEEE Pervasive Computing / IEEE Computer Society [and] IEEE Communications Society, n.d.*, 50–62.

Liu, T., & Martonosi, M. (2003). Impala: A middleware system for managing autonomic, parallel sensor systems. In *Proceedings of the 9th ACM SIGPLAN Symposium on Principles and Practice of Parallel Programming (PPoPP 2003)*, (p. 118). ACM Press.

Loo, B. T., Condie, T., Hellerstein, J. M., Maniatis, P., Roscoe, T., & Stoica, I. (2005). Implementing declarative overlays. *ACM SIGOPS Operating Systems Review, 39*(5), 90. doi:10.1145/1095809.1095818

Madden, S., & Franklin, M. (2002). Fjording the stream: An architecture for queries over streaming sensor data. In *Proceedings of the 18th International Conference on Data Engineering (ICDE 2002)*, (pp. 555-566). IEEE Press.

Madden, S., Franklin, M., Hellerstein, J., & Hong, W. (2002). Tag: A tiny aggregation service for ad-hoc sensor networks. *ACM SIGOPS Operating Systems Review, 36,* 131–146. doi:10.1145/844128.844142

Madden, S. R., Franklin, M. J., Hellerstein, J. M., & Hong, W. (2005). TinyDB: An acquisitional query processing system for sensor networks. *ACM Transactions on Database Systems, 30*(1), 173. doi:10.1145/1061318.1061322

Mainland, G., Morrisett, G., & Welsh, M. (2008). Flask: Staged functional programming for sensor networks. *ACM Sigplan Notices, 43*(9), 335–346. doi:10.1145/1411203.1411251

Marrón, P. J. (2006). *Embedded WiSeNts research roadmap*. Berlin, Germany: Logos-Verl.

Mottola, L., & Picco, G. (2006). Logical neighborhoods: A programming abstraction for wireless sensor networks. In Gibbons, P., Abdelzaher, T., Aspnes, J., & Rao, R. (Eds.), *Distributed Computing in Sensor Systems* (*Vol. 4026*, pp. 150–168). Berlin, Germany: Springer. doi:10.1007/11776178_10

Mottola, L., & Picco, G. (2006). Programming wireless sensor networks with logical neighborhoods. In *Proceedings of the 1st International Conference on Integrated Internet Ad-Hoc and Sensor Networks (InterSense 2006)*, (p. 8). IEEE Press.

Mottola, L., & Picco, G. P. (2010). Programming wireless sensor networks: Fundamental concepts and state of the art. *ACM Computing Surveys, 5*(3), 1–51.

Newton, R. Arvind., & Welsh, M. (2005). Building up to macroprogramming: an intermediate language for sensor networks. In *Proceedings of the 4th International Symposium on Information Processing in Sensor Networks*, (p. 6). IEEE Press.

Newton, R., Morrisett, G., & Welsh, M. (2007). The regiment macroprogramming system. In *Processions of the 6th International Conference on Information Processing in Sensor Networks (IPSN 2007)*, (p. 498). IEEE Press.

Newton, R., & Welsh, M. (2004). Region streams: Functional macroprogramming for sensor networks. In *Proceedings of the 1st International Conference on Data Management for Sensor Networks*, (pp. 78-87). IEEE Press.

Paek, J., Chintalapudi, K., Govindan, R., Caffrey, J., & Masri, S. (2005). A wireless sensor network for structural health monitoring: Performance and experience. In *Proceedings of the 2nd IEEE Workshop on Embedded Networked Sensors (EmNetS 2005)*, (pp. 1-10). IEEE Press.

Pathak, A., & Prasann, V. (2006). Issues in designing a compilation framework for macroprogrammed networked sensor systems. In *Proceedings of the 1st International Conference on Integrated Internet Ad-Hoc and Sensor Networks (InterSense 2006)*, (p. 7). IEEE Press.

Pathan, M., Taylor, K., & Compton, M. (2010). Semantics-based plug-and-play configuration of sensor network services. In *Proceedings of the 3rd International Workshop on Semantic Sensor Networks (SSN 2010)*. IEEE Press.

Perkins, C., Belding-Royer, E., & Das, S. (2003). *Ad hoc on-demand distance vector (AODV) routing*. Retrieved from http://www.ietf.org.

Ranganathan, A., & Campbell, R. (2003). An infrastructure for context-awareness based on first order logic. *Personal and Ubiquitous Computing, 7*(6), 353–364. doi:10.1007/s00779-003-0251-x

Reijers, N., & Langendoen, K. (2003). Efficient code distribution in wireless sensor networks. In *Proceedings of the 2nd ACM International Conference on Wireless Sensor Networks and Applicaitons*, (pp. 60-67). ACM Press.

Römer, K. (2004). Programming paradigms and middleware for sensor networks. In *Proceedings of the GI/ITG Workshop on Sensor Networks*, (pp. 49-54). IEEE Press.

Romer, K., & Mattern, F. (2004). The design space of wireless sensor networks. *IEEE Wireless Communications*, *11*(6), 54–61. doi:10.1109/MWC.2004.1368897

Rubio, B., Diaz, M., & Troya, J. M. (2007). Programming approaches and challenges for wireless sensor networks. In *Proceedings of the 2nd International Conference on Systems and Networks Communications (ICSNC 2007)*. IEEE Press.

Sen, S., & Cardell-Oliver, R. (2006). A rule-based language for programming wireless sensor actuator networks using frequency and communication. In *Proceedings of the Workshop on Embedded Networked Sensors (EMNETS 2006)*. IEEE Press.

Sikka, P., Corke, P., Overs, L., Valencia, P., & Wark, T. (2007). Fleck: A platform for real-world outdoor sensor networks. In *Proceedings of the IPSN/SPOTS 2007*, (pp. 709–714). IEEE Press.

Stathopoulos, T., Heidemann, J., & Estrin, D. (2003). *A remote code update mechanism for wireless sensor networks. Technical Report*. Washington, DC: US Government Press.

Sugihara, R., & Gupta, R. K. (2008). Programming models for sensor networks: A survey. *ACM Transactions on Sensor Networks*, *4*(2), 1–29. doi:10.1145/1340771.1340774

Tanin, E., Chen, S., Tatemura, J., & Hsiung, W. (2007). Application semantics in query optimization for WSNs. In *Proceedings of the 5th International Conference on Embeded Networked Sensor Systems (SenSys 2007)*, (p. 436). IEEE Press.

Tolle, G., & Culler, D. (2005). Design of an application-cooperative management system for wireless sensor networks. In *Proceedings of the Second European Workshop on WIreless Sensor Networks (EWSN 2005)*. IEEE Press.

Usländer, T. (2005). Reference model for the ORCHESTRA architecture (RM-OA). *Open Geospatial Consortium*. Retrieved from https://portal. opengeospatial. org/ files.

von Eicken, T., Culler, D., Goldstein, S., & Schauser, K. (1992). Active messages: A mechanism for integrated communication and computation. *ACM SIGARCH Computer Architecture News*, *20*(2), 256–266. doi:10.1145/146628.140382

Wan, C., Campbell, A., & Krishnamurthy, L. (2005). Pump-slowly, fetch-quickly (PSFQ): A reliable transport protocol for sensor networks. *IEEE Journal on Selected Areas in Communications*, *23*(4), 862–872. doi:10.1109/JSAC.2005.843554

Welsh, M., & Mainland, G. (2004). Programming sensor networks using abstract regions. In *Proceedings of the 1st International Symposium on Networked Systems Design and Implementation (NSDI 2004)*, (p. 3). IEEE Press.

Whitehouse, K., Sharp, C., Brewer, E., & Culler, D. (2004). Hood: A neighborhood abstraction for sensor networks. In *Proceedings of the 2nd International Conference on Mobile Systems, Applications and Services (MobiSys 2004)*, (pp. 99-110). IEEE Press.

Woo, A., Tong, T., & Culler, D. (2003). Taming the underlying challenges of reliable multihop routing in sensor networks. In *Proceedings of the 1st International Conference on Embedded Networked Sensor Systems (SenSys 2003)*, (p. 27). IEEE Press.

Yick, J., Mukherjee, B., & Ghosal, D. (2008). Wireless sensor network survey. *Computer Networks*, *52*(12), 2292–2330. doi:10.1016/j.comnet.2008.04.002

KEY TERMS AND DEFINITIONS

Database: An organized collection of data for one or more purposes, usually in digital form. It can be in distributed form when storage devices are not attached to a common processor and stored in multiple computers located in the same physical location or dispersed over a network of interconnected computers.

Macroprogramming: Macroprogramming involves writing a single program for the entire network, rather than for individual nodes in the network.

Metadata: It is defined as data that provides information about one or more aspects of the data, such as data origin, purpose, time of data creation, placement and standards.

Middleware: A software component consisting a set of services that allows multiple processes running on one or more machines to interact.

Programming Models: A development platform comprised of a compiler for a domain specific language and a set of services. Services introduced by a programming model are the ones that are commonly required by the applications in which the programming model is intended to be used.

Routing: A routing strategy specifies how messages are communicated within a sensor network. It adapts to the specific characteristics of a sensor network, such as unreliable and redundant nodes, limited energy, high node count and limited memory.

Sensor Networks: It is a constitution of distributed wireless sensors to monitor physical or environmental conditions such as air pressure, temperature, sound, vibration, motion and cooperatively pass the measured data to a central location through an established network.

Virtual Machine (VM): A VM is used to provide a consistent interface to heterogeneous hardware and provide the sort of memory and multitasking protections unavailable on most devices.

Chapter 7
Wireless Sensor Network Security Attacks:
A Survey

Dennis P. Mirante
Hofstra University, USA

Habib M. Ammari
University of Michigan – Dearborn, USA

ABSTRACT

Wireless Sensor Networks (WSNs) are a rapidly growing area for research and commercial development. Originally used in military applications, their commercialization offers potential low cost solutions for real-world monitoring and process control. Since they may be deployed in hostile, unattended, environments and may collect sensitive data, they may be prone to attack by entities that wish to interfere with their operation and/or usurp or alter the information they collect. While their low cost enhances their desirability as a monitoring solution, it also presents inherent resource and computing constraints. These constraints are major obstacles for the implementation of traditional security paradigms. Consequently, one of the most active areas of research in Wireless Sensor Networks is security. This chapter takes a representative survey of the types of security attacks WSNs may be subjected to. Additionally, steps that may be taken to mitigate these attacks are also discussed. Intrusion Detection Systems, a paradigm for monitoring network activities for malicious behavior, are introduced, and specific examples of them are discussed.

DOI: 10.4018/978-1-4666-0161-1.ch007

INTRODUCTION

Security in Wireless Sensor Networks (WSNs) presents a challenging problem. In military applications, such as battlefield surveillance, networks are typically injected into hostile environments. Applications of this type require that an adversary's ability to determine and interfere with the extent and type of monitoring must be minimized. In this case, it is obvious that security is paramount. Security may also be required in environments where physical threats do not exist, i.e., in the healthcare industry, where access to patient information obtained during health monitoring must be restricted and safeguarded. WSNs may also be deployed in applications where physical protection is lacking, such as traffic control, electrical power generation and distribution, and factory infrastructure and process management. Depending on the specific application at hand, such networks require security to preclude anarchists or terrorists from causing mayhem, competitors from obtaining knowledge of secret product formulations, competitors from disrupting product manufacture or surreptitiously introducing faults into products. As WSNs become increasingly assimilated into modern society, new types of applications will surface, each with their attendant security problems and requirements.

Security issues in WSNs are exacerbated by the constraints imposed on each individual node's resources. Available battery power (or energy), memory, and computational speed are limited. Hence, complex data processing and data encryption requiring significant processing power are not typically employed. In applications where data confidentiality is paramount, data encryption may be performed by special purpose hardware, designed to consume minimal energy. Such hardware may significantly increase the cost of each sensor node. Additionally, the increased energy consumption, despite being minimized, reduces the node's longevity. The tradeoff between performance, longevity, and security, must be carefully weighed by the network designer.

The objective of this chapter is to study the types of security attacks WSNs may be subjected to and the methodologies that may be employed to mitigate them. Most existing security research in the WSN arena has dealt with the prevention of particular types of classic attacks, such as Denial of Service (DoS), wormhole, Byzantine, injected false data, man-in-the-middle, replay, to name a few. This chapter surveys the latest literature concerning these attacks, and discusses the means by which these attacks, or hybrids of them, may be prevented. When pertinent, the attacks will be discussed relative to the communication layer in the Internet Model at which the attack takes place. For instance, DoS attacks may occur at the Physical Layer when RF (radio frequency) jamming is employed against a WSN containing non-frequency agile sensor nodes. Alternatively, the attack may take place at the Data Link Layer, when an attacker induces collisions by initiating a transmission of a bogus packet after detecting that a node has begun sending valid data. On detection of the collision, the node sending the valid data will typically execute a random back-off algorithm, then attempt to retransmit its data. The random back-off algorithm will have no effect on the attacker, who will continue to induce collisions. Ultimately, the battery power of the legitimate sensor node is not conserved and will be reduced to the point of failure.

The introduction of new types of WSN applications will result in new types of security attacks. It is impossible to know or predict the characteristics of these future attacks. As a result, it would seem that WSN researchers and designers will always be playing catch up in their attempts to find and plug the latest security holes used by attackers. New research into the area of cooperative intrusion detection indicates that generic algorithms for the detection of aberrant nodes may be definable. In some cases, the use of these algorithms may allow researchers and designers to dispense with having to find a specific solution to each new attack type. Using these algorithms, an attack may be detected and the sensors and operator may be alerted. Attacking nodes may then be identified and isolated from the WSN by such an Intrusion Detection System (IDS). Additionally, this chapter discusses intrusion detection and presents examples of past and current work in this area.

CHARACTERISTICS OF WIRELESS SENSOR NETWORKS AFFECTING SECURITY

The driving force behind sensor node construction is cost. Node designers strive to limit sensor node cost, and in doing so, implicitly place corresponding limitations on the node's resources. Thus, there are restraints on the node's computational capabilities, memory, communications bandwidth and range, and energy source. These factors greatly impact the security algorithms and features that may be implemented.

Security mechanisms implemented in sensor nodes induce added processing overhead that results in increased computation, energy use, and possible reduction of sensor energy lifetime and performance. For example, security mechanisms, such as cooperative intrusion detection, may require a sensor node to turn on its receiver to monitor the behavior of adjacent nodes in order to determine if an attacker is among them (Krontiris, et al., 2007; Wensheng, et al., 2003). The energy consumed by the receiver, as well as that consumed by the processor for analyzing the monitored node's behavior, results in a reduction of overall available energy One of intended or ancillary goal of an attacker may be to induce excessive consumption of the sensor node's energy, causing it to fail prematurely due to energy exhaustion. An attacker, for example, may cause interference on the communications channel, resulting in the sensor node's having to retransmit data. Since transmission is the most expensive process in terms of energy consumption, a significant number of induced retransmissions may profoundly impact

the sensor node's life. WSN lifetime is increased through the use of energy efficient security algorithms and protocol mechanisms.

WSNs are advantageous in that they may be deployed in hostile environments and require no direct human supervision. The fact that they can be remotely managed through the Base Station, sometimes referred to as the Sink, is an additional benefit. These advantages are offset by security issues that arise when the WSN is deployed in an area that is unsecured and subject to environmental factors or physical attack. Messages passed between network sensor nodes and the Sink must be protected from eavesdropping or alteration. Protection against false message injection by attackers must be provided. Unauthorized access to processing entities connected to the Sink via network sensor nodes must be also be prevented.

Since sensor nodes are designed to be as cheap as possible, they are not built to be tamper proof. Attackers may utilize this vulnerability via a direct physical attack on sensor nodes contained within an unsecured deployment area. This type of attack, called node capture, takes place when an adversary obtains a sensor node, analyzes its content, and uses the result of the analysis in an attempt to disrupt network operation. An attacker may extract encryption keys contained within a captured node's memory and subsequently utilize them to determine the content of messages flowing through the network. A large number of encryption keys are typically distributed throughout the WSN. If enough nodes are captured, key extraction and subsequent use by an attacker could compromise the integrity of the network. Attackers may also choose to modify the software of captured nodes to have it alter valid messages or inject false ones into the network. Sensor node software may also be modified to drop messages received from other nodes that are to be forwarded to the Sink cooperatively through other network nodes. After modifying nodes in this manner, the attacker can re-insert them into the deployment area. Using knowledge garnered from node capture, an attacker may also chose to manufacture his own nodes, outfit them with malicious software, and insert them into the area the target WSN is deployed in. Rogue nodes may also be equipped with out of band communications capability (with respect to the WSN being attacked) that facilitate more sophisticated attacks such as the wormhole attack discussed in a later section of this chapter. Becher et al. (2006) present an in-depth discussion on node capture and tampering.

SECURITY REQUIREMENTS

Security in WSNs should fulfill the following requirements (Wang & Zhang, 2009; Li & Gong, 2009):

- Availability, which ensures that the desired network services are available whenever required.
- Authentication, which ensures that the communication from one node to another node is genuine.
- Confidentiality, which provides the privacy of the wireless communication channels.
- Integrity, which ensures that the message or the entity under consideration is not altered.
- Non-repudiation, which prevents malicious nodes from hiding or denying their activities.
- Freshness, which implies that the data is recent and ensures that no adversary can replay old messages.
- Survivability, which ensures an acceptable level of network services even in the presence of node failures and malicious attacks.
- Self-security, which ensures that countermeasures introducing additional hardware and software infrastructures into the network must themselves be secure enough to withstand attacks.

GENERIC WSN ATTACKS

WSNs are susceptible to the following generic attacks:

- **Accidental Association:** Occurs when foreign computers or devices inadvertently connect to a neighboring company's overlapping wireless network without being aware that it is happening. Occurrences like this are a significant security breach and my expose proprietary company information and/or systems (Radmand, et al., 2010).
- **Malicious Association:** Occurs when hackers obtain access to the network. Access is obtained through protocol loopholes and/or weak security measures. Computers may be lured to log into imposter networks that impersonate a valid network. Users may be captured if the attacker has a connection to the network under attack, temporarily interrupts real network response, and simultaneously grants access to the imposter network. The imposter network can then transparently view future communication from the user to/from the real network. This capability facilitates password and data theft, trojan installation, and other attacks (Radmand, et al., 2010).
- **Byzantine:** Occurs when some subset of the WSN's sensor nodes have been compromised. The compromised nodes work in collusion and may carry out their attack by creating routing loops, forwarding packets via non-optimal routes, dropping packets, injecting fictitious packets, or by modifying sensor data in packets. This type of attack is difficult to detect, as network operation may appear normal to non-compromised nodes (Sen, 2010). Node replication attacks are a form of Byzantine attack. In this attack, the attacker captures a node from the deployment area, clones

its identity, and deploys it into the network to launch an attack. Chan & Perrig (2003) catalog attacks that may be launched using replicated nodes. An attacker can place replicated nodes at strategic locations in the network in an attempt to manipulate a segment of the network and possibly induce network partitioning (Sen, 2010).

- **Denial of Service (DoS):** Occurs when an attacker floods an access point or device with superfluous messages in order to reduce or stop its ability to perform its assigned functions (Wood, et al., 2003). Jamming the wireless communication channel also falls under this category. Message latency in WSNs providing time critical data may be significantly increased, perhaps to the point where the delivered data is rendered useless.
- **Environmental Tampering:** Occurs when the attacker affects the integrity of sensor node readings by altering the environment of the deployment area. For example, the attacker can use means to alter the temperature and/or humidity in the deployment around temperature/humidity sensor nodes (Radmand, et al., 2010).
- **Man-in-the-Middle:** Occurs when the attacker uses Malicious Association techniques to position himself between nodes or users in the network and transparently monitor traffic. The attacker may then remove, alter the contents of, or replace network packets to provide false information.
- **Network Injection:** Occurs when an attacker makes use of access points that are exposed to non-filtered network traffic to inject bogus network re-configuration commands. These commands may adversely affect routers, switches, and intelligent hubs to the point where the network crashes, requiring rebooting or perhaps even reprogramming of intelligent net-

working devices contained therein (Choi, et al., 2008; Radmand, et al., 2010).

- **Resource Depletion:** Occurs when an attacker node attempts to deplete the resources of legitimate nodes in the network. Typically targeted resources are battery power, computational power, and bandwidth. Of these, battery power is the most important, as it determines sensor node lifetime.

CLASSIFICATION OF SPECIFIC WSN ATTACKS

Specific WSN attacks may be classified according to their origin and nature. Origin classification divides WSN attacks into two classes—*internal* and *external*. Internal attacks are launched from within the WSN by authorized nodes that have been compromised or are malicious (Zhou, et al., 2008). For example, an internal attack can be facilitated by simply compromising nodes by environmental tampering or by introducing replicated nodes programmed for malicious behavior. External attacks are launched from outside the scope of the network by nodes that are not part of the WSN and are not authorized access to it. Nature based classification further divides the internal and external classes into *active* and *passive* subclasses. Figure 1 illustrates the classification of WSN attacks discussed in this chapter.

In addition, attacks may be further classified according to protocol layer(s) of the Internet Model that the attack exploits, if any. In the ensuing discussion, the attack name in the heading is followed by the origin of the attack in brackets, followed by the protocol layer(s) in the Internet Model that may be utilized by an attacker in parenthesis, ie., Attack Name [origin] (protocol layer).

Figure 1. Taxonomy of WSN attacks

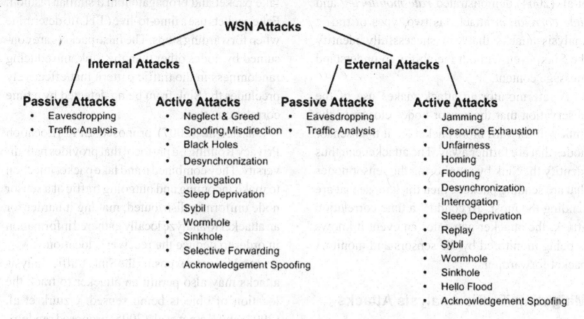

PASSIVE ATTACKS

An attacker's goal in a passive attack is to obtain information about the WSN and the sensor data it is collecting, without being discovered. Passive attacks may be internal or external in origin. They are much easier to carry out in the wireless environment than in the wired because of the inherent shared nature of the wireless communication medium (Zhou, et al., 2008). If the attacker knows the network protocol, it can parse the messages it overhears in the same manner as an authenticated node, and can glean information from them. By continually collecting information from one or more target nodes, the attacker may obtain knowledge that can be utilized at a later time to launch an active attack. There are two forms of passive attacks: *eavesdropping* and *traffic analysis*.

Eavesdropping: Internal and External (Physical Layer)

Eavesdropping may enable the attacker to intercept sensor data and routing information being exchanged between sensor nodes or between sensor nodes and the Sink. It is the easiest and most common form of attack on data confidentiality. If the messages being exchanged are not cryptographically protected, the attacker may easily ascertain the contents. Even if the messages are encrypted, the attacker may have previously obtained encryption keys via node capture and node tampering which allow him to decipher them. Sensitive information gained in this manner may be used for any number of illicit purposes. For example, it is feasible that patient information may be stolen in a healthcare scenario or that process control information may be illegally obtained and used in an attempt to recreate the formulation of a competitor's product.

Traffic Analysis: Internal and External (Data Link Layer)

Traffic analysis may permit the attacker to obtain knowledge of the network topology, the location of sensor nodes performing critical tasks, and the location of the Sink itself (Sen, 2010). If the attacker can compromise or destroy the Sink, then the whole network will be rendered useless. Deng et al. (2004) demonstrated *rate monitoring* and *time correlation* attacks as two types of traffic analysis attacks that can successfully identify the Sink, even without the ability to understand message content.

A rate monitoring attack makes use of the observation that the sensor nodes closest to the Sink will forward more packets to it than sensor nodes that are farther away. The attacker can thus identify the Sink by monitoring the sensor nodes that are sending packets, then track those that are sending the most. To conduct a time correlation attack, the attacker generates an event it knows is being monitored by the sensors and monitors packet forwarding.

Mitigating Traffic Analysis Attacks

Several strategies to mitigate traffic analysis attacks on the Sink by traffic de-patterning have been put forth. *Multi-Parent Routing* (Deng, et al., 2005) avoids consistent shortest path propagation of packets between sensor nodes. Multiple paths, between same source and destination sensor nodes, are randomly selected. The *Random Walk* technique (Deng, et al., 2005) visualizes the WSN as a tree with the Sink as its root. Packets are forwarded up the tree from a sensor node to its parent until they reach the Sink. To protect against traffic analysis, a packet is forwarded to both the parent node and a node other than the parent on occasion. This technique makes it hard for the attacker to find a particular path from the sensor node to the Base Station, thus affording protection from a rate monitoring attack. It does not, however, protect against a time correlation attack. Deng et al. (2005) proposed the *Fractal Propagation* method, which uses the generation of fake messages, to counter a time correlation attack. Under this method, a node senses that its neighbor is forwarding a packet to the Sink and generates (with some probability) a fake packet that is randomly sent to one of its neighboring sensor nodes. The neighbor may also generate a

fake packet and propagate it in a similar fashion. Fake packets use a time-to-live (TTL) to determine when forwarding stops. The false packets are consumed by nodes other than the Sink, introducing randomness in the traffic pattern that effectively precludes the Sink from being detected by a time correlation attack.

Jian et al. (2007) proposed LPR (Location Privacy Routing), a protocol that provides path diversity. They combined it and fake packet injection to make incoming and outgoing traffic at a sensor node uniformly distributed, making it harder for an attacker to analyze locally gathered information in order to deduce the receiver's location.

In addition to exposing the Sink, traffic analysis attacks may also permit an attacker to track the location of objects being sensed. Ozturk et al. (2004) and Kamat et al. (2005) proposed randomized data routing and phantom traffic generation as mechanisms used to mask real traffic and protect the identity of the source. Their methodology is based on flooding routing protocols. They define the following:

- **Baseline Flooding:** Every network sensor node forwards a packet once. No packet previously transmitted is retransmitted. If a packet has been transmitted previously, it is dropped, otherwise it is forwarded to all of the sensor node's neighbors.
- **Probabilistic Flooding:** Packet forwarding is limited to a subset of sensor nodes. Any sensor node not in the forwarding subset drops packets it receives. A concern in this approach is lost packets, resulting in degraded network connectivity. The authors, however, stated that this is not a significant reason for concern.
- **Flooding With Fake Packets:** Modifies the previously mentioned protocols by introducing the injection of fake packets into the network to further the objective of masking real traffic. Attackers capturing

packets have no way to determine whether or not they are real.

- **Phantom Flooding:** Phantom Flooding and Probabilistic Flooding have a common goal in that they both try to prevent an attacker from receiving a steady stream of packets that will enable it to determine the source. In order to accomplish this, they attempt to disperse packets to different locations in the network. Probabilistic Flooding is not effective in that shorter paths tend to deliver more messages. Realizing this, the authors put forth the notion of a fake source, the *Phantom Source*, which is used to lure the attacker away from the real source. Phantom Flooding is a two stage process for every packet: (1) the walking phase, which is a random walk or directed walk, and (2) the flooding phase, in which the message is delivered to the Sink. The source unicasts the packet in a random/directed manner for the first h_{walk} hops (random/directed walk phase), then the packet is flooded using Baseline Flooding (flooding phase).

Chen et al. (2009) propose that a purely random walk is inefficient at making the phantom source appear far from the real source and state that, for reasonable h_{walk} values, location privacy is not significantly enhanced. They conclude that bias should be introduced into the walking process to avoid random walks that cancel each other and introduce two directed walk techniques that accomplish that goal:

- A *Sector Based Directed Random Walk* requires each sensor node to partition the 2-dimensional plane into two half planes. In order to accomplish this, without the use of a sectional antenna, it is assumed that the network has landmark nodes. The authors give an example of where the west most node is the landmark node and is des-

ignated as such upon network deployment. This node then initiates a flood throughout the network. Each network sensor node then partitions its neighbors into two sets, S0 and S1 by determining whether each of them is west or east of it. If sensor node i forwards a packet to its neighbor j before it receives the same packet from j, then j is to the east, otherwise j is to the west. When the source starts the directed random walk, it randomly picks whether it is going to use set S0 or S1. After that, every node within the first h_{walk} hops that receives the packet randomly chooses a neighbor from the chosen set to forward the packet to.

- A *Hop-Based Directed Random Walk* requires that each sensor node must know the hop count between it and the Sink. It is similar to the *Sector Based Directed Random Walk* in that partitioning between neighbors is based on hop count to the Sink. One set includes neighbors whose hop counts are less than or equal to that of the node and the other set includes all the other neighbors. The selection process from the two partitions is the same.

GROW (Greedy Random Walk) was proposed by Xi et al. (2006) as another mechanism to preclude obtaining location information from traffic analysis. A two-way random walk strategy is used. The Sink initiates an N-hop random walk, followed by an M-hop random walk initiated by the source. When the source packet reaches the intersection of the paths, it is forwarded to the Sink via the N-hop path created by it. Backtracking is minimized in both directions by checking each intermediate node against those stored in a Bloom filter during the walk.

Note that all anti-traffic analysis mechanisms incur an energy cost as a result of their effort to support anonymity.

ACTIVE ATTACKS

Active attacks exploit security issues that may have been found in a prior passive attack or security holes in the network protocol. An active attack seeks to disrupt the normal functionality of the WSN. It may do this by interfering with the flow of information through the network, injecting false information into the network, modifying information flowing through the network, or replaying information obtained through eavesdropping at another time or place within the network (Zhou, Fang & Zhang, 2008). Since the attacker is actively involved in network communication, anomalies are present that can exhibit evidence of a malicious attack (Zhou, Fang & Zhang, 2008). As with passive attacks, active attacks can be classified as internal or external, depending on whether or not the attacking node(s) are part of the WSN. Attacks can be further classified according to the layers of the Internet Model at which they occur—Physical Layer, Data Link Layer, Network Layer, Transport Layer, or Application Layer. Some attacks are possible at multiple layers.

The following sections discuss specific types of active attacks in detail. All these attacks are forms of DoS attacks.

Jamming: External (Physical Layer/Data Link Layer)

Jamming is a mechanism used to disrupt communications between sensor nodes. It relies on the broadcast nature of the communications channel. The jammer's goal is to emit a signal that causes collisions with valid signals on the communications medium, rendering the information carried on the valid signals worthless. Jamming may occur at the Physical and Data Link Layers. Xu et al. (2005) proposed four generic jammer models:

- **Constant Jammer:** This jammer emits a continuous jamming signal, which has random data content. A constant jammer has an extremely large or infinite power source. Its goal is to interfere with any transmitting node so that packets at the receiver are corrupted and to make any transmitter not currently transmitting sense the channel is busy, thus precluding it from gaining access to the channel. Constant jamming prevents nodes from communicating with one another and reporting the attack to the Sink.

- **Deceptive Jammer:** Replays or fabricates valid signals. This jammer continually transmits bits like the constant jammer, except that the information transmitted is not random. Valid packets are transmitted without gaps between transmissions, giving listening nodes the impression that legitimate traffic is being sent. Listening nodes with packets to transmit will remain in the listening state. This type of jamming is harder to detect than constant jamming, because the packets look legitimate.

- **Random Jammer:** More power efficient jammer than the previous two. Sleeps for a random amount of time, then jams for a random amount of time, then sleeps again. By changing the sleep and jamming intervals, this jammer can alter its aggressiveness to permit power savings.

- **Reactive Jammer:** Smartest and most efficient jammer. Listens for activity on the communication channel. Upon detecting it, begins transmitting, causing packet collision and corruption at the receiver.

Implementations of the aforementioned jamming models cause packet loss through the deterioration of the communications channel. If the jammer does not have an infinite power supply, jamming must be performed in an energy-efficient manner, with the ultimate goal of having the jammer outlive the WSN. Preferable jamming techniques dictate that jamming occurs in such a manner that the WSN is not aware that it is happening. The WSN may detect a problem, but should not infer that it is being jammed. A continuous jammer advertises its presence, hence is easily discoverable, and prone to counterattack and destruction, something a sensible attacker would avoid (Law et al, 2005). Xu et al. (2005) showed that deceptive jammers and reactive jammers are effective in severely limiting packet delivery, but are energy inefficient with respect to their intended victims, when given comparable energy budgets. This means they would not meet the ultimate goal of surviving the WSN. Random jammers were found to be less effective, despite the fact that they save energy by sleeping. Signal strength, carrier sensing time, or the packet delivery ratio, taken individually, were shown as not sufficient enough metrics for use in detecting jamming. Consistency checking, based on signal strength or location information, according to them, can detect a jamming attack. Pelechrinis et al. (2010) show, however, that their schemes can only detect Constant and Deceptive Jammers, but not Reactive or Random Jammers.

Depending on network topology, a single jammer may be powerful enough to disrupt an entire WSN. Instead of using a single, high power jammer, an attacker may choose to distribute lower power jammers at strategic points in the network. Wood & Stankovic (2002) stated that an intermittent jammer may be capable of causing significantly untoward operation in a WSN dealing with time critical data. Wood et al. (2003) proposed a countermeasure that can be used when only a portion of the network is affected by jamming. In this method, sensor nodes on the perimeter of the jammed region collaborate with their neighbors to define the jammed region. All traffic is then routed around it.

Law et al. (2005; 2009) found that energy-efficient jamming can be achieved by exploiting knowledge of the communications protocol and Data Link Layer semantics. They examined three representative MAC protocols, B-MAC, S-MAC, and LMAC and stated that their results were appli-

cable to a wide range of protocols belonging to the same categories as these three. By an examination of packet structure and timing, they were able to ascertain the most critical point at which to start the jamming processes during packet transmission. This approach results in the jammer transmitting strategically timed, quick interference bursts, that conserve battery energy. The authors concluded that there were no effective measures against Data Link Layer jamming and recommended the following be used by WSNs requiring security against Data Link Layer jamming to minimize susceptibility:

- Encrypted Data Link Layer packets, ensuring a high entry barrier for jammers.
- Use of spread spectrum hardware - this hardware spreads the signal in the frequency domain, resulting in a higher bandwidth, and an increased resistance to jamming, detection, and interference. The signal is essentially hidden behind environmental noise. The downside for use of this additional hardware is its increased cost.
- Use of a TDMA protocol.
- Used of randomized transmission intervals.

Pelechrinis et al. (2010) present a detailed up-to-date discussion on jamming attacks, examine various techniques for detecting jammer presence, and survey protection mechanisms that may be used against jamming attacks. They categorize various jamming models with respect to implementation complexity, energy efficiency, stealthiness, level of DoS, and anti-jamming resistance. Like Law et al. (2009), they conclude that jamming is still an open and important research area.

While jamming has been viewed only as detrimental to WSN operation, Martinovic et al. (2009) propose a novel use of it for WSN protection. They purport that jamming can be used to destroy unauthenticated packets being transmitted. In doing so, sensor nodes will be precluded from having to receive and authenticate these packets, resulting in a lower overall energy consumption. This approach is in its nascent state and will require further research to determine whether or not jamming packets versus receiving and authenticating them is more cost effective in terms of energy usage. Additional research into developing mechanisms that ensure only invalid packets are targeted will also be required.

Resource Exhaustion: External (Data Link Layer)

WSNs utilizing Data Link Layer protocols that do not recognize a jamming attack will repeatedly attempt retransmission due to collisions. Random back off algorithms employed to obviate the occurrence of collisions are effective only when the collisions are random and not instituted by a jammer. Naive Data Link Layer protocols may cause a sensor node to continuously attempt retransmissions in the presence of the jammer. A smart reactive jammer will cause the collision late in the transmission, in order to maximize the transmitting node's energy usage. Repeated transmissions will ultimately lead to energy depletion and failure or degradation of the WSN (Wood & Stankovic, 2002).

Resource exhaustion may also take place when an attacker transmits a consistent, high volume of packets from one or more attack nodes. All sensor nodes that are within the communication range of the attack nodes are possible targets and their batteries are subject to intentional exhaustion. The degradation of the batteries is accelerated if the packets emanating from the attackers elicit a transmitted response from the target nodes. This would happen, for example, if the target node chooses to forward the packet to other nodes in the WSN. Resource exhaustion attacks executed in this manner are more severe than other DoS attacks, in that more sensor nodes will become unavailable at the same time and the WSN may be isolated into sub-networks that cannot communicate with one another (Tanabe & Aida, 2007).

Tanabe & Aida (2007) suggested three methods for mitigating a resource exhaustion attack:

- **Time Slot Method:** Each WSN sensor node is assigned a time slot and can only transmit packets during that slot time. Since the attacker does not belong to the network, it does not have an assigned time slot to transmit its packets. Legitimate sensor nodes can detect and discard illegitimate packets through knowledge of the time slot assignments, preventing their forwarding to other legitimate sensor nodes. The drawbacks from this method require all nodes to have a synchronized clock and temporal knowledge of the pre-assigned time slots for all the other sensor nodes they directly communicate with. While this scheme precludes expenditure of power in forwarding attack frames, the immediately attacked nodes still waste battery power receiving, validating, and discarding the illegitimate packets.

- **Token Method:** Each sensor node may only transmit its packets when it has received a token. Since the attack node cannot receive a token, it transmits its packets without one. Legitimate sensor nodes that receive attack packets directly from the attack node can determine packet validity by checking the packet header. Any packet found that does not contain the token in the header information is discarded, preventing it from being forwarded to other legitimate sensor nodes. Battery power is conserved to the same extent and for the same reasons as in the Time Slot method. The drawbacks from this method are that each sensor node may only transmit its packets when it has the token. The sensor node must also transfer the token to the next node when it is done transmitting its packets or after a timeout. Passing a token in the WSN environment is difficult.

- **Secret Key Method:** Each node in the network transmits its packets with a common secret key obtained when it joins the network. Since the attack node does not belong to the network, it does not have the secret key and transmits the packets without one. Legitimate sensor nodes that receive attack packets directly from the attack node can determine packet validity by checking the packet header for secret key information. Any packet found that does not contain the correct header information is discarded, preventing it from being forwarded to other legitimate sensor nodes. Battery power is conserved to the same extent and for the same reasons as in the Time Slot and Token methods. The drawbacks of this method is that each sensor node must obtain the secret key when it joins the network and that it must include the secret key in the header of each packet transmitted, introducing more overhead in the transmission process.

Tanabe & Aida (2007) concluded that the advantages of all three methods were almost the same, however, the secret key method was the easiest to implement. Their conclusion was based on the fact that the time slot method requires all nodes to synchronize their clocks, a difficult undertaking, and that token handling is also difficult and losing a token in the network can cause serious problems.

Unfairness: External (Data Link Layer)

Unfairness is a weak type of DoS attack (Wood & Stankovic, 2002) that degrades service rather than denying it. By intermittently causing collisions, or abusing a cooperative MAC sub-layer priority scheme, the attacker may cause degradation of applications running on other nodes. MAC protocol priority schemes are abused when the attacker cheats while negotiating channel access and monopolizes the channel for a long period, preventing legitimate nodes from transmitting (David, et al., 2010). The effects of this type of an attack may not prevent total access to the communications channel, but can cause real-time applications to miss deadlines because of increased latency (Wood & Stankovic, 2002). Wood & Stankovic (2002) proposed the use of small frames as a countermeasure for this type of attack.

David et al. (2010) present an overview of DoS attacks, including unfairness, that may be carried out against the MAC sub-layer and propose a trust model for mitigating them. In their model, coordinator nodes keep a running tally of MAC sub-layer operational data that sensor nodes measure by observing their neighbors. Each sensor node submits its collected neighbor node data to the coordinator, who calculates a trust value for every node data in the collected data set. This trust value is a measure of the probability of the node's being malicious or honest. Upon determining a node to be unfair or malicious, a coordinator can take defensive action, such as warning the legitimate nodes to stop routing packets from the misbehaving node.

Neglect and Green: Internal (Network Layer)

In this type of attack, a malicious node is neglectful if it arbitrarily neglects to route all or some packets. The malicious node will appear to participate in the lower-level protocols and may appear to be operating properly to the sender of the packet, who will receive an acknowledgement of reception from the malicious node (Wood & Stankovic, 2002). Greed comes in to play when a malicious node gives undue priority to packets generated by itself. Protocols that promote the same route to a destination may be degraded or blocked by a greedy node on the path. The use of multi-path routing and/or redundant messages are countermeasures that may be employed against these attacks (Wood & Stankovic, 2002). These countermeasures require the attacker to have commandeered more nodes, in order to be effective.

Probing, a test of network connectivity is a countermeasure that may be used to determine the presence of neglectful and greedy nodes, and black holes, which will be discussed in a later section. Networks that use geography-based routing schemes use their knowledge of the network's physical topology to detect anomalies via probing. Probes are periodic messages sent across the network topology that may be used to test for blackout regions due to black holes and dropped packets or high latency in packet delivery due to neglect and greed. These special purpose packets must be indistinguishable from normal traffic. Otherwise, neglectful or greedy nodes could evade detection by identifying them and behaving properly upon encountering them Distributed probing schemes may be used to detect malicious nodes. Cheung & Levitt (1997) described one of the first distributed cooperative intrusion detection schemes used for this purpose.

Homing: External (Network Layer)

Some WSNs have sensor nodes that are given special assignments, such as analyzing and aggregating data collected from other sensor nodes, managing cryptographic keys, the Sink, etc. A homing attack (Wood & Stankovic, 2002) begins with an attacker launching a passive attack to identify nodes within the WSN that have special responsibilities. Homing attacks are extremely dangerous for location-aware routing protocols relying on geographic information, as the passive attacker can easily learn the location of the special nodes. Once these nodes have been identified, the attacker launches an active attack to interfere with their normal operation. The techniques discussed in mitigating passive attacks may be used to prevent a homing attack.

Spoofing, Misdirection: Internal (Network Layer)

In this type of attack, packets are forwarded along wrong paths. A sender is targeted when traffic is diverted away from its intended destination. A receiver is targeted when many traffic flows are diverted in one direction to target a particular node. An attacker may be able to attract or repel network traffic, extend or shorten source routes, create routing loops, generate false error messages, partition the network, increase end-to-end latency, etc.

Countermeasures include egress filtering for use in hierarchical routing protocols, authorized exchange of routing information, verification of source addresses, and use of an intrusion detection scheme (Wood & Stankovic, 2002; Chen, et al., 2007).

Flooding: External (Transport Layer/Network Layer)

This attack is applicable where Transport Layer protocols are employed that require the maintenance of state at either end of a connection (Wood & Stankovic, 2002; Raymond & Midkiff, 2008). Connectionless protocols, inherently stateless, are not susceptible to this attack. The attacker repeatedly sends connection establishment requests to the victim, causing allocation of memory resources for state maintenance, until the resources are completely exhausted. There are two types of countermeasures for this attack - *limiting the number of connections* and *client puzzles*.

Limiting the number of connections prevents complete resource exhaustion, allowing the victim to continue work on other tasks that may be assigned to it. If a mechanism is not employed to recover resources allocated to connections that are not legitimately in use, then the establishments of legitimate connections with the victim are precluded when the limit is reached.

Figure 2. Black hole

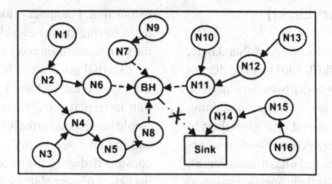

Client puzzles, introduced by Aura et al. (2001), employ the notion that a connecting node must demonstrate its commitment to the connection by solving a puzzle that is computationally intensive before the connection request is granted. This makes the attacker commit resources to the connection, with the assumption being that attacker will not be able to establish new connections fast enough to exhaust the resources of the victim. This assumption is true only if the attacker, like the victim, has limited resources. A disadvantage to this approach is that higher energy consumption is required for legitimate sensor nodes, in order to support the required computations. This, however, is less costly than the energy that would be wasted effecting the transmissions that would be induced by flooding in the absence of this countermeasure (Wood & Stankovic, 2002).

Black Holes: Internal (Network Layer)

The multi-hop nature of communication in WSNs facilitates DoS attacks based on a sensor node's desire to find the shortest path for packet delivery. In this attack (Wood & Stankovic, 2002), malicious nodes advertise zero-cost routes, making them attractive for traffic delivery. The attacker's goals are to make themselves part of many routes, increasing the potential damage they can inflict. As their advertisements propagate throughout the network, more traffic is routed in their direction.

The attacker will either drop or refuse all packets. This disrupts message delivery and causes intense resource contention in their neighbors, who are forced to compete for limited bandwidth. If the neighbor's resources are exhausted prematurely, a hole or partition of the network results. Figure 2 illustrates a black hole.

Black hole attacks are easier to detect than neglect and greed and misdirection attacks, but are more disruptive (Wood & Stankovic, 2002). Countermeasures include probing (previously discussed), authorized exchange of routing information, redundancy in the form of both sending duplicate messages along the same route or along a different path, and monitoring. In addition to using probes, sensor nodes having knowledge of network topology may monitor for inconsistent advertisements and take defensive steps to declare the advertiser as a malicious node to other nodes in the network. Marti et al. (2000) introduce the notion of a next hop watchdog and pathrater to monitor node behavior. The watchdog identifies misbehaving nodes by listening to traffic and determining whether its neighborhood nodes properly pass on received packets to the next hop, drop them, or route them improperly. The pathrater mitigates the impact of misbehaving nodes by helping protocol users avoid routing traffic through them.

Desynchronization: Internal and External (Transport Layer)

Desynchronization attacks (Wood & Stankovic, 2002; Raymond & Midkiff, 2008) seek to disrupt an existing connection between two endpoints. The attacker repeatedly forges messages containing phony sequence numbers and/or control flags to one or both ends of the connection. These messages cause the receiver to think that it has missed frames, resulting in a request for their retransmission to the other end. If the attacker can continue injecting these phony messages with the right timing, no useful information will ever be exchanged between the endpoints. Their battery energy will be squandered in a continuous attempt to obtain message synchronization via a synchronization-recovery protocol. Resource exhaustion and lack of availability may ultimately result.

A countermeasure for an external attack is the authentication of all packets, including the control fields in the transport header. This assumes the attacker has no knowledge of the authentication mechanism, which the endpoints will use to detect and discard the forged messages. The effectiveness of this countermeasure on an internal attack depends on the key management scheme in use. Since an internal attacker is able to authenticate itself to some of its neighbor nodes, this countermeasure would not preclude a desynchronization attack on them.

Interrogation: Internal and External (Data Link Layer)

An interrogation attack (Wood & Stankovic, 2002; Raymond & Midkiff, 2008) exploits the Request-To-Send/Clear-To-Send (RTS/CTS) handshake used by most MAC sub-layer protocols to reserve channel access. An attacker's goal is to induce exhaustion of the victim's power resource by constantly sending RTS in order to obtain CTS responses from the victim. If the attacker is a more powerful device, it will eventually cause unavailability of the victim node due to energy exhaustion. The attacker may also be a "sacrifice" node, having the same level of energy resources as the victim, and ultimately suffering the same fate.

External attacks can be somewhat mitigated through the use of Data Link Layer authentication and replay protection, as the intended victim would not respond to the RTS. Network bandwidth and the intended victim's energy would still be consumed during the reception of bogus RTS packets. An internal attacker would be unhindered in performing this attack.

Sleep Deprivation: Internal and External (Data Link Layer)

The goal of the attacker in a sleep deprivation attack (Zhu et al., 2006) is to prevent sensor nodes from entering sleep mode, which leads to energy depletion. It is another form of resource exhaustion attack. As previously discussed, the sensor node's transceiver is the most energy consuming module of the sensor node. Attacks that keep this module on continuously, even if only for reception, will eventually drain the batteries in an accelerated manner. MAC Protocols such as SMAC, are susceptible to this type of attack (Raymond & Midkiff, 2008). For this particular protocol, the attacker repeatedly sends malicious synchronization packets that cause the victim to stay awake in order to maintain synchronization with the attacker.

Countermeasures that may be employed against an external attacker include Data Link Layer authentication, replay protection, and broadcast attack protection (Raymond & Midkiff, 2008). Internal attackers may be dealt with by using detection and mitigations schemes, an example of which was given in the section on resource exhaustion attacks.

Replay: External (Data Link Layer, Network Layer, Application Layer)

A replay attack is facilitated by eavesdropping. Legitimate packets sent from one sensor node to another are recorded and replayed at another time. Attacks can be mounted at multiple layers in the Internet Model: Data Link Layer - data frames can be replayed; Network Layer - routing packets; Application Layer - report data.

Countermeasures include sequence number or timestamps used in combination with an authentication scheme, i.e. use of a Message Authentication Code.

Sybil: Internal and External (Physical Layer, Data Link Layer, Network Layer)

In a Sybil Attack (Douceur, 2002), a single sensor node presents multiple identities to other sensor nodes. It can forge completely false identities or impersonate other nodes. This attack can seriously reduce the effectiveness of fault tolerant schemes such as distributed storage, dispersity, multi-path routing, and topology maintenance (Karlof & Wagner, 2003). Data aggregation, voting schemes, resource allocation, and misbehavior detection are also susceptible to Sybil attacks (Newsome et al., 2004). Sybil attacks pose a significant threat to geographic routing protocols, as an attacker can appear to be in more than one place simultaneously.

Data Link Layer authentication is a countermeasure that can be employed to prevent an external attack. Internal attacks against sensor nodes for which the attacker possesses the keys will be possible. The attacker can use the keys to forge their identities and impersonate them. Additional countermeasures that may be employed to limit the effectiveness of an internal attacker are the use of a list of trusted neighbors (Parno, et al., 2006), radio resource testing, verification of key sets for random key pre-distribution, registration and position verification (Newsome, et al.,

2004). Note that radio resource testing involves a node assigning a unique channel to each neighbor, including the phony. The node then tests to determine that it can communicate with the neighbors through the assigned channel. Sensor nodes are not typically able to communicate simultaneously on two channels; therefore, the subsequent failure to communicate on one of the assigned channels may be an indication of a Sybil attack.

Wormhole: Internal and External (Network Layer)

Wormhole attacks (Hu, et al., 2003; Karlof & Wagner, 2003) are facilitated by two colluding attackers tunneling packets from one part of the network to a different part via a low latency, out-of-band, link. The attacker node at one end of wormhole advertises a high quality link and the attacker node at the other end receives the attracted packets. Additional attacks, such as sinkhole attacks and selective forwarding, may be launched through use of a wormhole. Figure 3 illustrates a wormhole.

Data Link Layer authentication cannot be used to prevent an external attack of this sort. The attacker, despite the fact that it is not part of the WSN, can still tunnel packets sent by legitimate nodes in one part of the network to legitimate nodes in the other part in order to convince them that they are neighbors.

A countermeasure to defend against wormhole attacks was introduced by Hu et al. (2003). It involves the use of two types of packet leashes, geographical and temporal.

Meghdadi et al. (2011) presents a comprehensive survey of wormhole attacks and countermeasures that may be employed to defend against them.

Sinkhole: Internal and External (Network Layer)

Sinkhole attacks (Karlof & Wagner, 2003) lure traffic form one area of the network through an

Figure 3. Wormhole

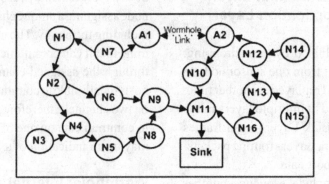

attacker node, creating a sinkhole with the attacker at the center. Wormhole attacks may be used to generate a sinkhole. The attacker node attracts traffic from its surrounding nodes by offering a lower latency link to some other destination area of the network. It can spoof or replay advertisements for a low latency route to the Sink, for example, attracting all nearby traffic. Network traffic will be routed towards the sinkhole node, causing resource contention and disruption of message delivery.

Sinkhole (Figure 4) attacks may be used as precursors for other attacks, such as selective forwarding. Selective forwarding becomes trivial in this case, as all traffic in the area will flow through the sinkhole node and packets originating from any node in the area can be modified or dropped by the attacker.

Data Link Layer authentication can prevent external attacks, but cannot stop an internal attacker that is able to authenticate through use of compromised keys.

Selective Forwarding: Internal (Network Layer)

A selective forwarding attack (Karlof & Wagner, 2003) is similar to the neglect and greed attack described earlier. In this attack, a compromised sensor node on the routing path refuses to forward certain packets or drops them, resulting in the packets not being propagated any further. If all packets were to be dropped, a black hole would be created. Since black holes are easy to detect, the attacker evades detection by selectively dropping packets and forwarding all other traffic. This will preclude neighboring sensor nodes from deciding

Figure 4. Sinkhole

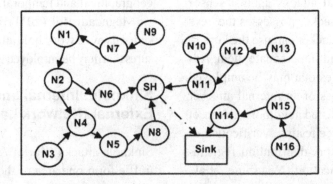

that the attacker node has failed or is compromised, hence choosing another route.

Countermeasures against an external attack include Data Link Layer authentication and encryption, which prevent the attacker from joining the network and selectively dropping messages based on content. Internal attacks may be thwarted through the use of watchdogs (Marti, et al., 2000), whose use was mentioned in the section on black holes, acknowledgement-based protocols (Zhang, et al., 2007), multi-path routing, routing messages over disjoint or braided paths (Ganesan, et al., 2001), and dynamically picking the next hop from set of candidates on a random basis.

Hello Flood: External (Network Layer)

Many routing protocols specify the broadcast of HELLO packets by sensor nodes, in order to announce their presence to their one hop neighbors. Sensor nodes receiving these packets assume that they are within range of the sensor. A HELLO flood attack (Karlof & Wagner, 2003) is perpetrated by high power attacker nodes in an attempt to trick nodes in another area of the network that they are neighbors of the attacker. It is an attack against minimum cost forwarding. An attacker with enough transmission power could convince every node in the network that it is a neighbor and begin packet exchange with those nodes (provided the attacker has a receiver sensitive enough to hear them). If the attacker broadcasts an attractive route to the Sink, the fooled nodes will attempt to pass traffic to the attacker. Messages will be lost, as the fooled nodes will most likely be out of communication range with the attacker. The attacker could also replay HELLO packets from other sensor nodes, causing further network disturbances.

One countermeasure against this type of attack is a test of the bi-directionality of the link. This, however, will be useless if the attacker has a sensitive receiver. External attacks can be prevented

through authentication. Internal attacks can only be successful if the attacker can authenticate itself to all intended victim nodes. If authentication involves the Base Station, an attacker claiming to be a neighbor of an unusually large number of nodes would raise an alarm (Karlof & Wagner, 2003). Routing protocols that do not maintain routing tables or use HELLO message are not susceptible to this type of attack.

Acknowledgement Spoofing: Internal and External (Data Link Layer)

Several routing protocols rely on explicit or implicit Data Link Layer acknowledgements. An attacker can spoof Data Link Layer acknowledgements to packets, overheard through eavesdropping, that are addressed to neighbor nodes. The attacker's goals may include convincing the sender that a weak link is strong or a dead node is alive. A selective forwarding attack may be mounted by spoofing acknowledgements for a node that is dead. Packets transmitted to the dead node will be lost. Protocols whose next hop link selection is based on link reliability may thus be fooled into using the dead link as a preferred link.

External attacks can be prevented through authentication and encryption. Internal attackers will still be able to spoof acknowledgments for nodes whose keys they possess.

INTRUSION DETECTION

WSN security paradigms, no matter how carefully designed, will never prevent all attackers from being able to find a way to break into the network and launch an active attack. This is observed in the wired world, where there is no end to zero day exploits. There is no reason to believe that it will be any different in the wireless arena. The introduction of new types of WSN applications will result in new types of security attacks. It is impossible to know or predict the characteristics of these future attacks. As a result, it would seem that WSN researchers and designers will always be playing catch up in their attempts to find and plug the latest security holes used by attackers. An additional issue here is that even if tamper-resistant devices are available for WSN use, they still cannot guarantee perfect security, thus node compromise is unavoidable (Zhou, et al., 2008). Intrusion Detection Systems (IDS) are a second line of network defense used when intrusion prevention techniques, such as authentication, and encryption have failed.

Passive attackers will most likely remain un-detected, as they exhibit no anomalous behavior. Active attackers, on the other hand, will cause anomalies that may indicate the existence of an attack. IDS may be used to monitor the network for such anomalies in an attempt to match them to activity patterns that confirm the presence of a malicious attack. Attack signatures may be pre-programmed or learned, depending on the IDS implementation (Wood & Stankovic, 2002).

IDS Agents

IDS Agents (Farooqi & Khan, 2009) are respon-sible for analyzing the network, detecting abnor-mal behavior, and taking actions to mitigate it. An IDS Agent works in three phases: the collection phase, during which network data is collected; the detection phase, during which some detection policy is applied to the collected network data to find intrusions; the response phase, during which alerts and defensive actions may be taken in the case where an anomaly is detected.

IDS Agents may be installed in three possible ways (Farooqi & Khan., 2009)—purely central-ized, purely distributed, and hybrid. They are used in centralized, distributed, and hierarchical/hybrid IDS architectures, respectively, and have the following characteristics:

- **Purely Centralized IDS Agent Installation:** The IDS Agent is installed at the Sink. It collects information from the sensor nodes concerning their observations on network behavior; their own and their neighbors. Centralized agents typically do not have issues with limited resources. They have a single point of failure, so the security of the Sink must be guaranteed. In addition, this approach has problems with scalability, as the addition of new nodes may affect performance.

- **Purely Distributed IDS Agent Installation:** The IDS Agent is contained in each node. It monitors each of its neigh-bor nodes that are in its communication range to determine their behavior. Two types of decision making are possible. *Individualized decision making*, in which every node that detects aberrant behavior of another node sends notification to the Sink and *cooperative decision making*, in which each node detecting aberrant behav-ior of any node votes with other nodes in its neighborhood to make a determination on whether not the node being observed is malicious. The use of distributed agents avoids single point of failure. In addition, scalability is supported.

- **Distributed-Centralized IDS Agent Installation, sometimes referred to as Hierarchical or Hybrid:** the network is divided into clusters, each one having a cluster-head. The IDS Agent is installed on the cluster-head, which has two func-tions—normal sensor operations as per-formed by the other sensor nodes and in-trusion detection. The cluster-head handles malicious actions of its own cluster and other cluster-heads. It acts as a local Base Station for the nodes within the cluster, aggregating information from its member nodes concerning malicious activities they have observed. The cluster heads can also cooperate with the Base Station, resulting in global IDS.

IDS Detection Techniques

Detection techniques used in IDS can be classified into three types (Abduvaliyev et al., 2010; Islam et al., 2010):

1. **Signature or Misuse Detection:** Intrusions are detected by comparing the actions and behaviors of nodes with signatures or behaviors of known attack patterns. The attack signatures are pre-defined and are distributed to the IDS Agents. This technique has the disadvantage that it requires knowledge of attack characteristics in order to build the attack pattern signature. It may exhibit low false positive rate, but is not able to detect previously unknown types of attacks. A disadvantage is the fact that the attack signature database must be updated to provide protection for new types of attack and the IDS Agents must be notified of the new attack signatures.

2. **Anomaly Detection:** Rather than using attack patterns, normal node behavior is defined in a profile and the behavior of the observed nodes is compared to the profile. Any deviation of behavior from the profile is classified as an intrusion. Normal behavior profiles are established by automated training. The normal behavior profile is updated as the system learns the behavior. This type of system can detect unknown attacks, but exhibits high false rates when encountering legitimate, but previously unobserved, behavior. In addition, this detection mechanism will not detect an intrusion that does not exhibit anomalous behavior (false negative).

3. **Specification Based Detection:** This technique is similar to anomaly detection, in that attacks are detected as deviations from a norm. It does not, however, rely on machine learning. Instead, it utilizes specifications that are manually developed and define legitimate (rather than previously observed)

behavior. Intrusion is indicated when a node's behavior deviates from the specification. This technique can detect unknown attacks. It is not subject to the high false alarm rate caused by legitimate but previously unobserved behavior that is characteristic of the anomaly detection technique. The disadvantage to this technique is that development of detailed specifications may be extremely time consuming. Typically, the IDS designer must trade off specification development with the possibility that some attacks may be missed (false negatives).

Examples of Centralized Intrusion Detection Architectures

In centralized IDS, all information pertaining to intrusion detection is transferred to a single entity, typically the Base Station. Intrusion detection is only performed by the Base Station, which is assumed to have orders of magnitude more memory and processing power than the sensor nodes. Superior resources allow the Base Station to perform more sophisticated detection analysis than can be accomplished by an individual sensor node. In addition, centralized implementations have a global view of the network that permits detection of attacks that would remain undiscovered in other architectures. Centralized approaches have several disadvantages, among them is that their architecture has a single point of failure and increased traffic. The challenge in a centralized architecture is to find a balance between detection accuracy and report rate.

Kaplantzis et al. (2007) propose a purely centralized intrusion detection scheme based on Support Vector Machines (SVM) and sliding windows. Their scheme detects black holes and selective forwarding attacks using routing information contained within the Base Station. Anomaly detection is used and alarms are generated based on the 2D feature vector (bandwidth, hop count). Data pattern classification is accomplished using a one-class SVM classifier. The authors claim that theirs was the first attempt to use an SVM for intrusion detection in WSNs and the first study to utilize a centralized IDS that had no implications on node power. Since the scheme is centralized, data processing and anomaly detection is carried out exclusively by the Base Station. Centralized intrusion detection shifts the processing burden off the sensor nodes, in order to preclude them from using their resources and, as a consequence, increases network lifetime.

A Minimum Transmission Energy (MTE) routing protocol is used. The goal of this class of protocol is to minimize the transmission energy required to forward a packet, in a attempt to extend each node's lifetime. $E(k,d) = E_{TX} * k + E_{AMP} * k *d^2$ defines the energy a node expends to transmit a packet of size k a distance d. E_{TX} is the energy needed to run the transmitter circuit and E_{AMP} is the energy used by the transmit amplifier. An examination of the equations shows the sensor should select the next hop based on minimum distance.

SVMs are supervised learning methods that analyze data and recognize patterns. A standard SVM is trained by taking a set of training samples whose elements are marked as belonging to the attack traffic class or the regular traffic class and using them to build a classifier model. This classifier model represents the training examples as points in space that are mapped so that samples of the separate classes are divided by a gap that is wide as possible. After the initial construction of the classifier model via training, the SVM extends the model by taking input and predicting the class the input belongs to, based on which side of the gap it falls on. The SVM used by the authors is a one-class SVM, which is trained using only normal traffic data. The main objective of the learning algorithm in this case is to learn normal behavior and subsequently detect deviations from it. This type of SVM was chosen over a standard one as the authors thought that it would be unlikely to a-priori know the form of any attack. Thus *any*

training set they envisioned constructing would not provide accurate representation of an actual attack.

During training and subsequent operation, the Base Station records the incoming bandwidth utilization and the number of hops each packet took to reach it. Data is smoothed using a sliding window with a width of 10 samples. The goal of the sensor network is to report the presence of a mobile intruder capable of inserting itself into a network path and dropping some or all packets flowing through it to the Base Station. A sensor node sends a packet to the Base Station when it detects the intruder's presence. Initial training is accomplished by having each node in the WSN send a packet when it detects the presence of the mobile intruder. During training, the intruder does not drop any packets. During the operational phase, tests were carried out with the intruder dropping some or all of the packets. The authors reported high efficiency of their algorithm using their simulation data. There may be some criticism of their work, however, due to the fact that the ability to train on attack-free data cannot be guaranteed in real world deployments.

Ngai et al. (2006) offer an algorithm that detects sinkhole attacks, even in the presence of node collusion. The first step of their algorithm consists of finding a list of suspect nodes. It is assumed that the Base Station has knowledge of the location of the sensor nodes that is obtainable via various localization methods. An estimate is made of the area under attack and nodes within that area form the list of suspect nodes. The Base Station estimates the attack area using statistical analysis of sensor data to detect nodes that have missing or inconsistent data. Let X_1, ..., X_n be sensing data collected in a sliding window and M be their mean. Define $f(X_i) =$ Square Root($(X_i - M)^2 / M$)). A given node i is suspect if $f(X_i) >$ some threshold, t, as data from this node differs from others in the same general area. Using this information, the Base Station circles a suspected attack area, using a circle with a radius that encompasses all suspected nodes. Traffic from nodes within the circle could be attracted by the sinkhole, hence these are also referred to as *affected* nodes.

The attacker is found by analyzing the routing pattern within the affected area. A time stamped request message containing the IDs of all affected nodes is broadcast by the Base Station. Time stamping prevents replay attacks. In addition, the request is signed with the private encryption key of the Base Station. Symmetric encryption is employed to prevent packet alteration. Every node has an individual key shared with the Base Station. When an affected node receives the request, it replies with an encoded message containing its ID, the ID of the next hop node and the routing cost (hop count) to that node. The reply is sent along the reverse path taken by the broadcast message, as the next hop and routing cost could be affected by the attack. Using the next hop information contained in the replies, the Base Station generates and analyzes a routing pattern tree. Some branches of the routing pattern tree may be broken, due to missing information. More than one tree of network flow information may also exist. A depth-first search is used to calculate the number of nodes in different trees, and the sinkhole is at the root of the biggest tree, as it attracts the most network traffic.

The authors also address the problem of multiple malicious nodes and offer solutions employing key establishment and path redundancy.

Few researchers have explored the potential of centralized schemes, perhaps due to the fact their architecture has a single point of failure.

Examples of Distributed Intrusion Detection Architectures

Some IDS utilize a cooperative detection scheme, wherein each node is monitored by its neighbors to determine whether or not it is behaving correctly. The monitoring nodes operate in promiscuous mode, listening to the packets being sent to and from the nodes under observation. Each monitoring node keeps a tally of the correct and aberrant action of each node being monitored. When the aberrant behavior exceeds some threshold, the observer will deduce that the node is malicious. Observer nodes periodically vote on the behavior of nodes being observed. An observed node is declared malicious if the vote tally indicates a majority of the observers have determined its behavior to be aberrant. Once a node has been declared as malicious, actions are taken to limit its affect on network operation.

Some of the active attacks previously discussed have had IDS schemes proposed for their detection and mitigation. These IDS schemes have typically been attack-specific and not general in nature. For example, Wensheng et al. (2003) proposed a scheme using cooperative detection as described in the preceding paragraph to detect selective forwarding. They observed that, in routing a node, the number of packets forwarded must equal the number received. When the number of packets the observed node fails to forward exceeds the specified threshold, the observer marks the observed mode as malicious and votes to that effect when voting occurs.

Krontiris et al. (2007) proposed a two rule IDS scheme similar to Wensheng et al. (2003) to detect black holes and selective forwarding attacks. When a node is sending packets, all of its neighbor nodes are required to monitor it. Assume node A transmits a packet to node B. The first rule requires monitoring nodes store the packet transmitted by node A and watch to determine whether or not node B forwards it. If node B does not forward it, a failure counter is incremented. When the failure counter is greater than a defined threshold value, an alarm is raised. The second rule states that if a majority of the monitoring nodes have raised an alarm, the monitored node is compromised.

A distributed mechanism was proposed for the detection of node replication attacks by Parno et al. (2005). Each node must send its location to a set of observer nodes. If an observer finds an anomaly in the location claims, then the node is assumed to be replicated.

Da Silva et al. (2005) proposed a three phase intrusion detection technique. During phase 1, the data acquisition phase, data is acquired. A monitor node listens in promiscuous mode and stores packet information required for analysis in phase 2. In phase 2, a set of rules are applied to the data collected in phase 1. If any packet fails any of the rules, a failure counter is incremented. The following are the IDS rules applied in phase 2:

1. **Interval Rule:** A failure occurs if two consecutive packet receptions are greater or smaller than the allocated time. This rule can detect DoS resource exhaustion attacks wherein the attacker sends frequent messages in an attempt to deplete energy.
2. **Retransmission Rule:** A failure occurs if the node does not forward the packet. (Detects black hole, sinkhole, and selective forwarding attacks).
3. **Integrity Rule:** A failure occurs if the packet payload is modified.
4. **Delay Rule:** A failure occurs if the packet is not delivered within a defined threshold time.
5. **Repetition Rule:** A failure occurs if the same packet is retransmitted by a node more times than specified by an allowable retransmit threshold value. (Detects resource exhaustion attack).
6. **Radio Range Rule:** A failure occurs if the packet is received from a node other than a neighbor node. The monitor node must receive only packets originated by one of its neighbors. This rule detects wormhole and HELLO flood attacks.
7. **Jamming Rule:** The number of collisions associated with a packet sent by the monitor node must be lower than the expected number of collisions occurring within the network.

In phase 3, the failure count is compared to a threshold value. If the threshold is exceeded, then an alarm is raised. The threshold value is based on failure history (there is an expected number of occasional failures) for each node in the neighborhood monitored by the monitor node. Note that the monitor nodes in this model are special nodes, and the authors offer no information on how these nodes are distributed within the WSN field.

Roman et al. (2006) first proposed general guidelines for applying IDS to WSNs. Up to that point, research in IDS was a mature subject area in wired networks, but little work had been published concerning the application of IDS to WSNs. They introduced *spontaneous watchdogs* as a technique for optimally monitoring neighbors. It is a cooperative scheme that detects the abnormal behavior using knowledge and an environmental database. IDS Agents are located on every node in the WSN and every node has a database used for storing security information collected by the IDS Agents. IDS Agents are composed of two parts, *local agents* and *global agents*. Local agents are responsible for monitoring the packets sent and received by the sensor, in order to detect an attack. Their overhead is minimal, as their analysis is performed only when the sensor node is active. Global agents operate in promiscuous mode and watch the communications of their immediate neighbor sensor nodes. Only a selected subset of global agents are active at any time, in order to reduce energy usage and the huge overhead that would occur if all global agents were activated simultaneously. Global agent activation depends on the routing architecture used by the WSN. In hierarchical routing architectures, global agents are activated in every cluster head. Since the combination of all cluster heads covers the entire WSN, total network coverage in terms of intrusion detection is assured. Flat routing architectures present a problem in the selection of global agents to activate, as it is not possible to know what agents cover the network. The author's solution avoided the use of clustering techniques within the flat architecture for IDS purposes only, as they wished to avoid incurring the additional network complexity and maintenance overhead. Spontaneous watchdogs, a distributed solution, was proposed to solve the problem. The goal of this solution is to activate only one global agent per packet circulating in the network. It attempts to accomplish this via a rules based algorithm that checks the destination of every packet. The solution does not, however, ensure that one and one global agent per packet is activated.

Bhuse and Gupta (2006) describe an IDS using anomaly detection applied at multiple layers of the Internet Model. Their model is based on the assumption that routing protocols for ad hoc networks are applicable to sensor networks. They utilized Dynamic Source Routing (DSR) and DSDV protocols in their model. For the most part, commercially available sensors do not support ad hoc routing algorithms such as these. Their model uses existing system information such as routing tables, neighbor lists, sleep and wake-up schedules, etc. to detect anomalous behavior at multiple layers. Using detection at multiple layers is advantageous, since it affords the opportunity to detect an attacker that may have escaped detection at a particular layer.

At the Physical Layer, they use the Received Signal Strength Indicator (RSSI) value to detect anomalies. Each node records the RSSI value received from each of its neighbors during neighbor discovery. Subsequently, any node receiving a packet with an unexpected RSSI value raises an alarm. There is a high positive false alarm rate using this technique, because RSSI value is affected by background noise and other factors.

At the Data Link Layer, if a TDM scheduling algorithm is used to allocate time slots to each node, an alarm is raised if a node A receives a packet from node B during a time slot when B is supposed to be asleep. If the SMAC protocol is used, any packet received from a source during its sleeping period is an anomaly.

At the Network Layer, they propose a protocol called Information Authentication for Sensor Network (IASN). In lieu of authenticating nodes,

this protocol authenticates information that is expected to be received from neighbors. Each node keeps track of its neighbors and the type of information expected to be received from them. If a node receives information from a node that it does not expect, an anomaly is declared.

At the Application Layer, they propose a mutual guarding technique and the use of round trip times. The use of round trip times is not very effective, as high false positive rates may be encountered, due to many factors.

Baig (2008) proposed a distributed scheme for the detection of Distributed DoS (DDoS) attacks in WSNs. DDoS attacks are launched from multiple ends of a WSN against legitimate sensor nodes with the goal of inducing energy resource exhaustion. He modeled DDoS detection as a pattern recognition problem, wherein topology-dependant patterns are defined to model normal network traffic and are used to differentiate between legitimate traffic packets and attack traffic packets. The techniques used for detection rely on distributed pattern recognition. Baig (2011) proposes a similar distributed scheme for the detection of resource exhaustion attacks.

As evidenced by the number of examples provided herein, distributed IDS architectures predominate intrusion detection schemes that have been postulated for use in WSN.

Examples of Hierarchical/Hybrid Intrusion Detection Architectures

Like centralized architectures, the use of distributed-centralized architectures, also referred to as hierarchical or hybrid architectures, has been explored by few researchers. Mamun & Kabir (2010) present a hierarchical IDS for use in Wireless Sensor Networks. They use a clustering mechanism to build a four level hierarchical network that utilizes both signature detection and anomaly detection techniques. In addition to intrusion detection, they introduce the use of a policy based response mechanism that takes action to isolate an attack node from the WSN. Their model uses what they term a Hierarchical Overlay Design (HOD). Each area of sensor nodes is divided into a hexagonal region similar to a GSM cell. The sensor nodes in each of the hexagonal regions are considered to be the first layer (leaf nodes) and are monitored by a cluster node. These cluster nodes form the second layer of the model. Each cluster node, in turn, is monitored by a regional node. Regional nodes form the third layer of the module and are controlled and monitored by the Base Station (the top layer).

Signatures of known attacks are propagated from the Base Station to the IDS modules in the cluster and regional nodes, for use in detecting attacks. Leaf nodes have no IDS modules installed, hence have no IDS functionality. They function primarily as sensing and routing entities. Facilities for detecting intrusion at multiple layers of the Internet Model are provided in the cluster and regional nodes.

Physical Layer attacks (jamming) are detected by use of the RSSI, the carrier sense time, and the packet delivery ratio (PDR). During initialization, the cluster node determines and stores the RSSI value for communication between it and the leaf level sensor nodes and for sensor node to sensor node. These values are used by the anomaly processor in the cluster node, along with the carrier sense time and PDR, to detect jamming.

Data Link Layer attacks are detected by using TDMA and SMAC to detect the anomaly. In a TDMA scheme used to access the radio channel, if an attacker sends a packet using the source address of a node that is not allocated to transmit in a given time slot, an anomaly is detected. If the SMAC protocol is used to assign wakeup and sleep times for the sensor nodes, an anomaly has occurred if a packet is received from its purported source node during the node's sleeping period.

Network Layer route tracing is used to detect whether a packet is really using the best route. If a packet comes to the destination via a path other than the desired path, then the anomaly processor

is invoked to detect a possible intrusion according to a set of predefined rules.

Application Layer monitoring is done by using three upper level watchdogs, which are located in the Base Station, regional node, and cluster node. Sensor nodes are monitored by a watchdog in the cluster node, while cluster nodes are monitored by a watchdog in the regional node, and the regional node is monitored by the top level watchdog in the Base Station. If any node is compromised by an attacker, the higher layer watchdog detects the attack and generates an alarm.

Intrusion response is determined by policy and the policy database may be modified at any time to create or modify rules, in order to prevent future attacks. The policy mechanism classifies nodes according to one of five classes, and places restrictions on their interactions with other nodes, depending on their observed behavior and class categorization. Nodes may be classified as *Fresh*, *Member*, *Unstable*, *Suspect*, or *Malicious*.

When a node is new, it is classified as Fresh and it is only permitted to forward and receive packets from other sensor nodes, but may not source its own packets. If, after a specified period of time, the node has not misbehaved, the node's classification changes to Member, otherwise, the classification is set to Suspect.

When in Member state, a node may create, send, receive, or forward packets. If the node misbehaves while in the Member state, its state will change to Unstable for a short period of time. While in the Unstable state, nodes can send and receive packets other than their own. If the node behaves well while in this state, it will transfer back to the Member state.

A node in the Unstable state transitions to the Suspect state under one of two conditions: the node transitioned back and forth between the Member and Unstable state for more than some threshold number of times within a specified time period, or the node was misbehaving for a long time.

A node in the Suspect state is isolated from the network for a short period of time. It may not send, receive, or forward packets and any packets that are received from it are discarded. After a specified period of time, the Suspect node is reconnected to the system and is monitored closely by the IDS Agents in all three layers. If the watchdogs determine that the node has not misbehaved during the extended monitoring period, then its classification is changed to Unstable. If the node continues to misbehave, then it is labeled as Malicious and is permanently banned from the network.

Islam et al. (2010) present a four level hierarchical clustering architecture similar to Mamun & Kabir (2010) using a specification based detection technique. The lowest level consists of all leaf sensor nodes collecting environmental data. The second and third levels contain monitor nodes. The second level monitors the behavior of the bottom level leaf sensor nodes, while the level three sensors monitor the behavior of the level two sensors. The top level is the Base Station. Their model requires a heterogeneous network with level two and three sensors having more power with respect to transmission range and battery life. Their intrusion detection algorithm is a modification of Da Silva et al. (2005) and is implemented in the level two and three nodes. No IDS Agent is incorporated in the leaf sensors. In phase 1, the leaf sensor nodes collect environmental information and report it to the level 2 sensor nodes. In phase 2, a layer based attack detection scheme similar to that described by Bhuse and Gupta (2006) is used to detect attacks, rather that the rules utilized by Da Silva et al. (2005). Phase 3 compares each result to the defined threshold value to determine whether or not an alarm should be raised. The layer based attack detection algorithm is as follows:

- **Physical Layer:** While receiving information from the leaf level sensors, the level 2 sensors record the RSSI value. Subsequent to that they compare the recorded RSSI value with the received value to detect anomalies. In a similar manner, level 3 sensor nodes record the RSSI value of level 2 sensors to detect an intrusion.
- **Data Link Layer:** TDMA is used to assign time slots for the leaf sensor nodes. SMAC is used for the wakeup and sleep scheduling in the leaf sensor and level 2 sensor nodes. Level 2 and level 3 sensor nodes can detect intrusion if data is received from some sensor node during a time slot not allocated to it.
- **Network Layer:** Uses the IASM protocol specified in Bhuse & Gupta (2006). This permits the level 2 and level 3 sensor nodes to easily detect whether or not a packet has been received from the correct source.
- **Application Layer:** The three level monitoring technique is used instead of mutual guarding, as proposed in Bhuse & Gupta (2006).

Evaluation of Learning Algorithms for Future Use in Anomaly Detection

There are many classes of learning algorithms that future researchers may wish to explore for use in anomaly detection. Becker et al. (2009) did a interesting study on several learning algorithms to evaluate their suitability. They discussed and evaluated bio-inspired approaches such as Neural Networks and Artificial Immune Systems, along with simpler classical algorithms such as Decision Trees, Bayes Classifier, Support Vector Machines, and k-Nearest Neighbors. They point out that Artificial Immune Systems (AIS) is one of the most recent approaches in computational intelligence and that motivations for its use are the efficiency of the human immune system when dealing with harmful bacteria, viruses or fungi. Previous work indicated that AIS could provide good detection with a low rate of false positives, however, only simplistic types of misbehavior had been examined. Their findings concluded that the simpler classification algorithms were as well suited for sensor networks as their more complex

Neural Network and AIS counterparts. The AIS algorithm was found to require three orders of magnitude more operations than the Neural Network algorithm, making it use undesirable because of its increased power consumption.

Towards a Formal Definition of Intrusion Detection

Krontiris et al. (2009) examine the problem of cooperative intrusion detection in WSN, where nodes are equipped with local detector modules and identify an intruder in a distributed fashion. They claim to be the first to formally define the problem of intrusion detection in WSN and offer the first formal proof and generic algorithm for its solution. In addition, they identify the necessary and sufficient conditions for solving the problem. They investigate only the case of a single attacker, which turns out to be complex, and give an algorithm that works under a general threat model. Their solution also identifies conditions and scenarios in which the cooperative intrusion detection problem is unsolvable. They concede that individual solutions to specific problems may be more efficient; however, their solution is lightweight enough to run on sensor nodes.

FUTURE RESEARCH DIRECTIONS

The problem of intrusion detection in WSNs is an interesting and viable research area. Cooperative intrusion detection techniques and proofs, as presented by Krontiris et al. (2009), formalize the problem and show the benefits and theoretical limitations of that scheme. Future research into the area of multiple attacker scenarios and formulation of proofs addressing them may lead to further insight into what is and is not solvable. Dynamic neighborhood topology adjustment in terms of node addition and deletion may be able to alter initially unsolvable scenarios to the point where they become solvable.

Performance of WSNs is typically degraded with the addition of security paradigms. Current work on security in WSNs focuses primarily on things like intrusion detection, secure data aggregation, secure routing, etc. Consideration of how to guarantee a particular level of Quality of Service (QoS) in combination with security needs to be addressed. With this in mind, the authors will be looking to perform further research into the area of secure connected k-coverage. Guaranteeing k-coverage while under attack is an area that has not been yet explored.

Development of hardware more suitable to supporting security constructs as proposed by Hu et al. (2010) is another interesting research area. The availability of cheap, more powerful hardware supporting Internet level security in WSNs would facilitate more powerful security primitives than are currently available.

Current works on security give little consideration to the security of the Sink. It is assumed, for the most part, that the Sink is trustworthy, while the sensor nodes are not. In real scenarios, however, like battlefield surveillance, it is quite plausible that the Sink may be compromised or destroyed. Therefore, new approaches to guarantee Sink and sensor node mutual security is another possible IDS research direction. In a battlefield application, it would seem advantageous to have sensor nodes cease reporting or generate erroneous reports to a compromised Sink. This would preclude an adversary from determining how much information is known about them via the WSN.

The use of game theory in IDS is another viable research area. Initial work into using game theory to promote coexistence with malicious nodes is explored in Wang et al. (2009). Rather than quarantine a misbehaving node from the WSN, it may be advantageous to let it handle some traffic, in order to improve network throughput and lifetime. This approach may be especially advantageous in circumstances where network resources are extremely limited. So long as the damage a misbehaving node invokes is less than the legitimate work it can do, coexistence may be a viable alternative to quarantining. This approach would require the development of metrics to detect and mechanisms to compensate for the malicious behavior of the errant node.

The application of game theory to all known attacks on the layers of the Internet Model is another possible area of research. Research has been accomplished in applying game theoretic approaches in preventing DoS attacks using non-cooperative game theory (Agah, et al., 2005), cooperative game theory (Agah et al., 2004), and repeated game theory (Agah & Das, 2007). Yu et al. (2011) state that game theory has yet to be applied to all known attack types on the layers of the Internet Model and support the view that doing so may yield useful results. They also purport that research into efficient learning mechanisms based on game theory, coupled with game history, may result in methodologies that permit sensor nodes to predict the behavior of errant nodes.

Current WSN security work focuses on the security of discrete events, such as temperature measurement. The authors have seen nothing in the literature that deals with the security of continuous data streams, such as video or audio. While video and audio sensors for use in WSNs may not be currently available, it is not too farfetched to believe a demand for them will occur in the future. Encryption, authentication, and data compression methodologies necessary to provide security for continuous data streams are quite different those required for discrete event security. The extension of current security protocols and implementation of IDS for protection of continuous data streams may be yet another interesting future research area.

LESSONS LEARNED

Our survey of WSN security has shown that WSNs present security challenges that are not encountered in mainstream wired or wireless networks. It is likely to remain a viable research area for some time to come. In particular, the areas of intrusion detection and response offer great challenges.

A wide variety of sophisticated learning algorithms have yet to be applied to anomaly detection. We have observed that the majority of solutions and results generated by researchers in IDS are theoretical or based on simulations. Empirical study of real world systems that gives insight on how to prevent, detect, respond, and co-exist with an attacker remains to be undertaken.

CONCLUSION

This chapter attempts to provide an overview of the security attacks WSNs are subject to. The characteristics of WSNs affecting their security were introduced, as were the security requirements required by WSNs. The two main categories of attacks, Passive and Active, were defined and specific examples of them were enumerated, along with actions that may be taken to mitigate them. The Intrusion Detection paradigm was introduced and illustrative examples of IDS architectures and detection techniques were presented. As the use of Wireless Sensor Networks continues to become more common place, we expect that Intrusion Detection Systems will play an important role in implementing security functionality.

Research into WSN security is ongoing and new work in this arena is being published on on-going basis. There are many fundamental security problems that must be solved before Wireless Sensor Networks can be considered secure. Our goal is to provide a general overview of the wide ranging and salient aspects of WSN capabilities and security issues. We strived to give citations that point an interested researcher in a direction where a further, more focused, review of relevant literature can be undertaken. In addition, a reader having no prior knowledge of WSN security should be able to garner considerable insight into it via a read of this work. Therefore, this chapter can be used as a starting point or a summary of some of the work accomplished so far.

ACKNOWLEDGMENT

The authors gratefully acknowledge the insightful comments of the anonymous reviewers which helped improve the quality and presentation of this book chapter significantly. The work of H.M. Ammari is partially supported by the US National Science Foundation (NSF) grant 0917089.

REFERENCES

Abduvaliyev, A., Lee, S., & Lee, Y. K. (2010). Energy efficient hybrid intrusion detection system for wireless sensor networks. In *Proceedings of the 2010 International Conference on Electronics and Information Engineering (ICEIE 2010)*, (pp. V2-25 – V2-29). Los Alamitos, CA: Conference Publishing Services.

Agah, A., Basu, K., & Das, S. K. (2005). Preventing DoS attack in sensor networks: A game theoretic approach. In *Proceedings of 2005 IEEE International Conference on Communications (ICC 2005)*, (pp. 3218-3222). Los Alamitos, CA: Conference Publishing Services.

Agah, A., & Das, S. K. (2007). Preventing DoS attacks in wireless sensor networks: A repeated game theory approach. *International Journal of Network Security*, 5, 259–263.

Agah, A., Das, S. K., & Basu, K. (2004). Preventing DoS attack in sensor networks: A game theoretic approach. In *Proceedings of IEEE International Conference on Performance, Computing, and Communications*, (pp. 259-263). Los Alamitos, CA: Conference Publishing Services.

Aura, T., Nikander, P., & Leiwo, J. (2001). DOS-resistant authentication with client puzzles. *Lecture Notes in Computer Science*, 2133, 171–177.

Baig, Z. A. (2008). *Distributed denial of service attack detection in wireless sensor networks*. Unpublished Doctoral Dissertation. Monash University.

Baig, Z. A. (2011). Pattern recognition for detecting distributed node exhaustion attacks in wireless sensor networks. *Computer Communications*, *34*(3), 468–484. doi:10.1016/j.comcom.2010.04.008

Becher, A., Benenson, Z., & Dornseif, M. (2006). Tampering with motes: Real-world physical attacks on wireless sensor networks. In *Proceedings of the 3rd International Conference on Security in Pervasive Computing (SPC)*, (pp. 104-118). Berlin, Germany: Springer.

Becker, M., Drozda, M., Schaust, S., Bohlmann, S., & Szczerbicka, H. (2009). On classification approaches for misbehavior detection in wireless sensor networks. *Journal of Computers*, *4*(5), 357–365. doi:10.4304/jcp.4.5.357-365

Bhuse, V., & Gupta, A. (2006). Anomaly intrusion detection in wireless sensor networks. *Journal of High Speed Networks*, *15*(1), 33–51.

Chan, H., & Perrig, A. (2003). Security and privacy in sensor networks. *Computer*, *36*(10), 103–105. doi:10.1109/MC.2003.1236475

Chen, H., Han, P., Zhou, X., & Gao, C. (2007). Lightweight anomaly intrusion detection in wireless sensor networks. In *Proceedings of the 2007 Pacific Asia conference on Intelligence and Security Informatics (PAISI 2007)*, (pp. 105-116). Berlin, Germany: Springer-Verlag.

Chen, Y., Xu, W., Trappe, W., & Zhang, Y. (2009). *Securing emerging wireless systems*. New York, NY: Springer. doi:10.1007/978-0-387-88491-2

Cheung, S., & Levitt, K. N. (1997). Protecting routing infrastructures from denial of service using cooperative intrusion detection. In *Proceedings of the New Security Paradigms Workshop (NSPW 1997)*, (pp. 94-106). New York, NY: ACM.

Choi, M., Rosslin, J. R., Hong, C., & Kim, T. (2008). Wireless network security: Vulnerabilities, threats, and countermeasures. *International Journal of Multimedia and Ubiquitous Engineering, 3*(3), 77–86.

Da Silva, A., Martins, M., Rocha, B., Loureiro, A., Ruiz, L., & Wong, H. (2005). Decentralized intrusion detection in wireless sensor networks. In *Proceedings of the 1st ACM International Workshop on Quality of Service & Security in Wireless and Mobile Networks (Q2SWinet 2005)*, (pp. 16-23). New York, NY: ACM.

David, B. M., Santana, B., Peotta, L., Holtz, M. D., & Timoteo de Sousa, R. Jr. (2010). A context-dependent trust model for the MAC layer in LR-WPANs. *International Journal on Computer Science and Engineering, 2*(9), 3007–3016.

Deng, J., Hun, R., & Mishra, S. (2004). *Countermeasures against traffic analysis in wireless sensor networks*. Technical Report CU-CS-987-04. Boulder, CO: University of Colorado at Boulder.

Deng, J., Hun, R., & Mishra, S. (2005). Countermeasures against traffic analysis attacks in wireless sensor networks. In *Proceedings of the First International Conference on Security and Privacy for Emerging Areas in Communications Networks (SECURECOMM 2005)*, (pp. 113-126). Los Alamitos, CA: Conference Publishing Services.

Douceur, J. R. (2002). The sybil attack. *Lecture Notes in Computer Science, 2429*, 251–260. doi:10.1007/3-540-45748-8_24

Farooqi, A. H., & Khan, F. A. (2009). Intrusion detection systems for wireless sensor networks: A survey. *Communications in Computer and Information Science, 56*, 234–241. doi:10.1007/978-3-642-10844-0_29

Ganesan, D., Govindan, R., Shenker, S., & Estrin, D. (2001). Highly-resilient, energy-efficient multipath routing in wireless sensor networks. *Mobile Computing and Communications Review, 4*(5), 1–13.

Hu, W., Tan, H., Corke, P., Shih, W. C., & Jha, S. (2010). Toward trusted wireless sensor networks. *ACM Transactions on Sensor Networks, 7*(1), 5:1 - 5:25.

Hu, Y. C., Perrig, A., & Johnson, D. (2003). Packet leashes: A defense against wormhole attacks in wireless ad hoc networks. In *Proceedings of Twenty-Second Annual Joint Conference of the IEEE Computer and Communications Societies (Infocom 2003)*, (pp. 1976-1986). Piscateway, NJ: IEEE Operations Center.

Islam, M. S., Khan, R. H., & Bappy, D. M. (2010). A hierarchical intrusion detection system in wireless sensor networks. *International Journal of Computer Science and Network Security, 10*(8), 21–26.

Jian, Y., Chen, S., Zhang, Z., & Zhang, L. (2007). Protecting receiver-location privacy in wireless sensor networks. In *26th IEEE International Conference on Computer Communications (INFOCOM 2007)*, (pp. 1955–1963). Los Alamitos, CA: Conference Publishing Services.

Kamat, P., Zhang, Y., Trappe, W., & Ozturk, C. (2005). Enhancing source-location privacy in sensor network routing. In *Proceedings of 25th IEEE International Conference on Distributed Computing Systems (ICDCS 2005)*, (pp. 599–608). Los Alamitos, CA: Conference Publishing Services.

Kaplantzis, S., Shilton, A., Mani, N., & Sekercioglu, Y. A. (2007). Detecting selective forwarding attacks in wireless sensor networks using support vector machines. In *Proceedings of the 2007 International Conference on Intelligent Sensors, Sensor Networks and Information Processing*, (pp. 335-340). Los Alamitos, CA: Conference Publishing Services.

Wireless Sensor Network Security Attacks

Karlof, C., & Wagner, D. (2003). Secure routing in wireless sensor networks: Attacks and countermeasures. In *Proceedings of the First IEEE International Workshop on Sensor Network Protocols and Applications,* (pp. 113-127). Los Alamitos, CA: Conference Publishing Services.

Krontiris, I., Benenson, Z., Freiling, F. C., Dimitriou, T., & Giannetsos, T. (2009). Cooperative intrusion detection in wireless sensor networks. In *Proceedings of the 6th European Conference on Wireless Sensor Networks (EWSN 2009),* (pp. 263–278). Berlin, Germany: Springer-Verlag.

Krontiris, I., Dimitriou, T., & Frieling, F. C. (2007). Towards intrusion detection in wireless sensor networks. In *Proceedings of the 13th European Wireless Conference (EW 2007)*. Paris, France. Retrieved April 1, 2011, from http://www.web-portal-system.de/ wps/ wse/ dl/ showfile/ rannenberg/ 5315/ krontiris-ew2007.pdf.

Law, Y. W., Palaniswami, M., van Hoesel, L., Doumen, J., Hartel, P., & Havinga, P. (2009). Energy-efficient link-layer jamming attacks against wireless sensor network MAC protocols. *ACM Transactions on Sensor Networks, 5*(1), 6:1-6:38

Law, Y. W., van Hoesel, L., Doumen, J., Hartel, P., & Havinga, P. (2005). Energy-efficient link-layer jamming attacks against wireless sensor network MAC protocols. In *Proceedings of the 3rd ACM Workshop on Security of Ad Hoc and Sensor Networks (SASN 2005),* (pp. 76-88). New York, NY: ACM.

Li, Z., & Gong, G. (2009). *A survey on security in wireless sensor networks*. Retrieved April 1, 2011 from http://www.cacr.math. uwaterloo.ca/ techreports/ 2008/ cacr2008-20.pdf.

Mamun, M., & Kabir, A. (2010). Hierarchical design based intrusion detection system for wireless ad hoc sensor network. *International Journal of Network Security and Its Applications, 2*(3), 102–117. doi:10.5121/ijnsa.2010.2307

Marti, S., Giuli, T. J., Lai, K., & Baker, M. (2000). Mitigating routing misbehavior in mobile ad hoc networks. In *Proceedings of the 6th Annual International Conference on Mobile Computing and Networking (MobiCom 2000),* (pp. 255-265). New York, NY: ACM.

Martinovic, I., Pichota, P., & Schmitt, J. B. (2009). Jamming for good: A fresh approach to authentic communication in WSNs. In *Proceedings of the Second ACM Conference on Wireless Network Security (WiSec 2009),* (pp. 161-168). New York, NY: ACM.

Meghdadi, M., Ozdemir, S., & Guler, I. (2011). A survey of wormhole-based attacks and their countermeasures in wireless sensor networks. *IETE Technical Review, 28*(2), 89–102. doi:10.4103/0256-4602.78089

Newsome, J., Shi, E., Song, D., & Perrig, A. (2004). The sybil attack in sensor networks: Analysis & defenses. In *Proceedings of the 3rd International Symposium on Information Processing in Sensor Networks (IPSN 2004),* (pp. 259-268). New York, NY: ACM.

Ngai, E. C. H., Liu, J., & Lyu, M. R. (2006). On the intruder detection for sinkhole attack in wireless sensor networks. In *Proceedings of the 2006 IEEE International Conference on Communications (ICC 2006),* (pp. 3383-3389). Los Alamitos, CA: Conference Publishing Services.

Ozturk, C., Zhang, Y., & Trappe, W. (2004). Source-location privacy in energy constrained sensor network routing. In *Proceedings of the 2nd ACM workshop on Security of Ad Hoc and Sensor Networks (SASN 2004)*, (pp. 88-93). New York, NY: ACM.

Parno, B., Luk, M., Gaustad, E., & Perrig, A. (2006). Secure sensor network routing: A clean slate approach. In *Proceedings of the 2006 ACM Co Next Conference (CoNEXT 2006),* (pp. 1-13). New York, NY: ACM.

Parno, B., Perrig, A., & Gligor, V. (2005). Distributed detection of node replication attacks in sensor networks. In *Proceedings of the 2005 IEEE Symposium of Security and Privacy (SP 2005)*, (pp. 49-63). Los Alamitos, CA: Conference Publishing Services.

Pelechrinis, P., Iliofontou, M., & Khrishnamurthy, S. V. (2010). Denial of service attacks in wireless networks: The case of jammers. *IEEE Communications Surveys & Tutorials*, *12*(4), 1–13.

Radmand, P., Talevski, A., Petersen, S., & Carlsen, S. (2010). Taxonomy of wireless sensor network cyber security attacks in the oil and gas industries. In *24th IEEE International Conference on Advanced Information Networking and Applications (AINA 2010)*, (pp. 949-957). Los Alamitos, CA: Conference Publishing Services.

Raymond, D. R., & Midkiff, S. F. (2008). Denial-of-service in wireless sensor networks: Attacks and defenses. *IEEE Pervasive Computing / IEEE Computer Society [and] IEEE Communications Society*, *7*(1), 74–81. doi:10.1109/MPRV.2008.6

Roman, R., Zhou, J., & Lopez, J. (2006). Applying intrusion detection systems to wireless sensor networks. In *Proceedings of 2006 IEEE Consumer Communications and Networking Conference (CCNC 2006)*, (pp. 640-644). Los Alamitos, CA: Conference Publishing Services.

Sen, J. (2010). Routing security issues in wireless sensor networks: Attacks and defenses. In Tan, Y. K. (Ed.), *Sustainable Wireless Sensor Networks* (pp. 279–309). Rijeka, Croatia: Intech.

Tanabe, M., & Aida, M. (2007). Preventing resource exhaustion attacks in ad hoc networks. In *Proceedings of the 8th International Symposium on Autonomous Decentralized Systems (ISADS 2007)*, (pp. 543-548). Los Alamitos, CA: Conference Publishing Services.

Wang, Q., & Zhang, T. (2009). A survey on security in wireless sensor networks. In Zhang, Y., & Kitsos, P. (Eds.), *Security in RFID and Sensor Networks* (pp. 293–317). Boca Raton, FL: CRC Press. doi:10.1201/9781420068405.pt2

Wang, W., Chatterjee, M., & Kwiat, K. (2009). Coexistence with malicious nodes: A game theoretic approach. In *Proceedings of the 9th International Conference on Game Theory for Networks (GameNets 2009)*, (pp.277-286). Los Alamitos, CA: Conference Publishing Services.

Wensheng, G. W., Wang, G., Zhang, W., Cao, G., & LaPorta, T. (2003). On supporting distributed collaboration in sensor networks. In *Proceedings of 2003 Military Communications Conference (MILCOM 2003)*, (pp.752-757). Los Alamitos, CA: Conference Publishing Services.

Wood, A., Stankovic, J., & Son, S. (2003). JAM: A mapping service for jammed regions in sensor networks. In *Proceedings of the 24th International IEEE Real-Time Systems Symposium (RTSS 2003)*, (pp. 286-297). Los Alamitos, CA: Conference Publishing Services.

Wood, A. D., & Stankovic, J. A. (2002). Denial of service in sensor networks. *IEEE Computer*, *35*(10), 54–62. doi:10.1109/MC.2002.1039518

Xi, Y., Schwiebert, L., & Shi, W. (2006). Preserving source location privacy in monitoring-based wireless sensor networks. In *Proceedings of the 20th IEEE International Parallel and Distributed Processing Symposium (IPDPS 2006)*. Los Alamitos, CA: Conference Publishing Services.

Xu, W., Trappe, W., Zhang, Y., & Wood. (2005). The feasibility of launching and detecting jamming attacks in wireless networks. In *Proceedings of the 6th ACM International Symposium on Mobile Ad Hoc Networking and Computing (MobiHoc 2005)*, (pp. 46-57). New York, NY: ACM Press.

Yu, F., Shen, S., Yue, G., & Cao, Q. (2011). A survey of game theory in wireless sensor networks security. *Journal of Networks, 6*(3), 521–532.

Zhang, X., Chan, H., Jain, A., & Perrig, A. (2007). *Bounding packet dropping and injection attacks in sensor networks.* Technical Report CMU-CyLab-07-019. Pittsburgh, PA: Carnegie Mellon University.

Zhou, Y., Fang, Y., & Zhang, Y. (2008). Securing wireless sensor networks: A survey. *IEEE Communications Surveys & Tutorials, 10*, 6–28. doi:10.1109/COMST.2008.4625802

Zhu, S., Narayanan, V., McDaniel, P., Kandemir, M., Brooks, R., & Pirretti, M. (2006). The sleep deprivation attack in sensor networks: Analysis and methods of defense. *International Journal of Distributed Sensor Networks, 2*(3), 267–287. doi:10.1080/15501320600642718

ADDITIONAL READING

Akyildiz, I. F., Su, W., Sankarsubramaniam, Y., & Cayirci, E. (2002). A survey on sensor networks. *IEEE Communications Magazine, 40*(8), 102–114. doi:10.1109/MCOM.2002.1024422

Al-Karaki, J. N., & Kamal, A. E. (2004). Routing techniques in wireless sensor networks: A survey. *IEEE Wireless Communications, 11*(6), 6–28. doi:10.1109/MWC.2004.1368893

Chen, R. C., Hsieh, C. F., & Huang, Y. F. (2009). A new method for intrusion detection on hierarchical wireless sensor networks. In *Proceedings of the 3rd International Conference on Ubiquitous Information Management and Communication (ICUIMC 2009),* (pp. 238-245). New York, NY: ACM.

Dai, T. T., & Agbinya, J. I. (2010). Early and lightweight distributed detection of node replication attack in sensor networks. In *Proceedings of the 2010 IEEE Wireless Communications and Networking Conference (WCNC 2010),* (pp. 1-6). Los Alamitos, CA: Conference Publishing Services.

Li, M., Lou, W., & Ren, K. (2010). Data security and privacy in wireless body area networks. *IEEE Wireless Communications, 17*(1), 51–58. doi:10.1109/MWC.2010.5416350

Liu, A., & Ning, P. (2008). TinyECC: A configurable library for elliptic curve cryptography in wireless sensor networks. In *Proceedings of the 7th International Conference on Information Processing in Sensor Networks (IPSN 2008),* (pp. 245-256). Los Alamitos, CA: IEEE Computer Society Press.

Loo, C. E., Ng, M. Y., Leckie, C., & Planiswami, M. (2006). Intrusion detection for routing attacks in sensor networks. *International Journal of Distributed Sensor Networks, 2*(4), 313–332. doi:10.1080/15501320600692044

Lopez, J., Roman, R., & Alcaraz, C. (2009). Analysis of security threats, requirements, technologies, and standards in wireless sensor networks. *Lecture Notes in Computer Science, 5705*, 289–338. doi:10.1007/978-3-642-03829-7_10

Machado, R., & Tekinay, S. (2008). A survey of game-theoretic approaches in wireless sensor networks. *Computer Networks, 53*, 3047–3061. doi:10.1016/j.gaceta.2008.07.003

Maheshwari, R., Gao, J., & Das, S. R. (2007). Detecting wormhole attacks in wireless networks using connectivity information. In *Proceedings of the 26th IEEE International Conference on Computer Communications (INFOCOM 2007),* (pp. 107-115). Los Alamitos, CA: Conference Publishing Services.

Meulenaer, G. D., Gosset, F., Standaert, F., & Pereira, O. (2008). On the cost of communication and cryptography in wireless sensor networks. In *Proceedings of the 4ᵗʰ IEEE International Conference on Wireless and Mobile Computing, Networking & Communication (WiMob 2008),* (pp. 580-585). Los Alamitos, CA: Conference Publishing Services.

Naït-Abdesselam, F. N., Bensaou, B., & Taleb, T. (2008). Detecting and avoiding wormhole attacks in WSNs. *IEEE Communications Magazine, 46*(4), 127–132. doi:10.1109/MCOM.2008.4481351

Ni, J., Zhou, L., & Ravishankar, C. V. (2010). Dealing with random and selective attacks in wireless sensor systems. *ACM Transactions on Sensor Networks, 6*(2), 15:1-15:40.

Onat, I., & Miri, A. (2005). An intrusion detection system for wireless sensor networks. In *Proceedings of the IEEE International Conference on Wireless and Mobile Computing, Networking, and Communications, 2005 (WiMob 2005),* (pp. 253-259). Los Alamitos, CA: Conference Publishing Services.

Roman, R., & Alcaraz, C. (2007). Applicability of public key infrastructures in wireless sensor networks. *Lecture Notes in Computer Science, 4582,* 313–320. doi:10.1007/978-3-540-73408-6_22

Roman, R., Alcaraz, C., & Lopez, J. (2007). A survey of cryptographic primitives and implementations for hardware-constrained sensor network nodes. *Mobile Networks and Applications, 12*(4), 231–244. doi:10.1007/s11036-007-0024-2

Roman, R., & Lopez, J. (2009). Integrating wireless sensor networks and the internet: A security analysis. *Internet Research, 19*(2), 246–259. doi:10.1108/10662240910952373

Stankovic, J. A., & Wood, A. D. (2005). A taxonomy for denial-of-service attacks in wireless sensor networks. In Ilyas, M., & Mahgoub, I. (Eds.), *Handbook of Sensor Networks: Compact Wireless and Wired Sensing Systems.* Boca Raton, FL: CRC Press.

Sun, K., Liu, A., Xu, R., Ning, P., & Maughan, W. D. (2009). Securing network access in wireless sensor networks. In *Proceedings of the Second ACM Conference on Wireless Network Security (WiSec 2009),* (pp. 261-268). New York, NY: ACM.

Xie, M., Han, S., Tian, B., & Parvin, S. (2011). Anomaly detection in wireless sensor networks: A survey. *Journal of Network and Computer Applications.*

Xiong, X., Wong, D. S., & Deng, X. (2010). TinyPairing: A fast and lightweight pairing-based cryptographic library for wireless sensor networks. In *Proceedings 2010 IEEE Wireless Communications and Networking Conference (WCNC 2010).* Los Alamitos, CA: Conference Publishing Services.

Ye, F., Luo, H., & Lu, S. (2005). Statistical en-route filtering of injected false data in sensor networks. *IEEE Journal on Selected Areas in Communications, 23*(4), 839–850. doi:10.1109/JSAC.2005.843561

Zhang, J., & Varadharajan, V. (2008). A new security scheme for wireless sensor networks. In *Proceedings 2008 IEEE Global Telecommunications Conference,* (pp. 128-132). Los Alamitos, CA: Conference Publishing Services.

Zhang, Q., Yu, T., & Ning, P. (2008). A framework for identifying compromised nodes in wireless sensor networks. *ACM Transactions on Information and System Security, 11*(3), 1–37. doi:10.1145/1341731.1341733

Zhu, S., Setia, S., Jajodia, S., & Ning, P. (2007). Interleaved hop-by-hop authentication against false data injection attacks in sensor networks. *ACM Transactions on Sensor Networks, 3*(3), 14:1-14:33.

KEY TERMS AND DEFINITIONS

Active Attack: An attack in which the attacker takes offensive action to disrupt the normal functionality of the WSN.

Denial of Service Attack: An active attack that seeks to make resources of a particular WSN node or group of WSN nodes, unavailable to their intended users.

Eavesdropping: The act of monitoring the communication channel in order to intercept sensor data and/or routing information being exchanged between sensor nodes or between sensor nodes and the Sink.

IDS Agent: Active component of an IDS, which may be resident in all sensor nodes or a specialized sensor node, that is used to implement the IDS paradigm. An IDS Agent works in three phases: the collection phase, during which network data is collected; the detection phase, during which some detection policy is applied to the collected network data to find intrusions; the response phase, during which alerts and defensive actions may be taken in the case where an anomaly is detected.

Intrusion Detection System (IDS): A system that monitors network activity for malicious behavior and takes actions to report and mitigate it.

Passive Attack: An attack in which the attacker attempts to obtain information about the WSN and the sensor data it is collecting, without being discovered.

Traffic Analysis: Analysis of data flowing through a WSN in order to obtain knowledge of the network topology, the location of sensor nodes performing critical tasks, and the location of the Sink itself.

Wireless Sensor Network (WSN): A wireless network consisting of spatially distributed autonomous sensors that monitor physical or environmental conditions and pass the collected data back to a central location, called the Base Station or Sink, in a cooperative manner.

Chapter 8
Clustering in Wireless Sensor Networks:
Context–Aware Approaches

Enamul Haque
Bangladesh Agricultural University, Bangladesh

Norihiko Yoshida
Saitama University, Japan

ABSTRACT

Applications of Wireless Sensor Networks (WSN) have been expanded from industrial operation to daily common use. With the pace of development, a good number of state-of-the-art routing protocols have been proposed for WSN. Among many of these protocols, hierarchical or cluster-based protocol technique is adopted from the wired network because of its scalability, better manageability, and implicit energy efficiency. In this chapter, the authors have surveyed Low Energy Adaptive Clustering Hierarchy, Power-Efficient Gathering in Sensor Information Systems, Adaptive Periodic Threshold-Sensitive Energy Efficient Sensor Network, and Hybrid Energy-Efficient Distributed Routing Protocols. These protocols exhibit notable characteristics and advantages compared to their contemporaries. Again, context aware computing and applications have been greatly emphasized in recent articles by renowned technologists. This approach is considered as a momentous technology that will change the way of interaction with information devices. Accordingly, context aware clustering technique carries a great deal of importance among WSN routing protocols. Therefore, the authors have investigated noteworthy context aware routing protocols such as: Context Adaptive Clustering, Data-Aware Clustering Hierarchy, Context-Aware Clustering Hierarchy, and Context-Aware Multilayer Hierarchical Protocol. Their investigation and analysis of these protocols has been included in this chapter with useful remarks. Context awareness is considered an integral part of Body Sensor Networks (BSN), which is one kind of WSN. Thus, the authors have also discussed issues related to context aware techniques used in BSN.

DOI: 10.4018/978-1-4666-0161-1.ch008

Figure 1. Sensor nodes of WSN. (Source: Crossbow Inc. [left & right], Sentilla Corp. [middle])

WIRELESS SENSOR NETWORKS (WSN): AN INTRODUCTION

Advancement of Micro-Electro-Mechanical Systems (MEMS) and wireless networking has led to a sort of revolution in the development of sensor technology. Sensor nodes are getting smaller in size and smarter in functionality. Each of these sensors generally includes one or more sensing units, a data processing unit and a wireless communication unit. The sensing unit or units of a sensor node measure ambient conditions of surrounding and transform those into an electrical signal. Such ambient conditions may be temperature, humidity, acoustic, seismographic data of the environment, or may be motion, direction of living beings. Based on application and capability, that electrical signal is processed to reveal some vicinity properties or compressed to reduce communication overhead. Then, the communication unit wirelessly sends such data towards a central control directly or via other sensors. This central control is often regarded as a sink or base station. In this way, these sensor nodes form an ad-hoc network which is referred as Wireless Sensor Networks (WSN).

Some physical characteristics of sensor nodes often differ depending on applications. However, a common characteristic of WSN is that the deployment is usually in physical environment. As the sensory range is quite limited, a large number of sensors are needed to be deployed to get complete area coverage or accurate information. Regarding the size and weight of sensor nodes,

they are needed to be as small as possible. There are commercially available sensors the size of a matchbox (Crossbow Inc., 2010) or even the size of a coin (Crossbow Inc., 2010) as shown in Figure 1. In the military domain, cheap and cubic centimeter sized sensor nodes are aimed to be developed which can be heavily deployed in larger areas (Warneke, et al., 2001). And, the weight is becoming more suitable for easy deployment and longer sustainment. For commercial applications, cost is a major issue. Costs already have fallen sharply compared to products a decade ago. With rapid technological advancement, it is expected that sensors will be cheaper and more affordable in the near future.

One of the key characteristics of sensor nodes is that they are energy constrained. Typically sensor nodes rely on finite energy sources like batteries. Due to the massive numbers deployed and remote, unattended positions, replacements of batteries are quite impossible. Harvesting energy from the environment is currently a promising but under-developed research area. Moreover, expectancy of longer lifetime of sensor nodes has put researchers to work on every possible aspect of sensor nodes in gaining energy efficiency. Other key characteristics include limited computation and communication capability. The processing unit usually has an 8-bit to 32-bit microcontroller with 256 Kbytes to 512 Kbytes programmable flash. Therefore, there are limitations in the amount of data to be processed and processing criteria. Some existing sensors use 2.4

GHz or 916 MHz channels and promise to provide a communication range between 75 to 150 meters outdoors and 20 to 30 meters indoors. However, in actual deployment, such communication range cannot be obtainable due to different overheads (Kim, et al., 2007). Another key issue is to make WSN data available to the human observers or control applications. Often it is possible by connecting WSN to a fixed communication infrastructure via wireless LAN, satellite network or cellular network. To do this, one or more gateways are necessary to carry the inter communication. Sometimes, one of the sensor nodes acts as a gateway or in other cases, specialized gateway devices such as PDAs and laptops are used. In either case, gateways have two interfaces, one with the WSN and another with the communication infrastructure. As gateways are expected to have more energy and communication capability, they sometimes carry the additional burden of the WSN. Due to the advancement of WSN, applications have been expanded to numerous diverse fields (Arampatzis, et al., 2005). These applications can be classified into two broad categories (Culler, et al., 2004), namely, monitoring space and monitoring targets. The first category includes applications such as habitat monitoring, precision agriculture, electronic surveillance, and intelligent security systems. The latter category is comprised of applications like object tracking, structural monitoring, terrain mapping, etc. There is another type of category that is hybrid WSN. In Hybrid WSN, interaction between targets and with surrounding environment facilitate in emergency management such as in nuclear plants, mining, etc. Some major applications of WSN are described below:

Environmental monitoring: WSN can be deployed to gather environmental data from a specific geographic region. Already there are many such deployments. For example, WSNs have been deployed in Ecuador to monitor volcanic activities at different times (Allen, et al., 2006).

Security applications: Key public infrastructures, nuclear power plants can be secured by integrating networks of video, acoustic, and other sensors. Due to availability and affordable price, smaller versions of such security systems are becoming more and more popular.

Military applications: Early WSN research actually started on the military domain first. In this domain, there are some wide categories of usage such as battlefield coordination and tracking enemy vehicles (Abdelzaher, et al., 2004).

Medical and health monitoring: In health care applications, individual sensors were used to get patients' physiological information such as electrocardiograms and electroencephalograms in real time. Another significant use in health care is providing basic medical services for elderly patients by collaborating between WSN and other appliances.

Industrial control management: Industrial applications have gotten much attention because WSN can be used as a means of lowering cost, improving machines, and providing better maintainability. Sensors can be implemented within and inside the machineries where human access in not possible.

Intelligent environment: WSN is applicable not only outside or as independent but also can be within existing systems. For example, motor vehicles are now manufactured with a number of sensors in components like the accelerator pedal and brake pedal that form a network to deliver precise vehicular status information.

ROUTING IN WSN

Routing in WSN is quite challenging due to its inherent constraints and basic characteristics that

Figure2. A typical cluster-based wireless sensor network scenario

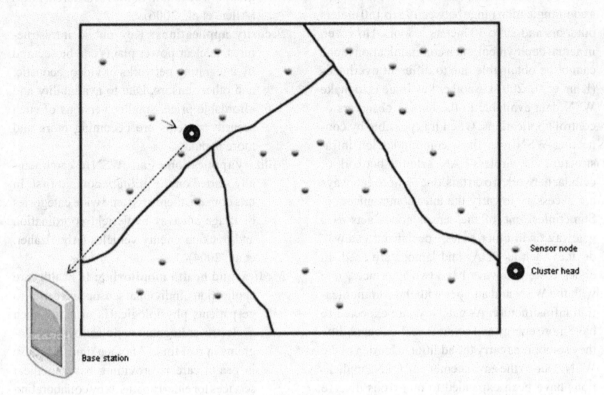

distinguish WSN from other wireless networks. The absence of a global addressing scheme, characteristic of data flow, a single destination, and resource constraints have made routing a difficult task. A handful of routing protocols have already been proposed for WSN. These protocols can be broadly categorized into four different types (Al-Karaki & Kamal, 2004), namely, data centric, hierarchical or cluster-based, location-aware, and data flow or Quality of Service (QoS) based.

Hierarchical or Cluster-Based Routing

In a hierarchical routing, sensor nodes are assembled into groups called clusters (Figure 2). Every node in a cluster has usually a single point of communication that is a Cluster Head (CH). Sometimes a normal node performs this duty or higher residual energy nodes are assigned. Such

a CH can be elected by the sensor nodes or pre-assigned by the network designer. Tasks of a CH include the processing of member node's data and long-range communication. CHs usually communicate with the Base Station (BS) directly or in multi-hop fashion. Cluster membership may or may not change during network lifetime. In some cases, CHs are further grouped for a higher level hierarchy.

The hierarchical or cluster-based protocol technique is originally derived from the wired network to wireless network because it offers a number of advantages. Such as:

1. Clustering keeps routing table of individual nodes quite short by localizing route setup within clusters (Akkaya, et al., 2005).
2. Clustering technique preserves bandwidth and avoids congestion by managing inter-

cluster communication only through cluster heads.

3. It is easier to maintain topology as nodes usually communicate with cluster head only. (Hou, 2005).

4. Cluster heads can aggregate a packet based on defined criteria. Thus, this technique reduces redundant packets (Dasgupta, et al., 2003).

5. Special node management strategies such as node activity optimization or scheduling scheme can be implemented which can make nodes energy efficient.

The formation of hierarchical structure significantly increases the overall system scalability, system lifetime, and energy efficiency. The activities of such protocols can be layered into two phases–first, selection of cluster heads and cluster boundary and second, routing activity. Among many proposed cluster-based protocols, Low Energy Adaptive Clustering Hierarchy (Heinzelman, et al., 2000), Power-Efficient Gathering in Sensor Information Systems (Lindsey & Raghavendra, 2002), Adaptive Periodic Threshold-Sensitive Energy Efficient Sensor Network Protocol (Manjeshwar & Agrawal, 2002), and the Hybrid Energy-Efficient Distributed Clustering (Younis & Fahmy, 2004) routing protocols have notable characteristics and advantages. Below three major hierarchical protocols are discussed.

Low Energy Adaptive Clustering Hierarchy (LEACH)

LEACH (Heinzelman, et al., 2000) is the first hierarchical protocol in WSN. In many recent studies, it has been considered as the benchmark for other protocols. It has some distinctive characteristics like self-reconfiguration, adjustment of communication range according to distance, schedule of data transmission of individual nodes, etc. Moreover, unlike most proposed protocols, LEACH has been implemented on actual hardware

(MICAz sensor nodes) (Obashi, et al., 2007). It has some assumptions like fixed-base station location, energy constrained homogeneous nodes, and predetermined ratio of cluster heads among all nodes. The operation of LEACH is separated into a series of equal length time spans. In each of these time spans, cluster head selection and cluster formation and scheduling procedures are completed, respectively, at the very beginning. Cluster heads are selected based on a probabilistic value satisfying the condition that those nodes have not played that role previously. Upon receiving broadcasted advertisement messages from a single or multiple cluster heads, a node sends a joining declaration to the nearest cluster head. Cluster heads then create a TDMA schedule and notify its member nodes. This distributed cluster formation technique is depicted in Figure 3. The following data transmission phase has the larger chunk of each span, which is also divided into a number of equal frames. In each frame, there is a slot for every member node. Member nodes send data to cluster heads at their slot time. The cluster head aggregates the data and send to the base station. Despite significant advantages, LEACH also has to deal with some drawbacks such as:

*   Cluster head is selected based on probabilistic value. So there is a possibility that cluster heads will be repeatedly selected from one part of the network.
*   Cluster head role is not uniformly distributed. Thus, some of the nodes might be out of service quickly.

To overcome these, LEACH-C (Heinzelman, et al., 2002) was proposed imposing centralized control. Nevertheless, none of these two versions is concerned about the context of the environment. The framework of LEACH has been utilized in the development of other protocols (Lindsey & Raghavendra, 2002; Muruganathan, et al., 2005). Power Efficient Gathering in Sensor Information System (PEGASIS) has been proposed by Lind-

Figure3. Distributed cluster formation in LEACH

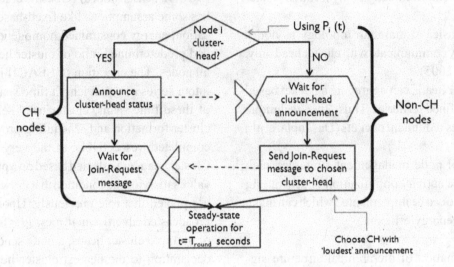

sey & Raghavendra (2002) that uses a greedy algorithm to construct a chain. Each node only transfers packets to the closest node on the same chain. But it inherits limitations of the multi hop model such as excessive delay for distant nodes. Again, a single leader can be a bottleneck for the whole network.

Threshold-Sensitive Energy Efficient Sensor Network (TEEN) and Adaptive TEEN (APTEEN) Protocol

Two protocols namely TEEN (Manjeshwar & Agrawal, 2001) and APTEEN (Manjeshwar & Agrawal, 2002) were proposed specifically for time critical applications. TEEN protocol forms clusters with closer nodes in a data centric approach. This approach continues until the BS has been reached. After cluster formation, CHs broadcast two thresholds, namely a hard threshold and a soft threshold. The hard threshold is the minimum possible threshold value of Sensed Value (SV). On the other hand, the soft threshold is the small change in SV that triggers the sending of SV. Thus, these thresholds reduce the number of transmissions significantly. Moreover, users can set the tradeoff ratio between energy efficiency

and data accuracy. Whenever CHs are changed, new threshold values have to be broadcast. The main drawback of TEEN is, if the threshold values are not received, nodes are out of communication. Again, this protocol is not very suitable for continuous monitoring, such as habitat monitoring. To overcome these drawbacks, TEEN was extended as APTEEN which combines both proactive and reactive policies. APTEEN CHs broadcast additional parameters such as Time Division Multiple Access (TDMA) schedules, count time, and desired attributes of the user's query. TDMA schedules contain a specific slot for each node. And, the count time is the maximum period between two successive SV reports. If the count time exceeds, the node will send the SV again whether the soft threshold has been reached or not. Despite the extension, there are some drawbacks to these two approaches such as overhead of threshold functions, complexity in multilevel hierarchies, and complicated attributed queries.

Hybrid Energy-Efficient Distributed Clustering (HEED)

HEED is a multi hop hybrid clustering protocol that utilizes residual energy information and node density to balance energy consumption within the network. This protocol has aimed to achieve longer network lifetime and lesser control overhead. HEED follows strict procedures to map nodes within non overlapping clusters. Energy consumption of each node is assumed not to be uniform. The protocol functionality is organized into three phases. At the initialization phase, the percentage of CHs has been set based on the residual energy to limit the number of CH announcements. In the subsequent repetition phase, every node goes through a number of iterations to find a CH with the least communication cost. Otherwise, the node declares itself as a CH. During this iterative state, a prospective CH continues with a 'tentative' status until a lower cost CH has been found. At the finalization phase, this status is changed to 'final' if the node can become a CH. Other nodes set their status appropriately. Thus, through these three phases, distributed CHs with non overlapping boundaries are selected based on residual energy and transmission cost. HEED protocol performs better in cases of longer network lifetimes. However, limited parameters in CH selection sometimes may impose constraints on the total system.

CONTEXT-AWARE APPROACHES IN WSN

The term "context-awareness" was introduced to the computational world more than a decade ago (Schilit, et al., 1994). Here, 'context' was referred to as location, identities of nearby people and objects, and changes to those objects. In the foremost application, software had been developed that could examine and react to an individual's changing context. The main purpose of such context awareness was to identify an individual's location, companion, and surrounding resources. Generally, context-awareness refers to linking changes in the environment with computer systems. This context awareness has not been utilized

in WSN until recently. A number of cluster-based routing protocols have been proposed based on the context aware approach. Moreover, this concept has gained much attention in other viable fields such as context aware computing and applications. In a keynote speech in September, 2010, at the Intel Developer Forum (Intel Newsroom, 2010), industry giant Intel's Chief Technology Officer greatly emphasized context aware computing as it will fundamentally change the nature of interaction with information devices. Such context aware computing can be defined as a system if it uses context to provide relevant information and/or services to the user, where relevancy depends on the user's task (Dey, 2001). Thus, context aware clustering carries a great deal of importance among WSN routing protocols. Exploitation of such context awareness in a WSN routing protocol has to meet some prerequisites during protocol development. These requirements include:

1. Autonomous or manual selection of context range for clustering has to be intelligent enough so that clusters are mutually exclusive and equally scattered as much as possible throughout the area.

2. If contextual data is not changing or changing by a negligible value, nodes should be aware of such patterns and utilize these patterns in sensor data traffic.

3. In case of creating multiple hierarchies based on context information, cluster heads have to be carefully selected to avoid multiple duties. Otherwise, multiple duties can be cause for early energy exhaustion of some nodes.

4. Context aware protocols have the competitive advantage of having data resemblance within a cluster. Thus, utilization of advances in node data processing techniques such as data fusion and data aggregation at the cluster heads can be considered an essential requirement of a smart context aware routing protocol in WSN.

Among proposed context aware protocols of such type, Context Adaptive Clustering (Jin & Park, 2006), Data-Aware Clustering Hierarchy – DACH (Wu, et al., 2008), Context-Aware Clustering Hierarchy (Haque, et al., 2009), and Context-Aware Multilayer Hierarchical Protocol (Haque, et al., 2010) are noteworthy for their features and applicability. Below these protocols are described briefly:

Context Adaptive Clustering (CAC)

CAC has been proposed with the aim for efficient data aggregation. CAC presents a simple, transparent, and decentralized algorithm and utilizes the high data correlation within clusters. In cluster formation, the number of initial clusters, tolerance parameter (range of context), and a threshold for re-clustering are manually determined. Authors have proposed a clustering mechanism that strives to form clusters of sensors with similar output data within the bounds of a given tolerance parameter. If a cluster head detects context value beyond the threshold, re-clustering is initiated. During the re-clustering operation, nearby nodes become a cluster head if they are on the list and broadcast re-clustering commands to their neighbors. In the other case, the nearby node joins if own context match with the new cluster head. If none of these two conditions matches, it stops propagating the re-clustering command. In the later data transmission phase, cluster heads aggregate data received from the nodes and send it to the base station. As clusters are formed with nodes gathering similar data, the simple data aggregation technique works well without introducing large errors. An expected benefit is to reduce energy consumption and to prolong network service life. This protocol shows impressive performance in an environment where the change of the surrounding context is quite gradual. On the contrary, the cluster head role has not been distributed, which might cause energy exhaustion of some nodes early. Again, there is no distinctness between the set-up and data

transmission phase. Besides, if the environmental phenomenon is changing rapidly, the algorithm might not be suitable. Thus, this algorithm's applicability is limited to certain fields only.

Data-Aware Clustering Hierarchy (DACH)

In DACH, authors have proposed a protocol that is data-aware, and cluster formation is based on distance between nodes. The protocol constructs a multilayer hierarchical structure and utilizes data similarities within clusters for query processing. Moreover, 'discrimination' functionality of data mining is effectively used in querying. It operates in three phases. At the initialization phase, the base station generates time series based on received data from all nodes. Based on time series, base station then calculates discrimination of each pair sensors. Lowest discrimination constitutes level 0 of the hierarchy of the structure. If the discrimination is higher than the specified threshold, nodes are included in the next higher level of the hierarchy. In the setup phase, base station receives energy information and generates paths in a bottom-up way. In this process, cluster heads are selected with highest residual energy. The data transmission phase is quite identical to previous two protocols. DACH shows better performance in the simulation. However, a closer look at this protocol reveals some unattended issues. In the selection of high residual cluster heads, the energy information must be shared among every node. Without having an active routing protocol, dissemination of such information is quite impossible unless being broadcasted. Broadcasting this information might significantly increase the traffic and ultimately will decrease energy efficiency. Moreover, the multilevel clustering hierarchy is not optimized in selecting cluster heads. As a result, in certain situations the cluster head role might be played by the same node in multiple levels, which may cause faster depletion of residual energy.

Figure4. Clustering algorithm in CACH

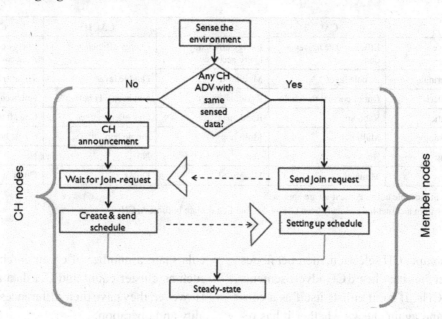

Context-Aware Clustering Hierarchy (CACH) and Context-Aware Multilayer Hierarchical Protocol (CAMHP)

CACH has been proposed with the aim to attain maximum energy efficiency. It forms clusters entirely based on the context of the environment and distribute cluster head role across the network symmetrically (Figure 4). In CACH, lifetime of the network is divided into some rounds like LEACH. After the initial deployment, nodes enter into the setup phase. Each node enlists itself to a cluster by exchanging advertisement messages with context information and join request messages. CH of each cluster is decided based on the earliest message propagation role among nodes. Next, CH sends a schedule for the current round to member nodes in a unidirectional manner. In the latter steady operation phase, each node sends its own data to the CH according to the slot time. In consecutive slots, upon sensing the environment, a node compares its current sensed value with the previous one. If there is no change in the value, the node does not send the data. CHs

sequentially aggregate data from member nodes into a single packet disregarding the empty slot. This aggregated packet is sent to the Base Station (BS) directly. On this end, BS keeps track of each member node in every cluster. So, an aggregated packet is being extracted and checked for any missing member node data. If so, BS assumes the current data content is the same as the previous one and continues its operation with the previous data. Upon forming a cluster in later rounds, a CH checks the role history of every member node. If all nodes within a cluster have already been a CH in previous rounds, this role history is erased; thus CHs become just like the initial stage. This technique ensures the CH role rotation that is responsible for uniform distribution of energy consumption across the network. Contrasting to other context aware protocols (Jin & Park, 2006, Wu, et al., 2008), CACH provides advantages like distinctive cluster formation, equal distribution of CH role, and data traffic optimization.

CAMHP is also context aware and utilizes a multilayer hierarchical structure to cover more area. After the initial deployment, nodes act the same as CACH for the selection of member nodes

Table 1. Comparison of context-aware protocol based on selected criteria

	CAC	DACH	CACH	CAMHP
Protocol objective	Efficient data aggregation	Energy efficiency + query accuracy	Energy efficiency	Energy efficiency + Area coverage
Degree of clustering	Double layer	Multilayer	Double layer	Tri layer
CH selection criteria*	Out of context threshold	Residual energy	Not been CH before**	Not been CH before**
CH role distribution	Random	Random	One after another	One after another
Inter-cluster topology	Multi hop	Multi hop	Single hop	Single hop
Query processing	No	Yes	No	No
Mobility	Minimal	Undefined	Quasi	Quasi

* All protocols in the table utilize context-aware approach.

** If all nodes within a cluster have already been CH, nodes that first declare becomes a CH.

and CHs. For super CH selection, member nodes check whether they have heard CH advertisements from all the CHs. If so, it enlists itself as a candidate node and again checks whether it has received any super CH advertisements or not. If so, the candidate proceeds with the duties of a member node. Otherwise, it declares itself as a super CH and broadcasts this message. This message is processed by the CHs only and assists them to identify the super CH. If a node has not heard CH advertisements from all the CHs, it proceeds with the normal duties of a member node. Thus CHs are hooked up with a single super CH to whom aggregated packets are sent. Duties of a super CH are same as CHs except it communicates directly to BS. CAMHP inherits all the advantages of CACH as well as covering more sensing area through additional hierarchy. However, in both CACH and CAMHP, the threshold for not sending sensed data in consecutive rounds is not well defined. Thus, prior measurement of environmental phenomena is needed before implementing these protocols. Moreover, in certain rounds, CHs with the farthest distance from super CHs or BSs were selected causing early energy exhaustion of those nodes. Thus, CH and super CH role distribution is not that effective sometimes.

Table 1 shows a comparison between CAC, DACH, CACH, and CAMHP based on selected criteria. These context-aware hierarchical protocols share a number of common characteristics such as cluster count and CH data aggregation. However, they have their differences in functionality and operation.

CONTEXT AWARENESS IN BODY SENSOR NETWORKS (BSN)

BSN has been on a peak of research effort in recent years due to the development of affordable sensors as well as urgency for early, accurate, and complete diagnosis. BSN, also known as Body Area Network (BAN), is one kind of WSN where sensors are wearable by humans. Typically BSN includes multiple miniature sensors that can measure the human body's physiological conditions such as blood pressure, temperature, glucose concentration, ph measurement, oxygen saturation level, etc. There is also a single Body Central Unit (BCU) or Local Processing Unit (LCU) that processes the sensory data, converts it to a readable format, and sends it to the health service infrastructure via Internet or cellular network (Ullah, et al., 2010). Compared to other types of WSN, BSN has some specific development criteria. As BSN is aimed to sense human body conditions, such sensing should be respectful and non invasive to human dignity as well as affordable and cost effective. Concurrent BSN research is dealing with a number of technical challenges like biosensor design, suitable power source, context awareness, and multi sensory data fusion (Lo & Yang, 2005). Among these challenges, context awareness plays a vital role for accurate and meaningful information extraction through BSN. Relying only on physiological information can often cause false detection due to motion artifacts and changes in the contextual environment. For example, a sudden heart beat increase may be due to jogging rather than cardiac arrest. Thus to acquire relevant information, context awareness must be incorporated with BSN.

Context Aware Techniques

To gather contextual information, classification of raw data is the first step. Raw data can be associated with a context profile through the means of user labels. Some classification techniques recognize context at a given instance in time and others utilize supervising layer to extract constant recognition of context. All together, context aware techniques can be categorized into three broad approaches (Korel & Koo, 2010):

Artificial Neural Network (ANN): Application of ANN in BSN is purely for clustering of sensed data. Generally two types of ANN are used such as: Kohonen Self-Organizing Map (KSOM) and KSOM with k-means. One of the notable advantages of using ANN is the capability of clustering despite the presence of noise in sensor data. Another advantage is inclusion of unsupervised training of input data. In the latter case, a BSN does not need to spend much time on training which makes BSN more feasible and adaptable in applications. There are numerous works on these two branches of ANN for utilization in BSN (Lagerholm, et al., 2000; Gao, et al., 2004; Thiemjarus, et al., 2006) and still ongoing to overcome limitations such as dealing with high dimension input data.

Bayesian Network (BN): BN is a directed graph model that can signify sensory data as random variables and directed arcs as their ca-

sual dependencies. BN follows an independence assumption between random variables that can promote higher accuracy in clustering. Advantages of using BN include computational efficiency, noise resiliency, and energy efficiency by feature selection. Researchers utilizing BN for deducing context in BSN have proposed systems based on either Naïve Bayes classifier (Korpipaa, et al., 2003; Tapia, et al., 2004) or BN with hidden node (Thiemjarus, et al., 2005).

Hidden Markov Models (HMM): In BSN context needs to be continually recognized throughout a time span not just at exact instances in time. With such requirements, HMM can be introduced at the supervising layer to build a model of context transition. Hence, HMM is more capable of modeling human behavior as it can recognize sequences of activities. The probabilistic model of HMM can also offer other advantages like handling of noisy sensor data and improved computational performance. Notable research works on HMM for BSN include Clarkson & Pentland (2000), Kautz et al. (2003), and Chen et al. (2005).

FUTURE SCOPE

Research on context aware routing protocols is a bit immature compared to other types of routing protocols of WSN. Therefore, many open issues still need to be addressed. Some key future scopes are described below:

1. As context-aware protocols are crucially dependent on different synchronous phases during operation, lightweight time synchronization is quite significant in real applications. Though, there are a good number of time synchronization protocols for WSN (Sundararaman, et al., 2005); yet there are still some critical open issues regarding accuracy, scalability, energy efficiency, and fault tolerance.

2. In the future, fewer nodes will be equipped with energy sources like batteries. Thus, it is expected that the majority of WSN nodes will rely either on powered mains or on energy harvesting. This will also profoundly affect any kind of routing design. Irrespective of routing protocol category, energy harvesting is definitely a significant challenge.

3. Actual deployment or real world implementation is quite important for WSN. Though simulation of protocols is an effective and reasonable way of testing, actual implementation can find many hidden design issues (Alippi, et al., 2008).

4. Prior measurement of environmental context for setting threshold is considered as an assumption in context aware protocols. Thus, there should be a suitable schemes to set and adjust threshold parameters upon initial deployment.

We have also discussed context awareness techniques in BSN. Future research issues in this domain include noise detection, adaptive learning, and appropriate feature selection (Korel & Koo, 2010). However, details of these issues are beyond the scope of this chapter.

CONCLUSION

In this chapter, we have first briefly focused on three prominent hierarchical protocols of WSN. As a recent trend, the context-aware technique has been applied in hierarchical protocols. Four such promising protocols are surveyed here and compared based on selected criteria. Designers of these protocols have discussed further development of their propositions in related publications. However, these protocols inherit various shortcomings which are concisely mentioned here. One of the most promising types of WSN is the BSN. Thus, context aware techniques of BSN are also briefly discussed according to the scope of this chapter.

It is expected that continual advancement of the context-aware approach will address the future issues and pave the way for smooth deployment of WSN in real world applications.

REFERENCES

Abdelzaher, T., Blum, B., Evans, D., George, J., George, S., & Gu, L. ... Wood, A. (2004). EnviroTrack: Towards an environmental computing paradigm for distributed sensor networks. In *Proceedings of the 24th International Conference on Distributed Computing Systems,* (pp. 582-589). IEEE Computer Society Press.

Al-Karaki, J. N., & Kamal, A. E. (2004). Routing techniques in wireless sensor networks: A survey. *IEEE Wireless Communications, 11*(6), 6–28. doi:10.1109/MWC.2004.1368893

Alippi, C., Camplani, R., Galperti, C., & Roveri, M. (2008). Effective design of WSNs: From the lab to the real world. In *Proceedings of the 3rd International Conference on Sensing Technology,* (pp. 1-9). IEEE Press.

Allen, G. W., Lorincz, K., Ruiz, M., Marcillo, O., Johnson, J., Lees, J., & Welsh, M. (2006). Deploying a Wireless sensor network on an active volcano. *IEEE Internet Computing,* 18–25. doi:10.1109/MIC.2006.26

Arampatzis, T., Lygeros, J., & Manesis, S. (2005). A survey of applications of wireless sensors and wireless sensor networks. In *Proceedings of the IEEE International Symposium on Intelligent Control,* (pp. 719-724). IEEE Press.

Chen, J., Kam, A. H., Zhang, J., Liu, N., & Shue, L. (2005). Bathroom activity monitoring based on sound. In *Proceedings of the 3rd International Conference on Pervasive Computing,* (pp. 47-61). Springer Publisher.

Clarkson, B., Mase, K., & Pentland, A. (2000). Recognizing user context via wearable sensors. In *Proceedings of the 4th International Symposium on Wearable Computers*, (pp. 69-76). IEEE Press.

Crossbow Inc. (2010a). *Product MicaZ*. Retrieved July 25, 2010, from http://www.xbow.com/Products/wproductsoverview.aspx.

Crossbow Inc. (2010b). *Product Mica2dot*. Retrieved July 25, 2010, from http://www.xbow.com/products/Product_pdf_files/Wireless_pdf/MICA2DOT_Datasheet.pdf.

Culler, D., Estrin, D., & Srivastava, M. (2004). Overview of sensor networks. In *Sensor Networks* (pp. 41–49). IEEE Computer Society Press.

Dey, A. K. (2001). Understanding and using context. *Personal and Ubiquitous Computing, 5*(1), 4–7. doi:10.1007/s007790170019

Gao, D., Madden, M., Schukat, M., Chambers, D., & Lyons, G. (2004). Arrhythmia identification from ECG signals with a neural network classifier based on a Bayesian framework. In *Proceedings of the 24th SGAI International Conference on Innovative Techniques and Applications of Artificial Intelligence*. IEEE Press.

Haque, M. E., Matsumoto, N., & Yoshida, N. (2009). Context-aware cluster-based hierarchical protocol for wireless sensor networks. *International Journal of Ad Hoc and Ubiquitous Computing, 4*(6), 23–37. doi:10.1504/IJAHUC.2009.028666

Haque, M. E., Matsumoto, N., & Yoshida, N. (2010). Utilizing multilayer hierarchical structure in context aware routing protocol for wireless sensor networks. *International Journal of Computational Science, 4*(1), 23–37.

Hartung, C., Han, R., Seielstad, C., & Holbrook, S. (2006). FireWxNet: A multitiered portable wireless system for monitoring weather conditions in wildland fire environments. In *Proceedings of the 4th International Conference on Mobile Systems*, (pp. 28-41). ACM Press.

Heinzelman, W. B., Chandrakasan, A. P., & Balakrishnan, H. (2000). Energy-efficient communication protocol for wireless microsensor networks. In *Proceedings of the 33rd Annual Hawaii International Conference on System Sciences*, (pp. 10). IEEE Computer Society Press.

Heinzelman, W. B., Chandrakasan, A. P., & Balakrishnan, H. (2002). An application-specific protocol architecture for wireless microsensor networks. *IEEE Transactions on Wireless Communications, 1*, 660–670. doi:10.1109/TWC.2002.804190

Hou, Y. T., Shi, Y., & Sherali, H. D. (2005). On energy provisioning and relay node placement for wireless sensor networks. *IEEE Transactions on Wireless Communications, 4*(5), 2579–2590. doi:10.1109/TWC.2005.853969

Intel. (2010). *Newsroom*. Retrieved December, 2010, http://newsroom.intel.com/community/intel_newsroom/blog/2010/09/15/context-awareness-to-radically-change-how-we-interact-with-technology.

Jin, G., & Park, M. (2006). CAC: Context adaptive clustering for efficient data aggregation in wireless sensor networks. *Lecture Notes in Computer Science, 3976*, 1132–1137. doi:10.1007/11753810_98

Kautz, H., Etzioni, O., Fox, D., & Weld, D. (2003). *Foundations of assisted cognition systems. Technical report CSE-02-AC-01*. Seattle, WA: University of Washington.

Kim, S., Pakzad, S., Culler, D., Demmel, J., Fenves, G., Glaser, S., & Turon, M. (2007). Health monitoring of civil infrastructures using wireless sensor networks. In *Proceedings of the 6th International Conference on Information Processing in Sensor Networks*, (pp. 254-263). ACM Press.

Korel, B. T., & Koo, S. G. M. (2010). A survey on context-aware sensing for body sensor networks. *Wireless Sensor Network, 2*(8), 571–583. doi:10.4236/wsn.2010.28069

Korpipaa, P., Koskinen, M., Peltola, J., Makela, S. M., & Seppanen, T. (2003). Bayesian approach to sensor-based context awareness. *Personal and Ubiquitous Computing, 7*(2), 113–124. doi:10.1007/s00779-003-0237-8

Lagerholm, M., Peterson, C., Braccini, G., Edenbrandt, L., & Sornmo, L. (2000). Clustering ECG complexes using her-mite functions and self-organizing maps. *IEEE Transactions on Bio-Medical Engineering, 47*(7), 838–848. doi:10.1109/10.846677

Lindsey, S., & Raghavendra, C. S. (2002). PEGASIS: Power efficient gathering in sensor information systems. In *Proceedings of the IEEE Aerospace Conference*, (pp. 1125-1130). IEEE Computer Society Press.

Lo, B., & Yang, G. Z. (2005). Key technical challenges and current implementations of body sensor networks. In *Proceedings of the 2nd International Workshop on Body Sensor Networks*, (pp. 1-5). IEEE Press.

Manjeshwar, A., & Agrawal, D. P. (2001). TEEN: A protocol for enhanced efficiency in wireless sensor networks. In *Proceedings of the 1st International Workshop on Parallel and Distributed Computing Issues in Wireless Networks and Mobile Computing*, (pp.2009-2015). IEEE Computer Society Press.

Manjeshwar, A., & Agrawal, D. P. (2002). APTEEN: A hybrid protocol for efficient routing and comprehensive information retrieval in wireless sensor networks. In *Proceedings of the Parallel and Distributed Processing Symposium*, (pp. 195-202). IEEE Computer Society Press.

Muruganathan, S. D., Ma, D. C. F., Bhasin, R. I., & Fapojuwo, A. O. (2005). A centralized energy-efficient routing protocol for wireless sensor networks. *IEEE Communications Magazine*, 8–13. doi:10.1109/MCOM.2005.1404592

Obashi, Y., Kokogawa, T., Zheng, Y., Chen, H., Mineno, H., & Mizuno, T. (2007). Evaluation of metadata-based data aggregation scheme in clustering wireless sensor networks. *Lecture Notes in Artificial Intelligence, 4694*, 477–483.

Schilit, B., Adams, N., & Want, R. (1994). Context-aware computing applications. In *Proceedings of the IEEE Workshop on Mobile Computing Systems and Applications*, (pp. 85-90). IEEE Press.

Sundararaman, B., Buy, U., & Kshemkalyani, A. (2005). Clock synchronization for wireless sensor networks: A survey. *Ad Hoc Networks, 3*(3), 281–323. doi:10.1016/j.adhoc.2005.01.002

Tapia, E. M., Intille, S. S., & Larson, K. (2004). Activity recognition in the home using simple and ubiquitous sensors. In *Proceedings of the 2nd International Conference on Pervasive Computing*, (pp. 158-175). Springer Publisher.

Thiemjarus, S., King, R., Lo, B., Gilles, D., & Yang, G. Z. (2005). A noise resilient distributed inference framework for body sensor networks. In *Proceedings of the 3rd International Conference on Pervasive Computing*, (pp. 13-18). Springer Publisher.

Thiemjarus, S., Lo, B. P. L., & Yang, G. Z. (2006). A spatio-temporal architecture for context-aware sensing. In *Proceedings of the IEEE International Workshop on Wearable and Implantable Body Sensor Networks,* (pp. 191-194). IEEE Computer Society Press.

Ullah, S., Higgins, H., Braem, B., Latre, B., Blondia, C., & Moerman, I. (2010). A comprehensive survey of wireless body area networks: On PHY, MAC, and network layers solutions. *Journal of Medical Systems*, 1–30.

Warneke, B., Last, M., Liebowitz, B., & Pister, K. S. J. (2001). Smartdust: Communicating with a cubic-millimeter computer. *IEEE Transactions on Computers*, *45*(1), 44–51.

Wu, X., Wang, P., Wang, W., & Shi, B. (2008). Data-aware clustering hierarchy for wireless sensor networks. *Lecture Notes in Computer Science*, *5012*, 795–802. doi:10.1007/978-3-540-68125-0_77

Younis, O., & Fahmy, S. (2004). HEED: A hybrid, energy-efficient, distributed clustering approach for ad-hoc sensor networks. *IEEE Transactions on Mobile Computing*, *3*(4), 366–379. doi:10.1109/TMC.2004.41

KEY TERMS AND DEFINITIONS

Body Sensor Networks: A specific class of WSN is Body Sensor Networks (BSN) that represents an emerging platform for many human-centered applications, spanning from medical to sports performance monitoring, gaming, and social networking.

Context-Aware Clustering: It is a clustering technique that is used in WSN routing protocols. Here, context' is referred as location, identities of nearby people and objects, and changes to those objects.

Context-Aware Computing: Context aware computing and applications have been greatly emphasized in recent articles by renowned technologist. This approach is considered as a momentous technology that will change the way of interaction with information devices.

Wireless Sensor Networks: Wireless Sensor Networks (WSN) are inherently distributed in nature and distributed across the globe. A WSN consists of spatially distributed sensor nodes to cooperatively monitor physical, environmental, or human conditions such as temperature, sound, vibration, pressure, motion, heart rate, and blood pressure.

Chapter 9
A Comparative Analysis of Hierarchical Routing Protocols in Wireless Sensor Networks

Anar Abdel Hady
Electronics Research Institute, Cairo, Egypt

Sherine M. Abd El-kader
Electronics Research Institute, Cairo, Egypt

Hussein S. Eissa
Electronics Research Institute, Cairo, Egypt

Ashraf Salem
Ain Shams University, Cairo, Egypt

Hossam M.A. Fahmy
Ain Shams University, Cairo, Egypt

ABSTRACT

Wireless Sensor Networks (WSNs) consist of small nodes with sensing, computation, and wireless communications capabilities. Many routing, power management, and data dissemination protocols have been specifically designed for WSNs. Routing protocols in WSNs might differ depending on the application and network architecture. However, wireless sensor networks have several restrictions, e.g. limited energy supply, limited computing power, and limited bandwidth, and hence, one of the main design goals of WSNs is to carry out data communication while trying to prolong the lifetime of the network and prevent connectivity degradation by employing efficient energy management techniques. This chapter will give a detailed description of the characteristics of routing in wireless sensor networks; it describes the routing protocols used in these networks pointing out the advantages and disadvantages of each.

DOI: 10.4018/978-1-4666-0161-1.ch009

INTRODUCTON

Due to the recent development in the field of Micro Electrical Mechanical Systems (MEMS) (Min, Cho, Shih, Bhardwaj, & Sinha, 2001; Rabaey, Patel, & Roundy, 2000) radio communication has made it possible to form small tiny nodes with the capability of sensing, computing, and communication in a short range. They are capable of forming an autonomous intelligent network which functions with unattended management. Technology reviews at MIT and Global Future say that sensor technology is one of the ten emerging technologies that will change the world (Werff, 2003). The network is capable of monitoring activities and phenomenon which cannot be monitored easily by human beings, such as the site of a nuclear accident, some chemical field monitoring, or environment monitoring for longer periods of time. Wireless sensor networks offer information about remote structures, widespread environmental changes, etc. in unknown and inhospitable terrains (Manjeshwar, Zeng, & Agrawal, 2002). Also, the low cost makes it possible to have a network of hundreds or thousands of these sensors, thereby enhancing the reliability and accuracy of data and the area coverage.

Networking unattended sensor nodes are expected to have significant impact on the efficiency of many military and civil applications such as combat field surveillance, security, and disaster management. These systems process data gathered from multiple sensors to monitor events in an area of interest. For example, in a disaster management setup, a large number of sensors can be dropped by a helicopter. Networking these sensors can assist rescue operations by locating survivors, identifying risky areas and making the rescue crew more aware of the overall situation. Such application of sensor networks not only can increase the efficiency of rescue operations but also ensure the safety of the rescue crew. On the military side, applications of sensor networks are numerous. For example, the use of networked

set of sensors can limit the need for personnel involvement in the usually dangerous reconnaissance missions. In addition, sensor networks can enable a more civic use of landmines by making them remotely controllable and target-specific in order to prevent harming civilians and animals. Security applications of sensor networks include intrusion detection and criminal hunting (Akkaya & Younis, 2005; AL-Karaki & Kamal, 2004).

There are a number of advantages of wireless sensor networks over wired ones such as ease of deployment (reducing installation cost), extended range (network of tiny sensors can be distributed over a wider region), fault-tolerance (failure of one node does not affect the network operation), self-organization (the nodes can have the capability to reconfigure themselves) But there are a few inherent limitations of wireless media such as low bandwidth, error prone transmissions, collision free channel access requirements etc. Also, since the wireless nodes are mostly mobile and are not connected in any way to a constant power supply, they derive energy from a personal battery. This limits the amount of energy available to the nodes. In addition, since these sensor nodes are deployed in places where it is difficult to either replace individual nodes or their batteries, it is desirable to increase the longevity of the network and preferable that all the nodes die together so that the whole area could be replenished by a new set of tiny nodes. Finding individual dead nodes and then replacing those nodes selectively would require pre-planned deployment and eliminate some advantages of these networks (Manjeshwar, Zeng, & Agrawal, 2002).

Routing protocols are the implementation of algorithms used to carry out the communication across an internetwork. A routing protocol uses specified metrics (energy, bandwidth, delay, etc) to determine which path to utilize to transmit a packet. Routing in wireless sensor networks is very challenging due to the following inherent characteristics that distinguish these networks from other wireless networks like mobile ad hoc networks or cellular networks:

- **Large number of sensor nodes:** This large number makes it impossible to build a global addressing scheme for deployment of sensor nodes as overhead of ID maintenance of sensor nodes will be high.
- **Numerous sources:** Almost all applications of sensor networks require flow of data from multiple sources to a particular base station.
- **Tight constraints:** Sensor nodes are tightly constrained in energy, processing, and storage capacities and thus, they require careful resource management.
- **Mobility:** Most sensor nodes in WSNs are stationary, however in some applications nodes may be allowed to move.
- **Sensor networks are application specific:** Design requirements of a sensor network change with application.
- **Position awareness:** Position awareness of sensor nodes is important since data collection is normally based on the location.
- **Data redundancy:** Data collected by many sensors in WSNs is typically based on common phenomena; hence there is a high probability that this data has some redundancy. Such redundancy needs to be exploited by the routing protocols to improve energy and bandwidth utilization.

And that is why routing in wireless sensor networks is a very important issue to be studied extensively so as to make the best use of such networks while confronting its limitations.

The rest of the chapter is organized as follows: Section 2 specifies the routing challenges and design constraints facing routing protocols in wireless sensor networks so as to carry out data communication while trying to prolong the lifetime of the network. Section 3 is the core of the chapter and will give a detailed survey on routing protocols in wireless sensor networks while focusing on hierarchical protocols as it has proved a lot of advantages in such networks. We will start this section by classifying most of the known protocols in wireless sensor networks under one of three classifications Flat networks routing, Hierarchical networks routing or Location based routing. Section 4 gives a comparative analysis for existing hierarchical routing protocols through a comparison table. Section 5 gives an overview on the recent approaches for research in hierarchical routing. Section 6 lists the lessons learnt from this chapter. Section 7 gives the future directions in this research area. Section 6 lists the conclusions extracted from this chapter.

Routing Challenges and Design Constraints in Wireless Sensor Networks

Wireless sensor networks have several restrictions, e.g. limited energy supply, limited computing power and limited bandwidth, and hence, one of the main design goals of WSNs is to carry out data communication while trying to prolong the lifetime of the network and prevent connectivity degradation by employing aggressive energy management techniques. The following are some design issues that affect routing process in WSNs: (Akkaya & Younis, 2005; AL-Karaki & Kamal, 2004)

1. Network Dynamics

There are three main components in a sensor network. These are the sensor nodes, sink and monitored events. Aside from the very few setups that utilize mobile sensors (Subramanian & Katz, 2000), most of the network architectures assume that sensor nodes are stationary. On the other hand, supporting the mobility of sinks or cluster-heads (gateways) is sometimes considered necessary (Ye, et al., 2002). Routing messages from or to moving nodes is more challenging since route stability becomes an important optimization factor, in addition to energy, bandwidth etc. The sensed event can be either dynamic or static depending on the application (Tilak, et al., 2002). For instance, in a target detection/tracking application, the event (phenomenon) is dynamic whereas forest monitoring for early fire prevention is an example of static events.

2. Node Deployment

Node deployment can be either deterministic or randomized. In deterministic deployment, the sensors are manually placed and data is routed through pre-determined paths. On the other hand, in random deployment, the sensors are scattered randomly in an ad hoc manner (Sohrabi, et al., 2000; Heinzelman, Chandrakasan, & Balakrishnan, 2000; Younis, Youssef, & Arisha, 2002; Manjeshwar & Agrawal, 2001).

3. Lowering energy consumption without losing accuracy

During the creation of network infrastructure, setting up the routes is greatly influenced by energy considerations. Since the transmission power of a wireless radio is proportional to distance squared or even higher order in the presence of obstacles, multi-hop routing will consume less energy than direct communication. However, multi-hop routing introduces significant overhead for topology management and medium access control. Therefore, direct routing would perform well enough if all the nodes were very close to the sink but most of the time sensors are scattered randomly over the area and multi-hop routing becomes unavoidable (Heinzelman, Chandrakasan, & Balakrishnan, 2000).

4. Data Delivery Models

The data delivery model to the sink can be continuous, event-driven, query-driven or hybrid depending on the application of the sensor network (Tilak, et al., 2002). In the continuous delivery model, each sensor sends data periodically. In event-driven and query driven models, the transmission of data is triggered when an event occurs or a query is generated by the sink. Some networks use a hybrid model proposing a combination of continuous, event driven and query-driven data delivery. The routing protocol is highly influenced by the data delivery model, especially with regard to the minimization of energy consumption and route stability.

5. Node Capabilities

In a sensor network, different functionalities can be associated with the sensor nodes. Depending on the application a node can be dedicated to a particular special function such as relaying, sensing and aggregation since engaging the three functionalities at the same time on a node might quickly drain the energy of that node. Some of the hierarchical protocols designate a cluster-head different from the normal sensors. While some networks have picked cluster-heads from the deployed sensors (Heinzelman, Chandrakasan, & Balakrishnan, 2000; Lindsey & Raghavendra, 2002; Lindsey, Raghavendra, & Sivalingam, 2001), in other applications a cluster-head is more powerful than the sensor nodes in terms of energy, bandwidth and memory (Subramanian & Katz, 2000; Younis, Youssef, & Arisha, 2002). In such cases, the burden of transmission to the sink and aggregation is handled by the cluster-head.

6. Fault Tolerance

The failure of sensor nodes should not affect the overall task of the sensor network, so, if many nodes fail, MAC and routing protocols must accommodate formation of new links and routes to the data collection base stations. This may require actively adjusting transmit powers and signaling rates on the existing links to reduce energy consumption, or rerouting packets through regions of the network where more energy is available. Therefore, multiple levels of redundancy may be needed in a fault-tolerant sensor network.

7. Scalability

The number of sensor nodes in a wireless sensor network may be in the order of hundreds or thousands, or more. Any routing scheme must be able to work with this huge number of sensor nodes. Also sensor network routing protocols should be able to scale enough to respond to events in the environment.

8. Transmission Media

Communicating nodes in sensor networks are linked by a wireless medium. And so it should deal with the traditional problems associated with a wireless channel (e.g., fading, high error rate) so that it doesn't affect the operation of the network. Related to the transmission media is the design of Medium Access Control (MAC). One approach of MAC design for sensor networks is to use TDMA based protocols that conserve more energy compared to contention based protocols like CSMA (e.g., IEEE 802.11). Bluetooth technology can also be used in sensor networks.

9. Connectivity

Sensor nodes are expected to be highly connected. However, the network topology may vary and the network size may shrink due to sensor node failures. Also, connectivity depends on the, usually random, distribution of nodes.

10. Area Coverage

Each sensor node in a wireless sensor network obtains a limited view of the environment both in range and in accuracy. Hence, it can only cover a limited physical area of the environment, some-

thing which has to be considered in designing a routing protocol.

11. Data Aggregation/Fusion

Since different sensor nodes may generate redundant data, similar packets from multiple nodes can be aggregated so that the number of transmissions is reduced. Data aggregation is the combination of data from different sources according to a certain aggregation function, e.g., duplicate suppression, minima, maxima and average (Krishnamachari, Estrin, Wicker, 2002). Also signal processing methods can also be used for data aggregation. In this case, it is referred to as data fusion where a node is capable of producing a more accurate output signal by using some techniques such as beamforming to combine the incoming signals and reducing the noise in these signals (Heinzelman, Chandrakasan, & Balakrishnan, 2000).

12. Quality of Service

In some applications bounded latency for data delivery is a condition for time-constrained applications. However, in many other applications, conservation of energy is considered more important than the quality of data sent. As the energy drains, the network may be required to reduce the quality of the results in order to reduce the energy dissipation in the sensor nodes and hence increase the total network lifetime and for such a purpose energy-aware routing protocols are proposed.

13. Network Topology

Network topology affects the quality of service of the network. Thus, it has to be very carefully chosen to make best use of the network. The available network topologies are shown in Figure 1.

Fully connected networks suffer from NP-complexity; mesh networks are regularly distributed networks that generally allow transmission only to a node's nearest neighbors. The nodes in

Figure 1. Basic network topologies

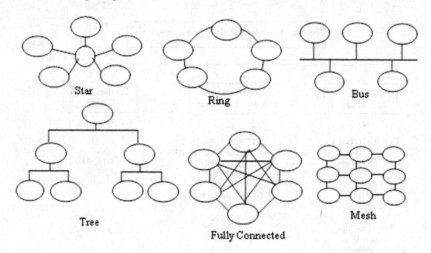

these networks are generally identical, so that mesh nets are also referred to as peer-to-peer nets. Mesh nets can be good models for large-scale networks of wireless sensors that are distributed over a geographic region, e.g. personnel or vehicle security surveillance systems.

All nodes of the star topology are connected to a single hub node. The hub requires greater message handling, routing, and decision-making capabilities than the other nodes. If a communication link is cut, it only affects one node. However, if the hub is incapacitated the network is destroyed. In the ring topology all nodes perform the same function and there is no leader node. Messages generally travel around the ring in a single direction. However, if the ring is cut, all communication is lost. In the bus topology, messages are broadcast on the bus to all nodes. Each node checks the destination address in the message header, and processes the messages addressed to it. The bus topology is passive in that each node simply listens for messages and is not responsible for retransmitting any messages.

ROUTING PROTOCOLS IN WIRELESS SENSOR NETWORKS

Routing in wireless sensor networks can be classified using one of the following three classifications either according to network structure, protocol structure or depending on how the source finds the destination. Firstly, it can be divided into flat based routing, hierarchical based routing, and location based routing depending on the network structure. In flat-based routing, all nodes are assigned equal roles, however, in hierarchical-based routing nodes will play different roles in the network while in location-based routing, sensor nodes' positions are exploited to route data in the network. Also, these protocols can be classified depending on the protocol operation into multipath-based where multiple paths are used rather than single paths in order to enhance network performance, query-based where the destination nodes propagate a query for data from a node through the network and the node having this data responds to the node initiating the query, negotiation-based where the protocols use high level data descriptors to eliminate redundant data transmissions through negotiation, QoS-based where the network has to balance between energy

Figure 2. Routing protocols in wireless sensor networks

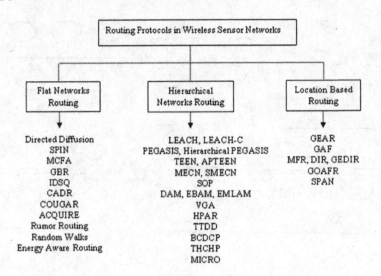

consumption and data quality, or coherent-based routing techniques where nodes cooperate in processing different data flooded in the network. Lastly, routing protocols can be classified into three categories depending on how the source finds a route to the destination proactive, reactive, and hybrid protocols. In proactive protocols, all routes are computed before they are needed, while in reactive protocols, routes are computed on demand. Hybrid protocols use a combination of these two ideas. When sensor nodes are static, it is preferable to have table driven routing protocols rather than using reactive protocols. A significant amount of energy is used in route discovery and setup of reactive protocols.

Existing routing protocols for wireless sensor networks can be classified based on their network structures and protocol operation are shown in Figure 2.

Flat Networks Routing

The first category of routing protocols is the flat routing protocols. In flat networks, all nodes play the same role and sensor nodes cooperate together to perform the sensing task. Due to the large number of such nodes, it is not feasible to assign a global identifier to each node. This consideration has led to data centric routing, where the base-station sends queries to certain regions and waits for data from the sensors located in the selected regions. Since data is being requested through queries, attribute-based naming is necessary to specify the properties of data (Al-Karaki & Kamal, 2004). In this section, we discuss Directed Diffusion protocol (Intanagonwiwat, Govindan, & Estrin, 2000) as an example of Flat Networks Routing.

Directed Diffusion

In Intanagonwiwat, Govindan, and Estrin (2000) a popular routing protocol for wireless sensor networks has been proposed called Directed Diffusion. The main idea aims at combining data through sensor nodes by using a naming scheme for the data in order to save energy. Direct Diffusion suggests the use of attribute-value pairs for the data and queries the sensors in an on demand basis by using those pairs. The base station requests data by broadcasting interests. Interest describes a task required to be done by the network. Interest

Figure 3. Directed diffusion protocol

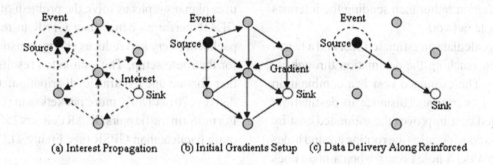

(a) Interest Propagation   (b) Initial Gradients Setup   (c) Data Delivery Along Reinforced

diffuses through the network hop-by-hop, and is broadcast by each node to its neighbors. As the interest is propagated throughout the network, gradients are setup to draw data satisfying the query towards the requesting node, i.e., a BS may query for data by disseminating interests and intermediate nodes propagate these interests. Each sensor that receives the interest setup a gradient toward the sensor nodes from which it receives the interest. This process continues until gradients are setup from the sources back to the BS. When a path between a source and the sink fails, a new or alternative path should be identified. For this, Directed Diffusion basically reinitiates reinforcement by searching among other paths, which are sending data in lower rates.

Directed diffusion cannot be applied to all sensor network applications since it is based on a query-driven data delivery model. The applications that require continuous data delivery to the sink will not work efficiently with a query-driven on demand data model. Therefore, Directed Diffusion is not a good choice as a routing protocol for the applications such as environmental monitoring. In addition, the naming schemes used in Directed Diffusion are application dependent and each time should be defined a priori. Moreover, the matching process for data and queries might require some extra overhead at the sensors (see Figure 3).

Location Based Routing

In Location Based Routing, sensor nodes are addressed by means of their locations. The distance between neighboring nodes can be estimated on the basis of incoming signal strengths. Relative coordinates of neighboring nodes can be obtained by exchanging such information between neighbors. Alternatively, the location of nodes may be available directly by communicating with a satellite, using GPS (Global Positioning System), if nodes are equipped with a small low power GPS receiver (Xu, Heidemann, & Estrin, 2001). To save energy, some location based schemes demand that nodes should go to sleep if there is no activity. More energy savings can be obtained by having as many sleeping nodes in the network as possible (Al-Karaki & Kamal, 2004). In this section, we discuss GEAR (Yu, Estrin, & Govindan, 2001) protocol as an example of Location Based Routing.

GEAR: Geographic and Energy Aware Routing

In Yu, Estrin, and Govindan (2001) a routing protocol for wireless sensor networks has been proposed called Geographic and Energy Aware Routing (GEAR). The protocol is based on energy aware and geographically informed neighbor selection heuristics to route a packet towards the destination region. This protocol conserves energy more than directed diffusion by restricting the number of interests by considering only a certain region rather than sending the interests to the whole network.

Nodes calculate an estimated cost and a learning cost of reaching the destination through its neighbors. The estimated cost is a combination of residual energy and distance to destination. The learned cost improves the estimated cost by taking into consideration the routing around holes in the network. A hole occurs when a node does not have any closer neighbor to the target region than itself. If there are no holes, the estimated cost is equal to the learned cost. There are two phases in the algorithm:

1. Forwarding packets towards the target region: On receiving a packet, a node checks its neighbors to see if there is one neighbor, which is closer to the target region than itself. If there is more than one, the nearest neighbor to the target region is selected as the next hop. If they are all further than the node itself, this means there is a hole. In this case, one of the neighbors is picked to forward the packet based on the learning cost function. This choice can then be updated according to the convergence of the learned cost during the delivery of packets.
2. Forwarding the packets within the region: If the packet has reached the region, it can be diffused in that region by either recursive geographic forwarding or restricted flooding. Recursive geographic flooding is better than restricted flooding in high-density networks, it is more energy efficient than restricted flooding. In that case, the region is divided into four sub regions and four copies of the packet are created. This splitting and forwarding process continues until the regions with only one node are left.

In Yu, Estrin, and Govindan (2001), GEAR was compared to a similar non-energy-aware routing protocol GPSR (Karp & Kung, 2000), which is one of the earlier works in geographic routing that uses planar graphs to solve the problem of holes. GEAR performs better than GPSR in terms of packet delivery and reduces energy consumption for the route setup. The simulation results show that for an uneven traffic distribution, GEAR delivers 70% to 80% more packets than (GPSR). For uniform traffic pairs GEAR delivers 25%-35% more packets than GPSR (see Figure 4).

Hierarchical Networks Routing

Hierarchical or cluster based routing, originally proposed in wireline networks, are well-known techniques used specially for scalability and efficient communication. And so the concept of hierarchical routing is also introduced to perform energy efficient routing in WSNs. In a hierarchical routing, higher energy nodes can be used to process and send the information while low energy nodes can be used to perform the sensing in the proximity of the target. The creation of clusters and assigning special tasks to cluster heads can greatly contribute to overall system scalability, lifetime, and energy efficiency. Data aggregation and fusion are used in hierarchical routing to lower energy consumption within a cluster by decreasing the number of transmitted messages to the base-station. Hierarchical routing is mainly two-layer routing where one layer is used to select cluster-heads and the other layer is used for routing (AL-Karaki & Kamal, 2004). In this section we explore hierarchical routing protocols elaborately as they are the focus of this chapter.

LEACH: Low-Energy Adaptive Clustering Hierarchy

LEACH (Heinzelman, 2004) is one of the most popular hierarchical routing algorithms for sensor networks and is a good example of a proactive network protocol. In LEACH, the nodes organize themselves into local clusters, with one node acting

Figure 4. Recursive geographic forwarding in GEAR

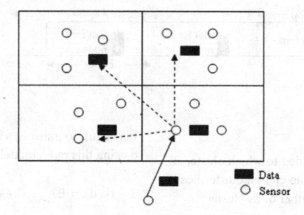

as the local base station or cluster-head. LEACH includes randomized rotation of the cluster-head position periodically such that the cluster-head role rotates among the various sensors so that the battery of a single sensor is not drained.

The three key features of LEACH are:

1. Localized coordination and control between nodes for cluster set-up and operation.
2. Randomized rotation of the cluster "cluster-heads" and the corresponding clusters periodically between nodes.
3. Local compression of data at cluster-heads to reduce global communication.

The operation of LEACH is broken up into rounds with each round including the following phases:

Advertisement Phase

Initially, when clusters are being created, each node decides whether or not to become a cluster-head for the current round based on the percentage of cluster heads determined a priori for the network and the number of times the node has been a cluster-head so far. This decision is made by the

node n choosing a random number between 0 and 1. If the number is less a certain threshold the node becomes a cluster-head for the current round. The threshold is set as:

$$
T(n) = \begin{cases} \dfrac{P}{1 - p * (r \bmod \frac{1}{p})} & \text{if } n \in G \\ 0 & \text{otherwise} \end{cases} \quad (1)
$$

where p is the desired percentage of cluster heads (e.g. 0.05), r is = the current round, and G is the set of nodes that have not been cluster heads in the last 1/p rounds. Optimal number of cluster-heads is estimated to be 5% of the total number of nodes.

Each node that has elected itself a cluster-head for the current round broadcasts an advertisement message to the rest of the nodes. Each non-cluster-head node decides the cluster to which it will belong for this round based on the strength of the received signal of the advertisement. The cluster-head advertisement heard with the largest signal strength is the cluster-head to whom a minimum amount of transmission energy is needed for communication.

Figure 5. LEACH operation

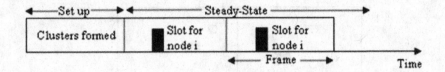

Cluster Set-Up Phase

After each node has decided to which cluster it belongs, it must inform the chosen cluster-head node that it will be a member of its cluster.

Schedule Phase

After the cluster-head node receives all the messages from nodes that would like to join the cluster it creates a TDMA schedule based on the number of nodes in the cluster telling each node when it can transmit. This schedule is broadcast back to the nodes in the cluster.

Data Transmission

Once the clusters are created and the TDMA schedule is fixed, data transmission can begin and thus the steady-state operation of LEACH networks. Assuming nodes always have data to send, they send it during their allocated transmission time to the cluster head using a minimal amount of energy (chosen based on the received strength of the cluster-head advertisement). Once the cluster-head has all the data from the nodes in its cluster, the cluster-head node aggregates the data and then transmits the compressed data to the base station. Since the base station is usually far away, this is a high energy transmission (see Figure 5).

Energy Analysis of LEACH Protocol

In LEACH it is assumed a simple radio model where the radio dissipates $E_{elec} = 50nJ / bit$ to run the transmitter or receiver circuitry and $\mu_{amp} = 100pJ / bit / m^2$ for the transmit ampli-

fier. Thus, to transmit a k-bit message a distance d using this radio model, the radio expends:

$$E_{Tx}(k, d) = E_{Tx-elec}(k) + E_{Tx-amp}(k, d)$$

$$E_{Tx}(k, d) = E_{elec} * k + \varepsilon_{amp} * k * d^2 \qquad (2)$$

and to receive this message, the radio expends:

$$E_{Rx}(k) = E_{Rx-elec}(k)$$

$$E_{Rx}(k) = E_{elec} * k \qquad (3)$$

It is assumed that the radio channel is symmetric such that the energy required to transmit a message from node A to node B is the same as the energy required to transmit a message from node B to node A.

LEACH achieves over a factor of 7 reduction in energy dissipation compared to direct communication and a factor of 4-8 compared to the minimum transmission energy routing protocol. Nodes die randomly as dynamic clustering increases lifetime of the system. LEACH is completely distributed and requires no global knowledge of network. However, LEACH uses single-hop routing where each node can transmit directly to the cluster-head and the base station. Therefore, it is not quite suitable to networks deployed in large regions. Furthermore, the idea of dynamic clustering brings extra overhead because of head changes, advertisements etc., which may diminish the gain in energy consumption (Akkaya & Younis,

2005). Also the cluster division in LEACH does not consider the distribution of event-detecting sensor nodes, when an event is detected by sensor nodes in two or more clusters; the sink may receive two or more reports on the same event. This greatly wastes sensor energy and thereby reduces network lifetime (Yin, Wang, & Øien, 2008). LEACH supposes that all nodes contain the same quantity of energy capacity at every election round, it is also presumed that every node has an adequate amount of transmission power in order to directly get in touch with the base station if required. Nevertheless, in most cases these hypotheses are unlikely. Also cluster-heads are not uniformly distributed so they may be located at the edges of the cluster (Kandris, Tsioumas, Tzes, Nikolakopoulos, & Vergados, 2009).

LEACH-C: LEACH-Centralized

Although there are advantages to using LEACH's distributed cluster formation algorithm, it offers no guarantee about the placement and/or number of cluster head nodes. Since the clusters are adaptive, obtaining a poor clustering set-up during a given round will not greatly affect overall performance. However, using a central control algorithm to form the clusters may produce better clusters by dispersing the cluster head nodes throughout the network. This is the basic idea for LEACH-centralized (LEACH-C) (Heinzelman, Chandrakasan & Balakrishnan, 2002) protocol, a protocol that uses a centralized clustering algorithm and otherwise the same functionality as LEACH as follows:

Base Station Cluster Formation

During the set-up phase of LEACH-C, each node sends information about its current location (possibly determined using a GPS receiver) and energy level to the base station. Not only does the base station need to determine good clusters it also has to ensure that the energy load is evenly distributed among all the nodes. To do this, the base station computes the average node energy, and any node having energy below this average cannot be a cluster head for the current round. Using the remaining nodes as possible cluster heads, the base station finds clusters using the simulated annealing algorithm to solve the NP-hard problem of finding optimal clusters. This algorithm attempts to minimize the amount of energy for the non-cluster head nodes to transmit their data to the cluster head, by minimizing the total sum of squared distances between all the non-cluster head nodes and the closest cluster head. Once the cluster heads and associated clusters are found, the base station broadcasts a message that contains the cluster head ID for each node. If a node's cluster head ID matches its own ID, the node is a cluster head; otherwise, the node determines its TDMA slot for data transmission and goes to sleep until it is time to transmit data.

Steady-State Phase

The steady-state phase of LEACH-C is identical to that of LEACH.

Energy Analysis of LEACH-C Protocol

In LEACH-C it is assumed a simple radio model where the radio dissipates $E_{elec} = 50nJ / bit$ to run the transmitter or receiver circuitry and $\mu_{amp} = 100pJ / bit / m^2$ for the transmit amplifier, both the free space (d^2 power loss) and the multipath fading (d^4 power loss) channel models were used, depending on the distance between the transmitter and receiver. Thus, to transmit an l-bit message a distance d using this radio model, the radio expends:

$$E_{Tx}(l, d) = E_{Tx-elec}(l) + E_{Tx-amp}(l, d)$$

$$= \begin{cases} lE_{elec} + 1_{\mu fs} d^2 & d < d_o \\ lE_{elec} + 1_{\mu mp} d^4 & d \geq d_o \end{cases}$$

$$(4)$$

and to receive this message, the radio expends:

$$E_{Rx}(l) = E_{Rx-elec}(l) = lE_{elec} \qquad (5)$$

LEACH-C is also an example of a proactive network protocol. LEACH is not as efficient as LEACH-C (LEACH-C delivers about 40% more data per unit energy than LEACH). This is because the base station has global knowledge of the location and energy of all the nodes in the network, so it can produce better clusters that require less energy for data transmission. The authors of (Heinzelman, Chandrakasan, & Balakrishnan, 2002) cite two key reasons for the improvement: configuration of better clusters and producing the optimal number of CHs. The number of cluster heads in each round of LEACH-C equals a predetermined optimal value, whereas for LEACH the number of cluster heads is randomly chosen from round to round. Although LEACH and LEACH-C provides significant energy saving, due to dense deployment in WSNs, redundant nodes exist in the network, in which sensing ranges are fully overlapped by their on-duty neighbors (Noh, Lee, & Kim, 2008).

TEEN: Threshold Sensitive Energy Efficient Sensor Network Protocol

TEEN (Manjeshwar & Agrawal, 2001) is targeted at reactive networks and is the first protocol developed for reactive networks. In this scheme, at every cluster change time, in addition to the attributes, the cluster-head broadcasts to its members two thresholds.

Hard Threshold (H_T): This is a threshold value for the sensed attribute. It is the absolute value of the attribute beyond which, the node sensing this value must switch on its transmitter and report to its cluster head.

Soft Threshold (S_T): This is a small change in the value of the sensed attribute which triggers the node to switch on its transmitter and transmit.

The nodes sense their environment continuously. The first time a parameter from the attribute set reaches its hard threshold value, the node switches on its transmitter and sends the sensed data. The sensed value is stored in an internal variable in the node, called the Sensed Value (SV). The nodes will next transmit data in the current cluster period, only when both the following conditions are true:

1. The current value of the sensed attribute is greater than the hard threshold.
2. The current value of the sensed attribute differs from SV by an amount equal to or greater than the soft threshold.

Whenever a node transmits data, SV is set equal to the current value of the sensed attribute. Thus, the hard threshold tries to reduce the number of transmissions by allowing the nodes to transmit only when the sensed attribute is in the range of interest. The soft threshold further reduces the number of transmissions by eliminating all the transmissions which might have otherwise occurred when there is little or no change in the sensed attribute once the hard threshold.

The main features of this scheme are as follows:

1. Time critical data reaches the user almost instantaneously. So, this scheme is eminently suited for time critical data sensing applications.
2. Message transmission consumes much more energy than data sensing. So, even though

Figure 6. Operation of TEEN

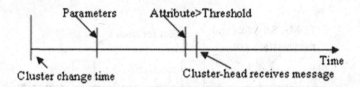

the nodes sense continuously, the energy consumption in this scheme can potentially be much less than in the proactive network, because data transmission is done less frequently.

3. The soft threshold can be varied, depending on the criticality of the sensed attribute and the target application.
4. A smaller value of the soft threshold gives a more accurate picture of the network, at the expense of increased energy consumption. Thus, the user can control the trade-off between energy efficiency and accuracy.
5. At every cluster change time, the attributes are broadcast afresh and so, the user can change them as required. The main drawback of this scheme is that, if the thresholds are not reached, the nodes will never communicate; the user will not get any data from the network at all and will not come to know even if all the nodes die (Barati, Movaghar, Barati, & Mazreah, 2008). Thus, this scheme is not well suited for applications where the user needs to get data on a regular basis.

Another possible problem with this scheme is that a practical implementation would have to ensure that there are no collisions in the cluster. TDMA scheduling of the nodes can be used to avoid this problem. This will however introduce a delay in the reporting of the time-critical data. CDMA is another possible solution to this problem. Also from the drawbacks are the overhead and complexity of forming clusters in multiple levels, implementing threshold-based functions

and dealing with attribute-based naming of queries (Akkaya & Younis, 2005) (see Figure 6).

APTEEN: Adaptive Periodic Threshold-Sensitive Energy Efficient Sensor Network Protocol

This protocol is a protocol developed for hybrid networks. APTEEN (Manjeshwar, Zeng, & Agrawal, 2002) is an extension to TEEN and aims at both capturing periodic data collections and reacting to time-critical events. The architecture is same as in TEEN. When the base station forms the clusters, the cluster heads broadcasts the following parameters:

*   **Attribute (A):** This is a set of physical parameters which the user is interested in obtaining data about.
*   **Thresholds:** This parameter consists of a Hard Threshold (HT) and a Soft Threshold (ST). HT is a particular value of an attribute beyond which a node can be triggered to transmit data. ST is a small change in the value of an attribute which can trigger a node to transmit data again.
*   **Schedule:** This is a TDMA schedule, assigning a slot to each node.
*   **Count Time** (TC): It is the maximum time period between two successive reports sent by a node. It can be a multiple of the TDMA schedule length and it accounts for the proactive component. In a sensor network, close-by nodes fall in the same cluster, sense similar data and try to send

Figure 7. Operation of APTEEN

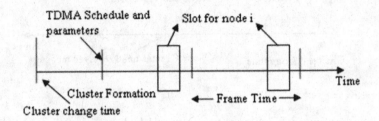

their data simultaneously, causing possible collisions. A TDMA schedule is introduced such that each node in the cluster is assigned a transmission slot.

Cluster heads also perform data aggregation in order to save energy. APTEEN supports three different query types: historical, to analyze past data values; one-time, to take a snapshot view of the network; and persistent to monitor an event for a period of time.

The main features of the scheme are:

1. By sending periodic data, it gives the user a complete picture of the network. It also responds immediately to drastic changes, thus making it responsive to time critical situations. Thus, it combines both proactive and reactive policies.
2. It offers a flexibility of allowing the user to set the time interval (TC) and the threshold values for the attributes.
3. Energy consumption can be controlled by the count time and the threshold values.
4. The hybrid network can emulate a proactive network or a reactive network, by suitably setting the count time and the threshold values.

The main drawbacks of this approach are the overhead and complexity of forming clusters in multiple levels, implementing threshold-based

functions and dealing with attribute-based naming of queries. Also the cluster heads in APTEEN broadcast e.g. the threshold values to the senor nodes, which is energy consuming (Hansen & Ewa, 2008) (see Figures 7 and 8).

PEGASIS: Power-Efficient Gathering in Sensor Information Systems

PEGASIS (Lindsey & Raghavendra, 2002) (Power-Efficient GAthering in Sensor Information Systems), a near optimal chain-based protocol that is an improvement over LEACH. The PEGASIS protocol achieves between 100 to 300% improvement when 1%, 20%, 50% and 100% of nodes die compared to the LEACH protocol.

The key idea in PEGASIS is to form a chain among the sensor nodes so that each node will receive from and transmit to a close neighbor. Gathered data moves from node to node, get fused, and eventually a designated node transmits to the BS. Nodes take turns transmitting to the BS so that the average energy spent by each node per round is reduced. When the round of all nodes communicating with the base-station ends, a new round will start and so on. This reduces the power required to transmit data per round as the power draining is spread uniformly over all nodes.

To locate the closest neighbor node in PEGA-SIS, each node uses the signal strength to measure the distance to all neighboring nodes and then adjusts the signal strength so that only one node

Figure 8. Hierarchical clustering in TEEN and APTEEN

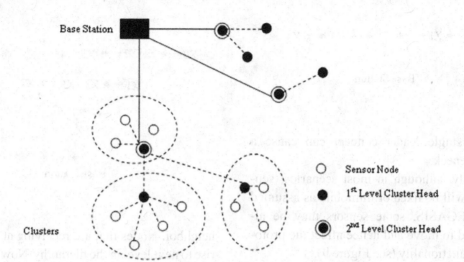

can be heard. The chain in PEGASIS will consist of those nodes that are closest to each other and form a path to the base-station. The aggregated form of the data will be sent to the base-station by any node in the chain and the nodes in the chain will take turns in sending to the base-station. The chain construction is performed in a greedy fashion.

In PEGASIS it is assumed a simple radio model as the one used in LEACH. PEGASIS has two main principles, first, to increase the lifetime of each node by using collaborative techniques and as a result the network lifetime will be increased. Second, to allow only local coordination between nodes that are close together so that the bandwidth consumed in communication is reduced. Unlike LEACH, PEGASIS avoids cluster formation and uses only one node in a chain to transmit to the BS instead of using multiple nodes.

Simulation results showed that PEGASIS is able to increase the lifetime of the network twice as much the lifetime of the network under the LEACH protocol. Such performance gain is achieved through the elimination of the overhead caused by dynamic cluster formation in LEACH and through decreasing the number of transmissions and reception by using data aggregation.

But although the clustering overhead is avoided, PEGASIS has some flaws that have fatal affect on the network performance:

- PEGASIS assumes that all nodes maintain a complete database about the location of all other nodes in the network. The method of which the node locations are obtained is not outlined in literature.
- PEGASIS assumes that all sensor nodes have the same level of energy and they are likely to die at the same time.
- PEGASIS requires dynamic topology adjustment as a sensor node needs to know about energy status of its neighbors in order to know where to route its data. Such topology adjustment can introduce significant overhead especially for highly utilized networks.
- PEGASIS assumes that each sensor node can be able to communicate with the BS directly. In practical cases, sensor nodes use multihop communication to reach the base-station.
- PEGASIS introduces excessive delay for distant node on the chain

Figure 9. Chaining in PEGASIS

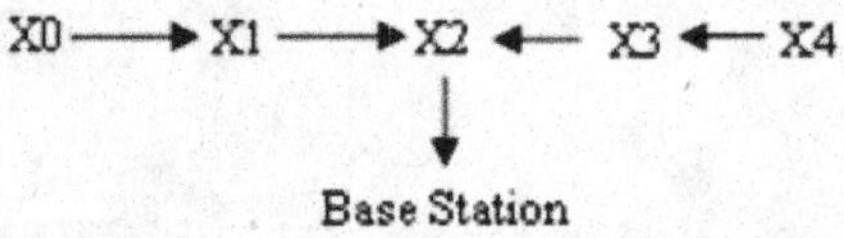

Figure 10. Data gathering in a chain based binary scheme

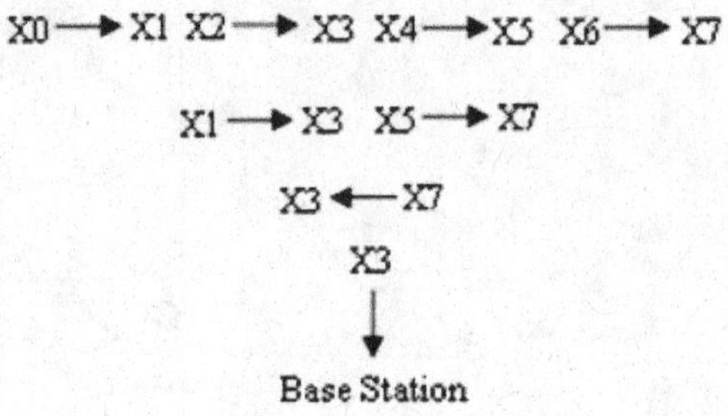

- The single leader concept can cause a bottleneck.
- Finally, although in most scenarios, sensors will be fixed or immobile as assumed in PEGASIS, some sensors may be allowed to move and hence affect the protocol functionality (see Figure 9).

Hierarchical-PEGASIS: Hierarchical Power-Efficient Gathering in Sensor Information Systems

Hierarchical-PEGASIS (Savvides, Han, & Srivastava, 2001) is an extension to PEGASIS, which improves PEGASIS by decreasing the delay incurred for packets during transmission to the base station and proposes a solution to the data gathering problem by pursuing simultaneous transmissions of data messages. Two approaches have been proposed to avoid collisions and possible signal interference among the sensors. The first approach uses signal coding, e.g. CDMA. And the second approach allows only spatially separated nodes to transmit at the same simultaneously.

The chain-based protocol with CDMA capable nodes, constructs a chain of nodes, that forms a tree like hierarchy, and each selected node in a particular level transmits data to the node in the upper level of the hierarchy. This method ensures data transmitting in parallel and reduces the delay significantly as shown in Figure 10 Node c3 is the designated leader for round 3. Since, node c3 is in position 3 (counting from 0) on the chain, all nodes in an even position will send to their right

neighbor. Nodes that are receiving at each level rise to next level in the hierarchy. Now at the next level, node c3 is still in an odd position (1). Again all nodes in an even position will aggregate its data with its received data and send to their right. At the third level, node c3 is not in an odd position, so node c7 will aggregate its data and transmit to c3. Finally, node c3 will aggregate its current data with that received from c7 and transmit the message to the base-station. The non-CDMA based approach creates a three-level hierarchy of the nodes and interference effects are reduced by carefully scheduling simultaneous transmissions.

Hierarchical-PEGASIS chain-based protocol has shown to perform better than the regular PEGASIS scheme by a factor of about 60.

MECN: Minimum Energy Communication Network

MECN (Rodoplu & Meng, 1999) protocol main idea is to compute an energy-efficient sub-network for a certain sensor network by utilizing low power GPS. This sub-network will have less number of nodes and requires less power for transmission between any two particular nodes. In this way, global minimum power paths are found without considering all the nodes in the network. This is performed using a localized search for each node considering its relay region that is identified for

Figure 11. Relay region of transmit-relay node pair (i, r) in MECN

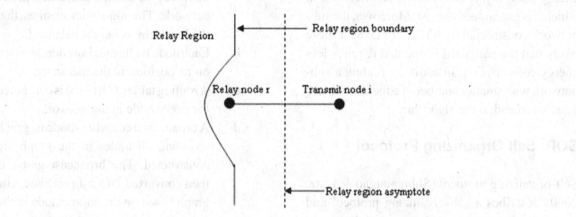

every node. The relay region consists of nodes in a surrounding area where transmitting through those nodes is more energy efficient than direct transmission. The relay region for node pair (i, r) is shown in Figure 11. The enclosure of a node i is then created by taking the union of all relay regions that node i can reach. MECN protocol first takes the positions of a two dimensional plane and constructs an enclosure graph, consisting of all the enclosures of each transmit node in the graph. This construction requires local computations in the nodes. The enclosure graph contains globally optimal links in terms of energy consumption. After that MECN finds optimal links on the enclosure graph, it uses distributed Belmann-Ford shortest path algorithm with power consumption as the cost metric. In case of mobility the position coordinates are updated using GPS.

MECN is self-reconfiguring and thus can dynamically adapt to node's failure or the deployment of new sensors. Between two successive wake-ups of the nodes, each node can execute the first phase of the algorithm and the minimum cost links are updated by considering leaving or newly joining nodes.

SMECN: Small Minimum Energy Communication Network

SMECN (Rodoplu & Meng, 2001) is an extension to MECN. In MECN, it is assumed that every node can transmit to every other node, which is not possible every time. In SMECN possible obstacles between any pair of nodes are considered. However, the network is still assumed to be fully connected as in the case of MECN. The subnetwork constructed by SMECN for minimum energy relaying is provably smaller (in terms of number of edges) than the one constructed in MECN. Hence, the sub-network (i.e., sub-graph G) constructed by SMECN is smaller than the one constructed by MECN if the broadcast region is circular around the broadcasting node for a given power setting. Sub-graph G of graph G, which represents the sensor network, minimizes the energy usage if it satisfies the following conditions; first the number of edges in G is less than in G while containing all nodes in G, second the energy required to transmit data from a node to all its neighbors in sub-graph G is less than the energy required to transmit to all its neighbors in graph G.

The sub-network computed by SMECN helps sending messages on minimum-energy paths. However, the proposed algorithm is local in the sense that it does not actually find the minimum-energy path; it just constructs a sub-network in which it is guaranteed to exist. Moreover, the sub-network constructed by SMECN makes it more likely that the path used is one that requires less energy consumption. In addition, finding a sub-network with smaller number of edges introduces more overhead in the algorithm.

SOP: Self Organizing Protocol

Self-organizing protocol (Subramanian & Katz, 2000) describes a self-organizing protocol and an application taxonomy that was used to build architecture used to support heterogeneous sensors which can be mobile or stationary. Some sensors probe the environment and forward the data to designated set of nodes that act as routers. Router nodes are stationary and form the backbone for communication. Collected data are forwarded through the routers to more powerful sink nodes. Each sensing node should be reachable to a router node in order to be part of the network. A routing architecture that requires addressing of each sensor node has been proposed. Sensing nodes are identifiable through the address of the router node it is connected to. The routing architecture is hierarchical where groups of nodes are formed and merge when needed. In order to support fault tolerance, Local Markov Loops (LML) algorithm, which performs a random walk on spanning trees of a graph, is used in broadcasting. The algorithm for self-organizing the router nodes and creating the routing tables consists of four phases:

- **Discovery phase:** Each node independently discovers its set of neighbors in the network and fixes its maximum radius of data transmission.
- **Organizational phase:** During this phase the network is organized and the following operations are performed:
  a. Nodes aggregate themselves into groups and groups are aggregated

to form larger groups. In this way, a hierarchy of groups is formed in the network. The algorithm ensures that the hierarchy is height balanced.
  b. Each node is allocated an address based on its position in the hierarchy.
  c. A routing table of $O(\log n)$ is computed for every node in the network.
  d. A broadcast tree and a broadcast graph spanning all nodes in the graph are constructed. The broadcast graph is then converted into a directed acyclic graph based on the source node in the network.

- **Maintenance phase:** In the maintenance phase the following operations are performed:
  a. In active monitoring, every node keeps track of its stored energy and constantly sends I am alive message to its neighbors once in 30 sec. In passive monitoring, a sensor node sends an activate message to its neighbors only on demand.
  b. Every node constantly updates its routing table about the next hop in the least power consuming path and the shortest delay path to the groups as dictated by the algorithm.
  c. Nodes also inform their neighbors of their routing tables and their energy levels to their neighboring nodes.
  d. Fault tolerant broadcast trees and broadcast graphs are maintained using Local Markov Loops (LML).

- **Self-Reorganization phase:** In this phase, a node may detect group partitions or node failures and change its routing table based on the new topology. If all neighbors of a node fail, then the node repeats the discovery phase. If a group partition occurs due to link or node failures, the sub groups reorganize and join with new groups. Group re-organization ensures that the hierarchy is still balanced.

The proposed algorithm utilizes the router nodes to keep all the sensors connected by forming a dominating set. The protocol achieves energy saving through utilization of a limited subset of nodes. Since sensor nodes can be addressed individually in the routing architecture, the proposed algorithm is suitable for applications such as parking-lot networks where communication to a particular node is required (Subramanian & Katz, 2000). The major advantage of using the algorithm is the small cost of maintaining routing tables and keeping routing hierarchy being strictly balanced. Moreover, the energy consumed for broadcasting a message is low due to the broadcast trees utilized in the algorithm. Fault tolerance is also achieved by using Local Markov Loops (LML) algorithm, LML, in broadcast trees. The problem is in the organization phase of algorithm, which is not on-demand, therefore introducing extra overhead. Another possible problem is in case of hierarchy forming when there are many cuts in the network. This will be expensive since network-cuts increase the probability of applying reorganization phase.

Sensor Aggregates Routing

In Fang, Zhao, and Guibas (2003), a set of algorithms with the aim of constructing and maintaining sensor aggregates were proposed. These algorithms are used in target tracking applications were they collectively monitor target activity in a certain environment. The sensor network is divided into clusters based on their sensed signal strength, so that there is only one peak per cluster. One peak may represent one target, multiple targets, or no target in case the peak is generated by noise sources. Cluster heads for each cluster are elected by exchanging packets with all its one-hop neighbors, the one that finds that it is higher than all its one-hop neighbors on the signal field landscape, it declares itself a leader. The cluster-head is assumed to know the geographical region of the collaboration. The following three algorithms are developed for low-cost, low-resolution wireless sensor nodes:

The first algorithm is a lightweight protocol, Distributed Aggregate Management (DAM) (Fang, Zhao, & Guibas, 2003), for forming sensor aggregates for a target monitoring task. The protocol comprises a decision predicate P for each node to decide if it should participate in an aggregate and a message exchange scheme M about how the grouping predicate is applied to nodes. A node determines if it belongs to an aggregate based on the result of applying the predicate to the data of the node as well as information from other nodes. Aggregates are formed when the process eventually converges.

The second algorithm, Energy-Based Activity Monitoring (EBAM) (Fang, Zhao, & Guibas, 2003) algorithm estimates the energy level at each node by computing the signal impact area, combining a weighted form of the detected target energy at each impacted sensor assuming that each target sensor has equal or constant energy level.

The third algorithm, Expectation-Maximization Like Activity Monitoring (EMLAM) (Fang, Zhao, & Guibas, 2003), removes the constant and equal target energy level assumption. EMLAM estimates the target positions and signal energy using received signals, and uses the resulting estimates to predict how signals from the targets may be mixed at each sensor. This process is iterated, until the estimate is sufficiently good.

The distributed track initiation management scheme, combined with the leader-based tracking algorithm described in Fang, Zhao, and Guibas (2003), form a scalable system. The system works well in tracking multiple targets when the targets are not interfering, and it can recover from inter-target interference once the targets move apart (Al-Karaki & Kamal, 2004).

Figure 12. Regular shape tessellation applied to the network area. In each zone, a cluster-head is selected for local aggregation. Subsets of those cluster-heads, called master nodes, are optimally selected to do global aggregation.

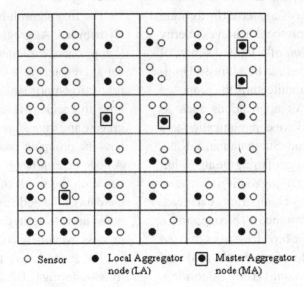

○ Sensor   ● Local Aggregator node (LA)   ▣ Master Aggregator node (MA)

VGA: Virtual Grid Architecture Routing

An energy-efficient routing paradigm is proposed in Al-Karaki, Ul-Mustafa, and Kamal (2004) that utilizes data aggregation and in-network processing to maximize the network lifetime. As nodes are stationary or have extremely low mobility in many applications in WSNs, an approach to arrange nodes in a fixed topology as was briefly mentioned in Xu, Heidemann, and Estrin (2001). A GPS-free approach (Savvides, Han, & Srivastava, 2001) is used to divide the network area into fixed, equal, adjacent, and non-overlapping symmetric shapes as clusters. In Al-Karaki, Ul-Mustafa, and Kamal (2004), square clusters were used to obtain a fixed rectilinear virtual topology. Inside each zone, a node is optimally selected to act as cluster-head. Data aggregation is performed locally and then globally. The set of cluster-heads, also called Local Aggregators (LAs), perform the local aggregation, while a subset of these LAs is used to perform

global aggregation. However, the determination of an optimal selection of global aggregation points, called Master Aggregators (MAs), is NP-hard problem. Figure 12 illustrates an example of fixed zoning and the resulting Virtual Grid Architecture (VGA) used to perform two level data aggregation. Note that the base station can be located at any arbitrary place in the network. Two solution strategies for the routing with data aggregation problem are presented in Al-Karaki, Ul-Mustafa, and Kamal (2004):

First using an exact algorithm using an Integer Linear Program (ILP) formulation and several near optimal, but simple and efficient, approximate algorithms, namely, genetics algorithms based heuristic, a k-means heuristic, and a greedy based heuristic.

Second, another efficient heuristic, called Clustering-Based Aggregation Heuristic (CBAH) (Al-Karaki, Ul-Mustafa, & Kamal, 2004), was also proposed to minimize energy consumption in the network, and hence prolong the network lifetime.

The main idea of all algorithms is to select a number of MAs out of the LAs that maximize the network lifetime.

It was noted in Al-Karaki, Ul-Mustafa, and Kamal (2004) that the problem of assigning MAs to LAs in CBAH is that neither the identities nor the amount of power that each MA will be using for different LAs are known. The approximate algorithms in Al-Karaki, Ul-Mustafa, and Kamal (2004) and Al-Karaki and Kamal (2004) produce results which are not far from the optimal solution, besides being fast and scalable to large sensor networks.

HPAR: Hierarchical Power-Aware Routing

In Li, Aslam, and Rus (2001), a hierarchical power-aware routing was proposed. The idea is to group together all the nodes that are in geographic proximity as a zone, treat the zone as an entity in the network, and allow each zone to decide how to route a message across the other zones such that the battery lives of the nodes in the system are maximized. Messages are routed along the path which has the maximum over all the minimum of the remaining power, called the max-min path that is because using nodes with high residual power may be expensive as compared to the path with the minimal power consumption. An approximation algorithm, called the max-min zP_{min} algorithm, was proposed in Li, Aslam, and Rus (2001). The main idea of the algorithm is based on the tradeoff between minimizing the total power consumption and maximizing the minimal residual power of the network. Hence, the algorithm tries to make power aware routing using the following solutions:

First, the algorithm computes the path with minimal power consumption (P_{min}) by using the Dijkstra algorithm. Second, the algorithm computes a path that maximizes the minimal residual power in the network. The proposed algorithm tries to optimize both solution criteria. This is achieved by relaxing the minimal power consumption for the message to be equal to zP_{min} with parameter z ≥ 1 to restrict the power consumption for sending one message to zP_{min}. The algorithm consumes at most zP_{min} while maximizing the minimal residual power fraction.

Zone-based routing algorithm is also proposed in Li, Aslam, and Rus (2001), it relies on max-min zP_{min}. It is a hierarchical approach where the area covered by the network is divided into a small number of zones. To send a message across the entire area, a global path from zone to zone is found. The sensors in a zone autonomously direct local routing and participate in estimating the zone power level. Each message is routed across the zones using information about the zone power estimates. A global controller for message routing is assigned the role of managing the zones which may be the node with the highest power. If the network can be divided into a relatively small number of zones, the scale for the global routing algorithm is reduced. The global information required to send each message across is summarized by the power level estimate of each zone.

TTDD: Two-Tier Data Dissemination

An approach in Ye et al. (2002), called Two-Tier Data Dissemination (TTDD), provides data delivery to multiple mobile base-stations. Each data source in TTDD proactively builds a grid structure which enables mobile base-stations to continuously receive data on the move by flooding queries within a local cell only. TTDD's design exploits the fact that sensor nodes are stationary and location-aware to construct and maintain the grid structures with low overhead.

Upon detection of an event, the data source proactively builds a grid structure throughout the sensor field and sets up the forwarding information at the sensors closest to grid points (called dissemination nodes). During this process, each intermediate node stores the source information and further forwards the message to its adjacent crossing points except the one from which the message comes from. This process continues until the message stops at the border of the network. When the message reaches a node that is closest to the crossing point (specified in the message) it will stop. With this grid structure in place, a query from the base-station traverses two tiers to reach a source. The lower tier is within the local grid square of the base-station's current location (called cells), and the higher tier is made of the dissemination nodes at grid points. The base-station floods its query within a cell. When the nearest dissemination node for the requested data receives the query, it forwards the query to its upstream dissemination node toward the source, which in turns further forwards the query, until it reaches either the source or a dissemination node that is already receiving data from the source (e.g. upon requests from other sinks). This query forwarding process lays information of the path to the base-station, to enable data from the source to traverse the same two tiers as the query but in the reverse order.

Although TTDD is an efficient routing approach, there are some concerns about how the algorithm obtains location information, which is required to set up the grid structure. The length of a forwarding path in TTDD is larger than the length of the shortest path. The authors of TTDD believe that the sub-optimality in the path length is worth the gain in scalability. Finally, how would TTDD perform if mobile sensor nodes are allowed to move in the network is still a problem. TTDD can achieve long lifetimes and good data delivery delays. However, the overhead associated with maintaining and recalculating the grid as network topology changes may be high. Furthermore, TTDD assumed the availability of very accurate positioning system which is not yet available for WSNs.

BCDCP: Base-Station Controlled Dynamic Clustering Protocol

In Muraganathan, Ma, Bhasin, and Fapojuwo (2005) new protocol that distributes the energy dissipation evenly among all sensor nodes to improve network lifetime and average energy savings has been proposed. The key ideas in BCDCP are the formation of balanced clusters where each cluster head serves an approximately equal number of member nodes to avoid cluster head overload, uniform placement of cluster heads throughout the whole sensor field, and utilization of cluster-head-to-cluster-head (CH-to-CH) routing to transfer the data to the base station. Thus, BCDCP utilizes the base station to control the coordinated sensing task performed by the sensor nodes. The sensor network model proposed has the following properties:

- A fixed base station is located far away from the sensor nodes.
- The sensor nodes are energy constrained with a uniform initial energy allocation.
- The nodes are equipped with power control capabilities to vary their transmitted power.
- Each node senses the environment at a fixed rate and always has data to send to the base station.
- All sensor nodes are immobile.

The two key elements considered in the design of BCDCP are the sensor nodes and base station. The sensor nodes are geographically grouped into clusters and capable of operating in two basic modes:

- The cluster head mode
- The sensing mode

In the sensing mode, the nodes perform sensing tasks and transmit the sensed data to the cluster head. In cluster head mode, a node gathers data from the other nodes within its cluster, performs data fusion, and routes the data to the base station through other cluster head nodes. The base station in turn performs the key tasks of cluster formation, randomized cluster head selection, and CH-to-CH routing path construction. BCDCP is a wireless sensor routing protocol with the base station being an essential component with complex computational abilities, thus making the sensor nodes very simple and cost effective. BCDCP operates in two major phases: setup and data communication.

The Setup Phase

The main activities in this phase are cluster setup, cluster head selection, CH-to-CH routing path formation, and schedule creation for each cluster. During each setup phase, the base station receives information on the current energy status from all the nodes in the network. Based on this feedback, the base station first computes the average energy level of all the nodes, and then chooses a set of nodes, denoted S, whose energy levels are above the average value. Cluster heads for the current round will be chosen from the set S, which ensures that only nodes with sufficient energy get selected as cluster heads, while those with low energy can prolong their lifetime by performing tasks that require low energy costs. The next major tasks for the base station are:

a. To identify cluster head nodes from the chosen set of nodes.
   b. To group the other nodes into clusters such that the overall energy consumption during the data communication phase is minimized.

The Data Communication Phase

The data communication phase consists of three major activities:

a. Data gathering.
b. Data fusion
c. Data routing

Using the TDMA schedule scheme, each sensor node transmits the sensed information to its cluster head. Since sensor nodes are geographically grouped into clusters, these transmissions consume minimal energy due to small spatial separations between the cluster head and the sensing nodes. Once data from all sensor nodes have been received, the cluster head performs data fusion on the collected data, and reduces the amount of raw data that needs to be sent to the base station. The compressed data, along with the information required by the base station to properly identify and decode the cluster data, are then routed back to the base station via the CH-to-CH routing path created by the base station. Besides, we also assume that the fused data from a given cluster head undergoes further processing as it hops along the CH-to-CH routing path.

Simulation results show that BCDCP outperforms LEACH, LEACH-C, PEGASIS by uniformly placing cluster heads throughout the whole sensor field, performing balanced clustering, and using a CH-to-CH routing scheme to transfer fused data to the base station. It is also observed that the performance gain of BCDCP increases with the area of the sensor field.

THCHP: Two-Level Hierarchical Clustering Based Hybrid Routing Protocol

In Muraganathan and Fapojuwo (2008) a Two-Level Hierarchical Clustering Based Hybrid Routing Protocol (THCHP) for wireless sensor networks is proposed. It is desirable to find the optimal number of clusters K_{opt} that minimizes the average sensor node energy dissipation (Heinzelman, Chandrakasan, & Balakrishnan, 2002). However, such a solution is not robust since different wireless sensor network applications possess varying degrees of sensed data correlation properties which do not permit the choice of an optimal number of clusters. For instance, consider a wireless sensor field which consists of K ($K \neq K_{opt}$) different regions where the sensed data in a given region are highly correlated. In this case, the choice of K clusters (as opposed to K_{opt}) will ensure efficient data aggregation at the CHs. To face this problem, THCHP presents a two-level hierarchical clustering based hybrid-routing protocol for applications that require periodic data monitoring as well as warnings about critical events. The use of a two-level clustering hierarchy enables us to fix the number of level 1 clusters K and to optimize the number of level 2 clusters so that the average sensor node energy dissipation is minimized.

The key network elements in the THCHP based network architecture are the wireless sensor nodes, Mobile User Nodes (MUN), and the BS.

The key steps involved in the two-level cluster setup of THCHP are as follows:

(1) The BS receives feedback from the sensor nodes on their current energy status prior to cluster setup. Using this feedback, the BS selects a set of candidate nodes to serve as L1-CHs for the next round of communication. The BS then chooses K nodes out of the candidates to be the L1-CHs and forms the L1 clusters.

(2) The BS identifies low energy peer-to-peer multi-hop routing paths for the L1-CHs via a minimum spanning tree (MST) approach (Muraganathan, Ma, Bhasin, & Fapojuwo, 2005). Following the multi-hop routing paths' selection, the BS elects the L1-CH node with the highest residual energy (amongst the K L1-CHs chosen in step 1) to serve as its direct point of contact (DPC). The DPC for the BS is not considered as a single point of failure since the role of L1-CH is randomly rotated among different sensor nodes over different communication rounds. If in case the node serving as the DPC L1-CH for the current communication round runs out of energy or gets damaged, a new DPC L1-CH node will be elected by the BS during the following communication round.

(3) Each L1 cluster is further split into k L2 clusters with the corresponding L2-CHs chosen following the procedure in step 1. However, no peer-to-peer multi-hop routing paths are utilized for the L2-CHs, as their destination node (i.e., the corresponding L1-CH) is located not too far away from them. This is opposite to the case in step 2 where the BS is located far away from the L1-CHs in which case a peer-to-peer multi-hop routing approach can yield notable energy savings. Thus, in THCHP, the L2-CHs transmit their data directly to the corresponding L1-CH.

(4) The BS creates TDMA schedules for the L1 and L2 clusters and sends the required information regarding the two-level cluster groupings to the sensor nodes.

THCHP operates in the following four major phases:

A. **Phase 1:** During phase 1, each NCH node in an L2 cluster is assigned a TDMA time-slot of duration to transmit its sensed data or route any queries it receives from the MUNs to the corresponding L2-CH.

B. **Phase 2:** The activities during phase 2 are similar to those of phase 1 with the roles of the NCH nodes and the L2-CHs replaced by the L2-CHs and the L1-CHs, respectively. However, a different TDMA schedule is utilized in phase 2, since each L1 cluster consists of κ L2-CHs.

C. **Phases 3 and 4:** During phase 3, each L1-CH transfers its aggregated data packet to the BS via a low energy peer-to-peer multi-hop routing path selected a-priori by the BS. We assume that a data packet corresponding to a given L1-CH does not undergo further data aggregations as it is routed through the other L1-CHs. Finally, a single time slot in phase 4 is reserved for the BS to respond to queries posed by the MUNs.

The simulation results show that the proposed THCHP scheme achieves significant energy savings when compared to APTEEN. In addition, comparisons between the average query response times of THCHP and APTEEN show that THCHP achieves a much lower query response time and can operate over a broad range of query arrival rates with minimal increases in response time. Hence, THCHP is a well suited routing protocol for energy efficient information retrieval in hybrid wireless sensor network applications with stringent query response time constraints.

MICRO: Minimum Cost Routing with Optimized Data Fusion

In Yin, Wang, and Øien (2008) a new routing protocol for event-driven dense wireless sensor networks is proposed, an improvement on LEACH and PEGASIS. The proposed MICRO protocol proposes a new cost function for routing, which considers the energy state of each sensor node as well as both the circuit energy consumption and the transmission energy consumption for each possible route. Moreover, the proposed routing protocol uses an iterative scheme with optimized data fusions to compute the minimum-cost route to the sink for each event-detecting sensor node.

As in the case of LEACH, the proposed protocol also divides the network into multiple clusters, each of which has one cluster head. The cluster head will store the location and the energy state information of each sensor node of its cluster. For an event message reporting, the cluster heads will perform routing computation and node-energy consumption calculation, but the event messages are not transmitted to these cluster heads as in LEACH it is transmitted like PEGASIS which performs a chain-like message transmission along the computed routes, and two or more messages representing reports on the same event will be fused into one message when they meet in a relay node.

A new cost metric for routing is proposed which considers the sensor energy states, the circuit energy consumption, and the transmission energy consumption for each possible transmission route. MICRO protocol operates in four steps as follows:

Step1
Upon the occurrence of an event, the proposed routing protocol uses an event-driven iterative scheme to compute the minimum-cost route for each event-detecting sensor nodes. MICRO computes the cost value for each edge with the following function:

$$\omega(s_i, s_j) =$$

$$(E_r(k) + E_t(k, d_{ij})) \cdot \pi / 4 / \arctan\left(\frac{ce(s_i)}{ie(s_i)}\right)$$

$$(8)$$

Here $\omega(s_i, s_j)$ is the cost value associated with the connection from sensor node s_i to node s_j, which consists of two factors. The first factor is the energy consumption associated with receiving and transmitting a k-bit message as when the node is used as a relay node. The second factor is the energy balancing factor, used to balance the energy consumption among sensor nodes. With this energy balancing factor, the cost of using edges starting from sensor nodes that have already consumed most of their available energy will increase greatly. As a result, the use of such nodes for relay transmission will be discouraged.

Step2
In the second step of the proposed routing algorithm, a minimum cost routing for all sensor nodes is performed with the cost metric computed in step 1 and using Dijkstra's algorithm. After the computation, every sensor node has a route, and an associated minimum cost value for transmitting messages, to the sink node. The routing algorithm then stays in a waiting state until one or more sensor

Figure 13. Comparison of flat and hierarchical routing in wireless sensor networks

Flat Routing	Hierarchical Routing
All nodes have the same role	Not all nodes have the same role
Non Scalable	Scalable
Collisions may occur	Efficient communication
Data aggregation by node on multi-hop path	Data aggregation and fusion by cluster head
Routes formed in region having data transmissions only	Overhead of cluster formation through network lifetime
Non uniform energy dissipation depending on traffic patterns	Uniform energy dissipation
Simple but non optimal	May be optimal but with added complexity

nodes report to their cluster heads that they have detected the occurrence of an event, and need to send an event message to the sink node.

Step3

In the third step these cluster heads communicate with each other to perform the routing computations.

Step4

In the fourth step the event-message transmission and fusion is done through the computed route. When one sensor node receives two or more event-messages, it fuses the messages into one message and transmits further the aggregated message. After transmission of the current event messages, the current energy of each cluster head is checked. If the current energy of one cluster head is lower than certain level (such as 1% of initial energy), another sensor node with the most residual energy is selected to be cluster-head.

Compared to the PEGASIS routing protocol, the MICRO protocol substantially improves the energy-efficiency of each route, by optimizing the trade-off between minimizing the total energy consumption of each route and balancing the energy state of each sensor node. It is demonstrated through simulations that the MICRO protocol outperforms the LEACH protocol and the PEGASIS protocol with respect to network lifetime with 100 - 300% and 10 - 100%, respectively.

COMPARITIVE ANALYSIS OF EXISTING HIERARCHICAL ROUTING PROTOCOLS IN WIRELESS SENSOR NETWORKS

We summarize recent research results on data routing in wireless sensor networks in the Tables shown in Figures 13 and 14. First we compare flat and hierarchical routing then we compare different hierarchical routing techniques according to many metrics.

The comparison shown in Figure 14 shows in the first field how protocols can be classified depending on how the source finds a route to the destination into proactive, reactive, and hybrid protocols, the classifications which have been discussed earlier in this chapter and we find that there are some protocols that did not focus on this issue and hence it was not known how it will perform according to this classification. In the following field we compare according to the best area size where the protocol could efficiently perform and we find that protocols that do not need a lot of direct transmission to other nodes or to the base station will perform well in small areas while other protocols work well in small areas if it needs small distances between nodes or between nodes and the base station. The next field of comparison is the energy consumption and we classify each protocol according to the energy analysis presented in its research study, if this protocol for example needs nodes to send

Figure 14. Comparison of routing protocols in wireless sensor networks

Protocol	Network Type	Area Size	Energy Consumption	Localized Coordination	Scalability	Network Knowledge Essentiality	Multipath	Query Based	Data Aggregation	Negotiation Based	Applications	Mobility
LEACH	Proactive	Small	High	Yes	Good	No	No	No	Yes	No		Fixed BS
LEACH-C	Proactive	Small	High	No	Good	No	No	No	Yes	No		Fixed BS
TEEN	Reactive	Large	Moderate	No	Good	Yes	No	No	Yes	No	Time critical data sensing	Fixed BS
APTEEN	Hybrid	Large	Moderate	No	Good	Yes	No	No	Yes	No		Fixed BS
PEGASIS	Proactive	Small	High	Yes	Limited	Yes	No	No	No	No		Fixed BS
MECN & SMECN	N/A	Small	High	Yes	Low	Yes	No	No	No	No		No
BCDCP	Proactive	Large	Moderate	No	Good	No	Possible	No	Yes	No		Fixed BS
THCHP	Hybrid	Large	Low	No	Good	No	Possible	No	Yes	No	Periodic data monitoring	Fixed BS
SOP	N/A	Small	Moderate	Yes	Low	Yes	No	No	No	No	Parking-lot Networks	No
HPAR	N/A	Small	Low	No	Good	Yes	No	No	No	No		No
VGA	N/A	Large	N/A	N/A	Good	Yes	Yes	No	Yes	Yes		No
Sensor Aggregates Routing	N/A	Large	Low	N/A	Good	No	No	Possible	Yes	No	Target Tracking	Limited
TTDD	Proactive	Large	High	N/A	Low	No	Possible	Possible	No	No		Yes
MICRO	Proactive	Small	Moderate	Yes	Good	No	Possible	No	Yes	No		Fixed BS

data to the base station directly without intermediate routing it will consume high energy whilst other protocols that use intermediate routing consume less energy. We compare also according to localized coordination, whether the nodes coordinate together for any decisions in the routing protocol like choosing the cluster head, forming routing trees, etc or not. Scalability of the protocol is also one of the important issues that need to be known for specific applications and whether increasing the number of nodes drains the performance or keeps it at an acceptable level. We also compare protocols by questioning the network knowledge essentiality, whether the nodes need to gather information about the network in any stage of the protocol, we find that in protocols where the base station takes all decisions and gives the final decision to nodes, nodes do not have to know anything about the network, while in protocols where nodes have to form trees by themselves, they will have to gather information about the network. The multipath field denotes whether in this protocol there may be multiple paths in routing or is there just a single possible route. Also in this comparison we point out if this protocol is query based or not where the destination nodes propagate a query for data from a node through the network and the node having this data responds to the node initiating the query. Also we denote whether protocols are negotiation based or not where the protocols use high level data descriptors to eliminate redundant data transmissions through negotiation. In this table we put light also on protocols that are most suited to special applications and we point out these applications. Mobility is always an open issue in discussing wireless networks and this is the last field we used in the shown comparison to show whether any of these protocols are good candidates for mobility or not.

Recent Approaches for Work in Hierarchical Routing Protocols

A lot of work has been presented recently in literature for improving performance of hierarchical routing protocols. For example researchers have given a lot of efforts in the field of choosing cluster heads like (Thein & Thein, 2010) which propose an energy efficient cluster-head selection algorithm for adapting clusters and rotating cluster head positions to evenly distribute the energy load among all the nodes. Also (Hao, Qiu, & Evans, 2009) propose an Improved Cluster-head Selection (ICS) approach. Firstly, they optimize the dynamic number of CHs. Then they obtain the suitable CHs via the improved selection procedures based on three selection phases by introducing the temporary clusters. ICS saves the energy consumption and prolongs the network lifetime. While the authors of Saadat, Saadat, and Mirjalily (2010) investigate a new threshold assignment for LEACH and xLEACH that improves energy consumption. They insert the distances of nodes from BS in threshold assignment in order to unbalance the CH selection to reduce energy consumption in the network. Also in Chen, Hong, Wang, and Jhuang (2010) they classify the lifetime into different types and give the corresponding CH selection method to achieve the lifetime extension objective. The simulation results demonstrate their study can enlarge the lifetime for different requests of the sensor networks.

A lot of work also has been done to increase the scalability and network lifetime as in Patel, Patel, and Patel (2011) where the authors focus on studying the communication routing protocol and its impact on both network lifetime and scalability. Also Tarigh and Sabaei (2011) propose an extension to LEACH by considering the number of neighbors and the remaining energy of each node in order to be chosen as a cluster-head and thus prolong the lifetime of the network.

An important issue that is also being studied in hierarchical protocols is the optimal number of cluster-heads as in Ranjan and Kar (2011) where they provide a method for determining the optimal number of cluster head for homogeneous sensor networks deployed in different scenario using a reasonable energy consumption model.

LESSONS LEARNED FROM THIS STUDY

1. Characteristics that distinguish wireless sensor networks from other wireless networks.
2. Design constraints for any proposals of routing protocols in wireless sensor networks.
3. The numerous present classifications of routing protocols in wireless sensor networks, also other more classifications could be contributed in literature.
4. Hierarchical routing protocols are one of the most promising kinds of protocols in this field where a lot of work could be done and a lot of gains could be achieved.
5. The objective analysis of the advantages and disadvantages of protocols gives a clear vision of the characteristics of each protocol.
6. Tradeoffs made in the design of protocols between all required gains are clarified like the tradeoff between energy and data accuracy, so as to try to understand that there are no gains except at cost and you have to decide if this cost is worth the gain or not and to which extent.
7. There is no absolute strong or weak protocol, depending on the application required and its characteristics, the suitable routing protocol is chosen and applied.
8. Lifetime is one of the most important issues in sensor networks and that is why it is addressed in numerous researches.
9. Addressing the proposal of any enhancement analytically besides simulations gives the results a great weight of confidence and trust.
10. Real world experimentation could give a more profound vision on the required design specifications and setup configurations. However, it could point out interesting point of views on applicability.

FUTURE DIRECTIONS FOR ROUTING IN WSNS

1. Extending Network Lifetime: Extending network lifetime is one of the main challenges confronting routing in wireless sensor networks and one of the hotspots for research in that field. Optimal routing techniques and data quality have to be balanced with power conservation and network lifetime.

2. Mobility: An important issue for routing is the consideration of mobility. Most of the current protocols assume that the sensor nodes and the sink are stationary. While, there might be situations such as battle environments where the sink and possibly the sensors may be mobile. In such cases, there must be a routing protocol that can deal with the frequent update of the position of the sink and the sensor nodes and the flow of data between them without draining the energy of nodes in such energy constrained environments.

3. Dealing with Heterogeneous Networks: Another possible future area of interest would be integrating sensor networks with other different networks like ad hoc networks that use different devices and different routing techniques. Also integrating with wired networks like the internet as most of the applications in security and environmental monitoring require the data collected from the sensor nodes to be transmitted to a server so that further analysis can be done. And in addition the requests from the end user should be made to the sink through Internet. Such integrations require routing protocols that can deal with it efficiently.

4. QoS: QoS of service is an area of research in WSNs that is still open and still needs further work as it will together with energy aware routing ensure guaranteed bandwidth through the duration of connection while using the most energy efficient path. QoS is essential for several applications like target tracking in battle fields and emergent event monitoring.

5. Using more Efficient Localization Techniques: The tradeoff between cost and accuracy is a major issue that still makes all the present localization techniques (techniques that need to estimate coordinates of nodes) not easily to be applied. Using GPS (Global Positioning system) is expensive is not able to deal with obstacles while other present techniques suffer from inaccuracy, something which makes this field an open field for future research and experiments.

6. Clustering Techniques: A very interesting issue for future research is clustering as it is a very broad area for proposing techniques depending on the demands of each application. Between optimization techniques of cluster numbers, extending the layers of clustering, cluster head selection, data aggregation techniques and covering all the network area with efficient distribution of clusters there is a lot of work to do.

7. Using Efficient Standard Naming Techniques: Efficient standard naming schemes are one of the new research areas in WSNs as many of the researchers name the data and query the nodes based on some attributes of the data in order to avoid the overhead of forming clusters, the use of specialized nodes etc.

8. Dealing with Uneven Node Distributions: Uneven node distributions in WSNs have to be dealt with carefully so that there are no uncovered areas in the network.

9. Using Intelligent Learning Techniques: Applying intelligent learning techniques to a lot of applications has proven a lot of advantages so applying it in hierarchical clusters techniques will would be a good plus.

10. Scalability: Scalability is always one of the most important issues in networking and especially in wireless networks. Inventing

routing schemes that can deal with scaled networks as the number of sensor nodes in real world sensor networks can reach hundreds or thousands of nodes is a very important point of research.

11. Real World Experiments: Research points proposed in literature may not prove that efficiency on applying in real world. Trying to apply such ideas in real world experiments may give results worth studying.

12. Security issues: Most of the present routing protocols in WSNs do not consider security issues although it is an important point in some situations like battle environments. Some aspects of the sensor networks complicate the design of a secure routing protocol, a problem which has to be addressed for application in real world.

CONCLUSION

This chapter has given an overview on routing in wireless sensor networks with all the design issues, challenges and constraints facing design in such networks. A number of classifications of routing protocols in WSNs are described in details. A comparative analysis of most hierarchical routing protocols presented in literature is given including the classical protocols and the ones added in the recent years to keep the reader updated with all contributions presented in the recent years .We chose to stress on hierarchical routing as it appears to be the most promising kind of routing and the richest for researchers to improve and apply.

We tried to highlight the advantages and disadvantages of each protocol so that they can be applied in the right places depending on the needs of each application. We end up by giving a comparison table to pinpoint easily the main features of each protocol.

Although a lot of these protocols have proven efficiency in some aspects there is still a lot of work to be done by researchers in the field and

we try to clarify some of these proposals in the future directions presented in the end.

REFERENCES

Akkaya, K., & Younis, M. (2005). A survey of routing protocols in wireless sensor networks. *Elsevier Ad Hoc Network Journal, 3*, 325–349. doi:10.1016/j.adhoc.2003.09.010

AL-Karaki, J. N., & Kamal, A. E. (2004). Routing techniques in wireless sensor networks: A survey. *IEEE Wireless Communications, 11*(6), 6-28.

Al-Karaki, J. N., & Kamal, A. E. (2004). On the correlated data gathering problem in wireless sensor networks. In *Proceedings of the Ninth IEEE Symposium on Computers and Communications*. Alexandria, Egypt: IEEE Press.

Al-Karaki, J. N., Ul-Mustafa, R., & Kamal, A. E. (2004). Data aggregation in wireless sensor networks - Exact and approximate algorithms. In *Proceedings of IEEE Workshop on High Performance Switching and Routing (HPSR)*. Phoenix, AZ: IEEE Press.

Barati, H., Movaghar, A., Barati, A., & Mazreah, A. A. (2008). A review of coverage and routing for wireless sensor networks, *37*.

Chen, J. S., Hong, Z. W., Wang, N. C., & Jhuang, S. H. (2010). Efficient cluster head selection methods for wireless sensor networks. *Journal of Networks, 5*(8), 964–970. doi:10.4304/jnw.5.8.964-970

Fang, Q., Zhao, F., & Guibas, L. (2003). Lightweight sensing and communication protocols for target enumeration and aggregation. In *Proceedings of the 4th ACM International Symposium on Mobile Ad Hoc Networking and Computing (MOBIHOC)*, (pp. 165-176). ACM Press.

Hansen, & Ewa. (2008). *Centralized routing for prolonged network lifetime in wireless sensor networks*. Mälardalen, Sweden: Mälardalen University Press.

Hao, P., Qiu, W., & Evans, R. (2009). *An improved cluster-head selection approach in wireless sensor networks*. Paper presented at the Intelligent Sensors Sensor Networks and Information Processing ISSNIP 2009 5th International Conference. Melbourne, Australia.

Heinzelman, W., Chandrakasan, A., & Balakrishnan, H. (2000). Energy-efficient communication protocol for wireless sensor networks. In *Proceeding of the Hawaii International Conference System Sciences*. Hawaii, HI: HICSS Press.

Heinzelman, W. B. (2000). *Application-specific protocol architectures for wireless networks*. PhD Thesis. Cambridge, MA: MIT Press.

Heinzelman, W. B., Chandrakasan, A. P., & Balakrishnan, H. (2002). An application-specific protocol architecture for wireless microsensor networks. *IEEE Transactions on Wireless Communications*, *1*(4), 660–670. doi:10.1109/TWC.2002.804190

Intanagonwiwat, C., Govindan, R., & Estrin, D. (2000). Directed diffusion: A scalable and robust communication paradigm for sensor networks. In *Proceedings of ACM MobiCom 2000*, (pp. 56-67). Boston, MA: ACM Press.

Kandris, D., Tsioumas, P., Tzes, A., Nikolakopoulos, G., & Vergados, D. (2009). Power conservation through energy efficient routing in wireless sensor networks. *Sensors (Basel, Switzerland)*, *9*(9), 7320–7342. doi:10.3390/s90907320

Karp, B., & Kung, H. T. (2000). GPSR: Greedy perimeter stateless routing for wireless sensor networks. In *Proceedings of the 6th Annual ACM/IEEE International Conference on Mobile Computing and Networking (MobiCom 2000)*. Boston, MA: ACM Press.

Krishnamachari, B., Estrin, D., & Wicker, S. (2002). Modeling data centric routing in wireless sensor networks. In *Proceedings of IEEE INFOCOM*. New York, NY: IEEE Press.

Li, L., & Halpern, J. Y. (2001). Minimum-energy mobile wireless networks revisited. *IEEE International Conference on Communications (ICC)*, *1*, 278-283.

Li, Q., Aslam, J., & Rus, D. (2001). Hierarchical power-aware routing in sensor networks. In *Proceedings of the DIMACS Workshop on Pervasive Networking*. IEEE Press.

Lindsey, S., & Raghavendra, C. S. (2002). PEGASIS: Power efficient gathering in sensor information systems. In *Proceedings of the IEEE Aerospace Conference*. Big Sky, MT: IEEE Press.

Lindsey, S., Raghavendra, C. S., & Sivalingam, K. (2001). Data gathering in sensor networks using the energy delay metric. *Proceedings of the IPDPS Workshop on Issues in Wireless Networks and Mobile Computing*. San Francisco, CA: IPDPS Press.

Manjeshwar, A., & Agrawal, D. P. (2001). TEEN: A protocol for enhanced efficiency in wireless sensor networks. In *Proceedings of the 1st International Workshop on Parallel and Distributed Computing Issues in Wireless Networks and Mobile Computing*, (pp. 23-27). San Francisco, CA: IEEE Press.

Manjeshwar, A., Zeng, Q. A., & Agrawal, D. P. (2002). An analytical model for information retrieval in wireless sensor networks using enhanced APTEEN protocol. *IEEE Transactions on Parallel and Distributed Systems*, *13*(12), 1290–1302. doi:10.1109/TPDS.2002.1158266

Min, R., Bhardwaj, M., Cho, S. H., Shih, E., Sinha, A., Wang, A., & Chandrakasan, A. (2001). Low-power wireless sensor networks. In *Proceedings of 14th International Conference on VLSI Design (VLSI DESIGN 2001)*, (pp. 205-210). VLSI Press.

Muraganathan, S. D., Bhasin, R. I., & Fapojuwo, A. O. (2005). A centralized energy-efficient routing protocol for wireless sensor networks. *IEEE Communications Magazine*, 8–13. doi:10.1109/MCOM.2005.1404592

Muruganathan, S. D., & Fapojuwo, A. O. (2008). A hybrid routing protocol for wireless sensor networks based on a two-level clustering hierarchy with enhanced energy efficiency. In *Proceedings of the Wireless Communications and Networking Conference, (WCNC 2008),* (pp. 2051-2056). IEEE Press.

Patel, D. K., Patel, M. P., & Patel, K. S. (2011). Scalability Analysis in wireless sensor network with LEACH routing protocol. In *Proceedings of the Computer and Management (CAMAN), 2011 International Conference,* (pp. 1-6). Wuhan, China: CAMAN Press.

Rabaey, J. M., Ammer, M. J., Patel, D., & Roundy, S. (2000). Pico radio support ad hoc ultra low power wireless networking. *IEEE Computer, 33,* 42–48. doi:10.1109/2.869369

Ranjan, R., & Kar, S. (2011). A novel approach for finding optimal number of cluster head in wireless sensor network. In *Proceedings of the NCC 2011,* (pp. 28-30). Bangalore, India: NCC Press.

Rodoplu, V., & Meng, T. H. (1999). Minimum energy mobile wireless networks. *IEEE Journal on Selected Areas in Communications, 17*(8), 133–344. doi:10.1109/49.779917

Saadat, M., Saadat, R., & Mirjalily, G. (2010) Improving threshold assignment for cluster head selection in hierarchical wireless sensor networks. In *Proceedings of the 5th International Symposium on Telecommunications (IST),* (pp.409-414). IST Press.

Savvides, A., Han, C. C., & Srivastava, M. (2001). Dynamic fine-grained localization in ad-hoc networks of sensors. In *Proceedings of the Seventh ACM Annual International Conference on Mobile Computing and Networking (MobiCom),* (pp. 166-179). ACM Press.

Sohrabi, K., & Pottie, G. (2000). Protocols for self-organization of a wireless sensor network. *IEEE Personal Communications, 7*(5), 16–27. doi:10.1109/98.878532

Subramanian, L., & Katz, R. H. (2000). An architecture for building self configurable systems. In *Proceedings of the 1st ACM International Symposium on Mobile Ad Hoc Networking & Computing,* (pp. 63-73). Boston, MA: IEEE Press.

Tarigh, H. D., & Sabaei, M. (2011). A new clustering method to prolong the lifetime of WSN. In *Proceedings of the Computer Research and Development (ICCRD), 2011 3rd International Conference,* (pp. 143-148). Shanghai, China: ICCRD Press.

Thein, M. C. M., & Thein, T. (2010). An energy efficient cluster-head selection for wireless sensor networks. In *Proceedings of the 1st International Conference on Intelligent Systems, Modelling and Simulation (ISMS 2010),* (pp. 287–291). ISMS Press.

Tilak, S., Abu-Ghazaleh, N. B., & Heinzelman, W. (2002). A two-tier data dissemination model for large-scale wireless sensor networks. *ACM Mobile Computing and Communications Review, 6*(2), 28–36. doi:10.1145/565702.565708

Werff, T. J. V. D. (2003). Global future report. *Technology Review.* Retrieved from http://www.globalfuture.com/mit-trends2003.htm.

Xu, Y., Heidemann, J., & Estrin, D. (2001). Geography-informed energy conservation for ad-hoc routing. In *Proceedings of the Seventh Annual ACM/IEEE International Conference on Mobile Computing and Networking,* (pp. 70-84). ACM Press.

Ye, F., Luo, H., Cheng, J., Lu, S., & Zhang, L. (2001). A two-tier data dissemination model for large-scale wireless sensor networks. In *Proceedings of Mobicon.* Atlanta, GA: ACM Press. doi:10.1145/570662.570664

Yin, L., Wang, C., & Øien, G. E. (2008). Minimum cost routing with optimized data fusion for event-driven dense wireless sensor networks. In *Proceedings of IEEE PIMRC.* IEEE Press.

Youngtae, N., Saewoom, L., & Kiseon, K. (2008). Basestation-aided coverage-aware energy-efficient routing protocol for wireless sensor networks. In *Proceedings of WCNC 2008, IEEE Wireless Communications & Networking Conference*, (pp. 2486-2491). Las Vegas, NV: IEEE Press.

Younis, M., Youssef, M., & Arisha, K. (2002). Energy-aware routing in cluster-based sensor networks. In *Proceedings of the 10th IEEE/ACM International Symposium on Modeling, Analysis and Simulation of Computer and Telecommunication Systems (MASCOTS 2002)*. Fort Worth, TX: ACM Press.

Yu, Y., Estrin, D., & Govindan, R. (2001). *Geographical and energy-aware routing: A recursive data dissemination protocol for wireless sensor networks. Technical Report*. Los Angeles, CA: UCLA Press.

ADDITIONAL READING

Akyildiz, I. F., Weilian, S., Sankarasubramaniam, Y., & Cayirci, E. (2002). A survey on sensor networks. *IEEE Communications Magazine, 40*(8), 102–114. doi:10.1109/MCOM.2002.1024422

Barati, H., Movaghar, A., Barati, A., & Azizi, M. A. (2008). A review of coverage and routing for wireless sensor networks. *World Academy of Science and Engineering Technology, 37*, 296–302.

Chamam, A., & Pierre, S. (2009). A distributed energy-efficient cluster formation protocol for wireless sensor networks. In *Proceedings of the 6th Annual IEEE Consumer Communications & Networking Conference, IEEE CCNC*, (pp. 10-13). Las Vegas, NV: IEEE Press.

Demirkol, I., Ersoy, C., & Alagöz, F. (2006). MAC protocols for wireless sensor networks: A survey. *IEEE Communications Magazine, 44*(4), 115–121. doi:10.1109/MCOM.2006.1632658

García-Hernández, C. F., Ibargüengoytia-González, P. H., García-Hernández, J., & Pérez-Díaz, J. A. (2007). Wireless sensor networks and applications: A survey. *International Journal of Computer Science Network Security, 7*, 264–273.

Ji, P., Wu, C., Zhang, Y., & Chu, H. (2009). A wireless sensor network routing protocol for fire estimation in building. In *Proceedings of the 2nd IEEE International Conference on Computer Science and Information Technology*, (pp.154-158). IEEE Press.

Jiang, C. F., Yuan, D. M., & Zhao, Y. H. (2009). Towards clustering algorithms in wireless sensor networks-A survey. In *Proceedings of IEEE Wireless Communications and Networking Conference (WCNC)*, (pp.1-6). Budapest, Hungary: IEEE Press.

Jiang, Z., Wu, J., Agah, A., & Lu, B. (2007). Topology control for secured coverage in wireless sensor networks. In *Proceedings of the IEEE International Conference on Mobile Ad hoc and Sensor Systems (MASS 2007)*. IEEE Press.

Kwon, T. J., & Gerla, M. (1999). Clustering with power control. In *Proceedings of IEEE MILCOM Conference*. IEEE Press.

Li, M., & Yang, B. (1999). A survey on topology issues in wireless sensor network. In *Proceedings of SPIE, the International Society for Optical Engineering*, (pp. 229–237). Orlando, FL: SPIE Press.

Li, W., & Shen, L. (2008). Optimal cluster number determination for clustered wireless sensor networks. In *Proceedings of the Global Communications Conference, GLOBECOM 2008*, (pp.251-254). New Orleans, LA: IEEE Press.

Liu, T., & Li, F. (2009). *Power-efficient clustering routing protocol based on applications in wireless sensor network*. Paper presented at the 5th International Conference on Wireless Communications Networking and Mobile Computing. Beijing, China.

Mhatre, V., & Rosenberg, C. (2004). Homogeneous vs. heterogeneous clustered sensor networks: A comparative study. In *Proceedings of IEEE International Conference on Communications (ICC 2004)*. IEEE Press.

Neander, J., Hansen, E., Nolin, M., & Bjorkman, M. (2006). Asymmetric multihop communication in large sensor networks. In *Proceedings of the 1st International Symposium on Wireless Pervasive Computing*, (p. 7). IEEE Press.

Noori, M., & Ardakani, M. (2008). A probabilistic lifetime analysis for clustered wireless sensor networks. In *Proceedings of the IEEE Wireless Communication and Networking Conference (WCNC)*, (pp. 2373-2378). Las Vegas, NV: IEEE Press.

Rai, V., & Mahapatra, R. N. (2005). Lifetime modeling of a sensor network. In *Proceedings of Design, Automation and Test in Europe* (pp. 202–203). Munich, Germany: IEEE Press. doi:10.1109/DATE.2005.196

Shafiq, U. Hashmi, Hussein, T., Mouftah, & Nicolas, D. G. (2007). Achieving reliability over cluster-based wireless sensor networks using backup cluster heads. In *Proceedings of GLOBECOM 2007*, (pp.1149-1153). IEEE Press.

Simek, M., Komosny, D., Moravek, P., Burget, R., Silva, R., & Silva, J. (2008). Data gathering model for wireless sensor networks based on the hierarchical aggregation algorithms for IP networks. *Journal of Computer Science*.

Subbu, K., & Li, X. (2010). *SFRP: A selective flooding-based routing protocol for clustered wireless sensor networks*. Paper presented at the IEEE Radio and Wireless Symposium (RWS). New Orleans, LA.

Tang, X., & Xu, J. (2006). Extending network lifetime for precision-constrained data aggregation in wireless sensor networks. In *Proceedings of the 25th IEEE INFOCOM 2006*. Barcelona, Spain: IEEE Press.

Tian, D., & Georganas, N. (2003). Energy efficient routing with guaranteed delivery in wireless sensor networks. In *Proceedings of IEEE Wireless Communications and Networking Conference*, (pp. 1923-1929). New Orleans, LA: IEEE Press.

Yassein, M. B., Al-zou'bi, A., Khamayseh, Y., & Mardini, W. (2009). Improvement on LEACH protocol of wireless sensor network (VLEACH). *International Journal of Digital Content Technology and its Applications, 3*(2), 132-136.

Younis, O., & Fahmy, S. (2004). Distributed clustering in ad-hoc sensor networks: A hybrid, energy efficient approach. In *Proceedings of IEEE INFOCOM* (pp. 629–640). IEEE Press. doi:10.1109/INFCOM.2004.1354534

Zhou, Y., Hart, M., Vadgama, S., & Rouz, A. (2007). A hierarchical clustering method in wireless ad hoc sensor networks. In *Proceedings of IEEE International Conference on Communications*, (pp. 3503-3509). IEEE Press.

KEY TERMS AND DEFINITIONS

Cluster: A group of nodes cooperating to perform a single task.

Connectivity: The degree of connection between nodes in a network.

Fault Tolerance: The failure of any part of the network does not cause the whole network failure.

Network Topology: The diagram form in which nodes are connected in a network.

Routing Protocol: Passing data packets from the source node to the destination node in a network following restrictions of that network.

Scalability: Increasing the number of nodes in a network without affecting its performance.

Wireless Sensor Network: A group of small nodes with sensing computational and wireless communications capabilities.

Chapter 10
Energy–Efficient MAC Protocols in Distributed Sensor Networks

Yupeng Hu
Hunan University, China

Rui Li
Hunan University, China

ABSTRACT

As an enabling network technology, energy efficient Medium Access Control (MAC) protocol plays a vital role in a battery-powered distributed sensor network. MAC protocols control how sensor nodes access a shared radio channel to communicate with each other. This chapter discusses the key elements of MAC design with an emphasis on energy efficiency. Furthermore, it reviews several typical MAC protocols proposed in the literature, comparing their energy conservation mechanism. Particularly, it presents a Collaborative Compression Based MAC (CCP-MAC) protocol, which takes advantage of the overheard data to achieve energy savings. Finally, it compares the performance of CCP-MAC with related MAC protocols, illustrating their advantages and disadvantages.

INTRODUCTION

Wireless Sensor Networks (WSNs) consist of large numbers of small, resource constrained senor nodes that communicate in a multi-hop network (Akyildiz, et al., 2002; Willig, 2006). By commanding these distributed sensor nodes, WSNs provide an economical solution for a variety of potential applications, including environmental

monitoring, enemy tracking, emergency alerting and so on (Zhang & Cao, 2003). Monitoring the volcanic activities is one of the representative applications for WSNs (Sohraby, et al., 2007). Figure 1 shows the WSNs' common communication architecture under field monitoring application.

Deployed far away from the permanent energy source available, WSNs depend on its own battery energy to carry out the information collecting and transmission. Differing from traditional wireless networks, WSNs have to take the

DOI: 10.4018/978-1-4666-0161-1.ch010

Figure1. WSNs' communication architecture for field surveillance application

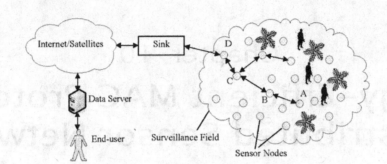

energy efficiency into account. Although the average power consumptions of sensor nodes are as little as 100mW given the state of arts in this domain, the operation efficiency are strongly depending on the specific application scenario and network deployment.

There are also quiet a few energy harvesting methods, including solar energy, wind energy and vibration energy. However, these methods can only provide a small amount of energy about 20mw or less to power these sensor nodes (Mainwaring, et al., 2002; Raghunathan, et al., 2002). The idea of maintaining and recharging these sensor nodes is impractical with regard to the expenses of keeping the massive distributed sensor network operational. Another alternative is to employ energy efficient data delivery and processing algorithms to manage the network operations. The energy efficient MAC protocols can help address this issue.

As an underlying protocol, energy conscious MAC protocols for WSNs have attracted a plethora of research interests, such as S-MAC (Ye et al, 2004), T-MAC (Dam & Langendoen, 2003), B-MAC (Polastre, et al., 2004), SCP-MAC (Ye, et al., 2006) and RI-MAC (Sun, et al., 2008), etc. However most of these contention based schemes still keep the root of traditional IEEE 802.11 protocol (Xu & Saadawi, 2002) and mainly focus on the energy-delay tradeoff (Demirkol, 2006; Muneeb, 2006). With regard to the data correla-

tion in WSN, an innovative protocol so-called CC-MAC (Vuran & Akyildiz, 2006) was proposed to reduce the data transmitted to the sink nodes under the help of a subset of representative sensor nodes. On the other hand, there are many traditional TDMA based protocols, like LEACH (Heinzelman, et al., 2000). This kind of MAC protocol has a natural advantage of energy conservation, since the duty cycle of the radio is reduced and there is no contention-introduced overhead and collisions. However, relying on the fundamental cluster based topology, TDMA protocols must restrict the nodes to communicate within the cluster. Managing inter-cluster communication and interference is an ad hoc task.

Depending on the coordinated sleep/wakeup mechanism at the underlying physical and link layer, almost all of contention based MAC protocols mainly utilize the overhearing avoidance technique to achieve significant energy savings. Actually when a sensor node overhears the data packets which do not intend for itself, before going back to sleep, it has to perform the RTS/CTS, MAC header or a long preamble check operation which already consumes considerable energy. Therefore the overhearing avoidance under a high deployment density and heavy load network also will result in a significant waste of energy. Quiet differing from prior works, CCP-MAC (Hu, et al., 2009; Hu, et al., 2011) which will be discussed in this chapter, acts as another class of MAC protocol. Instead of simply avoiding or discarding all overhearing, CCP-MAC takes advantage of the overheard data. Specifically it employs a collaborative compression method so as to reduce the data redundancy with the overheard data.

This chapter reviews energy efficient MAC protocols in wireless sensor networks. After explaining the key elements in MAC protocols design for distributed sensor networks in the second section, this chapter presents several representative MAC protocols and analysis their energy efficiency in the third section. The fourth section then introduces CCP-MAC as a case study of environment monitoring application of WSNs, detailing its design theory and channel contention mechanism. This chapter finally gives the future research directions of MAC protocols and concludes.

MAC PROTOCOL DESIGN FOR DISTRIBUTED SENSOR NETWORKS

This section discusses the key elements in MAC protocols design and how to balance them to meet the challenges of distributed sensor network and its applications. As one of the most important elements, the energy efficiency in MAC design is emphasized.

Key Elements in MAC Design

As the second layer of WSNs protocol stack, the MAC controls the sensor nodes when to access the medium and communicate with others. MAC protocols usually are influenced by a number of constraints in WSNs. Thus applications dependent MAC protocols in this domain are defined by varying the importance of the following key elements. This section first examines these key elements as well as illustrates how to make trade-offs among them in detail.

Energy efficiency is an important, almost the most concerned, element for sensor network MAC

protocols. Since WSNs are often battery constrained, it is very difficult to change or recharge batteries for sensor nodes. Actually there some design goals to build senor nodes that are as cheap as possible, so that it is beneficial to replace them rather than recharging them. Anyway prolonging the lifetime of sensor network is a critical issue. The radio is a major energy consumer on many hardware platforms. The MAC layer directly controls radio activities, and its energy savings significantly affect the overall node lifetime. More detailed discussion for energy efficiency is given below.

Scalability is the ability of MAC protocol that accommodates changes in network scale, node density and topology. In WSNs, some nodes may die and be replaced by new nodes; some nodes may move to different locations. It is very important to accommodate the changes gracefully for a good MAC protocol. Scalability is a important element, since distributed sensor networks are deployed in an ad hoc manner and operate in hostile or uncertain environments.

Collision avoidance is a fundamental task of MAC protocols in WSNs. It controls when and how a node can access the medium and send its data. Collisions are not necessary completely avoided in regular operation, e.g., contention-based MAC protocols accept certain level of collisions. The frequent collisions should be avoided yet. TDMA protocols are always free of collisions. Collision avoidance is important for energy constrained sensor networks with regard to the additional energy consumption for retransmissions. Also, collision probability can affect many other performance metrics, including latency, throughput, and delivery ratio.

Latency is the delay from when a sender has a packet to send until the packet is successfully received by the receiver. Latency importance basically depends on the applications. The detected events should be reported to the sink node as soon as possible so that the appropriate action could be taken immediately. However, in many applications such as surveillance or monitoring, nodes will be inactive with very low power consumption for a long time until something is detected. These applications are often delay tolerant, because the network speed is typically orders of magnitude faster than the speed of a physical object. The network speed has a lower bound according to the speed of the sensed object. Manipulating the operation of a MAC protocol can make a trade-off between energy consumption and message delay. When there is no sensing event in the area, the data flow in network is very light since the relevant sensor nodes are in low power sleeping mode. In this case, the latency for messages of initial and idle listen period may be less important than potential energy saving and longer active network lifetime. On the contrary, upon detecting something, the low-latency operation turns to be more important, and the sensing frequency may be faster.

Throughput refers to the amount of data (often referring to the payload data) successfully transmitted from a sender to a receiver in a unit time. Throughput in WSNs always only considers the payload data. To avoid the major data lost and retransmissions, in IEEE 802.15.4 (http://www.ieee802.org/15/pub/TG4.html), the data packet defined for MAC protocol has a short length of 40~100 bytes or so. The overhead is about 5~25 bytes long which actually occupies a large percentage of the message. In fact, considerable portion of the bandwidth is utilized by those control data, e.g., MAC header, RTS/CTS and beacon packet. Many factors influence the throughput, latency is one of the most closely related performance factors. Existing theoretical results show that longer latency indicates larger network throughput (Gupta & Kumar, 2000; Gamal, et al., 2004). While applications of WSNs demand longer lifetime would accept long latency and low data flow simultaneously.

Fairness implies the ability of different sensor node or applications to share the channel equally. It is an important attribute in traditional wireless networks, since each end point desire an equal opportunity to send or receive data for their own purposes. In many sensor network applications when bandwidth is limited, it is necessary to ensure that the sink node receives information from all sensor nodes fairly. However, at some particular time, some nodes detecting the event may have more data to send than other nodes. Rather than treating each senor node equally, collaborative operations among nodes for meeting the application requirements are first considered. Thus fairness is less important is sensor networks.

In summary, the above elements represent some major aspects must be considered in MAC design. Especially the energy efficiency, effective collision avoidance and scalability to density and network size are most important factors. Other elements are normally secondary.

Energy Efficiency in MAC Protocols

WSNs MAC protocols must place an emphasis on energy efficiency rather than balancing throughput, latency and scalability. Before explaining the resolution of energy efficiency, below we first list the major energy wastage sources in MAC protocols for WSNs.

Collision is the first major source of energy waste. It occurs when two or more nodes attempt to transmit simultaneously. As a result, the transmitted packets become corrupted and have to be discarded. The retransmissions increase the energy consumption. In massive distributed sensor networks, collisions normally are hard to be avoided and are controlled in certain extent.

Idle-listening is a second source. It occurs when the radio is listening to the channel to receive possible traffic that is not sent. The cost can be especially high in a periodic sample collecting operation if there is no sensory data. It is true in many WSNs applications that the sensor node will be in idle listening state for most of the time if nothing is sensed. Idle listening is a primary factor of radio energy consumption in these cases. While traditional MAC protocols in ad hoc wireless network always listen to the channel when active, and can turn off the device completely if there is no data to send. Generally the shortage radios in WSNs show listening costs of the same order of magnitude as receiving and transmission costs, often 50~100% of the energy needed for receiving. For example, on the Mica2 mote (www. xbow.com/pdf/XMesh_MOTEVIEW_PR.pdf), the ratios for radio power draw are 1:1:1.41 at 433MHz with RF signal power of 1mW in transmission mode. Saving the energy consumption of idle listening is one of common goals of most MAC protocol design.

Overhearing is a third source of waste. It happens when a sensor node receives packets that are destined for other nodes. Overhearing unnecessary data can be a dominant factor of energy waste when traffic load is heavy and node density is high. The overheard data is often useless and thus is discarded.

Control packet overhead is another source of waste. Control packet overheads are necessary for regulating access to the channel. Energy can be consumed in sending, receiving and listening various control packets. The effective throughput may be reduced since control packets do not directly convey sensory data. Also, additional control packets may lead to more collisions when the traffic load is heavy, and hence reduce the throughput.

Over-emitting is the last source of waste. It happens when the destination node is not ready to receive during the transmission procedure, and hence the packet is not correctly received.

Finally, the transition between different operation modes, such as sleep, idle, receive and transmit, can result in significant energy consumption. Limiting the number of transitions between sleep and active modes achieves a considerable energy savings.

A MAC protocol achieves energy savings by controlling the radio to avoid or reduce energy waste from the above sources. Generally, turning off the radio when it is not needed is an important strategy for energy conservation. A complete energy conversation scheme must consider all sources of energy consumption, not just the radio. For example, on the Mica2 mote, the 433MHz radio, when idle or receiving data, consumes about the same power draw as CPU when active.

MAC Protocol Performance Metrics

In order to evaluate and compare the performance of energy conscious MAC protocols, the following metrics are being used by the research community.

1. *Energy consumption per bit*: The energy efficiency of the sensor nodes can be defined as the total energy consumed/ total bits transmitted. The unit of energy efficiency is joules/bit. The lesser the number the better is the efficiency of a protocol in transmitting the information in the network. This performance metrics gets affected by all the major sources of energy waste in wireless sensor network such as idle listening, collisions, control packet overhead and overhearing.
2. *Average delivery ratio*: The average packet delivery ratio is the number of packets received to the number of packets sent averaged over all the nodes.
3. *Average packet latency*: The average packet latency is the average time taken by the packets to reach to the sink.
4. *Network throughput*: The network throughput is defined as the total number of packets delivered to the sink node per time unit. A related attribute is *goodput*, which refers to the network throughput measured only by data received by the sink without and errors.

REPRESENTATIVE WORK

MAC design for WSNs can be broadly divided into contention based and TDMA protocols:

Figure2. S-MAC frame format

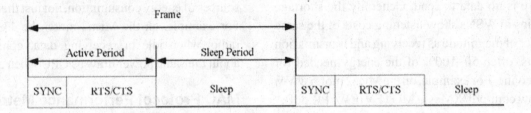

Contention Based MAC Protocols. The wireless nodes here contend to enter the wireless channel of connectivity and the winner node reserves the channel to itself until the end its transmission. Contention protocols of WSN mainly still inherit the CSMA (carried sense multiple access) mechanism concluded in the IEEE 802.11 standard.

TDMA (time division multiple access) Based MAC Protocols. The shared wireless channel here is divided into time slots, and each node knows its time slot when to enter the medium and conducts its operation.

Current literature on medium access in WSN focuses mainly on energy consumption management. In particular, the energy efficiency relies on a coordinated sleep/wakeup technique. Below we briefly discuss several popular MAC protocols in WSNs.

Contention Protocol

In WSNs, the contention based MAC protocol tries to avoid energy waste due to collisions, idle listening, overhearing and control packet overhead, by adjusting the coordinated sleep/wakeup technique. Based on this technique, contention protocol allocates the common channel for all nodes on-demand, offering a more scalability

and adaptivity to the changes on number of nodes than TDMA since TDMA requires slotting the time into slots to each node for channel access. We list some of the works in this area of research.

S-MAC (Ye, et al., 2004) is a contention based MAC protocol designed explicitly for wireless. While reducing energy consumption is the primary goal of this design. The energy efficiency of it relies on both a locally managed synchronization scheme and a periodic sleep/listen schedule. It uses synchronization to form virtual clusters of nodes on the same sleep schedule. These schedules coordinate nodes to avoid the over-emitting problem and minimize additional latency. Thus sensor nodes can awake to communicate if necessary while sleeping as much as possible. The energy efficient low-duty-cycle operation reduces the active time of nodes, meanwhile introducing a problem of latency when traffic load is high. To address this issue, S-MAC employs the adaptive listening technique, where nodes that overhear CTS can wake up at the end of the transmission to possibly act as the next hop. S-MAC also uses the same mechanism as IEEE 802.11 to avoid the overhearing, saving considerable energy. The frame format for S-MAC is shown in Figure 2.

T-MAC (Dam & Langendoen, 2003) aims to enhance the poor results of S-MAC under variable traffic load. In T-MAC, the listening period of T-MAC ends when no activation event has occurred for a time threshold. This way the nodes

Figure3. T-MAC frame format

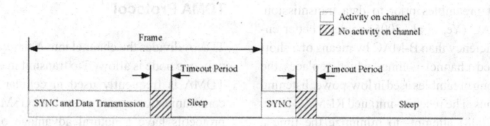

can save more energy by lowering the amount of time they spend in idle listening and also adapt to changes in traffic conditions. The decision for the time threshold is presented along with some solutions to the early-sleeping problem defined by the authors. Unlike S-MAC, T-MAC does not rely on a fixed duty cycle schedule. Instead, as shown in Figure 3, it uses a timer to indicate the end of the active period. Figure 3 also shows a T-MAC frame where the first active period has the sensor node involved in a message transmission and the second active period has only a SYNC transmission.

As a typical unscheduled MAC protocol, B-MAC (Polastre, et al., 2004) enables sensor nodes independently follow a sleeping schedule and uses a preamble to wakeup sleeping neighbors. Figure 4 shows the data transmission in B-MAC. As can be seen, prior to DATA frame transmission, a sender transmits a long wake-up signal, named a preamble, which lasts longer than the receiver's sleep interval. B-MAC is energy efficient only under light traffic since a node spends only a very short period of time in idle listening the channel activity. However, a node with B-MAC may wake up and remain awake due to channel activity, only to, in the end, receive one or more frames actually destined for other nodes. As the default MAC protocol of TinyOS (Culler, 2006), B-MAC relies on an adaptive bidirectional protocol interfaces so as to optimize performance for specific applications.

Figure4. B-MAC data transmission

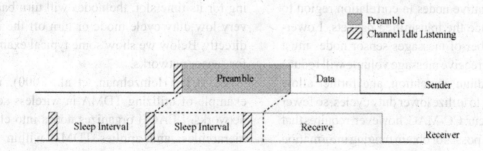

X-MAC (Michael, et al., 2006) solves the preamble overhearing problem in B-MAC by using a strobed preamble that consists of sequence of short preambles prior to data transmission. SCP-MAC (Ye, et al., 2006) achieve better energy efficiency than B-MAC by means of a short scheduled channel polling, which replaces the costly long preambles used in low-power listening operations. The receiver-initiated RI-MAC (Sun, et al., 2008) attempts to minimize the time a sender and its intended receiver occupy the channel to find a rendezvous time for exchanging data. In RI-MAC, each node periodically wakes up and broadcasts a beacon. When a node wants to send a data frame to a neighbor, it stays active silently and starts data transmission upon receiving a beacon from that neighbor. DSMAC (Lin, et al., 2004) adds dynamic duty cycle feature to S-MAC (Ye, et al., 2004). The aim is to decrease the latency for delay sensitive applications. The principal aim of DMAC (Lu, et al., 2004) is to achieve very low latency, but still to be energy efficient. It could be summarized as an improved slotted aloha algorithm where slots are assigned to the sets of nodes based on a data gathering tree.

CC-MAC (Vuran & Akyildiz, 2006) is proposed to reduce the number of packets transmitted to the sink nodes under the help of a subset of representative sensor nodes. It aims for event-centered wireless sensor network application. To achieve energy savings, CC-MAC filters sensory data from highly correlated sensor nodes in an effort to directly reduce the number of messages the sensor network must handle. Namely, it employs the representative nodes in correlation region to directly reduce the transmitted packets. Lowering the number of messages sensor nodes must transmit and receive message volume will reduce wireless medium contention, and further allow sensor nodes to utilize lower duty cycles, so fewer collisions occur. CC-MAC, however, requires that sensor nodes posses or obtain ranging information about their neighbors in order to filter data from correlated sensor nodes. The complicated nature of the CC-MAC protocol may also limit the application of itself.

TDMA Protocol

TDMA divides the channel into N time slots, and only one node is allowed to transmit in each slot. TDMA is frequently used in cellular wireless communication systems, such as GSM. TDMA protocols have a natural advantage of energy conservation compared to contention protocols, because the duty cycle of the radio is reduced and there is no contention-introduced overhead and collisions.

However, TDMA has some disadvantage that limits it use in wireless sensor networks. TDMA protocol usually requires the nodes to form real communication clusters, such as Bluetooth (Haartsen, 2000) and LEACH (Heinzelman, et al., 2000). Most nodes in a real cluster are restricted to communicate within the cluster; peer-to-peer communication is not directly supported. Thus its scalability and adaptivity is normally not as good as that of a contention-based protocol. When new nodes join or old nodes leave a cluster, the head or base station must adjust frame length or slot allocation. Also, TDMA protocols depend on distributed, fine-grained time synchronization to align slot boundaries.

There are many variations on basic TDMA protocol in the literature of WSNs. The major advantage of TDMA for WSNs is its energy efficiency, since it directly supports low power consumption operations on nodes. When waiting for its time slot, the nodes will turn back to very low duty cycle mode or turn off the radio directly. Below we show some typical examples for sensor networks.

LEACH (Heinzelman, et al., 2000), is an example of utilizing TDMA in wireless sensor networks. LEACH organizes nodes into cluster hierarchies, and applies TDMA within each cluster. Particularly, it rotates the cluster head within the cluster to distribute energy dissipation evenly throughout the nodes, enabling scalability and robustness locally. LEACH is an example that directly extends the cellular TDMA model to sensor network.

TRAMA (Rajendran, et al., 2003) is proposed to increase the utilization of classical TDMA in an energy-efficient manner. It is similar to NAMA (Bao & Garcia-Luna-Aceves, 2001), where for each time slot a distributed election algorithm is used to select one transmitter within two-hop neighborhood.

Designed for low rate wireless network applications, IEEE 802.15.4 introduces a superframe structure with two disjoint periods, i.e. contention access period and contention free period. But the network topology is also assumed to be cluster-based, requiring significant additional processing complexity and overhead in the overall sensor network.

CCP-MAC

CCP-MAC, proposed by Hu et al, is a spatial correlation based MAC protocol specifically designed for wireless sensor networks. The idea of compressing the data redundancy is not new in WSN. But we make the first attempt to compress the data in link layer by taking advantage of the overheard data.

There has been some related research effort to study the spatial correlation and in-networking data aggregation in WSN (Chalermek, et al., 2003; Pradhan, et al., 2003). While most of these data aggregation schemes only reduce the number of transmitted bits at cluster heads on the delivery route; from the network point of view, the amount of transmitted sensory data can be further minimized at the source nodes by regulating the channel access based on the overheard data. On the other hand, current literature on medium access in WSN focuses mainly on energy-latency tradeoff. Almost all of contention based MAC protocols mainly utilize the overhearing avoidance technique to improve energy efficiency. In fact, the overhearing avoidance under a high deployment density and heavy load network also incurs a significant waste of energy.

Motivated by the costly overhearing avoidance operations and inherent data correlation, we attempt to take advantage of the overheard data by compressing. Specifically we employ a collaborative compression method so as to reduce the data redundancy with the overheard data. Unlike prior MAC proposals, the event-centered CCP-MAC aims to collaboratively compress the spatial redundancy of observations by utilizing the overheard data, which is often treated useless.

CCP-MAC is suitable for latency insensitive applications such as precision agriculture, smart home and field monitoring, especially when high nodes density is required to provide sensing at a fine granularity. It is beneficial for sensor nodes to employ the CCP-MAC in MAC layer. The advantage is that, the redundancy of information pending in the link layer, can be eliminated at the source nodes. Afterwards, the forwarding nodes can further compress them in upper layer with a wide variety of existing in-networking processing or data aggregation schemes.

As a spatial correlation based protocol, CCP-MAC is proposed to co-exist with other MAC protocols like S-MAC, by importing a new channel contention mechanism below. To better describe the details of channel contention mechanism and MAC operations, we describe the related models and design goals first.

Correlation and Energy Models

In this subsection, we describe the correlation and energy consumption model used in our protocol. Many WSN systems have been developed for the specific applications such as environment monitoring, target tracking, disaster rescue, etc (Akyildiz, et al., 2002; Besma, et al., 2008). A representative sensor node for these applications, like Micaz node, has adequate memory to store the necessary protocol parameters. Because of high deployment density, the sensory data is spatially correlated. Moreover, we assume each node could measure the distance between the neighbor to itself by some means (For instance, at the system initialization stage, each node can control the sounder on its sensor board to broadcast a sound sample to the neighbors. This way all receivers are able to estimate the distance $D = T \cdot s$ between the sender to themselves according to the sound propagation delay T and speed s). Let's take an arbitrary monitoring node as the source node of the information. Suppose each node has been pre-installed certain spatial correlation model, which is only relevant to distance between sender and receiver. Assume that the sensory data gathered by a sensor node comprises a measurement value and a noise, and then a sensory sample S_i at time t can be expressed as:

$$S_i(t) = M(x_i, y_i, z_i, t) + N(x_i, y_i, z_i, t) \qquad (1)$$

where (x_i, y_i, z_i) denotes node i's position according to our coordinate system, M represents the measured value and N is the environment noise. We employ the commonly used model (Diggle, et al., 1998; Pattem & Krishnamachari, 2004), and assume the sensory data given in (1) are Joint Gaussian Random Variables (JGRVs) with zero mean and δ_M^2 variances, and noise N_i are variables with zero mean and δ_N^2 variances. In particular, the spatial correlation is inversely proportional to the distance between the nodes i and j:

$$\rho_{i,j}^{spatial} = \frac{E[S_i S_j]}{\delta_M^2 + \delta_N^2} = e^{-\varepsilon d_{i,j}} = e^{-\varepsilon \sqrt{(x_i - x_j)^2 + (y_i - y_j)^2 + (z_i - z_j)^2}}$$

$$(2)$$

where $\varepsilon > 0$ denotes a constant of intensity. Less value of ε will introduce larger correlation. By utilizing some entropy coding such as the Slepian-Wolf coding (Slepian & Wolf, 1973), sensor

nodes are able to estimate the condition entropy as well as the compression factor without extra communication cost. Hence we employ the spatial correlation factor in Equation (2) to calculate the compression factor in experiments for simplicity. In this chapter we will perform the collaborative compression method based on these prerequisites.

In addition, we also give an energy consumption model used in this chapter. The energy consumption for transmission and reception is specified as $E_{tx}(L) = P_{tx} \cdot L \cdot t_{byte}$ and $E_{rx}(L) = P_{rx} \cdot L \cdot t_{byte}$ respectively, where t_{byte} is the time cost for transmission a byte, L, is the data packet length, P_{tx} and P_{rx} denote the transmission and the reception power respectively. Similarly, the energy consumption for compression is specified as $E_{cp}(L) = P_{cp} \cdot L \cdot t_{cp}$, where P_{cp} denotes the compressing power which is almost negligible compared to transmission or reception power, $P_{tx} \gg P_{cp}$, $P_{rx} \gg P_{cp}$; t_{cp} denotes the time cost for compressing a single byte, $t_{cp} \ll t_{byte}$.

Design Goals

This subsection will explain our MAC design goals with an example shown in Figure 5. Figure 5 depicts a simplest network operation scenario of our method, where the network only consists of a single sink and two adjacent sensor nodes A and B, both nodes can simultaneously detect an event in a region. Suppose the amount of data on node B and A is L_B and L_A respectively. Let $L_{B|A}$ be the amount of data that B needs to transmit to sink if it compresses based on A. This way the compression ratio, i.e., $\dfrac{L_{B/A}}{L_B}$, can be calculated subject to the data compressing mechanism, based on the distance between them.

Since the energy for overhearing and compression operations may be even larger than the energy saved through compression, the first issue is when and how a sensor node to make use of

Figure 5. A simple operation scenario of our MAC protocol for event monitoring. By overhearing each other's data packets during the channel contention period, both A and B may perform data compressions before transmissions.

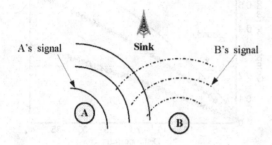

the overheard data. Assume the node A first accesses the channel and then sends a RTS packet to the sink. The node B should decide whether to overhear the following data packet or not, and the optional MAC operations are as follows.

- If node B decides not to overhear and then directly transmits its own sensory data with a length of L_B without compressing, the energy consumption of B should be $E_B = P_{tx} \cdot L_B \cdot t_{byte}$.

- By contrast, if B prefers to accept the following overheard data packets from A to the end, and further compresses them with its own sensory data using some compression algorithms; finally it sends the aggregated data packets with a length of $L_{B|A}$ to sink, thus the energy consumption of B is the sum of energy for overhearing, compressing and following transmission, i.e., $E_{B|A} = P_{rx} \cdot t_{byte} + P_{cp} \cdot L_B \cdot t_{cp} + P_{tx} \cdot L_{B|A} \cdot t_{byte}$.

To simplify the analysis, here assume that $L_B = L_A = L$, $L_{B|A} = L^*$, and $L^* \le L$. When $E_{B|A} < E_B$, we say the overhearing is effective, as the following condition, more energy will be saved if B decides to compress its data based on the overheard data packets before the transmission. Note that

$t_{cp} \ll t_{byte}$, $P_{rx} \gg P_{cp}$ and $P_{rx} < P_{tx}$ on common sensor node. Therefore when the compression ratio (L^*/L) is less than some threshold, it is beneficial for a node to compress before the transmission.

$$E_{B|A} < E_B \Rightarrow \frac{L^*}{L} < 1 - \frac{1}{P_{tx}}(P_{rx} + P_{cp} \cdot \frac{t_{cp}}{t_{byte}}) \quad (3)$$
$$< 1 - \frac{P_{rx}}{P_{tx}}$$

It is worth emphasizing that here the energy cost for being able to overhear is not considered, since our method does NOT incur additional node rendezvous operations. One goal of our MAC design is being able to co-exist with the existing schedule or synchronization schemes employed by other MAC protocols such as S-MAC. On the other hand, it is unnecessary for all surrounding nodes of the sender to remain awake, thus ineffective overhearing will be avoided in our MAC design as well.

Generally the compression ratio decreases when spatial correlation increases (Tharini & Vanaja, 2009; Tharini, 2010). In particular, we estimate compression ratio by $L^*/L = 1 - \rho^{spatial}$. Let $P_{tx} = 60$mW, $P_{rx} = 45$mW, and $\varepsilon = 0.01, 0.02, 0.03$. Figure 6 shows the boundary of region when it is beneficial for B to perform the compression. Specifically the upper boundary of compression ratio is 0.25, and the area below the boundary corresponds to the estimated value of (L^*/L) and transmission distance $d_{B,A}$ at which the B should compress based on A. It is easy to see the compression is more effective when B is closer to A. It is worth emphasizing that this estimation method is not very accurate but does work, we also evaluate its side effect in our experiments.

The remaining issue is to design a collaborative compression scheme, maximizing the nodes' lifetimes before node A or B dies. Below are two kinds of schemes:

- Scheme P_1. Let node A send data to sink at first, then node B will evaluate the possible compression factor. According to Equation (3), if the energy consumption can be reduced it will compress based on the overheard data sent by A before the transmission; otherwise, it will send to sink directly.
- Scheme P_2. Let node B send firstly, then node A will decide whether to sends data to sink directly or not, with respect to its estimated compression ratio.

In P_1, the energy consumption for each node is, $E_A^{P_1} = E_A = P_{tx} \cdot L_A \cdot t_{byte}$, $E_B^{P_1} = \min\{E_B, E_{B|A}\}$, respectively. In P_2, the energy consumption for each node is, $E_A^{P_1} = \min\{E_A, E_{A|B}\}, E_B^{P_1} = E_B = P_{tx} \cdot L_B \cdot t_{byte}$. Assume the P_1 and P_2 are employed r_1 and r_2 rounds for data-collecting respectively, before some node depleting its limited energy resource. Let e_A, e_B represent the initial energy of node A and B, respectively, the issue of maximizing the nodes lifetime until some node dies via collaborative compression scheme can be formulated as follows:

$$\arg\max_{r_1, r_2}\{r_1 + r_2\} \tag{4}$$

subject to

$$\begin{cases} r_1 \geq 0, r_2 \geq 0, \\ (E_A^{P_1} \cdot r_1 + E_A^{P_2} \cdot r_2) \leq e_A, \\ (E_B^{P_1} \cdot r_1 + E_B^{P_2} \cdot r_2) \leq e_B. \end{cases} \tag{5}$$

Since a node's lifetime is much longer compared to a data-gathering round in most applications, the r_1 and r_2 can be treated as real variables. Thus the above optimization problem is turned to be a linear programming problem which can be resolved with conventional standard methods.

Figure 6. Boundary of compression ratio for B to compress its own data based on A

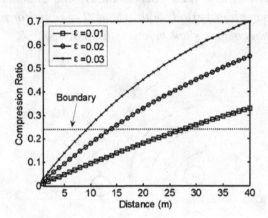

In conclusion, the following goals should be achieved in our MAC design.

- The first goal is being able to co-exist with other MAC protocols, without incurring additional node rendezvous operations.
- The second goal is to avoid ineffective overhearing. This way it is no need for all neighboring nodes of the sender to remain awake and overhear the whole packet until the end of transmission.
- The last, but most challenging goal, is being able to regulate the collaborative compressions among nodes in a distributed fashion.

With respect to above goals, we extend the linear programming model to a more complex network scenario, enabling the CCP-MAC protocol in a distributed environment. We describe the packet structures before presenting the details of CCP-MAC.

Packet Structure

We define the data packet structure of CCP-MAC for TinyOS1.X in Figure 7. CCP-MAC requires an additional field *cTag* in data packet. The RTS/CTS control packet also is used in CCP-MAC, as described in Figure7(a), the node receiving a RTS packet will reply a CTS packet piggybacking the same *cTag* value, so that the surrounding nodes overhearing the packet can decide whether to compress it or not. If the RTS/CTS mechanism is not employed, the *cTag* field should be defined in MAC layer header as shown in Figure7(b). Also, to avoid the ineffective overhearing of long preamble in B-MAC, employing raw bits stream based preamble for low power listening operation, the indicator *cTag* also can easily be embedded in the stream of preamble which is not presented here. Likewise, it also can be embedded into the sequence of short preambles used in X-MAC for the same purpose.

Protocol Design

This section will present the details of CCP-MAC, including its channel contention mechanism and MAC operations. By extending the simple collaborative compression scheme described previously to a general network scenario, the nodes participating the scheme in a data collecting round, will be divided into the following two types of subsets. One of basic task of CCP-MAC is to find out the nodes belong to subsets *U* and *V* respectively, and further coordinate them to perform the compressions.

- The first subset, denoted by *U*, consisting of the nodes that will not perform the compression and thus will be used by others for their compressions.
- On the contrary, the second subset, denoted by *V*, consisting of the nodes that will compress its own data based on the data of nodes in *U*.

Figure7. Packet structures defined in TinyOS1.X for RTS/CTS/ACK control, MAC header and MAC packet

```
// control packet -- RTS, CTS, ACK
typedef struct {
    PhyHeader phyHdr;
    char type;  //RTS/CTS/ACK
    uint8_t cTag;  //0,1,2
    uint16_t toAddr;
    uint16_t fromAddr;
    uint16_t duration;
    int16_t crc; //for CRC check
} __attribute__((packed)) MACCtrlPkt;
```

(a) Control packet

```
// MAC header
typedef struct {
    PhyHeader phyHdr;
    char type;
    uint8_t cTag;
    uint16_t toAddr;
    uint16_t fromAddr;
    uint16_t duration;
    uint8_t fragNo;
} __attribute__((packed)) MACHeader;
```

(b) MAC header

```
// MAC packet
typedef struct {
    MACHeader hdr;
    int8_t data[MAX_MAC_PAYLOAD];
    int16_t crc;
} MACPkt;
```

(c) MAC packet

Channel Contention Mechanism

With regard to the channel contention mechanism, CCP-MAC replaces the traditional random time slot selection mechanism used in S-MAC or other MAC protocols, with a new non-uniform time slot mechanism. The main idea of our mechanism is to enable the nodes that can't perform the compression or still having much residual energy to send at earlier time slot, meanwhile the other nodes with less energy to perform the compression before the transmissions. Each node n is able to calculate the compression ratio based on the distance to neighboring nodes. This way the nodes in subset U that node n can exploit for compression will be picked out. When no surrounding nodes can be used for compression, it means the node itself is not suitable to carry out compression, and should send at the earliest. Otherwise, every node will calculate the remaining energy when carrying out transmission without compression, and the nodes having more residual energy will transmit with higher priorities. To implement CCP-MAC, each node maintains a neighboring nodes information table which comprises the neighbors' ID, distance and residual energy. Notice that the R designates the frequency of renewing the information table, for instance, the information table can be updated every R events. Thus each node could find out the status and residual energy of neighboring nodes timely. Actually the value of residual energy could be indicated by the working voltage at that time.

Specifically, the CCP-MAC exploits a residual energy priority based contention window mechanism which utilizes non-uniform probability distribution function to determine the transmission sequence of nodes. In CCP-MAC, each node will select a time slot (like the one defined in a slotted CSMA) to send with certain probability. The more residual energy the node has, the higher probability it will select the former time slot to send. Note that the nodes which are unsuitable for carrying out compression will send firstly. Our contention window mechanism uses the so-called linear extension method, i.e., $CW_i = (i+1) \cdot CW_0$, every node is able to select the slot from $[1, CW_i]$. The reasons of using linear extension method rely on two sides: firstly, the former two time slots have the same size as in IEEE 802.11 MAC (Kanodia, et al., 2001; Xu & Saadawi, 2002); secondly, the probability of continuous three or more times collisions is negligible (Bottigliengo, et al., 2004), thereby the transmission delay will be reduced compared with the binary back-off mechanism. The probability of choosing time slot is,

$$\Pr(c) = \beta(\frac{1}{1 + e^{-\alpha(c+1)}} - \frac{1}{1 + e^{-\alpha c}}), c \in [1, CW_i]$$

(6)

where $\alpha(0 < \alpha \leq 1)$ is the ratio of residual energy to initial energy, β is a balance parameter.

Figure 8 depicts the α and β effect to transmission probability. The Y axis is the transmission probability and the X axis is the time slot number. As shown in Figure 8(a), α and β are fixed, the probabilities for former time slot are higher than posterior ones. When α is increasing, the transmission probabilities of former time slots become higher while the posterior turns to be lower. Consequently the parameter α is capable of controlling the transmission sequence well, enabling the nodes with more residual energy to send earlier. The Figure 8(b) depicts how the transmission probability is changing when $\alpha = 0.3$ and $\beta = 1, 2, 4$ respectively. The bigger β causes higher transmission probability for every time slot. We notice that α is set to 1 for the nodes which are unsuitable for carrying out compressions.

Notable, we constrain each node perform the compression based on only one optimal node's data. We will illustrate the purpose of this constraint in in the next subsection. Before selecting a time slot, via a simple analysis we stated earlier, every node can find out only one optimal node which it can compress to achieve maximum energy savings, even though there are several nodes that it can exploit. At the beginning each node will not know which nodes are suitable for compression and their residual energy, until the subsequent data-gathering rounds by checking the *cTag* value in overheard data packets. This way it takes it for granted that no nodes belongs can be used for compression by default. Furthermore the residual energy values of neighboring nodes will be obtained by updating the information table periodically.

Figure 8. Transmission probability for each time slot of slotted CSMA with different α and β

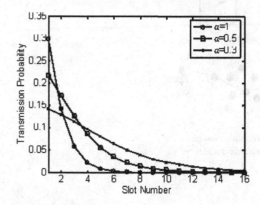

(a) Effects of different α

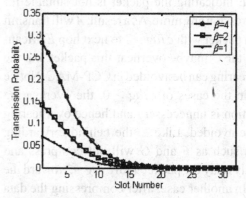

(b) Effects of different β

MAC Operations and Procedures

In addition to the new channel contention mechanism, CCP-MAC requires some extra operations for collaborative data compressions. The details of the operations and the procedures are as follows.

1. When waiting for the subsequent time slot, if a node n happens to overhear a RTS packet destined to others, then it will implement the following procedure based on the *cTag* value:

   ◦ Case 1: *cTag* = 0. It indicates that the following data packet will come from the source node with more re-

sidual energy or the node that is unsuitable for performing the compressions. If the source node happen to be the node suitable for compression, n will accept the overheard data packet and compress its own data based on it, meanwhile setting *cTag* = 1 in the new data packet which will be sent out when the channel is clear. Otherwise, if the node isn't suitable for compression, following the common overhearing avoidance procedure, n will go to sleep for a while so as to avoid the ineffective overhearing.

   ◦ Case 2: *cTag* = 1. It reflects that the coming data packet has been compressed, and n will return to sleep.

   ◦ Case 3: *cTag* = 2. It indicates that the coming data packet is forwarded by other nodes, the data correlation is relative low and thus the data will not be compressed. Then n goes back to sleep also.

2. If the node n listens a RTS packet destined to itself, it will accept the coming data packet, and then

   ◦ Case 1: *cTag* < 2, n will compress its data based on the received data packet and hence set *cTag* = 2. Afterwards, it will wait to send.

   ◦ Case 2: *cTag* = 2, it means that the data packet is a forwarded packet which will not be used for compression with regard to the low spatial correlation. Furthermore n sets α = 1 so as to send the packet next time with the highest priority.

3. If there is no data packet when the time slot is starting, it means that n itself belongs to *U*. Thus it will set *cTag* = 0 and send out its data packets immediately.

Besides the RTS/CTS mechanism, with respect to the beacon in RI-MAC or preamble in

Figure 9. An application of CCP-MAC in field monitoring

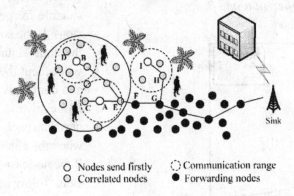

B-MAC, X-MAC, sensor nodes also can check the address and *cTag* field embedded in it, so as to decide whether to overhear the coming data packet or go back to sleep immediately. This way it is unnecessary for all surrounding nodes to keep awake to overhear a copy of the data packet. By replacing the traditional channel mechanism with the proposed channel contention mechanism and above procedures, CCP-MAC can co-exist with other MAC protocols. We provide some cases study in monitoring application below, illustrating the operational principles of CCP-MAC.

Case Study

The application of CCP-MAC in field monitoring is shown in Figure 9. Since the residual energy of the source nodes *A* and *B* located in event area is much more than that of others, they will success to obtain the channel to send data packets. According to the *fromAddr* field in these data packets, the neighboring nodes can decide whether to compress its own data based on these data packets or not.

In this case, the source nodes *C, D* may overhear the RTS of *A, B* respectively, thus will accept the following data packet to the end and compress them, setting *cTag* = 1 for transmission. On its delivery route, the compressed packet at source node *C* will be sent to *A* and further be compressed again with *A*'s new sensory data since *cTag* = 1.

Finally the indicator *cTag* in the packet becomes 2 at *A*, indicating the packet is not suitable for compression any more. As a result, *A* will transmit a data packet with *cTag* = 2 to next hop *E*. Meanwhile the *C* maybe overhear this packet, but the overhearing can be avoided in CCP-MAC. Notice that, in the cases of *cTag* > 0, the overhearing operation is unnecessary and hence overhearing can be avoided. Like *E*, the behind forwarding nodes such as *F* and *G* will not compress and directly relay the packet with *cTag* = 2 toward the sink. In another case, after compressing the data packet with *cTag* = 0 from source node *I*, node *H* will set *cTag* = 2. Forwarding node *G* on the route can find out *cTag* = 2, so as to send the data packet out right away.

CCP-MAC Performance

Network Parameters

This section presents the performance evaluation for CCP-MAC protocol. We develop a simulation system for testing the CCP-MAC protocol in large scale sensor network based on the OMNET testbed (Varga, 2001). According to Micaz sensor node's performance parameters, we use the following network scenario and protocol parameters:

Figure 10. Gain in lifetime when CCP-MAC is applied

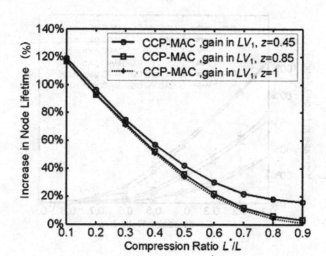

- 800 sensor nodes are randomly deployed over a 0.6km by 0.6km square area. The simulated events randomly occur in some regions periodically. Every event detecting node will sent five data packets with a length of 40 bytes each time. N is the number of event detecting nodes, $N \in [20, 100]$.
- The CCP-MAC is combined with S-MAC, B-MAC for evaluating lifetime of network respectively. The duty cycle is set to 5%, $P_{tx} = 60$mW, $P_{rx} = 45$mW, $P_{cp} = 20$mW, the data rate is 250Kbps, and the transmission range for a sensor node is 60 meters. Note that, for simplicity, we embed some raw bits in the preamble stream as the indicator *cTag* when testing CCP-MAC with B-MAC.
- The neighbors information table will be updated every R events, R v [500, 10000], and the compression ratio is $L*/L \in [0.1, 0.9]$.

Experiments and Analysis

The first experiment we carried out aims to investigate the gain in lifetime when perform the compression scheme based on the data of only one node and several other nodes respectively. Originally each node n needs to send out 200 bytes of data on detecting an event with CCP-MAC. Assume that node n needs to transmit $L*$ bytes of data after compressing its own data based on the data of one other node. If n continues to perform the compression based on the data of m other nodes, we suppose it needs to transmit $L*m^z$ bytes of data, and z denotes the compression ratio. As illustrated in Figure 10, this experiment shows the maximum gain of lifetime at the end of phase 1, denoted by LV_1, that is, the lifetime of node that will die first. We set $z = 0.45, 0.85, 1, L*/L \in [0.1, 0.9]$. $z = 1$ means at most one node is used for compression. As can be seen, when $z = 0.45$, compared with $z = 1$ the small gain is obtained when letting each node compress its own data based on multiple other nodes' data. Note that $z = 0.45$ is not very probable. However, when $z = 0.85$, there is almost no gain compared to constrain each node to compress its data based on only one

Figure 11. Gain in lifetime when z= 0.85

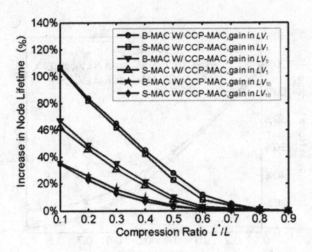

node's data. The reason is, compared with the energy gain via compressions much more reception energy will be wasted in this case. Therefore, multiple compressions are not worth the candle. This result just explains why we constrain each node perform the compression based on only one optimal node's data. In addition, since some nodes need to transmit uncompressed data and hence will not do the compression, the maximum gain is 120% although compression ratio equal to 0.1.

In Figure 11, we make a chart of the gain in lifetime when setting $z=0.85$. Specifically Figure 11 shows the gain in lifetime at the end of phase 1, 5 and 10, i.e, the lifetime of the nodes that dies first, 5th and 10th, denoted by LV_1, LV_5, LV_{10} respectively. Obviously, the lifetime improvements strongly depend on the compression ratio. In other words, when the spatial correlation is high, the gain of CCP-MAC is significant. As can be seen, gain achieved in LV_1 is most remarkable compared with the gain in LV_{10}. The result indicate that CCP-MAC strives to prolong the time period before first node dies so as to assure the in-net-working collaborative compression procedure works for a long time.

Our experiments combine the CCP-MAC with S-MAC as well as B-MAC, the results show that CCP-MAC can prolong the lifetimes of nodes

significantly. It also can be seen that the gain in B-MAC is larger relative to S-MAC, since original B-MAC suffers from the long preamble overhearing problem. When using CCP-MAC, the node can stop the progress and avoid accepting the whole preamble by checking the embedded *cTag* in the bits stream.

Figure 12 plots the performance when using different update frequency R. The maximum number of events a node can detect before using up its energy is set to 100,000. Notice that we set $R = 500$ when plotting Figure 10 and 11. As shown in Figure 12, heuristic algorithm still can keep nearly optimal performance with respect to the energy cost of the updating operations. It is interesting to see that gain of lifetime obtained by CCP-MAC is low when R is big. This is because the nodes will not know the neighboring nodes' exact statuses after a relative long time period. It is worth noticing that the compression ratio estimation method used previously will further reduce the accuracy of CCP-MAC. However, the gain of lifetime is still significant even though $R = 10,000$. Therefore the negative effect of the updating procedure in energy cost and inaccuracy are almost negligible.

Figure 13 plots the gain of lifetime versus the number of nodes N. Note that in Figure 10 to

Figure 12. Gain in lifetime vs varying R

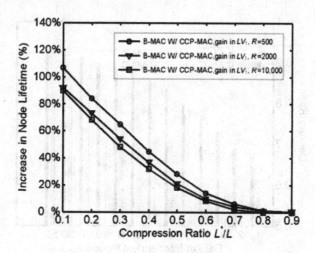

Figure 13. Gain in lifetime vs varying N

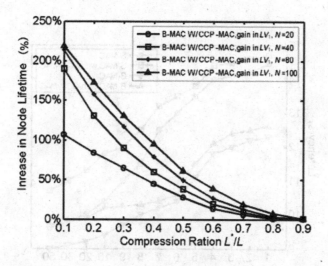

Figure 12, we set $N = 20$. As can be seen, the LV_1 becomes larger with the increase of N. The reason is that when N increases, each node could select the optimal node for compression from more neighboring nodes, so as to improve the performance. Meanwhile the speed of improvements slows down as N increasing. As shown in Figure 13, when $N = 100$ the improvements are not very significant relative to $N = 80$.

Figure 14 depicts the measured average fraction of non-repeated data received by sink. We notice that when the traffic load is heavy, the B-MAC has the lowest packet delivery due to the long preambles. S-MAC performs better than B-MAC but still a low percentage of data packets. Combining with CCP-MAC, both B-MAC and S-MAC will achieve higher delivery ratio. The reason is attributed to the light traffic load when the redundant data is eliminated. Notice that we

Figure 14. Delivery ratio

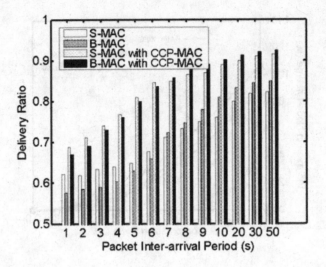

Figure 15. Latency

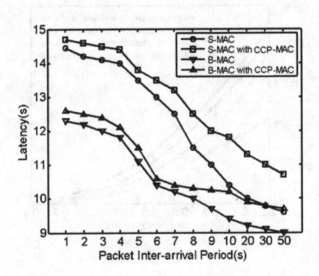

use a simple loss-less compression algorithm such that all data packets will be decompressed at sink.

As shown in Figure 15, due to the node selection and data compression operations, CCP-MAC has longer average delay compared to others. The latency performance is better when the traffic load is light in terms of the collision probability. Even though the slope of latency goes down, CCP-

MAC's performance is very close to B-MAC and S-MAC. Particularly the latency of CCP-MAC is almost equal to B-MAC and S-MAC under heavy traffic load.

FUTURE RESEARCH DIRECTIONS

We future research goal is implement the CCP-MAC on various types of sensor nodes, such as Micaz or IMote2 of Crossbow, trying not to incur additional complexity. We also are improving the compression ratio estimation method, so as to improve the accuracy of the spatial correlation model used in CCP-MAC. Developing energy efficient MAC protocols is still a critical issue for wireless sensor network, below we list some latest research directions on the literature:

- Energy efficient issue in some new applications scenario, such as underwater sensor network (Heidemann, et al., 2006). Designing energy efficient MAC protocol for underwater sensor network is challenging due to the uncertainty of data arrival caused by the long propagation delay, and the difficulty of synchronization in underwater environment. It is worth exploring efficient MAC protocols for underwater sensor network in the future.
- Energy efficient issue for multi-mode sensor networks with delay constraint (Rousselot & Decotignie, 2010). Rousselot & Decotignie propose WiseMAC-HA, a novel dual-mode MAC protocol, which combines the IEEE 802.15.4 non beacon enabled mode with the ultra low power MAC protocol WiseMAC, to offer both ultra low power consumption levels and low latency communications.
- Energy efficient issue for special communication architecture, such as asynchronous communication for WSNs (Hu, et al., 2011). Underlying communication of wireless sensor networks is mainly depending on coordinated sleep/wakeup mechanisms, and is still basing the link layer protocols upon the traditional 802.11. For wireless sensor networks usually having high node density and large scale, 802.11 pro-

tocol has tended to be not efficient in energy consumption, network throughput etc. Basing on the dynamic links in a large portion of monitoring applications of wireless sensor networks, Hu et al. propose a kind of weak connection-oriented asynchronous communication mechanism (ACM).

CONCLUSION

This chapter reviews energy efficient MAC protocols for distributed wireless sensor networks. Battery powered wireless sensor networks place an emphasis on the energy efficiency except for those traditional design elements. Depending on the coordinated sleep/wakeup mechanism at the underlying physical and link layer, most MAC protocols in this literature address the common energy issue. We have discussed the trade-offs in MAC design before reviewing several typical MAC protocols. Finally, we describe the CCP-MAC as an example.

ACKNOWLEDGMENT

This work is partially supported by the Hunan Provincial Natural Science Foundation of China under grant No.10JJ4042; the Chinese Central University Basic Research Foundation.

REFERENCES

Akyildiz, I. F., Su, W., Sankarasubramaniam, Y., & Cayirci, E. (2002). A survey on sensor networks. *IEEE Communications Magazine, 40*(8), 102–114. doi:10.1109/MCOM.2002.1024422

Bao, L., & Garcia-Luna-Aceves, J. J. (2001). A new approach to channel access scheduling for ad hoc networks. In *Proceedings of Seventh Annual International Conference on Mobile Computing and Networking,* (pp. 210-221). New York: ACM.

Besma, R. A., Nash, R. A., Yao, Y., & Mongi, A. A. (2008). Survey and analysis of multimodal sensor planning and integration for wide area surveillance. *ACM Computing Surveys, 41*(1), 1–36. doi:10.1145/1456650.1456657

Bottigliengo, M., Casetti, C., Chiasserini, C. F., & Meo, M. (2004). Short-term fairness for TCP flows in 802.11b WLANs. In *Proceedings of IEEE INFOCOM* (pp. 1383–1392). Piscataway, NJ: IEEE.

Culler, D. E. (2006). TinyOS: Operating system design for wireless sensor networks. *Sensor.* Retrieved January 10, 2011, from http://www.sensorsmag.com/networking-communications/tinyos-operating-system-design-wireless-sensor-networks-918.

Dam, T. V., & Langendoen, K. (2003). An adaptive energy-efficient MAC protocol for wireless sensor networks. In I. Akyildiz & D. Estrin (Eds.), *Proceedings of the 1st International Conference on Embedded Networked Sensor Systems,* (pp. 65-72). New York: ACM.

Demirkol, I., Ersoy, C., & Alagoz, F. (2006). MAC protocols for wireless sensor networks: A survey. *IEEE Communications Magazine, 44*(4), 115–121. doi:10.1109/MCOM.2006.1632658

Diggle, P. J., Tawn, J. A., & Moyeed, R. A. (1998). Model-based geostatistics. *Applied Statistics, 47*(3), 299–350. doi:10.1111/1467-9876.00113

El Gamal, A., Mammen, J., Prabhakar, B., & Shah, D. (2004). Throughput-delay trade-off in wireless networks. In V. O. K. Li (Ed.), *Proceedings of the 23th Annual Joint Conference of the IEEE Computer and Communications Societies,* (pp. 464-475). Hong Kong: IEEE.

Gupta, P., & Kumar, P. R. (2000). Capacity of wireless networks. *IEEE Transactions on Information Theory, 46*(2), 388–404. doi:10.1109/18.825799

Haartsen, J. C. (2000). The Bluetooth radio system. *IEEE Personal Communication Magazine, 7*(1), 28-36.

Heidemann, J., Li, Y., Syed, A., Wills, J., & Ye, W. (2006). Underwater sensor networking: Research challenges and potential applications. In *Proceedings of the IEEE Wireless Communications and Networking Conference,* (pp. 228-235). Las Vegas, NV: IEEE.

Heinzelman, W. R., Chandrakasan, A., & Balakrishnan, H. (2000). Energy efficient communication protocols for wireless microsensor networks. In *Proceedings of Hawaii International Conference on Systems Sciences,* (pp. 3005-3014). Washington, DC: IEEE.

Hu, Y. P., Li, R., Zhou, S. W., & Lin, Y. P. (2011). CCS-MAC: Exploiting the overheard data for compression in wireless sensor networks. *Computer Communications, 5*(2).

Hu, Y. P., Lin, Y. P., Jiang, H. Y., Li, X. L., & Zhou, S. W. (2009). MAC protocol for wireless sensor networks via collaborative compression. *Journal of Software, 20*(9), 2483–2494. doi:10.3724/SP.J.1001.2009.03316

Hu, Y. P., Lin, Y. P., Zhou, S. W., & Liu, Y. H. (2011). Asynchronous communication mechanism oriented wireless sensor networks and MAC protocols. *Chinese Journal of Computers, 34*(7).

Intanagonwiwat, C., Govindan, R., Estrin, D., Heidemann, J., & Silva, F. (2003). Directed diffusion for wireless sensor networking. *IEEE/ACM Transactions on Networking, 11*(1), 2–16. doi:10.1109/TNET.2002.808417

Kanodia, V., Li, C., Sabharwal, A., Sadeghi, B., & Knightly, E. (2001). Distributed multi-hop scheduling and medium access with delay and throughput constraints. In *Proceedings of ACM MOBICOM,* (pp. 200-209). New York: ACM.

Lin, P., Qiao, C., & Wang, X. (2004). Medium access control with a dynamic duty cycle for sensor networks. In *Proceedings of the IEEE Wireless Communications and Networking Conference,* (pp. 1534-1539). Atlanta, GA: IEEE.

Lu, G., Krishnamachari, B., & Raghavendra, C. S. (2004). An adaptive energy efficient and low-latency MAC for data gathering in wireless sensor networks. In *Proceedings of 18th International Parallel and Distributed Processing Symposium,* (pp. 3091-3098). Santa Fe, CA: IEEE.

Mainwaring, A., Polastre, J., Szewczyk, R., Culler, D., & Anderson, J. (2002). Wireless sensor networks for habitat monitoring. In C. S. Raghavendra & K. M. Sivalingam (Eds.), *Proceedings of the 1st ACM International Workshop on Wireless Sensor Networks and Applications,* (pp. 88-97). New York: ACM.

Michael, B., Gary, V. Y., Eric, A., & Richard, H. (2006). X-Mac: A short preamble MAC protocol for duty cycled wireless sensor networks. In *Proceedings of the 1st International Conference on Embedded Network Sensor Systems,* (pp. 307-320). New York: ACM.

Muneeb, A., Saif, U., & Dunkels. (2006). Medium access control issues in sensor networks. *ACM SIGCOMM Computer Communications Review, 36*(2), 33-36.

Pattem, S., & Krishnamachari, B. (2004). The impact of spatial correlation on routing with compression in wireless sensor networks. In *Proceedings of the IPSN,* (pp. 28-35). New York: ACM.

Polastre, J., Hill, J., & Culler, D. (2004). Versatile low power media access for wireless sensor networks. In J. A. Stankovic (Ed.), *Proceedings of the 2nd International Conference on Embedded Networked Sensor Systems,* (pp. 95-107). New York: ACM.

Pradhan, S. S., Kusuma, J., & Ramchandran, K. (2002). Distributed compression in a dense microsensor network. *IEEE Signal Processing Magazine, 19*(2), 51–60. doi:10.1109/79.985684

Raghunathan, V., Schurgers, C., Park, S., & Srivastava, M. B. (2002). Energy-aware wireless microsensor networks. *IEEE Signal Processing Magazine, 19*(2), 40–50. doi:10.1109/79.985679

Rajendran, V., Obraczka, K., & Garcia-Luna-Aceves, J. J. (2003). Energy-efficient, collision-free medium access control for wireless sensor networks. In *Proceedings of the 1st International Conference on Embedded Networked Sensor Systems,* (pp. 181-192). New York: ACM.

Rousselot, J., & Decotignie, J. (2010). When ultra low power meets high performance: The WiseMAC high availability protocol. In J. Beutel (Ed.), *Proceedings of the 8st International Conference on Embedded Networked Sensor Systems,* (pp. 441-442). New York: ACM

Sawyer, S., & Tapia, A. (2005). The sociotechnical nature of mobile computing work: Evidence from a study of policing in the United States. *International Journal of Technology and Human Interaction, 1*(3), 1–14. doi:10.4018/jthi.2005070101

Slepian, D., & Wolf, J. (1973). Noiseless coding of correlated information sources. *IEEE Transactions on Information Theory, 19*(4), 471–480. doi:10.1109/TIT.1973.1055037

Sohraby, K., Minoli, D., & Znati, T. (2007). *Wireless sensor networks: Technology, protocols, and applications.* Hoboken, NJ: John Wiley & Sons. doi:10.1002/047011276X

Sun, Y., Gurewitz, O., & Johnson, D. B. (2008). RI-MAC: A receiver initiated asynchronous duty cycle MAC protocol for dynamic traffic loads in wireless sensor networks. In T. Abdelzaher (Ed.), *Proceedings of the 6th International Conference on Embedded Networked Sensor Systems,* (pp. 1-14). New York: ACM.

Tharini, C. (2010). An efficient data gathering scheme for wireless sensor networks. *European Journal of Scientific Research, 43*(1), 148–155.

Tharini, C., & Vanaja, R. P. (2009). Design of modified adaptive huffman daata compression algorithm for wireless sensor network. *Journal of Computer Science, 5*(6), 466–470. doi:10.3844/jcssp.2009.466.470

Varga, A. (2001). The OMNeT++ discrete event simulation system. In *Proceedings of 15ᵗʰ European Simulation Multiconference,* (pp.319-324). Prague: SCS Europe.

Vuran, M. C., & Akyildiz, I. F. (2006). Spatial correlation-based collaborative medium access control in wireless sensor networks. *IEEE/ACM Transactions on Networking, 14*(2), 316–329. doi:10.1109/TNET.2006.872544

Willig, A. (2006). Wireless sensor networks: Concept, challenges and approaches. *Elektrotechnik & Informationstechnik, 123*(6), 224–231. doi:10.1007/s00502-006-0351-1

Xu, S., & Saadawi, T. (2002). Revealing the problems with 802.11 medium access control protocol in multi-hop wireless ad hoc networks. *Computer Networks, 38*(14), 531–548. doi:10.1016/S1389-1286(01)00273-0

Ye, W., Heidemann, J., & Estrin, D. (2004). Medium access control with coordinated adaptive sleeping for wireless sensor networks. *IEEE/ACM Transactions on Networking, 12*(3), 493–506. doi:10.1109/TNET.2004.828953

Ye, W., Silva, F., & Heidemann, J. (2006). Ultra-low duty cycle MAC with scheduled channel polling. In A. Campbell (Ed.), *Proceedings of the 4th International Conference on Embedded Networked Sensor Systems,* (pp. 321-334). New York: ACM.

Zhang, W., & Cao, G. (2003). Optimizing tree reconfiguration to track mobile targets in sensor networks. *ACM SIGMOBILE Mobile Computing and Communications Review, 7*(3), 39–40. doi:10.1145/961268.961282

KEY TERMS AND DEFINITIONS

Channel Contention Mechanism: Also known as channel access control mechanism, channel contention mechanism accounts for the allocation of the shared wireless medium for multiple sensor nodes competing to transmit.

Collaborative Compression: In this chapter, collaborative compression means the neighboring sensor nodes perform the data compressions in a cooperative way, based on the overheard data.

Energy Efficiency: Energy efficiency is a critical performance metric for battery powered wireless sensor network, it reflects the energy consumption level of a protocol or operation. An energy efficient protocol can prolong the lifetime of a wireless sensor network.

Medium Access Control: Medium access control (layer) is a sub-layer of the data link layer. In wireless sensor network, it provides addressing and channel access control mechanisms that make it possible for multiple sensor nodes to communicate through a shared wireless medium.

Overhearing: Overhearing happens when a sensor node receives packets which are destined for other nodes. Overhearing unnecessary data can be a dominant factor of energy waste when traffic load is heavy and node density is high. The overheard data is often useless and thus is discarded.

Spatial Correlation: Spatial correlation in wireless sensor network means that there is a correlation among the observations of different nodes that scattered in adjacent locations.

Wireless Sensor Network: A wireless sensor network consists of numerous sensor nodes with sensing, limited wireless communications and computing capabilities. The sensor nodes are distributed in an unattended environment, collaborating to collect physical or environment data, such as temperature, sound, vibration, motion or pollutants, and to deliver their data through the network to an end user.

Chapter 11

Low Loss Energy–Aware Routing Protocol for Data Gathering Applications in Wireless Sensor Network

Basma M. Mohammad El-Basioni
Electronics Research Institute, Egypt

Sherine M. Abd El-Kader
Electronics Research Institute, Egypt

Hussein S. Eissa
Electronics Research Institute, Egypt

Mohammed M. Zahra
Al-Azhar University, Egypt

ABSTRACT

As the Wireless Sensor Network is a form of the realization of the Ambient Intelligence system vision where computation, control, and communication are embedded into the physical environment such that the resulting interaction paradigms is person-to-physical world paradigm, the Wireless Sensor Network covers a wide range of applications. Current and future application areas include habitat and environment monitoring, disaster control and operation, military applications, object tracking, video surveillance, traffic control, industrial surveillance and automation, as well as health care, and home automation. One of the main functionalities of Wireless Sensor Network applications is gathering sensory data about the physical environment regardless of the application field and the nature of gathered data and the required processing on it.

When developing a Wireless Sensor Network, a number of design factors have to be considered in the design process, such as, fault tolerance, scalability, production cost, operating environment, network topology, hardware constraints, transmission media, and power consumption; the key challenge a Wireless Sensor Network has to deal with is energy efficiency because sensor nodes typically are battery-

DOI: 10.4018/978-1-4666-0161-1.ch011

powered, and it may not be possible to change or recharge batteries; so, the protocols and algorithms used should be energy-efficient.

But, as the energy-efficiency is critical for periodical data gathering applications in wireless sensor networks, it has the highest priority in algorithms design; also the latency, packet loss, and throughput are important factors and should be addressed. This chapter proposes a routing protocol inspired by an energy-efficient cluster-based routing protocol called Energy-Aware Routing Protocol (EAP). The new enhanced protocol that is called Low Loss Energy-Aware Routing Protocol (LLEAP) enhances the performance of EAP in terms of some quality of service parameters by adding a second iteration for constructing the tree structure for multi-hop communication among cluster heads, by modifying the used weights of the cluster heads and parent node selection, and finally by selecting suitable aggregation method to decrease losses and delay. Simulation results showed that LLEAP significantly outperforms EAP in terms of packet loss percentage by on average 93.4%.

INTRODUCTION

A Wireless Sensor Network (WSN) typically consists of a large number of low-cost, low-power, and multifunctional devices called sensor nodes and one or more sinks; sensor nodes are not just sensors, but sensors are one of their components. Sensor nodes consist of the components which make them eligible as network entities. These sensor nodes usually densely deployed in an ad hoc manner in a field of interest (this field is called a sensor field) to perform distributed sensing and information processing. Sensor nodes communicate over a short distance via a wireless medium and collaborate to accomplish a common task, for example, environment monitoring, battlefield surveillance, and industrial process control. A sink, on the other hand, does not generate any data by itself but collects data from sensor nodes. A sink can be regarded as a gateway between a sensor network and other networks such as the Internet, or an interface between a sensor network and the people who operate the sensor network (Wang, 2010, p. 9).

WSN routing especially won and still owns a large interest in the research field, particularly because the routing protocol may be different for different WSN applications while these applications are many and vary in their characteristics and requirements, and on top of that, the routing protocols used in traditional data networks whether wired or wireless (even Ad Hoc networks) are not suitable for use as they are for WSN applications to the WSN of differences, requirements, and constraints on the design. The key challenge WSN routing has to deal with is the energy efficiency and prolonging network lifetime.

Hierarchical communication among sensor nodes by clustering them is more scalable, energy-efficient, lower in latency, better in terms of network lifetime than flat communication. This chapter presents a routing protocol inspired by another energy-efficient hierarchical cluster-based routing protocol proposed already in literature; this protocol is called Energy-Aware routing Protocol (EAP). EAP meets several important requirements for a clustering algorithm. It was proved that EAP performance is better than Low-Energy Adaptive Clustering Hierarchy (LEACH) performance in terms of network lifetime. The new protocol that is called Low Loss Energy-Aware routing Protocol (LLEAP) enhances EAP in terms of packet loss percentage, throughput, and end to end delay.

WSN ROUTING CHALLENGES

This section will talk about some of the design issues, challenges, and mechanisms that should be taken into consideration in WSN routing protocols design and generally in WSN design:

Energy-efficiency and network lifetime: usually sensor nodes work with batteries and use their limited capacity in sensing, computation and communication. While sensor node lifetime shows a strong dependence on battery lifetime and therefore the network lifetime shows a strong dependence on it, WSN should use energy-efficient techniques in its operation to reduce node's energy consumption. But to increase network lifetime, a load-balance must exist among sensor nodes in addition to conserving the energy of every individual sensor node.

Computation capabilities: sensor nodes have limited computing power and therefore may not be able to run sophisticated network protocols. Therefore, new or light-weight and simple versions of traditional routing protocols are needed to fit in the WSN environment (Ilyas & Mahgoub, 2005).

Limited memory: sensor nodes usually have a small amount of memory; the size of a sensor node memory unit is ranging from hundreds of KB to hundreds of MB, so, the routing protocol shouldn't require the storage of large amount of routing state information.

Communication range: inter-sensor communication exhibits short transmission ranges. Therefore, it is most likely that a route will generally consist of multiple wireless hops (Ilyas & Mahgoub, 2005).

WSN highly dynamic nature: in addition to the physical topology of WSN is usually unstructured due to random deployment, it changes dynamically because of some reasons for example, in any point of time sensor nodes may be added or removed from the network due to the exhaustion of limited energy, environmental conditions, or mobility intended or unintended, the wireless links between sensor nodes can come and go

and its quality varies according to the presence of obstacles, weather conditions, radio interference, nodes mobility, etc. The physical topology dynamics cause the logical or communication topology dynamics. Even if the physical topology of nodes is stable, the communication topology should be time-varying for achieving the desired design goals such as energy-efficiency.

Fault tolerance: because of WSN dynamic nature, the protocols used in a sensor network should be able to detect and handle changes in network topology such as network partitioning. This is especially relevant to the routing protocol design, which has to ensure that alternate paths are available for rerouting of the packets. Therefore, multiple levels of redundancy may be needed in a fault-tolerant sensor network. Different deployment environments pose different fault tolerance requirements (Boukerche, 2009, p. 131).

Scalability: the number of deployed nodes in a WSN is usually big, but it may be redundant for achieving data accuracy, fault tolerance, or better area coverage, so WSN should accommodate a huge number of sensor nodes without fast degradation in network performance.

Control overhead: the routing protocol requires the exchange of control packets which are the packets that don't used in sending the actual data but used for sending control information in a periodic or an on-demand fashion for neighborhood discovery, route discovery, topology update, etc. Therefore, control overhead increases due to the increase in nodes count, node mobility, and periodic network setup. Excessive control overhead exhausts nodes' energy in something other than sending the required data and increases packets collisions, so the routing protocol should reduce the control overhead.

Locality: because sensor nodes have limited storage capacity, processing power, and other resources, the routing protocol shouldn't depend in its operation on a global knowledge of the network, but the node should be charged to collect only local data from its neighbors, such that the network become scalable to high node density.

Heterogeneous application requirements: some WSN applications may require, the deployment of different types of sensor nodes with different features and capabilities in terms of power, storage, processing, sensing and other resources, for example there may exist a mixture of mobile and static sensor nodes, also WSN application may need the existence of sensor nodes as well as actors in the network. WSN applications may require the use of more than one data reporting model from the continuous, query-driven or event-driven data reporting models. The heterogeneity in these requirements puts a burden on the routing protocol in how to deal with it.

Self-organization: regardless of the distribution of nodes, the nodes should form the logical structure among them and operate automatically without external intervention along the lifetime of the network.

Data-centric paradigm: the operating paradigm of WSNs is centered around information retrieval from the underlying network, usually referred to as a data-centric paradigm. Compared to the address-centric paradigm exhibited by traditional networks, the data-centric paradigm is unique in several ways. New communication patterns resemble a reversed multicast tree. In-network processing extracts information from raw data and removes redundancy among multiple source data. Also, cooperative strategies among sensor nodes are used to replace the non-cooperative strategies for most internet applications. The development of appropriate routing strategies that take the above factors into consideration is challenging (Yu, Prasanna, & Krishnamachari, 2006, p. 17).

Aggregation: it is to aggregate raw data packets from a number of nodes by eliminating redundancy or by expressing them with only one value (such as minimum, maximum, average, etc.) sent in one packet to the next-hop to reduce the energy consumed if every raw data packet

sent individually. Data fusion also refers to the aggregation of data but by using signal processing techniques.

Location-awareness: due to the data-centric nature of the WSN, addressing and data collection don't based on the node itself, but it based on the phenomena nodes sense and the properties of these phenomena (attribute-based addressing), also data collection may be according a property of the nodes themselves which is nodes location, i.e. the data may be required from a certain area on the network, or it may be required to know the location of the received data. Using the Global Positioning System (GPS) for every sensor node to determine its geographical position is infeasible because it is high consumer of energy and cost and its size increases the node size, so, localization algorithms are used in WSNs to aid nodes to approximate their positions.

Trade-offs: WSNs should exploit or deal with various inherent trade-offs between mutually contradictory goals, both during system/protocol design and at runtime. Examples for such trade-offs are the trade-off between energy-efficiency and data accuracy which represented by data aggregation process and the trade-off between network lifetime and data latency which represented by multi-hop communication.

Cross-layer design: which means that the design of each layer in the protocol stack is not a separate process, but all the layers are designed with each other, function with each other, and exchange the control information and the data about the status of the layers and the network, so all layers cooperate to achieve the design goals in a better manner under the same design constraints. This may result in; the cancellation of a function a certain layer performs it because another layer already performs the same function, the cancellation of a whole layer, or the concatenation of two layers, in addition, cross-layer design aids in capturing network dynamic nature, exploiting trade-offs, and the development and improvement of resource utilization and allocation techniques.

Cross-layer design must be a careful process and it may result in problems in security.

RELATED WORK

There are a lot of hierarchical clustering routing protocols proposed in literature; these protocols differ in many ways such as the basis on which the Cluster Heads (CHs) are selected, the used method for cluster formation, etc. These protocols such as:

Low-Energy Adaptive Clustering Hierarchy (LEACH) (Heinzelman, Chandrakasan, & Balakrishnan, 2000): LEACH is a distributed clustering routing protocol, in which, a predefined percentage of nodes are selected as CHs randomly and randomly rotated- with no probability of a CH to become again CH up to certain number of rounds- to evenly distribute the load of the head role among nodes. Each selected CH broadcasts a message to the remaining nodes to offer them joining its cluster; each node selects the closest head, then nodes send data to their CH using a Time Division Multiple Access (TDMA) schedule to aggregate and send it to the sink. This method of cluster formation doesn't consider the remaining energy of the selected CH, its distance from the sink, its distance from the other heads, and its distance from its members. All of these factors result in bad CH selection, bad CHs distribution, and instability in generated clusters number and size; this increases the load on CHs as well as on cluster members, which tends to the fast depletion of nodes energy and fast nodes death which indoors fasten the network death. In addition, sometimes the distance between the CH and its member may be very long, this leads to high energy consumption from the member node, as well as it takes a long time for data to reach the CH which implies widening the time slot of the TDMA schedule, and because of the instability in generated clusters number and size, sometimes the whole network formed in one cluster i.e. one CH and all the remaining nodes are its members, this

implies the lengthening of the TDMA schedule itself to be enough for all the nodes existing in the network minus one (the alone CH). This long TDMA schedule with its wide time slots increases the data latency.

LEACH-Centralized (LEACH-C) (Heinzelman, Chandrakasan, & Balakrishnan, 2002): is an improved scheme of LEACH in which a centralized algorithm at the Base Station (BS) makes cluster formation. Each node sends information about current location and energy level to BS, then the BS utilizes its global information of the network to produce better clusters that require less energy for data transmission. LEACH-C does not take into account a method to overcome the sensor node failure and it needs GPS or other location-tracking method.

Hybrid, Energy-Efficient, Distributed clustering approach (HEED) (Younis & Fahmy, 2004): for prolonging network lifetime, CH selection in this protocol is primarily based on the residual energy of each node, and to increase energy efficiency and further prolong network lifetime, a secondary clustering parameter considers intra-cluster "communication cost" which can be a function of neighbor proximity or cluster density. The main objectives of HEED are to distribute energy consumption to prolong network lifetime, minimize energy during the CH selection phase, and minimize the control overhead of the network, but HEED needs multiple broadcasting for cluster formation and thus consumes more energy.

Energy-Efficient Clustering Scheme (EECS) (Ye, Li, Chen, & Wu, 2005): a constant number of candidate nodes for CH role are elected with a probability T and compete according to the residual energy within range $R_{compete}$. The candidate will be a head if it didn't find another higher energy candidate, otherwise, it will give up competition with the first found higher energy candidate. The cluster size should be justified such that, the larger the distance between the CH and the BS is, the smaller cluster size the CH should accommodate. It is true that the CH selected is the candidate with larger residual energy in range $R_{compete}$, but the set of candidate nodes in the competition are selected randomly before the competition, this may result in non-optimal CH selection.

Partition Energy Balanced and Efficient Clustering Scheme (PEBECS) (Wang, Yang, & Zhang, 2009): PEBECS mitigates or avoids the hot spot problem, which occurs when CHs closer to the sink are burdened with heavier relay traffic and tend to die much faster, by dividing a WSN into several partitions with equal area and then grouping the nodes into unequally sized clusters. The shorter the distance between the partition and the sink, the more clusters are created within the partition. Further, the CH is selected by using the node's residual energy, degree difference and relative location in network. PEBECS achieves long network lifetime by better balancing node energy consumption.

Distributed Hierarchical Agglomerative Clustering (DHAC) algorithm (Lung & Zhou, 2010): with simple six-step clustering, DHAC provides a bottom-up clustering approach by grouping similar nodes together before the CH is selected. DHAC can accommodate both quantitative (e.g., location, Received Signal Strength [RSS]) or qualitative (e.g., connectivity of nodes) information types in clustering. DHAC performs clustering only once, at the initial stage because DHAC uses automatic CH rotation and re-scheduling. Hence, DHAC avoids the time and energy consumed by re-clustering, provides high energy efficiency, and achieves uniform energy dissipation through the whole network.

Context-Aware Multilayer Hierarchical Protocol (CAMHP) (Haque, Matsumoto, & Yoshida, 2010): it is a distributed context-aware cluster-based hierarchical protocol. The context-adaptive clustering forms clusters of sensor nodes with similar output data within the bound of given tolerance parameter. CAMHP consists of three layer hierarchies where nodes are grouped into a number of clusters (the ratio of CHs among other nodes is predetermined) and those clusters form a super cluster; multilayer hierarchical structure aids in covering more area and distributing energy-consumption across the network. For more optimization, the nodes always temporarily store their sensed data for a single round such that the packets containing the same value as previous iteration are not sent by the nodes; this reduces the data traffic between CHs and nodes significantly. Also each node keeps track of its role history and it checks its role history whether it has become a CH in previous rounds or not, if so, it restrains itself in becoming a CH (the same thing for the super CH role), so that, the CH role can be uniformly distributed among the member nodes of that cluster. The required aim from this protocol is less energy consumption and prolonging active service. This protocol has shown significant performance improvement where the environmental context is quite gradual. However, the CH role has not been effectively distributed which might cause early energy exhaustion of some nodes. Besides, if the environmental phenomenon is changing rapidly, this protocol might not be a feasible one.

Weighted Election Protocol (WEP) (Rashed & Kabir, 2010): is a clustered heterogeneous routing protocol for wireless sensor networks. Its main aim is to maintain well balanced energy consumption and improve the stable period which is defined as the time interval before the death of first node. It is based on the clustering hierarchy process using the characteristic parameters of heterogeneity, namely the fraction of advanced nodes and the additional energy factor between advanced and normal nodes. CHs are randomly selected from both advanced and normal nodes upon a probability based on the energy level and they establish a chain among them using a greedy algorithm and select its leader randomly among them. WEP achieves energy-efficiency and improve the stability region with reasonable amount of data delivery delay.

Multi-hop Data Communication Algorithm (MDCA) (Kumar & Patel, 2011): it is a distributed, randomized, multi-hop clustering algorithm to organize the sensor nodes in a heterogeneous WSN into clusters. The network is assumed to be composed of three types of nodes depending on the energy level, deployed uniformly in a square region, including normal nodes, advanced nodes, and a few super nodes. The selection probability of each node to become a CH is weighted by the initial energy of a node relative to that of the normal node in the network. A multi-hop communication approach is adopted between member nodes and their respective CH (intra-cluster communication) and also between CHs and the sink (inter-cluster communication) and the shortest path either between member nodes and the CH or between CH and the sink is selected to save the nodes' energy. It is proved that MDCA achieves balanced energy consumption and good characteristics in terms of lifetime and stability.

ENERGY-AWARE ROUTING PROTOCOL FOR WIRELESS SENSOR NETWORK

Energy-Aware routing Protocol (EAP) (Liu, Cao, Chen, & Wang, 2009) is an energy-aware dynamic distributed hierarchical clustering routing protocol for data gathering applications in WSN. It works in rounds as LEACH and each round consists of two main phases, set-up phase and data phase where the data gathered from sensors and sent to the sink. The set-up phase is subdivided into two phases, cluster formation phase and cluster heads tree construction phase.

EAP Operation

After the deployment of the network directly before the start of protocol operations there is a startup period, in which the sink node broadcasts to all nodes a message called *OK_Msg*, and the nodes receive this message, acquire the *RSS* (Received Signal Strength) as estimation to their distances from the sink. This *RSS* remains constant during

the network lifetime unless the sink varies its location or sensor nodes are mobile with intent or without.

Cluster Formation Phase

In this phase each node takes one of three states (roles), candidate, plain, or head. First, all nodes are CH candidates (i.e. occupy the candidate role); each node needs to maintain a neighborhood table to store the information about its neighbors, so each node broadcasts a message called *E_Msg* within radio range *r* (intra-cluster range); this message contains node IDentification number (ID) and node residual energy. After sending and receiving *E_Msg*, the time of CH selection comes. EAP consider in its CH selection method the heterogeneous energy circumstances which may arise from some conditions. From this view, making the probability of selecting a sensor node as a CH depends only on its residual energy ($E_{residual}$) doesn't help balance the energy load to the proper nodes in some special cases (Liu, Cao, Chen, & Wang, 2009), so this probability is better made to depend on the average residual energy (E_a) of all neighbors in the cluster range to choose the CH which will collect the nodes with low residual energies in its cluster as member nodes (i.e. occupy the plain role), and gives the other nodes with relatively higher residual energies the chance to become CHs (i.e. occupy the head role). E_a is computed from the neighborhood table information by using Equation (1).

$$E_a = \frac{\sum_{j=1}^{m} v_j . E_{residual}}{m} \qquad (1)$$

Where, *m* is the number of nodes within cluster range and v_j represents any node in this range. Every node waits a time delay equals (*t*) before it broadcasts a message *Compete_Msg* containing its weight to compete for the head role with other nodes, and then it waits a time delay equals to $(2 \times \Delta t)$ to make sure whether there exist other *Compete_Msgs* broadcasted by other nodes in its cluster range, where Δt denotes the time interval which can guarantee that all neighbors can receive the *Compete_Msg*, the time delay (t) is calculated according to Equation (2).

$$t = k \times \left(T_{clustering} \right) \times \left(\frac{E_a}{E_{residual}} \right) \qquad (2)$$

Where, k is a real value uniformly distributed between 0 and 1, and $T_{clustering}$ is the time duration for CHs election. The node that received a *Compete_Msg* during the delay time (t) (before it broadcasts its *Compete_Msg*) will give up competition and takes the plain role as a member of the first received *Compete_Msg* owner cluster. From that we can say that, the less the ratio of the average residual energy of all neighbors of the competing node to its residual energy, the less delay time t, the more likely the node to become a CH. Over $(2 \times \Delta t)$, if the node has not received any *Compete_Msg* from its neighbors it will take the head role, or else it will compare its weight with the weights received in *Compete_Msg* of other broadcasting neighbors. If its weight is the largest one, it will take the head role and other broadcasting neighbors give up competition, or else it will take the plain role, i.e. it will become a member node in the cluster of the node with the largest weight. Using the time delay (t) has an advantage of reducing control overhead, because the node that received a *Compete_Msg* during (t) will not send its *Compete_Msg*.

Tree Construction Phase

In this phase each CH takes additional role(s) to form the tree which represents the logical structure of inter-cluster communication, these roles are child, parent, and root, so that the CH may be a Child Cluster Head only (CCH), Parent Cluster Head (PCH) which indoors is a child, Root Cluster Head which may be a parent but not a child (RCH /RPCH). The CCH aggregates data from its members and sends it to its parent. The PCH aggregates data from its members and from its children CHs and sends it to its parent. The RPCH aggregates data from its members and from its children CHs and sends it to the sink. While the RCH has no children, so it aggregates data from its members only and sends it to the sink.

To construct this tree, after clusters formation, the selected CHs broadcast a message called *Root_Compting_Msg* within radius R (the inter-cluster range $R = 2.5r$) to compete with other CHs for the roles of parent and root. This message contains the CH weight and ID. Each CH compares its own weight and the weights contained in the *Root_Compting_Msg* messages received from its neighbor CHs. If it has smaller weight, it selects the node that has the largest weight as its parent and sends a *My_Parent* message to notify it. Finally, after a specified time, a routing tree will be constructed, with the root node has the largest weight among all CHs in the same independent connected component. In this protocol, the weight of a node i is computed by Equation (3).

$$\text{weight}_i = \left(\frac{D(RSS_i) \times E_a}{D(RSS_{max}) \times E_{residual}} \right) \qquad (3)$$

Where, RSS_i denotes node i's received signal strength of the signal broadcasted by the base station, RSS_{max} is a constant which is determined by the location of base station, and D is a function used for estimating the distance between node i and the base station. From Equation (3), it is obvious that the weight depends on the energy as well as on the distance from the sink. The previous method of tree construction may result in the formation of more than one tree especially when the node density is small and sometimes a CH is isolated from all the other CHs because it lies outside their inter-cluster ranges, so it takes the role of RCH and communicates with the sink directly although it may be far from it. After routing tree construction, CHs broadcast a TDMA schedule to their active member nodes to be ready for data gathering.

Data Phase

After the network set-up, the member nodes begin to send the sensed data to their CHs according to the TDMA schedule and the CHs send the aggregated data to their parents and so on until the aggregated data received at the root. Then the root sends the whole aggregated data from its tree to the sink.

PERFORMANCE ANALYSIS FOR EAP

In the following discussion the motivation of the presented work will be described. EAP achieves several important requirements for a clustering algorithm such as distributed operations, energy-efficiency, uniform CHs distribution, well-balanced energy consumption, efficient handling of heterogeneous energy circumstances, it deals with the heterogeneity in nodes' energies with a different and better treatment than other hierarchical routing protocols such as HEED and EECS. Also EAP achieves a good performance in terms of network lifetime by minimizing energy consumption for in-network communications; all the energy consumed for intra-cluster communications can be computed by free space model where the energy consumed to transmit a packet over a specified distance is only proportional to the square of this distance, also the energy consumed in in-network communications is reduced by using aggregation in intra-cluster and inter-cluster communications. EAP also increases the lifetime by balancing the energy load among all of the nodes by selecting in each round the appropriate node for the high energy consuming roles, head and root roles, thus this load is rotated among all of the nodes not relayed on specific nodes.

Figure 1. The two common root overload cases in EAP (a) There is one root and all of the CHs are its children directly (star topology) (b) The CH is isolated from the other CHs

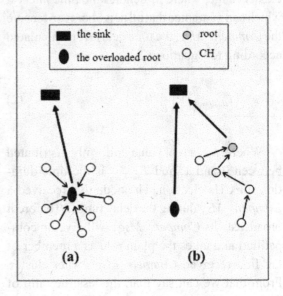

But the main disadvantage of EAP is that it lacks a mechanism that informs member nodes about their CH death and informs CHs about their parent death during the round. So, EAP leads to energy loss that is consumed in sending packets to a dead node and loss in the sent packets, and these losses continue until the end of the round. EAP authors concerned only in their study for that protocol on the network lifetime and they didn't consider other performance metrics of the protocol such as delay, packet loss, and throughput. By simulation, it was found that the common cause of EAP losses is the death of the root during the round when it is overloaded and there are two common cases of root overload; Figure 1 demonstrates these two cases. In Figure 1a, a CH is located in the range of all the remaining CHs and it has the largest weight among them, so all of them select it as a parent and it becomes a root constituting a star topology not a tree topology, this increases the aggregation load on it. Also in Figure 1b, a CH is far from the other CHs so it obliged to be a root although it is very far from the sink, this increases the transmission load on it.

But it should be mentioned that the most common case is the first one, this means that the constructed tree is not ideal, it doesn't aid in making a balance among the CHs in the load of data relaying. As a numerical illustrative example, Figure 2 shows the constructed tree in a round which composed of CHs numbers 63, 75, 90, 49, 56, 38, 20, and 66.

The corresponding parameters and weights of these CHs are shown in Table 1; by using the same simulation parameters' values of Table 3, CH 56 is in the inter-cluster range of the other CHs and it has the largest weight among them, so they choose it as parent and it becomes a root although it hasn't the largest residual energy and it isn't the nearest to the sink. The small residual energy with the large number of children and the far distance to the sink of root 56 make it dies during the round and all the data generated in the network until the end of the round is lost.

THE NEW PRESENTED ALGORITHM

To cure the previous mentioned limitation of EAP and eliminate or decrease these losses, a recovery method from CH (child, parent, or root) death or failure could be directly used, but this method will

exhaust a lot of energy and reduce the lifetime and may also affect the other performance metrics of EAP. So, the protection from losses cause is better than the cure from it; whenever the losses reduced, whenever the unwanted side effects of the recovery method reduced.

The protection manner used in the modified protocol Low Loss Energy-Aware routing Protocol (LLEAP) consists of two techniques, the first technique is used to increase the lifetime,

Figure 2. An example of the first case of root overload

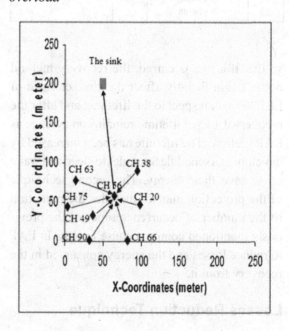

Table 1. Parameters and weights of CHs in Figure 2

CH ID	RSS/RSS_{max}	E_a	$E_{residual}$	weight computed by equation (3)
56	9.286367×10^{-13}	0.09664	0.03737	2.401455×10^{-12}
20	5.866963×10^{-13}	0.17703	0.34802	2.986284×10^{-13}
38	1.965002×10^{-12}	0.10121	0.28687	6.936457×10^{-13}
63	1.467638×10^{-12}	0.30708	0.34533	1.304730×10^{-12}
66	2.345462×10^{-13}	0.24390	0.40939	1.3979×10^{-13}
49	4.817408×10^{-13}	0.14959	0.07622	9.456572×10^{-13}
75	5.504609×10^{-13}	0.33084	0.38431	4.739468×10^{-13}
90	2.405633×10^{-13}	0.21551	0.59059	8.780560×10^{-14}

Table 2. Neighborhood tables of nodes 0 and 71

Node 0 table		Node 71 table	
ID	Residual Energy	ID	Residual Energy
0	1.023137	71	1.066552
81	1.003496	0	1.023137
49	1.071129	81	1.003496
71	1.066552	74	1.072991
65	0.925812	12	0.965689
74	1.072991	49	1.071129
12	0.965689	65	0.925812
38	1.157639	5	1.058009
96	0.913016	96	0.913016
22	0.952887	29	1.089093
2	0.944270	38	1.157639
59	0.992562	59	0.992562
31	0.909392		
84	0.935792		
43	0.853876		
85	0.878288		

Table 3. Simulation parameters

Parameters	Value
Network Field	(100,100)
Node numbers	100~500
Cluster radius r	30 m
Sensing radius r_s	10 m
Inter-cluster range R for EAP	$2.5 \times r$
Inter-cluster range R for LLEAP	$2 \times r$
Inter-cluster range RR	$3 \times r$
Sink position	(50,200)
Initial energy	2 J
Data packet size	525 Bytes
Broadcast packet size	25 Bytes
$E_{threshold}$	0.01 J
E_{elec}	50 nJ/bit
E_{fs}	10 pJ/bit/m^2
e_{amp}	0.0013 pJ/bit/m^4
E_{DA}	5 nJ/bit/signal
Threshold distance d_0	75 m
Coverage expectation	95%

so that if a loss occurred, the recovery method doesn't significantly affect the characteristic of LLEAP with respect to the lifetime, and after the recovery, LLEAP lifetime remains on average as EAP lifetime. The lifetime has been increased by developing a schedule for nodes to sleep and wake up to save their energy. The second technique of the protection manner includes the reduction of the number of occurrence times of the previously mentioned common cause for loss in EAP to reduce losses and the energy consumed in the recovery from it.

Losses Reduction Technique

The shape of the constructed tree should be controlled to reduce the occurrence of loss cause; to be more precise, the formation of star topology among CHs should be avoided, the maximum limit or the average value of the "branching factor" which can be defined as the variable number represents the number of children of each parent node should be decreased as much as possible especially the branching factor value of the root node, the branching factor values of all CHs should be convergent to distribute the tree aggregation load among them, and this will be done by modify-

ing the weight used in the tree construction phase because it is the best way by which the tree shape could be controlled.

Weight Modification

EAP uses the same weight for head selection and tree construction. To study this weight well, first it should be studied as a head selection weight. In clustering phase the weight used during the period $(2 \times \Delta t)$ for comparison among nodes to select a head from them, the node which has the largest weight will become the head, and since the target of the protocol is to choose the node with the smallest ($\dfrac{E_a}{E_{residual}}$) ratio to become CH, the weight equation should satisfy this relation among its parameters: the less ratio of the average residual energy of a node's neighbors to its residual energy ($\dfrac{E_a}{E_{residual}}$), the greater the node weight, the greater the likelihood of that node to become a CH, so that the selected CH will collect in its cluster the maximum number of small residual energy nodes decreasing the load on them and giving the other nodes which have relatively higher energy the chance to become CHs, this requires reversing the ratio $\dfrac{E_a}{E_{residual}}$ which used in the equation of head selection weight in EAP. For example, if nodes 71 and 0 received a *Compete_Msg* from each other during $(2 \times \Delta t)$, while the IDs, the residual energies of them and their neighbors are as shown in Table 2.

So,

$$\left.\frac{E_a}{E_{residual}}\right|_{node0} = 0.95415$$

and

$$\left.\frac{E_a}{E_{residual}}\right|_{node71} = 0.96083$$

If it is assumed that their distances from the sink are the same or node 71 has a smaller distance, then node 71 will be the head, including in its cluster a large number of nodes which have larger energies, leaving a larger number of nodes which have smaller energies, increasing the probability of these smaller energy nodes to become CHs. Although this condition may rarely happen, the weight used in LLEAP for head selection uses the reversed ratio as calculated from Equation (4)

$$\text{CH selection weight} = \left(\frac{D(RSS_i) \times E_{residual}}{D(RSS_{max}) \times E_a}\right) \tag{4}$$

For tree construction phase, the weight in Equation (4) is not applicable, E_a is used in level 0 of the hierarchy in clusters formation to increase the probability of low energy nodes to become member nodes and the probability of higher energy nodes to become heads, but in the tree construction in level 1 of the hierarchy where the network is summarized to the graph composed of CHs only, E_a which is the average residual energy of a CH neighbors has no meaning and no effect, rather, it may have a negative impact on the selection of inappropriate CH as a root (as in the example of Figure 2), the node 56 is not the best among its neighbor CHs with respect to the residual energy and the distance from the sink but it was selected as a root because it has the smallest E_a value), also using E_a in computing the weight used in parent selection increases the number of parameters upon which the parent node is selected and thus increases the probability of the selection of all CHs to only one CH (which satisfies all the parameters or the conditions required in the weight equation) to be their parent, this causes the formation of star topology; above that, E_a at the time of sending *Root_Compting_Msg* is no longer a correct estimation of the average residual energy at this time, because it is calculated at the start of the round before nodes send and/or receive different numbers of other messages. So, the tree construction weight in LLEAP is calculated as in Equation (5).

$$\text{Tree construction weight} = \left(\frac{D(RSS_i)}{D(RSS_{max})} \times E_{residual}\right) \tag{5}$$

By applying this weight in the example of Figure 2, two trees will constructed as shown in Figure 3. As shown in Figure 3, this weight decreased the branching factors of all CHs and made them convergent, reduced the load on the root node with respect to the number of children (i.e. with respect to the energy consumed in aggregation), select the appropriate CH for the root role which has the largest residual energy and smallest distance to the sink, and reduced the load of the root with respect to the energy consumed in the transmission to the sink. But it should be noted that the number of roots increased which resulted in a reduction in the lifetime while the losses were not decreased with a big percentage.

The problem of the increase in roots number has been solved by making a second iteration for tree construction.

The Second Iteration for CHs Tree Construction

In the second tree construction iteration, the root nodes formed in the first iteration broadcast *Root_Compting_Msg* message in larger transmission range *RR*. This message contains the weight of the root calculated as in the first iteration and also contains a list of the children of the sending root. After a specified period, each root compares the weights it received during this period with its own, if it has the largest weight, it remains a root; if not, before it chooses the root with the largest weight as parent, it considers the children of this root, if one of them or more are located in its transmission range *R* used in the first iteration, it chooses the child with the largest weight as parent, otherwise it chooses the root itself. This decreases the aggregation load on the selected root in iteration2, and decreases the transmission load on the root that joins with its tree the tree of the selected root in iteration2 because this method gives it the facility to transmit its data in the smaller range *R* used in iteration1, if that possible. By this method the constructed two trees in the previous example will concatenated into one tree as shown in Figure 4.

It should be noted that the algorithm is still has the previously mentioned advantages of using the modified tree construction weight; in addition to the number of roots has been reduced and the probability of the existence of an isolated root has been also reduced (The second common case of packets loss cause in EAP). The previous work reduces the occurrence of the loss cause.

It should be noted that, if the number of roots generated in the first iteration equals one, the second iteration becomes useless, but it wastes time and energy. In this case the second iteration

Figure 3. The network of Figure 2 after applying the new weight

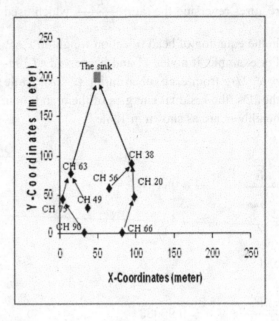

Figure 4. The constructed tree after adding the second tree construction iteration

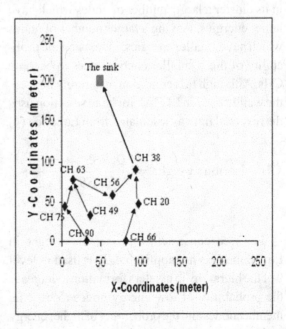

should be canceled and if it is canceled it should be canceled by all the nodes of the different types; candidate, plain, child, parent, and root; this to preserve the synchronization of protocol operations, all nodes begin and end all phases and rounds with each other, so the canceling decision cannot be taken by nodes upon a probability function because this function will generate random values for nodes.

Of course these nodes need to take the decision to cancel the second tree construction iteration to know the number of root nodes that have formed after the first iteration, and this information is not available to any node at that time, even the root node itself knows its role is root but it doesn't know whether there are other root nodes have formed. This knowledge can be conveyed to nodes by different means for example, after the first iteration every root floods or broadcasts in a large transmission range a control message informs about its existence, but all these means require sending control messages and thus consuming a lot of energy; that negates the used mean.

To deal with this shortcoming without sending or receiving any additional control messages, all nodes in the network take the decision to use the second iteration for a specified constant number of rounds and invert this decision for another specified constant number of rounds, taking into consideration that the error in the first decision-making is better than the error in the second decision-making because if the decision to cancel the second iteration is taken wrong, it will result in the existence of more than one root thus the lifetime decreases and losses increase, while the error in the decision of using the second iteration only results in consuming an amount of energy from the alone root to broadcast *Root_Compting_Msg* message in range *RR*, and consuming some time in the useless second iteration period.

As a result, the number of rounds in which the second iteration canceled is smaller than the number of rounds in which the second iteration used, and after another specified constant number

of rounds from the network deployment when nodes count decreased and roots count increased due to low node density, i.e. the probability of the formation of only one root decreased, the second iteration always used.

Aggregation Method Modification

When the target from designing a routing protocol for WSN is to decrease packet losses, the used method of aggregation can't be ignored, because it may be a cause of losses. So, a good aggregation method should be used. Up to now in EAP and LLEAP implementations, each parent waits after the frame time a period for its children to aggregate their aggregated data with its cluster members' data and send the total aggregated data to its parent once. This wait time has been set for every PCH equal to ($2\times$ expected number of CHs − 2) $\times T_{child\_aggre}$, but, the RPCH waits a period equals ($2\times$ expected number of CHs − 1) $\times T_{child\_aggre}$, where T_{child_aggre} is the maximum time needed for the data packet to propagate from children to parent, the RCH and CCH wait zero time. After frame time during this wait period, if a parent receives the data messages from all its children, it will cut this period, aggregate data, and send it to its parent.

This aggregation method can't deal with some situations, such as the situation when a parent waits for one of its children, while this child dead or it was a CCH with no members, i.e. has no data to send (this can happen when the delay times *t* and ($2\times\Delta t$) for a node are expired without receiving any *Compete_Msg*, so it becomes a head while all the nodes located in its intra-cluster range are located in the intra-cluster range of another node sent them a *Compete_Msg* during their time *t*, and they select it as a head). The parent of this waiting parent will wait it and so on. Because parents stay the same time waiting their children, each child will send its aggregated message to its parent after its parent sends its aggregated message to its parent, so its data will be lost.

Figure 5. Level and wait time for CHs

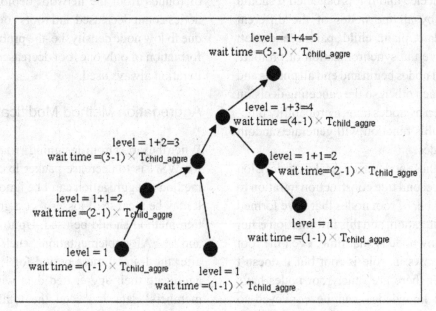

The solution of this problem is to differentiate the wait time for each parent according to its level in the tree, i.e. according to its position in the family, is it a father, a grandfather, a parental grandfather, or a forefather. This done by maintaining a variable for each CH represents its level in the tree, and initializing it to value "one" at the beginning of each cycle. The initial value of the wait time for every CH is set at or before the beginning of the first cycle and it is calculated as before. At the time for aggregation, each head sends the value of its level variable with the aggregated data message to its parent, and each parent updates its level variable value at the time for aggregation, and accordingly updates its wait time (see Figure 5) according to the following equations:

$$\text{level} = \text{level} + \text{maximum value of children levels} \quad (6)$$

$$\text{wait time} = (\text{level} - 1) \times T_{child\_aggre} \quad (7)$$

But the case when a parent has a child with no members or children will not completely solved by this method because each CH knows its level in the tree in the first cycle but this case exists before that during network setup, this causes the loss of data in the first cycle in the sub-tree containing that parent and its child and rooted at the CH which the root is its grandfather. To solve this problem, at the time for aggregation, if the CH finds that the number of its members and children equals zero, i.e. there is no data to relay or aggregate and send, it will send to its parent instead of an aggregated data message a control message called *I_Am_Inactive* to notify it about this so it will not wait for its data. Accordingly, the parent deletes it from its children list.

The Presented Schedule Technique

Dividing the operation of any protocol to time periods has the advantage of giving the facility to make a schedule organizes which nodes have to be awake and which nodes could sleep in each period. This saves nodes' energy, for example making the transceiver of some nodes asleep for a period of time, prevents them from spending energy in receiving broadcast messages they aren't its intended recipients because they make

Figure 6. The timeline of LLEAP

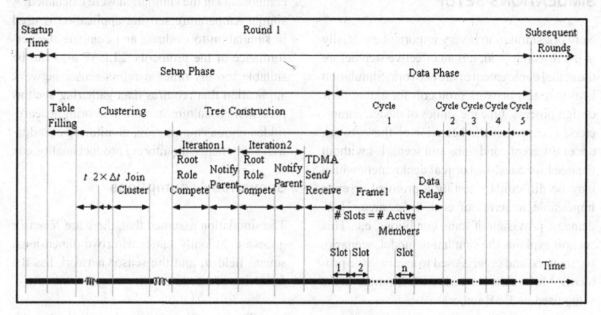

no use of it, only when it reaches the network layer they neglect it (overhearing). This message is as *Root_Compting_Msg* when received by plain nodes. The timeline of LLEAP operation is shown in Figure 6 and the details of the schedule are described below:

During Startup Time (which is the period required for nodes after deployment to receive the *OK* message from the sink to acquire the *RSS),* all nodes wake up receiving *OK* message. During Table Filling period all nodes are awake for sending and receiving *E_Msg* and filling the neighborhood table. During (*t*) all nodes are awake until a *Compete_Msg* received, after that they send *Join_Msg* message to their selected CH and sleep. During (2 ×Δ*t*), plain nodes sleep while head nodes awake receiving *Compete_Msg* or *Join_Msg*. In the remaining time in Clustering phase, plain nodes formed after time (2 ×Δ*t*) are awake for sending *Join_Msg* to their selected CH, and head nodes are still awake for receiving *Join_Msg*. Through Root Role Compete period in iteration1 plain nodes sleep, head nodes awake sending and receiving *Root_Compting_Msg*, and nodes which are still candidate sleep.

During Notify Parent period in iteration1, plain nodes sleep, head nodes awake sending and receiving *My_Parent* messages, and candidate nodes sleep Over Root Role Compete period in iteration2 plain nodes sleep, head nodes (children and parents) sleep, root nodes awake sending and receiving *Root_Compting_Msg*, and candidate nodes sleep Over Notify Parent period in iteration2 plain nodes sleep, head nodes awake sending and receiving *My_Parent* messages, and candidate nodes sleep.

During TDMA Send/Receive period plain nodes awake receiving *TDMA_Schedule* message, head nodes wake up sending *TDMA_Schedule* message, and candidate nodes sleep During each Slot period, one of the plain nodes in each cluster awake sending *Data_Msg*, head nodes awake receiving *Data_Msg*, and candidate nodes sleep Finally, during Data Relay period (which is the period required for the aggregated messages from all the constructed trees to reach the sink), plain nodes sleep, head nodes awake relaying the aggregated data to the sink, and candidate nodes sleep.

SIMULATIONS SETUP

Network simulation is very important especially in the research field; it is an effective step before the actual deployment of the network. Simulation is used to test network protocols for aiding their design process, tune the values of design parameters, and predict the behavior of the network under different conditions and scenarios without the need for a test-bed or real deployment which may be difficult for testing a protocol or even impossible in terms of cost, time, area, H.W. damage, provision of some conditions, etc. This section explains the simulation model, scenario, parameters, and criteria used to evaluate the protocols. Most of the network setup is similar to the setup used by EAP authors.

Network Model

To evaluate the performance of LEACH, EAP, and the modified version LLEAP and compare their performances, a set of simulation runs were carried out. The simulation was conducted using the discrete event simulator OMNeT++ (Varga, 2005) and SENSIM framework (Mallanda, et al., 2005; Sensor Networks Research Group, 2006) as the simulation platform to generate a network in 100×100 m² area in which sensor nodes are distributed statically and uniformly. The sink node is located at a fixed point (50,200) outside the area and it is assumed that it has infinite power and other resources. The signal propagation model used is the free space propagation model when the propagation distance is less than the threshold distance d_0 and the ground reflection (two-ray) propagation model when the propagation distance is greater than the threshold distance d_0.

As assumed in EAP paper, for simplicity, the probability of signal collision and interference in the wireless channel is ignorable and the radio transmitter, radio amplifier and data fusion unit are the main energy consumers of a sensor node, so only the energy consumption of these three

components in the simulation were calculated. A simple temperature sensing application is used in simulation to evaluate and compare the performance of the protocols. LLEAP also can be suitable for any other wireless sensor network application that requires data gathering such as precision agriculture, habitat monitoring, disease-ridden regions monitoring, monitoring of industrial equipments, monitoring product quality, etc.

Scenarios Assumptions

The simulation assumed that, there are N sensor nodes are randomly scattered in a two-dimensional square field A, and the sensor network has the following properties:

- The network is a static densely deployed.
- There is only one base station in the field, which is deployed at a fixed place outside A.
- The energy of sensor nodes cannot be recharged.
- Sensor nodes are location-unaware.
- The radio power can be controlled, i.e., a node can vary its transmission power depending on the distance to the receiver.
- For simplicity, it is assumed that the probability of signal collision and interference in the wireless channel is ignorable and the radio transmitter, radio amplifier and data fusion unit are the main energy consumers of a sensor node, so the two states (asleep and awake) used in the schedule technique are for the radio transceiver only, no need to consider these states for other energy consumers such as the sensing unit and the processor.
- Packet loss due to factors such as increased collisions due to the presence of hidden terminals, environmental disturbances, human interference, frequent path breaks due to mobility of nodes, and the inherent fad-

ing properties of the wireless channel don't exist or are ignorable.

- Processing, reception and state changing delays are neglected.
- Sensors always have data to send.
- The Radio H.W. energy dissipation model (Heinzelman, et al., 2002) used is: to transmit a *l*-bit message over a distance *d*, the transmitter consumes

$$
E_{Tx} = \begin{cases} l \times E_{elec} + l \times e_{fs} \times d^2, d < d_o \\ \\ l \times E_{elec} + l \times e_{amp} \times d^4, d \geq d_o \end{cases} \quad (8)
$$

And to receive that *l*-bit message, the receiver consumes

$$
E_{Rx} = l \times E_{elec} \quad (9)
$$

Where e_{fs} and e_{amp} are the energies dissipated in the transmitter amplifier for either a free-space channel or a multi-path fading channel respectively. E_{elec} is the Energy dissipated in transmitter and receiver electronics per bit.

- The consumed energy in aggregating *M l*-bit signals into a single representative *l*-bit signal = $M \times E_{DA} \times l$, where: E_{DA} denotes the energy consumed by data fusion.
- As assumed in EAP paper, there are five cycles in each round.
- A node considered to be dead or killed when it becomes not capable of transmitting data to the sink, and this occurs in three cases:
  1. The node residual energy becomes below a specified threshold (E_{death}). This threshold equals to the energy required for a member node to participate in a

round, so that it transmits at least one data packet.
  2. There is no head in its cluster range (this appears when the energies of all its neighbor nodes fall below a specified energy threshold ($E_{threshold}$) below which the node doesn't participate in the competition for the head role).
  3. There is no any node in its cluster range for any reason and it can't be a head.

Performance Metrics

The used metrics and how they are measured in simulation are as follows: because the packets received by the sink are resulted from the aggregation of other different number of raw data packets, it is not correct to use them in computing losses, delay, and throughput as noticed from the following definitions.

Packet loss percentage: the ratio of the number of packets lost due to node death (the number of raw data packets sent by nodes and received aggregated at the sink subtracted from the total number of raw data packets transmitted by all nodes) to the total number of raw data packets transmitted by all nodes in the network until its lifetime end.

Lifetime: for EAP and LLEAP, it is measured in terms of round when the Last Node Dies (LND). While the lifetime of LEACH network is measured in terms of round when all nodes goes below $E_{threshold}$.

Throughput: is the number of sent data bits by plain nodes which the sink benefit by per second and it can be considered as a measure to extent of sink benefit from the network lifetime because it determines whether the amount of data received to the sink is suitable with respect to the lifetime of the network and whether there is a lot of time lost in network setup and data relaying. The throughput of the network is computed as the total number of data bits sent by plain nodes and received at the sink during network lifetime regardless of the form in which they are received divided by network lifetime in seconds.

End to End delay: the average time it takes for raw data packets to traverse from the plain nodes to the sink regardless of the form in which they are received, in other words it is the average delay of the sink in benefiting from every raw data packet sent in the network until network lifetime end.

Simulation Parameters

Most of the parameters' values are selected as the same as those in EAP paper for comparing the protocols under the same conditions which EAP authors used, for example, the monitored area size, the position of the sink, the initial energy, $E_{threshold}$, the threshold distance, cluster radius, sensing radius, data packet size, and broadcast packet size. The inter-cluster range used in EAP is $2.5 \times r$, but in LLEAP there are two iterations for tree construction in the first iteration the inter-cluster range used (R) is $2 \times r$ this decreases the broadcasting load on CHs and also contributes on reducing the branching factor, in the second iteration the inter-cluster range used (RR) is $3 \times r$, although this range is greater than the range used in EAP, but this increases the broadcasting load on only a small number of nodes which are the previously formed roots, and also it decreases the probability of the existence of more than one root at the end of the tree construction phase. The parameters used in the simulation are reported in Table 3.

RESULTS AND ANALYSIS

A number of simulation runs were carried out by using the same network setup, model, scenario, parameters' values, performance metrics, and simulator mentioned before to evaluate the performance of LEACH, EAP, and LLEAP in terms of Quality of Service (QoS). Then the obtained results were compared with each other. In simula-

tion, the initial number of nodes deployed in the monitored area is increased from 100 to 500 node with step 100, and for each value the corresponding average value of each one of the previously mentioned performance metrics is calculated for each protocol. Most of the results were obtained by averaging multiple independent simulation runs with a 95% confidence interval, where each run uses a different randomly-generated topology of sensor nodes.

Performance Evaluation for EAP and LEACH

In this section, the results of EAP and LEACH evaluation are presented. Although the main drawback of EAP deduced from studying its operations is causing data losses, the results presented in this section are not only related to the performance of the protocols in terms of loss percentage, but it also represents the evaluation of the protocols in terms of other QoS parameters which are end to end delay, throughput, and lifetime. The results shown in the next four subsections prove that EAP really results in data loss and its average packet loss percentage is greater than that of LEACH, but it is better than LEACH in terms of the other QoS parameters.

End to End Delay

The average delay of EAP is not constant and it approximately increased slightly with the increases in the number of deployed nodes as shown in Figure 7. In EAP implementation, if the number of a member's neighbors in its sensing radius is greater than a threshold value related to the quality of coverage determined by specific application, it goes to be asleep with probability $(1 - \frac{1}{threshold})$ (Gong, Liu, Mao, Chen, & Xie, 2006), which means the more neighbors it has, the more probability to be asleep. This causes a reduction in the average number of active mem-

Figure 7. The avg. end to end delay for EAP vs. no. of nodes

Figure 8. The avg. count of members per cluster for EAP vs. no. of nodes

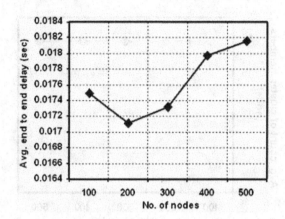

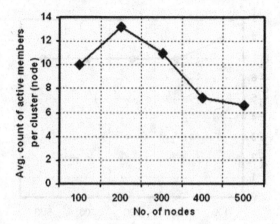

Figure 9. An illustrative example of the inverse relation between the average end to end delay and the count of active members per cluster

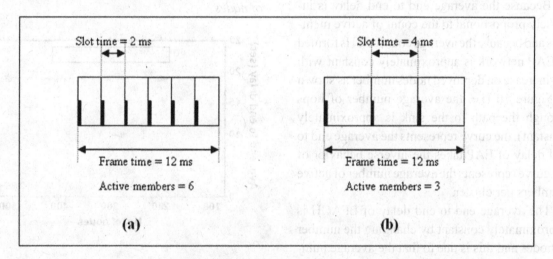

bers per cluster when the number of deployed nodes increases and reaches 300, then it continues to decrease as the number of deployed nodes increases as shown in Figure 8.

The average end to end delay is inversely proportional to the count of active members; the smaller the active members count, the larger the slot time, the more time most cluster members wait after sending the data message before the end of the frame and the beginning of data aggregation and relaying. For example, if we assume that the frame time equals 12 ms as shown in

Figure 9 and the transmission delay is neglected, the average time a raw data packet waits for the end of the frame when the number of active members equals six as shown in Figure 9a equals $\frac{12+10+8+6+4+2}{6} = 7$, while if the number of active members equals three as shown in Figure 9b the average time a raw data packet waits for the end of the frame equals $\frac{12+8+4}{3} = 8$.

Figure 10. Avg. count of CHs for EAP vs. no. of nodes

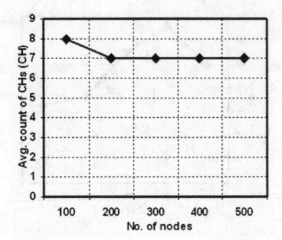

Figure 11. Avg. count of members per cluster for LEACH vs. no. of nodes

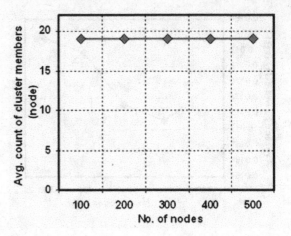

Figure 12. Average end to end delay vs. number of nodes

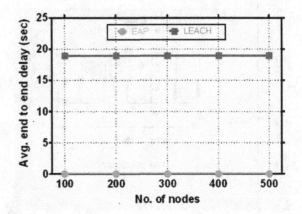

Because the average end to end delay is inversely proportional to the count of active members and because the average count of CHs formed in EAP network is approximately constant with the increase on deployed nodes number as shown in Figure 10 (i.e. the average number of hops through the path to the sink is approximately constant), the curve represents the average end to end delay of EAP takes the inverse behavior of the curve represents the average number of active members per cluster.

The average end to end delay of LEACH is approximately constant by changing the number of nodes and this is due to that the average number of cluster members in LEACH network is constant as shown in Figure 11 and every packet sent by member nodes in the network passes an equal number of hops (two hops) to reach the sink. The end to end delay in each hop equals to the packet transmission delay plus the packet propagation delay. It should be noted that the transmission delay is the same for all nodes because the length of the data packet is constant, and the propagation delay has very small value that will not greatly affect the value of the end to end delay.

Figure 12 demonstrates the average end to end delay for both EAP and LEACH. From Figure 12, it could be concluded that the average delay of EAP is less than that of LEACH by on average 99.9% although in EAP the packets from member nodes may go across more than two hops; this is mainly due to the previously mentioned requirement of LEACH for a wide TDMA schedule to accommodate all nodes expected to be deployed in the network minus one as members.

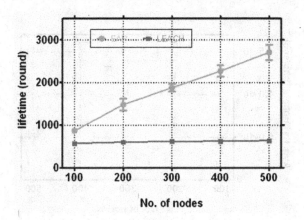

Figure 13. Network lifetime vs. number of nodes

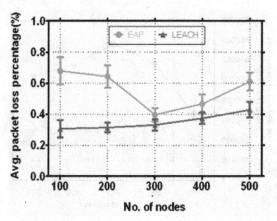

Figure 14. Average packet loss percentage vs. number of nodes

Lifetime

Figure 13 demonstrates the lifetime of both EAP and LEACH. From Figure 13, it is obvious that the lifetime of EAP increased with the number of deployed nodes and this relation is approximately linear due to the intra-cluster coverage method used. The lifetime of LEACH is less than the EAP lifetime by on average 61.5% because LEACH bear with load unbalance and high energy consumption from both CHs and members.

Packet Loss Percentage

Figure 14 demonstrates the average packet loss percentage for both EAP and LEACH. From Figure 14, it could be noticed that the packet loss percentage of EAP is higher than that of LEACH by 35%. As mentioned the reason of packet loss in EAP is the lack of a mechanism that informs about CH death. Although, LEACH has the same limitation and also in LEACH the probability of CH death is higher than in EAP because of higher CH energy consumption, the losses of LEACH is smaller than EAP as shown in the figure, this is due to that usually in each round of LEACH there are more than one CH and each CH is responsible only for its members, then the death of a CH means losses in its members data only, but

in EAP the network has only a single point of failure, i.e. if in a round the dead CH is a root, all the generated data in the whole network through this round will be lost.

Also the fact that the count of the generated packets in LEACH is redundant and higher than that of EAP specifically when the number of deployed nodes increases (from 300 to 500 deployed node) and accordingly the count of inactive members in EAP network increases can't be ignored, so the percentage of the lost packets to the generated packets in LEACH network is small. The generated packets in LEACH are redundant and more than the generated packets in EAP when the number of deployed nodes increases because LEACH doesn't use intra-cluster coverage method and all nodes are active in the same time that the intra-cluster coverage method used in EAP in addition to it causes the increase of inactive members when the number of deployed nodes increases, it causes the existence of a number of successive inactive rounds which do not used in sending data to the sink, rather these rounds consume nodes energy in sending control packets in the interval precedes activity test, so some nodes die quickly after these rounds or during it without benefiting from them in sending data. Due to these reasons at 400 and 500 deployed nodes where the

Figure 15. Average generated raw data packets count for EAP vs. number of nodes

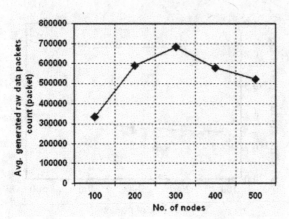

Figure 16. Average throughput vs. number of nodes

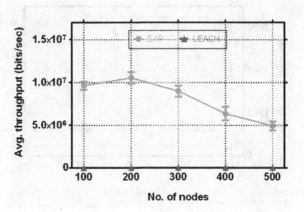

count of inactive members and successive inactive rounds increase, the average count of generated raw data packets decreases as shown in Figure 15.

From Figure 14, it could be noticed that the curve represents the average packet loss percentage of LEACH takes a stable behavior where the loss percentage increases with the number of deployed nodes. While the curve represents the average packet loss percentage of EAP changes its behavior after the 300 deployed node point from decrease to increase taking the inverse behavior of average generated raw data packets curve because it inversely proportional to it and directly proportional to the count of lost raw data packets which is not large and its change is small compared to the change in the generated raw data packets such that it can be considered constant.

Throughput

Figure 16 demonstrates the average throughput of both EAP and LEACH. From Figure 16, it could be noticed that the throughput of EAP is higher than that of LEACH by on average 99.6%. This is also because LEACH design requires a wide TDMA schedule to accommodate the circumstances when only one CH formed and the

remaining large number of nodes becomes its members, while the average number of cluster members in LEACH network is not large and constant as shown in Figure 11, i.e., in most cases the long TDMA frame divided of a small number of nodes, as a result the slot time dedicated to each node becomes longer than its need, it sends its data packet in a small percent of this slot time and the remaining of the slot represents wasted time. This increases the wasted time - that don't used in sending data - through network lifetime, thus the throughput decreased.

It is obvious from Figure 16 that the throughput of EAP decreased dramatically after the number deployed nodes increased over 200 nodes, but the difference between the lower point in EAP throughput curve and the higher point of LEACH throughput curve is still large and approximately equals to the percentage 99.1%. The throughput of EAP decreased mainly due to the appearance of a number of successive inactive rounds as mentioned before when the number of deployed nodes equals 300 and this number increased at 400 and 500 node, also because the throughput is directly proportional to the count of active members per cluster, it takes the same behavior as the curve represents the average count of active members per cluster shown in Figure 8.

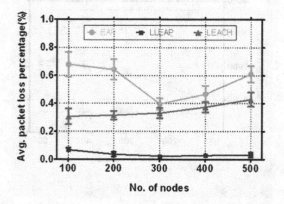

Figure 17. Average packet loss percentage vs. number of nodes

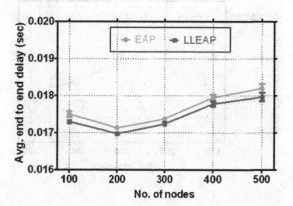

Figure 18. Average end to end delay vs. number of nodes

Performance Evaluation for LLEAP

This section shows the results obtained from LLEAP evaluation and compares these results with the results obtained from EAP and LEACH evaluation. The purpose of LLEAP evaluation is to prove that its average packet loss percentage is really less than EAP and LEACH average packet loss percentages, and give an approximate value of this reduction percent. Also the modified protocol LLEAP is evaluated in terms of end to end delay, throughput, and lifetime to study the impact of the modifications used on it on these performance metrics. The results showed that LLEAP significantly reduces EAP loss percentage and approximately preserves its characteristics in terms of lifetime, end to end delay, and throughput.

Packet Loss Percentage

The LLEAP still keeps the advantages of EAP, it throw up the load of the transmission to the sink to one node only in each round and distributes this load among all nodes through rounds (this advantage doesn't exist in LEACH which leads to less lifetime than EAP). In the same time, LLEAP also overcomes the disadvantage of EAP which is the single point of failure (which leads to high losses than LEACH) by reducing this failure i.e.,

reducing root death by reducing the aggregation and transmission loads on it.

In LLEAP generally the number of CH death is reduced and in case of CH death, the death is at the end of the round after the CH sends the last aggregated data message. Therefore, LLEAP will still retain lifetime higher than LEACH, and its losses become less than EAP, and also less than LEACH. As shown in Figure 17 the average loss percentage of the LLEAP is below the average loss percentage of EAP by on average 93.4%, and below the average loss percentage of LEACH by on average 89.3%.

End to End Delay

Although the number of hops is increased and the path to the sink is elongated in LLEAP, the delay is decreased as shown in Figure 18 by on average 1%, because the used method of aggregation made the waiting period for children data proportional to the level of the parent in the tree, also it canceled the wasted time in waiting an inactive child (CH with no children or members). From Figure 12, it is known that LEACH delay is higher than EAP delay with high percentage, so from both Figure 12 and 18 it is self-evident that LEACH delay is also higher than LLEAP with high percentage, so that in Figure 18, it was sufficient to zoom in EAP

Figure 19. Average throughput vs. number of nodes   *Figure 20. Network lifetime vs. number of nodes*

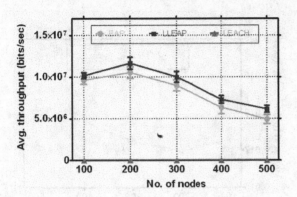

and LLEAP curves only to clarify the difference between them.

Throughput

As shown in Figure 19, the throughput of LLEAP is increased over the throughput of EAP by approximately 11.8% although the setup time increased. This is due to the decrease in the wasted time from LLEAP network lifetime, which untapped in sending data, as a result of the reduction of the successive inactive rounds count and at the same time the average number of generated data packets doesn't remain as it is in EAP, but it increased over it slightly, and packet losses decreased.

Lifetime

Without simulation it was difficult to expect whether the lifetime of LLEAP network will be less or more than EAP, because LLEAP uses a time schedule to save nodes energy and increase lifetime, in the same time, some modifications which used in LLEAP exhaust nodes energy; for example, the restoration of the lost packets increases the aggregation load on CHs, as well as sending and receiving the additional control packets *Root_Compting_Msg* and *My_Parent* in larger range *RR*, and the obligation of some CHs to send data messages in larger range *RR* increases

the transmission load on these nodes. By using the simulation as shown in Figure 20 the LND lifetime of the LLEAP is below the LND lifetime of EAP by approximately 7.8%.

The percentage of LLEAP lifetime reduction is small when the number of deployed nodes is 100, 200, or 300, but this percentage increased notably when the number of deployed nodes increased to 400 and 500 nodes. This may not be considered as a disadvantage of LLEAP, because the increase in the percentage of LLEAP lifetime reduction is accompanied by an approximately equal percent increase in LLEAP throughput over EAP; this means that most of the large increase in EAP lifetime over LLEAP when the number of deployed nodes is 400 and 500 are not exploited in data transmission (because this large increase caused by the large count of successive inactive rounds appear in EAP network when the number of deployed nodes is increased, while the count of these successive inactive rounds in LLEAP is decreased).

FUTURE RESEARCH DIRECTIONS

Several routing protocols for Wireless Sensor Networks continuously proposed in literature for overcoming the challenges face WSNs routing protocols design and for developing a routing protocol suitable to a wide range of applications, for example the protocol presented in this chapter which is called LLEAP deals with some challenges and techniques related to WSN routing such as energy-efficiency, lifetime, QoS, network clustering, data aggregation, and multi-hop communication. Interestingly, some of the proposed routing protocols lack the realism in its design and evaluation. More realistic simulation models should be developed and used in the design to reflect the impact of the highly dynamic nature of the WSNs and the harsh environment in which the WSN may deployed. It should be concentrated on the suitability of the protocol to the characteristics and the abilities of the available sensor nodes hardware to ensure that the processing required by the protocol is not beyond the processing unit capabilities and don't consume a considerable amount of energy that couldn't be ignored. The protocol shouldn't require the storage of a large amount of data that fills node's memory and exceeds its capacity. Also the protocol should be tested against the achievement of different applications' requirements such as node mobility, node addition, query-processing, event detection, security, etc.

For LLEAP, there are still several works that could be addressed in future such as: first, how to increase the network lifetime without affecting the other performance metrics of LLEAP. Second, using a best method for canceling the second tree construction iteration when only one root formed in the first iteration. Also EAP still has some disadvantages not considered in LLEAP such as, some nodes will be neither CHs nor plain nodes after the clustering phase and they will remain candidate nodes, also after the clustering phase, some nodes will be plain nodes of a certain CH but with no TDMA schedule i.e. useless nodes, these nodes can be called "deceived nodes" because they deceived by a *Compete_Msg* message was sent to them during their delay time (t) from a node they considered it as a CH while this node becomes a member node in the cluster of another node with a larger weight sent to it a *Compete_Msg* mes-

sage during its ($2 \times \Delta t$) period. It is expected that these disadvantages can be addressed by further modification in weight and time (t) equations and good selection of Δt value. Finally, an important work that could be addressed in future is the trial to get over the constraints imposed upon LLEAP by some of the suggested assumptions making the protocol satisfies other applications' requirements, and studying LLEAP impact on all the resources of the node such as computation and storage resources; this may be better done by implementing the protocol in a test-bed WSN.

CONCLUSION

This chapter presents an energy-efficient hierarchical cluster-based routing protocol for WSN called LLEAP inspired by another hierarchical cluster-based routing protocol called EAP. LLEAP enhances EAP in terms of some QoS parameters by modifying the weights equations, adding a second iteration for CHs tree construction, using schedule technique for nodes sleep and awakening to save nodes energy, and using an aggregation method decreases delay and packets loss. Simulation results showed that LLEAP offers improvements over EAP in loss percentage, throughput, and delay by on average 93.4%, 11.8%, and 1% respectively, while LND lifetime reduced by 7.8%. The following discussion lists in the form of points what could be understood and learned from this Chapter:

- Some of WSN applications require QoS metrics other than lifetime
- The trade-off between lifetime and other QoS parameters should be taken into consideration
- The protection from loss cause is better than the cure from it
- The method used in the formation of logical tree structure may result in star topology not tree

- The root node of the tree is a critical point; it represents a single point of failure, thus it shouldn't be overloaded
- The more criteria you choose things on which, the less the number of things selected (as appeared in the equation of parent node selection weight when the number of the parameters used to compute it increased and accordingly the conditions that should be satisfied in the selected parent node increased)
- The hierarchical structure summarizes the network to number of levels, in any operation performed in each level, only the level representative nodes should be considered
- Whenever it is possible, the parameters sent in control packets should be updated just before sending
- The higher the count of roots, the smaller the network lifetime, the greater the data losses
- The choice of the inter-cluster range is critical, it should be enough big to decrease the probability of CHs isolation from each other, in the same time it shouldn't be very big in such a way that makes CHs consume a lot of energy for constructing the multi-hop communication between them, but it already quite wastes the benefit of using multi-hop communication because with a large inter-cluster range the sink may be nearer to the CH from its next-hop CH; a possible solution to this problem is to use two different ranges in two iterations for CHs tree construction, as done in LLEAP
- It may result from CH death not only the loss of its members and children data, but also the loss of its parents' data if a bad data aggregation method used
- Each CH should wait its children data a time period suitable to its level in the tree of CHs
- Although the division of the protocol operation to successive specified time periods requires nodes to be synchronized, it gives the facility of using a time schedule to iteratively activate and deactivate nodes, so that their wasted energy in the long duty cycle and overhearing problem is reduced
- The number of nodes in each cluster should be bounded such that the time periods which constitute a protocol operations timeline can be designed bounded even though the density of nodes is infinitely too big
- The conversion of the network to one cluster in an early time when all nodes or a large number of nodes are still alive should be prevented
- If the protocol requires nodes to transmit additional control information, the control overhead and energy consumption can be reduced by including this information as a field in a control packet the protocol already uses, that is if there is no need to use a separate control packet to transmit this information
- It is better for the protocol to preserve through the most of network lifetime a uniform distribution of CHs and nodes suitable to the remaining nodes' number

REFERENCES

Boukerche, A. (Ed.). (2009). *Algorithms and protocols for wireless sensor networks*. Hoboken, NJ: John Wiley & Sons, Inc.

Gong, H., Liu, M., Mao, Y., Chen, L., & Xie, L. (2006). Distributed energy efficient data gathering with intra-cluster coverage in wireless sensor networks. In X. Zhou, et al. (Eds.). *8th Asia – Pacific Web,* (pp. 109-120). Harbin, China: Springer.

Haque, M. E., Matsumoto, N., & Yoshida, N. (2010). Utilizing multilayer hierarchical structure in context aware routing protocol for wireless sensor networks. *International Journal of Computational Science, 4*(1), 23–37.

Heinzelman, W. B., Chandrakasan, A. P., & Balakrishnan, H. (2002). An application specific protocol architecture for wireless microsensor networks. *IEEE Transactions on Wireless Communications*, *1*(4), 660–670. doi:10.1109/TWC.2002.804190

Heinzelman, W. R., Chandrakasan, A., & Balakrishnan, H. (2000). Energy-efficient communication protocol for wireless microsensor networks. In *Proceedings of the 33rd Annual Hawaii International Conference on System Sciences,* (pp. 1-10). HICSS Press.

Ilyas, M., & Mahgoub, I. (Eds.). (2005). *Handbook of sensor networks: Compact wireless and wired sensing systems*. Boca Raton, FL: CRC Press.

Kumar, D., & Patel, R. B. (2011). Multi-hop data communication algorithm for clustered wireless sensor networks. *International Journal of Distributed Sensor Networks*. Retrieved from http://www.hindawi.com/journals/ijdsn/2011/984795/.

Liu, M., Cao, J., Chen, G., & Wang, X. (2009). An energy-aware routing protocol in wireless sensor networks. *Sensors (Basel, Switzerland)*, *9*(1), 445–462. doi:10.3390/s90100445

Louisiana State University. (2006). *LSU Sensor-Simulator user manual*. Retrieved from http://csc.lsu.edu/sensor_web/LSU_SensorSimulator_manual.pdf.

Lung, C.-H., & Zhou, C. (2010). Using hierarchical agglomerative clustering in wireless sensor networks: An energy-efficient and flexible approach. *Ad Hoc Networks*, *8*, 328–344. doi:10.1016/j.adhoc.2009.09.004

Mallanda, C., Suri, A., Kunchakarra, V., Iyengar, S. S., Kannan, R., Durresi, A., & Sastry, S. (2005). *Simulating wireless sensor networks with OMNeT++*. Retrieved from http://csc.lsu.edu/sensor_web/sensor_simulator/SensorSimulator-ACM-Computers.pdf.

Rashed, M. G., & Kabir, M. H. (2010). Weighted election protocol for clustered heterogeneous wireless sensor networks. *Journal of Mobile Communication*, *4*(2), 38–42. doi:10.3923/jmcomm.2010.38.42

Varga, A. (2005). *Omnet++ discrete event simulation system (Version 3.2)*. [Software program]. Retrieved from http://www.omnetpp.org/omnetpp/doc_details/2105-omnet-32-win32-binary-exe.

Wang, B. (2010). *Coverage control in sensor networks*. New York: Springer.

Wang, Y., Yang, T. L. X., & Zhang, D. (2009). An energy efficient and balance hierarchical unequal clustering algorithm for large scale sensor networks. *Information Technology Journal*, *8*(1), 28–38. doi:10.3923/itj.2009.28.38

Ye, M., Li, C., Chen, G., & Wu, J. (2005). EECS: An energy efficient clustering scheme in wireless sensor networks. In *Proceedings of the 24th IEEE International Performance, Computing, and Communications Conference,* (pp. 535–540). IEEE Press.

Younis, O., & Fahmy, S. (2004). HEED: A hybrid, energy-efficient, distributed clustering approach for ad hoc sensor networks. *IEEE Transactions on Mobile Computing*, *3*(4), 366–379. doi:10.1109/TMC.2004.41

Yu, Y., Prasanna, V. K., & Krishnamachari, B. (2006). *Information processing and routing in wireless sensor networks*. Singapore: World Scientific Publishing. doi:10.1142/9789812772589

ADDITIONAL READING

Akyildiz, I. F., Su, W., Sankarasubramaniam, Y., & Cyirci, E. (2002). Wireless sensor networks: A survey. *Computer Networks*, *38*(4), 393–422. doi:10.1016/S1389-1286(01)00302-4

Aslam, N., Phillips, W., Robertson, W., & Sivakumar, S. C. (2007). Balancing energy dissipation in clustered wireless sensor networks. In Thulasiraman, P., He, X., Xu, T., Denko, M., Thulasiram, R., & Yang, L. (Eds.), *Frontiers of High Performance Computing and Networking ISPA 2007 Workshops* (pp. 465–474). Berlin, Germany: Springer. doi:10.1007/978-3-540-74767-3_48

Chakrabarty, K., & Iyengar, S. S. (2005). *Scalable infrastructure for distributed sensor networks*. Berlin, Germany: Springer-Verlag.

De, S., Qiao, C., & Wu, H. (2003). Meshed multipath routing with selective forwarding: An efficient strategy in wireless sensor networks. *Computer Networks, 43*(4), 481–497. doi:10.1016/S1389-1286(03)00355-4

Ganesan, D., Govindan, R., Shenker, S., & Estrin, D. (2001). Highly-resilient, energy-efficient multipath routing in wireless sensor networks. *ACM Mobile Computing Communication Review, 5*(4), 11–25. doi:10.1145/509506.509514

García-Hernando, A.-B., Martínez-Ortega, J.-F., López-Navarro, J.-M., Prayati, A., & Redondo-López, L. (2008). *Problem solving for wireless sensor networks*. London: Springer-Verlag.

Hoesel, L. V., Nieberg, T., Wu, J., & Havinga, P. J. M. (2004). Prolonging the lifetime of WSNs by cross-layer interaction. *IEEE Wireless Communications, 11*(6), 78–86. doi:10.1109/MWC.2004.1368900

Intanagonwiwat, C., Govindan, R., & Estrin, D. (2000). Directed diffusion: A scalable and robust communication paradigm for sensor networks. In *Proceedings of the 6th MobiCom*, (pp. 56–67). ACM Press.

Jurdak, R. (2007). *Wireless ad hoc and sensor networks: a cross-layer design perspective*. New York, NY: Springer.

Krishnamachari, B., Estrin, D., & Wicker, S. (2002). Impact of data aggregation in wireless sensor networks. In *Proceedings of the 22nd International Conference on Distributed Computing Systems Workshops*, (pp. 575-578). IEEE Press.

Kulik, J., Heinzelman, W. R., & Balakrishnan, H. (2002). Negotiation-based protocols for disseminating information in wireless sensor networks. *Wireless Networks, 8*(2), 169–185. doi:10.1023/A:1013715909417

Lee, G., Lee, M., Seok, W., Kong, J., & Byeon, O. (2006). A base station centralized simple clustering protocol for sensor networks. In Sha, E., Han, S.-K., Xu, C.-Z., Kim, M., Yang, L., & Xiao, B. (Eds.), *Embedded and Ubiquitous Computing* (pp. 682–691). Berlin, Germany: Springer. doi:10.1007/11802167_69

Li, Y., Thai, M. T., & Wu, W. (2008). *Wireless sensor networks and applications*. Berlin, Germany: Springer.

Lindsey, S., & Raghavendra, C. S. (2002). PEGASIS: Power-efficient gathering in sensor information systems. In *Proceedings of the IEEE Aerospace Conference*, (pp. 1125–1130). IEEE Press.

Madan, R., Cui, S., Lall, S., & Goldsmith, A. (2006). Cross-layer design for lifetime maximization in interference-limited wireless sensor networks. *IEEE Transactions on Wireless Communications, 5*(11), 3142–3152. doi:10.1109/TWC.2006.04770

Mahalik, N. P. (Ed.). (2007). *Sensor networks and configuration: Fundamentals, standards, platforms, and applications*. Berlin, Germany: Springer-Verlag.

Misra, S., Woungang, I., & Misra, S. C. (Eds.). (2009). *Guide to wireless sensor networks*. London: Springer-Verlag.

Papadopoulos, A. (2004). Towards the design of an energy-efficient, location-aware routing protocol for mobile, ad-hoc sensor networks. In *Proceedings of the 15th International Workshop on Database and Expert Systems Applications*, (pp. 705-709). IEEE Press.

Petrović, D., Shah, R. C., Ramchandran, K., & Rabaey, J. M. (2003). Data funneling: Routing with aggregation and compression for wireless sensor networks. In *Proceedings of the 1st IEEE International Workshop on Sensor Network Protocols and Applications*, (pp. 156–162). IEEE Press.

Phoha, S., LaPorta, T., & Griffin, C. (Eds.). (2006). *Sensor network operations*. Hoboken, NJ: John Wiley and Sons, Inc.doi:10.1002/0471784176

Sadagopan, N., Krishnamachari, B., & Helmy, A. (2003). The acquire mechanism for efficient querying in sensor networks. In *Proceedings of the 1st International Workshop on Sensor Network Protocol and Applications*, (pp. 149-155). IEEE Press.

Seada, K., Zuniga, M., Helmy, A., & Krishnamachari, B. (2004). Energy-efficient forwarding strategies for geographic routing in lossy wireless sensor networks. In *Proceedings of the* 2nd *International Conference on Embedded Networked Sensor Systems*, (pp. 108–121). IEEE Press.

Shah, R. C., & Rabaey, J. M. (2002). Energy-aware routing for low energy ad hoc sensor networks. In *Proceedings of the IEEE Wireless Communications and Networking conference, 1*, 350–355.

Sohraby, K., Minoli, D., & Znati, T. (2007). *Wireless sensor networks: Technology, protocols, and applications*. Hoboken, NJ: John Wiley and Sons. doi:10.1002/047011276X

Ye, F., Zhong, G., Lu, S., & Zhang, L. (2005). Gradient broadcast: A robust data delivery protocol for large scale sensor networks. *Wireless Networks, 11*(3), 285–298. doi:10.1007/s11276-005-6612-9

Zhao, F., & Guibas, L. J. (2004). *Wireless sensor networks:An information processing approach*. Boston, MA: Elsevier-Morgan Kaufmann.

Zheng, J., & Jamalipour, A. (Eds.). (2009). *Wireless sensor networks: A networking perspective*. Hoboken, NJ: John Wiley & Sons. doi:10.1002/9780470443521

KEY TERMS AND DEFINITIONS

Attribute-Based Addressing: In this addressing scheme, the destination of the packet is specified by a property of the phenomenon sensed by the node, i.e. the address will be in the form of attribute-value pair(s).

Energy-Efficiency: It is to expend less energy in performing a certain task. While saving energy is an advisable design goal for most systems, it represents a necessity for wireless sensor network because sensor nodes are usually battery-powered and operate unattended.

Flat Routing: It is the data routing method in which the network is flat, in other words, all the nodes constitute one level because all of them are assumed to be of the same type and capabilities, and do the same tasks. The natural topology for nodes communication in flat routing is the tree topolgy. Flat routing is not scalable to high node density because all the nodes especially the critical nodes and the sink itself become susceptible to overloading.

Hierarchical Routing: It is the data routing method in which the network is hierarchical, in other words, the nodes constitute multiple levels because they are assigned different roles. In each level of the hierarchicy reside the nodes which perform the same jobs. Hierarchical routing assigns the the role which consumes more energy to a small percent of nodes and to achieve load-balance this group of nodes is changed periodically.

Negotiation-Based Routing: In this routing, the node labels the data with high-level descriptions and before it sends its actual data to all of its neighbors, it exchanges control packets with smaller size than the data to determine if this data is really needed by these nodes.

Quality of Service: It means achieving better service for the traffic rather than just conveying it to the destination. The parameters defining the Quality of Service (QoS) for wireless sensor networks are for example, reliability, latency, data accuracy, throughput, and security. Usually improving these parameters affects the energy-efficiency and accordingly the network lifetime.

Wireless Sensor Network: It is a distributed system consists of a large number of small electronic devices called sensor nodes, each node performs a particular job depends on the used application which is based mainly on its work on the collection of information from the surrounding environment. Usually, sensor nodes are deployed randomly and communicate wirelessly.

Compilation of References

Abdelzaher, T., Blum, B., Evans, D., George, J., George, S., & Gu, L. … Wood, A. (2004). EnviroTrack: Towards an environmental computing paradigm for distributed sensor networks. In *Proceedings of the 24th International Conference on Distributed Computing Systems,* (pp. 582-589). IEEE Computer Society Press.

Abduvaliyev, A., Lee, S., & Lee, Y. K. (2010). Energy efficient hybrid intrusion detection system for wireless sensor networks. In *Proceedings of the 2010 International Conference on Electronics and Information Engineering (ICEIE 2010),* (pp. V2-25 – V2-29). Los Alamitos, CA: Conference Publishing Services.

Adomi, E. (2007). Overnight internet browsing among cybercafé users in Abraka, Nigeria. *Journal of Community Informatics, 3*(2). Retrieved February 20, 2010 from http://ci-journal.net/index.php/ciej/article/viewFile/322/351.

Adomi, E. (2008). Combating cybercrime in Nigeria. *The Electronic Library, 26*(5), 716–725. doi:10.1108/02640470810910738

Adorni, G., Battigelli, S., & Coccoli, M. (2007). Beyond learning management systems in lifelong learning. In *Proceedings of the 13rd International Conference on Distributed Multimedia Systems - Workshop on Distance Education Technologies, DMS-DET 2007,* (pp. 159-164). San Francisco, CA: IEEE Press.

Adorni, G., Coccoli, M., Fadda, C., & Veltri, L. (2007). Audio and video conferencing tools in learning management systems. In *Proceedings of the 3rd IEEE International Conference on Automatic Production of Cross Media Content for Multi-channel Distribution - AXMEDIS 2007,* (pp. 123-129). Barcelona, Spain: IEEE Press.

Agah, A., Basu, K., & Das, S. K. (2005). Preventing DoS attack in sensor networks: A game theoretic approach. In *Proceedings of 2005 IEEE International Conference on Communications (ICC 2005),* (pp. 3218-3222). Los Alamitos, CA: Conference Publishing Services.

Agah, A., Das, S. K., & Basu, K. (2004). Preventing DoS attack in sensor networks: A game theoretic approach. In *Proceedings of IEEE International Conference on Performance, Computing, and Communications,* (pp. 259-263). Los Alamitos, CA: Conference Publishing Services.

Agah, A., & Das, S. K. (2007). Preventing DoS attacks in wireless sensor networks: A repeated game theory approach. *International Journal of Network Security, 5,* 259–263.

Akkaya, K., & Younis, M. (2005). A survey of routing protocols in wireless sensor networks. *Elsevier Ad Hoc Network Journal, 3,* 325–349. doi:10.1016/j.adhoc.2003.09.010

Akyildiz, I. F., Su, W., Sankarasubramaniam, Y., & Cayirci, E. (2002). A survey on sensor networks. *IEEE Communications Magazine, 40*(8), 102–114. doi:10.1109/MCOM.2002.1024422

Alani, O., & Elmirghani, J. (2009). Mix queues approach for indoor network traffic modelling. In *Proceedings of the Fifth International Conference on Networking and Services,* (pp. 438-443). IEEE Press.

Alavi, M. (2004). Distributed learning environments. *Computer, 37*(1), 121–122. doi:10.1109/MC.2004.1260733

Alessi, S. M., & Trollip, S. R. (1991). *Computer based instruction: Methods and development.* New York: Prentice Hall.

Alippi, C., Camplani, R., Galperti, C., & Roveri, M. (2008). Effective design of WSNs: From the lab to the real world. In *Proceedings of the 3rd International Conference on Sensing Technology,* (pp. 1-9). IEEE Press.

Al-Karaki, J. N., & Kamal, A. E. (2004). On the correlated data gathering problem in wireless sensor networks. In *Proceedings of the Ninth IEEE Symposium on Computers and Communications.* Alexandria, Egypt: IEEE Press.

AL-Karaki, J. N., & Kamal, A. E. (2004). Routing techniques in wireless sensor networks: A survey. *IEEE Wireless Communications, 11*(6), 6-28.

Al-Karaki, J. N., Ul-Mustafa, R., & Kamal, A. E. (2004). Data aggregation in wireless sensor networks - Exact and approximate algorithms. In *Proceedings of IEEE Workshop on High Performance Switching and Routing (HPSR).* Phoenix, AZ: IEEE Press.

Al-Karaki, J. N., & Kamal, A. E. (2004). Routing techniques in wireless sensor networks: A survey. *IEEE Wireless Communications, 11*(6), 6–28. doi:10.1109/MWC.2004.1368893

Allen, G. W., Lorincz, K., Ruiz, M., Marcillo, O., Johnson, J., Lees, J., & Welsh, M. (2006). Deploying a Wireless sensor network on an active volcano. *IEEE Internet Computing,* 18–25. doi:10.1109/MIC.2006.26

Anantharaman, V., Park, S.-J., Sundaresan, K., & Sivakumar, R. (2004). TCP performance over mobile ad hoc networks: A quantitative study. *Journal of Wireless Communications and Mobile Computing, 4*(2), 203–222. doi:10.1002/wcm.172

Arampatzis, T., Lygeros, J., & Manesis, S. (2005). A survey of applications of wireless sensors and wireless sensor networks. In *Proceedings of the IEEE International Symposium on Intelligent Control,* (pp. 719-724). IEEE Press.

Armenio, F., Barthel, H., Burstein, L., Dietrich, P., Duker, J., Garrett, J., et al. Williams, J. (2007). *The EPCglobal architecture framework.* Retrieved February 12th, 2009, from http://www.epcglobalinc.org/ standards/ architecture/ architecture_ 1_2-framework- 20070910.pdf.

Asif, Z., & Mandviwalla, M. (2005). Integrating the supply chain with RFID: A technical and business analysis. *Communications of the Association for Information Systems, 15*(24), 393–426.

Aura, T., Nikander, P., & Leiwo, J. (2001). DOS-resistant authentication with client puzzles. *Lecture Notes in Computer Science, 2133,* 171–177.

Ayanoglu, E., Paul, S., LaPorta, T., Sabnani, K., & Gitlin, R. (1995). Airmail: A link-layer protocol for wireless networks. *Wireless Networks, 1*(1), 47–60. doi:10.1007/BF01196258

Ayoade, J. (2007). Roadmap to solving security and privacy concerns in RFID systems. *Computer Law & Security Report, 23*(6), 555–561. doi:10.1016/j.clsr.2007.09.005

Badrinath, B., Acharya, A., & Imielinski, T. (1993). Impact of mobility on distributed computations. *ACM Operating Systems Review, 27*(2), 15–20. doi:10.1145/155848.155853

Bai, Y., Wang, F., & Liu, P. (2006). Efficiently filtering RFID data streams. In *Proceedings of the CleanDB Workshop,* (pp. 50-57). IEEE Press.

Baig, Z. A. (2008). *Distributed denial of service attack detection in wireless sensor networks.* Unpublished Doctoral Dissertation. Monash University.

Baig, Z. A. (2011). Pattern recognition for detecting distributed node exhaustion attacks in wireless sensor networks. *Computer Communications, 34*(3), 468–484. doi:10.1016/j.comcom.2010.04.008

Bakre, A., & Badrinath, B. R. (1995). I-TCP: Indirect TCP for mobile hosts. In *Proceedings of the 15th International Conference on Distributed Computing Systems (ICDCS).* IEEE Press.

Bakshi, B., Krishna, P., Vaidya, N. H., & Pradhan, D. K. (1997). Improving performance of TCP over wireless networks. In *Proceedings of ICDCS.* Baltimore, MD: IEEE Press.

Balakrishnan, H., Padmanabhan, V. N., & Katz, R. H. (1997). The effects of asymmetry on TCP performance. In *Proceedings of ACM/IEEE Mobicom,* (pp. 77–89). IEEE Press.

Balakrishnan, H., Padmanabhan, V., Seshan, S., & Katz, R. H. (1997). A comparison of mechanisms for improving TCP performance over wireless links. *IEEE/ACM Transactions on Networking, 5*(6), 756–769. doi:10.1109/90.650137

Balakrishnan, H., Seshan, S., & Katz, R. (1995). Improving reliable transport and handoff performance in cellular wireless networks. *ACM Wireless Networks, 1,* 469–482. doi:10.1007/BF01985757

Bao, L., & Garcia-Luna-Aceves, J. J. (2001). A new approach to channel access scheduling for ad hoc networks. In *Proceedings of Seventh Annual International Conference on Mobile Computing and Networking,* (pp. 210-221). New York: ACM.

Baraka, H. (2009). *Empowerment and safety for children in a knowledge society: Egyptian experience.* Paper presented at the APEC-OECD Symposium. Singapore.

Barati, H., Movaghar, A., Barati, A., & Mazreah, A. A. (2008). A review of coverage and routing for wireless sensor networks, *37.*

Barton, P., & Nissanka, V. (2003). Cyber-crime criminal offence or civil wrong? *Computer Law & Security Report, 19*(5), 401–405. doi:10.1016/S0267-3649(03)00509-0

Bazelon, D. L., Choi, Y. J., & Conaty, J. F. (2006). Computer crimes. *The American Criminal Law Review, 43,* 259–310.

Becher, A., Benenson, Z., & Dornseif, M. (2006). Tampering with motes: Real-world physical attacks on wireless sensor networks. In *Proceedings of the 3rd International Conference on Security in Pervasive Computing (SPC),* (pp. 104-118). Berlin, Germany: Springer.

Bechler, M., Jaap, S., & Wolf, L. (2005). An optimized TCP for Internet access of vehicular ad hoc networks. *Lecture Notes in Computer Science, 3462,* 869–880. doi:10.1007/11422778_70

Becker, M., Drozda, M., Schaust, S., Bohlmann, S., & Szczerbicka, H. (2009). On classification approaches for misbehavior detection in wireless sensor networks. *Journal of Computers, 4*(5), 357–365. doi:10.4304/jcp.4.5.357-365

Bequai, A. (2001). Organised crime goes cyber. *Computers & Security, 20*(6), 475–478. doi:10.1016/S0167-4048(01)00604-6

Besma, R. A., Nash, R. A., Yao, Y., & Mongi, A. A. (2008). Survey and analysis of multimodal sensor planning and integration for wide area surveillance. *ACM Computing Surveys, 41*(1), 1–36. doi:10.1145/1456650.1456657

Bhuse, V., & Gupta, A. (2006). Anomaly intrusion detection in wireless sensor networks. *Journal of High Speed Networks, 15*(1), 33–51.

Bickel, G. (2010). *Inter/intra-vehicle wireless communication.* Retrieved from http://userfs.cec.wustl.edu/~gsb1/index.html#toc.

Bochicchio, M. A., & Longo, A. (2009). Hands-on remote labs: Collaborative web laboratories as a case study for it engineering classes. *IEEE Transactions on Learning Technologies, 2*(4), 320–330. doi:10.1109/TLT.2009.30

Bolettieri, P., Falchi, F., Gennaro, C., & Rabitti, F. (2007). A digital library framework for reusing e-learning video documents . In Duval, E., Klamma, R., & Wolpers, M. (Eds.), *EC-TEL 2007: Lecture Notes in Computer Science* (*Vol. 4753,* pp. 444–449). Berlin, Germany: Springer.

Bottigliengo, M., Casetti, C., Chiasserini, C. F., & Meo, M. (2004). Short-term fairness for TCP flows in 802.11b WLANs . In *Proceedings of IEEE INFOCOM* (pp. 1383–1392). Piscataway, NJ: IEEE.

Boukerche, A. (Ed.). (2009). *Algorithms and protocols for wireless sensor networks.* Hoboken, NJ: John Wiley & Sons, Inc.

Bradley, J. R., & Guerrero, H. H. (2010). A framework for RFID deployment in supply chains. *IT Professional, 12*(4), 44–50. doi:10.1109/MITP.2010.43

Brakmo, L. S., O'Malley, S. W., & Peterson, L. L. (1994). TCP Vegas: New techniques for congestion detection and avoidance. In *Proceedings of ACM SIGCOMM 1994,* (pp. 24-35). ACM Press.

Brenner, S. (2004). Cybercrime metrics: Old wine, new bottles. *Virginia Journal of Law and Technology, 9*(6), 537–584.

Bridge, P. D., Jackson, M., & Robinson, L. (2009). The effectiveness of streaming video on medical student learning: A case study. *Medical Education Online, 14.* Retrieved July 5, 2011, from http://www.med-ed-online.org.

Broisin, J., Vidal, P., Meire, M., & Duval, E. (2005). Bridging the gap between learning management systems and learning object repositories: Exploiting learning context information . In *Proceedings of Telecommunications* (pp. 478–483). IEEE Press.

Brown, K., & Singh, S. (1997). M-TCP: TCP for mobile cellular networks. *ACM Computer Communication Review, 27*(5).

Bulkowski, A., Nawarecki, E., & Duda, A. (2008). Peer-to-peer dissemination of learning objects for creating collaborative learning communities. In *Proceedings of the World Conference on Educational Multimedia, Hypermedia and Telecommunications,* (pp. 1874–1878). IEEE Press.

Burden, K., Palmer, C., & Lyde, B. (2003). Cyber-crime: A new breed of criminals? *Computer Law & Security Report, 19*(3), 222. doi:10.1016/S0267-3649(03)00306-6

Caceres, R., & Iftode, L. (2001). Improving the performance of reliable transport protocols in mobile computing environments. *IEEE Journal on Selected Areas in Communication, 19*(7).

Casey, E. (2004). *Digital evidence and computer crime.* St. Louis, MO: Elsevier Press.

Cassim, F. (2009). Formulating specialised legislation to address the growing spectre of cybercrime: A comparative study. *Preservation Education & Research, 12*(4), 35–79.

Caviglione, L. (2009c). Can satellites face trends? The case of Web 2.0. In *Proceedings of International Workshop on Satellite and Space Communications (IWSSC 2009),* (pp. 446-450). Siena, Italy: IEEE Press.

Caviglione, L., & Coccoli, M. (2010). Peer-to-peer infrastructures to support the delivery of learning objects. In *Proceedings of the 2nd International Conference on Education Technology and Computer (ICETC 2010),* (pp. 176 – 180). Shangai, China: IEEE Press.

Caviglione, L., & Veltri, L. (2006). A P2P framework for distributed and cooperative laboratories. In F. Davoli, S. Palazzo, & S. Zappatore (Ed.), *Distributed Cooperative Laboratories - Networking, Instrumentation and Measurements,* (pp. 309-319). Norwell, MA: Springer.

Caviglione, L., Coccoli, M., & Punta, E. (2010). *Education and training in grid-enabled laboratories and complex systems.* Paper presented at the INGRID 2010 Workshop, Instrumenting the grid. Poznań, Poland.

Caviglione, L., Collini-Nocker, B., & Fairhurst, G. (2008). FIRST: Future internet - A role for satellite technology. In *Proceedings of IEEE International Workshop on Satellite and Space Communications (IWSSC 2008),* (pp.160-164). IEEE Press.

Caviglione, L., Davoli, F., Asorey-Cacheda, R., & Gonzalez-Castaño, F. J. (2005). P2P in satellite networks: A tutorial on related problems and some possible solutions. In *Proceedings of 2nd International Symposium on Wireless Communication Systems,* (pp. 733-736). IEEE Press.

Caviglione, L. (2009a). *File-sharing applications engineering.* New York: Nova Science Publishers.

Caviglione, L. (2009b). Enabling cooperation of consumer devices through peer-to-peer overlays. *IEEE Transactions on Consumer Electronics, 55*(2), 414–421. doi:10.1109/TCE.2009.5174402

Caviglione, L., Berruti, L., Davoli, F., Polizzi, M., Vignola, S., & Zappatore, S. (2009). On the integration of telecommunication measurement devices within the framework of an instrumentation grid . In Davoli, F., Mayer, N., Pugliese, R., & Zappatore, S. (Eds.), *Grid Enabled Remote Instrumentation* (pp. 283–300). Norwell, MA: Springer.

Chandran, K., Raghunathan, S., Venkatesan, S., & Prakash, R. (2001). A feedback based scheme for improving TCP performance in ad-hoc wireless networks. *IEEE Journal on Personal Communications, 8*(1), 34–39. doi:10.1109/98.904897

Chan, H., & Perrig, A. (2003). Security and privacy in sensor networks. *Computer, 36*(10), 103–105. doi:10.1109/MC.2003.1236475

Chawki, M. (2009). Nigeria tackles advance fee fraud. *Journal of Information, Law and Technology,* 1361-4169.

Chawki, M., & Abdel-Wahab, M. (2006). Identity theft in cyberspace: Issues and solutions. *LexElectronica, 11*(1), 1–41.

Chen, H., Han, P., Zhou, X., & Gao, C. (2007). Lightweight anomaly intrusion detection in wireless sensor networks. In *Proceedings of the 2007 Pacific Asia conference on Intelligence and Security Informatics (PAISI 2007),* (pp. 105-116). Berlin, Germany: Springer-Verlag.

Chen, J., Kam, A. H., Zhang, J., Liu, N., & Shue, L. (2005). Bathroom activity monitoring based on sound. In *Proceedings of the 3rd International Conference on Pervasive Computing,* (pp. 47-61). Springer Publisher.

Cheng, P. F., & Soung, C. L. (2003). TCP Veno: TCP enhancement for transmission over wireless access networks. *IEEE Journal on Selected Areas in Communications, 21,* 216–228. doi:10.1109/JSAC.2002.807336

Chen, J. S., Hong, Z. W., Wang, N. C., & Jhuang, S. H. (2010). Efficient cluster head selection methods for wireless sensor networks. *Journal of Networks, 5*(8), 964–970. doi:10.4304/jnw.5.8.964-970

Chen, X., Zhai, H., Wang, J., & Fang, Y. (2002). A survey on improving TCP performance over wireless network. *ACM Computing Surveys, 34*(3), 357–374. doi:10.1145/568522.568524

Chen, Y., Xu, W., Trappe, W., & Zhang, Y. (2009). *Securing emerging wireless systems.* New York, NY: Springer. doi:10.1007/978-0-387-88491-2

Chetan, S., Ranganathan, A., & Campbell, R. (2005). Towards fault tolerance pervasive computing. *IEEE Technology and Society Magazine, 24*(1), 38–44. doi:10.1109/MTAS.2005.1407746

Cheung, S., & Levitt, K. N. (1997). Protecting routing infrastructures from denial of service using cooperative intrusion detection. In *Proceedings of the New Security Paradigms Workshop (NSPW 1997),* (pp. 94-106). New York, NY: ACM.

Chien, H.-Y. (2007). SASI: A new ultralightweight RFID authentication protocol providing strong authentication and strong integrity. *Transactions on Dependable and Secure Computing, 4*(4), 337–340. doi:10.1109/TDSC.2007.70226

Chigona, W., Bheekun, A., Spath, M., Derakhashani, S., & Van Belle, J. (2005). Perceptions on SPAM in a South African context. *Internet and Information Technology in Modern Organisations: Challenges and Answers.* Retrieved March 3, 2011 from http://www.commerce.uct. ac.za/ InformationSystems/ Staff/ PersonalPages/ jvbelle/ pubs/ IBIMA05% 20Cairo% 2069.pdf.

Choi, M., Rosslin, J. R., Hong, C., & Kim, T. (2008). Wireless network security: Vulnerabilities, threats, and countermeasures. *International Journal of Multimedia and Ubiquitous Engineering, 3*(3), 77–86.

Christian, F., & Matthias, L. (2005). RFID middleware design: Addressing application requirements and RFID constraints. In *Proceedings of the Joint Conference on Smart Objects and Ambient Intelligence: Innovative Context-Aware Services: Usages and Technologies,* (pp. 219 - 224). New York: ACM Press.

Christou, I. T., Efremidis, S., Tiropanis, T., & Kalis, A. (2007). Grid-based virtual laboratory experiments for a graduate course on sensor networks. *IEEE Transactions on Education, 50*(1), 17–26. doi:10.1109/TE.2006.886447

Chukwuemerie, A. (2006). Nigeria's money laundering (prohibition) act 2004: A tighter noose. *Journal of Money Laundering Control, 9*(2), 173–190. doi:10.1108/13685200610660989

Clampitt, H. G. (2006). *RFID certification textbook.* Houston, TX: PWD Group.

Clarkson, B., Mase, K., & Pentland, A. (2000). Recognizing user context via wearable sensors. In *Proceedings of the 4th International Symposium on Wearable Computers,* (pp. 69-76). IEEE Press.

Cole, K., Chetty, M., LaRosa, C., Rietta, F., Schmitt, D. K., & Goodman, S. E. (2008). *Cybersecurity in Africa: An assessment.* Unpublished.

Collier, D. (2004). Criminal law and the internet . In Buys, R. (Ed.), *Cyberlaw @ SA* (2nd ed.). Pretoria: Van Schaik Publishers.

Corchado, J. M., Bajo, J., de Paz, Y., & Tapia, D. I. (2008). Intelligent environment for monitoring Alzheimer patients, agent technology for health care. *Decision Support Systems, 44*(2), 382–396. doi:10.1016/j.dss.2007.04.008

Corter, J. E., Nickerson, J. V., Esche, S. K., Chassapis, C., Im, S., & Ma, J. (2007). Constructing reality: A study of remote, hands-on, and simulated laboratories. *ACM Transactions on Computer-Human Interaction, 14*(2).

Crossbow Inc. (2010a). *Product MicaZ.* Retrieved July 25, 2010, from http://www.xbow.com/Products/wproductsoverview.aspx.

Crossbow Inc. (2010b). *Product Mica2dot*. Retrieved July 25, 2010, from http://www.xbow.com/products/Product_pdf_files/Wireless_pdf/MICA2DOT_Datasheet.pdf.

Crow, B. P., Widjaja, I., Kim, L. G., & Sakai, P. T. (1997). IEEE 802.11 wireless local area networks. *IEEE Communications Magazine, 35*(9), 116–126. doi:10.1109/35.620533

Culler, D. E. (2006). TinyOS: Operating system design for wireless sensor networks. *Sensor*. Retrieved January 10, 2011, from http://www.sensorsmag.com/networking-communications/tinyos-operating-system-design-wireless-sensor-networks-918.

Culler, D., Estrin, D., & Srivastava, M. (2004). Overview of sensor networks . In *Sensor Networks* (pp. 41–49). IEEE Computer Society Press.

Da Silva, A., Martins, M., Rocha, B., Loureiro, A., Ruiz, L., & Wong, H. (2005). Decentralized intrusion detection in wireless sensor networks. In *Proceedings of the 1st ACM International Workshop on Quality of Service & Security in Wireless and Mobile Networks (Q2SWinet 2005),* (pp. 16-23). New York, NY: ACM.

Dabek, F., Brunskill, E., Kaashoek, M. F., Karger, D., Morris, R., Stoica, I., & Balakrishnan, H. (2001). Building peer-to-peer systems with chord: A distributed lookup service. In *Proceedings of the 8ᵗʰ Workshop on Hot Topics in Operating Systems,* (pp. 81-86). Elmau-Oberbayern, Germany: IEEE Press.

Dagiral, E., & Dauphin, F. (2005). P2P: From file sharing to meta-information pooling. *International Journal on Digital Economics, 59,* 35–51.

Dam, T. V., & Langendoen, K. (2003). An adaptive energy-efficient MAC protocol for wireless sensor networks. In I. Akyildiz & D. Estrin (Eds.), *Proceedings of the 1st International Conference on Embedded Networked Sensor Systems,* (pp. 65-72). New York: ACM.

Dang, Q., Hong, L., Liu, S., Su, Z., & Yu, J. (2009). RFID application in IT assets management. In *Proceedings of the International Conference on Microwave Technology and Computational Electromagnetics,* (pp. 29-32). IEEE Press.

Das, R., & Harrop, P. (2010). RFID forecasts, players and opportunities 2011-2021. *IDTechEx Inc Report*. Retrieved 10 December 2010 from http:// www.idtechex.com.

Dashevsky, V., & Sokolov, B. (2009). New concept of RFID reader networks structure: Hardware and software architecture. In *Proceedings of the International Conference on Ultra Modern Telecommunications & Workshops,* (pp. 1-4). IEEE Press.

David, B. M., Santana, B., Peotta, L., Holtz, M. D., & Timoteo de Sousa, R. Jr. (2010). A context-dependent trust model for the MAC layer in LR-WPANs. *International Journal on Computer Science and Engineering, 2*(9), 3007–3016.

Demirkol, I., Ersoy, C., & Alagoz, F. (2006). MAC protocols for wireless sensor networks: A survey. *IEEE Communications Magazine, 44*(4), 115–121. doi:10.1109/MCOM.2006.1632658

Deng, J., Hun, R., & Mishra, S. (2004). *Countermeasures against traffic analysis in wireless sensor networks*. Technical Report CU-CS-987-04. Boulder, CO: University of Colorado at Boulder.

Deng, J., Hun, R., & Mishra, S. (2005). Countermeasures against traffic analysis attacks in wireless sensor networks. In *Proceedings of the First International Conference on Security and Privacy for Emerging Areas in Communications Networks (SECURECOMM 2005),* (pp. 113-126). Los Alamitos, CA: Conference Publishing Services.

Derakhshan, R., Orlowska, M. E., & Li, X. (2007). RFID data management: Challenges and opportunities. *IEEE International Conference on RFID,* (pp. 175-182). IEEE Press.

Dey, A. K. (2001). Understanding and using context. *Personal and Ubiquitous Computing, 5*(1), 4–7. doi:10.1007/s007790170019

Diggle, P. J., Tawn, J. A., & Moyeed, R. A. (1998). Model-based geostatistics. *Applied Statistics, 47*(3), 299–350. doi:10.1111/1467-9876.00113

Ding, M., Liu, F., Thaeler, A., Chen, D., & Cheng, X. (2007). Fault-tolerant target localization in sensor networks. *EURASIP Journal on Wireless Communications and Networking, 1,* 19.

Douceur, J. R. (2002). The sybil attack. *Lecture Notes in Computer Science, 2429,* 251–260. doi:10.1007/3-540-45748-8_24

Downes, S. (2005). E-learning 2.0. *ACM eLearn Magazine, 10.*

Duval, E., Vandepitte, P., & Ternier, S. (2002). LOMster: Peer-to-peer learning object metadata. In P. Barker & S. Rebelsky (Eds.), *Proceedings of World Conference on Educational Multimedia, Hypermedia and Telecommunications 2002,* (pp. 1942–1943). IEEE Press.

Dyer, T., & Boppana, R. (2001). A comparison of TCP performance over three routing protocols for mobile ad hoc networks. In *Proceedings of ACM MOBIHOC,* (pp. 56–66). ACM Press.

El Gamal, A., Mammen, J., Prabhakar, B., & Shah, D. (2004). Throughput-delay trade-off in wireless networks. In V. O. K. Li (Ed.), *Proceedings of the 23th Annual Joint Conference of the IEEE Computer and Communications Societies,* (pp. 464-475). Hong Kong: IEEE.

Etges, R., & Sutcliffe, E. (2008). An overview of transnational organized cyber crime. *Information Security Journal: A Global Perspective, 17,* 87-94.

Evans, C. (2008). The effectiveness of m-learning in the form of podcast revision lectures in higher education. *Computers & Education, 50*(2), 491–498. doi:10.1016/j.compedu.2007.09.016

Fall, K., & Floyd, S. (1996). Simulation-based comparison of Tahoe, Reno, and SACK TCP. *ACM Computer Communications Review, 5*(3).

Fang, Q., Zhao, F., & Guibas, L. (2003). Lightweight sensing and communication protocols for target enumeration and aggregation. In *Proceedings of the 4th ACM International Symposium on Mobile Ad Hoc Networking and Computing (MOBIHOC),* (pp. 165-176). ACM Press.

Faria, J. A. E. (2004). E-commerce and international harmonization: Time to go beyond the functional equivalence. *Journal of Information, Law & Technology (JILT).* Retrieved February 22, 2011 from http://www2.warwick.ac.uk/fac/soc/law/elj/jilt/2008_2/sibanda/sibanda.pdf.

Farooqi, A. H., & Khan, F. A. (2009). Intrusion detection systems for wireless sensor networks: A survey. *Communications in Computer and Information Science, 56,* 234–241. doi:10.1007/978-3-642-10844-0_29

Fernando, H., & Abawajy, J. (2009). A RFID architecture framework for global supply chain applications. In *Proceedings of the 11th International Conference on Information Integration and Web Services,* (pp. 213-320). New York: ACM Press.

Fertalj, K., Hoić-Božić, N., & Jerković, H. (2009). Analysis of e-learning repository systems and frameworks with prepositions for improvements. In *Proceedings of the ITI 2009 31st International Conference on Information Technology Interfaces.* IEEE Press.

Flint, P. (2007). Baggage asphyxia. *Air Transport World, 44*(3), 5.

Floerkemeier, C., & Lampe, M. (2005). RFID middleware design: Addressing application requirements and RFID constraints. In *Proceedings of the 2005 Joint Conference on Smart Objects and Ambient Intelligence: Innovative Context-Aware Services: Usages and Technologies.* New York: ACM Press.

Floerkemeier, C., Lampe, M., & Roduner, C. (2007). Facilitating RFID development with the Accada prototyping platform. *IEEE Systems Journal, 1*(2), 495–500. doi:10.1109/JSYST.2007.909778

Floyd, S. (1994). TCP and explicit congestion notification. *ACM Computer Communication Review, 5*(5).

Floyd, S., Henderson, T., & Gurtov, A. (2004). The NewReno modification to TCP's fast recovery algorithm. *RFC 3782.* Retrieved from http://www.ietf.org.

Foster, I., & Kesselman, C. (1999). *The Grid: Blueprint for a new computing infrastructure.* San Francisco, CA: Morgan Kaufmann.

Friedland, G., Hrst, W., & Knipping, L. (2007). *Educational multimedia systems: The past, the present, and a glimpse into the future.* Paper presented at the ACM Workshop on Educational Multimedia and Multimedia Education. Augsburg, Germany.

Friesen, N. (2005). Interoperability and learning objects: An overview of e-learning standardization. *Interdisciplinary Journal of Knowledge and Learning Objects, 1,* 23–31.

Fritz, G., Beroulle, V., Nguyen, M. D., Aktouf, O., & Parissis, I. (2010). Read-error-rate evaluation for RFID system on-line testing. In *Proceedings of the IEEE 16th International Mixed-Signals, Sensors and Systems Test Workshop (IMS3TW)*, (pp. 1-6). IEEE Press.

Fu, P., Li, Y., & Tian, Y. (2010). Research on the compatibility of RFID middleware reader. In *Proceedings of the 2nd International Conference on Computer Engineering and Technology*, (vol 4), (pp. 16-18). IEEE Press.

Fu, Z., Meng, X., & Lu, S. (2002). How bad TCP can perform in mobile ad-hoc networks. In *Proceedings of IEEE ICNP 2002*. Paris, France: IEEE Press.

Fussler, H., Schnaufer, S., Transier, M., & Effelsberg, W. (2007). Vehicular ad-hoc networks: From vision to reality and back. In *Proceedings of IEEE Wireless on Demand Network Systems and Services*. IEEE Press.

Ganesan, D., Govindan, R., Shenker, S., & Estrin, D. (2001). Highly-resilient, energy-efficient multipath routing in wireless sensor networks. *Mobile Computing and Communications Review*, 4(5), 1–13.

Gao, D., Madden, M., Schukat, M., Chambers, D., & Lyons, G. (2004). Arrhythmia identification from ECG signals with a neural network classifier based on a Bayesian framework. In *Proceedings of the 24th SGAI International Conference on Innovative Techniques and Applications of Artificial Intelligence*. IEEE Press.

Gibson, W. (1984). *Neuromancer*. New York: Harper-Collins.

Glover, B., & Bhatt, H. (2006). *RFID essentials*. New York: O'Reilly Media.

Goff, T., Moronski, J., Phatak, D. S., & Gupta, V. (2003). *Freeze-TCP: A true end-to-end TCP enhancement mechanism for mobile environment*. Paper presented at IEEE INFOCOM 2000. Tel-Aviv, Israel.

Gong, H., Liu, M., Mao, Y., Chen, L., & Xie, L. (2006). Distributed energy efficient data gathering with intra-cluster coverage in wireless sensor networks. In X. Zhou, et al. (Eds.). *8th Asia–Pacific Web*, (pp. 109-120). Harbin, China: Springer.

Grobler, M., & van Vuuren, J. J. (2009). *Combating cyberspace fraud in Africa*. Johannesburg, South Africa: CSIR.

Gupta, P., & Kumar, P. R. (2000). Capacity of wireless networks. *IEEE Transactions on Information Theory*, 46(2), 388–404. doi:10.1109/18.825799

Haartsen, J. C. (2000). The Bluetooth radio system. *IEEE Personal Communication Magazine*, 7(1), 28-36.

Hale, C. (2002). Cybercrime: Facts and figures concerning the global dilemma. *Crime and Justice International*, 18(65), 5–26.

Halepovic, E., Wu, Q., Williamson, C. L., & Ghaderi, M. (2008). TCP over WiMAX: A measurement study. In *Proceedings of MASCOTS*, (pp. 327-336). IEEE Press.

Holland, G., & Vaidya, N. (1999). Analysis of TCP performance over mobile ad hoc networks. In *Proceedings of the 5th ACM/IEEE International Conference on Mobile Computing and Networking*, (pp. 219-230). IEEE Press.

Han, S., & Chao-Hsien, C. (2008). Tamper detection in RFID-enabled supply chains using fragile watermarking. In *Proceedings of the 2008 IEEE International Conference on RFID*, (pp. 111-117). IEEE Press.

Hansen, & Ewa. (2008). *Centralized routing for prolonged network lifetime in wireless sensor networks*. Mälardalen, Sweden: Mälardalen University Press.

Hao, P., Qiu, W., & Evans, R. (2009). *An improved cluster-head selection approach in wireless sensor networks*. Paper presented at the Intelligent Sensors Sensor Networks and Information Processing ISSNIP 2009 5th International Conference. Melbourne, Australia.

Haque, M. E., Matsumoto, N., & Yoshida, N. (2009). Context-aware cluster-based hierarchical protocol for wireless sensor networks. *International Journal of Ad Hoc and Ubiquitous Computing*, 4(6), 23–37. doi:10.1504/IJAHUC.2009.028666

Haque, M. E., Matsumoto, N., & Yoshida, N. (2010). Utilizing multilayer hierarchical structure in context aware routing protocol for wireless sensor networks. *International Journal of Computational Science*, 4(1), 23–37.

Harrison, J. (2010). Supply chain security and international terrorism . In Thomas, A. (Ed.), *Supply Chain Security* (*Vol. 1*, pp. 7–53). Santa Barbara, CA: ABC-CLIO.

Hartung, C., Han, R., Seielstad, C., & Holbrook, S. (2006). FireWxNet: A multitiered portable wireless system for monitoring weather conditions in wildland fire environments. In *Proceedings of the 4th International Conference on Mobile Systems,* (pp. 28-41). ACM Press.

Hashem, S. (2009). *Towards an Egyptian framework for cybersecurity.* PowerPoint presentation. Retrieved from http://www.itu.int/ITU-D/cyb/events/2009/tunis/docs/hashem-cybersecurity-framework-egypt-june-09.pdf.

Hassan, T., & Chatterjee, S. (2006). A taxonomy for RFID. In *Proceedings of the 39th Annual Hawaii International Conference on System Sciences,* (pp. 184b - 184b). IEEE Press.

Heidemann, J., Li, Y., Syed, A., Wills, J., & Ye, W. (2006). Underwater sensor networking: Research challenges and potential applications. In *Proceedings of the IEEE Wireless Communications and Networking Conference,* (pp. 228-235). Las Vegas, NV: IEEE.

Heinzelman, W. B. (2000). *Application-specific protocol architectures for wireless networks.* PhD Thesis. Cambridge, MA: MIT Press.

Heinzelman, W. B., Chandrakasan, A. P., & Balakrishnan, H. (2000). Energy-efficient communication protocol for wireless microsensor networks. In *Proceedings of the 33rd Annual Hawaii International Conference on System Sciences,* (pp. 10). IEEE Computer Society Press.

Heinzelman, W. R., Chandrakasan, A., & Balakrishnan, H. (2000). Energy efficient communication protocols for wireless microsensor networks. In *Proceedings of Hawaii International Conference on Systems Sciences,* (pp. 3005-3014). Washington, DC: IEEE.

Heinzelman, W. R., Chandrakasan, A., & Balakrishnan, H. (2000). Energy-efficient communication protocol for wireless microsensor networks. In *Proceedings of the 33rd Annual Hawaii International Conference on System Sciences,* (pp. 1-10). HICSS Press.

Heinzelman, W., Chandrakasan, A., & Balakrishnan, H. (2000). Energy-efficient communication protocol for wireless sensor networks. In *Proceeding of the Hawaii International Conference System Sciences.* Hawaii, HI: HICSS Press.

Heinzelman, W. B., Chandrakasan, A. P., & Balakrishnan, H. (2002). An application-specific protocol architecture for wireless microsensor networks. *IEEE Transactions on Wireless Communications, 1*(4), 660–670. doi:10.1109/TWC.2002.804190

Holt, T., & Graves, D. (2007). A qualitative analysis of advance fee fraud email schemes. *International Journal of Cyber Criminology, 1*(1), 137–154.

Hou, Y. T., Shi, Y., & Sherali, H. D. (2005). On energy provisioning and relay node placement for wireless sensor networks. *IEEE Transactions on Wireless Communications, 4*(5), 2579–2590. doi:10.1109/TWC.2005.853969

Hu, W., Tan, H., Corke, P., Shih, W. C., & Jha, S. (2010). Toward trusted wireless sensor networks. *ACM Transactions on Sensor Networks, 7*(1), 5:1 - 5:25.

Hu, Y. C., Perrig, A., & Johnson, D. (2003). Packet leashes: A defense against wormhole attacks in wireless ad hoc networks. In *Proceedings of Twenty-Second Annual Joint Conference of the IEEE Computer and Communications Societies (Infocom 2003),* (pp. 1976-1986). Piscateway, NJ: IEEE Operations Center.

Hu, Y. P., Lin, Y. P., Jiang, H. Y., Li, X. L., & Zhou, S. W. (2009). MAC protocol for wireless sensor networks via collaborative compression. *Journal of Software, 20*(9), 2483–2494. doi:10.3724/SP.J.1001.2009.03316

Hu, Y. P., Lin, Y. P., Zhou, S. W., & Liu, Y. H. (2011). Asynchronous communication mechanism oriented wireless sensor networks and MAC protocols. *Chinese Journal of Computers, 34*(7).

Hu, Y. P., Li, R., Zhou, S. W., & Lin, Y. P. (2011). CCS-MAC: Exploiting the overheard data for compression in wireless sensor networks. *Computer Communications, 5*(2).

Ilie-Zudor, E., Kemeny, Z., Blommestein, F. V., Monostori, L., & Meulen, A. V. D. (2011). A survey of applications and requirements of unique identification systems and RFID techniques. *Computers in Industry, 62*(3), 227–325. doi:10.1016/j.compind.2010.10.004

Ilyas, M., & Mahgoub, I. (Eds.). (2005). *Handbook of sensor networks: Compact wireless and wired sensing systems.* Boca Raton, FL: CRC Press.

Intanagonwiwat, C., Govindan, R., & Estrin, D. (2000). Directed diffusion: A scalable and robust communication paradigm for sensor networks. In *Proceedings of ACM MobiCom 2000,* (pp. 56-67). Boston, MA: ACM Press.

Intanagonwiwat, C., Govindan, R., Estrin, D., Heidemann, J., & Silva, F. (2003). Directed diffusion for wireless sensor networking. *IEEE/ACM Transactions on Networking, 11*(1), 2–16. doi:10.1109/TNET.2002.808417

Intel. (2010). *Newsroom.* Retrieved December, 2010, http://newsroom.intel.com/community/intel_newsroom/blog/2010/09/15/context-awareness-to-radically-change-how-we-interact-with-technology.

Ip, A., Morrison, I., & Currie, M. (2001). What is a learning object, technically? In *Proceedings of WebNet2001 Conference.* Orlando, FL: IEEE Press.

Islam, M. S., Khan, R. H., & Bappy, D. M. (2010). A hierarchical intrusion detection system in wireless sensor networks. *International Journal of Computer Science and Network Security, 10*(8), 21–26.

Issa, G. F., Hussain, S. M., & Al-Bahadili, H. (2010). A framework for building an interactive satellite TV based m-learning environment. *International Journal of Interactive Mobile Technologies, 4*(3).

Jeffery, S. R., Garofalakis, M., & Franklin, M. J. (2006). Adaptive cleaning for RFID data streams. In *Proceedings of the 32nd International Conference on Very Large Data Bases (VLDB 2006),* (pp. 163-174). IEEE Press.

Jeong, J., & Haas, Z. J. (2007). An integrated security framework for open wireless networking architecture. *IEEE Transactions on Wireless Communications, 14*(2), 10–18. doi:10.1109/MWC.2007.358959

Jian, Y., Chen, S., Zhang, Z., & Zhang, L. (2007). Protecting receiver-location privacy in wireless sensor networks. In *26th IEEE International Conference on Computer Communications (INFOCOM 2007),* (pp.1955–1963). Los Alamitos, CA: Conference Publishing Services.

Jin, H., Yin, Z., Yang, X., Wang, F., Ma, J., Wang, H., & Yin, J. (2005). APPLE: A novel P2P based e-learning environment. In *Distributed Computing, IWDC 2004: Lecture Notes in Computer Science,* (vol 3326), (pp. 52–62). Berlin, Germany: Springer.

Jin, G., & Park, M. (2006). CAC: Context adaptive clustering for efficient data aggregation in wireless sensor networks. *Lecture Notes in Computer Science, 3976,* 1132–1137. doi:10.1007/11753810_98

Johansson, P., Larsson, T., Hedman, N., Mielczarek, B., & Degermark, M. (1999). Scenario-based performance analysis of routing protocols for mobile ad hoc networks. In *Proceedings of the Fifth Annual ACM/IEEE International Conference on Mobile Computing and Networking,* (pp. 195–206). IEEE Press.

Johnson, D. R., & Post, D. G. (1996). Law and borders-the rise of law in cyberspace. *Stanford Law Review, 48,* 1367–1404. doi:10.2307/1229390

Johnstone, M., Creighton, D., & Nahavandi, S. (2010). Status-based routing in baggage handling systems: Searching verses learning. *IEEE Transactions on Systems, Man, and Cybernetics, 40*(2), 189–200.doi:10.1109/TSMCC.2009.2035519

Juels, A. (2006). RFID security and privacy: A research survey. *IEEE Journal on Selected Areas in Communications, 24*(2), 14. doi:10.1109/JSAC.2005.861395

Kamat, P., Zhang, Y., Trappe, W., & Ozturk, C. (2005). Enhancing source-location privacy in sensor network routing. In *Proceedings of 25th IEEE International Conference on Distributed Computing Systems (ICDCS 2005),* (pp. 599–608). Los Alamitos, CA: Conference Publishing Services.

Kamoun, F. (2009). RFID system management: State-of-the art and open research issues. *IEEE Transactions on Network and Service Management, 6*(3), 190–205. doi:10.1109/TNSM.2009.03.090305

Kandris, D., Tsioumas, P., Tzes, A., Nikolakopoulos, G., & Vergados, D. (2009). Power conservation through energy efficient routing in wireless sensor networks. *Sensors (Basel, Switzerland), 9*(9), 7320–7342. doi:10.3390/s90907320

Kanodia, V., Li, C., Sabharwal, A., Sadeghi, B., & Knightly, E. (2001). Distributed multi-hop scheduling and medium access with delay and throughput constraints. In *Proceedings of ACM MOBICOM,* (pp. 200-209). New York: ACM.

Kaplantzis, S., Shilton, A., Mani, N., & Sekercioglu, Y. A. (2007). Detecting selective forwarding attacks in wireless sensor networks using support vector machines. In *Proceedings of the 2007 International Conference on Intelligent Sensors, Sensor Networks and Information Processing,* (pp. 335-340). Los Alamitos, CA: Conference Publishing Services.

Karagiannis, T., Broido, A., Brownlee, N., Claffy, K. C., & Faloutsos, M. (2004). Is P2P dying or just hiding? In *Proceedings of IEEE Globecom 2004 - Global Internet and Next Generation,* (pp. 1532 – 1538). IEEE Press.

Karlof, C., & Wagner, D. (2003). Secure routing in wireless sensor networks: Attacks and countermeasures. In *Proceedings of the First IEEE International Workshop on Sensor Network Protocols and Applications,* (pp. 113-127). Los Alamitos, CA: Conference Publishing Services.

Karp, B., & Kung, H. T. (2000). GPSR: Greedy perimeter stateless routing for wireless sensor networks. In *Proceedings of the 6th Annual ACM/IEEE International Conference on Mobile Computing and Networking (MobiCom 2000).* Boston, MA: ACM Press.

Karygicmnis, A., Phillips, T., & Tsibertzopoulos, A. (2006). RFID security: A taxonomy of risk. In *Proceedings of the First International Conference on Communications and Networking in China,* (pp. 1-8). IEEE Press.

Kautz, H., Etzioni, O., Fox, D., & Weld, D. (2003). *Foundations of assisted cognition systems. Technical report CSE- 02-AC-01.* Seattle, WA: University of Washington.

Kim, S., Pakzad, S., Culler, D., Demmel, J., Fenves, G., Glaser, S., & Turon, M. (2007). Health monitoring of civil infrastructures using wireless sensor networks. In *Proceedings of the 6th International Conference on Information Processing in Sensor Networks,* (pp. 254-263). ACM Press.

Kim, S., & Garrison, G. (2010). Understanding users' behaviors regarding supply chain technology: Determinants impacting the adoption and implementation of RFID technology in South Korea. *International Journal of Information Management, 30*(5), 388–398. doi:10.1016/j.ijinfomgt.2010.02.008

Ko, C. C., Chen, B. M., Hu, S., Ramakrishnan, V., Cheng, C. D., Zhuang, Y., & Chen, J. (2001). A web-based virtual laboratory on a frequency modulation experiment. *IEEE Transactions on Systems, Man, and Cybernetics, 31*(3), 295–303. doi:10.1109/5326.971657

Kopparty, S., Krishnamurthy, S. V., Faloutsos, M., & Tripathi, S. K. (2002). Split TCP for mobile ad hoc networks. In *Proceedings of IEEE Global Communications Conference GLOBECOM,* (vol 1), (pp. 138- 142). IEEE Press.

Korel, B. T., & Koo, S. G. M. (2010). A survey on context-aware sensing for body sensor networks. *Wireless Sensor Network, 2*(8), 571–583. doi:10.4236/wsn.2010.28069

Korpipaa, P., Koskinen, M., Peltola, J., Makela, S. M., & Seppanen, T. (2003). Bayesian approach to sensor-based context awareness. *Personal and Ubiquitous Computing, 7*(2), 113–124. doi:10.1007/s00779-003-0237-8

Krishnamachari, B., Estrin, D., & Wicker, S. (2002). Modeling data centric routing in wireless sensor networks. In *Proceedings of IEEE INFOCOM.* New York, NY: IEEE Press.

Kronsteriner, R., Weippl, E. R., Ibrahim, I. K., & Kotsis, G. (2003). Can P2P deliver what web repositories promised: Global sharing of e-learning content? In *Proceedings of the 5th International Conference on Information and Web-Based Applications.* IEEE Press.

Krontiris, I., Benenson, Z., Freiling, F. C., Dimitriou, T., & Giannetsos, T. (2009). Cooperative intrusion detection in wireless sensor networks. In *Proceedings of the 6th European Conference on Wireless Sensor Networks (EWSN 2009),* (pp. 263–278). Berlin, Germany: Springer-Verlag.

Krontiris, I., Dimitriou, T., & Frieling, F. C. (2007). Towards intrusion detection in wireless sensor networks. In *Proceedings of the 13th European Wireless Conference (EW 2007).* Paris, France. Retrieved April 1, 2011, from http://www.web-portal-system.de/ wps/ wse/ dl/ showfile/ rannenberg/ 5315/ krontiris-ew2007.pdf.

Kshetri, N. (2006). The simple economics of cybercrimes. *IEEE Transactions on Security and Privacy, 4*(1), 33–39. doi:10.1109/MSP.2006.27

Kukulska-Hulme, A., Sharples, M., Milrad, M., Arnedillo-Sanchez, I., & Vavoula, G. (2009). Innovation in mobile learning: A European perspective. *International Journal of Mobile and Blended Learning, 1*(1), 13–35. doi:10.4018/jmbl.2009010102

Kumar, D., & Patel, R. B. (2011). Multi-hop data communication algorithm for clustered wireless sensor networks. *International Journal of Distributed Sensor Networks*. Retrieved from http://www.hindawi.com/journals/ijdsn/2011/984795/.

Lagerholm, M., Peterson, C., Braccini, G., Edenbrandt, L., & Sornmo, L. (2000). Clustering ECG complexes using her-mite functions and self-organizing maps. *IEEE Transactions on Bio-Medical Engineering, 47*(7), 838–848. doi:10.1109/10.846677

Lam, J., Yau, J., & Cheung, S. (2010). A review of mobile learning in the mobile age . In *Hybrid Learning, Lecture Notes in Computer Science* (Vol. 6248, pp. 306–315). Berlin, Germany: Springer.

Law, Y. W., Palaniswami, M., van Hoesel, L., Doumen, J., Hartel, P., & Havinga, P. (2009). Energy-efficient link-layer jamming attacks against wireless sensor network MAC protocols. *ACM Transactions on Sensor Networks, 5*(1), 6:1-6:38

Law, Y. W., van Hoesel, L., Doumen, J., Hartel, P., & Havinga, P. (2005). Energy-efficient link-layer jamming attacks against wireless sensor network MAC protocols. In *Proceedings of the 3rd ACM Workshop on Security of Ad Hoc and Sensor Networks (SASN 2005)*, (pp. 76-88). New York, NY: ACM.

Lee, K.-M., & Foong, S. (2008). Lateral optical sensor with slip detection of natural objects on moving conveyor. In *Proceedings of the IEEE International Conference on Robotics and Automation*, (pp. 329-334). IEEE Press.

Lewis, B. C. (2004). Prevention of computer crime amidst international anarchy. *The American Criminal Law Review, 41*, 1353–1356.

Li, G., Sun, H., Gao, H., Yu, H., & Cai, Y. (2009). A survey on wireless grids and clouds. In *Proceedings of International Conference on Grid and Cloud Computing*, (pp. 261- 267). IEEE Press.

Li, J., Chou, P. A., & Zhang, C. (2004). Mutualcast: An efficient mechanism for one-to-many content distribution. In *Proceedings of ACM SIGCOMM - Asia Workshop*. ACM Press.

Li, L., & Halpern, J. Y. (2001). Minimum-energy mobile wireless networks revisited. *IEEE International Conference on Communications (ICC), 1*, 278-283.

Li, Q., Aslam, J., & Rus, D. (2001). Hierarchical power-aware routing in sensor networks. In *Proceedings of the DIMACS Workshop on Pervasive Networking*. IEEE Press.

Li, T., & Deng, R. H. (2007). Vulnerability analysis of EMAP-An efficient RFID mutual authentication protocol. In *Proceedings of the International Conference on Availability, Reliability and Security*, (pp. 10-13). New York: ACM Press.

Li, Y., & Ding, X. (2007). Protecting RFID communications in supply chains. In *Proceedings of the 2nd ACM Symposium on Information, Computer and Communications Security*, (pp. 234-241). New York: ACM Press.

Li, Z., & Gong, G. (2009). *A survey on security in wireless sensor networks*. Retrieved April 1, 2011 from http://www.cacr.math. uwaterloo.ca/ techreports/ 2008/cacr2008-20.pdf.

Li, Z., Chu, C.-H., & Yao, W. (2008). SIP-RLTS: An RFID location tracking system based on SIP. In *Proceedings of the IEEE International Conference on RFID*, (pp. 173-182). IEEE Press.

Lien, Y.-N. (2009). Hop-by-hop TCP for sensor networks. *International Journal of Computer Networks & Communications*. IJCNC.

Lin, P., Qiao, C., & Wang, X. (2004). Medium access control with a dynamic duty cycle for sensor networks. In *Proceedings of the IEEE Wireless Communications and Networking Conference*, (pp. 1534-1539). Atlanta, GA: IEEE.

Lin, X., Pan, J., Liang, J., & Wang, D. (2009). An RFID reader coordination model for data process. In *Proceedings of the Second International Symposium on Computational Intelligence and Design*, (pp. 83-86). IEEE Press.

Lindsey, S., & Raghavendra, C. S. (2002). PEGASIS: Power efficient gathering in sensor information systems. In *Proceedings of the IEEE Aerospace Conference,* (pp. 1125-1130). IEEE Computer Society Press.

Lindsey, S., Raghavendra, C. S., & Sivalingam, K. (2001). Data gathering in sensor networks using the energy delay metric. *Proceedings of the IPDPS Workshop on Issues in Wireless Networks and Mobile Computing.* San Francisco, CA: IPDPS Press.

Li, S., & Visich, J. K. (2006). Radio frequency identification: Supply chain impact and implementation challenges. *International Journal of Integrated Supply Management,* 2(4), 407–424. doi:10.1504/IJISM.2006.009643

Littlejohn, A. (2004). *Reusing online resources: A substantial approach to e-learning.* London: Routledge Falmer.

Liu, L., Chen, Z., Yang, L., Lu, Y., & Wang, H. (2010a). Research on the security issues of RFID-based supply chain. In *Proceedings of the International Conference on E-Business and E-Government,* (pp. 3267-3270). IEEE Press.

Liu, W. N., Zheng, L. J., Sun, D. H., Liao, X. Y., Zhao, M., Su, J. M., et al. (2010b). RFID-enabled real-time production management system for Loncin motorcycle assembly line. *International Journal of Computer Integrated Manufacturing.*

Liu, J., & Singh, S. (2001). ATCP: TCP for mobile ad hoc networks. *IEEE Journal on Selected Areas in Communications,* 10(7).

Liu, M., Cao, J., Chen, G., & Wang, X. (2009). An energy-aware routing protocol in wireless sensor networks. *Sensors (Basel, Switzerland),* 9(1), 445–462. doi:10.3390/s90100445

Lo, B., & Yang, G. Z. (2005). Key technical challenges and current implementations of body sensor networks. In *Proceedings of the 2nd International Workshop on Body Sensor Networks,* (pp. 1-5). IEEE Press.

Longe, B., & Chiemeke, S. (2008). Cyber crime and criminality in Nigeria: What roles are internet access points playing? *European Journal of Social Science,* 6(4), 132–139.

Longe, O., Ngwa, O., Wada, F., Mbarika, V., & Kvasny, L. (2009). Criminal uses of information & communication technologies in sub-Saharan Africa: Trends, concerns and perspectives. *Journal of Information Technology Impact,* 9(3), 155–172.

Louisiana State University. (2006). *LSU SensorSimulator user manual.* Retrieved from http://csc.lsu.edu/sensor_web/LSU_SensorSimulator_manual.pdf.

Lovet, G. (2009). Fighting cybercrime: Technical, juridical and ethical challenges. In *Proceedings of the Virus Bulletin Conference,* (pp. 63-76). VBC Press.

Lowe, D., Murray, S., Lindsay, E., & Liu, D. (2009). Evolving remote laboratory architectures to leverage emerging Internet technologies. *IEEE Transactions on Learning Technologies,* 2(4), 289–294. doi:10.1109/TLT.2009.33

Lu, G., Krishnamachari, B., & Raghavendra, C. S. (2004). An adaptive energy efficient and low-latency MAC for data gathering in wireless sensor networks. In *Proceedings of 18th International Parallel and Distributed Processing Symposium,* (pp. 3091-3098). Santa Fe, CA: IEEE.

Lung, C.-H., & Zhou, C. (2010). Using hierarchical agglomerative clustering in wireless sensor networks: An energy-efficient and flexible approach. *Ad Hoc Networks,* 8, 328–344. doi:10.1016/j.adhoc.2009.09.004

Luo, H., Ramjee, R., Sinha, P., & Erran, L. (2003). Unified cellular and ad-hoc network. In *Proceedings of ACM Mobicom.* ACM Press.

Maarof, M. H. S., & Yahya, Y. (2008). LORIuMET: Learning object repositories interoperability using metadata. *International Symposium on Information Technology,* 3, 1–5.

Macgregor, G., & McCulloch, E. (2006). Collaborative tagging as a knowledge organization and resource discovery tool. *Library Review,* 55(5), 291–300. doi:10.1108/00242530610667558

Mainwaring, A., Polastre, J., Szewczyk, R., Culler, D., & Anderson, J. (2002). Wireless sensor networks for habitat monitoring. In C. S. Raghavendra & K. M. Sivalingam (Eds.), *Proceedings of the 1st ACM International Workshop on Wireless Sensor Networks and Applications,* (pp. 88-97). New York: ACM.

Ma, J., & Nickerson, J. V. (2006). Hands-on, simulated, and remote laboratories: A comparative literature review. *ACM Computing Surveys, n.d.,* 38.

Mallanda, C., Suri, A., Kunchakarra, V., Iyengar, S. S., Kannan, R., Durresi, A., & Sastry, S. (2005). *Simulating wireless sensor networks with OMNeT++.* Retrieved from http://csc.lsu.edu/sensor_web/sensor_simulator/SensorSimulator-ACM-Computers.pdf.

Mamun, M., & Kabir, A. (2010). Hierarchical design based intrusion detection system for wireless ad hoc sensor network. *International Journal of Network Security and Its Applications, 2*(3), 102–117. doi:10.5121/ijnsa.2010.2307

Manjeshwar, A., & Agrawal, D. P. (2001). TEEN: A protocol for enhanced efficiency in wireless sensor networks. In *Proceedings of the 1st International Workshop on Parallel and Distributed Computing Issues in Wireless Networks and Mobile Computing,* (pp. 23-27). San Francisco, CA: IEEE Press.

Manjeshwar, A., & Agrawal, D. P. (2001). TEEN: A protocol for enhanced efficiency in wireless sensor networks. In *Proceedings of the 1st International Workshop on Parallel and Distributed Computing Issues in Wireless Networks and Mobile Computing,* (pp.2009-2015). IEEE Computer Society Press.

Manjeshwar, A., & Agrawal, D. P. (2002). APTEEN: A hybrid protocol for efficient routing and comprehensive information retrieval in wireless sensor networks. In *Proceedings of the Parallel and Distributed Processing Symposium,* (pp. 195-202). IEEE Computer Society Press.

Manjeshwar, A., Zeng, Q. A., & Agrawal, D. P. (2002). An analytical model for information retrieval in wireless sensor networks using enhanced APTEEN protocol. *IEEE Transactions on Parallel and Distributed Systems, 13*(12), 1290–1302. doi:10.1109/TPDS.2002.1158266

Marti, S., Giuli, T. J., Lai, K., & Baker, M. (2000). Mitigating routing misbehavior in mobile ad hoc networks. In *Proceedings of the 6th Annual International Conference on Mobile Computing and Networking (MobiCom 2000),* (pp. 255-265). New York, NY: ACM.

Martinovic, I., Pichota, P., & Schmitt, J. B. (2009). Jamming for good: A fresh approach to authentic communication in WSNs. In *Proceedings of the Second ACM Conference on Wireless Network Security (WiSec 2009),* (pp. 161-168). New York, NY: ACM.

Marzullo, K. (1990). Tolerating failures of continuous-valued sensors. *ACM Transactions on Computer Systems, 8*(4), 284–304.doi:10.1145/128733.128735

Mascolo, S., Casetti, C., Gerla, M., Sanadidi, M. Y., & Wang, R. (2001). *TCP Westwood: Bandwidth estimation for enhanced transport over wireless links.* Paper presented at the 7th Annual International Conference on Mobile Computing and Networking. Rome, Italy.

Maymounkov, P., & Mazieres, D. (2002). Kademlia: A peer-to-peer information system based on the XOR metric. In *Proceedings of the 1st International Workshop of Peer-to-Peer Systems.* IEEE Press.

McGee, A. R., Vasireddy, S. R., Xie, C., Picklesimer, D. D., Chandrashekhar, U., & Richman, S. H. (2004). A framework for ensuring network security. *Bell Labs Technical Journal, 8*(4), 7–27. doi:10.1002/bltj.10083

Meghdadi, M., Ozdemir, S., & Guler, I. (2011). A survey of wormhole-based attacks and their countermeasures in wireless sensor networks. *IETE Technical Review, 28*(2), 89–102. doi:10.4103/0256-4602.78089

Michael, B., Gary, V. Y., Eric, A., & Richard, H. (2006). X-Mac: A short preamble MAC protocol for duty cycled wireless sensor networks. In *Proceedings of the 1st International Conference on Embedded Network Sensor Systems,* (pp. 307-320). New York: ACM.

Michel, M., Nelson, L. S., & José, F. (2003). On the performance of TCP loss recovery mechanisms. In *Proceedings of IEEE International Conference on Communications,* (vol. 3), (pp. 1812- 1816). IEEE Press.

Mills, D. (2003). A brief history of NTP time: Confessions of an internet timekeeper. *ACM Computer Communications Review.* Retrieved from http:// www.eecis.udel.edu/~mills/ database/ papers/ history.pdf.

Min, R., Bhardwaj, M., Cho, S. H., Shih, E., Sinha, A., Wang, A., & Chandrakasan, A. (2001). Low-power wireless sensor networks. In *Proceedings of 14th International Conference on VLSI Design (VLSI DESIGN 2001)*, (pp. 205-210). VLSI Press.

Mitrokotsa, A., Rieback, M. R., & Tanenbaum, A. S. (2010). Classification of RFID attacks. *Information Systems Frontiers*. Retrieved from http://www.cs.vu.nl/~ast/ publications/ iwrt-2008.pdf.

Mohan, M., Potdar, V., Chang, E., & Perth, W. A. (2006). Recovering and restoring tampered RFID data using steganographic principles. In *Proceedings of the IEEE International Conference on Industrial Technology (ICIT 2006)*, (pp. 15-17). IEEE Press.

Monks, J., Sinha, P., & Bharghavan, V. (2000). *Limitations of TCP-ELFN for ad hoc networks*. In Proceedings of Mobile and Multimedia Communications. ACM Press.

Muneeb, A., Saif, U., & Dunkels. (2006). Medium access control issues in sensor networks. *ACM SIGCOMM Computer Communications Review, 36*(2), 33-36.

Muraganathan, S. D., Bhasin, R. I., & Fapojuwo, A. O. (2005). A centralized energy-efficient routing protocol for wireless sensor networks. *IEEE Communications Magazine,* ▪▪▪, 8–13. doi:10.1109/MCOM.2005.1404592

Muruganathan, S. D., & Fapojuwo, A. O. (2008). A hybrid routing protocol for wireless sensor networks based on a two-level clustering hierarchy with enhanced energy efficiency. In *Proceedings of the Wireless Communications and Networking Conference, (WCNC 2008)*, (pp. 2051-2056). IEEE Press.

Muruganathan, S. D., Ma, D. C. F., Bhasin, R. I., & Fapojuwo, A. O. (2005). A centralized energy-efficient routing protocol for wireless sensor networks. *IEEE Communications Magazine*, 8–13. doi:10.1109/MCOM.2005.1404592

Nejdl, W., Wolf, B., Qu, C., Decker, S., Sintek, M., & Naeve, A. … Riscj, T. (2002). EDUTELLA: A P2P networking infrastructure based on RDF. In *Proceedings of the 11th International Conference on World Wide Web*, (pp. 604–615). IEEE Press.

Newsome, J., Shi, E., Song, D., & Perrig, A. (2004). The sybil attack in sensor networks: Analysis & defenses. In *Proceedings of the 3rd International Symposium on Information Processing in Sensor Networks (IPSN 2004)*, (pp. 259-268). New York, NY: ACM.

Ng'ang'a, A. M. (2009). Toward a regional ITC hub: Need for cyber laws in Kenya. *Information Security Journal: A Global Perspective, 18*, 47-50.

Ngai, E. C. H., Liu, J., & Lyu, M. R. (2006). On the intruder detection for sinkhole attack in wireless sensor networks. In *Proceedings of the 2006 IEEE International Conference on Communications (ICC 2006)*, (pp. 3383-3389). Los Alamitos, CA: Conference Publishing Services.

Ni, K., Ramanathan, N., Chehade, M. N. H., Balzano, L., Nair, S., Zahedi, S., … Srivastava, M. (2009). Sensor network data fault types. *ACM Transaction on Sensor Networks, 5*(3).

Ni, L. M., Liu, Y., Lau, Y. C., & Patil, A. P. (2003). *LANDMARC: Indoor location sensing using active RFID*. Paper presented at First IEEE International Conference on Pervasive Computing and Communications. Dallas-Fort Worth, TX.

Obashi, Y., Kokogawa, T., Zheng, Y., Chen, H., Mineno, H., & Mizuno, T. (2007). Evaluation of metadata-based data aggregation scheme in clustering wireless sensor networks. *Lecture Notes in Artificial Intelligence, 4694*, 477–483.

Ojedokun, A. A. (2005). The evolving sophistication of Internet abuses in Africa. *The International Information & Library Review, 37*(1), 11–17. doi:10.1016/j.iilr.2005.01.002

Okon, M., Kaliszan, D., Lawenda, M., Stoklosa, D., Rajtar, T., Meyer, N., & Stroinski, M. (2006). Virtual laboratory as a remote and interactive access to the scientific instrumentation embedded in grid environment. In *Proceedings of 2nd IEEE International Conference on e-Science and Grid Computing*, (pp. 124-128). IEEE Press.

Olowu, D. (2009). Cyber-crimes and the boundaries of domestic legal responses: Case for an inclusionary framework for Africa. *Journal of Information, Law & Technology*. Retrieved February 2, 2011 from http://www2.warwick.ac.uk/ fac/ soc/ law/ elj/ jilt/ 2009_1/ olowu/ olowu.pdf.

Or-Bach, R. (2005). Educational benefits of metadata creation by students. *SIGCSE Bulletin, 37*(4), 93–97. doi:10.1145/1113847.1113885

Oriola, T. (2005). Advance fee fraud on the internet: Nigeria's regulatory response. *Computer Law & Security Review, 21*(3), 237–248. doi:10.1016/j.clsr.2005.02.006

Ouyang, Y., Hou, Y., Pang, L., Wang, D., & Xiong, Z. (2008). An intelligent RFID reader and its application in airport baggage handling system. In *Proceedings of the International Conference on Wireless Communications, Networking and Mobile Computing*, (pp. 1-4). IEEE Press.

Ozturk, C., Zhang, Y., & Trappe, W. (2004). Source-location privacy in energy constrained sensor network routing. In *Proceedings of the 2nd ACM workshop on Security of Ad Hoc and Sensor Networks (SASN 2004)*, (pp. 88-93). New York, NY: ACM.

Panda, M., Panigrahi, T., Khilar, P. M., & Panda, G. (2010). Learning with distributed data in wireless sensor network. In *Proceedings of 1ˢᵗ International Conference on Parallel Distributed and Grid Computing*, (pp. 256-259). IEEE Press.

Papadopouli, M., & Schulzrinne, H. (2001). A performance analysis of 7DS a peer-to-peer data dissemination and prefetching tool for mobile users. In *Advances in Wired and Wireless Communications: IEEE Sarnoff Symposium Digest*. Ewing, NJ: IEEE Press.

Park, E. C., Kim, J. Y., Kim, H., & Kim, H. S. (2008). *Bidirectional bandwidth allocation for TCP performance enhancement in IEEE 802.16 broadband wireless access networks*. Paper presented at the IEEE 19th International Symposium on Personal, Indoor and Mobile Radio Communications, PIMRC 2008. Cannes, France.

Park, N., Song, Y., Won, D., & Kim, H. (2008). Multilateral approaches to the mobile RFID security problem using web service. In *Proceedings of APWeb 2008*, (vol 4976), (pp. 331–341). IEEE Press.

Parno, B., Luk, M., Gaustad, E., & Perrig, A. (2006). Secure sensor network routing: A clean slate approach. In *Proceedings of the 2006 ACM Co Next Conference (CoNEXT 2006)*, (pp. 1-13). New York, NY: ACM.

Parno, B., Perrig, A., & Gligor, V. (2005). Distributed detection of node replication attacks in sensor networks. In *Proceedings of the 2005 IEEE Symposium of Security and Privacy (SP 2005)*, (pp. 49-63). Los Alamitos, CA: Conference Publishing Services.

Parsa, C., & Garcia-Luna-Aceves, J. J. (1999). TULIP: A link-level protocol for improving TCP over wireless links. In *Proceedings of the Wireless Communications and Networking Conference*, (pp. 1253-1257). New Orleans, LA: IEEE Press.

Parsa, C., & Garcia-Luna-Aceves, J. J. (2000). Improving TCP performance over wireless networks at the link layer. *ACM Mobile Networks and Applications, 5*.

Patel, D. K., Patel, M. P., & Patel, K. S. (2011). Scalability Analysis in wireless sensor network with LEACH routing protocol. In *Proceedings of the Computer and Management (CAMAN), 2011 International Conference*, (pp. 1-6). Wuhan, China: CAMAN Press.

Pattem, S., & Krishnamachari, B. (2004). The impact of spatial correlation on routing with compression in wireless sensor networks. In *Proceedings of the IPSN*, (pp. 28-35). New York: ACM.

Pelechrinis, P., Iliofontou, M., & Khrishnamurthy, S. V. (2010). Denial of service attacks in wireless networks: The case of jammers. *IEEE Communications Surveys & Tutorials, 12*(4), 1–13.

Peng, X. Z. Ji, Z., Luo, Z., Wong, E. C., & Tan, C. J. (2008). *A P2P collaborative RFID data cleaning model*. Paper presented at the 3rd International Conference on Grid and Pervasive Computing – Workshops. Kunming, China.

Peris-Lopez, P., Hernandez-Castro, J. C., Estevez-Tapiador, J. M., & Ribagorda, A. (2006). RFID systems: A survey on security threats and proposed solutions. In *Proceedings of the 11th International Conference on Personal Wireless Communications*, (pp. 159 - 170). Berlin, Germany: Springer.

Peris-Lopez, P., Hernandez-Castro, J. C., Tapiador, J. M. E., & Ribagorda, A. (2008). Advances in ultralightweight cryptography for low-cost RFID tags: Gossamer protocol. In *Lecture Notes in Computer Science* (pp. 56–68). Berlin, Germany: Springer.

Pfleeger, C. (1997). *Security in computing*. Upper Saddle River, NJ: Prentice Hall.

Polastre, J., Hill, J., & Culler, D. (2004). Versatile low power media access for wireless sensor networks. In J. A. Stankovic (Ed.), *Proceedings of the 2nd International Conference on Embedded Networked Sensor Systems,* (pp. 95-107). New York: ACM.

Pradhan, S. S., Kusuma, J., & Ramchandran, K. (2002). Distributed compression in a dense microsensor network. *IEEE Signal Processing Magazine, 19*(2), 51–60. doi:10.1109/79.985684

Rabaey, J. M., Ammer, M. J., Patel, D., & Roundy, S. (2000). Pico radio support ad hoc ultra low power wireless networking. *IEEE Computer, 33,* 42–48. doi:10.1109/2.869369

Radmand, P., Talevski, A., Petersen, S., & Carlsen, S. (2010). Taxonomy of wireless sensor network cyber security attacks in the oil and gas industries. In *24th IEEE International Conference on Advanced Information Networking and Applications (AINA 2010)*, (pp. 949-957). Los Alamitos, CA: Conference Publishing Services.

Raghunathan, V., Schurgers, C., Park, S., & Srivastava, M. B. (2002). Energy-aware wireless microsensor networks. *IEEE Signal Processing Magazine, 19*(2), 40–50. doi:10.1109/79.985679

Rajasegarar, S., Leckie, C., Bezdek, J. C., & Palaniswami, M. (2010). Centered hyperspherical and hyperellipsoidal one-class support vector machines for anomaly detection in sensor networks. *IEEE Transactions on Information Forensics and Security, 5*(3), 518–533.doi:10.1109/TIFS.2010.2051543

Rajendran, V., Obraczka, K., & Garcia-Luna-Aceves, J. J. (2003). Energy-efficient, collision-free medium access control for wireless sensor networks. In *Proceedings of the 1st International Conference on Embedded Networked Sensor Systems,* (pp. 181-192). New York: ACM.

Ramachandran, K., Buddhikot, M. M., Chandranmenon, G., Miller, S., Belding-Royer, E., & Almeroth, K. (2005). On the design and implementation of infrastructure mesh networks . In *Proceedings of WiMesh 2005*. Santa Clara, CA: IEEE Press.

Ramakrishnan, K., Floyd, S., & Black, D. (2001). The addition of explicit congestion notification (ECN) to IP. *RFC 3168.* Retrieved from http://www.ietf.org.

Ranasinghe, D. C., Leong, K. S., Ng, M. L., Engels, D. W., & Cole, P. H. (2005). A distributed architecture for a ubiquitous RFID sensing network. In *Proceedings of the Second International Conference on Intelligent Sensors, Sensor Networks and Information Processing,* (pp. 7-12). IEEE Press.

Ranjan, R., & Kar, S. (2011). A novel approach for finding optimal number of cluster head in wireless sensor network. In *Proceedings of the NCC 2011,* (pp. 28-30). Bangalore, India: NCC Press.

Rao, K. S., & Chandranr, K. R. (2009). Efficient method for identifying location and removal of data redundancy for RFID data. *International Journal of Recent Trends in Engineering, 2*(1).

Rashed, M. G., & Kabir, M. H. (2010). Weighted election protocol for clustered heterogeneous wireless sensor networks. *Journal of Mobile Communication, 4*(2), 38–42. doi:10.3923/jmcomm.2010.38.42

Raymond, D. R., & Midkiff, S. F. (2008). Denial-of-service in wireless sensor networks: Attacks and defenses. *IEEE Pervasive Computing / IEEE Computer Society [and] IEEE Communications Society, 7*(1), 74–81. doi:10.1109/MPRV.2008.6

Richards, G., & Hatala, M. (2005). Linking learning object repositories. *International Journal of Learning Technology Molecular Biology, 1*(4), 399–410. doi:10.1504/IJLT.2005.007151

Rieback, M., Tanenbaum, A., & Crispo, B. (2006). Is your cat infected with a computer virus? In *Proceedings of the Fourth Annual IEEE International Conference on Pervasive Computing and Communications,* (p. 10). IEEE Press.

Roach, K. (2011). The Air India report and the regulation of charities and terrorism financing. *The University of Toronto Law Journal, 6*(1), 45–57.doi:10.3138/utlj.61.1.045

Rodoplu, V., & Meng, T. H. (1999). Minimum energy mobile wireless networks. *IEEE Journal on Selected Areas in Communications, 17*(8), 133–344. doi:10.1109/49.779917

Roman, R., Zhou, J., & Lopez, J. (2006). Applying intrusion detection systems to wireless sensor networks. In *Proceedings of 2006 IEEE Consumer Communications and Networking Conference (CCNC 2006)*, (pp. 640-644). Los Alamitos, CA: Conference Publishing Services.

Rosenberg, M. (2001). *E-learning: Strategies for delivering knowledge in the digital age*. New York: McGraw Hill.

Rotter, P. (2008). A framework for assessing RFID system security and privacy risks. *IEEE Pervasive Computing / IEEE Computer Society [and] IEEE Communications Society, 7*(2), 70–77. doi:10.1109/MPRV.2008.22

Rousselot, J., & Decotignie, J. (2010). When ultra low power meets high performance: The WiseMAC high availability protocol. In J. Beutel (Ed.), *Proceedings of the 8st International Conference on Embedded Networked Sensor Systems,* (pp. 441-442). New York: ACM

Saadat, M., Saadat, R., & Mirjalily, G. (2010) Improving threshold assignment for cluster head selection in hierarchical wireless sensor networks. In *Proceedings of the 5th International Symposium on Telecommunications (IST),* (pp.409-414). IST Press.

Savvides, A., Han, C. C., & Srivastava, M. (2001). Dynamic fine-grained localization in ad-hoc networks of sensors. In *Proceedings of the Seventh ACM Annual International Conference on Mobile Computing and Networking (MobiCom),* (pp. 166-179). ACM Press.

Sawyer, S., & Tapia, A. (2005). The sociotechnical nature of mobile computing work: Evidence from a study of policing in the United States. *International Journal of Technology and Human Interaction, 1*(3), 1–14. doi:10.4018/jthi.2005070101

Saygin, C., & Natarajan, B. (2010). RFID-based baggage-handling system design. *Sensor Review, 30*(4), 324–335. doi:10.1108/02602281011072215

Schilit, B., Adams, N., & Want, R. (1994). Context-aware computing applications. In *Proceedings of the IEEE Workshop on Mobile Computing Systems and Applications,* (pp. 85-90). IEEE Press.

Schjolberg, S. (2010). *A cyberspace: A United Nations convention or protocol on cybersecurity and cybercrime.* Paper presented at the Twelfth United Nations Congress on Crime Prevention and Criminal Justice. Salvador, Brazil: United Nations Press.

Schuster, E. W., Allen, S. J., & Brock, D. L. (2007). *Global RFID.* Berlin, Germany: Springer.

Seddik Ghaleb, A., Ghamri Doudane, Y. M., & Senouci, S. M. (2009). TCP WELCOME: TCP variant for wireless environment, link losses, and congestion packet loss models. In *Proceedings of the 1st International Conference on Communication Systems and Networks, COMSNETS 2009.* Bangalore, India: IEEE Press.

Sen, J. (2010). Routing security issues in wireless sensor networks: Attacks and defenses . In Tan, Y. K. (Ed.), *Sustainable Wireless Sensor Networks* (pp. 279–309). Rijeka, Croatia: Intech.

Sen, S., & Wang, J. (2004). Analysing peer-to-peer traffic across large networks. *IEEE/ACM Transactions on Networking, 12*(2), 219–232. doi:10.1109/TNET.2004.826277

Shin, I. S., Nam, S.-H., Roberts, R., & Moon, S. (2009). A minimum-time algorithm for intercepting an object on a conveyor belt. Industrial Robot . *International Journal (Toronto, Ont.), 36*(2), 127–137. doi:10.1108/01439910910932586

Sibanda, O. S. (2009). *Anti-spam: A comparative appraisal of Canadian, European Union, and South African regulatory regimes.* Paper presented at the Lex Informatica Conference. Pretoria, South Africa. Retrieved February 02, 2011 from http://www.thefreelibrary.com/Anti-spam: a comparative appraisal of Canadian, European Union, and...-a0197857850.

Sinha, P., Venkitaraman, N., Sivakumar, R., & Bhargavan, V. (1999). WTCP: A reliable transport protocol for wireless wide-area networks. In *Proceedings ACM MOBICOM,* (pp. 231–241). ACM Press.

Siror, J. K., Guangun, L., Kaifang, P., Huanye, S., & Dong, W. (2010). Impact of RFID technology on tracking of export goods in Kenya. *Journal of Convergence Information Technology, 5*(9).

Slepian, D., & Wolf, J. (1973). Noiseless coding of correlated information sources. *IEEE Transactions on Information Theory, 19*(4), 471–480. doi:10.1109/TIT.1973.1055037

Snail, S. L. (2008). Cyber crime in context of the electronic communications act. *Juta Business Law, 6*(2), 65. Retrieved February 20, 2011 from http://www.all-business.com/crime-law/criminal-offenses-cybercrime/12956172-1.html.

Sohrabi, K., & Pottie, G. (2000). Protocols for self-organization of a wireless sensor network. *IEEE Personal Communications, 7*(5), 16–27. doi:10.1109/98.878532

Sohraby, K., Minoli, D., & Znati, T. (2007). *Wireless sensor networks: Technology, protocols, and applications*. Hoboken, NJ: John Wiley & Sons. doi:10.1002/047011276X

Sosteric, M., & Hesemeier, S. (2002). When is a learning object not an object: A first step towards a theory of learning objects. *International Review of Research in Open and Distance Learning, 3*(2).

Subramanian, L., & Katz, R. H. (2000). An architecture for building self configurable systems. In *Proceedings of the 1st ACM International Symposium on Mobile Ad Hoc Networking & Computing*, (pp. 63-73). Boston, MA: IEEE Press.

Sun, Y., Gurewitz, O., & Johnson, D. B. (2008). RI-MAC: A receiver initiated asynchronous duty cycle MAC protocol for dynamic traffic loads in wireless sensor networks. In T. Abdelzaher (Ed.), *Proceedings of the 6th International Conference on Embedded Networked Sensor Systems*, (pp. 1-14). New York: ACM.

Sundararaman, B., Buy, U., & Kshemkalyani, A. (2005). Clock synchronization for wireless sensor networks: A survey. *Ad Hoc Networks, 3*(3), 281–323. doi:10.1016/j.adhoc.2005.01.002

Szczytowski, P., & Schmid, C. (2006). Grid technologies for virtual control laboratories. In *Proceedings of 2006 IEEE International Conference on Control Applications*, (pp. 2286-2291). IEEE Press.

Tajima, M. (2007). Strategic value of RFID in supply chain management. *Journal of Purchasing and Supply Management, 13*(4), 261–273. doi:10.1016/j.pursup.2007.11.001

Tan, J., Wang, H., Li, D., & Wang, Q. (2008). A RFID architecture built in production and manufacturing fields. *International Conference on Convergence and Hybrid Information Technology, 1*, 1118-1120.

Tanabe, M., & Aida, M. (2007). Preventing resource exhaustion attacks in ad hoc networks. In *Proceedings of the 8th International Symposium on Autonomous Decentralized Systems (ISADS 2007)*, (pp. 543-548). Los Alamitos, CA: Conference Publishing Services.

Tang, S., Yuan, J., Li, X.-Y., Chen, G., Liu, Y., & Zhao, J. (2009). RASPberry: A stable reader activation scheduling protocol in multi-reader RFID systems. In *Proceedings of the 17th IEEE International Conference on Network Protocols*, (pp. 304-313). IEEE Press.

Tapia, E. M., Intille, S. S., & Larson, K. (2004). Activity recognition in the home using simple and ubiquitous sensors. In *Proceedings of the 2nd International Conference on Pervasive Computing*, (pp. 158-175). Springer Publisher.

Tarigh, H. D., & Sabaei, M. (2011). A new clustering method to prolong the lifetime of WSN. In *Proceedings of the Computer Research and Development (ICCRD), 2011 3rd International Conference*, (pp. 143-148). Shanghai, China: ICCRD Press.

Tharini, C. (2010). An efficient data gathering scheme for wireless sensor networks. *European Journal of Scientific Research, 43*(1), 148–155.

Tharini, C., & Vanaja, R. P. (2009). Design of modified adaptive huffman daata compression algorithm for wireless sensor network. *Journal of Computer Science, 5*(6), 466–470. doi:10.3844/jcssp.2009.466.470

Thein, M. C. M., & Thein, T. (2010). An energy efficient cluster-head selection for wireless sensor networks. In *Proceedings of the 1st International Conference on Intelligent Systems, Modelling and Simulation (ISMS 2010)*, (pp. 287–291). ISMS Press.

Thiemjarus, S., King, R., Lo, B., Gilles, D., & Yang, G. Z. (2005). A noise resilient distributed inference framework for body sensor networks. In *Proceedings of the 3rd International Conference on Pervasive Computing*, (pp. 13-18). Springer Publisher.

Thiemjarus, S., Lo, B. P. L., & Yang, G. Z. (2006). A spatio-temporal architecture for context-aware sensing. In *Proceedings of the IEEE International Workshop on Wearable and Implantable Body Sensor Networks,* (pp. 191-194). IEEE Computer Society Press.

Thiesse, F., Al-Kassab, J., & Fleisch, E. (2009). Understanding the value of integrated RFID systems: A case study from apparel retail. *European Journal of Information Systems, 18,* 592–614.doi:10.1057/ejis.2009.33

Tilak, S., Abu-Ghazaleh, N. B., & Heinzelman, W. (2002). A two-tier data dissemination model for large-scale wireless sensor networks. *ACM Mobile Computing and Communications Review, 6*(2), 28–36. doi:10.1145/565702.565708

Tladi, S. (2008). The regulation of unsolicited commercial communications (SPAM): Is the opt-out mechanism effective? *South African Law Journal, n.d.,* 178–183.

Tushabe, F., & Baryamureeba, V. (2005). Cyber crime in Uganda: Myth or reality? In *Proceedings of World Academy of Science, Engineering and Technology.* WASET Press.

Ullah, S., Higgins, H., Braem, B., Latre, B., Blondia, C., & Moerman, I. (2010). A comprehensive survey of wireless body area networks: On PHY, MAC, and network layers solutions. *Journal of Medical Systems,* 1–30.

UNECA. (2009). *ECA cooperative actions on cybersecurity.* Paper presented at the ITU Regional Cybersecurity Forum for Africa and Arab States. Tunisia, Tunis.

Varga, A. (2001). The OMNeT++ discrete event simulation system. In *Proceedings of 15th European Simulation Multiconference,* (pp.319-324). Prague: SCS Europe.

Varga, A. (2005). *Omnet++ discrete event simulation system (Version 3.2).* [Software program]. Retrieved from http://www.omnetpp.org/omnetpp/doc_details/2105-omnet-32-win32-binary-exe.

Vuran, M. C., & Akyildiz, I. F. (2006). Spatial correlation-based collaborative medium access control in wireless sensor networks. *IEEE/ACM Transactions on Networking, 14*(2), 316–329. doi:10.1109/TNET.2006.872544

Wall, D. (2007). *Cybercrime: The transformation of crime in the Information age.* Cambridge: Polity Publishers.

Wang, R., Valla, M., Sanadidi, M. Y., Ng, B. K. F., & Gerla, M. (2002). Efficiency/friendliness tradeoffs in TCP Westwood. In *Proceedings of the Seventh IEEE Symposium on Computers and Communications.* IEEE Press.

Wang, W., Chatterjee, M., & Kwiat, K. (2009). Coexistence with malicious nodes: A game theoretic approach. In *Proceedings of the 9th International Conference on Game Theory for Networks (GameNets 2009),* (pp.277-286). Los Alamitos, CA: Conference Publishing Services.

Wang, B. (2010). *Coverage control in sensor networks.* New York: Springer.

Wang, C., Sohraby, K., & Li, B. (2005). SenTCP: A hop-by-hop congestion control protocol for wireless sensor networks . In *Proceedings of IEEE INFOCOM 2005.* Miami, FL: IEEE Press.

Wang, J., Luo, Z., & Wong, E. C. (2010). RFID-enabled tracking in flexible assembly line. *International Journal of Advanced Manufacturing Technology, 46,* 351–360. doi:10.1007/s00170-009-2102-z

Wang, Q., & Zhang, T. (2009). A survey on security in wireless sensor networks . In Zhang, Y., & Kitsos, P. (Eds.), *Security in RFID and Sensor Networks* (pp. 293–317). Boca Raton, FL: CRC Press. doi:10.1201/9781420068405.pt2

Wang, Y., Yang, T. L. X., & Zhang, D. (2009). An energy efficient and balance hierarchical unequal clustering algorithm for large scale sensor networks. *Information Technology Journal, 8*(1), 28–38. doi:10.3923/itj.2009.28.38

Warneke, B., Last, M., Liebowitz, B., & Pister, K. S. J. (2001). Smartdust: Communicating with a cubic-millimeter computer. *IEEE Transactions on Computers, 45*(1), 44–51.

Weis, S. A., Sarma, S. E., Rivest, R. L., & Engels, D. W. (2003). Security and privacy aspects of low-cost radio frequency identification systems. *Lecture Notes in Computer Science, 28*(8), 201–212.

Wensheng, G. W., Wang, G., Zhang, W., Cao, G., & LaPorta, T. (2003). On supporting distributed collaboration in sensor networks. In *Proceedings of 2003 Military Communications Conference (MILCOM 2003),* (pp.752-757). Los Alamitos, CA: Conference Publishing Services.

Werff, T. J. V. D. (2003). Global future report. *Technology Review*. Retrieved from http://www.globalfuture.com/mit-trends2003.htm.

Westin, O. (2003). TCP performance in wireless mobile multi-hop ad hoc networks. *SICS Technical Report T2003:24*. Stockholm, Sweden: Swedish Institute of Computer Science.

Willig, A. (2006). Wireless sensor networks: Concept, challenges and approaches. *Elektrotechnik & Informationstechnik*, *123*(6), 224–231. doi:10.1007/s00502-006-0351-1

Wood, A., Stankovic, J., & Son, S. (2003). JAM: A mapping service for jammed regions in sensor networks. In *Proceedings of the 24th International IEEE Real-Time Systems* Symposium (*RTSS 2003*), (pp. 286-297). Los Alamitos, CA: Conference Publishing Services.

Wood, A. D., & Stankovic, J. A. (2002). Denial of service in sensor networks. *IEEE Computer*, *35*(10), 54–62. doi:10.1109/MC.2002.1039518

World Bank. (2008). *Global monitoring report 2008*. Washington, DC: World Bank.

Wu, X., Wang, P., Wang, W., & Shi, B. (2008). Data-aware clustering hierarchy for wireless sensor networks. *Lecture Notes in Computer Science*, *5012*, 795–802. doi:10.1007/978-3-540-68125-0_77

Xi, Y., Schwiebert, L., & Shi, W. (2006). Preserving source location privacy in monitoring-based wireless sensor networks. In *Proceedings of the 20th IEEE International Parallel and Distributed Processing Symposium (IPDPS 2006)*. Los Alamitos, CA: Conference Publishing Services.

Xu, W., Trappe, W., Zhang, Y., & Wood. (2005). The feasibility of launching and detecting jamming attacks in wireless networks. In *Proceedings of the 6th ACM International Symposium on Mobile Ad Hoc Networking and Computing (MobiHoc 2005)*, (pp. 46-57). New York, NY: ACM Press.

Xu, Y., Heidemann, J., & Estrin, D. (2001). Geography-informed energy conservation for ad-hoc routing. In *Proceedings of the Seventh Annual ACM/IEEE International Conference on Mobile Computing and Networking*, (pp. 70-84). ACM Press.

Xu, K., Tian, Y., & Ansari, N. (2004). tcp-jersey for wireless ip communications. *IEEE Journal on Selected Areas in Communications*, *22*(4), 747–756. doi:10.1109/JSAC.2004.825989

Xu, S., & Saadawi, T. (2002). Revealing the problems with 802.11 medium access control protocol in multi-hop wireless ad hoc networks. *Computer Networks*, *38*(14), 531–548. doi:10.1016/S1389-1286(01)00273-0

Yamamoto, A., Suzuki, S., Hada, H., Mitsugi, J., Teraoka, F., & Nakamura, O. (2008). A tamper detection method for RFID tag data. In *Proceedings of the IEEE International Conference on RFID*, (pp. 51-57). IEEE Press.

Yang, X., & de Veciana, G. (2004). Service capacity of peer to peer networks. In *Proceedings of the 23rd Annual Joint Conference of the IEEE Computer and Communications Societies*, (pp. 2242–2252). IEEE Press.

Yan, Z., & Holtmanns, S. (2007). Trust modeling and management: From social trust to digital trust . In *Computer Security, Privacy and Politics: Current Issues, Challenges and Solutions*. Hershey, PA: IGI Global.

Ye, M., Li, C., Chen, G., & Wu, J. (2005). EECS: An energy efficient clustering scheme in wireless sensor networks. In *Proceedings of the 24th IEEE International Performance, Computing, and Communications Conference*, (pp. 535–540). IEEE Press.

Ye, W., Silva, F., & Heidemann, J. (2006). Ultra-low duty cycle MAC with scheduled channel polling. In A. Campbell (Ed.), *Proceedings of the 4th International Conference on Embedded Networked Sensor Systems*, (pp. 321-334). New York: ACM.

Ye, F., Luo, H., Cheng, J., Lu, S., & Zhang, L. (2001). A two-tier data dissemination model for large-scale wireless sensor networks . In *Proceedings of Mobicon*. Atlanta, GA: ACM Press. doi:10.1145/570662.570664

Ye, W., Heidemann, J., & Estrin, D. (2004). Medium access control with coordinated adaptive sleeping for wireless sensor networks. *IEEE/ACM Transactions on Networking*, *12*(3), 493–506. doi:10.1109/TNET.2004.828953

Yin, L., Wang, C., & Øien, G. E. (2008). Minimum cost routing with optimized data fusion for event-driven dense wireless sensor networks. In *Proceedings of IEEE PIMRC*. IEEE Press.

Youngtae, N., Saewoom, L., & Kiseon, K. (2008). Basestation-aided coverage-aware energy-efficient routing protocol for wireless sensor networks. In *Proceedings of WCNC 2008, IEEE Wireless Communications & Networking Conference,* (pp. 2486-2491). Las Vegas, NV: IEEE Press.

Younis, M., Youssef, M., & Arisha, K. (2002). Energy-aware routing in cluster-based sensor networks. In *Proceedings of the 10th IEEE/ACM International Symposium on Modeling, Analysis and Simulation of Computer and Telecommunication Systems (MASCOTS 2002).* Fort Worth, TX: ACM Press.

Younis, O., & Fahmy, S. (2004). HEED: A hybrid, energy-efficient, distributed clustering approach for ad hoc sensor networks. *IEEE Transactions on Mobile Computing, 3*(4), 366–379. doi:10.1109/TMC.2004.41

Yu, F., Shen, S., Yue, G., & Cao, Q. (2011). A survey of game theory in wireless sensor networks security. *Journal of Networks, 6*(3), 521–532.

Yu, Y., Estrin, D., & Govindan, R. (2001). *Geographical and energy-aware routing: A recursive data dissemination protocol for wireless sensor networks. Technical Report.* Los Angeles, CA: UCLA Press.

Yu, Y., Prasanna, V. K., & Krishnamachari, B. (2006). *Information processing and routing in wireless sensor networks.* Singapore: World Scientific Publishing. doi:10.1142/9789812772589

Zhang, P., Liu, W., & Zou, X. (2008). A study of video-on-demand learning system in e-learning platform. In *Proceedings of the 2008 International Conference on Computer Science and Software Engineering,* (pp. 793–796). IEEE Press.

Zhang, X., & Baciu, G. (2008). Low cost minimal mutual authentication protocol for RFID. In *Proceedings of the IEEE International Conference on Networking, Sensing and Control,* (pp. 620-624). IEEE Press.

Zhang, X., Chan, H., Jain, A., & Perrig, A. (2007). *Bounding packet dropping and injection attacks in sensor networks.* Technical Report CMU-CyLab-07-019. Pittsburgh, PA: Carnegie Mellon University.

Zhang, X., Liu, J., Li, B., & Yum, T.-S. P. (2005). Coolstreaming/donet: A data-driven overlay network for efficient media streaming. In *Proceedings of IEEE INFOCOM.* IEEE Press.

Zhang, M., Zhang, Q., Sun, L., & Yang, S. (2007). Understanding the power of pull-based streaming protocols: Can we do better? *IEEE Journal on Selected Areas in Communications, 25*(9), 1678–1694. doi:10.1109/JSAC.2007.071207

Zhang, T., Ouyang, Y., & He, Y. (2008). Traceable air baggage handling system based on RFID tags in the airport. *Journal of Theoretical and Applied Electronic Commercial Research, 3*(1), 106–115.

Zhang, W., & Cao, G. (2003). Optimizing tree reconfiguration to track mobile targets in sensor networks. *ACM SIGMOBILE Mobile Computing and Communications Review, 7*(3), 39–40. doi:10.1145/961268.961282

Zhao, W., Ammar, M., & Zegura, E. (2004). A message ferrying approach for data delivery in sparse mobile ad hoc networks. In *Proceedings of ACM Mobihoc 2004.* Tokyo, Japan: ACM Press.

Zhou, S., Luo, Z., Wong, E., Tan, C. J., & Luo, J. (2007). Interconnected RFID reader collision model and its application in reader anti-collision. In *Proceedings of the IEEE International Conference on RFID,* (pp. 212-219). IEEE Press.

Zhou, Y., Fang, Y., & Zhang, Y. (2008). Securing wireless sensor networks: A survey. *IEEE Communications Surveys & Tutorials, 10,* 6–28. doi:10.1109/COMST.2008.4625802

Zhu, S., Narayanan, V., McDaniel, P., Kandemir, M., Brooks, R., & Pirretti, M. (2006). The sleep deprivation attack in sensor networks: Analysis and methods of defense. *International Journal of Distributed Sensor Networks, 2*(3), 267–287. doi:10.1080/15501320600642718

Zualkernan, I. A. (2005). HYDRA: A light-weight, SCORM-based P2P e-learning architecture. In *Proceedings of the 5th IEEE International Conference on Advanced Learning Technologies,* (pp. 484–486). IEEE Press.

Zug, S., Dietrich, A., & Kaiser, J. (2011). An architecture for a dependable distributed sensor system. *IEEE Transactions on Instrumentation and Measurement, 60*(2), 408–419. doi:10.1109/TIM.2010.2085871

About the Contributors

Jemal Abawajy is a faculty member at Deakin University and has published more than 100 articles in refereed journals and conferences as well as a number of technical reports. He is on the editorial board of several international journals and edited several international journals and conference proceedings. He has also been a member of the organizing committee for over 60 international conferences and workshops serving in various capacities including best paper award chair, general co-chair, publication chair, vice-chair, and program committee. He is actively involved in funded research in building secure, efficient, and reliable infrastructures for large-scale distributed systems. Towards this vision, he is working in several areas including: pervasive and networked systems (mobile, wireless network, sensor networks, grid, cluster, and P2P), e-science and e-business technologies and applications, and performance analysis and evaluation.

Mukaddim Pathan is a Research Scientist at CSIRO, the national government body of scientific research in Australia. He also holds the position of an Adjunct Lecturer at the Australian National University. His research interests include data management, resource allocation, load balancing, and coordination policies in wide-area distributed systems such as content delivery networks, cloud computing, and sensor networks. He is the editor of *Content Delivery Networks*, published by Springer. He has authored and co-authored a number of research papers in internationally recognized journals and conferences. He is involved in the organization of the UPGRADE-CN and IDCS workshops and is a PC member of several international conferences. He has edited a few research issues in reputed international journals and also serves as a reviewer and editorial board member of several renowned journals. He is a member of IEEE, IEEE Computer Society, and ACM. For further information, please visit: http://www.ict.csiro.au/staff/mukaddim.pathan.

Mustafizur Rahman is a Consultant of Business Analytics and Optimization Service Line at IBM Australia. He also worked as Endeavour Research Fellow at the Institute of High Performance Computing, Agency for Science Technology and Research (A*STAR), Singapore. He received PhD degree from Department of Computer Science and Software Engineering at the University of Melbourne, Australia. His research interests include workflow scheduling and resource management in grid/cloud computing systems as well as fault-tolerance and load balancing in P2P and self-managing systems. He has been actively engaged in the research and development projects of CLOUDS Lab at the University of Melbourne and received the 2010 Endeavour Research Fellowship Award from the Australian Government. He has authored and co-authored several research papers in internationally recognized journals and conferences. He is a member of IEEE, IEEE Computer Society, and ACM. He has been involved in the organization of several international workshops and conferences. He also serves as the reviewer of renowned journals, including *Future Generation Computer Systems (FGCS)* and *Concurrency & Computation: Practice & Experience (CCPE)*.

Al-Sakib Khan Pathan received the Ph.D. degree in Computer Engineering in 2009 from Kyung Hee University (KHU), South Korea. He received B.Sc. degree in Computer Science and Information Technology from Islamic University of Technology (IUT), Bangladesh, in 2003. He is currently an Assistant Professor and FYP Coordinator of the Computer Science Department in International Islamic University Malaysia (IIUM), Malaysia. Till June 2010, he served as an Assistant Professor of the Computer Science and Engineering Department in BRAC University, Bangladesh. Prior to holding this position, he worked as a Researcher at Networking Lab, KHU, South Korea, till August 2009. His research interests include wireless sensor networks, network security, and e-services technologies. He has served as a Chair and a PC member in numerous international conferences/workshops. He is currently serving as the Editor-in-Chief of *IJIDCS*, an Area Editor of *IJCNIS*, and Editor of several other well-known journals and books. He also serves as a referee of a few renowned journals. He is a member of IEEE, IEEE ComSoc Bangladesh Chapter, and several other international organizations.

Mustafa Mat Deris received the Ph.D degree in Computer Science in 2002 from University Putra, Malaysia. He is currently a Professor in the Faculty of Computer Science and Information Technology, Universiti Tun Hussein Onn, Malaysia. He has published more than 150 articles in refereed journals and proceedings. He is on the editorial board of several international journals and conferences and also Guest Editor of *International Journal of BioMedical Soft Computing and Human Science* for Special Issue on "Soft Computing Methodologies and Its Applications" a reviewer of several international journals such as *IEEE Transaction on Parallel and Distributed Computing, Journal of Parallel and Distributed Databases, Journal of Future Generation on Computer Systems, Elsevier Journal of Cluster Computing, Kluwer Journal of Computer Mathematics, Taylor & Francis IEEE Conference on Cluster and Grid Computing*. He has served as a program committee member and co-organizer for numerous international conferences/workshops including Grid and Peer-to-Peer Computing, (GP2P, 2005, 2006), Autonomic Distributed Data and Storage Systems Management (ADSM, 2005, 2006, 2007), and Grid Pervasive Computing Security, organizer for Rough and Soft Sets Theories and Applications (RSAA, 2010), Fukuoka, Japan, and Soft Computing and Data Engineering (SCDE, 2010), Jeju, Korea. His research interests include distributed databases, data grid, soft computing and data mining.

* * *

Sherine M. Abd El-Kader has her M.Sc. and Ph.D. degrees from the Electronics & Communications Dept. & Computers Dept., Faculty of Engineering, Cairo University, in 1998 and 2003, respectively. Dr. Abd El-Kader is an Associate Professor of the Computers & Systems Dept., Electronics Research Institute (ERI). She is supervising three Ph.D students, and 5 M.Sc. students. Dr. Abd El-Kader had published more than 15 papers in the computer networking area. She is working in many computer networking hot topics such as Wi-MAX, Wi-Fi, IP mobility, active queue management, QoS, wireless sensors networks, ad-hoc networking, real-time traffics, Bluetooth, and IPv6. She is an Associate Professor of the Faculty of Engineering, Akhbar El Yom Academy from 2007 till now. Also she is a Technical Reviewer for many international Journals. She has headed the Internet and Networking unit at ERI since 2003. Dr. Abd El-Kader is supervising many automation and Web projects for ERI. She is supervising many Graduation Projects from 2006 till now. Finally, Dr. Abd El-Kader is the main researcher at two US-EG joint funded projects with the University of California at Irvine.

Anar Abdel Hady received her B.Sc. degree from Computer Dept., Faculty of Engineering, Ain Shams University, 2002, and the M.Sc. degree from the Computers Dept., Faculty of Engineering, Cairo University, 2007. She is currently a Ph.D. student at from Computer Dept., Faculty of Engineering, Ain Shams University. Anar Abdel Hady is an Assistant Researcher in the Computers & Systems Dept., Electronics Research Institute (ERI). Her research interests include ad hoc networks and wireless sensor networks.

Habib M. Ammari is an Associate Professor in the Department of Computer and Information Science, College of Engineering and Computer Science, University of Michigan-Dearborn, and the Founding Director of Wireless Sensor and Mobile Ad-hoc Networks (WiSeMAN) Research Lab at the University of Michigan-Dearborn since September 2011. Prior to that, he was on the faculty of the Department of Computer Science, Hofstra University from September 2008 – August 2011. Also, he was on the faculty of the Superior School of Communications of Tunis (Sup'Com Tunis), Tunisia, from 1992 to 2005 (Engineer of Computer Science, 1992-1993; Lecturer of Computer Science, 1993-1997; Assistant Professor of Computer Science, 1997-2005; received tenure in 1998). He obtained his second Ph.D. degree in Computer Science and Engineering from the Department of Computer Science and Engineering, University of Texas at Arlington in May 2008, and his second Master's degree in Computer Science from the Department of Computer Science and Engineering, Southern Methodist University in December 2004. Also, he obtained his first Ph.D. (Highly Honorable with Praise) and Master's degrees in Computer Science from the Department of Computer Science, Faculty of Sciences of Tunis in December 1996 and July 1992, respectively.

Luca Caviglione has a PhD in Electronic and Computer Engineering from the University of Genova, and participated in many research projects funded by the European Union (EU), and by the Italian Ministry of Research (MIUR). He is author or coauthor of more than seventy academic publications (conferences, journals, and book chapters) about TCP/IP networking, P2P systems, QoS architectures, and wireless networks. In 2006 he was with the Genoa Research Unit of the Italian National Consortium for Telecommunications. Since 2007, he works at the Genoa Branch of the Istituto di Studi sui Sistemi Intelligenti per l'Automazione of the Italian National Research Council. He is a Work Group Leader of the Italian IPv6 Task Force and he has filed, as a coauthor, several patents in the field of P2P. He is also a professional engineer.

Mauro Coccoli received the Italian Master-level degree in Electronic Engineering in 1995 and the PhD in Electronic Engineering and Computer Science in 2000, from the University of Genoa. He is with the DIST, Dept. of Communication, Computer and Systems Science, University of Genoa, where he has been a temporary researcher since 1995. In the period 2003-2005, he was Sole Director of a small ICT consulting company. Now, he is Assistant Professor with the University of Genoa, Faculty of Education Science, since December 2005. He is course lecturer for: Data Base since 2005, Laboratory of Computer Science since 2007, and Computer Science Fundamentals since 2008, at the University of Genoa, Faculty of Education Science. He is author of about 80 publications (including journals, edited books, and international conferences). His research interests are on technologies for e-learning, knowledge representation, and multi-agent systems.

Hussein S. Eissa received his B.Sc. and M.Sc. degrees from the Electronics & Communications Dept., Faculty of Engineering, Cairo University in 1993 and 1996. Dr. Eissa received his Ph.D degree from the Electronics & Communications Dept., Faculty of Engineering, Cairo University in cooperation with the Electrical Engineering Dept., University of Pennsylvania, Philadelphia, in 2000. He received an International Certificate in Business & Management from IESES Business School, University of Navarra, Spain, in 2004. Dr. Eissa is an Associate Professor of the Computers & Systems Dept., Electronics Research Institute. He has published 22 papers in the computer networking area. Dr. Eissa is the Director of the R&D Sector for the Egyptian IPv6 task force (E-IPv6 TF) since 2004. He is the director of Information System Dept. at Ministry of Communications & Information Technology.

Bellarmine Ezumah is an Assistant Professor in the Department of Journalism and Mass Communication at Murray State University, KY, where she teaches undergraduate and graduate courses including International Communications, New Technologies, Mass Media Effects, Mass Communication Theory and Contemporary Mass Media. She graduated from Howard University as a Frederick Douglass Scholar in August 2010 with a dual degree of PhD in Mass Communication and Media Studies and a Graduate Certificate in International Studies. She has conducted research both in the United States and internationally including Ghana and Nigeria. Some of her research interests comprise effective design and implementation of emergent technologies in classrooms, international/intercultural communications/cross-cultural research, monitoring and evaluation of educational technology programs, social media, and participatory action model. Dr. Ezumah has published book chapters and articles as well as presented numerous papers at national and international conferences and is active in various professional associations.

Hossam M. A. Fahmy is the Chair of Computer Engineering & Systems Department, Faculty of Engineering at Ain Shams University, Cairo, Egypt. He has published and refereed in international refereed journals and conferences. He works on computer networks, MANETs, fault tolerance, software and web engineering. He has chaired the IEEE International Conference on Computer Engineering and Systems since 2006. He is a senior IEEE member.

Yacine Ghamri-Doudane is currently an Associate Professor (Maître de Conferences) at the Ecole Nationale Supérieure d'Informatique pour l'Industrie et l'Entreprise (ENSIIE), a major French postgraduate school located in Evry, France, and member of the Computer Science Laboratory of the Gaspard Monge Institut (LIGM – UMR 8049) at Marne-la-Vallée, France. Since February 2011, he is a Visiting Research Fellow at the University College Dublin, Ireland. Yacine received an engineering degree in Computer Science from the National Institute of Computer Science (INI), Algiers, Algeria, in 1998, an M.S. degree in Signal, Image and Speech Processing from the National Institute of Applied Sciences (INSA), Lyon, France, a Ph.D. degree in Computer Networks from the Pierre & Marie Curie University, Paris 6, France, and an Habilitation to Direct Research (HDR) from the University Paris-Est, Marne-la-Vallée, France, in 1999, 2003, and 2010, respectively. His current research interests include Wireless

Sensor Networks (WSN), vehicular networks, TCP and multimedia over wireless, QoS in WLAN/WMAN, mobility management in 4G mobile networks, management of wireless/mobile networks.

Alaa Ghaleb-Seddik is the inventor of TCP-Welcome, the first TCP protocol specifically designed for wireless mobile ad hoc networks. Her area of research is focused on TCP applications and solutions for the industry. Alaa holds two international patents and she authored 8 peer-reviewed publications in international conferences and journals. She started her career after graduating as a Telecom Engineer from the renowned Helwan University in Cairo, Egypt, in 1998. She was one of the Egyptian telecom engineers of her generation who pioneered the introduction of the Internet infrastructure in Egypt. After working for several years in major Egyptian technological firms, she moved to France to pursue an R&D career where she achieved a Masters degree in Telcoms from Paris VI University, in 2004, and a Ph.D. from the University of Evry, in 2009. She worked on research projects in collaboration with LRSM, ENSIIE research laboratories, as well Orange and Philips.

Enamul Haque received B.Sc. degree in Computer Science from East West University, Bangladesh, in 2003 and M.IT degree in Information Technology from University of Dhaka, Bangladesh, in 2005. From April 2007, he was a Graduate Researcher at University of Trento, Italy, for five months. He received his Ph.D. in Wireless Sensor Networks from Saitama University, Japan, in 2010. Since 2003, he has been a permanent Faculty Member of the Department of Computer Science and Mathematics, Bangladesh Agricultural University, Bangladesh. Currently he is a Postdoctoral Researcher at National Institute of Informatics, Japan. His research interests include wireless sensor networks, agricultural information systems, and next generation networks.

Yupeng Hu was born in Qidong of Hunan Province of China in 1981. He received his B.S. degree in Computer Science and Technology from Hunan University in 2002, and his M.S. degree and Ph.D in Computer Application Technology from Hunan University in 2005 and 2008, respectively. He is the recipient of the Excellent Dissertation Award of Hunan University (2010); Second prize of Hunan Province Excellent Paper Award (2010). He possesses several patents and software copyrights on wireless sensor networks. He is currently an Associate Professor in the Information Science and Engineering College of Hunan University. His current major research interests focus on areas of sensor networks and social network computing.

Rui Li was born in Yueyang of Hunan Province of China in 1975. He received his B.S. degree in Computer Science from Xi'an Architecture Technology University in 1998, and M.S. degree in Computer Application Technology from Central South University in 2004. Now he is a Doctoral Candidate in Hunan University. He is also currently a teacher in the Information Science and Engineering College of Hunan University. His current major research interests focus on areas of wireless sensor networks.

Hairulnizam Mahdin is a Lecturer, University of Tun Hussein Onn, Malaysia. He is currently taking study leave to do Ph.D. under the supervision of Assoc. Prof. Jemal Abawajy at Deakin University, Australia. His research topic is on RFID Data Filtering Problems. He has published his Ph.D research in a number of conferences and journals internationally.

Dennis P. Mirante received the B.S. degree in Chemistry from Hofstra University, Hempstead, NY, in 1972. He has studied Computer Science at the NYU Courant Institute of Mathematical Science, NY, at the graduate level and is currently involved in research in the Wireless Sensor and Mobile Ad-Hoc Networks (WiSeMAN) Research Lab at Hofstra University. Since 1975, he has worked in the computer industry as a consultant and has led and participated in many industrial research projects and industry standards committees. His research interests include wireless sensor networks, communication and security in computer networks, and distributed systems and their applications.

Basma M. Mohammad El-Basioni is a Research Assistant in the Computers and Systems Department at the Electronics Research Institute (ERI) in Egypt. In May 2005, she completed her B.S. in Computers and Control, Science, Faculty of Engineering, Zagazig University. During the 2005-2006 year, she joined the Professional Training Project (Network Management & Infrastructure [Tivoli] Track), which is organized by the Egyptian Ministry of Electricity And Information Technology; during this period she took some courses such as Network Essentials, Linux, Security+, SCP (Security Certified Program), IBM Tivoli Products, and Berlitz English courses. In November 2006, she finished her training after obtaining some international certifications, which are LPI (Linux Professional Institute) level 1, SCNP (Security Certified Network Professional), IBM Tivoli Enterprise Console, IBM Tivoli Storage Manager 5.3.2 Implementation, and Berlitz English (levels 1, 2, 3, and 4), and certification for Dale Carnegie Training (Busines Correspondence, Soft Skills, Marketing & Advertising). At the beginning of 2007, she took her current position in the Electronics Research Institute. Her current research interests focus on networks, especially on Wireless Sensor Networks (WSN). Now, she is studying for M.Sc. degree and its subject area is Routing in WSN.

Suraj Olunifesi Adekunle is a Lecturer in the Department of Broadcasting and Communication Technology, Adebola Adegunwa School of Communication, Lagos State University, Nigeria. Prior to joining academics, he had worked with several consultancy and ICT firms, the last being the Computer WareHouse Group where he was appointed as the Head of Technical and Presales (Training). He has been a Knowledge Management and Communication Consultant to many Telecommunications and ICT companies. Dr. Suraj is a distinguished scholar with so many publications to his credit. He holds his master and doctoral degrees in Information Science from the prestigious University of Ibadan, Nigeria. His research interests among others include knowledge management, mobile applications, new media, new broadcasting technology, and multimedia applications. He is the director of an organization called Treasured Intelligence (a knowledge management consultancy and training firm) and presently serves as a board member of the university senate committee on curriculum.

Doug Palmer has worked in the software industry for over 25 years, in areas as diverse as archaeology, video games, and finance. He gained his PhD in 1997 from the University of Melbourne and has worked at CSIRO as a research engineer for 10 years. His current area of interest is sensor network data management. He used to be able to say that he understood how computers work at every level, from fundamental particle physics to very high level languages, but somewhere along the way something broke and he can't work out how a modern PC works.

Harinda Sahadeva Fernando has completed a diploma in Computer Information System (CIS) from the Institute of Technological Studies (ITS), Sri Lanka, and a bachelor's degree in Business Information Technology (BBIT Hon) from Deakin University, Australia. He has been awarded a number of academic awards during his career including being placed on the Dean's List for his undergraduate degree. He is currently a Post Graduate Student at Deakin University in the school of IT. His research is in the general area of IT security and pervasive computing. His current research focuses on enhancing the security and performance of networked RFID systems using low cost RFID tags. He has published several papers in international peer reviewed conferences and a number of technical reports. He has also acted as a guest reviewer for a number of journals.

Ali Salehi has a Ph.D. in Computer Science from École Polytechnique Fédérale de Lausanne (EPFL), Switzerland. His research interests are data stream processing, cloud computing, and financial markets. Ali is founder of Global Sensor Networks (http://gsn.sf.net), NexTick (http://nextick.sf.net), and Phenonet (http://phenonet.com). He is currently engaged in the Sensor Informatics project, developing an information processing middleware for sensor networks.

Ashraf Salem is a Professor of Computer Engineering in Ain Shams University. He obtained his PhD from Grenoble University and M. Sc. and B. Sc. from Ain Shams University in 1992, 1987, and 1983, respectively. His research areas are computer aided design of digital circuit, formal verification, and hardware description languages. He has published more than 80 articles in these fields.

Sidi-Mohammed Senouci was born in Nédroma, Tlemcen, Algeria, on May 26, 1972. He received in 1995 the B.S. degree in Computer Science Engineering from the University of Science and Technology of Oran (USTO), Algeria, and in 1999 the M.S. degree in Artificial Intelligence from the University of Paris 13, France. In his master, he developed several works in the area of optical networks. After that, he joined the Network and Performance (RP) Group of the LIP6 Laboratory (LIP6), University Pierre and Marie Curie (Paris VI), France, where he started his Ph.D. thesis under the supervision of Pr. Guy Pujolle. During this period, he was involved in several projects including industrial and academic researchers, in an international context. In particular, he was the main LIP6 representative in the ITEA AMBIENCE project. He is a Member of IEEE and the Communications Society and Expert Senior of the French society SEE (Society of Electricity and Electronics).

Norihiko Yoshida received the Dr. Eng. degree in Computer Science and Communication Engineering in 1990 from Kyushu University, Japan. He is Professor of Computer Systems in Saitama University, Japan, since 2002, and also Director of Information Technology Center, since 2008. His research interests include system design methodologies and parallel and distributed computation.

Mohammed M. Zahra received the B. S. and M. S. degrees from Al-Azhar University, Cairo, Egypt, in 1979 and 1987, respectively, all in Electrical Engineering. He received the Ph. D. degree from AGH, Krakow, Poland, in 1993. His doctoral research focused on bandwidth allocation techniques in ATM networks. He was an Assistance Professor of Communication Networks from 1993 to 2006 and Associate Professor from 2006 to present in Al-Azhar University. He is an IEEE member.

Index